PENGUIN BOOKS

PANZER LEADER

Heinz Guderian was born in 1888, the son of a Prussian General. He attended the War School at Metz and was then commissioned into the German Army. He spent the First World War as a technical and staff officer. After the war he remained with the small army that Germany was allowed to retain under the Treaty of Versailles. At this time he specialized in military transport technology, working on the secret development of tanks, which had been prohibited by the Treaty. When Hitler repudiated the restrictions of the Treaty in 1937, Guderian was created General of Panzer Troops, and in 1938 published a book on armoured warfare entitled *Achtung! Panzer!*

During the Second World War Guderian commanded forces invading Poland, France and the Soviet Union, successfully employing the *blitzkrieg* warfare method of massed firepower. His military career was, however, chequered by clashes with Hitler and General von Kluge, and he was dismissed and reinstated a number of times. Hitler made him Army Chief of Staff in 1944, but finally dismissed him in March 1945. After the Second World War, Guderian was interrogated about war crimes by the Nuremberg Tribunal. He was released without being indicted after it was decided he did not have direct responsibility or knowledge of the atrocities committed during the war. *Panzer Leader* was published in 1952. Guderian died in 1953.

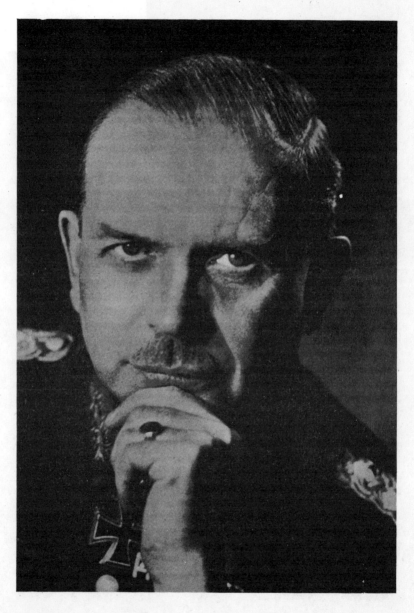

GENERAL HEINZ GUDERIAN

*

PANZER LEADER

*

Foreword by
CAPTAIN B. H. LIDDELL HART

Translated from the German by
CONSTANTINE FITZGIBBON

PENGUIN BOOKS

PENGUIN BOOKS

Published by the Penguin Group
Penguin Books Ltd, 80 Strand, London WC2R 0RL, England
Penguin Putnam Inc., 375 Hudson Street, New York, New York 10014, USA
Penguin Books Australia Ltd, Ringwood, Victoria, Australia
Penguin Books Canada Ltd, 10 Alcorn Avenue, Toronto, Ontario, Canada M4V 3B2
Penguin Books India (P) Ltd, 11 Community Centre, Panchsheel Park,
New Delhi – 110 017, India
Penguin Books (NZ) Ltd, Cnr Rosedale and Airborne Roads, Albany, Auckland,
New Zealand
Penguin Books (South Africa) (Pty) Ltd, 24 Sturdee Avenue, Rosebank 2196, South Africa

Penguin Books Ltd, Registered Offices: 80 Strand, London WC2R 0RL, England

www.penguin.com

This translation first published in the USA by Dutton 1952
Published in Great Britain by Michael Joseph 1952
Published with a new introduction in the USA by Da Capo Press 1996
Published as a Classic Penguin 2000
8

Printed in Great Britain by Clays Ltd, St Ives plc

CONTENTS

	PAGE
List of appendices	1
List of illustrations	2
List of sketch maps	3
Introduction	5
Foreword	11
1. Background and Youth	16
2. The Creation of the German Armoured Force	18
3. Hitler at the Peak of his Power	47
1938. The Blomberg–Fritsch crisis	47
The Incorporation of Austria into the Reich	49
The Incorporation of the Sudetenland into the Reich	57
The Situation Deteriorates Once Again	60
4. The Beginning of the Disaster	64
The Drift to War	64
The Polish Campaign	65
Between the Campaigns	84
5. The Campaign in the West	89
Preparations for the Campaign	89
The Break-through to the Channel	98
The Capture of the Channel Ports	114
Hitler's Momentous Order to Stop	117
The Break-through to the Swiss Border	120
The Armistice	135
6. The Campaign in Russia, 1941	140
The Background	140
Preparations	145
Opening Operations	152
Crossing the Dnieper	167
Smolensk—Elnya—Roslavl	174
Moscow or Kiev?	189
The Battle of Kiev	202

PAGE

The Battles of Orel and Bryansk 226
The Advance to Tula and Moscow 242
My First Dismissal 264

7. On Inactive Service 272

8. The Development of the Armoured Force, January 1942
   to February 1943 276

9. Inspector-General of Armoured Troops 284
   Appointment and First Actions 284
   Dr. Goerdeler's Visits 300
   'Operation Citadel' 302
   Disagreements during the Second Half of 1943 . . 312
   The Year of Decision 327

10. July 20th and its Sequel 338

11. Chief of the General Staff 351
    Operations on the Eastern Front 373
    The Ardennes Offensive 379
    Defensive Preparations in the East 381
    The Russian Offensive 389

12. The Final Collapse 425

13. Leading Personalities of the Third Reich . . . 430
    Hitler 430
    The Party 444
    The National and District Controllers 449
    Hitler's Intimate Circle 451
    The Government 452

14. The German General Staff 454
    'To Be or Not to Be, That is the Question!' . . . 466

   Index 525

APPENDICES

1. My Military Appointments 467

2. O.K.W. Directive No. 1 for the Prosecution of the War
(31.8.1939) 470

3. Report by the Inspector-General of Armoured Troops on
the Organisation and Strength of the Armoured Troops
in the Western Campaign 472

4. XIX Army Corps, Corps Order (12.5.40) 474

5. XIX Army Corps, Warning Order for the Meuse Crossing
(12.5.40) 476
1st Panzer Division, Divisional Order No. 4 (12.5.40) . . 477
10th Panzer Division, Warning Order for the Meuse
Crossing (12.5.40) 477

6. XIX Army Corps, Corps Order No. 3 for the Attack across
the Meuse (13.5.40) 478
1st Panzer Division, Divisional Order No. 5 for the Attack
across the Meuse (13.5.40) 480
10th Panzer Division, Divisional Order for the Attack across
the Meuse (13.5.40) 484

7. XIX Army Corps, Corps Order, 13.5.40, 22.30 hrs. . . 487

8. XIX Army Corps, Corps Order No. 5, 14.5.40 . . . 488

9. XIX Army Corps, Corps Order No. 7, 16.5.40 . . . 490

10. XIX Army Corps, Corps Order No. 8, 18.5.40 . . . 491

11. XIX Army Corps, Corps Order No. 9, 18.5.40 . . . 493

12. XIX Army Corps, Corps Order, 18.5.40, 13.00 hrs. . . 496

13. XIX Army Corps, Corps Order No. 10, 19.5.40 . . . 497

14. XIX Army Corps, Corps Order 20.5.40, 16.30 hrs. . . 499

15. XIX Army Corps, Corps Order No. 11, 20.5.40 . . . 500

16. XIX Army Corps, Preliminary Order No. 12, 21.5.40 . . 502
Group von Kleist, Group Order No. 12, 21.5.40 . . . 503

17. Group von Kleist, Group Order No. 13, 22.5.40 . . . 505

18. XIX Army Corps, Corps Order No. 13, 25.5.40 . . . 506

PAGE

19. XIX Army Corps, Order for the Relief of 1st Panzer Division by 20th (Motorised) Infantry Division, 26.5.40   508

20. XIX Army Corps, Corps Order No. 14, 26.5.40 .   .   .   509

21. XIX Army Corps, Corps Order No. 15, 28.5.40 .   .   .   511

22. A Hitler Order: Directive No. 21, 'Operation Barbarossa,' 18.12.40 513

23. The Organisation of the Command of the Armed Forces, 1944 517

24. War Establishment of a Panzer Division as of 15.10.35 . 518

25. War Establishment of a Panzer Division as of 9.5.40 . . 519

ILLUSTRATIONS

Portrait of the author .   .   .   .   .   *Frontispiece*

1. At an artillery observation post .   .   .   . *facing* 64

2. Polish summer landscape 65

3. Battle for an emplacement near Vizna 65

4. Brest-Litovsk: The Russians take over 96

5. In an armoured command vehicle 97

6. Boulogne: The assault on the town wall . . . 128

7. The attack rolls on 129

8. Advancing as though on manœuvres: tanks move forward (Champagne, June 1940) 160

9. Lieutenant-Colonel Balck handing over a flag captured at Juniville. 161

10. Dawn, June 22, 1941 192

11. Russia: The road forward 192

12. Bridge-building over the Dnieper near Kopys . . 193

13. The Battle of Shklov 193

14. Crossing the Dnieper near Kopys 224

15. With General Marras on the banks of the Dnieper near Kopys 225

PAGE

16. Before the attack . . . . *facing* 256

17. An anti-tank ditch in the Stalin Line 256

18. Near Roslavl, August 5, 1941 257

19. Panzer Regiment 35 advancing before the Battle of Goro-
    dishtche 257

20. The outskirts of Orel on the Oka: a typical Russian town . 288

21. Dmitrovsk: early winter 289

22. Night battle before Moscow, 1941 289

SKETCH MAPS

1. General Sketch Map 1: The advance into Poland. Situation
   31.8–5.9.39 67

2. Sketch Map 1: The battle of Tuchel Heath, 2–3.9.39 . . 69

3. General Sketch Map 2: The advance into Poland. Situation
   9.9–18.9.39 77

4. Sketch Map 2: Advance of XXI Army Corps to Brest-
   Litovsk. Situation 8.9–17.9.39 79

5. Sketch Map 3a: Advance of XIX Army Corps through the
   Ardennes 93

6. Sketch Map 3b: Advance of XIX Army Corps to the Channel
   Coast 95

7. Sketch Map 4: Battle for the Meuse Crossings. Situation
   13.5–15.5.40 103

8. Sketch Map 5: Battle for the Channel Ports. Situation
   24.5–28/29.5.40 115

9. Sketch Map 6: Break through the Weygand Line to the
   Plateau de Langres. Situation 11.6–15.6.40 . . . 121

10. Sketch Map 7: Break through to the Swiss Border and into
    Upper Alsace. Situation 16.6–20.6.40 131

11. Sketch Map 8: Advance eastwards of Panzer Group
    Guderian. Situation 22.6–28.6.41 155

12. Sketch Map 9: Developments 28.6–2.7.41 163

13. Sketch Map 10: Developments 3.7–10.7.41 165

A*

PAGE

14. Sketch Map 11: Crossing the Dnieper and Smolensk. Situation 11.7–16.7.41 173

15. Sketch Map 12: Elnya. Situation 17.7–20.7.41 . . . 177

16. Sketch Map 13: Roslavl. Situation 30.7–3.8.41 . . . 187

17. Sketch Map 14: Krichev—Miloslavitchi. Situation 9.8.41 . 191

18. Sketch Map 15: Situation on 17.8.41 197

19. Sketch Map 16: Situation on 24.8.41 (Conference with Hitler) 201

20. Sketch Map 17: Situation 26.8.41. Developments to 31.8.41 205

21. Sketch Map 18: The Battle of Kiev. Situation 4.9–14.9.41 . 211

22. Sketch Map 19: Crisis at Romny—Putivl. Situation 18.9.41 217

23. Sketch Map 20: Developments 19.9–22.9.41 221

24. Sketch Map 21: Situation on 23.9.41 223

25. Sketch Map 22: Situation on 30.9.41 229

26. Sketch Map 23: Orel. Situation on 5.10.41 231

27. Sketch Map 24: Situation on 14.10.41 241

28. Sketch Map 25: Advance to Tula. Situation 27.10–14.11.41 243

29. Sketch Map 26: The Battle for Moscow. Situation 1.12–5.12.41 253

30. Sketch Map 27: Developments in the East, 22.2.43–4.3.44 . 305

31. Sketch Map 27a: Operations by 25 Panzer Division, November 1943 321

32. Sketch Map 28: The Destruction of Army Group Centre. Situation 22.6–1.8.44 335

33. Sketch Map 29: Developments in the Baltic States. Situation 23.7–4.10.44 353

34. Sketch Map 30: The Cutting-off of Army Group North. Situation 5.10–25.10.44 357

35. Sketch Map 31: The Loss of Rumania. Situation 16.3–4.10.44 363

36. Sketch Map 32: The Battles in Hungary. Situation 5.10–21.12.44 375

37. Sketch Map 33: The Catastrophe in January 1945. Situation 12.1–25.1.45 391

INTRODUCTION

In the fantasy world of Adolf Hitler's Germany very few General Staff Corps generals received a hero's treatment from Josef Goebbels's propagandists. Fewer still were also sacked by the Führer, only to be reinstated later. One such—and, indeed, the first to receive major public acclaim—was Heinz Guderian. He began to attract public notice in 1937 when his best-selling book about tanks, *Achtung! Panzer!*, was published. It not only established him as a forceful writer and personality, but also made clear that, as the brains behind the newly created *Panzertruppe*, he was a soldier to be reckoned with in any future war. Between September 1939 and November 1941 Guderian's reputation grew further as he displayed colossal verve and brilliant fighting in the campaigns against Poland, France, and Soviet Russia. The striking successes of his blitzkrieg technique not only enhanced his professional standing as a soldier, but also vindicated the revolutionary principles underlying this new type of "lightning" warfare that Guderian had developed and would reaffirm in 1942 with his little-known book, *Mit den Panzern in Ost und West*.

After the war he indelibly recorded for history his role in the Third Reich's rise and fall in *Erinnerungen eines Soldaten* (*Memoirs of a Soldier*), of which *Panzer Leader* is a translation. When first published in Germany, *Erinnerungen* received muted, though fair, notices from the critics, but was read with intense interest by the public. For this was the first book by a general to give authentic insight into the German war effort and campaigns, and into the author's own relations with the High Command and with Hitler. By 1953 it was a bestseller. This edition is but the latest of the many in different languages which have since been published—a clear indication of its enduring value as a standard work of reference.

Panzer Leader is about one man's endeavor, at a moment of institutional change, to defend his country by the modernization of its army. It has no pretensions to being an autobiography, although there are numerous passages which reveal the innermost thoughts and workings of an honest, outspoken patriot of passionate beliefs. Only two pages are allocated to an outline of his life prior to 1922, when he was pitched into a General Staff post with the Inspectorate of Transport Troops. It was an appointment that ideally suited his dynamic, innovative temperament, and one that led him to understand the vital importance of mechanization and the tank in restoring armored mobility for combat troops engaged in maneuver warfare.

Guderian was a modest person who, as I discovered while writing his biography, *Guderian: Panzer General*, was uncomfortable in the glare of publicity. In letters to his wife, this outstanding modern leader (as Field Marshal Kesselring rated him) deprecated the adulation of General Erwin Rommel generated by Goebbels's Propaganda Ministry. As a fervent believer in the rules of the old great General Staff, he adhered to the tradition of "Achieve much, appear little" by maintaining a low profile while a staff officer. Yet, once given command, he was quite unable to suppress his natural charisma and strong opinions when thrusting ahead with revolutionary matters, regardless of controversy and, sometimes, obedience.

Nevertheless, it was the ingrained low profile of the General Staff officer that probably led Guderian in *Panzer Leader* to play down certain fundamental reasons why he was so effective and intuitive an innovator. For unlike many ex-infantry General Staff officers, he was by the end of the First World War (as a result of his training and experience) a technologist. He had trained as a signals specialist; had come to understand air power by flying on reconnaissance missions as an observer; had gained practical experience as a logistician when serving as a supply staff officer; and, as a light infantryman (and the son of one), was ever imbued with the need for quick thinking, speed, and mobility in combat. More than that, as a rapid learner trained to draw conclusions from every fact and opinion, he was impatient with intellects slower than his own. Guderian did not always suffer fools gladly. For example, after the Battle of the Marne in 1914, as a mere 2nd Lieutenant in command of the 5th Cavalry Division's wireless station, he took the divisional commander to task for misemploying his detachment and nearly, incidentally, landing him in a French prisoner-of-war camp!

Guderian was a Prussian who sometimes seemed more Prussian than the Prussians. He was proud, dignified, honorable, kind, and courtly, with a twinkling sense of humor. Major Kenneth Hechler, an American interrogating officer, wrote after the war: "I did not have the feeling that he twisted any of his real opinions in order to say what he felt an American would like to hear. He responded quickly to all the questions and I do not believe that he was trying to make any particular impression or grind an axe."

Hechler's high opinion laid the foundations for *Panzer Leader*. It was he who recommended that, while in captivity between May 1945 and June 1948, Guderian should be an important contributor among the 2,000 or more German officers selected to record their experiences and opinions of Germany's conduct of World War Two. A previous Chief of the General Staff, General Franz Halder, designed this stupendous project as a trilogy dealing with OKH (the Army High Command) as it was; OKH as it should have been; and OKH as it should be. Guderian, the last Chief of the General Staff, and at loggerheads with Halder, was given the task of commenting on the first two parts and running the third. This was an indication of the special regard in which the Americans held him, particularly for his prejudices and pride intermingled with caustic shafts aimed at adversaries. Hundreds of documents, some of considerable length, were compiled to create a remarkable, comprehensive archive. Among the contributors were several who, like Guderian, seized on the opportunity, as a sideline, to assemble material for their own memoirs.

Panzer Leader concentrates on four main themes:

1. The struggle to create and develop the *Panzertruppe* and panzer formations, including the acquisition of good equipment.
2. The brilliant campaigns of 1939, 1940, and 1941.
3. The attempt to rebuild the *Panzertruppe* and the army after the disasters in Russia and North Africa at the start of 1943.
4. The efforts to save Germany, when on the brink of defeat in 1944, by attempting to create conditions for peace on reasonable terms.

Until August 23, 1941, when he was suggested for Army Commander in Chief in place of the weak Field Marshal Werner von Brauchitsch, Guderian's star was very much in the ascendant. He was his own man. When in 1929 he became convinced that tanks in combination with other weapons would revolutionize land warfare, it was from deep studies of history, recent British experiments, and the writings chiefly of British General J. F. C. Fuller; not to the same extent as those of B. H. Liddell Hart, regardless of the third paragraph on page 20 (inserted in the English-language edition of *Panzer Leader* at Liddell Hart's own dogged suggestion) where Guderian acknowledges his "debt" to Liddell Hart.

Throughout the 1930s Guderian worked skillfully and with considerable success, both as a staff officer and a commander, to modernize the army. It was a struggle against conservatism within an organization divided by factions. There were those who could not visualize the psychological and physical effects created by fast-moving armored forces, coordinated by radio and led by a commander from the front. Others feared that an almost defenseless Germany might again be drawn into war and defeated by old enemies from both east and west. Interwoven with the military factions was that other insidious force with which but few generals knew how to cope: the Nazi Party with all its evil militias and ideologies, led by the criminally-minded Adolf Hitler.

From 1933 onwards, the dilemmas posed by that war-loving demagogue dominated Guderian's career. As one among many Germans who yearned for a savior for a nation whose power and influence had lain in the doldrums since 1919, he believed Hitler was the right politician for the job. From 1934 Guderian supported him with special enthusiasm after the demonstration at Kummersdorf, when he managed to convince the Führer of the revolutionary potential of armored forces in battle.

Yet his letters revealed misgivings about a politician who cleverly managed to be all things to all men. Along with the rest of the army, he was compelled to swear a personal oath of allegiance to Hitler on August 2, 1934. Nobody refused (at a mere 48 hours notice were they likely to?), though in a letter to his wife he entered a thoughtful caveat: "The army is accustomed to keep its oath. May the army be able, in honor, to do so this time." Unfortunately, the army's leaders, caught off balance by Hitler's craftiness, had already sold out to him by forfeiting the decisive political power they had once wielded.

The oath posed the most intractable dilemma in the years to come as he contributed strongly to rebuilding an army which, almost unprecedented by 1940, was perfectly designed and trained to overcome every other army in the world. How could he satisfy honor while conducting unprovoked campaigns of aggression with the knowledge that, in the aftermath of each victory, the people of Poland, Yugoslavia, and Soviet Russia were to be treated as inferior and exterminated? Guderian never was comfortable with this problem, so he chose to ignore it. Presented with an opportunity to defy Hitler over a crisis of opinion in Russia in August 1941, he chose to obey on the excuse that it was wrong, by tradition, to oppose a superior officer's resolved decision. Not even after he was sacked for disobeying Hitler's unsound orders in December 1941 would he join the handful of resisters plotting against the Head of State. But, after all, those few Germans who eventually did rebel still held back until it became evident in 1942 that Germany might lose the war.

The third part of the story, the rebuilding of the *Panzertruppe* and the army after Stalingrad, must be seen in the context of the fourth—the attempt to save Germany, on the brink of defeat, from her own excesses. There is very little doubt that by then Guderian saw no hope of victory and had already formulated a resolve to do all he could, within the meaning of the oath of allegiance, to save the nation from extinction. His fortuitous recall in February 1943 to serve as Inspector of Armored Forces, reporting directly to Hitler, presented unique opportunities to pursue that aim.

With that in mind, the remainder of the book should be read as the description of a long, drawn-out, psychological, as well as military, withdrawal, phased to win time for a miraculous salvation—rather in the way Prussia had been saved from defeat in the Seven Years War by the fortuitous withdrawal of Russia in 1762.

How he attempted the virtually impossible is perhaps among the most fascinating passages of *Panzer Leader*. Crisis by crisis, until July 20, 1944, when a handful of blundering plotters failed to blow up Hitler and seize power, he skillfully, but mostly unavailingly, endeavored to divert Hitler from perpetrating heinous errors. He continued deftly to sidestep involvement with the plotters, whom he neither approved of nor had confidence in. Without admitting knowledge of the assassination's imminence, Guderian managed, most uncharacteristically, to be out of contact while taking a long walk around his estate; thus, again without admitting it, he was poised either to side with the plotters if successful or fill a gap if they failed. This is a gray area. Nowhere else in *Panzer Leader* is he so evasive or so far below his normal standards of behavior.

The outcome of this sleight of hand, for which he was later maligned by some Germans, was elevation to Chief of Staff (acting), the one post which, so he hoped, might make possible the achievement of his aim. Might he not "with the Führer's close confidence" be able to tackle the dreaded task of ending the war that Guderian and his wife often discussed as a possibility, even as the enemy drew close to Germany's frontiers on two fronts? Rumors that he had betrayed the plotters were bandied about, but easily disposed of, if only because no general was likely to relish the dangerous nightmare of becoming Chief of Staff to a Commander in Chief who was ferociously hunting down, torturing, and killing generals, or anybody else, remotely suspected of disloyalty.

Throughout the ensuing eight dramatic months Guderian rose to his greatest heights of patriotism and courage by daily opposing Hitler's outrageous decisions. Official records, besides his own testimony, make clear his struggle until in early February 1945 he did what no general had done before—outface Hitler in a (literally) stand-up row over yet another ludicrous order. The unimaginable had happened! With admiration Albert Speer watched Hitler, "with flashing eyes and the hairs on his moustache literally standing on end," being intimidated by Guderian's assault.

Prior to that, however, Guderian had taken his life in his hands by collaborating with Speer in attempting to limit further damage to German industry and by trying to persuade Foreign Minister Joachim von Ribbentrop to end the war by diplomacy before the rest of the country was destroyed. But a terrified Ribbentrop failed him, as did the equally frightened head of the SS, Heinrich Himmler. It was all far too late, of course. But at least Guderian had shown what might have been done if in the early 1930s a general of commanding stature had stood up to Hitler and stopped the Nazi rot before it took hold.

For even at this late hour, one or two among Hitler's sycophants drew courage from Guderian's example, belatedly preventing the last of Hitler's wild excesses. On March 28 a belligerent and still-protesting Guderian escaped with his life when sent on four weeks convalescent leave. It was a clear sign that the last Chief of Staff of the German Army had achieved what no other surviving general had managed. Guderian had actually fought and won the respect of a thoroughly anti-general Supreme Commander, and then outlived the monster to tell his tale with dignity, honesty, and insight.

KENNETH MACKSEY
Dorset, England
April 1996

Kenneth Macksey served as an officer in the Royal Tank Regiment during World War II. The author of more than forty books on military history, including biographies of Field Marshals Kesselring and Rommel and Generals Guderian and Hobart, Macksey has also edited The Penguin Encyclopedia of Modern War, The Penguin Encyclopedia of Weapons and Military Technology, *and* The Hitler Options.

FOREWORD

by

CAPTAIN B. H. LIDDELL HART

In this book a man who has made history—on a great scale—gives us his own story of how he shaped it by means of a new idea, and how it led to an end he had not foreseen. Guderian had a tremendous impact on the course of events in our time. Without him, it is probable that Hitler would have met early frustration in his offensive efforts when he embarked on war. For in 1939–40 Germany's forces in general were not sufficient to overcome any major Power. Her opening run of victory in the Second World War was only made possible by the panzer forces that Guderian had created and trained, *and* by his audacious leading of those forces in disregard of his superiors' caution as well as Hitler's fears. Guderian's break-through at Sedan and lightning drive to the Channel coast virtually decided the issue of the Battle of France.

A year later, the drive he led into the East came close to producing the complete collapse of Russia's armies, but this time renewed hesitancy on top imposed a delay that spun out the campaign until winter intervened, and gave the Russians a breathing-space for recovery. Stalin was able to raise fresh armies and develop new arms factories to replace those that had been captured. Russia's strength went on increasing, while Germany was never again as strong as in that first campaign. Hitler's 1942 effort, though dangerous, was a more limited one than in the previous year. After the failure at Stalingrad the decline of the Germans' power became manifest to all, while America's entry into the war definitely ensured their downfall.

Thus the victories that Guderian had made possible proved more fatal than if no victory had been gained. Early blossom turned into bitter fruit.

He himself had an early foretaste of its juice, since at the end of 1941 he was dismissed for taking a timely step-back instead of pandering to Hitler's illusions. He was recalled to service only when Germany's situation had become desperate, and was eventually made Chief of the General Staff when it had become hopeless. So he was doomed to swallow the full bitterness of the dregs.

That retributive sequel to his work, however, does not affect his historical significance—in the moulding of history by the application of a new idea, of which he was both the exponent and executant. The conquest of the West did not last, but it changed the shape of Europe and has profoundly affected the future of the whole world. That is clear, although we cannot yet tell what will emerge.

Guderian's book is also of great interest as a self-exposition of the specialist mind and how it works. He had far more imagination than most specialists, but it was exercised almost entirely within the bounds of his professional subject, and burning enthusiasm increased the intensity of his concentration.

Guderian was a single-minded soldier, professional in the truest sense—the quintessence of the craftsman in the way he devoted himself to the progress of a technique. In that pursuit he showed as little regard for careerist ambition, and the tact which it requires, as for the purpose such technical progress might serve. To understand him one must be capable of understanding the passion of pure craftsmanship. There one can find a natural explanation of his attitude to Hitler—clearly more favourable than that of most of the generals brought up in the old tradition. Hitler manifested a liking for new military ideas, and for the tank idea in particular, so Guderian was naturally disposed to like him. Hitler showed an inclination to back that revolutionary idea, so Guderian was inclined to back him. Hitler was in conflict with the General Staff and with established conventions; so was Guderian in his sphere—and thus the more ready to think well of Hitler, until disillusioned by what he saw for himself when he eventually came into close contact with the Führer.

It will be apparent to those who read his memoirs that he did not question the cause which he and his troops were serving, or the duty of fighting for their country. It was sufficient for him that she was at war, and thus in danger, however it had come about. The fulfilment of duty was not compatible with doubts. As a dutiful soldier he had to assume that his country's cause was just, and that she was defending herself against would-be conquerors. His evident assumptions on that score may jar on readers outside Germany—conscious of the menace that their countries had to meet, from Germany. But his assumptions are similar to those of most soldiers of any country at any time. Few qualms of conscience are to be found in the memoirs of those who exercised command in the wars for highly questionable causes that Britain and the U.S.A. waged in the nineteenth century. There is a markedly 'Victorian' flavour about Guderian's turn of phrase and thought.

Moreover, soldiers everywhere are accustomed to accept the time-honoured dictum that 'attack is the best defence,' so that they become apt to regard the difference between attack and defence as a tactical

distinction between two interchangeable forms of action, with little
or no bearing on the question of aggression. The greatest experts in the
field of international law have found it difficult to frame an irrefutable
definition of aggression, and aggressively minded statesmen have always
found it easy to shift the blame on to the shoulders of their foreign
opponents. An appeal to patriotism can befog the clearest issue, and
those who are most imbued with the sense of duty to country are, and
are bound to be, the easiest to deceive and to silence. Soldiers are not
trained to explore the truth behind international disputes, and if they
try to wrestle with the resulting questions they are likely to become
incapable of performing their task. There is a place, and a need, for the
military philosopher in the study and guidance of war, but a profoundly
reflective mind does not fit easily into the service itself.

As a practical necessity a commander in the field often has to take
action without reflection, and, even when he has the time for it, a habit
of reflecting on the remote consequences of the action ordered would
tend to induce paralysis—save in a man with the most uncommon
power of detachment (Wellington was one of these rare exceptions).
So long as fighting services continue, it is essential for the performance
of their task that they should be composed of those who confine their
thinking to the effective execution of that task. 'Theirs not to reason
why, theirs but to do and die.' No nation that maintains fighting
services can afford to revoke that rule of experience. Where soldiers
begin to question the rightness of the cause for which they are fighting,
armies soon collapse.

It is easy to condemn Guderian's attitude as evidence of 'unrepentant
militarism'—but wiser to recognise that his basic assumptions were a
necessity of military service. That he makes no pretence of discarding
them now, to court favour, is typical of his brusque honesty—which so
often brought him in conflict with his superiors, and with Hitler—as
well as of the pugnacity that made him such a dynamic military reformer
and commander.

Anyone who is 'put off' Guderian's memoirs by dislike of his attitude
will be foolish—as were those superiors who let irritation prejudice
them against the value of his military ideas. This book is the fullest,
most factual, and most revealing personal account of the war from the
German side that has yet emerged. The fullness of detail, which is
valuable for the record, is lightened in the reading by the vigour and
frankness of the comment.

Guderian's revelations, in the opening chapters, about the opposition
he met in developing the panzer forces and the blitzkrieg technique will
come as a surprise to many readers here who have a picture of the
German General Staff as a far-sighted and united body of planners

ceaselessly seeking to get a march ahead in preparation for the next war. (What he reveals will be less unexpected to those who know the nature of armies and their halting course throughout history.)

His story of the 1940 campaign not only brings out the hazards and uncertainties of the assault on the Meuse near Sedan, but conveys the pace and tempo of the follow-up drive to the Channel coast. It is almost like having a seat in Guderian's car in that breathless race, and being able to watch him handling his panzer divisions. For me it was like the repetition of a dream, as it was just the way that in pre-war years I had pictured such a force being handled by a leader who grasped the new idea—only to be told, then, that the picture was unrealistic. When Hobart gave a demonstration of it in the 1934 exercises on Salisbury Plain, orthodox soldiers retorted that such a method would not work in war.

Guderian's account of the 1941 advance into Russia provides by far the most detailed account yet available of that invasion. If the detail tends to slow down the tempo, his revelations about the conflicts within the German Command are very illuminating, and his picture of the ghastly final stages of the winter push for Moscow in mud and snow is extraordinarily vivid. Then comes the story of his own dismissal, and recall in 1943 to reorganise the panzer forces after the Stalingrad disaster. In the later chapters he throws new light on the breakdown of the plans to meet the Allied landing in Normandy.

When the situation became desperate he was summoned to take over the post of Chief of the General Staff, a post which was by that time limited to dealing with the Eastern Front, and further restricted by Hitler's desire to control everything himself. While these limitations of function left Guderian little scope for effective influence, his appointment gave him ample opportunity for close observation of Hitler's mind and emotions during the last stage of the war. Nothing could be more dramatic than his sober account of the disintegration of a demented dictator and a demoralised entourage. Guderian completes the story with character-sketches of Hitler and the other 'Leading Personalities of the Third Reich'—and that chapter is the most interesting of all.

The acuteness and balance of these character sketches is notable. Those qualities may owe much to a characteristic of his which does not often appear directly in the book, but which strikes anyone who meets him—his sense of humour. It is the more refreshing because it is uncommon in his circle.

Although Guderian could do little to check the downslide he had done enough earlier, when in a nominally lower position, to establish his military fame for all time. With men of action, the place they fill in history is usually determined by the extent to which they have shaped history. Guderian's achievements—his effect on the Second World War, and on warfare—put him on the top level as a soldier. Although he never enjoyed the nominal qualification of independent command, he applied the idea of the independent use of armoured forces so fully and decisively that he brought about victories which, measured by any standard, have hardly been matched in the records of warfare.

It is clear, too, that he possessed most of the qualities that distinguished the 'Great Captains' of history—*coup d'œil*, a blend of acute observation with swift-sure intuition; the ability to create surprise and throw the opponent off balance; the speed of thought and action that allows the opponent no chance of recovery; the combination of strategic and tactical sense; the power to win the devotion of troops, and get the utmost out of them. It is not so clear, because of differing evidence, whether he had another of the classic qualities: a sense of what is possible. But Guderian had an amazing knack of making 'the impossible' possible.

Beyond these qualities Guderian had creative imagination—the basic characteristic of genius, in the military sphere as well as in others. Most of the recognised masters of the art of war have been content to use the familiar tools and technique of their time. Only a few set out to provide themselves with new means and methods. Developments in weapons have usually been due to some 'outside' inventor, often a civilian. Developments in tactics have usually been due to some original military thinker and his gradually spreading influence on progressive-minded officers of the rising generation. Innovators have rarely had the chance to put into practice themselves the theories they have expounded. Guderian, however, was able to gain that opportunity. And as he coupled creative imagination with dynamic energy he was able to exploit the opportunity—with revolutionary results.

1. BACKGROUND AND YOUTH

I first saw the light of day at Kulm on the Vistula, one Sunday morning, the 17th of June, 1888. My father, Friedrich Guderian, was at that time Senior Lieutenant in the 2nd Pomeranian Jaeger Battalion: he had been born on the 3rd of August, 1858, at Gross-Klonia in the district of Tuchel. My mother, *née* Clara Kirchhoff, was born on the 26th of February, 1865, at Niemczyk in the district of Kulm. Both my grandfathers were landed gentry and, for so far back as I can trace my family, all my ancestors were either landowners or lawyers in the Warthegau or in East or West Prussia. My father was the only regular army officer to whom I was at all closely related.

On the 2nd of October, 1890, my brother Fritz was born.

In 1891 my father's military duties took him to Colmar, in Alsace, and from the age of six, until his transfer to Saint-Avold in Lorraine in 1900, I attended school there. Saint-Avold, however, is too small to boast a high school of its own, so my parents had to send us away to boarding school. My father's limited means, and the expressed wishes of both his sons to become officers, made him choose a cadet school for our further education. So my brother and I were sent to the Karlsruhe cadet school in Baden, on April 1st, 1901, where l remained until the 1st of April, 1903, on which date I was transferred to the chief cadet school at Gross-Lichterfelde, near Berlin, my brother following me thither two years later. In February of 1907 I took my final examinations, the *Reifeprüfung*. When I remember my instructors and teachers from these formative years it is with emotions of deep gratitude and respect. Our education in the cadet corps was of course one of military austerity and simplicity. But it was founded on kindness and justice. Our course of studies was based on that of the up-to-date civilian schools, the *Realgymnasium*, the main emphasis being on modern languages, mathematics and history. This provided a good preparation for life, and the standards reached by the cadets were in no way inferior to those of similar civilian institutions.

In February 1907 I was sent, as ensign-cadet, *Fähnrich*, to the 10th Hanoverian Jaeger Battalion at Bitche in Lorraine, which my father commanded until December 1908. This was a stroke of good fortune, since I could now once again enjoy the pleasures of living in my parents' home after my six years' absence at the cadet schools. After attending the War School at Metz from April to December 1907 I was commissioned Second Lieutenant on the 27th of January, 1908, with seniority as of the 22nd of June, 1906. From then, until the beginning of the First World War, I lived the happy life of a junior officer. On October 1st, 1909, our Jaeger Battalion was sent to its home district, the province of Hanover, and was employed on garrison duty at Goslar in the Harz mountains. It was there that I became engaged to Margarete Goerne, my dear wife. We were married on October 1st, 1913, and she has been a true helpmate to me ever since, sharing with me all the pleasures and the pains of a long, eventful, and by no means always easy military career.

Our newly found happiness was rudely interrupted by the outbreak of war on August the 2nd, 1914, and during the next four years it was only very occasionally that I managed to spend a short leave with my wife and our little family. On August 23rd, 1914, God gave us a son, Heinz Günter, and on the 17th of September, 1918, a second son, Kurt.

My dear father died at the beginning of the war as the result of a serious operation that he had had to undergo the previous May and that had necessitated his leaving the service as physically unfit. With his death I lost a man whom I regarded as a model of soldierly and human virtue. My mother survived him for over sixteen years. She departed this life in March of 1931 after a life filled with kindness and love.

When the armistice of 1918 was signed I participated in frontier defence in the East, first in Silesia and later in the Baltic States. At the end of this book will be found a detailed list of my various military appointments together with relevant facts concerning my personal life. From this it can be seen that my career up to 1922 alternated between regimental and staff duties, that I was by training an infantry man, but that an attachment to the 3rd Telegraph Battalion at Koblenz and an assignment involving work with radio during the early months of the First World War enabled me to acquire a certain knowledge of signal matters which was to stand me in good stead in the years to come when I was to be engaged in building up a new arm of the service.

2. THE CREATION OF THE GERMAN ARMOURED FORCE

My main activity during the period between the two wars was connected with the creation of a German armoured force. Although originally a Jaeger (light infantry) officer and without any technical training, I was destined to find myself deeply involved in the problem of motorisation.

After returning from the Baltic in the autumn of 1919, I was for a short time employed with the 10th Reichswehr Brigade at Hanover. In January of 1920 I was given command of a company in my old Jaeger Battalion at Goslar. I had no thought at that time of returning to General Staff work, on which I had been engaged until January 1920; in the first place, my departure from the Baltic had been in circumstances not of the happiest, and, in the second, the small size of the 100,000-man army made any rapid advancement extremely unlikely. I was therefore all the more surprised when, in the autumn of 1921, my deeply respected regimental commander, Colonel von Amsberg, asked me if I felt any inclination to go back to General Staff duty. I replied that I did, but for a long time I heard nothing more on the subject. It was not until January 1922 that Lieutenant-Colonel Joachim von Stülpnagel telephoned me from the *Truppenamt* (the General Staff of the Army) of the Defence Ministry (*RWM*) in Berlin to ask why I had not yet reported to Munich. I learned from him that I was to be transferred to the Inspectorate of Transport Troops, Motorised Transport Department, since the Inspector, General von Tschischwitz, had requested the assignment of a General Staff officer to his staff. My transfer was to become effective on April 1st, but it was considered advisable for me to acquire some practical knowledge of regimental duty with transport troops before taking up my staff appointment, and I was therefore to be attached at once to the 7th (Bavarian) Motorised Transport Battalion, Munich; I was to leave immediately.

Delighted with my new job, I set off and reported in Munich to the battalion commander, Major Lutz. In the years to come I was to work closely with this officer, for whom I was to have great respect and who was always most helpful and kind in his attitude towards me. I was stationed in Munich and assigned to the 1st Company, which was at that time commanded by Wimmer, an ex-air force officer who was later to fly again. Major Lutz explained to me on arrival that I was eventually to work at the Ministry in connection with the organisation and employment of motorised transport troops. My activities in Munich were to be primarily a preparation for this assignment. Major Lutz and Captain Wimmer did all they could to teach me something about their branch of the service, and I learned a great deal.

On April 1st, 1922, I reported to General von Tschischwitz in Berlin, very keen to receive his instructions concerning my new General Staff duties. He explained that he had originally intended to assign me the employment of motorised transport troops as my field of work. But meanwhile his Chief of Staff, Major Petter, had ordered otherwise: I was to be engaged on the problems of M.T. workshops, fuel depots, constructional work, and technical officials, my duties ultimately to include also road and other communication facilities. I was astonished by this and I informed the general that I was in no way prepared for such primarily technical work and that I did not believe that I had sufficient specialist knowledge of these subjects for employment at the Ministry. General von Tschischwitz replied that he had originally wished to employ me along the lines of which Major Lutz had spoken to me. His Chief of Staff, however, had produced an order of procedure originating from the Royal Prussian War Ministry, dated 1873 and of course amplified by a small pile of amendments and corrections; the Chief of Staff had pointed out that according to this document it was the responsibility of the Chief of Staff and not of the Inspector to decide on the employment of Staff Officers; the Inspector therefore regretted that he was unable to effect any alteration to his Chief of Staff's instruction; he would, however, do his best to ensure that I participate in the studies that he had planned. I requested that I be returned to my Jaeger company: my request was refused.

So there I was, embarked on a technical career in which I must try to find my way about. Apart from a few documents in his pending tray, my predecessor had left nothing worth mentioning behind. My sole support consisted of a number of elderly employees of the Ministry who knew their way about the files, who understood how our business was transacted and who did their best to help me. My work was certainly instructive and what I learned in that office was to be useful to me later on. However, its principal value consisted in a study undertaken by General von Tschischwitz concerning the transport of troops by motorised vehicles. As a result of this study, which had been preceded by a small practical exercise in the Harz, I became for the first time aware of the possibility of employing motorised troops, and I was thus compelled to form my own opinions on this subject. General von Tschischwitz was a highly critical superior; he noticed the slightest mistakes, and he laid great stress on accuracy. Working for him was good training.

During the First World War there had been very many examples of
the transport of troops by motorised vehicles. Such troop movements
had always taken place behind a more or less static front line; they
had never been used directly against the enemy in a war of movement.
Germany now was undefended, and it therefore seemed improbable
that any new war would start in the form of positional warfare behind
fixed fronts. We must rely on mobile defence in case of war. The
problem of the transport of motorised troops in mobile warfare soon
raised the question of the protection of such transports. This could only
be satisfactorily provided by armoured vehicles. I therefore looked for
precedents from which I might learn about the experiments that had
been made with armoured vehicles. This brought me in touch with
Lieutenant Volckheim, who was then engaged in collating information
concerning the very limited use of German armoured vehicles, and the
incomparably greater employment of enemy tank forces during the
war, as a staff study for our little army. He provided me with a certain
amount of literature on the subject; though weak in theory it gave me
something to go on. The English and French had had far greater
experience in this field and had written much more about it. I got hold
of their books and I learned.

It was principally the books and articles of the Englishmen, Fuller,
Liddell Hart and Martel, that excited my interest and gave me food for
thought. These far-sighted soldiers were even then trying to make of
the tank something more than just an infantry support weapon. They
envisaged it in relationship to the growing motorisation of our age,
and thus they became the pioneers of a new type of warfare on the
largest scale.

I learned from them the concentration of armour, as employed in
the battle of Cambrai. Further, it was Liddell Hart who emphasised the
use of armoured forces for long-range strokes, operations against the
opposing army's communications, and also proposed a type of armoured
division combining panzer and panzer-infantry units. Deeply impressed
by these ideas I tried to develop them in a sense practicable for our
own army. So I owe many suggestions of our further development to
Captain Liddell Hart.

In the country of the blind, the one-eyed man is king. Since nobody
else busied himself with this material, I was soon by way of being an
expert. A few small articles that I contributed to the *Militär-Wochenblatt*
('The Military Weekly') served to enhance my reputation: its editor,
General von Altrock, visited me frequently and encouraged me to
write more on the subject. He was a first-class soldier and was anxious
that his paper should publish material dealing with contemporary
problems.

These activities also brought me the acquaintance of the Austrian, Fritz Heigl, the author of the *Taschenbuch der Tanks* ('The Handbook of the Tank'). I was able to supply him with a certain amount of information concerning tactical matters, and I learned to value him as an upright German gentleman.

During the winter of 1923–24 Lieutenant-Colonel von Brauchitsch, who was later to be Commander-in-Chief of the Army, organised manœuvres to test the possibilities of employing motorised troops in co-operation with aeroplanes: this exercise attracted the attention of the Army Training Department, and resulted in my being proposed as an instructor in tactics and military history. After passing a test, I was sent on a so-called 'instructor's tour of duty.' As part of this tour I was assigned, in the autumn of 1924, to the staff of the 2nd Division at Stettin, now under General von Tschischwitz, who thus became my commanding officer for the second time.

Before going there, however, I had been responsible, under Colonel von Natzmer, Tschischwitz's successor as Inspector, for a whole series of exercises, both on the ground and on paper, intended to explore the possibilities of the employment of tanks, particularly for reconnaissance duties in connection with cavalry. All we had for these purposes were the 'armoured troop carriers,' a clumsy vehicle which the Versailles Treaty had allowed us to keep. It was provided with a four-wheel drive, but owing to its weight it was to all intents and purposes road-bound. I was satisfied with the results of my exercises, and in a closing address I expressed the hope that as a result of our efforts we were on the way to transforming our motorised units from supply troops into combat troops. My inspector, however, held a contrary opinion, and informed me bluntly: 'To hell with combat! They're supposed to carry flour!' And that was that.

So I set off for Stettin in order to instruct the officers destined for future staff work in tactics and military history. My new post entailed a great deal of work; my audiences, too, were highly critical in their attitude, so that the exercises I set them had to be very thoroughly thought out, the solutions most carefully considered, and the lectures I gave clear and thorough. So far as the military history went, I concentrated on Napoleon's 1806 campaign, a campaign which in Germany at least had never received the attention it deserved, doubtless on account of the painful German defeat in which it culminated; as regards the command of troops in conditions of mobile warfare it is, however, a very instructive campaign. I also dealt with the history of the German and French army cavalry in the autumn of 1914. This thorough study of cavalry tactics in 1914 was to prove very useful to the development of my theories which were becoming ever increasingly preoccupied with the tactical and operational[1] use of movement.

Since I had frequent opportunities to propound my ideas in tactical exercises and war games, my immediate superior, Major Höring, became aware of them and referred to these interests of mine in his report on me. As a result of this I was, after three years as an instructor, transferred back to the War Ministry, where I was assigned to the Transport Department of the *Truppenamt* under Colonel Halm, later under Lieutenant-Colonels Wäger and Kühne, and which at that time formed part of the Operations Department. My post had been newly created: I was to deal with the subject of troop transportation by lorry. Indeed that was then all we had at our disposal. My studies along these lines soon made plain the difficulties involved in troop movements of this sort. It is true that the French, particularly in the First World War, had achieved great successes in this field—for example at Verdun— but then their problem had been one of movement behind the cover of a more or less static front: in such conditions a division does not need to have all its horse-drawn and mechanised transport immediately available, and notably not its artillery transports. But in mobile warfare, when the whole of a division's equipment including its artillery horses would have to be loaded on lorries, the number required would be enormous. There were many heated discussions of this problem, and more sceptics than believers in the possibility of finding a workable solution.

In the autumn of 1928 I was approached by Colonel Stottmeister, of the M.T. Instructional Staff, with the request that I teach his people something about tank tactics. My superiors approved my undertaking this additional activity. So I returned to my preoccupation with tanks, though still only from the theoretical angle. I was totally lacking in all practical experience of tanks; at that time I had never even seen the inside of one. And now I was supposed to give instruction about them. This required first of all the most careful preparation and a detailed study of the material available. Literature dealing with the last war was by now available in great quantities and in foreign armies considerable subsequent developments had taken place which were already apparent from their service manuals.[2] This made the study of tank theory an easier task than it had been when first I was employed at the War Ministry. So far as practical experience went we had at first to rely on

[1] There is no true English equivalent to the German military concept of which the adjective is *operativ*, and which might be described as lying mid-way between the *tactical* and the *strategic*. I have translated it as *operational* throughout this work.—*Tr.*

[2] The current English handbook on armoured fighting vehicles was translated into German and for many years served as the theoretical manual for our developing ideas.

exercises carried out with dummies: originally these had been canvas dummies pushed about by men on foot, but now at least they were motorised dummies of sheet metal. Thus we did manage to have tactical exercises with our dummies, thanks to the willing help of Lieutenant-Colonels Busch and Liese and the IIIrd (Spandau) Battalion of the 9th Infantry Regiment which they successively commanded. It was during these exercises that I made the acquaintance of a man with whom I was later to work very closely, Wenck, who was then Adjutant of IIIrd Battalion, 9th Infantry Regiment. We set to work systematically and explored the possibilities of the tank as a unit, of the tank platoon, the tank company and the tank battalion.

Limited though our chances of practical exercises might be, they yet sufficed to give us a gradually clearer appreciation of the prospects of the tank in modern warfare. I was particularly delighted when I was sent to Sweden for four weeks and had the opportunity there to see the latest German tank, the LK II, in action, and even to drive it myself. (The German LK II was manufactured towards the end of World War I, but was not used at the front during the war. The components of this tank were sold to Sweden and formed the first Swedish tank unit in 1918.)

My wife and I went to Sweden by way of Denmark, where we passed a few interesting days in Copenhagen and its lovely surroundings. We were deeply impressed by the beauty of Thorwaldsen's sculpture. And standing on the terrace at Elsinore we could not but recall Hamlet

There are more things in heaven and earth, Horatio,
Than are dreamt of in your philosophy.

Be that as it may, when we stood on that terrace while the sunshine glittered on the straits and made the old bronze cannons glow green, no ghost appeared.

We went by ship from Motala through the Gota canal and the Swedish lakes. One night we left the ship to visit the beautiful old monastery at Vreta Chyrka. The next day Stockholm lay before us with its beautiful buildings, the Venice of the North, a proud sight.

I was assigned to the Strijdsvagn Battalion, the IInd Battalion of the Gota Guards, and the commander, Colonel Burén, gave me a most friendly welcome. I was to be with the company commanded by Captain Klingspor, an officer with whom I soon struck up a close friendship which was to last until the day of his death. The Swedish officers whom I got to know adopted a frank and amiable attitude towards their German guests. Their hospitality was offered to us as something to be taken for granted. When we were out on exercises we were invited to share their quarters in the friendliest possible way.

I shall always remember with pleasure and gratitude the lovely and instructive time that I was fortunate enough to spend in Sweden.

In this year, 1929, I became convinced that tanks working on their own or in conjunction with infantry could never achieve decisive importance. My historical studies, the exercises carried out in England and our own experiences with mock-ups had persuaded me that tanks would never be able to produce their full effect until the other weapons on whose support they must inevitably rely were brought up to their standard of speed and of cross-country performance. In such a formation of all arms, the tanks must play the primary role, the other weapons being subordinated to the requirements of the armour. It would be wrong to include tanks in infantry divisions: what was needed were armoured divisions which would include all the supporting arms needed to allow the tanks to fight with full effect.

During the summer field exercises without troops of 1929, I based one exercise on the employment of part of one of these imaginary armoured divisions. The exercise was a success, and I was convinced that I was on the right track. But the Inspector of Transport Troops, who was now General Otto von Stülpnagel, forbade the theoretical employment of tanks in units of greater than regimental strength. It was his opinion that Panzer Divisions were a Utopian dream.

In the autumn of 1929 the Chief of Staff to the Inspectorate of Motorised Troops, my old friend from Munich days, Colonel Lutz, asked me if I would like to command a motorised battalion. I said I would and on the 1st of February, 1931, I was given the 3rd (Prussian) Motorised Battalion at Berlin-Lankwitz. This battalion consisted of four companies: Nos. 1 and 4 were with the battalion staff at Berlin-Lankwitz, No. 2 was at the military training area Döberitz-Elsgrund, No. 3 was at Neisse. No. 4 Company had been formed from a squadron of the 3rd Horse Transport Battalion. As soon as I had taken up my command, Colonel Lutz helped me to re-equip my unit: No. 1 Company was given armoured reconnaissance cars and No. 4 was equipped with motor-cycles, so that together they provided the nucleus of an Armoured Reconnaissance Battalion. No. 2 Company received dummy tanks, and No. 3 at Neisse was reorganised as an anti-tank company, again with dummy weapons, in this case wooden guns. It is true that No. 1 Company did possess a complement of the old armoured troop-carrying vehicles that the Treaty of Versailles had allowed us to keep, but in order not to wear them out we used dummies on exercises. Only the motor-cycle company had its proper equipment and was armed with machine guns.

With this very improvised unit I now proceeded to concentrate on field exercises. I was delighted at long last to be my own master, even though my command was such a small one. Both officers and other ranks took to their new tasks with enthusiasm, and doubtless these provided welcome relief after the day-by-day monotony of serving as supply troops in the 100,000-man army. My superiors, however, were less encouraging. The Inspector of Transport Troops, indeed, had so little faith in this new unit that he forbade us to carry out combined exercises with other battalions stationed in the area. When the 3rd Division, of which we formed a part, went on manœuvres, we were not allowed to be employed in units of over platoon strength. An exception in our favour was made, it is true, by the commander of the 3rd Division, General Joachim von Stülpnagel, the same officer who years before had telephoned me about my appointment in Munich. This outstanding general officer was interested in what we were attempting to do and was kindly disposed towards us. He helped us a great deal. His sense of fair play made him insist on just criticism of our efforts after exercises were over. Unfortunately, in the spring of 1931, General von Stülpnagel decided to retire from the Army as a result of a disagreement with the War Ministry.

In that same spring our Inspector, General Otto von Stülpnagel, left us as well. His parting words to me were: 'You're too impetuous. Believe me, neither of us will ever see German tanks in operation in our lifetime.' He was a clever man, but his scepticism was a hindrance to him and stopped him from acting with all the determination of which he was capable. He could recognise problems but could not find the point of departure from which to set about solving them.

He was succeeded by his former Chief of Staff, General Lutz. He too was a clever man with great technical knowledge and brilliant powers of organisation. He recognised the advantages of the new tactical developments for which I was struggling, and he took my side entirely. He made me his Chief of Staff, and in the autumn of 1931 I took up my new appointment. There followed years of hard work and, at times, of considerable stress, but years that were after all to prove highly fruitful. This was the time when our armoured force was brought into existence.

We were quite convinced that the future development of our armoured troops must be directed at making them into an operationally decisive weapon. They must, therefore, be organised in the form of Panzer Divisions and later of Panzer Corps. Now the problem was to persuade the other arms of the service and the Commander-in-Chief of the Army that our way was the correct way. This was difficult since no one then believed that the motorised troops—who were only service troops, after all—were capable of producing new and fruitful ideas in the tactical and even the operational field. The older arms of the service, particularly the infantry and cavalry, regarded themselves as the most important elements of the army. The infantry still considered itself to be 'the queen of battle.' Since the 100,000-man army was not allowed to possess tanks, nobody had actually seen these weapons of which we spoke so highly: and when we appeared on manœuvres with our sheet-metal dummies, these wretched mock-ups struck the old soldiers from the First World War as so utterly ridiculous that they tended to feel sorry for us and were certainly not inclined to take us seriously. The result of all this was that while they were quite prepared to accept tanks as infantry support weapons, they would not agree to the concept of the tank as a new principal arm of the service.

Our main adversary was the Inspectorate of Cavalry. My general enquired of the cavalrymen whether in their future development they envisaged their role as one of reconnaissance troops for other units or whether they were planning to organise as heavy cavalry, prepared to fight battles on its own. The Inspector of Cavalry, General von Hirschberg, replied that heavy cavalry was envisaged. He was willing to hand over the job of operational reconnaissance to the motorised troops. We thereupon decided to train our Panzer Reconnaissance Battalions for this task. Apart from this we were striving for the creation of Panzer Divisions in which to employ our tanks. Finally, we wished to see the establishment of a Motorised Anti-Tank Battalion in every Infantry Division, because we were convinced that in order to be effective against tanks, anti-tank weapons must be capable of equal speed and mobility.

General von Hirschberg, however, was succeeded by General Knochenhauer, who came from the infantry, and this officer proved unwilling to regard as lost the ground which his predecessor had already surrendered to us. Out of the three Cavalry Divisions in the 100,000-man army he built up a Cavalry Corps, and he attempted to make operational reconnaissance once again the responsibility of the cavalry, which would result in his taking over our new invention. With this purpose in mind our young units were to be impregnated by an invasion of cavalry officers. The arguments often became extremely heated. But finally the creators of the fresh ideas won their battle against the reactionaries; the combustion engine defeated the horse; and the cannon, the lance.

Equal in importance to organisation and employment was the problem of the equipment which would enable us to abandon the theoretical for the practical. A certain amount of preparatory work had been done on the technical side. Since 1926 a testing station had been in existence abroad where new German tanks could be tried out.

The Army Ordnance Office had given contracts to various firms for the production of two types of medium and three of light tanks—as they were then classified. Two specimens of each type were produced, so that there was a total of ten tanks in existence. The mediums were armed with a 75 mm., the light tanks with a 37 mm. gun. These specimens were not built of armour plate but of mild steel. The maximum speed of all these types was approximately 12 miles per hour.

The officer responsible for this production, Captain Pirner, had taken pains to include a number of modern requirements in the new models, including gas-proofing, a good engine-efficiency rate, an all-round field of fire both for the turret gun and for the machine-guns, a sufficiently high ground-clearance, and excellent manœuvrability. He had to a great extent succeeded in achieving all this. On the other hand one great disadvantage was that the tank commander had to sit in the body of the tank, next to the driver, whence he had of course no field of vision whatever towards the rear and that towards the sides was partially blocked by the forward ends of the tracks and further limited by his low position in relationship to the ground. Wireless equipment was not yet available. So although tank construction in the 'twenties was marked by great technical improvements over the tanks built during the First World War, it was still inadequate to fill the tactical requirements of the tanks to be employed in the new role which we had envisaged for them. It was not possible simply to order the mass-production of the experimental models then available. The construction of new models was essential.

Our opinion then was that for the eventual equipment of Panzer Divisions we would need two types of tank: a light tank with an armour-piercing gun and two machine-guns, one in the turret and the other in the body: and a medium tank with a large calibre gun, and two machine-guns as before. The light tanks would equip the three light companies of the tank battalion: the medium tanks would enable the medium company of the battalion to perform its dual role of, first, supporting the light tanks in action, and, secondly, of shooting at targets out of range of the light tanks' smaller calibre guns. We had differences of opinion on the subject of gun calibre with the Chief of the Ordnance Office and with the Inspector of Artillery. Both these gentlemen were of the opinion that a 37 mm. gun would suffice for the light tanks, while I was anxious that they be equipped with a 50 mm. weapon since this would give them the advantage over the heavier armour plate which we expected soon to see incorporated in the construction of foreign tanks. Since, however, the infantry was already being equipped with 37 mm. anti-tank guns, and since for reasons of productive simplicity it was not considered desirable to produce more than one type of light anti-tank gun and shell, General Lutz and I had to give in. A gun of 75 mm. calibre was agreed on for the mediums. The total weight of this tank was not to exceed 24 tons. The limiting factor here was the carrying capacity of the German road bridges. The speed requirement was settled at 25 m.p.h. The crew of each type of tank was to consist of five men; the gunner, loader and tank commander in the turret (the commander to sit above the gunner and to be provided with a special small command turret with all-round field of vision), the driver and wireless operator in the body of the tank. The crew would receive their orders by means of larynx microphones. Facilities for wireless communication from tank to tank that would function while the tanks were in motion were to be installed. A comparison of these constructional demands with previous requirements as exemplified by the tank models then in existence will show the changes necessitated by the newly envisaged tactical and operational role that tanks were to play.

When we drew up these long-range plans we were well aware that years must pass before our new tanks would be ready for action. In the meantime we had to build a training tank. The Carden-Loyd chassis, which we purchased in England, was suited to this purpose; it was actually intended as a carrier for a 20 mm. anti-aircraft gun. It was true that nothing larger than machine-guns could be mounted in any turret that this vehicle could carry. But with this disadvantage, it could be made ready for action by 1934 and it would at least serve as a training tank until our real combat tanks began to appear. So the supply of this item of equipment, which was designated the Panzer I, was ordered. Nobody in 1932 could have guessed that one day we should have to go into action with this little training tank.

Production difficulties of the main types of tank which we had ordered dragged on longer than we had originally hoped. In consequence General Lutz decided on a second stop-gap: this was the Panzer II, equipped with a 20 mm. gun and one machine-gun, and manufactured by the MAN company.

During the summer of 1932 General Lutz for the first time organised exercises involving both reinforced infantry regiments and tank battalions—the latter, of course, equipped with dummies—at the training areas of Grafenwöhr and Jüterbog. For the first time since the signing of the Treaty of Versailles there appeared at that year's manœuvres German armoured reconnaissance cars built, according to our specifications, of steel armour plate mounted on the chassis of a six-wheel lorry. School children, accustomed to stick their pencils through the canvas walls of our dummies in order to have a look at the inside, were disappointed this time; so, too, were the infantrymen who usually defended themselves against our 'tanks' with sticks and stones and who now found themselves ruled out of action by the despised panzers. Even the bayonet was proved to be an ineffective weapon against armoured fighting vehicles.

During these manœuvres the possibility of operations by armoured and motorised units was put to the test. There was considerable unobjective criticism on the part of the cavalry, but our success was so obvious that not much notice was taken of this petulance. Indeed many of the more wideawake and younger cavalry officers began to show keen interest in this new development; and numbers of them came over to our side—realising that in our day and age the true and tried principles of cavalry warfare were only still valid if the cavalry were equipped with new weapons and methods.

The 1932 manœuvres were the last at which the aged Field-Marshal von Hindenburg was present. During the critical discussion after they were over he made a short speech, and I was amazed at the clarity with which the old gentleman pointed out the mistakes that had been made. Mentioning the leadership of the Cavalry Corps, the old gentleman had this to say: 'In war only what is simple can succeed. I visited the staff of the Cavalry Corps. What I saw there was not simple.' He was quite right.

In 1933 Hitler became Chancellor and both the external and internal politics of the Reich were entirely changed. I saw and heard Hitler for the first time at the opening of the Berlin Automobile Exhibition, at the beginning of February. It was unusual for the Chancellor himself to open the exhibition. And what he had to say was in striking contrast to the customary speeches of Ministers and Chancellors on such occasions. He announced the abolition of the tax on cars and spoke of the new national roads that were to be built and of the *Volkswagen*, the cheap 'People's Car,' that was to be mass-produced.

The appointment of General von Blomberg as War Minister and of General von Reichenau as Chief of the Ministerial Office (*Chef des Ministeramtes*) was to have an immediate effect on my work. Both these generals favoured modern ideas, and so I now found considerable sympathy for the ideas of the armoured force, at least at the highest levels of the *Wehrmacht* (the Armed Forces). In addition, it soon became apparent that Hitler himself was interested in the problem of motorisation and armour. The first proof I had of this was at Kummersdorf, where a meeting was held under the aegis of the Army Ordnance Office to demonstrate recent weapon development: I was allotted half an hour in which to show the Chancellor the position as far as motorised troops were concerned. I was able to demonstrate a motor-cycle platoon, an anti-tank platoon, a platoon of Panzer I's in the experimental form of the time, and one platoon of light and one of heavy armoured reconnaissance cars. Hitler was much impressed by the speed and precision of movement of our units, and said repeatedly: 'That's what I need! That's what I want to have!' As a result of this demonstration I was convinced that the head of the government would approve my proposals for the organisation of an up-to-date *Wehrmacht*, if only I could manage to lay my views before him. The rigidity of procedure in our army, and the opposition of the persons in authority over me—the General Staff Officers who stood between Blomberg and me—were the principal obstacle to this plan.

Incidentally, it is an interesting sidelight on German politics since 1890 that Prince Bismarck was the last Chancellor who had shown sufficient interest in the development of military equipment to pay a visit to Kummersdorf; from then, until this visit of Hitler's, no Chancellor had ever taken the trouble to set foot inside the place. The visitors' book of the Army Ordnance Office proved this when the Head of that Office, General Becker, asked Hitler for his signature. This surely makes it plain that German policy had not been 'militaristic.'

On the 21st of March, 1933, the Reichstag was opened with a religious service in the Garrison Church at Potsdam.

The state ceremony in the Garrison Church was followed, on the 23rd of March, 1933, by the notorious Authorisation Act, which was passed with the approval of the 'National Front' and the Central Party and which gave the new Chancellor full dictatorial powers. With laudable courage the Social-Democrat Party voted against this bill; few politicians realised at the time what misfortunes the Act was to cause in years to come. The politicians who voted for the Authorisation Act cannot escape the responsibility for what was later to happen.

In the summer of 1933 the head of the National-Socialist Motor Corps, Adolf Hühnlein, invited me to a festive meeting of the leaders of his organisation at which Adolf Hitler had promised to be present. I thought that it might be interesting to see Hitler among his faithful followers. Since Hühnlein was also a decent, upright man with whom it was easy to work, I accepted. Hitler made a speech dealing with the history of revolutions; the speaker showed considerable knowledge of history, and in a speech lasting for several hours he demonstrated how any revolution must, after a certain time and when it has achieved its aims, become a process of evolution. That point in its history had now been reached by the National-Socialist revolution. He urged his followers to bear this thought in mind for the future. It was only to be hoped and prayed that these indications of his would be fulfilled.

An armoured force was now in process of being created, and the year 1933 was one of considerable progress. A series of experimental and training exercises with dummy tanks did much to clarify the relationship between various weapons and served to strengthen me in my convictions that tanks would only be able to play their full part within the framework of a modern army when they were treated as that army's principal weapon and were supplied with fully motorised supporting arms.

If the tactical developments were not unsatisfactory, the equipment side was by contrast all the more worrying. One of the results of our disarmament after the Versailles Treaty was that for many years our industry had produced no war materials; consequently it lacked not only the skilled labour but also the very machines with which to turn our intentions into facts. In particular the production of a sufficiently tough armour plating proved very difficult. The first sheets delivered splintered like glass. It similarly took a considerable time before our requirements in the wireless and optical field—which, it must be admitted, were technically very advanced—could be filled. However, I have never regretted my insistence at that time on our tanks being equipped with first-class visual and command facilities. So far as the latter is concerned, we were at all times superior to our enemies and this was to compensate for many other subsequent inferiorities that necessarily arose.

In the autumn of 1933 General Freiherr von Fritsch became Commander-in-Chief of the Army (*Chef der Heeresleitung*). In him the army had at its head a soldier in whom the officer corps had complete confidence. His was a fine, chivalrous nature, and he was a clever, careful soldier with sound tactical and operational views. He had not a great deal of technical knowledge, but he was always ready to try out new ideas without prejudice and, if they seemed to him good, to adopt them. As a result of this my official dealings with him concerning the development of the armoured force were easier and more agreeable than with any of the other members of the Army High Command. As head of the 1st Department of the *Truppenamt* in the 100,000-man army he had already been interested in the questions of motorisation and of armour, and had devoted a period of detached service to the study of the Panzer Division. In the high office which he now filled he continued to show the same interest in our doings. The following little incident is typical of the way he used to do things. I had laid some technical question before him concerning tank development. He seemed doubtful, and he said to me: 'You should realise that all technicians are liars.' I replied: 'I admit they do tell lies, but their lies are generally found out after a year or two when their technical ideas can't be put into concrete shape. Tacticians tell lies too, but in their case the lies only become evident after the next war has been lost and by then it's too late to do anything about it.' Fritsch, as was his custom, twisted his monocle in his fingers before replying: 'You may be right.' Though he was extremely reserved and even shy at large gatherings, when he was among friends whom he trusted he proved himself to be open-hearted and affable. He was possessed of a fine wit when he wished to use it and of a most attractively charming manner.

A more difficult personality was that of the new Chief of the General Staff, General Beck. His was an upright character, a calm, almost too calm, and thoughtful man of the old school, a disciple of Moltke; it was Beck's intention to form a General Staff for the new army of the Third Reich of which Moltke would have approved. He had no under-standing for modern technical matters. Since he inevitably chose men with much of his own attitude to fill the more important General Staff posts, and even more so to form his own close circle, as time went on he erected—without wishing to do so—a barrier of reaction at the very centre of the army which was to prove very difficult to overcome. He disapproved of the plans of the armoured force: he wanted the tanks to be employed primarily as infantry support weapons, and the largest tank unit that he would agree to was the Panzer Brigade. He was not interested in the formation of Panzer Divisions.

I had to win a long-drawn-out fight with General Beck before he would agree to the setting up of the Panzer Divisions and to the publication of the training manuals for armoured troops. Finally he went so far as to agree to the establishment of two Panzer Divisions, while I was already insisting on three. I described the advantages of these new formations to him in the most glowing terms, and in par-ticular their operational significance. He replied: 'No, no, I don't want to have anything to do with you people. You move too fast for me.' When I maintained that, thanks to the recent developments of wireless, command could still be maintained despite great speed of advance, he did not believe me. It was frequently repeated in our training manuals that all unit commanders should be as far forward as possible, and he did not like this at all. 'But you can't command without maps and telephones. Haven't you ever read Schlieffen?' That even a divisional commander should be as far forward as ever he could without actually bumping into the enemy was too much for him.

Leaving the whole argument of armoured troops aside, however, Beck was above all a procrastinator in military as in political matters.

He was a paralysing element wherever he appeared. He always foresaw all the difficulties and required time to think everything over. Significant of his way of thought was his much-boosted method of fighting which he called 'delaying defence.' Even before the First World War we had heard in our manuals of 'the delaying battle': in the 100,000-man army this delaying defence became the cardinal principle. Beck's 'delaying defence' was envisaged and practised down to and including rifle sections. This method of fighting a battle is invariably marked by extreme confusion, and I have never seen an example of it that was anything but unsatisfactory. After the formation of the Panzer Divisions Fritsch scrapped the whole concept.

In the spring of 1934 a Motorised Troops Command Staff was set up: General Lutz was appointed head of this office and I took over the duties of his Chief of Staff. Lutz remained, in addition, Inspector of Motorised Troops and also Chief of Weapon Department 6 in the General Army Office of the Defence Ministry (*Waffenabteilung In 6 im Allgemeinen Heeresamt des RWM.*)

At the same period Hitler paid his first visit to Mussolini, in Venice, with results that were apparently not very satisfactory. After his return he addressed a meeting of generals, party chiefs and SA leaders in Berlin. The response of the SA leaders to his oratory was noticeably cool. As I was leaving the hall I overheard remarks such as: 'Adolf's got quite a bit to unlearn.' It amazed me to discover in this way that there were grave differences of opinion within the Party itself. On the 30th of June the riddle was solved. Roehm, the Chief of Staff of the SA, and a large number of SA leaders were shot out of hand, and not only they, but also numerous men and women who had had nothing to do with the SA and whose only crime—as we know now—was at some time or other in some way to have opposed the Party. Among those murdered was the former Defence Minister and Chancellor, General von Schleicher, together with his wife and his friend and colleague, General von Bredow. Attempts to secure an open vindication of the two generals led to no satisfactory results. Only old Field-Marshal von Mackensen made it clear, on the occasion of the Schlieffen Dinner of 1935 (a yearly reunion of active and retired General Staff Corps Officers), that the honour of the two men was unsullied. Hitler's statement to the Reichstag concerning these events was insufficient. It was hoped at that time that the Party would soon get over its growing pains. Looking back now, it is to be regretted that the leaders of the army did not insist on receiving full satisfaction. Had they only done so they would have rendered a great service not only to themselves but also to the armed forces and to the German people.

On the 2nd of August, 1934, Germany suffered a grievous loss. Field-Marshal von Hindenburg died, leaving his people in the midst of an internal revolution, the outcome of which no man could foresee. I wrote on that day to my wife:

'The old gentleman is no more. We are all saddened by this irreplaceable loss. He was like a father to the whole nation and particularly to the armed forces, and it will be a long and hard time before the great gap that he leaves in our national life can be filled. His existence alone meant more to foreign powers than any numbers of written agreements and fine words. He possessed the confidence of the world. We, who loved and honoured him, are become much poorer for his death.

'To-morrow we swear the oath to Hitler. An oath heavy with consequence! Pray God that both sides may abide by it equally for the welfare of Germany. The army is accustomed to keep its oaths. May the army be able, in honour, to do so this time.

'You are right. It would be a fine thing if the leaders of all the various organisations were to make use of this opportunity to postpone all ceremonies and celebrations indefinitely and to stop making speeches. . . . What is needed now is honest hard work and modest talk.'

These words, written on the 2nd of August, 1934, show the mood, not only of myself, but also of many of my comrades and of a huge section of our people at this time.

On the 7th of August, 1934, German soldiers carried the mortal remains of the immortal Field-Marshal and President to be laid to rest in the Tannenberg Memorial. Hitler's final words rang out: 'Dead warrior! Go now to Valhalla!'

Already on August 1st, on the strength of the Authorisation Bill, the Chancellor and his Cabinet had declared that in the event of Hindenburg's death the office of President would be merged in that of Chancellor. As a result Hitler, on August 2nd, became simultaneously Head of the State and Commander-in-Chief of its armed forces. Since he retained his position as Chancellor he thus united all the power in Germany in his own hand. From now on the dictatorship was for all intents and purposes unlimited.

After a winter of hard work we learned in March of 1935 that our right to military self-determination was to be re-established. Every soldier greeted this news, which meant the cancelling of a humiliating portion of the Versailles Treaty, with delight. On Heroes' Memorial Day, which opened with a march past in Field-Marshal von Mackensen's presence of units from all arms of the services, there were to be seen for the first time a few battalions of the new panzer troops, mostly, it is true, without their equipment—since this was a foot parade. In the preparations for the parade the participation of panzer troops was originally looked on rather askance, because—as the responsible staff officer explained to me—'with those short carbines of theirs they won't be able to present arms properly.' Despite this 'serious' disadvantage I managed to arrange for quite a number of our men to take part in the ceremony.

On the 16th of March of that year the English Military Attaché had invited me to his house for the evening. Shortly before I left my own home I switched on the wireless and heard the broadcast of a government announcement. This was the order for the reintroduction of universal military service in Germany. The conversation with my English friend, and with his Swedish colleague who was also present, took a lively turn that evening. Both those gentlemen showed understanding for the satisfaction that I felt at hearing this excellent news for the German Army.

Our theoretical aim in the accelerated rearmament that ensued was to achieve equality with our highly armed neighbours. Practically speaking—at least so far as the panzer troops were concerned—there could be no question for the time being of even approaching their standard of equipment either in quality or in quantity. We had therefore to attempt to make up those deficiencies by means of superior organisation and leadership. A tight concentration of our limited forces in large units, in divisions to be precise, and the organisation of those units as a Panzer Corps would, we hoped, compensate for our numerical inferiority.

First of all we had to convince our military superiors that our way was not only feasible but also the correct one. With this end in view the Motorised Troops Command, set up in June 1934 under the leadership of General Lutz, had arranged for four weeks' training of a panzer division improvised from the units then available: this was to take place during the summer of 1935. The training division was to be commanded by General Freiherr von Weichs. It was to be assembled at the military training area Munster-Lager, and was to be systematically exercised in four distinct tactical roles. It was not our intention on this occasion to instruct the subordinate unit commanders in the appreciation of and reaction to their individual tactical problems, but rather simply to demonstrate that the movement and commitment in action of large masses of tanks, together with supporting weapons, was in fact possible. Generals von Blomberg and Freiherr von Fritsch followed these exercises with great interest. The attendance of Hitler, whom General Lutz had also invited to be present, was prevented by the passive resistance of his military adjutant.

The results of the experimental exercises and the demonstrations there carried out were highly satisfactory. When the yellow balloon that marked the end of the exercises floated upwards, Colonel-General von Fritsch remarked jokingly: 'There's only one thing missing. The balloon should have *Guderian's Panzers are Best* marked on it.' General Lutz was appointed Commander of the new Armoured Troops Command. We expected this command to have the authority of a General Command (*Generalkommando*), analogous to those in existence for the other major arms, but this was prevented by the Chief of the Army General Staff, General Beck.

On the 15th of October, 1935, three Panzer Divisions were formed:

1st Panzer Division under General Freiherr von Weichs at Weimar;
2nd Panzer Division under Colonel Guderian at Würzburg;
3rd Panzer Division under General Fessmann at Berlin.

For the establishment of a Panzer Division in 1935, see Appendix XXIV.

At the beginning of October I left Berlin, exchanging my position at the centre of activities for practical service with troops. I knew that I was leaving the Armoured Troops Command in the safe hands of General Lutz. All the same we could rely on growing opposition from certain elements within the General Staff, and it was not certain whether my successor as Chief of Staff would be tough enough to withstand their pressure.[1] Similarly it was doubtful whether the Inspectorate for Armoured Troops at the Army High Command (*OKH*), which was responsible for looking after our interests with the chief of the General Army Office (*Chef des Allgemeinen Heeresamt*), would be able to carry on with our plans along the original lines laid down. In both these offices what I had feared soon came about: the Chief of the General Staff won the day, and Panzer Brigades were formed for the purpose of providing close support for the infantry. As early as 1936 the 4th Panzer Brigade was set up to carry out this role. Next, owing to agitation on the part of the cavalry for greater control over motorised troops, three so-called Light Divisions were formed in place of further Panzer Divisions envisaged: these Light Divisions consisted each of two Motorised Rifle Regiments, a Reconnaissance Regiment, an Artillery Regiment, a Tank Battalion and numerous supporting units. Apart from the Light Divisions four Motorised Infantry Divisions were also formed; these were normal Infantry Divisions which were fully motorised and which required a very considerable complement of M.T. Thus the XIV Army Corps for the Motorised Infantry Divisions, and the XV Army Corps for the Light Divisions came into

---

[1] The new Chief of Staff to General Lutz was Colonel (later Field-Marshal) Paulus—who commanded the forces in the attack on Stalingrad in 1942, and was captured there.

existence, while the Armoured Troops Command became the XVI Army Corps with under it the three Panzer Divisions. Finally, these three corps were all subordinated to Group Command 4 with headquarters at Leipzig and commanded by General von Brauchitsch, who became responsible for all further training and development.

The various arms of the service each had its own particular colour, which was worn on the shoulder tabs, etc. Up to this time the colour for all panzer troops had been pink, and pink remained the colour for the Panzer Regiments and the Anti-tank Battalions. The Armoured Reconnaissance Battalions were changed, first to yellow and then to brown: the Rifle Regiments and the Motor-Cycle Riflemen in the Panzer Divisions received the colour green: the Cavalry Rifle Regiments in the Light Divisions wore the cavalry yellow: while the Motorised Infantry Regiments continued to wear the infantry white. And of course all this led to much argument with the Weapon Inspectorates of the infantry and of the cavalry.

I deeply regretted this splitting up of our motorised and armoured strength but there was nothing I could do at the time to prevent events following this course. The damage then done could only be partially put to rights later on.

Our limited resources in the sphere of motorisation were further squandered owing to various organisational errors committed by other arms of the service. For example, the Chief of the General Army Office, General Fromm, ordered that the 14th (anti-tank) Company of all Infantry Regiments be motorised. When I maintained that these companies, since they would be working with foot soldiers, would do better to remain horse-drawn, he replied 'The infantry's got to have a few cars too.' My request that, instead of the 14th Companies, the Heavy Artillery Battalions be motorised was turned down. The heavy guns remained horse-drawn, with unfortunate results during the war, particularly in Russia.

The development of tracked vehicles for the tank supporting arms never went as fast as we wished. It was clear that the effectiveness of the tanks would gain in proportion to the ability of the infantry, artillery and other divisional arms to follow them in an advance across country. We wanted lightly armoured half-tracks for the riflemen, combat engineers and medical services, armoured self-propelled guns for the artillery and the anti-tank battalions, and various types of tank for the reconnaissance and signals battalions. The equipment of the divisions with these vehicles was never fully completed. Despite all increases in productivity the limited facilities of German industry never succeeded in catching up with the vastly expanded requirements of the motorised *Wehrmacht* and *Waffen-SS* formations and of industry itself. Despite all the warnings of the specialists, the supreme command never imposed limitations to the greed of certain politically powerful individuals. I will have occasion to refer to this matter again when I deal with military events in 1941.

Meanwhile I was with my division in Würzburg and only indirectly concerned with these problems. My work consisted of the setting-up and training of my new formation whose component units came from such diverse military backgrounds. The winter of 1935–36 passed uneventfully. I was accepted in a friendly fashion by the old Würzburg garrison, under General Brandt, and also by the inhabitants of the town and of the surrounding countryside. I managed to procure a small house in the Boelckestrasse with a wonderful view over the town stretched out below in the valley of the Main: we could also see from our windows the Marienfeste and the Käppele, one of the pearls of the baroque period.

In the spring of 1936 we were surprised by Hitler's decision to re-occupy the Rhineland. Since the occupation was intended simply as a military gesture, no tank troops were to be employed. It is true that my division was alerted and transferred to the troop training area at Münsingen, but without its Tank Brigade, which remained behind at its normal station in order to avoid unnecessary increase of tension. After a few weeks we all returned to our peace-time station.

On the 1st of August of that year I was promoted Major-General.

The only panzer unit to take part in that year's autumn manœuvres was the 4th Panzer Regiment from Schweinfurt. The employment of this single regiment within the framework of an infantry division failed to give any clear idea of our combat capabilities.

One of the guests at these manœuvres was Colonel-General von Seeckt, recently returned from the Far East; I had the honour to tell him about this new armoured force, which was something previously quite unknown to him. Also I was able to speak to the representatives of the Press, who had been invited, concerning the organisation and combat methods of this new arm of the service.

The year 1937 passed peacefully. We were busily engaged in a training programme which culminated in manœuvres at divisional strength in the troop training area Grafenwöhr. Under the instructions of General Lutz I prepared a book during the winter of 1936–37 which was published with the title *Achtung! Panzer!*; it told the story of the development of armoured forces and outlined our basic ideas as to how the German armoured force should be built up. We hoped by this book to interest a wider public in our plans than could be reached through normal Service channels. In addition I took some trouble to see that our point of view was made clear through the specialist military

Press and thus to counteract the arguments of the very vocal opposition. Shortly afterwards an article expressing our views appeared in the journal of the National Union of German Officers, dated the 15th of October, 1937. I should like to quote this, since it gives a good picture of our efforts and of the differences of opinion that were rife at the time.

Tank Attack by Fire and Movement

'The layman, when thinking of a tank attack, tends to envisage the steel monsters of Cambrai and Amiens as pictured in the war reports of that period. He thinks of vast wire entanglements being crushed like so much straw; he remembers how the tanks crashed through dug-outs, smashing machine-guns to splinters beneath their weight; he recalls the terror that they inspired as they ploughed through the battlefield, flames darting from their exhaust pipes, and how this "tank terror" was described as the cause of our collapse on the 8th of August, 1918. Such steam-roller tactics are one—though not the most important—of the things tanks can do; but the events of the last war have so impressed themselves on the minds of many critics, that they have built up an entirely fanciful idea of a tank attack in which vast numbers of tanks massed together roll steadily forward to crush the enemy beneath their tracks (thus providing a magnificent target for artillery and anti-tank fire) whenever and wherever ordered by the high command, regardless of the nature of the ground. The fire-power of the tanks is under-estimated: the tank is thought to be both blind and deaf: it is denied the ability to hold ground that it has captured. On the other hand every advantage is ascribed to anti-tank defence: it is alleged that the defence will no longer be susceptible to surprise by tanks; anti-tank guns and artillery always find their mark regardless of their own casualties, of smoke, fog, trees or other obstacles and ground contours; the defence, too, is always located exactly where the tanks are going to attack; with their powerful binoculars they can easily see through smoke screens and darkness, and despite their steel helmets they can hear every word that is said.

'As a result of this picture it follows that tank attacks have no future. Should tanks therefore be scrapped and—as one critic has suggested— the tank period be simply by-passed? If this were done all our worries about new tactics for old arms of the service could be scrapped at the same time and we could settle down comfortably once again to positional warfare as practised in 1914–15. Only it is not very sensible to leap into the dark if you have no idea where you are going to land. *It follows that until our critics can produce some new and better method of making a successful land attack other than self-massacre, we shall con-*

tinue to maintain our belief that tanks—properly employed, needless to say—are today the best means available for a land attack. But in order to make it easier to judge the prospects of tank attacks, here are some of the significant characteristics of tanks today.

Armour Plating

'All tanks intended for serious action are at least sufficiently armoured to be impervious to armour-piercing bullets fired from machine-guns. For fighting against anti-tank weapons and enemy tanks, such protection is insufficient; therefore the tanks so far ordered by the so-called victorious nations of the World War are considerably more strongly armoured. For example, to penetrate the shell of the French Char 2C a gun of at least 75 mm. calibre is required. If an army can in the first wave commit to the attack tanks which are invulnerable to the mass of the enemy's defensive weapons, then those tanks will inevitably overcome this their most dangerous adversary: and this must lead to the destruction of the enemy's infantry and engineers, since the latter, being shot at by tanks and with their defensive weapons eliminated, can easily be mopped up even by light tanks. However, should the defence succeed in producing a defensive weapon which can penetrate the armour of all the attacker's available tanks, and should he manage to deploy such weapons at the right time and in the decisive place, then the tanks will have to pay heavily for their successes or may even fail altogether if the defence is sufficiently concentrated and sufficiently deep. The struggle for mastery between missile and armour has been going on for thousands of years, and panzer troops have to reckon with it even as do fortress troops, sailors and, recently, airmen. The fact that such a struggle exists, with results that continually vary, is no reason for denigrating tanks as a land weapon: for if we do, we shall be reduced to sending men into the attack with no more protection than the woollen uniforms of the World War which, even then, were regarded as insufficient.

Movement

'It has been said, "only movement brings victory."[1] We agree with this proposition and wish to employ the technical means of our time to prove its truth. Movement serves to bring the troops in contact with the enemy: for this purpose one can use the legs of men or of horses, the railways or—recently—the automobile and the aeroplane engine. Once contact with the enemy has been made, movement is generally

[1] The numerals 1–10 refer to the remarks made by our adversaries in the *Militär-Wissenschaftliche Rundschau* (*The Review of Military Science*), 1937, vol. 3, pp. 326, 362, 364, 368, 369, 372, 373, and 374. This publication was put out by the Army General Staff.

THE CREATION OF THE GERMAN ARMOURED FORCE

paralysed by hostile fire. In order to permit the relaxation of this paralysis, the enemy must either be destroyed or made inoperative or driven from his positions. This can be done by employing fire-power so superior that his powers of resistance collapse. Fire-power from fixed positions has an effective range corresponding exactly to the observed range of the mass of the weapons employed. That is as far as the infantry can make use of its covering fire; when that point is reached the heavy weapons and the artillery must change their position in order to permit a further advance under cover of their fire-power. Vast numbers of weapons and an even vaster quantity of ammunition are needed to fight this sort of battle. The preparations for an attack of this sort require considerable time and are difficult to conceal. Surprise, that important element of success, is very hard to achieve. And even if the original attack does catch the enemy unawares, the moment it is launched the attacking force will have shown its hand, and the reserves of the defence will converge on the point of attack and block it; since reserve forces will now be motorised, the building up of new defensive fronts is easier than it used to be; *the chances of an offensive based on the timetable of artillery and infantry co-operation are, as a result, even slighter today than they were in the last war.*

'*Everything is therefore dependent on this: to be able to move faster than has hitherto been done: to keep moving despite the enemy's defensive fire and thus to make it harder for him to build up fresh defensive positions: and finally to carry the attack deep into the enemy's defences.* The proponents of tank warfare believe that, in favourable circumstances, they possess the means for achieving this; the sceptics, on the other hand, say that since the element of surprise can no longer be produced as in 1918 "conditions for a successful tank attack can no longer be anticipated."[2] But is it true that a tank attack can no longer take the enemy by surprise? How then does it happen that surprises have been achieved in warfare regardless of whether new or old methods were employed to bring them about? In 1916 General von Kuhl proposed to the High Command that in order to make a break-through primary importance must be attached to the element of surprise in launching the attack;[3] and yet at that time he had no new methods or weapons at his disposal. As a result of surprise achieved, the March Offensive of 1918 was outstandingly successful, despite the fact that no new types of weapons were employed. If, in addition to the normal methods of achieving surprise, new weapons are also employed, then the effects of the surprise will be greatly increased; but the new weapons are not a prerequisite to those effects. *We believe that by attacking with tanks we can achieve a higher rate of movement than has been hitherto obtainable, and—what is perhaps even more important—*

B*

that we can keep moving once a break-through has been made. We
believe that movement can be kept up if certain conditions, on which
the success of a tank attack today depend, exist: these include among
others, concentration of force in suitable terrain, gaps in the enemy's
defence, and an inferior enemy tank force. When we are blamed because
we cannot successfully attack in all and any conditions, because we
cannot storm fortifications with tanks armed only with machine-guns,
then we can only say that we are sorry and point out that other arms of
the service possess in many respects even less attacking power than we
do. We do not claim to be omnipotent.

'It has been maintained that a weapon only achieves its maximum
effectiveness while it is new and before it need fear defensive counter-
measures.[4] Pity the artillery! it is already hundreds of years old. Pity
the air force! Age is creeping up on it in the form of anti-aircraft. We
believe that the effectiveness of any weapon is a relative quality,
depending on the effectiveness of the counter weapons employed
against it. If tanks run into a superior enemy—whether in the form of
hostile tanks or of anti-tank weapons—they will be beaten; their
effectiveness will be reduced; if conditions are reversed, then they will
achieve startling success. Every weapon is dependent not only on the
strength of the opposition but also on its own willingness to make
immediate, maximum use of the latest technical developments and
thus to remain at the summit of its period. From this point of view the
tank will not admit that it has been surpassed by any other weapon.
It has been said: "The shells of the defensive artillery travel faster than
the tanks that are attacking that artillery."[5] Nobody, up to now, has
questioned this fact. Yet as long ago as 1917 and 1918 hundreds of
tanks could be moved up to a concentration area immediately behind
the front lines of the infantry: could penetrate in their swarms the
enemy's line of defensive fire: could clear a way for dozens of infantry
and even of cavalry divisions: and what is more could do all this without
any preliminary artillery bombardment, that is to say in the teeth of
an intact enemy artillery. It is only in unusually unfavourable conditions
that the hostile artillery can have any serious effect on the movement
of tanks: and once the tanks have succeeded in breaking through to the
gun lines, the batteries will soon fall silent and will thus be no longer
capable even of hurting the following infantry. Even the immutable
artillery tactics of having guns registered on all localities of possible
danger proved a failure in the last war. The defensive fire will throw
up columns of earth, dust, smoke and so on and this will limit the
vision of the tank crews; but such limitation is not intolerable; even
in peacetime we have learned how to overcome that. In fact tanks can
now advance through night and fog on compass bearings.

'*In an attack that is based on a successful tank action the "architect of victory" is not the infantry but the tanks themselves, for if the tank attack fails then the whole operation is a failure, whereas if the tanks succeed, then victory follows.*

Fire

'Armour and movement are only two of the combat characteristics of the tank weapon; the third and the most important is fire-power.

'Tank guns can be fired whether the tank is stationary or on the move. In both cases the gun is laid by direct observation. If the tank is stationary range can be quickly adjusted and the target destroyed with a minimum expenditure of ammunition. When the tank is in motion the recognition of targets becomes harder owing to difficulties in observation, but this is compensated for to a certain extent by the fact that the gun is situated comparatively high above ground, which is particularly useful if the terrain is overgrown; thus the high silhouette, which has been so frequently the cause of adverse comment as presenting the enemy with an easy target, is not without a certain advantage for the tank gunner. If it is necessary to shoot while in movement the chances of short-range accuracy are good; they decrease with longer range, higher speed and when travelling over uneven ground.

'In any event, in land battles the tank possesses the unique quality of being able to bring its fire-power to bear while actually advancing against the enemy, and it can do this even though all the defence's guns and machine-guns have not been silenced. We do not doubt that guns fired from stationary positions are more accurate than guns fired in motion; we are well able to judge this, since we are capable of both types of engagement. However: "Only movement brings victory." Now should a tank attack be envisaged simply as a means of steam-rolling a path through thick and deep defensive positions held by infantry and artillery fully equipped with anti-tank weapons,[6] as was done during the battles of *matériel* of the last war? Certainly not. A man who would attempt this would be thinking purely in terms of the infantry tank, a weapon whose sole function was the closest co-operation with the infantry, a weapon adjusted to the foot-soldier's scale of time and space values. This was a concept which we hung on to for far too long. We neither can nor wish to devote weeks or even months to reconnaissance; we have no desire to rely on an enormous expenditure of ammunition; *what we do want to do is, for a short period of time, to dominate the enemy's defence in all its depth.* We are well aware that with the limited fire-power of our tanks we cannot mount a "planned artillery preparation" or achieve a "concentrated artillery bombardment"; our intention is exactly the contrary, it is to knock out our targets with single, surely aimed shells. For we have not forgotten how during the war week-long barrages by the most powerful artillery on earth failed to enable the infantry to achieve victory. *We have been taught by our enemies to believe that a successful, rapid tank attack, in sufficient width and depth to penetrate all the way through the opposing defence system, can achieve more towards ensuring victory than the system of limited advances as practised in the World War.* Our shells, being aimed at specific targets, will not whistle over the enemy's heads as they did during those costly though pointless creeping barrages: rather if the attack is carried out with sufficient concentration, width and depth we shall destroy recognisable targets as they present themselves and thus drive a hole in the enemy's defences through which our reserves can follow more speedily than was possible in 1918. *We want these reserves to be available in the form of Panzer Divisions, since we no longer believe that other formations have the fighting ability, the speed and the manœuvrability necessary for full exploitation of the attack and break-through.* Therefore we do not regard the tank force as "an additional means for winning battles, which on many forseeable occasions could, in co-operation with other weapons, help the infantry to advance."[7] If that were all that tanks were for, the situation would be the same now as in 1916; and if that were true then one might as well be resigned to positional warfare from the very beginning and give up all hope of quick decisions in the future. But neither the alleged superiority in armaments of our enemy in any future war, nor the increased accuracy and range of guns of all calibres, nor the technical advances made in the employment of artillery suffice to shake our beliefs. On the contrary! In the tank we see the finest weapon for the attack now available: we will not change our minds until such time as the technicians can show us something better. We will in no circumstances agree to time-wasting artillery preparation and the consequent danger of losing the element of surprise, simply because the old maxim says that "only fire can open the way to movement."[8] We believe, on the contrary, that the combination of the internal combustion engine and armour plate enable us to take our fire to the enemy without any artillery preparation, provided always that the important conditions for such an operation are fulfilled: suitable terrain, surprise and mass commitment.

'The idea of mass commitment gives our critics cold feet. They write: "There is also the question of organisation: of whether the massing of all tank strength in one striking force is a sound basic idea, or whether the alternative theory of allotting tanks organically to the infantry, in order to enable it to attack, is not worthy of equally serious consideration."[9] We assume from this remark that the infantry without tanks is at present incapable of attacking; it follows that the weapon which can attack, and which can enable other arms of the Service to advance, must indubitably be the principal weapon. The question of whether or not tanks should be allotted to infantry can be clarified by the following imaginary story:

'Red and Blue are at war. Each side has 100 Infantry Divisions and 100 Tank Battalions. Red has split up its tanks among its Infantry Divisions: Blue has massed them in Panzer Divisions under direct control of supreme headquarters. On a front of, shall we say, 300 miles, 100 are tank-proof, 100 are difficult for tanks and 100 are good tank country. So in battle the following picture emerges: Red has deployed a sizeable proportion of its divisions, along with their tank components, opposite the Blue positions in country where tanks cannot operate and are therefore useless, while a further portion are in difficult tank country where, though not entirely wasted, their chances of successful action are small. Whatever happens, only a fraction of Red's tank forces can be employed in the country for which they are suited. Blue, on the other hand, has collected all its armour in the one place where a decision can be reached and where the ground can be made use of; he therefore has the opportunity of going into battle with at least double his adversary's tank strength while assuming the defensive along the rest of the front against Red's very small-scale tank attacks. An Infantry Division with, say, 50 anti-tank weapons can stand up far more easily to an attack by 50 tanks than to an attack by 200. We conclude that the suggestion that our tanks be divided among Infantry Divisions is nothing but a return to the original English tactics of 1916–17, which were even then a failure, for the English tanks were not successful until they were used in mass at Cambrai.

'By carrying the attack quickly into the enemy's midst, by firing our motorised guns with their protective armour direct into the target, we intend to achieve victory. It is said: "The motor is not a new weapon: it is simply a new method of carrying old weapons forward."[10] It is fairly well known that combustion engines do not fire bullets; if we speak of the tank as a new weapon, we mean thereby that it necessitates a new arm of the service, as happened for example in the navy in the case of the U-boat; that too is called a weapon. *We are convinced that we are a weapon and one whose successes in the future will leave an indelible mark on battles yet to be fought*. If our attacks are to succeed then the other weapons must be adjusted to fit in with our scale of time and space in those attacks. We therefore demand that in order to exploit our successes the necessary supporting arms be made as mobile as we are, and that even in peace-time those arms be placed

under our command. *For to carry out great decisive operations it is
not the mass of the infantry but the mass of the tanks that must be on
the spot.'*

In the late autumn of 1937 large army manœuvres were held at
which Hitler and, towards the end, a number of foreign guests were
present: these latter included Mussolini, the English Field-Marshal
Sir Cyril Deverell, the Italian Marshal Badoglio, and a Hungarian
military mission. The panzer troops taking part were the 3rd Panzer
Division, commanded by General Fessmann, and the 1st Panzer
Brigade. I was in charge of the staff of umpires dealing with the panzer
exercises.

The positive result of these manœuvres was the proof that the Panzer
Division could be employed as a unit. Supply and repair facilities were
found to be insufficient. Rapid improvement was needed here. I made a
few suggestions on these matters to the Armoured Corps Command.
Unfortunately they were not immediately adopted, so that weaknesses
which had become apparent during the manœuvres were to recur in the
full glare of publicity during the spring of 1938.

On the last day of the manœuvres a final attack was mounted for
the benefit of the foreign guests; all the available tanks took part in
this, under my command. It was an impressive spectacle even though
the only tanks we then had were the Panzer I.

After the manœuvres there was a parade in Berlin, followed by a
luncheon party which Colonel-General von Fritsch gave in honour of
the foreign guests. I was invited to this. It was an opportunity for a
number of interesting conversations and I talked, among others, with
Field-Marshal Sir Cyril Deverell and the Italian Marshal Badoglio.
Badoglio spoke of his experiences during the Abyssinian campaign.
Sir Cyril Deverell asked me my opinion concerning motorisation.
Younger British officers were interested in the problem of whether it
was possible to employ as many tanks on a battlefield in wartime as
were accustomed to appear before Mussolini on manœuvres. They
seemed reluctant to believe that it was so and appeared to tend towards
the theory of the tank as an infantry support weapon. At all events the
conversation was an animated one.

3. HITLER AT THE PEAK OF HIS POWER

1938. The Blomberg–Fritsch crisis. The incorporation of Austria and the Sudetenland into the Reich

The eventful year of 1938 began with my unexpected promotion to lieutenant-general. I received information of this during the night of February 2nd–3rd, together with an order to appear at a meeting presided over by Hitler on February 4th in Berlin. As I was walking along the street in Berlin early that morning an acquaintance in a passing tram hailed me with the information that I had been appointed Commanding General of the XVI Army Corps. This was a complete surprise to me; I quickly got hold of a morning paper where I read with amazement the news that a whole group of senior officers had been dismissed, including Blomberg and Fritsch and my good friend General Lutz. The reasons for this were given, at least partially, during the conference at the Chancellery. All the Commanding Generals of the armed forces were assembled in a semicircle in a large hall; Hitler came in and informed us that he had relieved the War Minister, Field-Marshal von Blomberg, of his post because of his marriage and that, simultaneously, he had been obliged to dismiss the Commander-in-Chief of the Army, Colonel-General von Fritsch, on account of a criminal offence. He said nothing about the other dismissals. We were flabbergasted. These serious allegations against our most senior officers, whom we knew to be men of spotless honour, cut us to the quick. They were quite incredible, and yet our immediate reaction was that the first magistrate of the German State could not simply have invented these stories out of thin air. After Hitler had spoken he left the room and we were dismissed. Not one of us had a word to say. Indeed what was there to say at such a moment of shock, since we had no way of judging what had happened?

The Blomberg affair was quite clear. His retention of ministerial office was obviously out of the question. But the case of Colonel-General Freiherr von Fritsch was very different. This was a matter for a military court to investigate. A court was set up, over which Goering presided, and despite its president it returned a verdict of complete innocence. The foul slander put out against the general was proved to be entirely without foundation. Months after this infamous calumny was nailed as a lie, we were assembled again—this time at an aerodrome—to hear the president of the supreme military court, General Heitz, read out the verdict together with an exhaustive preamble. The announcement of the verdict was preceded by a short statement by Hitler in which he announced regret and promised us that there would be no repetition of such occurrences in the future. We demanded complete rehabilitation for Colonel-General Freiherr von Fritsch. However, the new Commander-in-Chief of the Army, Colonel-General von Brauchitsch —whom Blomberg had himself suggested for this position—succeeded only in getting Colonel-General Freiherr von Fritsch appointed honorary colonel of Artillery Regiment No. 12 in Schwerin and thus once more placed on the active list. He never received a command. This was grossly insufficient compensation for the great harm that had been done him. The wicked man who had borne false witness against him was, it is true, put on trial by Hitler's orders, but the far more dangerous figures behind the cowardly act went unpunished. The condemnation to death of the slanderer served only as a smoke-screen. On August 11th, at the military training area Gross-Born, Colonel-General Freiherr von Fritsch took over command of Artillery Regiment No. 12. On the 13th of August Hitler attended an exercise at this very place. The two men did not meet.

The dignified reticence with which Colonel-General Freiherr von Fritsch behaved during the ensuing months compelled admiration. Whether in fact it was the correct attitude to adopt towards his political enemies is another matter. Yet this opinion is inevitably based on subsequent knowledge of the issues and personalities involved.

On the 4th of February, 1938, Hitler himself assumed the title of Commander-in-Chief Armed Forces. The post of War Minister remained unfilled. The Chief of the Ministerial Office, General Wilhelm Keitel, took over the Minister's duties in so far as these were not subdivided among the commanders of the three services. Keitel, however, did not have command powers. He called himself Chief of the High Command of the Armed Services (*Chef des Ober-kommandos der Wehrmacht*, abbreviated to *OKW*). The new commander of Group Command 4, which controlled the three motorised corps, was General von Reichenau, a progressively minded and intelligent soldier for whom I soon felt a comradely friendship.

The 4th of February, 1938, was the second black day for the army high command, the first having been the 30th of June, 1934. The corps of German generals has been subsequently severely blamed for its failure to do anything on these two occasions. But blame can only be apportioned to the few individuals in authority at the very top. For the majority, the true state of affairs remained obscure. Even in the

case of Fritsch, which from the very beginning seemed not only improbable but unthinkable, it was necessary to wait for the promulgation
of the court's findings before any serious steps could be taken. The
new Commander-in-Chief of the Army was asked, and even urged, to
take these steps, but he could not make up his mind to do so. Meanwhile the whole business was overshadowed by developments of the
greatest importance in the field of foreign affairs, namely the Austrian
anschluss. The fruitful moment for action had passed. But the Fritsch
case did prove the existence of a serious lack of trust between the head
of the Reich and the leaders of the army; I was aware of this though
I was not in a position to understand what lay behind it all.

From my honoured predecessor, General of Panzer Troops[1] Lutz,
I took over my new command. The Chief of Staff of XVI Army Corps
was Colonel Paulus whom I had known for many years; he was the
finest type of brilliantly clever, conscientious, hard-working, original
and talented General Staff officer, and it is impossible to doubt his
pure-minded and lofty patriotism. In later years the foulest slanders
and accusations were to be levelled at the unfortunate commander of
the Sixth Army destroyed at Stalingrad. Until such time as Paulus is
himself capable of speaking in his own defence, I cannot accept any of
the charges made against him.

Meanwhile the Panzer Divisions had received new commanding
generals, as follows:
1st Panzer Division, General Rudolf Schmidt.
2nd Panzer Division, General Veiel.
3rd Panzer Division, General Freiherr Geyr von Schweppenburg.

The Incorporation of Austria into the Reich

On the 10th of March at 16.00 hrs. I was sent for by the Chief of the
General Staff of the Army, General Beck, and learned from him as a
matter of the greatest secrecy that Hitler was contemplating the incorporation of Austria into the Reich and that in consequence a
number of formations must reckon on receiving marching orders.
'You'll have to take over your old 2nd Panzer Division once again,'
he said to me. I pointed out that this might well offend my successor
in that command, General Veiel, who was in any case a thoroughly
competent general officer. 'All the same,' Beck replied, 'it is imperative

[1] Full generals in the German Army carried in their military title the arm of the service
from which they originally came or, in arms more lately created, with which they were
most closely connected: i.e. General of Infantry, General of Artillery, etc. This rank,
though nominally equivalent to that of British general, was actually closer to that of
British lieutenant-general. A German colonel-general was more nearly equivalent to a
British full general.—*Tr.*

that you command the motorised units taking part in this operation.'
I thereupon suggested that XVI Army Corps be made mobile and be
put in control of some other formation besides 2nd Panzer Division.
General Beck agreed and proposed the Waffen-SS Division, *SS-Leibstandarte 'Adolf-Hitler,'* which was also scheduled to form part of the
occupying force. He finished by saying: 'If the *anschluss* is to be carried
out, this is probably the best moment to do it.'

I returned to my office, gave orders for such preparations as the
situation required, and contemplated what measures should be taken
in order to carry out the operation. At about 20.00 hrs. Beck sent for
me again and after a short wait I was instructed, between 21.00 and
22.00 hrs., to alert 2nd Panzer Division and *SS-Leibstandarte 'Adolf
Hitler'* and to assemble the two units in the neighbourhood of
Passau. I now learned that the formations detailed to march into Austria
were to be commanded by Colonel-General von Bock. Infantry divisions south of my Army Corps were to cross the River Inn; other units
were to go to the Tyrol.

Between 23.00 and 24.00 hrs. I alerted the 2nd Panzer Division by
telephone; Sepp Dietrich, the commander of the *Liebstandarte*, I saw
personally. All units were to move off at once with destination Passau.
There was no difficulty in the *Leibstandarte* carrying out its orders; with
the 2nd Panzer Division it was not so simple, since a number of its staff
officers, together with the divisional commander, were on a training
trip to Trier in the Moselle. They had first of all to be fetched back by
car. Despite this complication, orders were quickly carried out and the
troops were soon on the move.

The distance from 2nd Panzer Division's station at Würzburg to
Passau averaged 250 miles, from Passau to Vienna a further 170 miles.
It is 598 miles from Berlin to Vienna.

Before Sepp Dietrich left me he informed me that he was going at
once to see Hitler. Now it seemed to me that the *anschluss* should be
completed without any fighting. I felt that for both countries it was an
occasion of rejoicing. It therefore occurred to me that as a sign of our
friendly feelings the tanks might well be beflagged and decked with
greenery. I asked Sepp Dietrich to inquire if Hitler would give his
approval for this, and half an hour later I was informed that he did.

XVI Army Corps staff arrived at Passau at about 20.00 hrs. on the
11th of March. There we received orders to march into Austria at
08.00 hrs. on the 12th. Towards midnight General Veiel arrived in
Passau at the head of his troops. He neither had maps of Austria nor
fuel for a further advance. In place of a map I supplied him with an
ordinary tourist's Baedeker's Guide. The fuel problem was a little more
difficult to solve. It is true that there was an army fuel depot at Passau,

but it was earmarked for the deployment of troops in the West and for the defence of the West Wall (the so-called Siegfried Line); it was under orders only to distribute its fuel in the event of mobilisation and for this sole purpose. The officers in authority here had not been informed of our operation and could not be reached in the middle of the night. The man in charge of the depot, faithful to the orders he had received, refused to let me have any of his precious fuel, and eventually I had to threaten to use force before he would give in.

Since we had no mobile supply columns, we had to improvise. The mayor of Passau helped by providing us with a number of lorries out of which we rapidly built up the necessary fuel columns. For the rest, the Austrian petrol stations along our road of advance were requested to keep open.

Despite all General Veiel's efforts it was not possible to cross the frontier punctually at eight. It was not until 9 o'clock that the first units of the 2nd Panzer Division drove past the upraised frontier barriers, to be received with joy by the population on the Austrian side. The division's advanced guard consisted of the 5th (Kornwestheim) and 7th (Munich) Armoured Reconnaissance Battalions and the 2nd (Kissingen) Motor-cycle Rifle Battalion. This advanced guard moved fast through Linz, which was reached at noon, towards St. Pölten.

I went with the main body of the 2nd Panzer Division, while the *Leibstandarte 'Adolf Hitler,'* which had now joined us after its long drive from Berlin, brought up the rear. The flags and decorations on the tanks proved highly successful. The populace saw that we came as friends, and we were everywhere joyfully received. Old soldiers from the First World War had pinned their decorations to their chests and saluted us as we drove by. At every halt the tanks were decked with flowers and food was pressed on the soldiers. Their hands were shaken, they were kissed, and there were tears of joy. No untoward incident marred the occasion that had for so many years been longed for by both sides, the much postponed *anschluss*. Children of one nation, split by unfortunate politics into two during so many decades, were now happily united at last.

We advanced along one road, the road that leads through Linz. Shortly before twelve I arrived in Linz, paid my respects to the local authorities and partook of a quick luncheon. Just as I was leaving the town in the direction of St. Pölten I met the Reich leader of the SS, Himmler, who was accompanied by the Austrian ministers Seiss-Inquart and von Glaise-Horstenau. They informed me that the Führer was due to arrive in Linz at about 15.00 hrs., and they asked me to arrange for the closing of the roads into the town and of the market-place. I therefore ordered my advance guard to stop in St. Pölten, while with the troops available from my main body I made the necessary preparations in and about Linz. The garrison troops of the Austrian Army asked permission to participate in these duties, which was granted. Soon the streets and squares were filled with some 60,000 people. The crowd was enormously enthusiastic and excited. The German soldiers were loudly and repeatedly cheered.

It was almost dark by the time Hitler entered Linz. I was waiting for him just outside the city limits and was thus a witness to the triumphal nature of his entry into that town. I also heard his speech from the balcony of the town hall. Neither before nor since have I ever seen such tremendous enthusiasm as was shown during those few hours. After his speech Hitler visited a few men who had been wounded in the riots that preceded the *anschluss* and then repaired to his hotel, where I reported to him to announce the continuation of my march on Vienna. It was plain that he was deeply moved by the way the crowd in the market-place had received him.

I left Linz at about 21.00 hrs., arriving in St. Pölten at midnight. I ordered my advanced guard to move off again at once, and going myself at the head of the column drove through a blinding snowstorm into Vienna, which we reached at approximately 01.00 hrs. on the 13th of March.

In Vienna a great torch-light procession in celebration of the *anschluss* had just ended, and the streets were full of excited and happy people. So it was no wonder that the appearance of the first German soldiers was the signal for frantic rejoicing. The advanced guard marched past the Opera House behind an Austrian military band and in the presence of the commander of the Vienna Division of the Austrian Army, General Stumpfl. After the march past was over renewed cheering and rejoicing broke out once again. I was carried to my quarters. The buttons of my greatcoat were instantly transformed into prized souvenirs. We were treated with great friendliness.

After a short rest I set off, early in the morning of the 13th of March, on a round of visits to the commanders of the Austrian Army, by all of whom I was most courteously received.

The 14th of March was fully occupied by preparations for the great parade ordered for the 15th. I was put in charge of these arrangements and so had the pleasure of working for the first time in co-operation with our new comrades. We had soon come to agreement as to how the parade was to be organised and the next day we had the satisfaction of seeing how well this first public demonstration went off in a Vienna that was now part of the German Reich. Formations of the Austrian Army opened the march past. They were followed by alternate German and Austrian units. The enthusiasm of the crowd was enormous.

On one of the following evenings I invited a number of the Austrian generals whom I had met in the past few days to a small dinner party at the Hotel Bristol, hoping thus privately to strengthen our new public comradeship. I then set out on a tour of the country to visit the various mechanised units of the Austrian Army and to decide how best they could be incorporated in our new united army. I recall with particular vividness two visits I then made. One was to Neusiedel-am-See, where a Motorised Jaeger Battalion was in garrison. The second took me to Bruck an der Leitha where the Austrian Army's Tank Battalion was stationed. This latter was commanded by Lieutenant-Colonel Theiss, a particularly fine officer who had suffered considerable physical injury as a result of a severe tank accident. His troops made a first-class impression and I soon struck up an easy relationship with his young officers and men. Both morale and discipline in these two units were so excellent that their incorporation into the Reich Army could be anticipated as both profitable and pleasant.

We wished to show the Austrians Germany besides showing the Germans Austria, thus strengthening the feeling of unity. So a number of soldiers from the old Austrian Army were sent on short visits to the original Reich. One of these formations went to my former garrison town of Würzburg, where my wife arranged that they be received and entertained.

Shortly afterwards my dear wife managed to come to Vienna, so we were able to celebrate her birthday, March the 25th, together.

The German armoured troops learned a number of important lessons from the occupation of Austria.

The march had been carried out, in general, smoothly enough. Breakdowns among the wheeled vehicles were few, but among the tanks rather more numerous. I can no longer recall the exact figures, but they were certainly not as high as 30 per cent. Until the 15th of March parade almost all the tanks were in good condition. In view of the great distances that they had then travelled and the speed of the march past, the number of breakdowns was not disproportionately high; but to those who knew nothing of tanks, and also to Colonel-General von Bock, it seemed so. Therefore after the parade the young armoured force was subjected to much harsh criticism from certain quarters. It was alleged that tanks were now proved incapable of performing any lengthy and sustained advance. In fact the proper targets for criticism were quite different. In order correctly to evaluate the performance of the panzer troops on their march to Vienna, the following points must be borne in mind:

(a) The troops were in no way prepared for this operation. At the beginning of the march they were just starting company training. The theoretical training of staff officers, which had been intensively carried out within the 2nd Panzer Division during the previous winter, was to have been completed by the exercises in the Moselle previously mentioned. Nobody had contemplated an unexpected winter operation of divisional size.

(b) The higher command was equally unprepared. The decision was taken purely on Hitler's initiative. It was all a matter of improvisation; for the Panzer Divisions, which had only been in existence since the autumn of 1935, this was bound to be very difficult.

(c) The improvised march to Vienna meant that the 2nd Panzer Division had to cover about 420 miles, the SS-Leibstandarte 'Adolf Hitler' about 600 miles, within the space of some forty-eight hours. In general these tasks were performed satisfactorily.

(d) The most important weakness to make itself felt was the insufficiency of maintenance facilities, particularly for the tanks. This weakness had already become apparent during the autumn manœuvres of 1937. Proposals to remedy this state of affairs had, however, not yet been fulfilled by March of 1938. This mistake was never made again.

(e) Fuel supply had been shown to be a fundamental problem. Shortages which here became apparent were immediately put to rights. Since no ammunition had been used, our ammunition supply system could only be judged by analogy with the fuel supply. This sufficed, however, to make us take various precautions.

(f) It was in any case proved that our theoretical belief concerning the operational possibilities of panzer divisions was justified.

(g) The march had taught us that it was possible without difficulty to move more than one motorised division along one road. Our views concerning the setting up and the operational employment of motorised corps had prevailed.

(h) It must, however, be stressed that the experience gained applied only to the alerting, moving and supplying of tank units; we had added nothing to our knowledge of tank warfare. Still, the future was to show that here, too, the German armoured troops were on the right course.

In his valuable and highly significant Memoirs, Winston Churchill gives a very different picture of the *anschluss*.[1] It is worth quoting in full:

A triumphal entry into Vienna had been the Austrian Corporal's dream. On the night of Saturday, March 12, the Nazi Party in the capital had planned a torchlight procession to welcome the conquering hero. But nobody arrived. Three bewildered Bavarians of the supply services who had come by

[1] Winston Churchill, *The Second World War*, vol. 1. *The Gathering Storm*, p. 242. Cassell and Co., Ltd., London, 1948.

train to make billeting arrangements for the invading army had therefore to be carried shoulder-high through the streets. . . . The cause of this hitch leaked out slowly. The German war machine had lumbered falteringly over the frontier and come to a standstill near Linz. In spite of perfect weather and road conditions the majority of the tanks broke down. Defects appeared in the motorised heavy artillery. The road from Linz to Vienna was blocked with heavy vehicles at a standstill. General von Reichenau, Hitler's special favourite, Commander of Army Group IV, was deemed responsible for a breakdown which exposed the unripe condition of the German Army at this stage in its reconstruction.

Hitler himself, motoring through Linz, saw the traffic jam, and was infuriated. The light tanks were disengaged from confusion and straggled into Vienna in the early hours of Sunday morning. The armoured vehicles and motorised heavy artillery were loaded on to the railway trucks, and only thus arrived in time for the ceremony. The pictures of Hitler driving through Vienna amid exultant or terrified crowds are well known. But this moment of mystic glory had an unquiet background. The Fuehrer was in fact convulsed with anger at the obvious short-comings of his military machine. He rated his generals, and they answered back. They reminded him of his refusal to listen to Fritsch and his warnings that Germany was not in a position to undertake the risk of a major conflict. Appearances were preserved. The official celebrations and parades took place. . . .

Winston Churchill was evidently misinformed. So far as I know, no trains ran from Bavaria to Vienna on March 12.[1] The 'three bewildered Bavarians' must therefore have flown there. The German war machine was held up in Linz by my orders for the reception of Hitler, and for no other reason. In any event, it reached Vienna that same afternoon. The weather was bad; it began to rain during the afternoon, and that night there was a violent snowstorm. The single road from Linz to Vienna was in process of being relaid; in consequence it was torn up for miles on end while other parts of it were in very poor condition. The majority of the tanks arrived safely in Vienna. Defects in the heavy artillery could not have appeared since we did not possess any heavy artillery. At no time was the road blocked. General von Reichenau had only assumed command of Army Group 4 on the 4th of February, 1938, and could therefore hardly be held responsible for the equipment of troops whom he had only commanded for five weeks. Also his predecessor, Colonel-

[1] The railway authorities at Munich have been good enough to inform me that, according to the unanimous statements of employees engaged there at the time of the march into Austria, no special trains with military personnel or equipment left Germany for Vienna. In any case such a move would have required unified control of the German and Austrian railways, which at that time did not exist. On the day before the march in, the infantry divisions detrained in the frontier area near Berchtesgaden, Freilassing and Simbach, the empty trains returning immediately to Germany to pick up other units. On the second day of the operation troop trains could go as far as Salzburg; it was not until the third day that they could proceed all the way to Vienna.

General von Brauchitsch, had only held that post for so short a time
that even he could not be made to bear any blame either.

As described above, I met Hitler in Linz. He showed not the slightest
signs of being infuriated. It was perhaps the only occasion on which I
ever saw him deeply moved. While he addressed the enthusiastic crowd
below, I was standing next to him on the balcony of Linz town hall and
I was able to observe him closely. Tears were running down his cheeks,
and this was certainly not play-acting.

At the time we only possessed light tanks. Heavy tanks were as non-
existent as heavy artillery, and therefore could not have been loaded on
to railway trucks.

No general was 'rated,' at least not to my knowledge. The alleged
retorts could thus hardly have been given; or if they were, I know
nothing about this either. For myself, I was treated with uniform
politeness by Hitler during these March days, both in Linz and in
Vienna. The only person to find fault with me was Colonel-General
von Bock, the commander-in-chief of the occupying forces; this was
because of the decorations which I had ordered to be put on the tanks
and which he regarded as contrary to regulations. When I explained
that Hitler had given his permission for this, the matter was instantly
dropped.

This same war machine, which now 'lumbered falteringly over the
frontier,' proved itself capable in the spring of 1940, after only minor
improvements, of giving very short shrift indeed to the out-of-date
armies of the Western Powers. It is apparent from Winston Churchill's
Memoirs that he is anxious to prove that the political leaders of Great
Britain and France could have gone to war in 1938 with a good prospect
of achieving victory. The military leaders of those countries were considerably more sceptical, and with reason. They knew the weaknesses of
their own armies, though they could not see the way to building up
their strength afresh. The German generals wanted peace too; not,
however, out of weakness or fear of new inventions, but because they
believed that their country could peacefully achieve its national aims.

2nd Panzer Division remained in the Vienna area, and from the
autumn of that year began to receive Austrian replacements. The
SS-Leibstandarte and the staff of XVI Army Corps returned to Berlin
in April. The area around Würzburg was now empty, and it was here
that in the autumn of 1938 a new Panzer Division, the 4th, was set up
under General Reinhardt. In addition, the 5th Panzer Division and the
4th Light Division were also formed.

During the summer months of 1938 I carried out the peacetime duties
of a Corps Commander. These consisted principally in visiting the troops

under my command. In this way I managed to get to know both officers and other ranks and to lay the foundations for that sentiment of mutual trust in wartime of which I have always been particularly proud.

In August I was able to occupy the house in Berlin which was allotted to the commander of XVI Army Corps. In that same month occurred the visit of the Hungarian Regent, Admiral Horthy, who was accompanied by his wife and by the Prime Minister, Imredy. I took part in the reception at the station, the parade, the dinner party which Hitler gave, and the gala presentation at the opera. After dinner Hitler sat down for a time at my table and discussed tank problems with me.

Hitler was disappointed by the political results of Horthy's visit. He had doubtless hoped to persuade the Regent to sign a military pact, but in this he was not successful. Unfortunately he made his disappointment fairly obvious, both during the speech he made and by his behaviour after dinner.

From September 10th to 13th my wife and I were present at the National Party Day (the *Reichsparteitag*) at Nuremberg. During this month the tension between Germany and Czechoslovakia had reached its climax. The atmosphere was heavy and threatening. This was most vividly expressed in Hitler's great closing address in the Nuremberg congress hall. The immediate future looked ominous indeed.

I had to go straight from the *Parteitag* to the troop-training area Grafenwöhr, where the 1st Panzer Division and the *SS-Leibstandarte* were located. The next few weeks were filled with training exercises and inspections. Towards the end of the month we began to prepare for the march into the Sudetenland. In view of the refusal of the Czechs to agree to any concessions, the danger of war increased. The situation grew more and more serious.

The Munich conference, however, cleared a way for a peaceful solution, and so the incorporation of the Sudetenland into the Reich took place without bloodshed.

I had to make one personal sacrifice to the political situation. October 1st marked my wife's and my silver wedding anniversary. I spent the day alone at Grafenwöhr, while she was equally alone in Berlin, since both our sons were with their regiments on the border. But we received the finest possible present—the fact that peace had been preserved.

The Incorporation of the Sudetenland into the Reich

For the march into the Sudetenland, XVI Army Corps had the 1st Panzer Division and the 13th and 20th (Motorised) Infantry Divisions under command. The occupation was to be carried out in three stages. On the 3rd of October the 13th (Motorised) Infantry Division,

commanded by General Otto, occupied Eger, Asch and Franzensbad;
on the 4th of October the 1st Panzer Division entered Carlsbad; and on
the 5th all three divisions moved up to the demarcation line.

Adolf Hitler spent the first two days of the occupation with my corps.
The 1st Panzer and the 13th (Motorised) Infantry Divisions had moved
up during the nights of the 30th–1st and 1st–2nd, the former covering a
distance of 170 miles from Cham to Eibenstock in Saxony, the latter
coming from Grafenwöhr so as to be on time for the bloodless occupation of the Egerland. From the marching point of view this was a fine
performance.

On October the 3rd I met Hitler at the frontier near Asch and was
able to inform him of the successful move forward by my divisions.
Then I drove through Asch to a field kitchen immediately in front of
Eger where I had a meal, as did Hitler. It was the normal soldiers'
field rations, a thick stew with pork in it. When Hitler realised that
the stew contained meat he contented himself with eating a few apples;
he also asked me to arrange for the field kitchen to prepare a meatless
meal for the following day. Our entry into Eger was a gay and joyful
occasion. The majority of the population were dressed in the pretty
and becoming Egerland national dress and they gave Hitler a most
enthusiastic ovation.

On the 4th of October I met Hitler at the field kitchen of 1st Panzer
Division staff. I sat opposite him while we ate and took part in a very
friendly conversation, in which all present expressed their deep satisfaction that we had managed to avoid war. There were troops all
along the road down which Hitler now drove. He saluted them and
was impressed by their smart appearance. Everything was gay. As in
March in Austria the tanks were covered over and over again with
flowers and branches of greenery. I drove on to Carlsbad, where a
guard of honour was waiting before the theatre, consisting of three
companies, one each from the 1st Panzer Regiment, the 1st Rifle
Regiment and the *SS-Leibstandarte*. On the right flank of the Panzer
Company, next to his C.O., stood my elder son, who was Adjutant
of the 1st Battalion of the 1st Panzer Regiment.

There was only just sufficient time to close the side roads before
Adolf Hitler arrived. He walked through the ranks of the guard of
honour into the theatre, where he was greeted by the populace. Outside
the rain poured down in sheets, but inside the theatre the most touching
scenes now took place. The women and young girls in their national
costume burst into tears, many knelt down, and the cheers were
deafening. The Sudeten Germans had had to go through a great deal,
endless poverty, unemployment and persecution. Many had lost all
hope. Now a new day had dawned. We immediately set to work

distributing food from the field kitchens until such time as the charitable organisations could take over this task.

Between the 7th and the 10th of October a further German-inhabited zone was occupied. I drove through Kaaden and Saatz to Teplitz-Schönau. Everywhere our soldiers were greeted with the same pathetic joy. A wreath of flowers hung on every tank and every motor vehicle. The dense crowds of young men and girls in the streets sometimes made it difficult for us to move forwards. Thousands of soldiers of German blood, released from the Czech Army, were marching homewards on foot, most of them still wearing their Czech uniforms, carrying a box or a kitbag on their backs—an army defeated without a blow having been struck. We passed through the first lines of the Czech fortifications. These were not so strong as we had expected them to be; all the same we were glad that we did not have to capture them in bloody battle.

But our greatest joy was the peaceful turn the political situation had taken. A war would have hit this strip of German land particularly hard, and the German mothers would have had to make many sacrifices.

In Teplitz I took up my quarters in the *Kurhaus* that belonged to Prince Clary-Aldringen. The Prince and Princess received us in the most friendly and gracious fashion. We got to know numerous members of the German-Bohemian aristocracy and rejoiced to discover how truly German they had remained. I believe that Lord Runciman judged the situation in Czechoslovakia correctly and that his views had a great deal to do with the preservation of peace at this time.

In any event the political tension was for a while relaxed, a matter of rejoicing for all of us. I had the opportunity to go deer stalking, and in two weeks I managed to account for quite a few good animals.

The hectic year of 1938 was nearing its close and soldiers who, like me, had no connection with politics were hoping that despite past storms a period of peaceful progress would ensue. We thought that Germany would now settle down to the lengthy business of assimilating its newly-acquired territories and populations: we believed that once it had strengthened the positions gained, Germany would be so powerful in Europe that it would be able peacefully to achieve its national aims. I had seen Austria and the Sudetenland with my own eyes; despite all the enthusiasm with which the populations greeted their incorporation into the Reich, the economic situation in both territories was so bad, and the differences between their administration and that of the old Reich so great, that a long period of peace appeared to me essential to carry out a successful and durable amalgamation of the German lands. The Munich agreement seemed to offer the possibility of this.

Hitler's great achievements in the field of foreign policy had, furthermore, dissipated the evil impressions made by the crisis of the previous February. Even the replacement of Beck by Halder as Chief of the General Staff in September lost its significance in view of the success in the Sudetenland. General Beck had resigned because he could not subscribe to Hitler's foreign policy, which he regarded as dangerous. When he proposed that the whole corps of generals should make a unanimous declaration in favour of peace, Brauchitsch unfortunately turned the proposal down and the generals were never told of this suggestion. So when I returned from the Sudetenland to Berlin, it was with the anticipation of a long period of peace that I set to work again. Unfortunately I was to be proved wrong.

The Situation Deteriorates Once Again

Towards the end of October a district Party celebration (*Gautag*) took place on the occasion of the opening of a new wing of the Elephant Hotel at Weimar. Hitler was present and I, as Commanding General of the XVI Army Corps and senior officer of the Weimar district, was also invited to attend. The *Gautag* was officially opened in the *Stadtschloss* and reached its climax with an open-air speech by Hitler to a mass audience. In this speech Hitler spoke sharply against England, being particularly bitter about Churchill and Eden. Owing to being in the Sudetenland at the time, I had not heard his previous speech at Saarbrücken and so was extremely surprised to note this new, tense atmosphere. After Hitler's speech there was a tea-party at the Elephant. Hitler invited me to sit at his table and I was able to have a two-hour conversation with him. In the course of this I asked him why he had spoken so sharply against England. His attitude, I discovered, was based on what he took to be the improper behaviour towards himself of Chamberlain at Godesberg and the deliberate rudeness of certain prominent visitors who had come to see him. He had informed Ambassador Henderson: 'The next time one of your people comes to see me sloppily dressed, I'll tell my ambassador to call on your king in his pullover. Tell that to your Government.' He went on angrily to describe what he regarded as the rebuffs that he had received, and he said that the English were not really interested in honestly establishing friendly relations with Germany. He felt this all the more deeply since he had originally had great respect for England and had cherished the dream of close co-operation between the two countries.

Despite the Munich conference Germany was confronted with a very tense and anxious state of affairs. This disappointing and worrying fact had to be faced.

On the evening of the *Gautag* a performance of *Aïda* was given in the Weimar theatre. I sat in the Führer's box and was invited to dine at his table during the dinner party which marked the end of the celebrations. Conversation was on general and artistic matters. Hitler spoke of his trip to Italy and of a performance of *Aïda* which he had seen at Naples. At two o'clock he moved over to the actors' table.

When I returned to Berlin I was sent for by the Commander-in-Chief of the Army. He told me of his intention to create a post controlling both the motorised troops and cavalry, a sort of superior inspectorate for these two arms of the service, which he referred to collectively as 'mobile troops.' He had himself composed a draft of the duties and responsibilities which this post would carry with it, and he gave me this document to read. This draft outlined the authority that the officer in charge would have, which included the right of inspection and the making out of a yearly report. He was to have no command powers, no control over the preparation and issuing of service manuals, no authority in matters of organisation or personnel. I declined this dummy appointment.

A few days later the Chief of the Army Personnel Office—General Bodewin Keitel, younger brother to the head of the *OKW*—came to see me and urged me on behalf of the Commander-in-Chief of the Army to reconsider my decision and to accept the appointment. I declined once again, fully stating my reasons. Then Keitel confided to me that the creation of this new post was not in fact Brauchitsch's idea but had originated with Hitler. I could not therefore properly refuse it. I was unable to conceal my disappointment that the Commander-in-Chief of the Army had not told me in the very first place where the orders for this new appointment originated; but I still declined to accept it and I asked Keitel to give the reasons for my refusal to Hitler and to say that I was prepared to explain them personally to him if that were desired.

A few days later Hitler sent for me. He saw me alone and I was able to give him my views on the matter. I described the command organisation of the Army High Command and I told him of the proposed functions of the new post as outlined by the Commander-in-Chief of the Army in the draft that he had shown me. Meanwhile, in my present position as Commanding General of three Panzer Divisions, I was able to exert more influence on the development of panzer troops than I would ever be able to do in the proposed new appointment. In view of my detailed knowledge of the important personalities in the Army High Command, and of their varying attitudes towards the problem of developing the armoured force as a large-scale weapon for offensive operations, I was forced to regard this suggested innovation as a step in the wrong direction. I explained the ruling tendency in the Army High Command to subdivide the tank force among the infantry, and I said that in view of past conflicts on this score I could not be convinced that future progress might not be blocked. Furthermore, this proposed coupling of the armoured force with the cavalry would inevitably be against the wishes of the older arm of the Service, since they regarded me as their adversary and must view this new dispensation with distrust. Modernisation of the cavalry was urgently required, but even on this subject strong resistance was likely to be encountered from the Army High Command and from the senior cavalry officers. I ended my detailed exposition with the words: 'The proposed powers that would be vested in this appointment would be insufficient to enable me to overcome that resistance and the consequence would be continual friction and argument. I must therefore beg you to allow me to retain my present position.'

Hitler had let me talk for some twenty minutes without interruption. When I had finished he told me that he intended the new post to have all the necessary authority for exercising centralised control over the development of all motorised and cavalry troops; he therefore declined my request and ordered me to take up the new appointment. He finished: 'If you feel that you are being in any way hindered in the exercise of your functions by the resistance of which you spoke, you are to make a direct report to me personally. Together we'll see that the necessary modernisation is carried through. I therefore order you to accept the new appointment.'

Naturally there was never any question of my writing a direct report, despite the difficulties that immediately arose.

So I was promoted General of Panzer Troops and appointed Chief of 'Mobile Troops' and as such supplied with modest office accommodation in the Bendlerstrasse. I was alloted two General Staff Corps officers, Lieutenant-Colonel von le Suire and Captain Röttiger; my adjutant was Lieutenant-Colonel Riebel. I received a clerk for each branch of the Services entrusted to me. And then I went to work. It was a labour of Hercules. Up to that time the panzer troops possessed hardly any training manuals. We drew them up and submitted the drafts for the approval of the Army Training Department. This department did not contain a single tank officer. So our drafts were not judged according to the needs of the panzer troops but from quite other points of view. They were usually returned with the annotation: 'The subject-matter is not arranged according to the pattern adopted by the infantry manuals. The draft is therefore unacceptable.' Uniformity in the arrangement of subject-matter and 'nomenclature,' those were the two vital aspects according to which our work was judged. The needs of the troops played no part in all this whatever.

I regarded it as essential that the cavalry be reorganised into easily handled divisions with modern weapons. I therefore proposed a new organisation which was promptly turned down by the head of the General Army Office, General Fromm, since it involved the acquiring of 2,000 horses which that officer did not feel justified in purchasing. In consequence the cavalry retained its old unsatisfactory organisation until the outbreak of war. As a result of this, save for a single brigade that was stationed in East Prussia, the cavalry could only be used for the creation of mixed Reconnaissance Battalions for Infantry Divisions; these consisted of each one horse squadron, one motor-cycle squadron, and one motorised squadron with an insufficient number of armoured cars, of anti-tank guns and of cavalry weapons all mixed up together. To command this remarkable conglomeration was well-nigh impossible. On mobilisation, moreover, the cavalry would only be capable of providing these Reconnaissance Battalions for the regular peace-time divisions. The newly formed ones would have to make do as best they could with motor-cyclists. It was therefore urgent that an altogether fresh approach to the problem be made. The cavalry had reached this hopeless position despite the fact that all its senior officers felt a particularly deep love for their arm of the Service. Such is the difference between theory and practice.

One other incidental circumstance may serve to throw light on the situation as it then was: my mobilisation order informed me that in the event of mobilisation the Chief of Mobile Troops was to take command of a Reserve Infantry Corps. It was only after considerable trouble that I managed to get this changed for a command of armoured troops.

4. THE BEGINNING OF THE DISASTER

The Drift to War

In March of 1939 the Czechs were incorporated into the Reich in the name of a Protectorate. This led to a serious aggravation of the international situation. Hitler was exclusively responsible for the taking of this step.

On the morning of the occupation, the Commander-in-Chief of the Army sent for me; he informed me of the accomplished fact and ordered me to go at once to Prague, where I was to collect data concerning the advance made in wintry weather by our panzer units and to examine the Czech armoured equipment.

In Prague I found my successor as commanding general of XVI Army Corps, General Hoeppner, who informed me of his experiences during the advance. I also visited various units in order to collect first-hand impressions. In Brno I examined the Czech armoured equipment and found it serviceable. It was to prove useful to us during the Polish and French campaigns. During the Russian campaign it was finally replaced by heavier German equipment.

After Czechoslovakia, Memel was incorporated into the Reich without a blow being struck.

On April 20th Hitler celebrated his fiftieth birthday with a huge parade. All the colours of the armed forces were assembled into one colours battalion and the massed flags were dipped before him. He was now at the pinnacle of his success. Would he have the necessary self-control to consolidate it, or would he overreach himself? The situation was highly inflammable.

On the 28th of April he repudiated the Anglo-German Naval Agreement and announced the signature of a Non-aggression Pact with Poland.

On the 28th of May the Italian Foreign Minister, Count Ciano, visited Berlin. The German Foreign Minister gave a great reception in his honour. In order to make more room, two huge tents were set up which almost filled his garden. But that was a cold May, and so the tents had to be heated, a difficult undertaking. Hitler was present at this reception. The guests were entertained by cabaret turns, including dances by the Höpfner Sisters; this took place inside one of the tents in which a stage had been erected. There was a wait before the performance could begin, since Hitler wanted to sit next to Olga Chekova

Fig. 1.   At an artillery observation post

FIG. 2.   Polish summer landscape

FIG. 3.   Battle for an emplacement near Vizna

and this lady had first to be found. Hitler was partial to artistes and enjoyed their company. The political motive of Ciano's visit was clearly to warn Hitler against the danger of war. I am not capable of judging whether he possessed sufficient continuity of purpose and tact to carry out Mussolini's instructions up to the end of his visit.

June brought the visit to Berlin of the Prince Regent Paul of Yugoslavia and his beautiful bride. Again there was a great parade, mostly of motorised troops; so many units took part in this march past that the effect was more exhausting than impressive. It was significant that the Prince Regent went on to London from Berlin. So far as I know Hitler did not achieve the results that he had hoped for from this visit.

There was no lack of political warnings. But Hitler and his Foreign Minister, Ribbentrop, had persuaded themselves that the Western Powers would never risk war with Germany, and that they therefore had a free hand in Eastern Europe.

During the summer months of 1939 I was engaged in preparing for the large-scale manœuvres of motorised troops that were to be held in the autumn. They were to take place in the Erz Mountains and the Sudetenland. The considerable work involved was to be in vain.

The Polish Campaign

On the 22nd of August, 1939, I was ordered to the military training area Gross-Born to take command of the newly created XIX Army Corps staff which was to be re-christened 'Fortification Staff Pomerania.' This staff was to be responsible for the construction of field fortifications along the German border as protection against any possible Polish attack. The XIX Army Corps had under command the 3rd Panzer Division and the 2nd and 20th (Motorised) Infantry Divisions, together with corps troops. The 3rd Panzer Division was reinforced by the Panzer Demonstration Battalion, which was equipped with our newest tanks, the Panzer III and the Panzer IV. Among the corps troops was included the Reconnaissance Demonstration Battalion from Döberitz-Krampnitz. These demonstration units from our training schools were attached at my request, so that they might learn by practical experience. This was to stand them in good stead when they later returned to their primary functions.

It was only after a conference between the army commanders and Hitler at Obersalzburg, at which I was not present, that the commander of the Fourth Army, Colonel General von Kluge, told me what my mission really was. I then learned that my XIX Army Corps formed part of the Fourth Army. On my right, that is to the south, was General Strauss's II Corps and on my left were frontier defence units under

General Kaupisch: in the event of hostilities breaking out these latter were to be strengthened by the 10th Panzer Division which since March had been engaged on occupation duties in Prague and its neighbourhood. Behind my corps was stationed the army reserve, the 23rd Infantry Division from Potsdam. (*See Appendix* II.)

My task was to cross the River Brahe, with my right boundary the Zempolno and my left boundary running through Konitz, and to advance with all speed to the Vistula, thus cutting off and destroying the Polish forces in the so-called Polish Corridor. Strauss's Corps on my right was similarly to advance to the Vistula, while General Kaupisch, on my left, was to move on Danzig.

Polish forces in the Corridor were estimated at three infantry divisions and the *Pomorska* Cavalry Brigade. They were reckoned to possess a limited number of Fiat-Ansaldo tanks. The Polish side of the border was fortified. We had good observation of their field works. A secondary line of defensive positions was to be anticipated along the River Brahe.

The attack was to take place early on the 26th of August.

By means of a secret agreement with the Russians during these days Hitler had ensured the protection of his rear in the event of war. Owing to Ribbentrop's disastrous influence, illusions were still being cherished concerning the probable reactions of the Western Powers; it was considered unlikely that they would declare war.

In any case it is not with the knowledge of hindsight that I can declare that the attitude of the army was very grave indeed and that, had it not been for the Russian pact, there is no telling what the Army's reactions might not have been. We did not go light-heartedly to war and there was not one general who would not have advocated peace. The older officers, and many thousands of men, had been through the First World War. They knew what war would mean if it were not simply confined to a campaign against the Poles. There was every reason to fear that this would not be the case, since after the creation of the Bohemian Protectorate the British had guaranteed Poland's integrity. Each of us thought of the mothers and wives of our German soldiers and of the heavy sacrifices that they must be called upon to bear even if the outcome of the war were a successful one. Our own sons were on active service. My elder boy, Heinz Günter, was regimental adjutant of Panzer Regiment 35: my younger son, Kurt, had been commissioned Second Lieutenant in the 3rd Armoured Reconnaissance Battalion of the 3rd Panzer Division and so was in my Army Corps.

My last billet before the outbreak of war was at Dobrin near Preussisch-Friedland, where we were thoroughly spoiled by our dear hosts, the von Wilkens.

General Sketch Map 1.
The Advance into Poland
Situation 31.8 – 5.9.39.

During the night of 25th–26th August the attack was cancelled. Certain troops had already begun to move forward and had to be recalled. It was plain that diplomatic manœuvres were in progress. There was a last flicker of hope that peace might yet be preserved. But nothing positive reached the troops at the front. On the 31st of August there was a new alert. This time it was serious. The divisions moved up to the forward positions from which they would attack across the frontier. The order of battle of my XIX Army Corps was as follows:

On the right, 3rd Panzer Division under General Freiherr Geyr von Schweppenburg, with the task of advancing between two streams—the Zempolno and the Kamionka—to the Brahe, of crossing the Brahe east of Pruszcz in the neighbourhood of Hammermühle, and of pushing on to the Vistula in the direction of Schwetz.

In the centre, the 2nd (Motorised) Infantry Division under General Bader, located north of the Kamionka between Grunau and Firchau, with the task of breaking through the Polish frontier defences and of advancing on Tuchel.

On the left, the 20th (Motorised) Infantry Division under General Wiktorin, located west of Konitz, with the task of occupying that town and then of advancing across the Tuchel Heath towards Osche and Graudenz.

The main effort was to be carried out by the 3rd Panzer Division reinforced by corps troops, with the Army reserve (23rd Infantry Division) following behind.

On the 1st of September at 04.45 hrs. the whole corps moved simultaneously over the frontier. There was a thick ground mist at first which prevented the air force from giving us any support. I accompanied the 3rd Panzer Brigade, in the first wave, as far as the area north of Zempelburg where the preliminary fighting took place. Unfortunately the heavy artillery of the 3rd Panzer Division felt itself compelled to fire into the mist, despite having received precise orders not to do so. The first shell landed 50 yards ahead of my command vehicle, the second 50 yards behind it. I reckoned that the next one was bound to be a direct hit and ordered my driver to turn about and drive off. The unaccustomed noise had made him nervous, however, and he drove straight into a ditch at full speed. The front axle of the half-tracked vehicle was bent so that the steering mechanism was put out of action. This marked the end of my drive. I made my way to my corps command post, procured myself a fresh vehicle and had a word with the over-eager artillerymen. Incidentally it may be noted that I was the first corps commander ever to use armoured command vehicles in order to accompany tanks on to the battlefield.

Sketch Map 1

The Battle of Tuchel Heath.

2 - 3. 9. 39

They were equipped with radio, so that I was able to keep in constant touch with my corps headquarters and with the divisions under my command.

The first serious fighting took place north of Zempelburg in and around Gross-Klonia, where the mist suddenly lifted and the leading tanks found themselves face to face with Polish defensive positions. The Polish anti-tank gunners scored many direct hits. One officer, one officer cadet and eight other ranks were killed.

Gross-Klonia had once belonged to my great-grandfather, Freiherr Hiller von Gärtringen. Here, too, was buried my grandfather Guderian. My father had been born in this place. This was the first time I had ever set eyes on the estate, once so beloved by my family.

After successfully changing vehicles, I rejoined the 3rd Panzer Division whose most forward troops had now reached the Brahe. The bulk of the division was between Pruszcz and Klein-Klonia and was about to settle down for a rest. The divisional commander had been sent for by the Commander-in-Chief of the Army Group, Colonel-General von Bock, and was therefore absent. I asked the officers of the 6th Panzer Regiment who were there to tell me about the situation on the Brahe. The regimental commander did not believe that a passage of the river could be forced on that day, and he was eager to carry out the welcome orders for a rest. The corps order—that the Brahe should be crossed during the first day of the attack—had been forgotten. I walked angrily away and tried to decide what measures I should take to improve this unhappy state of affairs. A young Lieutenant Felix came over to where I was standing. He had taken off his tunic, his shirt sleeves were rolled up, and his arms were black with powder. 'Herr General,' he said, 'I've just come from the Brahe. The enemy forces on the far bank are weak. The Poles set fire to the bridge at Hammermühle, but I put the fire out from my tank. The bridge is crossable. The advance has only stopped because there's no one to lead it. You must go there yourself, sir.' I looked at the young man in amazement. He made a very good impression and his eyes inspired confidence. Why should not this young lieutenant have done the trick of Columbus and the egg? I followed his advice and drove through a confusion of German and Polish vehicles along the narrow sandy track that led through the woods to Hammermühle, where I arrived between 16.00 and 17.00 hrs. A group of staff officers were standing behind a stout oak tree about 100 yards from the water's edge. They greeted me with the cry: 'Herr General, they're shooting here!' They were indeed, both the tank guns of the 6th Panzer Regiment and the rifles of the 3rd Rifle Regiment blazing away. The enemy on the far bank sat in his trenches and was invisible. First of all I put a stop to the idiotic firing, in which I was ably assisted by the newly arrived commander of the 3rd Rifle Brigade, Colonel Angern. Then I ordered that the extent of the enemy's defensive positions be established. Motor-cycle Battalion 3, which had not yet been in action, was sent across the river in rubber boats at a point that was not under enemy fire. When they had crossed successfully, I ordered the tanks over the bridge. They took the Polish bicycle company, which was defending this sector of the stream, prisoner. Casualties were negligible.

All available troops were immediately employed on building up a bridgehead. Armoured Reconnaissance Battalion 3 was ordered to push forward straight across the Tuchel Heath until it reached the River Vistula near Schwetz, with the mission of locating the main Polish forces and their reserves, if any. At about 18.00 hrs. the crossing of the Brahe was completed. During the night the 3rd Panzer Division reached its objective, Sviekatovo.

I returned to my corps headquarters at Zahn, which I reached at dusk.

The long road was deserted. Not a shot was to be heard. I was therefore all the more amazed to be stopped on the outskirts of Zahn by men of my own staff, whom I found busily engaged in setting up an anti-tank gun, steel helmets on their heads. When I enquired what the purpose of this was, I was informed that Polish cavalry was advancing towards us and would be upon us at any minute. I calmed them down and proceeded to get on with my work at headquarters.

Messages from the 2nd (Motorised) Infantry Division stated that their attack on the Polish wire entanglements had bogged down. All three infantry regiments had made a frontal attack. The division was now without reserves. I ordered that the regiment on the left be withdrawn during the night and moved to the right wing, from where it was to advance next day behind the 3rd Panzer Division and make an encircling movement in the direction of Tuchel.

The 20th (Motorised) Division had taken Konitz with some difficulty, but had not advanced any appreciable distance beyond that town. It was ordered to continue its attack on the next day.

During the night the nervousness of the first day of battle made itself felt more than once. Shortly after midnight the 2nd (Motorised) Division informed me that they were being compelled to withdraw by Polish cavalry. I was speechless for a moment; when I regained the use of my voice I asked the divisional commander if he had ever heard of Pomeranian grenadiers being broken by hostile cavalry. He replied that he had not and now assured me that he could hold his positions. I decided all the same that I must visit this division the next morning.

At about five o'clock I found the divisional staff still all at sea I placed myself at the head of the regiment which had been withdrawn during the night and led it personally as far as the crossing of the Kamionka to the north of Gross-Klonia, where I sent it off in the direction of Tuchel. The 2nd (Motorised) Division's attack now began to make rapid progress. The panic of the first day's fighting was past.

Armoured Reconnaissance Battalion 3 had reached the Vistula during the night. At the farm of Poledno, near Schwetz, it had unfortunately through carelessness sustained considerable officer casualties. The main body of the 3rd Panzer Division was split into two by the Brahe and during the morning the Poles attacked the units on the eastern bank. It was noon before a counter-attack could be launched and the division could continue its fighting advance through the woods. The 23rd Infantry Division followed behind the 3rd Panzer Division by means of forced marches. Both the motorised infantry divisions were making good progress across the Tuchel Heath.

On the 3rd of September the 23rd Infantry Division, under General Graf Brockdorff, was committed between the 3rd Panzer Division, which had pushed on to the Vistula, and the 20th (Motorised) Infantry Division: by this manœuvre, after many critical moments and some heavy fighting, we succeeded in totally encircling the enemy on our front in the wooded country north of Schwetz and west of Graudenz. The Polish *Pomorska* Cavalry Brigade, in ignorance of the nature of our tanks, had charged them with swords and lances and had suffered tremendous losses. A Polish artillery regiment on the march towards the Vistula was overrun by our tanks and destroyed; only two of its guns managed to fire at all. The Polish infantry had had heavy casualties too. A portion of their supply and bridging columns was caught while withdrawing and annihilated.

On the 4th of September the noose was tightened about the encircled enemy. The battle for the Corridor was approaching its end. For a short time the 23rd Infantry Division was in trouble, but a regiment detached from the 32nd Infantry Division of General Strauss's Corps soon cleared up the situation here.

The troops had fought brilliantly and were in good spirits. The casualties among our other ranks were small, but our losses of officers had been disproportionately heavy, for they had thrown themselves into battle with the greatest devotion to duty. General Adam, State Secretary von Weizsäcker and Colonel Freiherr von Funk had each lost a son.

On the 3rd of September I had visited the 23rd Infantry and 3rd Panzer Divisions and had thus had the opportunity of seeing my son Kurt and also the towers of Kulm, my birthplace, glittering in the sunshine on the far bank of the Vistula. On the 4th I watched the 2nd and

20th (Motorised) Infantry Divisions fight their way forwards through the woods; towards the end of the day I arrived at the former German military training area of Gruppe, west of Graudenz. That night I was with the 3rd Panzer Division which, with its back to the Vistula, was advancing westward for the final elimination of the enemy's remnants in the pocket.

The Corridor was pierced. We were available for fresh employment. While we had been fighting hard, the political situation had taken a serious turn for the worse. England and, under pressure from England, France had declared war on the Reich; this destroyed our hope of an early peace. We found ourselves engaged in a second World War. It was plain that it must last a long time and that we would need all the fortitude of which we were capable.

On the 5th of September our corps had a surprise visit from Adolf Hitler. I met him near Plevno on the Tuchel–Schwetz road, got into his car and drove with him along the line of our previous advance. We passed the destroyed Polish artillery, went through Schwetz, and then, following closely behind our encircling troops, drove to Graudenz where he stopped and gazed for some time at the blown bridges over the Vistula. At the sight of the smashed artillery regiment, Hitler had asked me: 'Our dive bombers did that?' When I replied, 'No, our panzers!' he was plainly astonished. Between Schwetz and Graudenz those elements of the 3rd Panzer Division not needed for the encirclement of the Poles were drawn up: these included the 6th Panzer Regiment and the 3rd Armoured Reconnaissance Battalion with my son Kurt. We drove back through parts of the 23rd and 2nd (Motorised) Infantry Divisions. During the drive we discussed at first the course of events in my corps area. Hitler asked about casualties. I gave him the latest figures that I had received, some 150 dead and 700 wounded for all the four divisions under my command during the Battle of the Corridor. He was amazed at the smallness of these figures and contrasted them with the casualties of his own old regiment, the *List* Regiment, during the First World War: on the first day of battle that one regiment alone had lost more than 2,000 dead and wounded. I was able to show him that the smallness of our casualties in this battle against a tough and courageous enemy was primarily due to the effectiveness of our tanks. Tanks are a life-saving weapon. The men's belief in the superiority of their armoured equipment had been greatly strengthened by their successes in the Corridor. The enemy had suffered the total destruction of between two and three infantry divisions and one cavalry brigade. Thousands of prisoners and hundreds of guns had fallen into our hands.

As we neared the Vistula we could see the silhouette of a town

C*

against the sky across the river. Hitler asked if that was Kulm. I replied:
'Yes, that is Kulm. In March of last year I had the privilege of greeting
you in your birthplace; today you are with me in mine. I was born in
Kulm.' Many years later Hitler was to recall this scene.

Our conversation turned on technical matters. Hitler wanted to know
what had proved particularly satisfactory about our tanks and what
was still in need of improvement. I told him that the most important
thing now was to hasten the delivery of Panzers III and IV to the
fighting troops and to increase the production of these tanks. For their
further development their present speed was sufficient, but they needed
to be more heavily armoured, particularly in front; the range and
power of penetration of their guns also needed to be increased, which
would mean longer barrels and a shell with a heavier charge. This
applied equally to our anti-tank guns.

With a word of recognition for the troops' achievements Hitler left
us as dusk was falling and returned to his headquarters.

It was noteworthy that the civilian population, which was re-emerging
from its hiding-places now that the fighting was over, cheered as Hitler
drove past and brought him flowers. The town of Schwetz was decorated
with our national colours. The impression made by his visit on the
troops was a very good one. Unfortunately as the war went on Hitler
visited the front less and less frequently, and in the final stages not
at all. By so doing he lost contact with the feelings of the troops and
was no longer able to understand their achievements and their sufferings.

On the 6th of September the corps staff and the advance guards of
the divisions crossed the Vistula. Corps headquarters was set up in
Finkenstein, in the very beautiful castle that belonged to Count
Dohna-Finckenstein and which Frederick the Great had given to his
minister, Count von Finckenstein. Napoleon had twice used this castle
as his headquarters. The Emperor first came there in 1807, when he
took the war against Prussia and Russia over the Vistula and into
East Prussia. After crossing the poor and monotonous Tuchel Heath,
Napoleon exclaimed at the sight of the castle: '*Enfin un château!*' His
feelings are understandable. It was there that he had planned his advance
towards Preussisch-Eylau. A mark of his presence was still to be seen
in the scratches left by his spurs on the wooden floor. He was there
for the second time before the Russian campaign of 1812; he spent
a few weeks in the castle in the company of the beautiful Countess
Walewska.

I slept in the room that had been Napoleon's.

Unfortunately our host, Count Dohna, was sick in a Berlin clinic,
so that I had not the honour of meeting him or his countess. He was
kind enough to write telling me to make free of his deer. Since we had

not yet received orders concerning our future employment, and only knew that we were to be detached from Fourth Army and placed immediately under the command of Army Group von Bock, I thought that I could accept his kind offer without detriment to the performance of my military duties. While my divisions were crossing the river during the night of the 7th and early morning of the 8th, I therefore went hunting and had the good fortune to bag a large twelve-pointer. The conscientious bailiff responsible for the administration of the Count's forest lands insisted on personally acting as my guide.

On the 8th of September all my divisions were across the river at Mewe and Käsemark, and events began to develop more rapidly. In the evening I was told to go to the Army Group headquarters at Allenstein to receive my orders. I left Finkenstein at about 19.30 hrs. and between 21.30 and 22.30 hrs. I was given my new instructions.

The Army Group's original intention was to attach my corps to General von Küchler's Third Army: it was to operate in close co-ordination with his left flank and to advance from the Arys area, through Lomsha, towards the eastern side of Warsaw. It seemed to me that such close co-operation with an infantry army was not in accordance with the full potentialities of my troops. I pointed out that the proposed operation would not enable me to make use of the speed of my motorised divisions, and that a slow advance on our part would give the Poles in the Warsaw area the chance of withdrawing eastwards and of establishing a new defensive line along the River Bug. I therefore suggested to the Chief of Staff of the Army Group, General von Salmuth, that my Panzer Corps remain under direct Army Group control and be pushed forward on the left of Küchler's army, through Vizna, along the east bank of the Bug, with Brest-Litovsk as its objective. This would frustrate any attempt on the part of the Poles now in and around Warsaw to establish new defensive positions. Salmuth and Colonel-General von Bock agreed to my suggestion; I received the necessary orders and went at once to the military training area Arys, where I told the corps order group to assemble (to receive fresh orders for the advance on the Narev River). Of my old divisions, I was to retain the 3rd Panzer Division and the 20th (Motorised) Infantry Division. The 2nd (Motorised) Infantry Division was for the time being withdrawn from my command into Army Group reserve. The 10th Panzer Division, which up to then had formed part of Küchler's army, together with the Fortress Infantry Brigade *Lötzen*, a newly formed unit of men from the older age-groups, were now subordinated to my XIX Corps: both these units were at present in action along the Narev in the neighbourhood of Vizna.

Orders were issued to the two divisions which had previously formed part of the corps. This took place at Arys between 02.00 and 04.30 hrs. on September 9th. I then drove to Korzeniste, 11 miles north of Lomsha, to visit General von Falkenhorst, the commander of XXI Army Corps which was now on my right; I wished to find out what his situation was and to hear what he might have to say about the units which I was now to command. I arrived there between 05.00 and 06.00 hrs., woke the officers and let them describe to me the previous battles on their front. I now learned that an attempt to capture Lomsha by means of a *coup de main* had failed, partly owing to the stubborn defence offered by the Poles, but partly also due to the inexperience of our own troops. XXI Army Corps was immobilised on the northern bank of the Narev.

At 08.00 hrs. I arrived at Vizna where I found the staff of the 10th Panzer Division. Its commander, General Schaal, had had an accident and the division was now under General Stumpff. The latter informed me that his infantry was over the river and had reported the capture of the Polish fortified positions dominating this sector. The battle was continuing. Reassured by this news I next visited the *Lötzen* Brigade; originally this unit had been intended to garrison these fortifications, but now had to cross the Narev in open battle. The brigade and its commander, Colonel Gall, made an excellent impression on me. They crossed the river and went into the attack. Quite satisfied with the measures that the brigade commander was taking, I returned to the 10th Panzer Division.

When I arrived back in Vizna I found to my disappointment that the morning's report on the successes of the division's infantry was based on a misapprehension. They were across the river but they had not reached the concrete defence emplacements on the far bank. For the time being nothing was happening. I therefore crossed the river myself to see the regimental commander. I did not succeed in discovering his command post. The battalion's headquarters were very well hidden, too. I found myself in the front line. There was no sign of the division's tanks, which were in fact all still on the north bank of the Narev. I therefore sent back my adjutant to order them across. In the front line an extraordinary performance was going on; when I asked what was happening I was told that the foremost companies were being relieved. It looked like nothing so much as a guard-mounting parade. The troops knew nothing about any order to attack. An artillery observer from the heavy artillery was located in the middle of the infantry and had no idea what he was supposed to be doing there. No one knew where the enemy was; there was no sort of reconnaissance being carried out. I first put a stop to the remarkable

General Sketch Map No 2.
The Advance into Poland.
Situation 9.9.—18.9.39.

manœuvre of company reliefs, and then ordered that the regimental and battalion commanders be brought to me. I next gave the artillery observer orders to lay down fire on the Polish positions. When the regimental commander at last turned up I immediately set out to find the enemy's front line and he and I went forward until we came under fire. We were by this time immediately in front of the concrete emplacements, where we stumbled on a German anti-tank gun, whose brave commander had advanced this far on his own. It was from here that we mounted the attack. I cannot pretend that I was anything but very disappointed by what had so far happened.

When I returned to the Narev, I found the tank regiment still on the northern bank. The regimental commander was ordered to cross the river with all speed. Since the bridges were not yet ready the tanks had to be ferried across. It was 18.00 hrs. before the attack could at last be launched. It was immediately successful and our casualties were very light. An energetic and determined leadership could easily have secured these results in the morning.

Before going to my corps headquarters, which was now established in Vizna, I gave both verbal and written orders to the engineer officer responsible for bridge-building; bridges over the Narev were to be built with all possible speed since they were urgently needed for transporting the 10th and ultimately the 3rd Panzer Divisions to the far side.

When I arrived at my headquarters I drew up orders for the following day: the 20th (Motorised) Infantry Division was to cross the Narev on the right of the 10th Panzer Division, while the 3rd Panzer Division was to follow behind the 10th. We slept in the newly built vicarage of Vizna, an uncompleted and almost uninhabitable building, but all the others were worse.

It was not until 05.00 hrs. on the 10th of September that I discovered that the bridges over the Narev, which were to have been ready by midnight, had been dismantled on the orders of the 20th (Motorised) Infantry Division's commander and moved downstream where they were to be put up anew for his division to cross. The two panzer divisions were therefore compelled to go on using ferries and nothing but ferries. It was desperate. The engineer officer had not informed the divisional commander of my order. The latter had acted in all good faith. Now we had to wait till evening before a new bridge was built for the tanks.

On this day General Wiktorin's 20th (Motorised) Infantry Division became involved in heavy fighting near Zambrov. Strong elements of the division were marching towards the Bug in the direction of Nur. I had sent the Reconnaissance Demonstration Battalion ahead of the

Sketch Map 2

Advance of XXI Army Corps
to Brest-Litovsk
Situation 8. 9. –17. 9. 39.

division to this crossing-place over the Bug, and the battalion had arrived there without encountering any resistance. The 10th Panzer Division pushed on to Bransk, fighting a number of engagements on the way. I followed this division towards evening and spent the night in the burning village of Vysokie-Masovieski. My corps staff, which had crossed the Narev that evening and was following behind me, could not get through a small village that was on fire north of Vysokie-Masovieski, and so we were compelled to spend the night in separate villages, a bad state of affairs from the command point of view. I had ordered the move of the headquarters prematurely; we would have done better to have spent another night in Vizna.

I passed the morning of September 11th impatiently awaiting the arrival of my staff. Polish forces, trying to withdraw south-east from Lomsha, had cut across the route of advance of the 20th (Motorised) Division at a point south of Zambrov and were causing that division considerable trouble. The divisional commander decided to order the portion of his command which was beyond the Poles, advancing on the Bug, to turn round in order that he might encircle the enemy and destroy him. I moved a part of the 10th Panzer Division across to help in this manœuvre. Meanwhile a rumour had spread through the 3rd Panzer Division, which was moving up on the left of the 10th, that I was myself in danger of being surrounded by Poles in Vysokie-Masovieski. Motorcycle Rifle Battalion 3 therefore turned off towards Vysokie to get me out. The men were very pleased when they found me standing safe and sound in the middle of the village street. This often-shown feeling of comradeship which the motor-cyclists displayed was good to see.

Corps headquarters spent the night at Vysokie-Masovieski.

On the 12th of September the 20th (Motorised) Division, together with those elements of the 10th Panzer Division sent to its assistance, succeeded in surrounding the Poles near Andrzeievo. The 10th Panzer Division reached Vysokie-Litovsk, the 3rd Panzer Division Bielsk. I myself had driven to Bielsk with the foremost troops of the reconnaissance battalion, and was thus able to receive their signal by hand. In the afternoon I saw my son Kurt.

The corps headquarters was moved to Bielsk. The 2nd (Motorised) Infantry Division was freed from Army Group reserve and once again placed under my command. It was ordered to advance along the line Lomsha–Bielsk and thus rejoin the rest of the corps. The order contained the words 'the divisional commander to come on ahead.' When, in the morning of the 13th, General Bader, in accordance to this order, was advancing well in front of his division, accompanied only by a wireless signals truck, he ran into Polish troops between Bransk and Bielsk who had managed to escape from the Andrzeievo pocket; he had to spend a few uncomfortable hours under fire before his competent wireless operator managed to let us know what had happened so that we could get them out. This accident was a lesson to us.

On this date the Poles near Andrzeievo surrendered. The commander of the 18th Polish Division was among the prisoners. The 3rd Panzer Division reached Kaminiec-Litovsk. They had reconnoitred as far as Brest-Litovsk. Orders for the attack on that fortress were given. We spent the night in Bielsk.

We knew that Polish forces had reached the famous forest of Bielovieza. I wanted to avoid a battle in the forest since this would have distracted us from our main objective—the capture of Brest-Litovsk—and would have tied up a sizeable portion of our force. I therefore contented myself with leaving troops to observe the edge of the forest.

On the 14th of September elements of the 10th Panzer Division, consisting of the Reconnaissance Battalion and of Panzer Regiment 8, broke through the line of fortified positions outside Brest. I immediately ordered the whole corps to advance with all speed on Brest in order to exploit this surprise success.

We spent the night in Vysokie-Litovsk.

On the 15th of September the ring was closed around Brest on the east bank of the Bug. An attempt to capture the citadel by means of a surprise tank attack failed, owing to the Poles having blocked the entrance gate by parking an old Renault tank at an angle across it, so that our tanks could not force their way in.

Corps headquarters that night was at Kaminiec-Litovsk.

The 20th (Motorised) Division and the 10th Panzer Division were deployed for a concerted attack on the citadel to take place on the 16th. They stormed the encircling wall but there the attack faltered owing to the failure of the infantry regiment of the 10th Panzer Division to advance, as ordered, immediately behind the creeping barrage that the artillery was putting down. When the regiment, in whose front line I myself was, did at last attack too late and without orders, it suffered sadly heavy casualties without reaching its objective. My adjutant, Lieutenant-Colonel Braubach, was severely wounded on this occasion, and died of his wounds a few days later. Fire from troops to the rear had been falling among our own advanced units; he had gone back in an attempt to stop this. A Polish sniper on the top of the rampart shot him at a range of 100 yards. His was a painful loss.

The 3rd Panzer Division, skirting Brest on the east, headed south towards Vlodava; the 2nd (Motorised) Division, following behind, moved east in the direction of Kobryn.

Corps headquarters remained in Kaminiec-Litovsk.

Early on September 17th the citadel was captured by the 76th Infantry Regiment under Colonel Gollnik, which had crossed over to the west bank of the Bug during the night. They captured it at the exact moment when the Polish garrison was about to attempt to break out westwards across the undamaged bridge over the Bug. This marked in a way the end of the campaign. Corps headquarters was transferred to Brest and established itself in the Voivodschaft. We learned that the Russians were advancing from the east.

The Polish campaign was the baptism of fire for my armoured formations. I was convinced that they had fully proved their value and that the work which had gone into building them up had been well spent. We were standing along the Bug, facing west, ready to receive the rest of the Polish Army. The corps' rear was covered by the 2nd (Motorised) Division, which still had heavy fighting to do before Kobryn. We were expecting at any moment to establish contact with the armoured forces moving up from the south. Our most forward reconnaissance troops reached Luboml.

Meanwhile the Fourth Army under Colonel-General von Kluge had caught up with us, and we were once again placed under its command. The Fortress Brigade *Lötzen*, which had fought so bravely on the Narev, had continued for a few days to be our left wing before it was subordinated to Fourth Army. Fourth Army now ordered that XIX Army Corps move forward, one division to go south, one to go east towards Kobryn, and one to go north-east towards Bialystok. Such a move would have split the corps and would have made all attempts at command impossible. The appearance of the Russians rendered these orders obsolete before they could be carried out.

As forerunner of the Russians there appeared a young officer in an armoured reconnaissance car, who informed us that a Russian Tank Brigade was on its way. Then we received information concerning the demarcation line which the Foreign Ministry had agreed; this surrendered Brest to the Russians, since the Bug was to be the boundary. We did not regard this as a very advantageous decision; and finally we were informed that we only had until the 22nd of September in which to evacuate the territory east of the line of demarcation. This was so little time that we could not even move all our wounded or recover our damaged tanks. It seems unlikely that any soldier was present when the agreement about the demarcation line and the cease fire was drawn up.

There is one more small incident that occurred in Brest-Litovsk and that seems to me worth recording. The Bishop of Danzig, O'Rourq, together with the Primate of Poland, Cardinal Hlond, had fled east-

wards from Warsaw. When the two princes of the Church arrived at
Brest they were much surprised to find the Germans already installed.
The Cardinal slipped away to the south-east and managed to reach
Rumania. The Bishop of Danzig decided to go north-east and thus fell
straight into our hands. He asked for an interview with me, which I
willingly gave him in Brest. Since he did not know where he could find
safety, and since in no circumstances did he wish to be handed over to
the Russians, I suggested that he travel back with one of my supply
columns which brought our stuff down from Koenigsberg. Once there
he could easily get in touch with the Bishop of Ermland and place
himself under the latter's protection. The Bishop accepted my suggestion,
and he and his entourage thus escaped without harm from the war zone.
He wrote me a charming letter, in which he spoke of the chivalrous
traditions of the German officer corps, to thank me for the assistance I
had been able to give him.

On the day for handing over to the Russians a Brigadier-General
Krivochin appeared, a tank man who had some knowledge of French,
and with whom I could therefore converse. What the instructions of the
Foreign Ministry had left undecided I now settled in a friendly fashion
directly with the Russians. All our equipment could be carried away:
only supplies captured from the Poles had to be left behind, since in
the short time at our disposal we had not been able to organise the transport necessary for their removal. A farewell parade and salutes to the
two flags in the presence of General Krivochin marked the end of our
stay in Brest-Litovsk.

Before leaving the fortress whose capture had cost us so much blood,
I accompanied my adjutant, Lieutenant-Colonel Braubach, to his last
resting-place on September 21st. I deeply regretted the loss of this brave
and capable colleague. The wound which he had received was not in
itself mortal, but it had become septic, and this, working on an already
weakened heart, had proved fatal.

On the evening of the 22nd of September we arrived at Zambrov.
The 3rd Panzer Division had already set off for East Prussia, with the
other divisions echeloned behind. The corps was now dissolved.

On the 23rd of September we occupied quarters in Gallingen, the
beautiful estate of Count Botho-Wend zu Eulenburg. The count himself
was on active service. We were therefore entertained by the countess and
her pretty daughter, and we enjoyed several peaceful days' rest, which
did us all good after the excitements and exhaustion of the campaign.

My son Kurt had survived the battles in good condition. I had had
no news of my elder son, Heinz; in fact during the whole campaign the
troops never once received any field post from home. This was a considerable hardship. Now we all hoped for an early transfer to our home

stations, so that we might get our units into good shape again as soon as possible.

We also hoped at that time that the speed of our Polish victory would bear political fruit, and that the Western Powers might now feel inclined to make a sensible peace. We imagined that if this were not the case, Hitler would quickly decide on a campaign in the West. Unfortunately both hopes were to prove groundless. We were entering the period which Churchill has described as the *drôle de guerre*.

I spent the leisure that was now granted me in visiting my East Prussian relatives, with whom I also found a nephew from West Prussia who had been compelled to join the Polish Army and who had now been released from captivity in order to serve his own nation.

On the 9th of October my corps staff was transferred to Berlin. On the way I stopped to see my relations in West Prussia once again; they had been through hard times, including the notorious Bromberg 'Bloody Sunday.' I also paid a short visit to my birthplace, Kulm, and found the houses in which my parents and my grandmother had lived. It was the last time I was ever to visit my first home.

Back in Berlin I soon had the great joy of seeing my elder son once again, who had been decorated with the Iron Cross, both First and Second Class. He had fought in the fierce battles for Warsaw.

I cannot end my story of the Polish campaign without mentioning my staff which, under its chief, Colonel Nehring, did such splendid work, and which by its intelligence and its first-class command technique contributed so immeasurably to the successes of my corps.

Between the Campaigns

On October 27th I was ordered to appear at the Chancellery. There I found myself to be one of the twenty-four officers who were to be decorated with the Knight's Cross of the Iron Cross. It was very pleasant to receive this order so early, and it seemed to me to be primarily a vindication of my long struggle for the creation of the new armoured force. That force had undoubtedly been principally responsible for the speed with which the campaign was won and for the smallness of the casualties that we had sustained while winning it. During the luncheon which followed the investiture, I was seated at Hitler's right and we had an animated conversation about the development of the armoured force and the experience we had gained during the campaign. Towards the end of the meal he asked me a direct question: 'I should like to know how the people and the army reacted to the Russian pact.' I could only reply that we soldiers had breathed a sigh of relief when we heard the news of its signature at the end of August. It had given us a feeling of security in our rear, and we were happy to think that we would be spared the two-front war of which we were frightened and which had proved our undoing in the long run during the previous World War. Hitler stared at me in amazement, and I felt that he was not pleased with my answer. However, he said nothing further on this matter, and indeed changed the subject. It was only much later that I realised how deep was Hitler's hatred of Soviet Russia. He had doubtless expected me to express astonishment at his having ever agreed to sign a pact with Stalin.

A short leave which I spent at home was saddened by the death of my mother-in-law, who passed on in our Berlin house on the 4th of November. We accompanied her coffin to Goslar and laid her in her final resting-place beside my late father-in-law. Then new orders took me away from home once again.

In the middle of November my staff was transferred, first to Dusseldorf, and then, as a result of a sudden change of plan, to Koblenz. There I was subordinate to Colonel-General von Rundstedt, the Commander-in-Chief of Army Group A.

In order to strengthen the political attitude of the officer corps, and particularly of the general officers, a series of lectures was now organised in Berlin, to be given, among others, by Goebbels, Goering and finally, on the 23rd of November, by Hitler himself. The audiences consisted in the main of generals and admirals, but also included some instructors and supervisors from War Schools down to the rank of lieutenant.

In the speeches of the three persons mentioned above, an almost identical train of thought was apparent, as follows: 'The Luftwaffe generals, under the purposeful leadership of party comrade Goering, are entirely reliable; the admirals can be trusted to follow the Hitlerite line; but the Party cannot place unconditional trust in the good faith of the army generals.' In view of the success of the recently concluded campaign in Poland, this insinuation struck us all as incomprehensible. When I was back in Koblenz I went to see the Chief of Staff of the Army Group, General von Manstein, whom I knew well, and discussed with him what should be done about this. He agreed with me that the corps of generals could not simply ignore the allegations that had been made. He had already talked to his Commander-in-Chief on the subject, but had found the latter disinclined to take any steps. He urged me to see if I could persuade Rundstedt to do something. I went to see him at once. Colonel-General von Rundstedt already knew all about this business, but said he was not willing to go farther than to visit the Commander-in-Chief of the Army and to draw that officer's attention to the allegations that had been made. I pointed out that as the allegations were directed primarily against the Commander-in-Chief of the Army and that as that officer had himself been present when they were made, the proper course to take was to approach Hitler from some other angle in order to urge on him the withdrawal of these unjustified accusations. General von Rundstedt was unwilling to take any further action in the matter. In the next few days I visited a number of senior generals in an attempt to urge them to do something, but in vain. The last one I saw was Colonel-General von Reichenau, whose good standing with both Hitler and the Party was well known. Reichenau informed me to my surprise that, on the contrary, his relations with Hitler were anything but good, that he had in fact had serious quarrels with him. Consequently there would be nothing to be gained by his going to see the Führer. He felt, however, that it was essential Hitler be informed of the sentiments of the corps of generals in this matter, and he suggested that I myself undertake this task. When I replied that I was among the most junior corps commanders, and therefore scarcely in a position to speak on behalf of so many of my superiors, he would not accept this argument and maintained that this very fact might be all to the good. He sent a signal to the Chancellery, requesting an interview for me, and the next day I received an order to report to Hitler in Berlin. During the conversation which resulted I made some remarkable discoveries.

Hitler received me alone and let me talk for some twenty minutes without interruption. I described the three speeches which I had heard in Berlin and the allegations that all these contained against the army generals, and then I went on to say: 'I have since talked to a number of generals. They have all expressed their astonishment and indignation that so outspoken a distrust of themselves should exist among the leading personalities of the government, despite the fact that they have only recently proved their ability and risked their lives for Germany in the Polish campaign which they brought to a victorious conclusion in little more than three weeks. In view of the serious war against the Western Powers that lies ahead of us all, they believe it essential that so important a breach in the supreme leadership be closed. You will perhaps be surprised that I, one of the juniors among commanding generals, should be the one to approach you on this matter. I asked a number of my seniors to undertake this duty, but none was willing. However, you must not later be in a position to say: "I told the army generals that I did not trust them and they accepted my distrust. Not one protested." That is why I have come to see you today, in order to protest against remarks that have been made which we feel to be both unfair and insulting. If there are individual generals —and it cannot be more than a question of individuals—whom you do not believe that you can trust, then you must dismiss them; the war that lies ahead will be a long one; we cannot afford such a breach in our military leadership, and mutual confidence must be restored before a critical situation arises comparable to the crisis of 1916 in the First World War prior to the appointment of Hindenburg and Ludendorff to the supreme command. On that occasion the solution was reached too late. Our highest leadership must be careful that it does not once again take the necessary measures too late.'

Hitler listened with great seriousness to all I had to say. When I had finished he replied brusquely: 'It's a question of the Commander-in-Chief of the Army.' I then said: 'If you feel you cannot trust the present Commander-in-Chief of the Army, then you must get rid of him and appoint a general in his place in whom you have complete confidence.' Then came the question which I had dreaded: 'Whom do you suggest?' I had thought up a whole list of general officers, who, in my opinion, were capable of filling that difficult appointment. I mentioned, first, Colonel-General von Reichenau. Hitler refused this suggestion with the words: 'Quite out of the question.' His expression was unusually disagreeable as he said this, and I realised that Reichenau had in no way been exaggerating during our conversation at Dusseldorf when he described his relations with Hitler as bad. A whole series of further suggestions, starting with Colonel-General von Rundstedt, proved equally unacceptable. Finally, I had exhausted my list of names and I fell silent.

Now Hitler began to talk. He described in detail the background of his mistrust of the generals; he started with the trouble Fritsch and Beck had caused him when he began the rearmament of Germany. He had wanted the immediate formation of 36 divisions, but they had told him that he must be satisfied for the time being with 21. The generals had warned him against the re-occupation of the Rhineland; indeed they had all been ready, at the first sign of a frown from the French, to withdraw their troops at once and only the active intervention of the Foreign Minister had prevented this act of capitulation from taking place. Then Field-Marshal von Blomberg had proved a great disappointment to him, and the Fritsch incident had left a bitter taste in his mouth. Beck had opposed him during the Czech crisis and had therefore gone. The present Commander-in-Chief of the Army had made proposals on the subject of further re-armament that were totally insufficient; a crass example of this were the completely inadequate figures for the increase in light field howitzer production, figures that were frankly ridiculously small. Already in the Polish campaign differences of opinion had arisen between himself and his generals concerning the prosecution of the offensive; as for the pending operations in the West, he did not feel that his ideas were in accordance with those of the Commander-in-Chief of the Army on this subject either.

Hitler thanked me for my frankness—and our conversation was over without anything having been achieved. It had lasted about one hour. I returned to Koblenz, deeply depressed by the insight that I had gained.

5. THE CAMPAIGN IN THE WEST

Preparations for the Campaign

Before embarking on the campaign against the Western Powers—which we would gladly have avoided—we carefully evaluated the lessons learned in Poland. These proved that the Light Divisions were an anomalous mixture, a discovery which did not take me by surprise. It was therefore ordered that they be changed into panzer divisions, bearing the numbers 6 to 9. The motorised infantry divisions had turned out to be too large and unwieldy. They were made smaller by the removal of one of their infantry regiments. The very urgent business of re-equipping the tank regiments with Panzers III and IV only went forward slowly, partially owing to the limited production capacity of the industry, but also because of a tendency by the Army High Command to hoard the new tanks.

I was given command of a few panzer divisions and the Infantry Regiment *Gross-Deutschland* for training purposes. Apart from this I was mainly occupied with plans and appreciations for the future operations in the West.

The Army High Command, spurred on by Hitler to mount an offensive, was intending to use, once again, the so-called 'Schlieffen Plan' of 1914. It is true that this had the advantage of simplicity, though hardly the charm of novelty. Thoughts therefore soon turned to alternative solutions. One day in November Manstein asked me to come to see him and outlined his ideas on the subject to me; these involved a strong tank thrust through southern Belgium and Luxembourg towards Sedan, a break-through of the prolongation of the Maginot Line in that area and a consequent splitting in two of the whole French front. He asked me to examine this plan of his from the point of view of a tank man. After a lengthy study of maps and making use of my own memories of the terrain from the First World War, I was able to assure Manstein that the operation he had planned could in fact be carried out. The only condition I attached was that a sufficient number of armoured and motorised divisions must be employed, if possible all of them.

Manstein thereupon wrote a memorandum which, with the approval and signature of Colonel-General von Rundstedt, was sent to the Army High Command on the 4th of December, 1939. There it was by no means joyfully received. To start with, the High Command only

wanted to use one or two panzer divisions for the attack through
Arlon. I held such a force to be too weak and therefore pointless.
Any subdivision of our already weak tank forces would have been
the greatest mistake that we could make. But it was precisely this that
the High Command was intent on doing. Manstein became insistent
and by so doing aroused such animosity in the High Command that
he was appointed commanding general of an Infantry Corps. He
requested that he be at least given a Panzer Corps: his request was not
granted. As a result our finest operational brain took the field as
commander of a corps in the third wave of the attack, though it was
largely thanks to his brilliant initiative that the operation was to be
such an outstanding success. His successor with Colonel-General
von Rundstedt was the more prosaic General von Sodenstern.

Meanwhile an aeroplane accident compelled our masters to abandon
the Schlieffen Plan. A Luftwaffe officer-courier who, contrary to
standing orders, was flying by night with important papers containing
references to the proposed Schlieffen Plan operation, crossed the
Belgian frontier and was compelled to make a forced landing on
Belgian soil. It was not known whether he had succeeded in destroying
his papers. In any case it had to be assumed that the Belgians, and
probably also the French and British, knew all about our proposed
operation.

Apart from this, when Manstein reported to Hitler on assuming
command of his corps, he took the opportunity to express his views
on the forthcoming operations. This resulted in the Manstein Plan
now becoming the object of serious study: a war game that took place
at Koblenz on the 7th of February, 1940, seemed to me decisive in its
favour. During the course of this map exercise I proposed that on the
fifth day of the campaign an attack be made with strong armoured and
motorised forces to force a crossing of the Meuse near Sedan with the
objective of achieving a break-through which would then be expanded
towards Amiens. The Chief of the Army General Staff, Halder, who
was present, pronounced these ideas 'senseless.' He envisaged tank
forces reaching the Meuse and even securing bridgeheads across it, and
then waiting for the infantry armies to catch up; after this a 'unified
attack' would be launched, which could not be mounted before the
ninth or tenth day of the campaign. He called this '*einen yangierten
Gesamtangriff*' ('a properly marshalled attack in mass'). I contradicted
him strongly and repeated that the essential was that we use all the
available limited offensive power of our armour in one surprise blow
at one decisive point; to drive a wedge so deep and wide that we need
not worry about our flanks; and then immediately to exploit any
successes gained without bothering to wait for the infantry corps.

My opinions concerning the value of the French frontier fortifications were strengthened by the very detailed studies of Major von Stiotta, the engineer adviser at Army Group headquarters. Major von Stiotta's conclusions were based principally on a microscopic evaluation of air photographs; his arguments were therefore not to be ignored.

On the 14th of February another war game took place at Mayen, the headquarters of Colonel-General List's Twelfth Army; again Halder was present and once again the battle for the Meuse crossing was the subject under study. The main questions that were put to me boiled down to this: could the panzer divisions attempt to force a river crossing on their own, or should they not rather wait until the infantry had caught up with them: in the latter case, should they take part in the initial river crossing or should this be left to the infantry? This last solution was impossible in view of the difficult terrain in the Ardennes north of the Meuse. The whole tone grew more and more depressing until at last General von Wietersheim—whose motorised XIV Army Corps was supposed to follow behind mine—and I eventually declared that in these circumstances we could have no confidence in the leadership of the operation. We declared that the proposed employment of the armour was incorrect and that in the event of its commitment in this fashion a crisis must arise.

The situation became even tenser when it became clear that not even Colonel-General von Rundstedt had any clear idea about the potentialities of tanks, and declared himself in favour of the more cautious solution. Now was the time when we needed Manstein!

There was endless discussion and worry about how the many armoured units should be commanded. After much chopping and changing it was decided that General von Kleist, who up to now had not shown himself particularly well disposed to the armoured force, should be placed in command. When it was at last settled that in any case my Panzer Corps should form the van of the attack through the Ardennes, I settled down busily to train my generals and staff officers for their forthcoming tasks. I was given the 1st, 2nd and 10th Panzer Divisions, the Infantry Regiment *Gross-Deutschland*, and a quantity of corps troops, including a mortar battalion. With the exception of Infantry Regiment 'G.D.' I knew my troops well both from peace and war and I had unbounded faith in their ability. Now I had the opportunity to prepare them for their hard task ahead, in whose successful outcome nobody at that time actually believed, with the exception of Hitler, Manstein and myself. The struggle to get our ideas accepted had proved exhausting in the extreme. I was in need of a little rest, and was granted short leave in the second half of March.

Before that, however, a conference took place attended by the army and army group commanders of Army Group A, accompanied by General von Kleist and myself, in the Reich Chancellery. Hitler was there. Each of us generals outlined what his task was and how he intended to carry it out. I was the last to speak. My task was as follows: on the day ordered I would cross the Luxembourg frontier, drive through Southern Belgium towards Sedan, cross the Meuse and establish a bridgehead on the far side so that the infantry corps following behind could get across. I explained briefly that my corps would advance through Luxembourg and Southern Belgium in three columns; I reckoned on reaching the Belgian frontier posts on the first day and I hoped to break through them on that same day; on the second day I would advance as far as Neufchâteau; on the third day I would reach Bouillon and cross the Semois; on the fourth day I would arrive at the Meuse; on the fifth day I would cross it. By the evening of the fifth day I hoped to have established a bridgehead on the far bank. Hitler asked: 'And then what are you going to do?' He was the first person who had thought to ask me this vital question. I replied: 'Unless I receive orders to the contrary, I intend on the next day to continue my advance westwards. The supreme leadership must decide whether my objective is to be Amiens or Paris. In my opinion the correct course is to drive past Amiens to the English Channel. Hitler nodded and said nothing more. Only General Busch, who commanded the Sixteenth Army on my left, cried out: 'Well, I don't think you'll cross the river in the first place!' Hitler, the tension visible in his face, looked at me to see what I would reply. I said: 'There's no need for you to do so, in any case.' Hitler made no comment.

I never received any further orders as to what I was to do once the bridgehead over the Meuse was captured. All my decisions, until I reached the Atlantic seaboard at Abbéville, were taken by me and me alone. The Supreme Command's influence on my actions was merely restrictive throughout.

After my short leave was over I returned to my preparations for the great undertaking. The long winter had become a delicious spring and the continual trial alerts threatened now to become serious. Before I turn to describe the events to come, I think I should explain why I looked forward to the pending operations with such confidence. To do so I must go back somewhat in time.

The First World War on the Western Front, after being for a short time a war of movement, soon settled down to positional warfare. No massing of war material, on no matter how vast a scale, had succeeded in getting the armies moving again until, in November 1916, the enemy's tanks appeared on the battlefield. With their armour plating, their tracks, their guns and their machine-guns, they succeeded in

Sketch Map 3a

Advance of XIX Army Corps
through the Ardennes.

XIX. A.K.

Koblenz
Rhine
Trèves
Bitburg
Wallendorf
Vianden
Sauer
Echternach
Cruchten
Luxembourg
Moselle
Tintange
Marlelange
Redingen
Arlon
Bellefontaine
Langwy
Verdun
Meuse
Bastogne
Neufchâteau
5. Col.D. Rossignol
Florenville
Libramont
Bouillon
Sedan
Semois
Namur
Charleville
Mézières

2. Army (Huntziger)
3.C.
71.
X.
55
9. Army (Corap)
XXXXI
61
102
53

carrying their crews, alive and capable of fighting, through artillery barrages and wire entanglements, over trench systems and shell craters, into the centre of the German lines. The power of the offensive had come back into its own.

The true importance of tanks was proved by the fact that the Versailles Treaty forbade Germany the possession or construction of armoured vehicles, tanks or any similar equipment which might be employed in war, under pain of punishment.

So our enemies regarded the tank as a decisive weapon which we must not be allowed to have. I therefore decided carefully to study the history of this decisive weapon and to follow its future development. For someone observing tank theory from afar, unburdened by tradition, there were lessons to be learned in the employment, organisation and construction of armour and of armoured units that went beyond the doctrines then accepted abroad. After years of hard struggle, I had succeeded in putting my theories into practice before the other armies had arrived at the same conclusions. The advance we had made in the organisation and employment of tanks was the primary factor on which my belief in our forthcoming success was based. Even in 1940 this belief was shared by scarcely anybody in the German Army.

A profound study of the First World War had given me considerable insight into the psychology of the combatants. I already, from personal experience, knew a considerable amount about our own army. I had also formed certain opinions about our Western adversaries which the events of 1940 were to prove correct. Despite the tank weapons to which our enemies owed in large measure their 1918 victory, they were preoccupied with the concepts of positional warfare.

France possessed the strongest land army in Western Europe. France possessed the numerically strongest tank force in Western Europe.

The combined Anglo-French forces in the West in May 1940 disposed of some 4,000 armoured vehicles: the German Army at that time had 2,800, including armoured reconnaissance cars, and when the attack was launched only 2,200 of these were available for the operation. We thus faced superiority in numbers, to which was added the fact that the French tanks were superior to the German ones both in armour and in gun-calibre, though admittedly inferior in control facilities and in speed. (*See Appendix* III.) Despite possessing the strongest forces for mobile warfare the French had also built the strongest line of fortifications in the world, the Maginot Line. Why was the money spent on the construction of those fortifications not used for the modernisation and strengthening of France's mobile forces?

The proposals of de Gaulle, Daladier and others along these lines

Sketch Map 3b

Advance of XIX Army Corps
to the Channel Coast.

had been ignored. From this it must be concluded that the highest
French leadership either would not or could not grasp the significance
of the tank in mobile warfare. In any case all the manœuvres and large-
scale exercises of which I had heard led to the conclusion that the
French command wanted its troops to be trained in such a way that
careful movement and planned measures for attack or for defence
could be based on definite, pre-arranged circumstances. They wanted
a complete picture of the enemy's order of battle and intentions before
deciding on any undertaking. Once the decision was taken it would be
carried out according to plan, one might almost say methodically, not
only during the approach march and the deployment of troops, but
also during the artillery preparation and the launching of the attack or
the construction of the defence as the case might be. This mania for
planned control, in which nothing should be left to chance, led to the
organisation of the armoured forces within the army in a form that
would not destroy the general scheme, that is to say their assignment
in detail to the infantry divisions. Only a fraction of the French armour
was organised for operational employment.

So far as the French were concerned the German leadership could
safely rely on the defence of France being systematically based on
fortifications and carried out according to a rigid doctrine: this doctrine
was the result of the lessons that the French had learned from the First
World War, their experience of positional warfare, of the high value
they attached to fire power, and of their underestimation of movement.

These French strategic and tactical principles, well known to us in
1940 and the exact contrary of my own theories of warfare, were the
second factor on which my belief in victory was founded.

By the spring of 1940 we Germans had gained a clear picture of
the enemy's dispositions, and of his fortifications. We knew that somewhere between Montmédy and Sedan the Maginot Line changed from
being very strong indeed to being rather weaker. We called the fortifications from Sedan to the Channel 'the prolonged Maginot Line.' We
knew about the locations and, usually, about the strength of the Belgian
and Dutch fortifications. They all faced only towards Germany.

While the Maginot Line was thinly held, the mass of the French
army together with the British Expeditionary Force was assembled in
Flanders, between the Meuse and the English Channel, facing north-
east; the Belgian and Dutch troops, on the other hand, were deployed
to defend their frontiers against an attack from the east.

From their order of battle it was plain that the enemy expected the
Germans to attempt the Schlieffen Plan once again, and that they
intended to bring the bulk of the allied armies against this anticipated
outflanking movement through Holland and Belgium. A sufficient

Fig. 4. Brest-Litovsk: The Russians take over

Fig. 5. In an armoured command vehicle

safeguard of the hinge of their proposed advance into Belgium by reserve units—in the area, say, of Charleville and Verdun—was not apparent. It seemed that the French High Command did not regard any alternative to the old Schlieffen Plan as even conceivable.

Our knowledge of the enemy's order of battle and of his predictable reactions at the beginning of the German advance was the third factor that contributed to my belief in victory.

In addition there were a number of other aspects in our general evaluation of the enemy which, though of less reliability, were still worth taking into consideration.

We knew and respected the French soldier from the First World War as a brave and tough fighter who had defended his country with stubborn energy. We did not doubt that he would show the same spirit this time. But so far as the French leaders were concerned, we were amazed that they had not taken advantage of their favourable situation during the autumn of 1939 to attack, while the bulk of the German forces, including the entire armoured force, was engaged in Poland. Their reasons for such restraint were at the time hard to see. We could only guess. Be that as it may, the caution shown by the French leaders led us to believe that our adversaries hoped somehow to avoid a serious clash of arms. The rather inactive behaviour of the French during the winter of 1939–40 seemed to indicate a limited enthusiasm for the war on their part.

From all this I concluded that a determined and forcibly led attack by strong armoured forces through Sedan and Amiens, with the Atlantic coast as its objective, would hit the enemy deep in the flank of his forces advancing into Belgium; I did not think that he disposed of sufficient reserves to parry this thrust; and I therefore believed it had a great chance of succeeding and, if the initial success were fully exploited, might lead to the cutting off of all the main enemy forces moving up into Belgium.

My next task was to persuade my superiors and equally the men under my command that my ideas were correct and thus to achieve freedom of decision from above and confident collaboration from below. The former endeavour was only partially successful, the latter much more so.

In the event of the attack, XIX Army Corps was ordered to advance through Luxembourg and the southern corner of Belgium, to win a bridgehead over the Meuse at Sedan and thus to help the infantry divisions that would be following to cross that river. No instructions were given as to what was to be done in the event of a surprise success.

Co-operation with the Luftwaffe was arranged. I was to be in touch with the leader of the close support planes, that exceptionally brave

D

man, General von Stutterheim, and simultaneously with the *Fliegerkorps* (roughly: air group) commanded by General Lörzer. In order to establish a sound basis for co-operation as quickly as possible, I had invited the airmen to my planning exercises and I also took part in an air exercise that General Lörzer organised. The principal matter discussed was the Meuse crossing. After detailed study we agreed that the air force could best be employed in giving the ground forces continuous support during the crossing; that meant no concentrated attack by bombers and dive bombers, but rather, from the very beginning of the crossing and throughout the whole operation, perpetual attacks and threats of attack against the enemy batteries in open emplacements; this should force the enemy gunners to take cover both from the bombs that were dropped and from the bombs that they expected to be dropped. The time schedules for these attacks, together with the targets, were marked on a map.

Shortly before the operation was due to start it was decided, in accordance with Goering's wish, that a battalion of Infantry Regiment 'G.D.' be loaded in 'Stork' aircraft and landed, on the first morning of the attack, behind the Belgians at Witry, west of Martelange, with the aim of spreading alarm among their frontier defence force.

For the rapid thrust through Luxembourg and southern Belgium, the three panzer divisions of the corps were drawn up in line. In the centre was the 1st Panzer Division, with behind it the corps artillery, the corps headquarters and the mass of our anti-aircraft artillery; here, to start with, was to be our point of main effort. On the right of the 1st Panzer was the 2nd Panzer Division: on its left the 10th Panzer Division and Infantry Regiment 'G.D.' The 1st Panzer Division was commanded by General Kirchner, the 2nd by General Veiel, and the 10th by General Schaal. I knew all three of them well. I had complete trust in their competence and reliability. They knew my views and shared my belief that once armoured formations are out on the loose they must be given the green light to the very end of the road. In our case this was—the Channel! That was a clear inspiration to every one of our soldiers, and he could follow it even though he might receive no orders for long periods of time once the attack was launched.

The Break-through to the Channel

We were alerted at 13.30 hrs. on the 9th of May, 1940. I left Koblenz at 16.00 hrs. and arrived at my corps headquarters, the Sonnenhof near Bitburg, that evening. The troops, as ordered, were drawn up along the frontier between Vianden and Echternach.

At 05.30 hrs. I crossed the Luxembourg frontier with the 1st Panzer Division near Wallendorf and headed for Martelange. By the evening of that first day the advance guard of the division was already through the Belgian frontier defences and had established contact with the air-borne troops of Infantry Regiment 'G.D.' but had not been able to advance deep into Belgium owing to extensive road-demolitions which could not be by-passed in that mountainous terrain. The roads were to be cleared during the night. The 2nd Panzer Division was fighting near Strainchamps, while the 10th Panzer Division, advancing through Habay-la-Neuve and Étalle, was in contact with French units (the 2nd Cavalry Division and the 3rd Colonial Infantry Division). Corps headquarters was established at Rambruch, west of Martelange.

In the morning of the 11th the demolitions and minefields along the Belgian frontier were broken through. Towards noon the 1st Panzer Division began to move forward. With its tanks leading, it headed for the fortifications on either side of Neufchâteau, which were held by the Belgian *Chasseurs Ardennais*, withdrawn from the frontier, and by French cavalry. After a short fight, with only light casualties, the enemy positions were broken and Neufchâteau taken. 1st Panzer Division immediately drove on, took Bertrix, and as dusk was falling reached Bouillon, but the French managed to hold that town throughout the night. The other two divisions had advanced exactly according to plan in the face of only slight opposition. The 2nd Panzer Division took Libramont. The 10th Panzer Division had had a few casualties near Habay-la-Neuve; the commander of Rifle Regiment 69, Lieutenant-Colonel Ehlermann, had fallen on the 10th of May near Sainte-Marie.

During the night of the 10th–11th Panzer Group von Kleist, which was in control of the operation, ordered the 10th Panzer Division on the left flank to change direction at once and move on Longwy, since French cavalry were reported to be advancing from that direction. I asked for the cancellation of these orders; the detachment of one-third of my force to meet the hypothetical threat of enemy cavalry would endanger the success of the Meuse crossing and therefore of the whole operation. In order to anticipate any difficulties that might be engendered by this curious fear of hostile cavalry, I ordered 10th Panzer Division to move along a parallel road north of its previous line of advance and to go through Rulles towards the sector of the Semois between Cugnon and Mortehan. The advance went on. The immediate danger of a halt and a change of direction was passed. The Panzer Group finally agreed to this. The French cavalry did not in fact appear. (*See Appendix* IV.)

Infantry Regiment 'G.D.' was withdrawn into corps reserve at Saint-Médard. Corps headquarters spent the night in Neufchâteau.

On Whitsun, the 12th of May, at 05.00 hrs., I drove with my staff through Bertrix–Fays les Veneurs–Bellevaux to Bouillon against which town the 1st Rifle Regiment under Lieutenant-Colonel Balck launched an attack at 07.45 hrs., which soon carried its objective. The French had blown the bridges over the Semois, but the stream was fordable for tanks at a number of points. The divisional engineers began the immediate construction of a new bridge. After I had satisfied myself concerning the measures taken I followed the tanks across the stream in the direction of Sedan, but mined roads compelled me to return to Bouillon. Here, in the southern part of the town, I experienced an enemy air attack for the first time; they were after 1st Panzer Division's bridge. Luckily the bridge remained undamaged, but a few houses were set on fire.

I now drove through the woods to 10th Panzer Division, which had crossed the Semois in the sector Cugnon–Herbeumont. When I reached their road of advance I witnessed an attack by the Reconnaissance Battalion on the frontier defences; the riflemen advanced immediately behind the reconnaissance unit, with the brave brigade commander, Colonel Fischer, at their head, followed closely by the divisional commander, General Schaal. The steady way the division moved forward under the command of its officers was an impressive sight. The defensive positions in the woods were soon captured; the advance through La Chapelle towards Bazeilles-Balan continued. I could return without anxiety to my corps headquarters at Bouillon.

Colonel Nehring, my Chief of Staff, had meanwhile established himself in the Hôtel Panorama, from whose windows there was a splendid view over the valley of the Semois. In the office that we shared my desk was in an alcove much decorated with trophies of the chase.

We went to work. Suddenly there was a series of explosions in rapid succession; another air attack. As though that were not enough, an engineer supply column, carrying fuses, explosives, mines and hand grenades, caught fire and there was one detonation after the other. A boar's head, attached to the wall immediately above my desk, broke loose and missed me by a hair's breadth; the other trophies came tumbling down and the fine window in front of which I was seated was smashed to smithereens and splinters of glass whistled about my ears. It had in fact become very unpleasant where we were and we decided to move elsewhere. We chose a small hotel to the north of Bouillon which had served as regimental headquarters for the 1st Panzer Regiment. When we went to look at it the commander of our air support, General von Stutterheim, who happened to be present, warned me that it was very exposed. Even while we were talking a squadron of Belgian planes appeared and bombed the bivouacs of the tank regiment. Our casualties were negligible, but we were now prepared to listen to Stutterheim's advice; we moved farther north, to the next village, Bellevaux-Noirefontaine.

Before this second move could be carried out a Fieseler-Storch aeroplane appeared to fetch me to General von Kleist's headquarters for orders. The order I received was to attack across the Meuse on the next day, the 13th of May, at 16.00 hrs. My 1st and 10th Panzer Divisions should be in position by that time, but the 2nd Panzer Division, which had run into difficulties along the Semois, would certainly not be. I reported this fact, which was of importance in view of the weakness of our attacking force. General von Kleist would not modify his orders, however, and I felt obliged to admit that there were probably advantages in thrusting forwards immediately without waiting for all our troops to be ready. A further order was far less pleasant. Unaware of the arrangements I had come to with Lörzer, General von Kleist and the air force General Sperrle had decided on a mass bombing attack, to be co-ordinated with the beginning of the artillery preparation. My whole attack plan was thus placed in jeopardy, since if such an attack were carried out the long-drawn-out neutralisation of the enemy batteries could no longer be achieved. I argued strongly against this and asked that my original plan, on which the whole attack was founded, be followed. General von Kleist refused this request too, and I flew back in the Fieseler-Storch, with a new pilot, to my corps headquarters. The young man maintained he knew exactly where the landing strip from which I had set off was located, but he could not find it in the fading light and the next thing I knew we were on the other side of the Meuse, flying in a slow and unarmed plane over the French positions. An unpleasant moment. I gave my pilot emphatic orders to turn north and find my landing strip; we just made it.

Back at corps headquarters I settled down at once to drawing up orders. In view of the very short time at our disposal, we were forced to take the orders used in the war games at Koblenz from our files and, after changing the dates and times, issue these as the orders for the attack. They were perfectly fitted to the reality of the situation. The only change that had to be made was that at Koblenz we had imagined the attack going in at 10.00 instead of 16.00 hrs. 1st and 10th Panzer Divisions copied this procedure and so the issuing of orders was an agreeably quick and simple business. (*See Appendix* V.)

By the evening of May 12th the 1st and 10th Panzer Divisions had occupied the northern bank of the Meuse and had captured the historic city and fortress of Sedan. The night was spent in making final preparations for the assault and in moving the Corps and Panzer Group

artillery into position. The point of main effort lay in the sector of the
1st Panzer Division, which was reinforced by the Infantry Regiment
'G.D.', the corps artillery and the heavy artillery battalions of the two
flanking divisions. When judging the achievements of the two flanking
divisions on the following day, this weakening of their artillery strength
must be borne in mind.

The transfer of corps headquarters to La Chapelle was ordered for
the 13th of May. (*See Appendix* VI.)

In the morning I first visited the headquarters of the 1st Panzer
Division to see how far advanced their preparations were; then,
driving across partially mined ground, which my staff drivers cleared,
and under artillery fire put down by the French defence from the far
bank, I went on to the 2nd Panzer Division at Sugny. The head of the
division had reached the French frontier. At midday I returned to my
corps headquarters, by now installed at La Chapelle.

At 15.30 hrs. I went through French shell fire to an advanced
artillery O.P. of 10th Panzer Division in order personally to observe
the effects of my artillery and of the Luftwaffe's contribution. At
16.00 hrs. the battle began with a display of artillery fire which, to us at
least, seemed magnificent. Tensely I waited for the air force. It arrived
punctually but my astonishment was great to see only a few squadrons
of bombers and dive-bombers, under fighter cover; they adopted the
tactics which Lörzer and I had agreed on during our war games. Had
General von Kleist changed his mind, or had the new orders for the
attack not got through to the squadrons in time? In any event the
flyers were doing exactly what I believed to be most advantageous for
our attack and I sighed with relief.

I was now anxious to take part in the assault across the Meuse by
the riflemen. The actual ferrying must be nearly over by now, so I went
to St. Menges and from there to Floing, which was the proposed
crossing-place of 1st Panzer Division. I went over in the first assault
boat. On the far bank I found the efficient and brave commander of
the 1st Rifle Regiment, Lieutenant-Colonel Balck, together with his
staff. He greeted me cheerfully with the cry: 'Joy riding in canoes on
the Meuse is forbidden!' I had in fact used those words myself in one
of the exercises that we had had in preparation for this operation, since
the attitude of some of the younger officers had struck me as rather
too light-hearted. I now realised that they had judged the situation
correctly.

The attack by the 1st Rifle Regiment and by Infantry Regiment
'G.D.'was developing as though it were being carried out on manœuvres.
The French artillery was almost paralysed by the unceasing threat of

Sketch Map 4.
Battle for the Meuse Crossings.
Situation 13.5. – 15.5. 40.

Bridgehead	13.5. 40.
"	14.5. 40
"	15.5. 40.
(in each case in the evening)	

Maginot-Line

attack by Stukas and bombers. The concrete emplacements along the Meuse had been put out of action by our anti-tank and anti-aircraft artillery, and the enemy machine-gunners were forced to keep down by the fire of our heavy weapons and artillery. Despite the completely open nature of the ground, our casualties remained light. By the time night fell a considerable penetration of the enemy's defences had been made. The troops had been ordered to keep up the attack without pause throughout the night, and I could rely on this important order being obeyed. By 23.00 hrs. they had captured Cheveuges and part of the Bois de la Marfée and west of Wadelincourt had reached the French main line of defence. Pleased and proud of what I had seen, I returned to my corps headquarters in the Bois de la Garenne, arriving at La Chapelle just in time for another air attack, and settled down to study the reports from the flanks.

Only the advance elements of the 2nd Panzer Division, the Reconnaissance Battalion and the Motor-cycle Battalion together with the heavy artillery, had been in action. With such few troops they had not succeeded in forcing a crossing. The whole of 1st Panzer Division's Rifle Brigade was over on the left bank of the Meuse by now: the division's tanks and artillery were ready to follow just as soon as a bridge could be thrown across. The 10th Panzer Division had crossed the river and established a small bridgehead on the far side; owing to lack of artillery support this division had had a hard day. Flanking fire from the Maginot Line south of Douzy-Carignan had been particularly worrying. The next morning, however, should bring relief both to them and to the 2nd Panzer Division. The corps heavy anti-aircraft was to be brought up to the near bank of the river during the night, since from the 14th no more support could be expected from the Luftwaffe, which was to be employed elsewhere.

During the night I telephoned Lörzer to inquire what the reason was for the change in the plan of air support and also to thank him for the splendid nature of that support which had contributed so markedly to our success. I learned that Sperrle's order had in fact arrived too late to be passed on to the squadrons and that Lörzer had therefore quite correctly made no modifications to the existing plan. I then sent a signal to Busch, who during the Hitler conference in Berlin had questioned my ability to cross the Meuse, informing him of my troops' success; he sent me a very cordial reply. Finally, I thanked my colleagues on my staff for their devoted help. (*See Appendix* VII.)

Early on the 14th of May the brave 1st Panzer Division signalled that they had managed to increase their penetration considerably during

the night and were now through Chémery. So off to Chémery I went.
On the banks of the Meuse were thousands of prisoners. At Chémery
the commander of the 1st Panzer Division was giving orders to
his subordinate commanders and I listened while he did so. There
was a report of strong French armoured forces moving up, and he
sent the tanks of 1st Panzer Division into the attack towards Stonne
to head them off; then I returned to the Meuse bridge, where I had
arranged for my command staff to await me, and ordered that
2nd Panzer Brigade move across the river immediately behind the 1st,
so that there would be sufficient armour available on the far side to
meet the French attack when it came in. This attack was stopped at
Bulson with the destruction of 20 tanks, and at Chémery with the
destruction of 50 more. Infantry Regiment 'G.D.' took Bulson and
advanced from there on Villers-Maisoncelle. Unfortunately shortly
after my departure German dive bombers attacked our troop concentration in Chémery, causing us heavy casualties.

Meanwhile the 2nd Panzer Division had crossed the Meuse near
Donchéry and was engaged in fighting its way up the southern bank.
I drove there to see how they were getting on and found the responsible
commanders, Colonels von Vaerst and von Prittwitz, at the head of
their troops, so I was able to return to the Meuse. There was now a
most violent air attack by the enemy. The extremely brave French
and English pilots did not succeed in knocking out the bridges, despite
the heavy casualties that they suffered. Our anti-aircraft gunners proved
themselves on this day, and shot superbly. By evening they calculated
that they had accounted for 150 enemy aeroplanes. The regimental
commander, Colonel von Hippel, later received the Knight's Cross
for this.

Meanwhile the 2nd Panzer Brigade continued to cross the river in
uninterrupted flow. Towards midday, to our general delight, the Army
Group commander, Colonel-General von Rundstedt, arrived to have
a look at the situation for himself. I reported our position to him in
the very middle of the bridge, while an air-raid was actually in progress.
He asked drily: 'Is it always like this here?' I could reply with a clear
conscience that it was. He then spoke a few deeply felt words in
appreciation of the achievements of our gallant soldiers.

Once again to the 1st Panzer Division, where I found the divisional
commander accompanied by his first general staff officer, Major
Wenck; I asked him whether his whole division could be turned
westwards or whether a flank guard should be left facing south on
the east bank of the Ardennes Canal. Wenck saw fit to interject a
somewhat slangy expression of mine '*Klotzen, nicht Kleckern*' (the sense
of it being to strike concentrated, not dispersed—it might be translated

D*

roughly as 'Boot 'em, don't spatter 'em'), and that really answered my question. 1st and 2nd Panzer Divisions received orders immediately to change direction with all their forces, to cross the Ardennes Canal, and to head west with the objective of breaking clear through the French defences. That I might co-ordinate the movements of the two divisions I next went to the command post of the 2nd Panzer Division, which was in the Château Rocan, on the heights above Donchéry. From that vantage-point a good view could be obtained over the ground across which 2nd Panzer Division had advanced and attacked on the 13th and 14th of May. I was surprised that the French long-range artillery in the Maginot Line and its westerly extension had not laid down heavier fire and caused us more trouble during our advance. At this moment, as I looked at the ground we had come over, the success of our attack struck me as almost a miracle.

In the afternoon I returned to my headquarters to arrange for the co-ordination of my divisions for the 15th of May. Immediately north of my corps was XLI Army Corps (Reinhardt), which had originally been following behind me and which, since the 12th, had been committed on the right of XIX Army Corps in the direction of Mézières–Charleville. On the 13th this corps had forced a crossing of the Meuse (at Monthermé) and was making a fighting advance westwards. General von Wietersheim's XIV Army Corps was now in my immediate rear and must soon reach the Meuse.

By evening the 1st Panzer Division had strong elements across the Ardennes Canal and had taken Singly and Vendresse despite strenuous enemy resistance. The tanks of the 10th Panzer Division had crossed the line Maisoncelle–Raucourt-et-Flabas, while the bulk of the division had reached the high ground south of Bulson-Thélonne, where they had captured more than forty guns.

The principal task of XIX Army Corps had been to secure the dominating heights around Stonne, thus depriving the enemy of any chance of breaking into our bridgehead, and assuring the formations that were moving up behind us a safe river crossing. The attack on the heights had involved the Infantry Regiment 'G.D.' and the 10th Panzer Division in heavy fighting on the 14th. The village of Stonne had changed hands several times. On the 15th these attacks were to be carried through to a successful conclusion. (*See Appendix* VIII.)

At 04.00 hrs. on the 15th of May I met General von Wietersheim at my corps headquarters to discuss with him the relief by his troops of my units now in the Meuse bridgehead south of Sedan. After briefly summarising the situation we set off together for the headquarters of the 10th Panzer Division near Bulson. General Schaal was forward with his troops. The first general staff officer of the division, the excellent Lieutenant-Colonel Freiherr von Liebenstein, explained the difficulties of the situation and answered patiently the many detailed questions of the general who was to take over from us. Finally we agreed that, for the duration of the relief, 10th Panzer Division and the Infantry Regiment 'G.D.' would be placed under command of XIV Army Corps until such time as units of that corps could take over from them. So I found my command limited, for the next few days, to the 1st and 2nd Panzer Divisions.

The 10th Panzer Division, with the Infantry Regiment 'G.D.' under command, was ordered to cover the southern flank of XIX Army Corps along the line Ardennes Canal—the high ground by Stonne—the bend in the Meuse south of Villemontry. In the course of the 15th of May it was already being strengthened by the advance units of the 29th (Motorised) Infantry Division.

From the headquarters of the 10th Panzer Division I drove to the headquarters of the Infantry Regiment 'G.D.' in Stonne. A French attack was actually in progress when I arrived and I could not find anyone. A certain nervous tension was noticeable, but finally the positions were held. I then went to my new corps headquarters, which was in a small wood near Sapogne on the southern bank of the Meuse.

Contrary to expectations the night was one of confusion, not owing to the activity of the enemy but on account of command difficulties with our superiors. Panzer Group von Kleist ordered a halt to all further advance and to any extension of the bridgehead. I neither would nor could agree to these orders, which involved the sacrifice of the element of surprise we had gained and of the whole initial success that we had achieved. I therefore got in touch, personally, first with the Chief of Staff of the Panzer Group, Colonel Zeitzler, and since this was not enough with General von Kleist himself, and requested that the order to stop be cancelled. The conversation became very heated and we repeated our various arguments several times. Finally, General von Kleist approved of the advance being continued for another twenty-four hours so that sufficient space be acquired for the infantry corps that were following. I had finally had to mention the Hentzsch Mission and thus remind him of the 'Miracle of the Marne,' a reminder that was no doubt not very well received by the Panzer Group.

I was pleased to have retained my freedom of movement when, early on the 16th of May, I went to the headquarters of the 1st Panzer Division. I drove through Vendresse to Omont. The situation at the front was not yet clear. All that was known was that there had been heavy fighting during the night in the neighbourhood of Bouvellemont. So on to Bouvellemont. In the main street of the burning village I found the regimental commander, Lieutenant-Colonel Balck, and let

him describe the events of the previous night to me. The troops were
over-tired, having had no real rest since the 9th of May. Ammunition
was running low. The men in the front line were falling asleep in their
slit trenches. Balck himself, in wind jacket and with a knotty stick in
his hand, told me that the capture of the village had only succeeded
because, when his officers complained against the continuation of the
attack, he had replied: 'In that case I'll take the place on my own!'
and had moved off. His men had thereupon followed him. His dirty
face and his red-rimmed eyes showed that he had spent a hard day
and a sleepless night. For his doings on that day he was to receive
the Knight's Cross. His opponents—a good Norman infantry division
and a brigade of Spahis—had fought bravely. The enemy's machine-
guns were still firing into the village street, but for some time now
there had been no artillery fire and Balck shared my opinion that
resistance was almost over.

Now on the previous day we had captured a French order, originating
if I am not mistaken from General Gamelin himself, which contained
the words: 'The torrent of German tanks must finally be stopped!'
This order had strengthened me in my conviction that the attack must
be pressed forward with all possible strength, since the defensive
capabilities of the French was obviously causing their high command
serious anxiety. This was no time for hesitancy, still less for calling
a halt.

I sent for the troops by companies and read them the captured order,
making plain its significance and the importance of continuing the
attack at once. I thanked them for their achievements to date and told
them that they must now strike with all their power to complete our
victory. I then ordered them to return to their vehicles and to continue
the advance.

The fog of war that had confused us soon lifted. We were in the
open now, with results that were rapidly to be seen. In Poix-Terron
I found the first general staff officer of the 2nd Panzer Division, told
him what the position was and drove on to Novion-Porcien and from
there to Montcornet. On this drive I passed an advancing column of
the 1st Panzer Division. The men were wide awake now and aware
that we had achieved a complete victory, a break-through. They cheered
and shouted remarks which often could only be heard by the staff
officers in the second car: 'Well done, old boy,' and 'There's our old
man,' and 'Did you see him? That was hurrying Heinz,' and so on.
All this was indicative.

In the market-place of Montcornet I found General Kempff, the
commander of the 6th Panzer Division of the Corps Reinhardt, whose
troops, after crossing the Meuse, had arrived in this town at the same

moment as my own. Now roads had to be allotted among the three panzer divisions—the 6th, 2nd and 1st—which were pouring through the town in their headlong drive towards the west. Since the Panzer Group had laid down no boundary between the two corps, we soon agreed on one among ourselves and ordered the advance to go on until the last drop of petrol was used up. My foremost units reached Marle and Dercy (over 40 miles from that morning's starting-point, and 55 miles from Sedan).

Meanwhile I told the men who were with me to go through the houses on the market-place. Within a few minutes they had collected several hundred prisoners, Frenchmen from various units, whose amazement at our being there was plain to see on their faces. An enemy tank company, which tried to enter the town from the south-west, was taken prisoner. It belonged to General de Gaulle's division, of whose presence in the area north of Laon we had already heard. We set up our corps headquarters in the little village of Soize, east of Montcornet. I was in contact with the staffs of the 1st and 2nd Panzer Divisions. The Panzer Group was informed by wireless of the day's events and I announced my intention of continuing the pursuit on the 17th of May. (*See Appendix* IX *and Sketch Map* 3*b*.)

After our splendid success on the 16th of May and the simultaneous victory won by XLI Army Corps, it did not occur to me that my superiors could possibly still hold the same views as before, nor that they would now be satisfied with simply holding the bridgehead we had established across the Meuse while awaiting the arrival of the infantry corps. I was completely filled with the ideas that I had expressed during our conference with Hitler in March, that is to say to complete our break-through and not to stop until we had reached the English Channel. It certainly never occurred to me that Hitler himself, who had approved the boldest aspects of the Manstein plan and had not uttered a word against my proposals concerning exploitation of the break-through, would now be the one to be frightened by his own temerity and would order our advance to be stopped at once. Here I was making a great mistake, as I was to discover on the following morning.

Early on the 17th of May I received a message from the Panzer Group: the advance was to be halted at once and 1 was personally to report to General von Kleist, who would come to see me at my airstrip at 07.00 hrs. He was there punctually and, without even wishing me a good morning, began in very violent terms to berate me for having disobeyed orders. He did not see fit to waste a word of praise on the performance of the troops. When the first storm was passed, and he had stopped to draw breath, I asked that I might be relieved of my command. General von Kleist was momentarily taken aback, but then he nodded and ordered me to hand over my command to the most senior general of my corps. And that was the end of our conversation. I returned to my corps headquarters and asked General Veiel to come to see me, that I might hand over to him.

I then sent a message to Army Group von Rundstedt by wireless in which I said that after I had handed over my command at noon I would be flying to the Army Group headquarters to make a report on what had happened. I received an answer almost at once: I was to remain at my headquarters and await the arrival of Colonel-General List, who was in command of the Twelfth Army that was following behind us and who had been instructed to clear this matter up. Until the arrival of Colonel-General List all units were to be ordered to remain where they were. Major Wenck, who came to receive these orders, was shot at by a French tank while returning to his division and was wounded in the foot. General Veiel now appeared and I explained the situation to him. Early that afternoon Colonel-General List arrived and asked me at once what on earth was going on here. Acting on instructions from Colonel-General von Rundstedt he informed me that I would not resign my command and explained that the order to halt the advance came from the Army High Command (the *OKH*) and therefore must be obeyed. He quite understood my reasons, however, for wishing to go on with the advance and therefore, with the Army Group's approval, he ordered: 'Reconnaissance in force to be carried out. Corps headquarters must in all circumstances remain where it is, so that it may be easily reached.' This was at least something, and I was grateful to Colonel-General List for what he had done. I asked him to clear up the misunderstanding between General von Kleist and myself. Then I set the 'reconnaissance in force' in motion. Corps headquarters remained at its old location in Soize; a wire was laid from there to my advanced headquarters, so that I need not communicate with my staff by wireless and my orders could therefore not be monitored by the wireless intercept units of the *OKH* and the *OKW*.

Before receiving the order to halt early on the 17th, 1st Panzer Division had taken Ribémont on the Oise and Crécy on the Serre. The advanced units of 10th Panzer Division, released from the area south of Sedan, had reached Fraillicourt and Saulces-Monclin. On the evening of the 17th of May a bridgehead was satisfactorily established across the Oise near Moy (15 miles from Dercy and 70 miles from Sedan). (*See Appendix* X.)

At 09.00 hrs. on the 18th of May the 2nd Panzer Division reached

St. Quentin. On its left the 1st Panzer Division was also across the
Oise, advancing on Péronne. Early on the 19th the 1st Panzer Division
succeeded in forcing a bridgehead across the Somme near this town.
Several French staffs, who had arrived at Péronne in an attempt to find
out what was happening, were captured. (*See Appendixes* XI *and* XII.)
Advanced corps headquarters moved to Villers-le-Sec.

On the 19th of May we crossed the old Somme battlefield of the
First World War. Until now we had been advancing north of the
Aisne, the Serre and the Somme, and those rivers had served to guard
our open left flank, which was also covered by reconnaissance troops,
anti-tank units and combat engineers. The danger from this flank was
slight; we knew about the French 4th Armoured Division, a new
formation under General de Gaulle, which had been reported on the
16th of May and had first appeared, as already stated, at Montcornet.
During the next few days de Gaulle stayed with us and on the 19th
a few of his tanks succeeded in penetrating to within a mile of my
advanced headquarters in Holnon wood. The headquarters had only
some 20 mm. anti-aircraft guns for protection, and I passed a few
uncomfortable hours until at last the threatening visitors moved off
in another direction. Also we were aware of the existence of a French
reserve army, some eight infantry divisions strong, which was being
set up in the Paris area. We did not imagine that General Frère would
advance against us so long as we kept on moving ourselves. According to the basic French formula, he would wait until he had exact
information about his enemy's position before doing anything. So
we had to keep him guessing; this could best be done by continuing to
push on.

By the evening of May 19th XIX Army Corps had reached the line
Cambrai–Péronne–Ham. 10th Panzer Division took over the protection
of our increasingly extended left flank, relieving the units of 1st Panzer
Division, which had previously been engaged on this task. During the
night of the 19–20th corps headquarters moved forward to Marleville.
On this day the corps at last received its freedom of movement once
again, with the authorisation to move on Amiens as from the 20th.
10th Panzer Division was now entrusted with the defence of our left
flank as far as Corbie, to the east of Amiens. Its previous sector was
taken over by the 29th (Motorised) Infantry Division. 1st Panzer
Division was to advance towards Amiens and to establish a bridgehead
on the south bank of the Somme with all speed. 2nd Panzer Division
was ordered to move through Albert to Abbéville, there to seize another
bridgehead across the Somme and to clean up any enemy troops

between Abbéville and the sea. The boundary between the 2nd and
1st Panzer Division was fixed as Combles–Longueval–Pozières–
Varennes–Puchevillers–Canaples–Flixécourt–the Somme.

Defensive sectors along the Somme were:

2nd Panzer Division: the mouth of the Somme to Flixécourt
(exclusive),

1st Panzer Division: Flixécourt to the junction of the Avre and the
Somme (east of Amiens),

10th Panzer Division: the Avre–Somme junction to Péronne.

I reckoned that the 1st Panzer Division should be in a position to
attack Amiens at about 09.00 hrs. I therefore ordered my car for
05.00 hrs., since I wished to participate in this historic event. My
officers maintained that this was too early and suggested a later start,
but I stuck to my original schedule and was proved right. (*See
Appendixes* XIII *and* XIV.)

When I reached the northern outskirts of Amiens at 08.45 hrs. on
the 20th of May, 1st Panzer Division was just moving into the attack.
On my way there I had visited Péronne to make sure that the 10th Panzer
Division was in position and there heard, in very strong terms, how
1st Panzer Division had been relieved. It seems that the units of
1st Panzer Division which were holding the bridgehead had not waited
for the relieving force to arrive before pulling out, because the officer
in charge, Lieutenant-Colonel Balck, had feared that otherwise he
would be late for the attack on Amiens, which he regarded as more
important than the holding of the bridgehead. His successor, Colonel
Landgraf, was extremely angry at such casual behaviour and even
more infuriated by Balck's answer to his remonstrances: 'If we lose
it you can always take it again. I had to capture it in the first place,
didn't I?' Luckily the enemy allowed Landgraf sufficient time to
re-occupy the empty ground without having to fight for it. I drove
around Albert, which was still held by the enemy, and passed endless
columns of refugees on my way to Amiens.

1st Panzer Division's attack went well, and by about noon we had
taken the city and forced a bridgehead to a depth of some 4 miles.
I had a quick look over the ground we had seized and also the city
with its beautiful cathedral, before hurrying back to Albert where I
expected to find the 2nd Panzer Division. I met the columns of my
advancing troops and had to drive through crowds of fleeing refugees.
I also ran into a number of enemy vehicles which, thick with dust,
had joined the German columns and hoped in this fashion to reach
Paris and avoid being taken prisoner. I thus quickly captured some
fifteen Englishmen. (*See Appendix* XV.)

In Albert I found General Veiel. The 2nd Panzer Division had captured an English artillery battery, drawn up on the barrack square and equipped only with training ammunition, since nobody had reckoned on our appearance that day. Prisoners of all nationalities filled the market-place and the adjoining streets. 2nd Panzer Division were almost out of fuel and were therefore proposing to stop where they were, but they were soon disillusioned.[1] I ordered them to advance at once to Abbéville and by 19.00 hrs. they had reached this objective, passing through Doullens–Bernaville–Beaumetz–Saint Riquier. Once there, a bombing attack by a few enemy bombers caused them a certain discomfort. After visiting the nimble commander of the 2nd Panzer Brigade, Colonel von Prittwitz, to make sure he understood about advancing on Abbéville, I made my way to Querrieu, to the north-east of Amiens, which was the new location of my corps headquarters. Here we were attacked by our own aeroplanes. It was perhaps an unfriendly action on our part, but our flak opened fire and brought down one of the careless machines. The crew of two floated down by parachute and were unpleasantly surprised to find me waiting for them on the ground. When the more disagreeable part of our conversation was over, I fortified the two young men with a glass of champagne. Unfortunately the destroyed machine was a brand-new reconnaissance plane.

During that night the Spitta Battalion[2] of the 2nd Panzer Division passed through Noyelles and was thus the first German unit to reach the Atlantic coast.

On the evening of this remarkable day we did not know in what direction our advance should continue; nor had Panzer Group von Kleist received any instructions concerning the further prosecution of our offensive. So the 21st of May was wasted while we waited for orders. I spent the day visiting Abbéville and our crossings and bridge-heads over the Somme. On the way I asked my men how they had enjoyed the operations up to date. 'Not bad,' said an Austrian of the 2nd Panzer Division, 'but we wasted two whole days.' Unfortunately he was right.

---

[1] The divisional commander was mistaken in thinking that his troops were out of fuel. After regulating the fuel stocks in the hands of the troops it proved possible to continue the advance. One must always distrust the report of troop commanders: 'We have no fuel.' Generally they have. But if they become tired they lack fuel. That is a common experience of war with the forward troops. During the campaign in France there was no lack of fuel— good staff work can avoid this calamity. Later in the war we often had a real scarcity of fuel because of the destruction of our industry. But in 1940 it was only a question of transport and easy to solve.

[2] Spitta was the name of the Battalion Commander.

The Capture of the Channel Ports

On the 21st of May I received orders to continue the advance in a northerly direction with the capture of the Channel ports as objective. I wanted the 10th Panzer Division to advance on Dunkirk by way of Hesdin and St. Omer, the 1st Panzer Division to move on Calais and the 2nd on Boulogne. But I had to abandon this plan since the 10th Panzer Division was withdrawn from my command by an order of the Panzer Group dated the 22nd of May, 06.00 hrs., and was held back as Panzer Group reserve. So when the advance began on the 22nd the only divisions I commanded were the 1st and 2nd Panzer. My request that I be allowed to continue in control of all three of my divisions in order quickly to capture the Channel ports was unfortunately refused. As a result the immediate move of the 10th Panzer Division on Dunkirk could not now be carried out. It was with a heavy heart that I changed my plan. 1st Panzer Division, together with Infantry Regiment 'G.D.', which had meanwhile arrived from Sedan, was to go by Samer–Desvres–Calais, while the 2nd Panzer Division moved along the coast to Boulogne.

On the 21st of May a noteworthy event occurred to the north of us: English tanks attempted to break through in the direction of Paris. At Arras they came up against the SS Division *Totenkopf*, which had not been in action before and which showed signs of panic. The English did not succeed in breaking through, but they did make a considerable impression on the staff of Panzer Group von Kleist, which suddenly became remarkably nervous. Subordinate units, however, were not infected by this. On the 21st of May the 8th Panzer Division of the XLI Army Corps reached Hesdin while the 6th Panzer Division of the same corps took Boisle.

Our new advance began early on the 22nd of May. At 08.00 hrs. the Authie was crossed in a northerly direction. Neither the 1st nor the 2nd Panzer Division could move in full strength since units of both divisions, and particularly of the 2nd, had to be left behind to secure our Somme bridgeheads until such time as they could be relieved by General von Wietersheim's XIV Army Corps which was following after us in the same role as at Sedan. (*See Appendixes* XVI *and* XVII.)

In the afternoon of the 22nd there was fierce fighting at Desvres, Samer and to the south of Boulogne. Our opponents were mostly Frenchmen, but included a number of English and Belgian units and even an occasional Dutchman. Their resistance was broken. But the enemy air force was very active, bombing us and firing their guns at us too, while we saw little of our own Luftwaffe. The bases from which our planes were operating were now a long way away and apparently

Sketch Map 5.

Battle for the Channel Ports.
Situation 24.5. – 28/29.5. 40.

could not be moved forward with sufficient speed. All the same, we managed to force a way into Boulogne.

Corps headquarters was moved to Recques.

The 10th Panzer Division was now once again placed under my command. I decided to move the 1st Panzer Division, which was already close to Calais, on to Dunkirk at once, while the 10th Panzer Division, advancing from Doullens through Samer, replaced it in front of Calais. There was no particular urgency about capturing this port. At midnight I sent my orders to the 1st Panzer Division by wireless: 'Assemble north of the Canche by 07.00 hrs. 23rd May, as 10th Panzer Division is following up behind you. 2nd Panzer Division has fought its way into Boulogne. 1st Panzer Division to move at once to line Audruicq–Ardres–Calais and then swing eastwards to advance east through Bourbourg-ville–Gravelines to Bergues and Dunkirk. 10th Panzer Division will be to the south. Carry out instructions on receipt of code-word "East-wards advance." Move off 10.00 hrs.'

Early on the 23rd I supplemented these instructions with a wireless order. 'Eastwards advance 10.00 hrs. Attack south of Calais towards St. Pierre–Brouck and Gravelines.'

On the 23rd of May the 1st Panzer Division set off towards Grave-lines against strong resistance, while the 2nd Panzer Division was involved in heavy fighting in and around Boulogne. The attack on the town itself assumed a curious form, since for some time neither our tanks nor our guns managed to penetrate the old town walls. By the use of a ladder from the kitchen of a nearby house, and with the powerful assistance of an 88 mm. flak gun, a breach was at last made in the wall near the cathedral and an entry forced into the town itself. There was fighting in the harbour area, during the course of which a tank managed to sink one British motor torpedo boat and damage several others.

On the 24th of May the 1st Panzer Division reached the Aa Canal between Holque and the coast and secured bridgeheads across it at Holque, St. Pierre-Brouck, St. Nicholas and Bourbourgville; the 2nd Panzer Division cleared up Boulogne; the bulk of the 10th Panzer Division reached the line Desvres–Samer.

The SS Division *Leibstandarte Adolf Hitler* was now placed under my corps command. I ordered this division to advance on Watten, thus giving more power to 1st Panzer Division's drive on Dunkirk. The 2nd Panzer Division was ordered to withdraw all the troops it could spare from Boulogne and to send them off too in the direction of Watten. The 10th Panzer Division encircled Calais and prepared to attack the old sea fortress. I visited the division during the afternoon and ordered it to advance carefully, so as to avoid casualties. On the

25th of May it was to be reinforced by the heavy artillery that was no longer needed at Boulogne.

Reinhardt's XLI Army Corps had meanwhile secured a bridgehead over the Aa at St. Omer.

Hitler's Momentous Order to Stop

On this day (the 24th) the Supreme Command intervened in the operations in progress, with results which were to have a most disastrous influence on the whole future course of the war. *Hitler ordered the left wing to stop on the Aa.* It was forbidden to cross that stream. We were not informed of the reasons for this. The order contained the words: 'Dunkirk is to be left to the Luftwaffe. Should the capture of Calais prove difficult, this port too is to be left to the Luftwaffe.' (I quote here from memory.) We were utterly speechless. But since we were not informed of the reasons for this order, it was difficult to argue against it. The panzer divisions were therefore instructed: 'Hold the line of the canal. Make use of the period of rest for general recuperation.'[1]

Fierce enemy air activity met little opposition from our air force.

Early on the 25th of May I went to Watten to visit the *Leibstandarte* and to make sure that they were obeying the order to halt. When I arrived there I found the *Leibstandarte* engaged in crossing the Aa. On the far bank was Mont Watten, a height of only some 235 feet, but that was enough in this flat marshland to dominate the whole surrounding countryside. On top of the hillock, among the ruins of an old castle, I found the divisional commander, Sepp Dietrich. When I asked why he was disobeying orders, he replied that the enemy on Mont Watten could 'look right down the throat' of anybody on the far bank of the canal. Sepp Dietrich had therefore decided on the 24th of May to take it on his own initiative. The *Leibstandarte* and the Infantry Regiment 'G.D.' on its left were now continuing their advance in the direction of Wormhoudt and Bergues. In view of the success that they were having I approved the decision taken by the commander on the spot and made up my mind to order the 2nd Panzer Division to move up in their support.

On this day we completed the capture of Boulogne. 10th Panzer Division was fighting outside the Calais citadel. When a demand that he surrender was addressed to the English commandant, Brigadier Nicholson sent the laconic reply: 'The answer is no, as it is the British

---

[1] Compare von Lossberg *Im Wehrmachtsführungstab*, page 81 (H. H. Nölke-Verlag, Hamburg).

Army's duty to fight as well as it is the German's.'[1] So we had to take it by assault. (*See Appendix* XVIII.)

On the 26th of May the 10th Panzer Division captured Calais. At noon I was at the divisional headquarters and according to the orders I had received I asked Schaal whether he wanted to leave Calais to the Luftwaffe. He replied that he did not, since he did not believe that our bombs would be effective against the thick walls and earthworks of the old fortifications. Furthermore, if the Luftwaffe were to attack them it would mean that he would have to withdraw his troops from their advanced positions on the edge of the citadel, which would then have to be captured all over again. I was bound to agree with this. At 16.45 hrs. the English surrendered. We took 20,000 prisoners, including 3–4,000 British, the remainder being French, Belgian and Dutch, of whom the majority had not wanted to go on fighting and whom the English had therefore locked up in cellars.

In Calais, for the first time since the 17th of May, I met General von Kleist, who expressed his appreciation for the achievements of my troops.

On this day we attempted once again to attack towards Dunkirk and to close the ring about that sea fortress. But renewed orders to halt arrived. We were stopped within sight of Dunkirk! We watched the Luftwaffe attack. We also saw the armada of great and little ships by means of which the British were evacuating their forces.

General von Wietersheim appeared at my headquarters during the course of the day to discuss with me arrangements for the relief of XIX Army Corps by his XIV Army Corps. The advanced division of this corps, the 20th (Motorised) Infantry Division, was placed under my command. I put it in on the right of the *Leibstandarte 'Adolf Hitler.'* Before this discussion was over, a small incident occurred. The commander of the *Leibstandarte*, Sepp Dietrich, while driving from the front came under machine-gun fire from a party of Englishmen who were still holding out in a solitary house behind our lines. They set his car on fire and compelled him and his companions to take shelter in the ditch. Dietrich and his adjutant crawled into a large drain pipe, where the ditch ran under a cross road, and in order to protect himself from the burning petrol of his car covered his face and hands with damp mud. A wireless truck following his command car signalled for help and we were able to send part of the 3rd Panzer Regiment of the 2nd Panzer Division, whose sector this was, to get him out of his unpleasant predicament. He soon appeared at my headquarters covered from head to foot in mud and had to accept some very ribald comments on our part. (*See Appendix* XIX.)

[1] Quoted in English in the original.—*Tr.*

It was not until the afternoon of May the 26th that Hitler gave permission for the advance on Dunkirk to be resumed. By then it was too late to achieve a great victory. (*See Appendix* XX.)

The corps was sent into the attack during the night of the 26–27th. The 20th (Motorised) Infantry Division, with the *Leibstandarte 'Adolf Hitler'* and the Infantry Regiment 'G.D.' under command and reinforced by heavy artillery, was given Wormhoudt as its objective. 1st Panzer Division on its left was ordered to push forward, with point of main effort its right wing, in accordance with the progress that that attack should make.

The Infantry Regiment 'G.D.' received useful support from the 4th Panzer Brigade of the 10th Panzer Division and secured its objective, the high ground Crochte–Pitgam. The Armoured Reconnaissance Battalion of the 1st Panzer Division took Brouckerque.

Heavy enemy movement of transport ships from Dunkirk was observed.

On the 28th of May we reached Wormhoudt and Bourgbourgville. On the 29th Gravelines fell to the 1st Panzer Division. But the capture of Dunkirk was after all completed without us. On the 29th of May XIX Army Corps was relieved by XIV Army Corps.(*See Appendix* XXI.)

The operation would have been completed very much more quickly if Supreme Headquarters had not kept ordering XIX Army Corps to stop and thus hindered its rapid and successful advance. What the future course of the war would have been if we had succeeded at that time in taking the British Expeditionary Force prisoner at Dunkirk, it is now impossible to guess. In any event a military victory on that scale would have offered a great chance to capable diplomats. Unfortunately the opportunity was wasted owing to Hitler's nervousness. The reason he subsequently gave for holding back my corps—that the ground in Flanders with its many ditches and canals was not suited to tanks—was a poor one.

On May 26th I was anxious to express my gratitude to the brave troops under my command. This took the form of the following corps order:

Soldiers of the XIX Army Corps!

For seventeen days we have been fighting in Belgium and France. We have covered a good 400 miles since crossing the German border: we have reached the Channel Coast and the Atlantic Ocean. On the way here you have thrust through the Belgian fortifications, forced a passage of the Meuse, broken the Maginot Line extension in the memorable Battle of Sedan, captured the important heights at Stonne and then, without halt, fought your way through St. Quentin and Péronne to the lower Somme at Amiens and Abbéville. You have set the crown on your achievements by the capture of the Channel Coast and of the sea fortresses at Boulogne and Calais.

I asked you to go without sleep for 48 hours. You have gone for 17 days. I compelled you to accept risks to your flanks and rear. You never faltered.

With masterly self-confidence and believing in the fulfillment of your mission, you carried out every order with devotion.

Germany is proud of her Panzer Divisions and I am happy to be your commander.

We remember our fallen comrades with honour and respect, sure in the knowledge that their sacrifice was not in vain.

Now we shall arm ourselves for new deeds.

For Germany and for our leader, Adolf Hitler!

signed, GUDERIAN.

Winston Churchill, in his memoirs of the Second World War, says that some of the German generals suggested that by holding up his tanks outside Dunkirk Hitler was hoping either to give the English an opportunity to sue for peace or to increase Germany's chances of negotiating a settlement. Neither then nor at any later period did I ever hear anything to substantiate this suggestion. Churchill's guess that Rundstedt may have himself decided to hold up the armour is also wide of the mark. As the commander on the spot I am able, moreover, definitely to state that the heroic defence of Calais, although worthy of the highest praise, yet had no influence on the development of events outside Dunkirk. Churchill assumes, quite correctly, that Hitler and above all Goering believed German air supremacy to be strong enough to prevent the evacuation of the British forces by sea. This belief was a mistake pregnant with consequence, for only the capture of the British Expeditionary Force could have influenced the English towards making peace with Hitler or could have created the conditions necessary for a successful German invasion of Great Britain.

In Flanders I received news that my elder son had been wounded, though mercifully the wound was not mortal. My second son was decorated in France with the Iron Cross, both First and Second Class. Despite being in action with an armoured reconnaissance battalion, he had survived all his engagements unhurt.

The Break-through to the Swiss Border

On the 28th of May Hitler ordered that a Panzer Group be set up under my command. My corps headquarters moved to Signy-le-Petit, south-west of Charleville, to make preparations for the next phase of the campaign. It arrived there on the 1st of June. The assembly of 'Panzer Group Guderian' took place during the first days of June in the area south-west of Charleville. Its staff was formed from the staff of my old XIX Army Corps. The trusty Colonel Nehring remained Chief of Staff, the operations officer (*I a*) was Major Bayerlein, and

Sketch Map 6

Break through the Weygand Line
to the Plateau de Langres.
Situation 11.6. — 15.6.40.

the adjutant Lieutenant-Colonel Riebel. The Panzer Group consisted of:

The XXXIX Army Corps (General Schmidt), with the 1st and 2nd Panzer Divisions and the 29th (Motorised) Infantry Division.

The XLI Army Corps (General Reinhardt), with the 6th and 8th Panzer Divisions and the 20th (Motorised) Infantry Division,

and a number of formations under direct command of the Group.

The Panzer Group itself was subordinate to Colonel-General List's Twelfth Army.

The march to our new assembly area was a considerable one, particularly for the 1st and 2nd Panzer Divisions coming from the Channel coast. The distance amounted to some 150 miles, but owing to detours necessitated by bridge demolitions some units had to cover a further 60 miles. Signs of extreme fatigue on the part of the troops and of wear to their vehicles began to be apparent. Fortunately the troops were enabled to have a few days for rest and maintenance, so that both they and, to a certain extent, their equipment were in better condition for the tasks ahead.

The success of the first phase of the Campaign in the West had resulted in the elimination of the enemy's forces in Holland, Belgium and Northern France. Our rear was now clear for the prosecution of operations southwards. We had already succeeded in destroying the bulk of the enemy's armoured and motorised strength. So the second phase of the campaign would simply involve the defeating of the remainder of the French Army—some 70 divisions, including two British—and making an advantageous peace. That at least is what we thought at the time.

Deployment for the renewal of the battle was completed more quickly by our right wing, along the Somme, than by our centre, along the Serre and the Aisne. Consequently Army Group von Bock could launch its attack on the 5th of June, while that of Army Group von Rundstedt did not start until June 9th.

In the sector of Army Group von Rundstedt, Twelfth Army had the task of crossing the Aisne and the Aisne Canal between Château-Porcien and Attigny and of then pushing on towards the south. The infantry corps were to be responsible for crossing the river and its accompanying canal at eight points. After the bridgeheads had been established and the bridges thrown across, the panzer divisions of my Group were to attack through the infantry, to fight their way into the open, and then—depending on the situation—advance either towards Paris or Langres or Verdun. Our first objective was to be the Plateau de Langres; there, at the latest, we were to receive further orders.

I asked the commander of the Twelfth Army to assign certain crossing-places to my divisions from the beginning and to let them capture those bridgeheads on the Aisne themselves. I did not care for the idea of attacking through the infantry divisions, since their numerous and large supply columns tended to block the roads and I was worried about possible command difficulties arising. However, the Army Commander wished to save the panzer divisions for the decisive break-through and therefore refused my request. The Panzer Group was consequently assembled behind the infantry corps and the four panzer divisions were ready to advance through the eight different bridgeheads as soon as those were established. The two motorised divisions were to follow behind the panzer divisions of their respective corps. In order that the plan should succeed it was of course essential that the infantry manage to cross the river and seize the bridgeheads.

The boundary between the XXXIX and the XLI Army Corps ran from Wasigny through Rethel–Juniville–Hauviné–Aubérive–Suippes–St. Rémy–Tilloy (all inclusive to XXXIX Army Corps)–Vanault–Sogny–Pargny (all inclusive to XLI Army Corps).

On the 8th of June the Panzer Group headquarters was moved to Bégny.

On the 9th of June, the first day of Twelfth Army's attack, I went to an observation post north-east of Rethel so that I might personally watch the progress of the infantry attack and thus not miss the moment for the commitment of my forces. From 05.00 hrs. to 10.00 hrs. there was nothing to see. I therefore sent my orderly officer to the next point of attack in order to find out if the infantry were over the Aisne there. At 12.00 hrs. I received messages from the front on either side of Rethel that the Rethel attacks had failed. My observers from the other fronts reported that the infantry had only succeeded in establishing a single bridgehead, a small one a mile to a mile and a half deep, in the neighbourhood of Château-Porcien. I got into communication with the chief of staff of Twelfth Army, my friend General von Mackensen, and asked him to tell his commander that in view of this I suggested that the tanks be moved into the single bridgehead during the hours of darkness so that they might be in a position to break out of it the following morning. I then went to Château-Porcien, by way of the headquarters of General Haase's III Army Corps, where I stopped briefly to find out what the situation was. After having a look at the bridgehead I went to see the commander of my XXXIX Army Corps, General Schmidt, who with General Kirchner was immediately to the north of that little town. I discussed with them the move forward of 1st Panzer Division and its commitment in the Château-Porcien bridgehead. The movement was to start at dusk.

Shortly afterwards I met the Army Commander, Colonel-General List, who had motored down from the north. On his way he had passed elements of the 1st Panzer Division and had noted with displeasure that a number of the tank men had taken off their jackets, while some were actually bathing in a nearby stream. He took me violently to task and wanted to know why my troops were not already advancing through the bridgeheads. Having just examined the situation for myself I was able to tell him that it was plainly impossible to advance through bridgeheads that had either not yet been captured or were not sufficiently extended. Furthermore, I pointed out that the capture of the bridgeheads was not the responsibility of my panzer troops. It was typical of Colonel-General List's chivalrous nature that he immediately offered me his hand and proceeded calmly to discuss the future development of the attack with me.

After spending a short time at my Group headquarters I returned to the Château-Porcien bridgehead in order to supervise the commitment of my tanks and to establish contact with the commander of the infantry division there engaged. I found General Loch, of the 17th Infantry Division, on the far bank and we were able to co-ordinate the measures we were taking. I remained at the front until 01.00 hrs., then visited the wounded from my tank and reconnaissance units who were waiting for transport back through the bridgehead, thanked them for their brave performance, and drove back to my headquarters at Bégny in order to issue my orders.

In the course of the afternoon two shallow bridgeheads had been formed to the west and east of Château-Porcien. These could be used for getting the 2nd Panzer Divisions over the river, together with further elements of the 1st.

The attack by my tanks was to start at 06.30 hrs. on the 10th of June. I was at the front by then and managed to get the 1st Rifle Brigade, which was too far back, moving forwards. I was surprised to be recognised by the front-line infantry, and when I asked how they knew my name, I discovered I was amongst the 55th Infantry Regiment, whose home station was Würzburg; the officers and men remembered me from the days when I commanded the 2nd Panzer Division in that once beautiful but now totally ruined city. We were delighted to see each other. The attack by the tanks and the infantry went in simultaneously and both arms had confidence in the other. The advance was rapid through Avançon and Tagnon to Neuflize on the Retourne. Once in the open the tanks met hardly any resistance, since the new French tactics concentrated on the defence of woods and villages, while the open ground was abandoned out of respect for our tanks. Consequently our infantry had to fight hard for the barricaded streets and houses of the villages, while the tanks, only slightly inconvenienced by the French artillery firing to the rear from the positions they still held on the Rethel front, broke straight through to the Retourne and crossed that swampy stream, which had been dammed, at Neuflize. 1st Panzer Division now pressed forward, attacking along both banks of the Retourne, with the 1st Panzer Brigade to the south and Balck's riflemen to the north of the stream. Juniville was reached in the early afternoon, where the enemy counter-attacked with strong armoured forces. A tank battle developed to the south of Juniville, which lasted for some two hours before being eventually decided in our favour. In the course of the afternoon Juniville itself was taken. There Balck managed personally to capture the colours of a French regiment. The enemy withdrew to La Neuville. While the tank battle was in progress I attempted, in vain, to destroy a Char B with a captured 47 mm. anti-tank gun; all the shells I fired at it simply bounced harmlessly off its thick armour. Our 37 mm. and 20 mm. guns were equally ineffective against this adversary. As a result, we inevitably suffered sadly heavy casualties.

In the late afternoon another heavy engagement with enemy tanks took place, this time to the north of Juniville. The French were advancing from the direction of Annelles towards Perthe with the intention of mounting a counter-attack, but we managed to beat them off.

Meanwhile the 2nd Panzer Division was across the Aisne to the west of Château-Porcien and was advancing southward. By evening it had reached Houdilcourt–St. Étienne. Parts of Reinhardt's corps, which had not yet been able to cross at the points allotted it, were sent over behind 1st Panzer Division. However, we reckoned that the capture of Juniville would soon bring the enemy resistance at Rethel to an end. Reinhardt's corps would then have freedom of movement once again.

Group headquarters was set up in the Bois de Sévigny, on the Aisne, south-east of Château-Porcien. I spent the night there. I was completely exhausted, and throwing myself down on a bundle of straw, without even taking my cap off, fell instantly asleep. Riebel, considerate as always, had a tent put up around me and posted guards so as to ensure that I had at least three hours' undisturbed sleep.

Early on June 11th I was at La Neuville for the attack by the 1st Panzer Division. The attack went forward as though this were a manœuvre: artillery preparation, advance by the tanks and riflemen, the encirclement of the village and break-through towards Béthéniville— this latter a village well known to me from the First World War. The enemy's resistance was stiffer along the Suippes. He counter-attacked in

vain, using some 50 tanks that probably belonged to the French 7th
Light Division. The villages of Nauroy, Beine, and St. Hilaire-le-Petit
were captured.

The 2nd Panzer Division reached Époye, the 29th (Motorised)
Infantry Division the wood to the south-west of this village.

Reinhardt's XLI Army Corps, advancing to the east of the XXXIX
Army Corps, had to beat off an attack on its flank by the French 3rd
Mechanised and 3rd Armoured Divisions, which came in from the
Argonnes. When these had been successfully repelled, it resumed its
advance towards the south.

In the afternoon I received a message that the Commander-in-Chief
of the Army intended to visit the Panzer Group, and I therefore
returned to my headquarters. I found Colonel-General von Brauchitsch
already there and I explained to him the position at the front and told
him what we anticipated for the future. I received no new instructions.
In the evening my headquarters moved to Juniville.

The attack was resumed on the 12th June. XXXIX Army Corps was
ordered to move on Châlons-sur-Marne with the 2nd Panzer Division,
and on Vitry-le-François with the 1st Panzer Division and the 29th
(Motorised) Infantry Division. XLI Army Corps was to push its right
wing through Somme–Py to Suippes.

Our progress was made more difficult through confusion that arose
from the impetuous advance of the infantry following behind us. The
infantry units were now over the Aisne and in some cases they had by
this time caught up with the panzer units which were fighting their way
forwards. Divisional boundaries had not been drawn with sufficient
clarity and units overlapped. A request was made to Army headquarters
that this be sorted out, but in vain. At points along the Suippes there
were a number of animated scenes. Both arms of the Service wanted to
lead the advance. The gallant infantrymen had marched day and night,
so keen were they to get at the enemy. On the morning of this day we
passed the Heights of Champagne, well known to me from the autumn
of 1917. I visited the 29th (Motorised) Infantry Division, commanded
by General Freiherr von Langermann, which was now appearing at the
front for the first time, near the northern edge of the camp of Mour-
melon-le-Grand. He was engaged in giving orders for an attack on the
camp by the reconnaissance battalion when I arrived. All his unit
commanders were present, well forward. The orders were short and to
the point. It all made a first-class impression. I could drive without
anxiety to the 2nd Panzer Division at Châlons-sur-Marne.

When I arrived there, Châlons had just been reached. Our foremost
reconnaissance troops had captured the Marne bridge intact but had
unfortunately failed to examine it at once for demolition charges,

although they had received very explicit orders always to do this. As a result the bridge blew up while our troops were actually crossing it with consequent, quite unnecessary casualties.

While I was discussing the further prosecution of his advance with General Veiel, I was summoned back to my Group headquarters, where the Commander-in-Chief of the Army Group, Colonel-General von Rundstedt, was expected.

By evening the 1st Panzer Division had reached Bussy-le-Château. They were ordered to move on Étrépy, on the Rhine–Marne Canal.

During the course of this day Reinhardt's Corps had fought a defensive battle against enemy troops attacking westwards from the Argonnes. I visited the divisions of that corps during the afternoon, in the neighbourhood of Machault, and was thus able, personally, to approve the measures that had been taken. We captured Souain, Tahure, and Manre. On my way back to my Group headquarters I came across renewed confusion caused by infantry units moving across our line of advance. Again I tried in vain to get Twelfth Army command to do something about this.

From now on the Panzer Group received every day many mutually contradictory orders, some ordering a swing towards the east, others a continuation of the advance southward. First of all Verdun was to be taken by means of a surprise attack, then the southward advance was to go on, then we were to swing east on St. Mihiel, then again we were to move south once more. Reinhardt's Corps was the one which suffered from all this vacillation; I kept Schmidt's Corps on a steady course, southwards, so that at least half of my Panzer Group was assured of continuity of purpose.

On the 13th of June I first visited the Reinhardt Corps and its 6th and 8th Panzer Division which were still engaged in battle with the enemy forces from Verdun and the Argonnes. Towards evening I set off to find the headquarters of the 1st Panzer Division, which had reached the Rhine–Marne Canal near Étrépy. XXXIX Army Corps had ordered the division not to cross this canal. I knew nothing of this order; nor would I have approved it if I had. Outside Étrépy I found Balck, the inexhaustible commander of the leading elements of 1st Panzer Division, and asked him whether he had secured the bridge over the canal. He replied that he had. I asked him if he had also established a bridgehead on the far side. After a pause he answered that he had done that too. His reticence surprised me. Was it possible, I asked, to drive over to his bridgehead by car? Looking at me with deep distrust, he rather timidly said that it was. So over we went. In the bridgehead I found a capital

engineer officer, Lieutenant Weber, who had risked his life to prevent
the demolition of the bridge, and the commander of the rifle battalion
which had formed the bridgehead, a Captain Eckinger. I was delighted
to be able to decorate these two brave officers with the Iron Cross,
First Class, on the spot. I then asked Balck why he had not pushed
farther forward; it was only then I learned of XXXIX Army Corps'
order to stop. This was the explanation of Balck's extraordinary reticence: he had already gone farther than he should and he expected me
to reprimand him for doing so.

Once again, as at Bouvellemont, our break-through was almost completed. Once again this was no time for hesitancy or delay. Balck gave
me his impressions of the enemy: opposite his sector the canal was
being defended by black troops with very little artillery support. He
received my order to advance directly on St. Dizier. I promised, myself,
to inform his divisional and corps commanders of this order. So Balck
set to. I went back to divisional headquarters and ordered that the
whole division be put in motion at once. I then informed General
Schmidt of the orders I had given to the 1st Panzer Division.

Finally, as dusk was falling, after driving through the area of the
29th (Motorised) Infantry Division, which had reached the canal at
Brusson, I found Reconnaissance Battalion 5 of the 2nd Panzer
Division just north of Vitry-le-François and learned from them
the situation in this sector and what progress their division had
made.

At 09.00 hrs., on the 14th of June, German troops began to enter
Paris.

My 1st Panzer Division reached St. Dizier during the course of the
night. French prisoners taken belonged to their 3rd Armoured Division,
as well as to the 3rd North African Division and the 6th Colonial
Infantry Division; they gave the impression of being utterly exhausted.
Farther west the remainder of XXXIX Army Corps crossed the canal.
East of Étrépy Reinhardt's Corps reached the Rhine–Marne Canal near
Revigny.

At midday, after a conversation with the commander of the 1st Panzer
Division, I entered St. Dizier. The first person I saw was my friend,
Balck, seated on a chair in the market-place. He was looking forward to
a few quiet hours after all the effort of the last few days and nights. I
had to disappoint him in this. The faster we could now continue our
advance, the greater must our victory be. Balck was ordered to set off
at once and to head straight for Langres. The rest of the 1st Panzer
Division was following behind. The advance was completed during the
night, and early on the morning of the 15th of June the old fortress
surrendered. Three thousand prisoners were taken.

Fig. 6. Boulogne: The assault on the town wall

Fig. 7. The attack rolls on

The 29th (Motorised) Infantry Division was sent through Wassy to Juzenencourt: the 2nd Panzer Division through Montierender–Soulaines to Bar-sur-Aube. Reinhardt's Corps was ordered to keep on moving south.

The intentions of the *OKH* that the Panzer Group should turn off towards Nancy by way of Joinville–Neufchâteau had already been issued as orders to the units: but there was still time for alternative orders to reach the troops.

Early on the 15th June I set of for Langres, arriving at about noon. I told the 1st Panzer Division to head for Gray-sur-Saône and Besançon, the 29th (Motorised) Infantry Division to advance towards the Saône, south-west of Gray, the 2nd Panzer Division to move on Til-Châtel, while the XLI Army Corps was to hold to its line of advance southwards, east of the Marne. On our right the XVI Army Corps of the Kleist Group was advancing towards Dijon. 1st Panzer Division moved off at 13.00 hrs. Then I sat down with my little combat staff in the French officers' mess, whose garden commanded a fine view towards the east, and anxiously considered my left flank; it was very long by this time and very open, and now reports were coming in of French forces advancing against it from the east. In the course of the afternoon General Wiktorin's 20th (Motorised) Infantry Division arrived at Langres; it moved off at once towards Vesoul, thus giving us protection on that section of our flank. The 29th (Motorised) Infantry Division was continuing to advance west of Langres. The situation was developing rapidly from hour to hour. By evening Bar-sur-Aube, Gray-sur-Saône and Bar-le-Duc had all been captured.

The French commandant of Gray fell in the defence of that town.

Group headquarters was moved in the evening to Langres. Since no orders had been received from the Army High Command concerning the future employment of the Panzer Group, I sent the *OKH* liaison officer attached to my staff back by plane to offer my suggestion that the advance be continued to the Swiss frontier.

We billeted ourselves in friendly, middle-class houses in Langres; we enjoyed the comfort of our quarters after the really strenuous time that we had had during the past few days. The 29th (Motorised) Infantry Division reached Pontaillier-sur-Saône; on the 16th it was to go to Pontarlier and the 2nd Panzer Division to Auxonne-Dôle. XLI Army Corps was to continue to advance, with the 20th (Motorised) Infantry Division moving ahead of the two panzer divisions.

On the 16th of June the 1st Panzer Division managed to capture a bridge over the Saône intact, at Quitteur to the north of Gray. German planes bombed the bridge that was being built at Gray, for hours on end, and caused us considerable delay as a result. Since they apparently came from Army Group Leeb, there was no way we could get in touch with them to tell them of their mistake. Luckily they did not cause us any casualties.

During the afternoon XXXIX Army Corps reached Besançon–Avanne; XLI Army Corps, with the 20th (Motorised) Infantry Division leading, moved through Port-sur-Saône, Vesoul, and Bourbonne. Thousands of prisoners were taken including, for the first time, Poles. Thirty tanks were captured at Besançon.

On the 17th of June my most efficient chief of staff, Colonel Nehring, collected all the staff together on the little terrace between our quarters and the wall of the old fortress, to wish me a happy birthday. As a birthday present he was able to hand me a message which stated that the 29th (Motorised) Infantry Division had reached the Swiss frontier. We were all delighted by this success, and I set off at once in order personally to congratulate the brave troops on the day of their great achievement. At about 12.00 hrs. I met General Freiherr von Langermann in Pontarlier, after a long drive during the course of which I passed most of his division advancing along my road. The men were in good spirits and waved cheerfully as I went by. We sent a message to supreme headquarters informing them that we had reached the Swiss border at Pontarlier, to which Hitler signalled back: 'Your signal based on an error. Assume you mean Pontailler-sur-Saône.' My reply, 'No error. Am myself in Pontarlier on Swiss border,' finally satisfied the distrustful *OKW*.

I paid a short visit to the frontier and had a word with the leaders of the reconnaissance battalion. It was thanks to their tireless efforts that we had had such superb intelligence of the enemy. Among the best of those officers was Lieutenant von Bünau, who was later to lose his life in the service of Germany.

From Pontarlier I sent a wireless signal, ordering XXXIX Army Corps immediately to change direction and to advance north-east. The 29th (Motorised) Infantry Division was to move along the border until it reached the frontier bend near Pruntrut and to clear the Jura of stragglers: 1st Panzer Division was to advance from Besançon through Montbéliard to Belfort: 2nd Panzer Division, advancing across what had been the line of march of those two divisions, was to go to Remiremont on the upper Moselle. At the same time the XLI Army Corps was to turn left towards Épinal and Charme.

Boundary between XXXIX and XLI Army Corps: the road fork south-west of Langres–Chalindrey–Pierrecourt–Membrey–Mailley–Vellefaux–Lure–Plancher (all inclusive to XLI Army Corps).

Sketch Map 7.
Break through to the Swiss Border and into Upper Alsace.
Situation 16. 6. — 20. 6. 40.

The purpose of this manœuvre was to establish contact with General Dollmann's Seventh Army, which was advancing from Upper Alsace, and cut the communication of the French forces in Alsace-Lorraine with the rest of France. The difficult business of making a 90-degree turn was carried out with the same precision that my panzer divisions had shown in all their movements up to date. The crossed lines of advance which I had ordered did not result in any confusion. I had the satisfaction, that evening at my headquarters, of receiving a signal from Army Group Leeb in which I was informed that my Group was now subordinated to that Army Group and was to advance in the direction of Belfort–Épinal. I could reply that these orders were already being carried out.

Six years later I was to share a cell in Nuremberg prison with Field-Marshal Ritter von Leeb. While sitting in that gloomy place we happened to discuss the events of 1940. Field-Marshal Ritter von Leeb told me that he had never understood how I managed to carry out his orders for the advance on Belfort–Épinal so quickly. I was able, belatedly enough, to give him the explanation. As a result of its operational role, the Panzer Group was able to see the situation from the same perspective as that of the Army Group and thus reach the same conclusions.

We had taken up our quarters in Avanne, a beautiful place, with a lovely view over the River Doubs, near Besançon. At dinner there I had the pleasure of seeing my younger son, Kurt, once again. He had just been transferred from the 3rd Armoured Reconnaissance Battalion to Hitler's bodyguard, the Führer Escort Battalion, and he took advantage of a courier mission to visit me here on my birthday.

Towards midnight the operations officer of the 1st Panzer Division, Major Wenck, signalled that his division had just reached Montbéliard, which was the objective assigned to it by XXXIX Army Corps. The troops, however, still had plenty of fuel and there was no reason why they should not go on. Since he could not reach his corps commander he wanted to know whether I would approve of the continuation of the division's advance. They could reach Belfort during the night. Naturally I approved his request, particularly as I had never envisaged the division stopping in Montbéliard; XXXIX Army Corps, imagining that the division could not reach Belfort in one march as I had ordered, had given them Montbéliard as intermediary objective. At the critical moment the corps headquarters was on the move and could not, therefore, be reached by the division. It was the old story of giving armour the green light to the end of the road. The enemy was completely taken by surprise.

After a short rest I set off early on the 18th of June for Belfort, where

I arrived at about 08.00 hours. Between Montbéliard and Belfort long columns of French vehicles, including much heavy artillery, were parked along the road. They had already surrendered. Thousands of prisoners were camped outside the entrance to the old fortress. But there were no German flags to be seen on the towers of the forts, and there was still shooting to be heard inside the town. I stopped a motor-cycle despatch rider of the 1st Panzer Division on the open space in front of the Lion de Belfort, and asked him where his divisional headquarters was located. The alert young man knew that his general was at the Hôtel de Paris and led me there. I found Wenck, who was very surprised to see me so early in the morning, and when I asked for the divisional commander he told me that that officer was in the act of taking a hot bath. I could well understand that this staff might well want a good wash after the terrific race which they had been running for the last few days, and I took advantage of the wait until Kirchner should appear to sample the breakfast that French cooks had prepared for French officers. Then I inquired about the position here and learned that the division was at present only in control of a part of the town, while the French still held the forts. Only the troops in the barracks had agreed to surrender. The forts refused to capitulate without a fight and must, therefore, be assaulted.

The division organised an assault group for the attack on the forts and on the citadel. The battle began at about noon. The first fort to be captured was Basses-Perches, followed by Hautes-Perches, near where I was standing, and the citadel itself. The tactics employed were extremely simple: first, a short bombardment by the artillery of 1st Panzer Division; then Eckinger's rifle battalion, in armoured troop-carrying vehicles, and an 88 mm. anti-aircraft gun drove right up to the fort, the latter taking up position immediately in front of the gorge; the riflemen thus reached the glacis without suffering any casualties, climbed up it, clambered over the entrenchments and scaled the wall, while the 88 mm. anti-aircraft gun fired into the gorge at point-blank range. The fort was then summoned to surrender, which under the impact of the rapid attack it did. Our ensign was hoisted to mark the completion of the surrender, and the assault troops turned to their next task. Our casualties were very light.

On this day other elements of 1st Panzer Division, under the command of Colonel Nedtwig, reached Giromagny to the north of Belfort. They captured 10,000 prisoners as well as 40 mortars and 7 aeroplanes, besides a great deal of other equipment.

Panzer Group moved its headquarters to Montbéliard.

Meanwhile, the French Government had resigned and the veteran Marshal Pétain had formed a new Cabinet which began to negotiate for an armistice on the 16th of June.

Our main task now was to establish contact with General Dollmann and to complete the encirclement of the enemy forces in Alsace Lorraine.

While the 29th (Motorised) Infantry Division was fighting its way forward through the Jura, towards Lomont and the Pruntrut corner, the 2nd Panzer Division reached the upper Moselle at Rupt and Remiremont. The 6th Panzer Division, under General Kempff, took Épinal in much the same way that the 1st Panzer Division had captured Belfort. In each of these fortresses we made some 40,000 prisoners.

Advance units of the Seventh Army reached Nieder-Asbach, to the south of Sennheim, in Upper Alsace.

On the 19th of June the advance was resumed and contact made with Seventh Army at La Chapelle, to the north-east of Belfort. We had a certain amount of trouble with the eastern Belfort forts, but finally these too surrendered. 1st Panzer Division stormed the heights of Belchen and the Ballon de Servance and at about midnight captured Le Tillot. The 2nd Panzer Division took Fort Rupt on the Moselle. The advance through the Vosges was carried out on a broad front. The infantry divisions of I Army Corps, advancing towards Épinal from the north, had to be halted, since the roads were already overloaded with panzer troops and the arrival of infantry formations as well would have brought all movement to a standstill. The infantry complained loudly at Army Group headquarters about what they regarded as this ill-treatment; they too wanted to have a go at the enemy. I sent my operations officer, Major Bayerlein, with all speed by aeroplane to Colonel-General Ritter von Leeb, since I wished the Army Group commander to know my reasons for halting the infantry. Bayerlein arrived just in time to prevent any unpleasantness.

The headquarters of the Panzer Group was now moved to the resort town of Plombières, an old spa well known to the Romans. We spent three very agreeable days there.

The collapse of the French was complete. On the 20th of June Cornimont fell, and on the 21st Bussang in the Vosges. The 2nd Panzer Division reached St. Amé and Tholy, the 29th (Motorised) Infantry Division Delle and Belfort. We took 150,000 prisoners. Arguments had developed between the generals of Army Group C concerning the numbers of prisoners captured by their respective troops; which prisoners belonged to whom? Colonel-General Ritter von Leeb had to sit in judgment like Solomon. He allotted the figure of 150,000 to me and added the flattering comment that had it not been for the encircling movement of my Panzer Group through Belfort and Épinal the totals for all units would have been considerably smaller.

Since the crossing of the Aisne the Panzer Group had taken in all approximately 250,000 prisoners, besides an incalculable quantity of equipment of all sorts.

On the 22nd of June the French Government agreed to an armistice. We were not immediately informed of its conditions. On the 23rd I drove through the Vosges, by way of Schlucht and Kaysersberg, to visit General Dollmann in his headquarters at Colmar. I saw once again the town in which I had spent my happy childhood.

My staff was moved to Besançon where we lived at first in a hotel, afterwards moving into the building which had previously housed the French area command. Now that the fighting was over I had the opportunity to thank my generals and general staff officers for their superb performance. Our work together had been marred by no misunderstandings whatever. The brave soldiers had carried out their very heavy duties with the greatest devotion. They could well be proud of their achievements.

On the 30th of June I said farewell to them with the following order of the day:

Group Guderian.   Besançon, 30.6.40.
   At this moment, when Group Guderian is about to be dissolved, I want to express to all commands and units who are about to depart for fresh tasks, my very best wishes.
   The victorious advance from the Aisne to the Swiss border and the Vosges will go down in history as an heroic example of a break-through by mobile troops.
   I thank you for what you have done. It has been the finest fulfillment to my labours and struggles of more than a decade's duration.
   On to fresh tasks, with the same spirit and the same success, until the final victory of Greater Germany is complete!
   Heil dem Führer!

                                        signed, GUDERIAN

The Armistice

I recall two visitors who came to see me while I was in Besançon. On the evening of the 27th General Ritter von Epp appeared, the honorary Colonel of the 19th Infantry Regiment, who was passing through Besançon while looking for his regiment: I knew him from the old days when we used to go hunting together in the Spessart. We had a long conversation in which we thoroughly discussed our armistice with

France and the future prosecution of the war against England. I enjoyed this conversation all the more since, isolated as I was, I had had no opportunity for an interchange of views on these subjects.

My second visitor, with whom I discussed the same matters on the 5th of July, was the Minister for Armaments and War Production, Dr. Todt. He had come to collect at first hand the opinion of front-line soldiers which might modify the planned developments in the field of tank production.

The German people were rejoicing and Hitler was satisfied with the armistice that had been signed. I felt less enthusiastic about it. In view of the totality of our victory there were several courses open to us. We could have insisted on complete French disarmament, on the occupation by our forces of the entire country, on the handing over to us of the French fleet and colonies. We could, alternatively, have chosen an entirely different approach: we could have offered the French the integrity of their country and colonies and their national independence in exchange for their assistance in securing a rapid peace with the English. Between these extremes there lay a host of variants. No matter what course was adopted, the object must be to produce circumstances favourable to Germany for bringing the war to an end, including the war with England. In order to make peace with England the first requirement must be an attempt to reopen diplomatic relations. Hitler's offer from the Reichstag tribunal cannot be counted as such. I am now aware that it is highly problematical whether Great Britain would, in fact, have agreed at that time to negotiate with Hitler. Nevertheless, the attempt had to be made, if only so that we could not later be accused of having neglected any possibility of a peaceful settlement. If diplomacy should not produce the desired results, then military methods would have to be used, immediately and with all available strength. Of course, Hitler and his staff considered the future prosecution of the war against Great Britain; the well-known plan for the invasion of England, *Operation Sea-lion*, is sufficient proof of that. But in view of the insufficiency of our preparations in the air and on the sea, which were far below what would be needed to invade, other means would have to be found of so damaging our enemy that he would accept a negotiated peace.

It seemed to me, then, that we could ensure peace in the near future by, first of all, advancing at once to the mouth of the Rhône: then, having captured the French Mediterranean bases in conjunction with the Italians, by landing in Africa, while the Luftwaffe's first-class parachute troops seized Malta. Should the French be willing to participate in these operations, so much the better. Should they refuse, then the war must be carried on by the Italians and ourselves on our own, and carried on at once. The weakness of the British in Egypt at that time was known to us. The Italians still had strong forces in Abyssinia. The defences of Malta against air attack were inadequate. Everything seemed to me to be in favour of further operations along these lines, and I could see no disadvantages. The presence of four to six panzer divisions in North Africa would have given us such overwhelming superiority that any British reinforcements would inevitably have arrived too late. It would plainly have been far more advantageous to make a German–Italian landing in North Africa in 1940 than it was in 1941, after the initial Italian defeat in that theatre.

It is possible that Italian distrust prevented Hitler from carrying the war into Africa at that time. But it is more likely that Hitler, thinking within the limited framework of continental ideas, failed properly to grasp the decisive importance of the Mediterranean to the British.

Be that as it may, I heard nothing more of my proposals at that time. It was not until 1950 that I learned that General Ritter von Epp did find an opportunity to lay these ideas before Hitler. According to Captain Wenig, who had accompanied Epp to see him, Hitler was not interested in exploring the possibilities involved.

My stay at Besançon enabled me to get to know the Jura. On the 1st of July I gazed from the top of Mont Rond down across the famous Lake of Geneva. I also visited Lyons to see my elder son, who had been wounded for the second time during the Campaign in the West. He received an advance of seniority as a reward for the bravery he had shown.

Our relations with the prefect and the mayor of Besançon were correct. Both these gentlemen were consistently courteous and polite.

At the beginning of July my Panzer Group was dissolved, some divisions returning to Germany while others were moved to the Paris area. The staff also went to Paris. We were supposed to organise a great parade at which the Führer was to have been present; fortunately this never took place.

While in Paris I visited Versailles and Fontainebleau, the latter a wonderful old castle full of historical memories and beautiful objects. I was particularly interested by the Napoleonic Museum at Malmaison. The aged and dignified director was kind enough to show me around himself, and I had a most instructive and interesting conversation about the great Corsican with that scholarly historian. Needless to say I visited all the sights of Paris, so far as military conditions permitted. I stayed first at the Hôtel Lancaster: later I was given very comfortable quarters in a private house in the Bois de Boulogne.

My stay in Paris was interrupted by the Reichstag session of the

19th July at which I, as well as the majority of the other general officers, was ordered to be present. Here Hitler announced my promotion to Colonel-General.

Since the parade was not to take place, there was no point in the staff of the Panzer Group remaining in Paris. We were, therefore, transferred to Berlin in early August, where we enjoyed a period of leisure and relaxation.

Meanwhile, the units that had remained behind in France were busy with the preparations for *Operation Sea-lion*. Even from the very beginning this operation was never taken seriously. In my opinion the lack of a sufficiently strong air force and of adequate shipping—not to mention the escape of the British Expeditionary Force from Dunkirk— made it a completely hopeless undertaking. Those two weaknesses— air power and shipping—are surely the best possible proof that Germany had neither intended nor made any preparations for a war against the Western Powers. When in September the autumn storms set in, *Operation Sea-lion*, which was already dead, was finally buried.

Sea-lion had one result for the tank troops, in that it led to experiments with underwater tanks, for which purpose Panzers III and IV were adapted. Those vehicles were made ready for operational employment at the tank gunnery school at Putlos, in Holstein, by the 10th of August. They were to be used in Russia during the crossing of the Bug in 1941.

On the basis of experience gained during the Western Campaign, Hitler ordered a tank production of 800 to 1,000 units per month. However, the Army Ordnance Office reckoned that the cost of this programme would be about two milliards of marks, and that it would involve the employment of 100,000 skilled workers and specialists. In view of these heavy expenses Hitler unfortunately agreed to the abandonment of this plan for the time being.

Hitler also ordered that the 37 mm. gun in the Panzer III be replaced by a 50 mm. L60. In fact it was the 50 mm. L42 which was used, a gun, therefore, with a considerably shorter barrel. Hitler was apparently not immediately informed of this modification to his directive on the part of the Ordnance Office; when, in February of 1941, he learned that his instructions were not being carried out even though all the technical requirements were to hand, he became extremely angry and he never forgave the responsible officers of the Ordnance Office for this high-handed act. Years later he was to refer to it.

After the campaign Hitler ordered a considerable increase in the number of panzer and motorised infantry divisions. The number of panzer divisions was soon doubled, though this involved a halving of the tank strength of each division. Thus the German Army, though doubling its nominal strength in armoured divisions, did not acquire double the number of tanks, which was after all what counted. The simultaneous doubling of the motorised infantry divisions placed such a terrific burden on the motor vehicle industry that Hitler's orders could only be carried out by making full use of all available supplies, including the material captured in the countries of Western Europe. These captured vehicles were markedly inferior in quality to the German ones and were particularly ill-suited for any employment that might be foreseen in the eastern or African theatres.

I was responsible for supervising the organisation and training of a number of panzer and motorised infantry divisions. This kept me fully occupied. During my rare hours of leisure I meditated about the apparent future course of the war, which somehow must eventually be brought to an end. My thoughts turned increasingly towards the south. I believed, as my conversations in Besançon already showed, that the end of the war with Great Britain was the most important, indeed the only important thing.

I had no contact with the Army High Command or with the General Staff. My opinions were not sought, either concerning the reorganisation of the armoured force or as to the future prosecution of the war.

A clear light was first thrown on this latter problem by M. Molotov's visit to Berlin on the 14th of November, 1940. A terrifyingly clear light.

6. THE CAMPAIGN IN RUSSIA, 1941

The Background. Preparations. Opening operations. Crossing the Dnieper. Smolensk–Elnya–Roslavl. Moscow or Kiev? The Battle of Kiev. The Battles of Orel and Bryansk. The advance to Tula and Moscow. My first dismissal.

On May 3rd, 1939, Molotov had been appointed Soviet Foreign Commissar in place of Litvinov. He played a prominent part in negotiating the non-aggression pact with Germany of August 23rd, 1939, which enabled Hitler to attack Poland. The Russians helped in the destruction of Poland by invading the eastern portions of that country on September 18th, 1939. On September 29th, 1939, Russia signed a pact of friendship with Germany and at the same time made a trade agreement that was to be of considerable value to the Germans in the economic prosecution of the war. Meanwhile, the Russians also made the most of the international situation. They seized the Baltic States and, on the 30th of November, 1939, launched an attack on Finland. While Germany's armed forces were occupied in the West, the Russians compelled the Rumanians to surrender Bessarabia; as a result of this move Hitler, on the 30th of August 1940, felt himself bound to guarantee Rumania's independence.

In October of 1940 Hitler had discussions with the French leaders and with Franco concerning the future course of the war. In connection with these conversations he next went to meet his friend Mussolini in Florence. It was while on his way to this meeting, on Bologna station to be exact, that he learned, to his surprise, of his ally's declaration of a private war against Greece: this had been done without Hitler's connivance and he did not approve of it. By this act of Mussolini's the Balkan problem was reopened and the war took a new direction which, for Germany at least, was highly undesirable.

The first result of Mussolini's arbitrary gesture—according to what Hitler told me—was that Franco immediately withdrew from any sort of collaboration with the Axis powers. He plainly had no intention of becoming involved in a common policy with such unpredictable partners.

The next sequel was increasing tension between Germany and the Soviet Union. Such tension already existed as a result of a number of incidents that had occurred during the past few months, mainly in connection with German policy in Rumania and on the Danube. It was to lessen this that Molotov was invited to Berlin.

In Berlin Molotov made the following claims:

1. Finland was to be regarded as belonging within the Soviets' sphere of interest.

2. An agreement was to be made concerning the future of Poland.

3. Soviet interests in Rumania and Bulgaria must be recognised.

4. Soviet interests in the Dardanelles must also be acknowledged.

After Molotov had returned to Moscow the Russians restated these demands, in more precise form, in writing.

Hitler was highly incensed by the Russian claims and expressed his displeasure at length during the Berlin conversations, while simply ignoring the subsequent Russian note. The conclusion he drew from Molotov's visit and its results was a belief that war with the Soviet Union must sooner or later be inevitable. He was to describe to me repeatedly the course that the Berlin conference took; I have given his version here. It is true that he never talked to me about this matter before 1943, but later on he did so several times and always in exactly the same terms. I have no reason to believe that what he said to me was not a repetition of his opinions at the time in question.

Angered as he was by the Russian claims, he expressed his annoyance with the Italian policy of October 1940 in even stronger words; from his point of view he was, I think, quite right to do so. The Italian attack on Greece was as fatuous in execution as it was unnecessary in design. The Italian offensive had already been brought to a halt by the 30th of October. On the 6th of November the initiative passed to the Greeks. As is usually the case when bad policy results in military catastrophe, Mussolini turned in anger against his generals, and in particular against Badoglio who had warned him against bellicose escapades, though unfortunately in vain. In the middle of November the Italians suffered a sharp defeat. Badoglio was therefore an enemy of the régime and a traitor. On the 26th of November he tendered his resignation. On December 6th Cavallero was appointed to succeed him.

On December 10th the Italians were heavily defeated in North Africa, near Sidi Barrani. It would have been more in the common interest of Germany and Italy to desist from the Greek adventure and in its place to strengthen the position in North Africa. Now Marshal Graziani began asking for German aeroplanes; Mussolini decided to request the despatch to Libya of two German panzer divisions. During the course of the winter Bardia, Derna and Tobruk were lost. Rommel's German troops finally put the situation in order once again.

Italy's unco-ordinated action and mistakes in the Balkans resulted in strong German forces being committed in Africa and Bulgaria, and subsequently in Greece and Serbia. This led to a weakening of our strength in the decisive theatres of the war.

It had now been shown that the principle by which the Alps were accepted as the boundary between the spheres of interest of the Axis powers was quite inapplicable to the real needs of wartime leadership. Co-operation between the two allies was so faulty that it might just as well not have existed at all.

Shortly after Molotov's visit my new Chief of Staff, Lieutenant-Colonel Freiherr von Liebenstein, and my first general staff officer,[1] Major Bayerlein, were summoned to a conference by the Chief of the Army General Staff; there they heard for the first time about the proposed campaign against Soviet Russia, *Operation Barbarossa*. They returned from this conference and reported to me: when they spread out a map of Russia before me I could scarcely believe my eyes. Was something which I had held to be utterly impossible now to become a fact? Hitler had criticised the leaders of German policy of 1914 in the strongest possible words for their failure to avoid a war on two fronts; was he now, on his own initiative and before the war with England had been decided, to open this second-front war against the Russians? All his soldiers had warned him repeatedly and urgently against this very error, and he had himself agreed with them.

I made no attempt to conceal my disappointment and disgust. My two staff officers, who had been entirely convinced by the arguments put forth by the *OKH*, were surprised by the vehemence of my language. They explained to me how the Chief of the Army General Staff, Halder, had calculated that Russia would be defeated in a campaign of eight to ten weeks' duration. Three army groups, each of approximately the same strength, were to attack with diverging objectives; no single clear operational objective seemed to be envisaged. Looked at from a professional point of view this did not appear at all promising. I arranged for my Chief of Staff to convey my views to the *OKH*, where they produced absolutely no effect.

As one of the uninitiated, I could only now hope that Hitler was not seriously planning an attack on the Soviet Union, and that all these preparations were a bluff. The winter and spring of 1941 passed as in a nightmare. Renewed study of the campaigns of Charles XII of Sweden and of Napoleon I clearly revealed all the difficulties of the theatre to which we threatened to be committed; it also became increasingly plain to see how inadequate were our preparations for so enormous an undertaking. Our successes to date, however, and in particular the surprising speed of our victory in the West, had so befuddled the minds of our supreme commanders that they had eliminated the word 'impossible' from their vocabulary. All the men of the *OKW* and the

---

[1] The First General Staff Officer (*Ia*) at a German headquarters held a position approximately equivalent to that of the General Staff Officer I (Operations) at a British headquarters.

OKH with whom I spoke evinced an unshakable optimism and were quite impervious to criticism or objections.

In view of the heavy task that lay ahead, I concentrated with especial energy on the training and equipping of the divisions for which I was responsible. I made it quite clear to my troops that the campaign ahead of them would be a far more difficult one than those which they had fought in Poland and the West. For security reasons I could not be more specific. I wanted, however, to make sure that my soldiers did not embark on this new and infinitely difficult task in a spirit of frivolity.

Unfortunately most of the vehicles of the new divisions which Hitler had ordered to be set up were, as already stated, French. This equipment was in no way capable of meeting the demands of warfare in eastern Europe. German vehicle production was insufficient to meet our greatly increased requirements; we could not therefore replace the palpably inferior captured vehicles with German ones.

The decrease in strength of the tank element within the panzer division has already been mentioned. The smaller number of tanks per division was compensated for, to a certain extent, by the fact that the old Panzers I and II had been almost completely replaced by Panzers III and IV. We believed that at the beginning of the new war we could reckon on our tanks being technically better than all known Russian types; we thought that this would more or less cancel out the Russians' vast numerical superiority, for when the campaign opened our tank strength amounted only to some 3,200 units. But one curious incident made me at least slightly dubious concerning the relative superiority of our armoured equipment. In the spring of 1941 Hitler had specifically ordered that a Russian military commission be shown over our tank schools and factories; in this order he had insisted that nothing be concealed from them. The Russian officers in question firmly refused to believe that the Panzer IV was in fact our heaviest tank. They said repeatedly that we must be hiding our newest models from them, and complained that we were not carrying out Hitler's order to show them everything. The military commission was so insistent on this point that eventually our manufacturers and Ordnance Office officials concluded: 'It seems that the Russians must already possess better and heavier tanks than we do.' It was at the end of July, 1941, that the T34 tank appeared at the front and the riddle of the new Russian model was solved.

Hitler attended a demonstration of armoured equipment on the 18th of April, at which I was present. It was on this occasion that he noticed that the Panzer III had been re-equipped by the Army Ordnance Office with a 50 mm. L42 cannon instead of with a 50 mm. L60 as he had ordered. This independent act on the part of the Ordnance Office infuriated him all the more since it involved a weakening of his original intentions. The firm of Alkett in Spandau was able, by the end of April, to produce the guns Hitler wanted, which made the excuses of the Army Ordnance Office appear even more feeble. Years later he was to refer to this disobedient inefficiency whenever an attempt was made to defend the Army Ordnance Office in his presence.

At this time our yearly tank production scarcely amounted to more than 1,000 of all types. In view of our enemies' production figures this was very small. As far back as 1933 I had visited a single Russian tank factory which was producing 22 tanks per day of the Christie-Russki type.

On March 1st Bulgaria joined the Triple Alliance, and on March 25th Yugoslavia followed suit. However, on March 27th a *coup d'état* in Belgrade upset the Axis plans. On April 5th Russia and Yugoslavia signed a pact of friendship; on April 6th the Balkan Campaign began. I took no part in this. The panzer troops engaged proved themselves once again and contributed greatly to our rapid victory.

Only one man was pleased by this new extension of the theatre of war: Mussolini. This was his own war, on which he had embarked without Hitler's permission. However, the pact of friendship signed between Russia and Yugoslavia made it clear to us that we were heading for trouble with our powerful eastern neighbour, and that the smash could not be long delayed.

Belgrade fell on April 13th. On April 17th the Yugoslav Army surrendered. The Greek Army did likewise on April 23rd, despite British assistance. At the end of May airborne troops made possible the capture of Crete, though unfortunately not of Malta. Germany, Italy, Hungary, Bulgaria and Albania all took slices of Yugoslav territory. An independent state of Croatia was formed; its king was to be the Italian Duke of Spoleto, but he never sat on his rather shaky throne. In accordance with a request of the King of Italy Montenegro was also reconstituted as an independent state.

Since the frontiers of the newly created Croatia did not correspond to the ethnological borders of that nation, there was from the very beginning constant friction with the Italians. Bitter disagreement further poisoned the atmosphere in this already turbulent corner of Europe.

In May and June of 1941 the British succeeded in occupying Syria and Abyssinia. A German attempt to secure a foothold in Iraq was carried out with insufficient force and failed. It could only have succeeded if it had been part of the logical and sensible Mediterranean policy which we could and should have adopted in the summer of 1940. By now it was too late for isolated actions of this type.

Preparations

The Balkan Campaign had been concluded with all the speed desired, and the troops there engaged which were now needed for Russia were withdrawn according to plan and very fast. But all the same there was a definite delay in the opening of our Russian Campaign. Furthermore we had had a very wet spring; the Bug and its tributaries were at flood level until well into May and the nearby ground was swampy and almost impassable. I was in a position personally to observe this during my tours of inspection in Poland.

Three army groups were formed for the attack on Soviet Russia:

Army Group South, under Field-Marshal von Rundstedt, to the south of the Pripet Marshes.

Army Group Centre, under Field-Marshal von Bock, between the Pripet Marshes and the Suvalki Peak.

Army Group North, under Field-Marshal Ritter von Leeb, in East Prussia.

The intention was that these three army groups should break through the Russian forces stationed near the frontier, then encircle and destroy them. The panzer groups were to push forward deep into Russia and thus prevent the forming of new defensive fronts. No area of main effort was laid down. The three army groups were of approximately equal strength, though Army Group Centre had two panzer groups allotted to it, while Army Groups South and North had only one each.

I commanded Panzer Group 2. General Hoth, immediately to my north, had Panzer Group 3. These were the two groups subordinated to Army Group Centre.

Panzer Group 2 was established as follows:

Commander: Colonel-General Guderian.

Chief of Staff: Lieutenant-Colonel Freiherr von Liebenstein.

XXIV Panzer Corps: General of Panzer Troops Freiherr Geyr von Schweppenburg.

3rd Panzer Division: Lieutenant-General Model.

4th Panzer Division: Major-General Freiherr von Langermann und Erlencamp.

10th (Motorised) Infantry Division: Major-General von Loeper.

1st Cavalry Division: Lieutenant-General Feldt.

XLVI Panzer Corps: General of Panzer Troops Freiherr von Vietinghoff genannt Scheel.

10th Panzer Division: Lieutenant-General Schaal.

SS Infantry Division (Motorised) *Das Reich:* Lieutenant-General Hausser.

Infantry Regiment *Gross-Deutschland:* Major-General von Stockhausen.
XLVII Panzer Corps: General of Panzer Troops Lemelsen.
17th Panzer Division: Major-General von Arnim.
18th Panzer Division: Major-General Nehring.
29th (Motorised) Infantry Division: Major-General von Boltenstern.
The Panzer Group also had under command a number of army
troops including:
A wing of close support planes under General Viebig.
The Anti-Aircraft Regiment *Hermann Goering* under General
von Axthelm.
The artillery was commanded by General Heinemann, the engineers
by General Bacher, the signal troops by Colonel Praun, the reconnaissance planes by Lieutenant-Colonel von Barsewisch (originally
by Colonel von Gerlach, but this gallant officer was shot down on the
third day of the attack). Fighter protection operating in the area of the
Panzer Group was under command, during the first few weeks, of
Colonel Mölders. (*See Appendix* XXII.)

My Panzer Group was assigned the following task: on the first day
of the offensive it was to cross the Bug on either side of Brest-Litovsk;
it was to break through the Russian defensive positions, then it was
quickly to exploit the success gained and advance to the area Roslavl–
Elnya–Smolensk. The intention was to prevent the enemy from regrouping and forming a new front, and thus to lay the groundwork
for a decisive victory during the 1941 campaign. My Panzer Group was
to receive further instructions when its objective had been reached.
Preliminary orders as issued by the *OKH* indicated that the plan was
then probably to switch Hoth's 3rd and my 2nd Panzer Groups due
north to capture Leningrad.
The border between the German controlled General-Gouvernement
of Poland and the Soviet Russian zone was the River Bug; thus the
fortress of Brest-Litovsk was split, the citadel being occupied by the
Russians. Only the old forts on the west bank were in German hands.
I had already captured the fortress once during the Polish Campaign;
I now had the same task to perform a second time, though in more
difficult circumstances.
Despite the very plain lessons of the Western Campaign, the supreme
German command did not hold uniform views about the employment
of armoured forces. This became evident during the various war games
that were held in preparation for the operation and for the purpose of
training the commanders for their missions. The generals who came
from arms of the Service other than the panzer troops were inclined

to the opinion that the initial assault should be made by infantry divisions after heavy artillery preparation and that the tanks should only be sent in to complete the break-through after a penetration to a specified depth had been made. The panzer generals held the contrary view. They wanted the panzer divisions to be in the forefront of the attack from the very beginning, because they regarded their arm as the most powerful attacking weapon. They expected the armour would thus achieve a deep and rapid break-through, which initial success could be immediately exploited by the tanks' speed of advance. The panzer generals knew from experience in France what happens when the other system is employed: at the critical moment of success the roads are covered with the endless, slow-moving, horse-drawn columns of the infantry divisions, and the panzers as a result are blocked and slowed up. So they wished the panzer divisions to be put in front on those sectors where a break-through was desired: on other sectors, where the tasks were different, as for example in the storming of fortresses, the infantry should lead the assault.

This situation arose in the sector of Panzer Group 2's attack. The fortifications of Brest-Litovsk were out of date, it is true, but the combination of the Bug, the Muchaviec and water-filled ditches made them immune to tank attack. Tanks could only have captured the citadel by means of a surprise attack, as had been attempted in 1939. The requisite conditions for such an attack did not exist in 1941.

I therefore decided to attack with my panzer divisions across the Bug on either side of Brest-Litovsk, and I asked that an infantry corps be placed under my command for the assault on the fortress. This corps would have to come from Fourth Army, which was to follow behind my Panzer Group. The Fourth Army would also have to provide further infantry to assist in the initial river crossings as well as a considerable amount of artillery support. In order to ensure unity of command, I asked that these troops be temporarily subordinated to me, and expressed my willingness to place myself under the command of Fourth Army's commander, Field-Marshal von Kluge, during this time. These command arrangements proved acceptable to the Army Group. They involved a sacrifice on my part; Field-Marshal von Kluge was a hard man to work under. But I held them to be important for the success of the undertaking.

The area for the attack was bounded on the front by the River Bug. Our first task was to secure crossings in the face of the enemy. This would be much easier if some degree of surprise could be obtained. I could not reckon on an immediate capture of the fortress of Brest-Litovsk, so my attacking armour would initially be split into two; I had therefore to ensure that my group did not suffer in consequence of this and also to secure the two open flanks of the Panzer Group. Once the Bug was crossed the right wing of the Group would be advancing along the edge of the Pripet Marshes, which are impassable to vehicles and very heavy going on foot: weak infantry forces of Fourth Army were to move through them. To the left of the Panzer Group there would be elements of Fourth Army attacking and, beyond them, the infantry of the Ninth Army. It was this left flank which was particularly threatened, since strong Soviet forces were known to be massing in the Bialystok area. It must be assumed that once these forces were aware of the danger to their rear from our panzer divisions, they would attempt to extricate themselves from encirclement along the line of the main road Volkovisk–Slonim.

This double threat to the flanks was parried by two counter-measures:

(a) through arranging our forces in depth, particularly on the more dangerously threatened left flank, and

(b) by sending the Panzer Group's 1st Cavalry Division through the marshes on our right which were wellnigh impassable to motorised formations.

Further security was provided by the Fourth Army's infantry divisions advancing behind the Panzer Group and by widespread air reconnaissance.

In consequence of all this, the order of battle of the Panzer Group for the attack was as follows:

Right Wing.

XXIV Panzer Corps (General von Geyr), with:

255th Infantry Division (under command only during the Bug crossing), from Vlodava to Maloryta,

1st Cavalry Division, from Slavatycze through Maloryta to Pinsk,

4th Panzer Division, from Koden to advance towards the Brest-Kobryn road,

3rd Panzer Division, from north of Koden to advance towards the Brest-Kobryn road,

10th (Motorised) Infantry Division, to advance behind as second wave of the assault.

Centre.

XII Army Corps (General Schroth), under command only during the initial phase, with:

45th Infantry Division and

31st Infantry Division, to advance between north of Koden and

Neple, with objective the encirclement of Brest-Litovsk. All forces of the corps not needed for this purpose were to advance between the two roads Brest-Litovsk–Kobryn–Beresa Kartuska and Motykaly–Piliszcze–Pruzana, with the task of mopping up between XXIV Panzer Corps on their right and XLVII Panzer Corps on their left and of securing the internal flanks of the two panzer corps.

Left Wing.

XLVII Panzer Corps (General Lemelsen), with:

18th Panzer Division and

17th Panzer Division, between Legi and Pratulin, with the task of crossing the Rivers Bug and Lesna and advancing Vidomla–Pruzana–Slonim,

29th (Motorised) Infantry Division advancing behind as second wave of the assault,

167th Infantry Division (under command only during the Bug crossing), to the west of Pratulin.

Panzer Group Reserve.

XLVI Panzer Corps (General von Vietinghoff), with

10th Panzer Division

SS Division *Das Reich*, and

Infantry Regiment *Gross-Deutschland*, to be held back in the area Radzyn–Lukov–Deblin until XLVII Panzer Corps was clear of the Bug bridges, when it would move forward behind the left wing of the Panzer Group.

On June 6th the Chief of the Army General Staff paid a visit to the Panzer Group. He expressed an opinion that in order to be in fit condition for performing their principal task of thrusting deep into the enemy's defences, the panzer divisions should be kept back during the initial phase, while infantry divisions carried out the first assault. For the reasons I have already given I could not agree to this alteration to the plan.

I received at my headquarters only bare indications of the Supreme Command's intentions for the second phase of the operation after the first objectives (in the case of my corps the area Roslavl–Elnya–Smolensk) had been reached. These envisaged first of all the capture of Leningrad and the Baltic coast, so that contact might be established with the Finns and Army Group North safely supplied by sea. A proof that such plans were being seriously studied is supplied by the operational instructions which were issued; in these it was stated that

Colonel-General Hoth's 3rd Panzer Group and possibly also my Group were to halt in the Smolensk area and prepare to swing north in support of the operations of Army Group North. This operation would have had one great advantage; it would once and for all have secured the left wing of the German armies fighting in Russia. In my opinion this was the best plan that could have been devised in the circumstances, but unfortunately I never heard anything more about it.

On June 14th Hitler assembled all the commanders of Army Groups, Armies and Panzer Groups in Berlin in order to explain his reasons for attacking Russia and to receive final reports on the preparations that had been made. He spoke on the following lines. He could not defeat England. Therefore in order to bring the war to a close he must win a complete victory on the Continent. Germany's position on the mainland would only be unassailable when Russia had been defeated. His detailed exposition of the reasons that led him to fight a preventive war against the Russians was unconvincing. The tension that had arisen as a result of German penetration of the Balkans, the intervention of the Russians in Finland, the occupation of the Baltic states, such were the political reasons; these were as insufficient causes for taking a resolve of such drastic dimensions as were the ideological theories of National-Socialist dogma and certain reports of preparations for attack on the part of the Russians that had come in. So long as the war in the West was still undecided, any new undertaking must result in a war on two fronts; and Adolf Hitler's Germany was even less capable of fighting such a war than had been the Germany of 1914. The assembled company listened to Hitler's speech in silence and then, since there was to be no discussion, dispersed, still in silence and with heavy hearts.

During the afternoon, at the military conference concerning the preparations that had been made, I was asked only one question. How long would it take me to reach Minsk? I replied: 'Five to six days.' The attack began on the 22nd of June and I arrived at Minsk on the 27th, while Hoth, advancing from Suvalki, had already occupied that city from the north on the 26th.

Before I turn to describing the operations of my Panzer Group, I should like to outline the general situation of the German Army at the beginning of this decisive campaign in Russia.

According to the information available to me, the German Army on the 22nd of June, 1941, consisted of 205 divisions as follows:

38 divisions in the West,
12 divisions in Norway,
 1 division in Denmark,
 7 divisions in the Balkans,

2 divisions in Libya, and therefore
145 divisions available for operations in the East.

This dispersal of strength involved an unpleasant dissipation. The figure of 38 divisions in the West appeared particularly high. 12 divisions for Norway also formed an unnecessarily large garrison.

A consequence of the Balkan campaign was that the Russian offensive could not be launched until late in the summer.

Far more significant, however, than either of these facts was the underestimate of the Russian as an enemy. Our outstanding military attaché in Moscow, General Köstring, had reported on the military strength of that gigantic country: Hitler attached as little importance to these reports as he did to others concerning the production capacity of Russian industry or the stability of the Russian political system. On the contrary, he had succeeded in infecting his immediate military entourage with his own baseless optimism. The *OKW* and *OKH* were so serenely confident of victory before winter set in that winter clothing had only been prepared for every fifth man in the army.

It was not until August 30th, 1941, that the *OKH* became seriously concerned with the problem of supplying major portions of the army with winter clothing. On this day an entry made in an *OKH* diary reads: "In view of recent developments which are likely to necessitate operations against limited objectives even during the winter, the Operations Department will draft a report on the winter clothing that will be required for this purpose. After approval by the Chief of the Army General Staff, this report will be passed to the Organisation Department for necessary action."

It is frequently maintained nowadays that Hitler and only Hitler was responsible for the lack of winter clothing in the army in 1941. I can in no way subscribe to this belief. Proof of this is that the Luftwaffe and the Waffen-SS were well and adequately equipped and had laid in the necessary stocks in plenty of time. But the supreme command was sunk in its dream of defeating the Russian Army in eight or ten weeks; this defeat would result, they thought, in the political collapse of the Soviets. So confident were they of this that in the autumn of 1941 a considerable portion of Germany's industry was switched from war production to other purposes. It was even proposed to move 60 to 80 of the divisions in the east back to Germany at the beginning of winter: what remained would suffice to control Russia until spring came. Those remaining divisions were to occupy comfortable quarters in a well-prepared defensive line to be built during the autumn. It all seemed to be very well thought out and delightfully simple. A description of events as they occurred will show how far these ideas were divorced from the cruel reality.

Finally, an allusion must be made to an event which was to leave a deep stain on Germany's reputation.

Shortly before the opening of hostilities the *OKW* sent an order direct to all corps and divisions concerning the treatment that was to be given to the civilian population and to prisoners of war in Russia. It specified that in the event of excesses being committed against civilians or prisoners, the responsible soldier was not automatically to be tried and punished according to military law; disciplinary action was only to be taken at the discretion of the man's immediate unit commander. This order was obviously likely to have the most unfortunate effect on the preservation of discipline. The Commander-in-Chief of the Army had apparently realised this himself, for an appendix to the order, signed by Field-Marshal von Brauchitsch, stated that the order would only be carried out if there was no danger of discipline suffering thereby. Since both I and my corps commanders were immediately convinced that discipline must suffer if the order were published, I forbade its forwarding to the divisions and ordered that it be returned to Berlin. This order, which was to play an important part in the post-war trials of German generals by our former enemies, was consequently never carried out in my Panzer Group. At the time I dutifully informed the Commander-in-Chief of the Army Group that I was not publishing or obeying this order.

The equally notorious, so-called 'Commissar Order' never even reached my Panzer Group. No doubt Army Group Centre had already decided not to forward it. Therefore the 'Commissar Order' was never carried out by my troops either.

Looking back, one can only deeply regret that neither the *OKW* nor the *OKH* blocked these two orders in the first place. Many brave and innocent soldiers would have thus been saved bitter suffering, and the good name of Germany would have been spared a great shame. Regardless of whether the Russians had signed the Hague Agreement or not, whether or not they had approved the Geneva Convention, German soldiers must accept their international obligations and must behave according to the dictates of a Christian conscience. Even without harsh orders the effects of war on the population of an enemy country are cruel enough, and the Russian civilians were as innocent of causing this war as were our own.

Opening Operations

In describing the events which now took place I have in places given an exact description of how my time was spent. I have done this in order to show the spiritual and physical demands that were made on the commander of a Panzer Group during the Russian Campaign.

After Hitler's speech to the generals on June 14th I flew to Warsaw, on the 15th, where my staff was quartered. The days until the opening of the attack on June 22nd I spent visiting the troops and their jumping-off places and also the neighbouring units in order to ensure full co-operation. The march to the assembly areas and the final preparations for the attack passed smoothly enough. On June 17th I examined the course of the River Bug, which was our front line. On the 19th I visited General von Mackensen's III Army Corps, which was immediately to the right of my Panzer Group. On the 20th and 21st I visited the forward units of my corps to make sure that all preparations for the attack were satisfactorily completed. Detailed study of the behaviour of the Russians convinced me that they knew nothing of our intentions. We had observation of the courtyard of Brest-Litovsk citadel and could see them drilling by platoons to the music of a military band. The strong points along their bank of the Bug were unoccupied. They had made scarcely any noticeable progress in strengthening their fortified positions during the past few weeks. So the prospects of our attack achieving surprise were good and the question therefore arose whether the one hour's artillery preparation which had been planned was now necessary after all. I finally decided not to cancel it; this was simply a precaution lest unexpected Russian counter-measures cause us avoidable casualties.

On the fateful day of June 22nd, 1941, I went at 02.10 hrs. to my Group command post which was located in an observation tower south of Bohukaly, 9 miles north-west of Brest-Litovsk. It was still dark when I arrived there at 03.10 hrs. At 03.15 hrs. our artillery opened up. At 03.40 hrs. the first dive-bomber attack went in. At 04.15 hrs. advance units of the 17th and 18th Panzer Divisions began to cross the Bug. At 04.45 hrs. the leading tanks of the 18th Panzer Division forded the river. For this they were equipped with the waterproofing that had been tested for *Operation Sea-lion*, which enabled them to move through 13 feet of water.

At 06.50 hrs. I crossed the Bug in an assault boat in the neighbourhood of Kolodno. My command staff, consisting of two armoured wireless trucks, a number of cross-country vehicles and some motorcyclists, followed at 08.30 hrs. I began by following the tank tracks of 18th Panzer Division and soon reached the bridge over the Lesna, whose capture was important for the advance of XLVII Panzer Corps; there I found nobody except some Russian pickets. The Russians took to their heels when they saw my vehicles. Two of my orderly officers set off after them, against my wishes; unfortunately they both lost their lives as a result.

At 10.25 hrs. the leading tank company reached the Lesna and crossed

the bridge. Next to arrive was the divisional commander, General
Nehring. I accompanied the 18th Panzer Division in their advance
until mid-afternoon. At 16.30 hrs. I returned to the bridgehead at
Kolodno and from there I went at 18.30 hrs. to my command post.

We had managed to take the enemy by surprise along the entire
Panzer Group front. To the south of Brest-Litovsk the XXIV Panzer
Corps had captured the bridges over the Bug intact. To the north-west
of the fortress our bridges were being built according to plan. The
enemy, however, soon recovered from his initial surprise and put up
a tough defence in his prepared positions. The important citadel of
Brest-Litovsk held out with remarkable stubbornness for several days,
thus depriving us of the use of the road and rail communications across
the Bug and Muchaviec.

In the evening the Panzer Group was fighting around Maloryta,
Kobryn, Brest-Litovsk, and Pruzana. At the last-named place the
18th Panzer Division became involved in the first tank battle of the
campaign.

On June 23rd I left my headquarters at 04.10 hrs. and went first to
XII Army Corps where General Schroth informed me about the
fighting in and around Brest-Litovsk. I then drove to XLVII Panzer
Corps at the village of Bildeiki, some 14 miles north-north-east of
Brest-Litovsk. There I talked to General Lemelsen and also spoke on
the telephone to my headquarters in order to receive the latest information about the general situation. I went on to 17th Panzer Division,
where I arrived at 08.00 hrs.; the commander of the division's rifle
brigade, General Ritter von Weber, described to me what his men were
doing. At 08.30 hrs. I met General Nehring of the 18th Panzer Division
and then returned to see General Lemelsen once again. I next drove to
Pruzana, where the headquarters of my Panzer Group was now to be
located. The command portion of the staff arrived there at 19.00 hrs.

On this day the XXIV Panzer Corps was fighting its way forward
towards Sluzk along the Kobryn–Beresa–Kartuska road.

I gained the impression that the XLVII Panzer Corps was likely
soon to be heavily engaged with Russian forces moving south-east
from the direction of Bialystok, and I therefore resolved to spend the
next day once again with this corps.

On June 24th I left my headquarters at 08.25 hrs. and drove towards
Slonim. The 17th Panzer Division had meanwhile arrived at this town.
Between Rozana and Slonim I ran into Russian infantry which was
laying down fire on the main road. A battery of the 17th Panzer
Division and dismounted motor-cyclists were returning the enemy fire

Sketch Map 8.

Advance eastwards of Panzer Group
Guderian.

Situation 22.6.–28.6.41.

10 5 0 10 20 30 40 50 60

Cherven

Bobruisk

Osipovitchi 28.6.

Beresina →

Sluzk 27.6.

17.6. 26.6. 25.6.

17.Pz. 26.6. 27.6.

Skolpce Niesweiz 18.Pz.

17.Pz.

Baranovicze

Grodno Lesna

Shtchara Zewa Hołinka Slonim 18.Pz.

Bialystok Volkovisk Byten Ivacevicze

Niemen Tavian Rozana Beresa Kartuska

28.6. 23.6.

24.6.

25.6. Pruzana 22.6.

Linovo 22.6. Kobryn

Warsaw Vistule ←Bug

Molodur Vidomla Malaryta

←Bug

Mokrany ←Bug

17.Pz.162 Brest Lit.

XXXXVII.Pz.K. Kodeni

29.m. 11. XXIV.Pz.K.4.Pz.

Vistule Slavatycse 10.m.–1.Kb.

26.6.

Vlodava

Lukov ←Bug

XXXXVI. Radzyn

Pz.K.

Deblin ←San

Pinsk ←Pripet

Oginski Canal

Krolevski—Canal

without any particular success. I joined in this action and by firing the machine-gun in my armoured command vehicle succeeded in dislodging the enemy from his position; I was then able to drive on. At 11.30 hrs. I arrived at the headquarters of the 17th Panzer Division, at that time located in the western outskirts of Slonim, where I found not only the divisional commander, General von Arnim, but also the corps commander, General Lemelsen. While we were discussing the situation there was a sudden outburst of lively rifle and machine-gun fire in our rear; our view of the road from Bialystok was blocked by a burning lorry, so that we were in ignorance of what was going on until two Russian tanks appeared from out of the smoke. They were attempting to force their way into Slonim, with cannons and machine-guns blazing, and were pursued by German Panzer IV's which were also firing heavily. The Russian tanks noticed the group of officers, of which I was one, and we were immediately subjected to a rain of shells, which, fired at such extremely close range, both deafened and blinded us for a few moments. Being old soldiers we had immediately thrown ourselves to the ground; only poor Lieutenant-Colonel Feller, who had come to us on a mission from the Commander of the Training Army, and who was unaccustomed to active service, was too slow and suffered a very painful wound in consequence. Also the commander of an anti-tank battalion, Lieutenant-Colonel Dallmer-Zerbe, received a severe wound from which, I regret to say, he died a few days later. The Russian tanks succeeded in forcing their way into the town where they were eventually put out of action.

I next visited the front line in Slonim and then drove in a Panzer IV through no-man's-land to the 18th Panzer Division. At 15.30 hrs. I was back in Slonim, having ordered the 18th Panzer Division to push on in the direction of Baranovicze, while the 29th (Motorised) Infantry Division was instructed to hasten its advance towards Slonim. I then returned to my Group command post. This drive took me unexpectedly through the middle of Russian infantry, which had come up in lorries to the very outskirts of Slonim and was on the point of dismounting. I ordered my driver, who was next to me, to go full-speed ahead and we drove straight through the Russians; they were so surprised by this unexpected encounter that they did not even have time to fire their guns. All the same they must have recognised me, because the Russian press later announced my death; I felt bound to inform them of their mistake by means of the German wireless.

I rejoined my staff at 20.15 hrs. There I found messages waiting for me concerning fierce fighting on our deep right flank, where LIII Army Corps had been successfully defeating Russian attacks in the Maloryta area since June 23rd. Between the XXIV and XLVII Panzer Corps elements of the XII Army Corps had managed to establish loose contact. The left flank of the Panzer Group was seriously threatened by an intensification of the attacks on the part of the Russian forces pouring back from Bialystok. To secure this flank rapid commitment of the 29th (Motorised) Infantry Division and of the XLVI Panzer Corps was necessary.

Fortunately, we were unaware that on this day Hitler had become nervous for fear lest the strong Russian forces succeed in breaking out of our encirclement at some point. He wanted to halt the panzer groups and turn them against the Russians in and about Bialystok. On this occasion, however, the *OKH* proved strong enough to insist on adherence to the original plan and on the completion of the encirclement by a continuation of our advance to Minsk.

Vilna was captured, as was Kovno.

The Finns occupied the Aaland Islands. The German I Mountain Corps seized the rich nickel area around Petsamo. Neither of these operations involved any fighting.

Early on the morning of the 25th I visited the wounded in our hospital. These were the victims of an air attack the previous day on my headquarters which I had escaped as I was away at the front at the time. At 09.40 hrs.I drove to XII Army Corps, at Linovo, 5 miles south of Pruzana, where I examined the situation in that sector. I then went on to the XXIV Panzer Corps, whose headquarters was at Zarzeczne, 22 miles south of Slonim. After talking with General Freiherr von Geyr I visited the 4th Panzer Division, returning to my headquarters at 16.30 hrs.

Fresh enemy units, including tanks, had appeared on this day, driving from Bialystok towards Slonim. The 29th (Motorised) Infantry Division arrived on the battlefield and took over the task of barring the Russians' advance on Slonim. Thus the main strength of 17th and 18th Panzer Divisions was freed to continue the advance on Minsk. The latter division was already fighting its way towards Baranovicze.

Early on the morning of June 26th I visited the front in the area of XLVII Panzer Corps as I wished to observe the progress of our advance on Baranovicze and Stolpce. XXIV Panzer Corps was instructed to support the advance of its northern neighbour.

At 07.50 hrs. I arrived at the 17th Panzer Division which I ordered to push on directly for Stolpce. By 09.00 hrs. I was at the headquarters of the 18th Panzer Division where I found the corps commander as well as the divisional commander. This headquarters was located at Lesna, on the Slonim–Baranovicze road, some 3 miles behind the division's forward elements. From here I got into wireless communication with

XXIV Panzer Corps in order to confirm my orders concerning the support that that corps was to give to the attack on Baranovicze. This support was to be supplied by elements of the 4th Panzer Division which had been formed into a battle group and had been advancing northwards since 06.00 hrs.

At 12.30 hrs. XXIV Panzer Corps informed me of the capture of Sluzk. This represented a fine performance on the part of both commanders and troops. I sent the corps commander a message of congratulation by wireless and then set off at once for the front of the 18th Panzer Division at Tartak. In the early afternoon a message was received that Hoth had reached a point 18 miles to the north of Minsk.

At 14.30 hrs. I received orders from the Army Group: the mass of my forces was to advance on Minsk, while XXIV Panzer Corps was to move on Bobruisk. I was able to signal back that XXIV Panzer Corps had already been given orders to capture Bobruisk and that XLVII Panzer Corps was attacking through Baranovicze, towards Minsk. I then ordered that my command staff move forward to Tartak, where it arrived at 23.30 hrs.

During the afternoon the 17th Panzer Division had signalled that they were advancing along a passable road, towards Stolpce. They reached their objective that evening. Unfortunately the divisional commander, General von Arnim, was wounded during the day's fighting and had to hand over his command to General Ritter von Weber.

My Panzer Group was now subordinated to Fourth Army, from which it received the order to occupy the line Zadvorze (5 miles north of Slonim)–Holynka–Zelva–the River Zelvianka, and to hold that line against the enemy advancing from Bialystok.

On this day advance elements of the XLVI Panzer Corps reached the battlefield near Tartak and took over the task of providing the link between the XXIV and XLVII Panzer Corps. The whole of the XXIV Panzer Corps was thereby freed to carry out its principal mission, the advance to Bobruisk.

In Army Group North, 8th Panzer Division succeeded in capturing Dünaburg and its bridges over the Dvina.

On June 27th the 17th Panzer Division reached the southern outskirts of Minsk and thus established contact with Panzer Group 3, which had already on the 26th penetrated into the town that the Russians had largely demolished. The Russian forces which had been in the Bialystok area and had since been attempting in vain to break through our encircling pincers were now completely surrounded. Only weak elements had succeeded in slipping through to the east before the pincers met. The foundations had been laid for the first great victory of the campaign.

My views concerning the next stage of the operations were as follows: to detach the minimum amount of the Panzer Group for the destruction of the Russians in the Bialystok pocket, while leaving the major part of this operation to the following infantry armies: thus our rapidly mobile, motorised forces would be able to push forward and seize the first operational objective of the campaign, the area Smolensk–Elnya–Roslavl. All my actions during the next few days had this end in view. I was thus in agreement with the original orders that had been issued. It seemed to me of decisive importance for the success of the whole campaign that the initial plan be adhered to despite the accidents and unexpected developments of battle. I was well aware that this plan involved taking certain risks.

These convictions of mine caused me to drive once again to the XLVII Panzer Corps on June 28th. This was the most immediately threatened of my formations; I therefore wished to be close at hand in case a crisis arose, so that I should be able quickly to arrange for its support. I found the corps commander at Svoiaticze (14 miles south-west of Nieswiez), where I examined the situation of his divisions; I then instructed my staff by wireless to hasten the northward move of the 29th (Motorised) Infantry Division and to arrange for air reconnaissance of the roads Novogrodek–Minsk and Novogrodek–Baranovicze–Turzec. I next visited the 18th Panzer Division; one column of this division had gone slightly astray and the division's advance had been somewhat held up in consequence, though not seriously so.

My chief of staff, Liebenstein, had meanwhile laid down defensive sectors for the divisions of the various corps against the threatened attempt at a break-out by enemy forces along the line Koidanov–Piaseczna (north-west of Mir)–Horodyszcze–Polonka. I approved the measures he had taken.

On this day XXIV Panzer Corps reached the outskirts of Bobruisk. Since the 25th its headquarters had been in Filipovicze.

On June 28th the headquarters of my Panzer Group moved to Nieswiez, taking up its quarters in an old castle that had once belonged to the Radziwill family and which had previously been occupied by a senior Russian staff. The only relic of the castle's previous contents was a photograph of a hunting party, at which Kaiser William I had been present, that was discovered in an attic. The population of Nieswiez asked permission to hold a Thanksgiving Service in celebration of their liberation; I was happy to be able to grant them this request.

On this day units reached the following places:
3rd Panzer Division, Bobruisk; 4th Panzer Division, Sluzk; 10th

(Motorised) Infantry Division, Siniavka; 1st Cavalry Division, the area east of Drohiczyn.

17th Panzer Division, Koidanov; 18th Panzer Division, Nieswiez; 29th (Motorised) Infantry Division, the Zelvianka.

Elements of 10th Panzer Division, the Zelvianka; the bulk of that division, Siniavka; *SS-Das Reich*, Beresa–Kartuska; Infantry Regiment *Gross-Deutschland*, the area north-east of Pruzana.

Panzer Group Hoth now had the 7th and 20th Panzer Divisions in the Minsk area. Far to the south, LIII Army Corps, on my right wing, had brought its battles in the Maloryta area to a successful conclusion. The danger to this flank was now finally eliminated.

On June 29th the battles continued along the entire front of my Panzer Group. There was particularly severe fighting in the sector along the Zelvianka, which caused Fourth Army considerable anxiety. This resulted in Army attempting to take a hand in my battle, a measure which was rather ungraciously received by me, since I was to a great extent unaware that they were doing this.

Army Group North captured Jakobstadt, Liewenhof and the southern portion of Riga, together with its railway bridge over the Dvina.

I spent the next day, June 30th, flying to Panzer Group 3, where I saw Hoth with whom I discussed the future co-ordination of our activities. Lieutenant-Colonel von Barsewisch piloted me himself, in a bomber, and we passed over the Puszcza Nalibocka, a large forest, from which Fourth Army was continually anticipating the Russians to attempt a break-out. I gained the impression that there were no considerable enemy forces in the forest and that there was, therefore, no danger from this quarter. I agreed with Hoth that my 18th Panzer Division should work closely with his right wing during the advance to Borissov and the securing of a bridgehead over the Beresina near this town.

On this date the *OKH* ordered that combat units advance to the line of the Dnieper.

The *OKH* informed the Army Group that a development of the operations towards Smolensk would be of decisive importance; it was, therefore, desired that crossings of the Dnieper in the areas of Rogachev, Mogilev, and Orsha, and of the Dvina at Vitebsk and Polotsk, be secured as quickly as possible.

On the next day, July 1st, I flew to XXIV Panzer Corps; our only normal means of communication with this headquarters was by wireless, which was insufficient for any length of time. Geyr's opinion of the enemy on his front was favourable to our future intentions. He was

FIG. 8. Advancing as though on manoeuvres: Tanks move forward (Champagne, June 1940)

Fig. 9. Lieutenant-Colonel Balck handing over a flag captured at Juniville

mainly opposed by units that had been hastily thrown together. The enemy's rail activity was slight. An air battle fought over Bobruisk on the previous day had ended in the defeat of the Russians. All the same the enemy continued, as always, to resist stubbornly. His battle technique, particularly his camouflage, was excellent; on the other hand he did not seem to have re-established a unified command as yet. The corps had succeeded in capturing the bridges over the Beresina, near Svisloch. At 09.30 hrs. a reinforced reconnaissance battalion had moved off from this Beresina bridgehead, eastwards of Bobruisk, in the direction of Mogilev, and was being followed by the mass of the 3rd Panzer Division; according to the way the situation developed General Freiherr von Geyr would decide whether to make his point of main effort towards Rogachev or Mogilev, both of which were on the Dnieper. At 10.55 hrs. strong elements of the 4th Panzer Division also moved off eastwards from Svisloch. The fuel situation was well in hand; ammunition, supply and medical services were all functioning smoothly. Casualties up to now were happily light. But there was a lack of bridging columns and construction troops. Co-operation with Colonel Mölders' fighters was excellent. Liaison with General Viebig's close-support planes was not, however, sufficiently rapid. The 1st Cavalry Division had shown itself to be a good unit in action.

Apart from all this, air reconnaissance during these days revealed clearly that the Russians were assembling fresh forces in the area Smolensk–Orsha–Mogilev. If the line of the Dnieper was to be captured without waiting for the arrival of the infantry, which would mean the loss of weeks, we would have to hurry.

Meanwhile, very fierce fighting went on around the Bialystok pocket. During the period 26th–30th June, one regiment, the 71st Infantry of the 29th (Motorised) Infantry Division, alone had brought in the considerable total of 36,000 prisoners—a proof of the massive scale of the Russians' attempts to break out. This fact made such a deep impression on Fourth Army that they insisted, henceforth, on the pocket being surrounded by strongly occupied and continuous lines. Field-Marshal von Kluge consequently forbade the departure of the 17th Panzer Division in the direction of Borissov which I had already ordered; he did this despite the fact that the 18th Panzer Division had already reached that town and had secured a bridgehead over the Beresina and that on the consolidation of this bridgehead depended to a large extent the further advance of XLVII Panzer Corps to the Dnieper. Although I disagreed with this order of Fourth Army I forwarded it to the troops under my command.

The 5th Machine-gun Battalion had the task of maintaining contact between 17th Panzer and 29th (Motorised) Infantry Divisions along the edge of the pocket. On July 2nd I visited this battalion in order, personally, to observe conditions along this front and to get the opinions of the officers on the spot concerning the encircled enemy. I was thus able to form a clear idea of the situation. I next drove to General Lemelsen and ordered him and the commander of the 29th (Motorised) Infantry Division, who was also present, to make sure that the pocket remained closed, and then went on at once to the 17th Panzer Division at Koidanov. General Ritter von Weber reported that enemy attempts to break through had been successfully beaten off. From there I drove to the new command post of my Panzer Group, which was at Sinilo, to the south-east of Minsk. When I arrived there I found that a mishap had occurred in the transmission of orders to 17th Panzer Division; part of the division had not received the order to remain on the encirclement front and had, therefore, set off for Borissov. I immediately despatched a signal to Fourth Army informing them of this. It was too late to do anything about it. I was then summoned to appear at Field-Marshal von Kluge's headquarters in Minsk, at 08.00 hrs. next morning. When I arrived there I was strongly taken to task for the accident that had occured. After I had given an ample explanation of how it had happened, Field-Marshal von Kluge informed me that he had actually intended to have Hoth and myself court-martialled, since exactly the same mishap had occurred in Hoth's Panzer Group and Kluge had, therefore, been led to believe that he was confronted by a generals' conspiracy. At least I could put his mind at rest on that score. After this interview I drove to XLVII Panzer Corps at Smolevicze (21 miles north-east of Minsk), but since I could not find the corps headquarters I went on to the 18th Panzer Division at Borissov. There I visited the Beresina bridgehead and had a word with the assembled unit commanders of the division. The division sent off an advance party to Tolochino. On my way back I found the corps commander at Smolevicze and discussed with him the next operations by the 17th and 18th Panzer Division. While this conversation was going on the wireless operators in my armoured command vehicle heard news of an attack by Russian tanks and aircraft on the Beresina crossing at Borissov. XLVII Panzer Corps was informed. The attacks were beaten off with heavy losses to the Russians, but not before a considerable impression had been made on the 18th Panzer Division; this was hardly surprising since here, for the first time, the enemy employed his T34 tank, a tank against which our guns at that time were largely ineffective.

On July 2nd the Panzer Group was disposed as follows:
1st Cavalry Division, south of Sluzk; 3rd Panzer Division, Bobruisk

Sketch Map 9.

Developments 26.6.–2.7.1941

advance line Hoth and Guderian		28.6.41.
" " "	"	29.6.41.
" " "	"	30.6.41.
" " "	"	1.7.41.
" " "	"	2.7.41.

Vitebsk
Dorogobush
Elnya
Smolensk
Roslavl
Orsha
Mogilev
Senno
Tolochino
St. Bychov
Krupki
Lepel
Novy Borissov
Rogachev
Shlobin
Els
4.Pz.
Els.3.Pz.
Bobruisk
10.Pz.
Cherven
4.R.
4.Pz.
3.Pz.
Osipovitchi
XXIV.Pz.K.
Minsk
23.J.D.
Hoth
Nieswiez
Sluzk
4.Pz.
Koidanov
Stolpce
9.m.
10.m.
Baranowitschi
Novogrodek
29.m.
10.Pz.
Guderian
Volkovisk
Slonim
1.K.D.
I.R.G.D.
Pruzana
4.Bttn.

Miles
40
30
20
10
0
10
20

with advance units outside Rogachev; 4th Panzer Division, Svisloch; 10th (Motorised) Infantry Division, east of Sluzk.

SS-Das Reich, to the north of Balusevicz, on the Beresina; 10th Panzer Division, Cherven; Infantry Regiment *Gross-Deutschland*, to the north of Baranovicze.

18th Panzer Division, Borissov; 17th Panzer Division, Koidanov; 29th (Motorised) Infantry Division, Stolpce; Machine-gun Battalion 5, south-east of Baranovicze.

On July 3rd the Russians inside the Bialystok pocket surrendered. I could now concentrate my attention on the advance to the Dnieper.

I spent July 4th visiting the XLVI Panzer Corps. I drove from Silino, through Smolevicze–Cherven–Slobodka, to the headquarters of the 10th Panzer Division and thence to the command post of the division *SS-Das Reich*. On my way I found the corps commander, who asked where the Infantry Regiment *Gross-Deutschland* was located; I could only reply that it was being held back by Fourth Army as army reserve in the area of Baranovicze. Then to *SS-Das Reich* at St. Rechki. General Hausser informed me that his motor-cyclists, after stiff fighting, had managed to secure a bridgehead over the Beresina, near Brodets, 10 miles to the south of Beresino. The Beresina bridge at Yakchizy had been blown and vehicles could not be got across. The engineers were still engaged in making the swampy approaches to the bridge passable for vehicles. I drove there and found the engineers hard at work; they promised to have completed the job by early on the 5th of July.

On this day XXIV Panzer Corps reached the Dnieper, near Rogachev, and fought for and secured further crossings over the Beresina. The divisions of the Panzer Group were now disposed as follows:

1st Cavalry Division, to the east of Sluzk; 3rd Panzer Division, outside Rogachev; 4th Panzer Division, at Starye–Bychov; 10th (Motorised) Infantry Division, Bobruisk.

SS-Das Reich, Balusevicy; 10th Panzer Division, Beresino; Infantry Regiment *Gross-Deutschland*, to the east of Stolpce.

18th Panzer Division, to the east of the Natcha; elements of 17th Panzer Division, Borissov, with the mass of the division at Minsk; 29th (Motorised) Infantry Division, Koidanova–Stolpce; Machine-gun Battalion 5, to the west of Stolpce.

On July 6th strong Russian forces crossed the Dnieper, near Shlobin, and attacked the right wing of XXIV Panzer Corps. They were thrown back by the 10th (Motorised) Infantry Division. Our air reconnaissance reported further enemy forces advancing in the direction of Gomel, from the area Orel–Bryansk. Wireless intercept picked up a new Russian

Sketch Map 10

Developments 3.7.–10.7.41.

army headquarters in the Orsha area. It seemed as though a fresh
defensive front was being built up along the Dnieper. We would have
to hurry.

By July 7th the following places had been reached:

Panzer Group headquarters was at Borissov.

XXIV Panzer Corps was at Bortniki.

1st Cavalry Division, Bobruisk; 10th (Motorised) Infantry Division,
Shlobin; 3rd Panzer Division, Rogachev–Novye Bychov; 4th Panzer
Division, Starye–Bychov.

10th Panzer Division, Bialynicy; *SS-Das Reich*, Beresino; Infantry
Regiment *Gross-Deutschland*, Cherven.

18th Panzer Division, Tolochino; 17th Panzer Division, Senno;
29th (Motorised) Infantry Division, Borissov.

The 17th Panzer Division was held up near Senno in a fierce battle
with strong enemy forces which included an unusually large number of
tanks. The 18th Panzer Division was also involved in heavy fighting.
Since XXIV Panzer Corps had already reached the Dnieper a decision
would have to be taken concerning the future course of the operations.
I had received no fresh instructions from my superiors and so I could
only assume that the original intention by which Panzer Group 2 was
to drive for the area Smolensk–Elnya–Roslavl remained unaltered.
Nor could I see any reason why this plan should be modified. I had no
way of knowing at that time of the widening gulf between Hitler's
opinions and those of the *OKH*. I only learned of this state of affairs
with its far-reaching results considerably later. The friction and confusion that had arisen in the leadership of operations up to date is
inexplicable unless a glance is first cast at the true condition of the
German Supreme Command during those days.

Hitler had forgotten that it was he himself who had ordered a rapid
offensive with objective Smolensk. During the past few days he had
concentrated his attention solely on the Bialystok encirclement. Field-
Marshal von Brauchitsch did not dare express his own differing point
of view to Army Group Centre, since he knew that Hitler was opposed
to it. According to his own statement, Field-Marshal von Bock was
anxious that Panzer Groups 2 and 3 be subordinated to Field-Marshal
von Kluge, for thus Bock would avoid being directly responsible for
their operations. Field-Marshal von Kluge—in agreement with the
official Hitlerian attitude—wanted to organise a strongly held ring
around the encircled Russians and to wait until they capitulated before
once again starting to move eastwards. Hoth and myself—in contradiction to this—were anxious to continue the advance eastwards with
our panzer forces according to the original, expressed intentions of the

supreme command, and to capture the objective initially assigned us. As already stated, we wished to use a minimum of panzer force for keeping the Russians encircled in the Bialystok area and to leave the final elimination of that pocket to the infantry armies which were following behind us. And while the *OKH* was secretly hoping that the commanders of the panzer groups would continue to go for their original objectives, whether without orders or even against orders, the *OKH* yet did not dare to drop a suggestion to the commanders of the army groups which might encourage them to carry out the previously accepted plan.

This is how it came about that while, on the one hand, Panzer Group 2 ordered that a minimum force be left behind to hold the ring at Bialystok and that all available troops be sent in pursuit of the enemy across the Beresina and the Dnieper, Field-Marshal von Kluge was simultaneously issuing contradictory orders by which all units were to remain in position about the encircled Russians and the advance eastwards was not to be resumed until further instructions were received. A number of units did not receive these orders in time and so continued their advance to the Beresina. It is lucky that no damage to the army as a whole resulted from this state of affairs; but the sequel was to be unpleasantly tense and a considerable amount of ill-feeling was engendered as a result.

Crossing the Dnieper

On July 7th I was faced with the necessity of taking a decision. Was I to continue my advance as rapidly as heretofore, to cross the Dnieper with panzer forces only, and attempt to reach my primary objective as quickly as possible according to the original plan of campaign? Or should I, in view of the measures that the Russians were taking to construct a defensive front along the line of the river, break off my advance and await the arrival of the infantry armies before launching the battle for the river?

At the moment the Russian defence was only beginning to be set up, and was therefore weak: this fact spoke in favour of an immediate attack. However, the enemy held strong bridgeheads at Rogachev, Mogilev, and Orsha, and attempts to take Rogachev and Mogilev by surprise had, in consequence, failed. It was true, too, that the approach of Russian reinforcements had been reported: there was a heavy enemy concentration in the Gomel area, and a weaker one around Senno, to the north of Orsha, where severe fighting was already in progress. But it would be some fourteen days before our infantry could arrive on the scene. By that time the Russian defences would be considerably stronger. Whether the infantry would then be able to smash a well-organised river defensive line so that mobile warfare might once again be possible seemed doubtful. Even more problematical, in this case, seemed the achievement of our first operational objectives, and the ending of the campaign in the autumn of 1941. And this was the real point.

I was well aware of the importance of the decision to be taken. I calculated the dangers of heavy counter-attacks against the open flanks of all three panzer corps once they were across the river. On the other hand I was so convinced of the vital importance and of the feasibility of the task assigned me, and at the same time so sure of the proved ability and attacking strength of my panzer troops, that I ordered an immediate attack across the Dnieper and a continuation of the advance towards Smolensk.

I therefore ordered that the battles on either flank—at Shlobin and Senno—be broken off, and that the commanders responsible be satisfied with keeping the enemy there under observation.

Owing to the strong Russian bridgeheads on our side of the river, the places available for forcing a crossing were limited: after a discussion with General Freiherr von Geyr we decided on Starye Bychov for his XXIV Panzer Corps and on July 10th as the day: XLVI Panzer Corps was to cross at Shklov and XLVII Panzer Corps at Kopys, between Mogilev and Orsha, both on July 11th. All movements and preparations for the crossings were to be most carefully concealed: there would be no marching, except by night. The fighter planes of gallant Colonel Mölders promised us air supremacy over our concentration areas, and for this purpose air strips were laid out immediately behind the front line. Wherever Mölders appeared the air was soon free of the enemy.

On July 7th I visited XLVII Panzer Corps in order verbally to explain my intentions for the Dnieper crossing. On the way there I stopped to examine a captured Russian armoured train. Then I went on to the corps headquarters which was at Natsha, 18 miles to the east of Borrissov. I next visited Tolochino, where 18th Panzer Division was engaged in a battle with enemy tanks. I told General Nehring of the necessity of clearing the enemy from the Kochanovo area, west of Orsha, and of the importance of confining the Russians in that area to a narrow bridgehead: this was essential for the success of the forthcoming operation. Our troops here once again made a splendid impression, and I was able to express my deep appreciation to them.

On July 8th I visited the XLVI Panzer Corps for the same purpose that had taken me to XLVII Panzer Corps on the previous day. The SS Division *Das Reich* of this corps was still fighting on the western bank of the Dnieper.

July 9th was marked by exceptionally heated conversations concerning the intended operation. First of all Field-Marshal von Kluge appeared at my headquarters early in the morning in order to hear what my situation and intentions were. He was absolutely opposed to my decision concerning an immediate crossing of the Dnieper, and ordered that the operation be broken off and the troops halted to await the arrival of the infantry. I felt this deeply and defended my plan with obstinacy. Finally, after explaining my reasons as given above, I told him that my preparations had already gone too far to be cancelled: that the troops of the XXIV and XLVI Panzer Corps were already, to a large extent, massed on their jumping-off positions: and that I could only keep them there for a limited length of time before the Russian air force must find them and attack them. I was, furthermore, convinced that the attack would succeed and I expected that this operation would decide the Russian campaign in this very year, if such a decision were at all possible. Field-Marshal von Kluge was clearly impressed by my objective explanation. With the words: "Your operations always hang by a thread!" he unwillingly gave his approval to my plan.

After this animated conversation I drove straight to XLVII Panzer Corps. They were in a difficult situation and seemed in need of special support. I reached General Lemelsen's headquarters at Krupka at 12.15 hrs. He expressed doubts whether the 18th Panzer Division and a battle group formed of anti-tank and reconnaissance units, under General Streich, would succeed in capturing the Kochanovo area, since the troops were becoming exhausted. I stood by my original orders and added that when 18th Panzer Division had completed its task it was to turn south-east towards the Dnieper. 17th Panzer Division, when it had shaken free of the enemy at Senno, was to do likewise. I drove from the corps headquarters to the front. On the way I met General Streich and gave him the necessary instructions. I then found Nehring who, contrary to his corps commander, declared that the capture of the desired assembly area could be carried out without difficulty. I next spoke to the commander of the 29th (Motorised) Infantry Division who similarly expressed his ability to reach his objective, Kopys, in short order. I impressed on the divisions the necessity of reaching the Dnieper, and their respective assembly areas, during the course of the coming night.

17th Panzer Division was engaged during the day in heavy fighting with hostile tanks. 100 Russian tanks were destroyed, a fine achievement on the part of this brave division.

Order of battle on the evening of July 9th:

Group headquarters, Borissov (to move on July 10th to Tolochino).

1st Cavalry Division, flank guard to the south-east of Bobruisk; 3rd Panzer Division, assembling in the area Shlobin–Rogachev–Novye

Bychov and moving north; 4th Panzer Division, area Starye Bychov; 10th (Motorised) Infantry Division, in its crossing-place near Starye Bychov.

10th Panzer Division, south of Shklov; *SS-Das Reich*, area Pavlovo with elements providing flank guard on the right, southwards of Mogilev; Infantry Regiment *Gross-Deutschland*, area Bialynicy.

18th Panzer Division, to the south of Tolochino; 17th Panzer Division, area Zamosia; 29th (Motorised) Infantry Division, south-west of Tolochino, assembling towards Kopys.

The infantry following behind us had reached the line Bobruisk–Svisloch–Borissov with weak advance guards, while the main body had arrived at the line Sluzk–Minsk.

Hoth had taken Vitebsk, and Hoeppner Pleskau.

On July 10th and 11th the Dnieper was crossed according to plan and at the cost of only light casualties.

During the morning of the 10th XXIV Panzer Corps reported that it had achieved its crossing near Starye Bychov. In the afternoon of that day I visited the XLVII Panzer Corps once again to make sure that the preparations were completed and the troops in good fighting condition. General Streich had reached his covering line, opposite the Russian bridgehead, west of Orsha. To the north-west of that town another battle group, under Colonel Usinger, was also covering the bridgehead. The reconnaissance battalion of the 29th (Motorised) Infantry Division had established contact with *SS-Das Reich* on its right. 18th Panzer Division was in its jumping-off area. Advance units of the 17th Panzer Division had reached the main road, near Kochanovo, at 10.00 hrs. Elements of this division were already fighting on the west bank of the Dnieper to the south-west of Orsha. The 29th (Motorised) Infantry Division had arrived in its area. I once again impressed on the divisional commander how extremely vital it was that Smolensk be reached with all speed as soon as the Dnieper was successfully crossed. So in XLVII Panzer Corps, too, the difficult business of assembly and preparation had been successfully carried out, and I therefore anticipated the events of the next few days with confidence.

For the further advance after the Dnieper was crossed the following tasks were assigned:

XXIV Panzer Corps was to head for the Propoisk–Roslavl road. It was to take care to guard its right flank against any attacks from the Shlobin–Rogachev area, and its left flank against the enemy in Mogilev.

XLVI Panzer Corps was to advance through Gorki–Pochinok to Elnya, while guarding its right flank against Mogilev.

XLVII Panzer Corps was assigned Smolensk as its main objective, while guarding its left flank along the line of the Dnieper, from Orsha to Smolensk, and not forgetting the enemy still inside Orsha. Battle groups Streich and Usinger would, meanwhile, continue to cover the enemy bridgehead at Orsha on the west and north-west of the Dnieper.

On the evening of July 10th the Italian military attaché, General Marras, whom I already knew from Berlin, visited my headquarters. He was accompanied by the naval Captain Bürkner. I invited these two gentlemen to accompany me to the Dnieper crossing, in the neighbourhood of Kopys, on the following day. Apart from these visitors Hitler's air adjutant, Lieutenant-Colonel von Below, also arrived during the course of this evening in order to find out the situation of my Panzer Group.

On July 11th I left my headquarters at Tolochino in beautiful sunshine, at 06.10 hrs., accompanied by my two guests. This place, incidentally, had been Napoleon's headquarters in 1812. We made for Kopys to watch the crossing by XLVII Panzer Corps. In view of the dense clouds of dust put up by our advancing columns the drive along the river bank was most unpleasant. This dust, endured now for weeks on end, was equally hard on men, weapons, and engines. In particular the cylinders of the tanks became so clogged that their efficiency was considerably affected. At the headquarters of the 29th (Motorised) Infantry Division, near Kopys, I found both the corps and divisional commanders and was briefed on the situation. Regiments 15 and 71 were already over the river and had reached the edge of the woods east of Kopys; we watched them advance against two enemy divisions (the Russian LXVI Army Corps, consisting of the 18th and 54th Rifle Divisions). The enemy was laying down weak harassing fire on the area around the divisional headquarters, which was also mined. We had good observation of the advance of our infantry and of the bridge-building that was being carried on immediately beneath where we were standing. After the departure of the Italian attaché I had myself ferried over to the east bank in an assault boat in order to make sure of our forces' further progress. I had originally intended to drive on to XLVI Panzer Corps, but had to abandon this idea since there was as yet no safe way of reaching Shklov by land.

Meanwhile, it had transpired that the 17th Panzer Division had run into such strong enemy forces to the south of Orsha that there seemed no point in the division making further attempts to enlarge the small bridgehead that had been secured on the eastern bank. The regimental commander on the spot, Colonel Licht, had therefore rightly decided to evacuate the bridgehead. The 17th Panzer Division was now ordered to cross at Kopys, behind the 29th (Motorised) Infantry Division.

On the way back to my headquarters I met Field-Marshal von Kluge to whom I was able to describe the latest developments. He approved the orders I had given and I, for my part, asked him to hasten the move of the leading infantry to the Dnieper so that they might take over as soon as possible the task of holding the strong Russian forces on the west bank, confined within their bridgeheads. At my headquarters I found Hitler's principal adjutant, Colonel Schmundt, with whom I had a conversation.

I was only at Tolochino for a short time before setting off, at 18.15 hrs.. for the XLVI Panzer Corps at Shklov. The roads were bad but the essential bridges were in order again. I arrived at 21.30 hrs. Heavy artillery fire and repeated bombing attacks on 10th Panzer Division's crossing-place had made the operation more difficult here than in XLVII Panzer Corp's area. The bridges in SS-Das Reich's sector had also been damaged by air attack. Nevertheless, the crossing had succeeded and advance elements got orders to push on to Gorki. I instructed the corps that it was necessary to continue their advance during the night in order to exploit the advantage of surprise which we had gained over the enemy. I then drove on to 10th Panzer Division in order to make sure that the advance guard was in movement. This visit turned out to be well worth while, since when I got there I found that the troops had not yet actually started.

After a difficult night drive I arrived back at Tolochino at 04.30 hrs. on the 12th.

On July 11th the divisions of my Panzer Group reached the following areas:

1st Cavalry Division, Shlobin–Rogachev; 4th Panzer Division and 10th (Motorised) Infantry Division, a bridgehead near and to the north of Starye Bychov, on the east bank of the Dnieper; 3rd Panzer Division, the area south of Mogilev, where it was acting as flank guard against the Russian bridgehead.

10th Panzer Division and Infantry Regiment Gross-Deutschland, south of Shklov; SS-Das Reich, a bridgehead, east of the Dnieper, in the Shklov area.

29th (Motorised) Infantry Division, a bridgehead over the Dnieper, east of Kopys; 18th Panzer Division, west of Kopys; 17th Panzer Division, south-west of Orsha.

Battlegroups Streich and Usinger were guarding the western and north-western approaches to the Russian bridgehead at Orsha.

The mass of the following infantry had reached a line east of Sluzk–east of Minsk, with advance units along the line of the Beresina. Hoth was near Vitebsk.

On July 12th the crossing continued. I flew on this day to XXIV

Crossing the Dnieper
and Smolensk

Sketch Map 11

10 5 0   10   20   30 MILES

▬▬▬ Situation 11.7.41.
➤ Developments up to 13.7.41.
••••> Marches up to 16.7.41.

Dorogobush

Smolensk

Elnya

Gusino

29. m.

Usinger

Streich

Orsha

17.Pz.

18.Pz.

Dnieper

18.Pz.

Krasnyi

13.7.

Pochinok

XXXXVII

17.Pz.

18.Pz.

Kop*s

29. m.

29. m.

Lenino

"R"

Gori

Gorki

Tatarsk
Shamovo

10.Pz.

Reich

Chislavitchi

10.Pz.

XXXXVI

10.Pz.

13.7.

Shklov

I.R.
G.D.

10.Pz.

I.R.
G.D.

13.7.

Mstislavl

Roslavl

to Moscow

Schumiatchi

Mogilev

13.7.

3.Pz.

3.Pz.

Chaussy

Krichev

Miloslavitchi

3.Pz.

3.Pz.

13.7.

4.Pz.

XXIV.

1.m.

10.m.

Cherikov

4.Pz.

Sosh

10.m.
4.Pz.

Propoisk

St. Bychov

10.m.
4.Pz.

1.K.D.13.7.

20 Divisions

Maglin

Surash

Rogachev

1.
K.D.

from Gomel

Chercherck

Timoshenko's Counterattack begun
13.7.41.

Klinzy

Shlobln

Panzer Corps where I remained for eight hours. Later on I saw
Schmundt.

The *OKH* did not at this time have a clear picture as to whether the
enemy was still capable of offering stubborn resistance to the panzer
groups of Army Group Centre, or whether he would withdraw. In any
event some sort of a defensive front was in process of being built up
before Smolensk, and it was the desire of the *OKH* that the panzer
groups should do their best to smash it and to destroy the enemy forces
in the area. Apart from this it was proposed that elements of Hoth's
3rd Panzer Group should swing north-east, and thus encircle and destroy
the enemy forces that were opposing the advance of Sixteenth Army's
right wing.

Smolensk–Elnya–Roslavl

On July 13th I transferred my headquarters to Siachody, on the east
bank of the Dnieper, some 4 miles to the south-east of Shklov. On the
same day I visited 17th Panzer Division on the bank of the river; since
the beginning of the campaign this brave division had destroyed 502
enemy tanks. I also watched elements of *SS-Das Reich* crossing the
river and talked to Generals Hausser and von Vietinghoff. The advance
of the SS troops in the direction of Monastirshtchino would have to be
fast and would need careful reconnaissance since reports from the air
force indicated that the Russians might attempt to break through to
the Dnieper in the area south-west of Gorki.

The magnificently led 29th (Motorised) Infantry Division managed,
during the course of the day, to reach a point only 11 miles from
Smolensk.

Our new headquarters, which I reached at 17.00 hrs., had the advantage
of being very near the front. Lively fire from the south indicated heavy
fighting on the part of Infantry Regiment *Gross-Deutschland*, which
was covering our flank against Mogilev. During the night we received
a cry for help: *Gross-Deutschland* had fired off all its ammunition. The
regiment, unaccustomed as yet to the conditions of Russian warfare,
wanted a fresh delivery. It did not get one, and with that the nervous
firing stopped and we had some quiet.

This was the date on which the *OKH* first thought of swinging Panzer
Group 2 in a south or south-easterly direction. The reason behind this
idea was the recent developments in Army Group South, which had
now reached the Dniester. On this same day the *OKH* was also preoccupied with the strategy of Rommel's African Campaign and future
operations in Libya: these were to be co-ordinated with an attack on
the Suez Canal, through Turkey and Syria. Preliminary studies for an
operation through the Caucasus, towards the Persian Gulf, were also
started.

On July 14th I sent the XLVI Panzer Corps with *SS-Das Reich* towards Gorki and accompanied them myself. 10th Panzer Division reached Gorki and Mstislavl after bitter fighting and sadly heavy casualties, particularly to the artillery. The 29th (Motorised) Infantry Division was making good progress towards Smolensk: the 18th Panzer Division had crossed the Dnieper and was moving forward to protect the 29th (Motorised) Infantry Division's left flank from Krasnyi to the north and north-west.

XXIV Panzer Corps had widened its bridgehead towards Volkovitchi and had moved the 1st Cavalry Division across the river at Starye Bychov.

On this day the *OKH* prepared its first staff study of the strength and organisation of the units that would be left behind in the East as occu-pation troops. The basic idea was to station for this purpose strong mobile forces in the principal industrial and communication centres: each group, besides its normal occupation duties, would be able to send out fast battle groups into the unoccupied hinterland to destroy any attempts at resistance before these could become dangerous. At the same time, a study was made of the future dispositions of the German Army in Europe after the conclusion of *Operation Barbarossa*, and of the consequent reorganisation and reduction in strength of the army.

Such trains of thought take a man far from reality. The primary task was to bring *Operation Barbarossa* to a speedy and successful end and to concentrate all efforts on this purpose.

Early on July 15th Field-Marshal von Kluge visited me at my headquarters. I then drove to Gorki, to XLVII Panzer Corps, and from there to XLVI Panzer Corps at Svierovitch, 8 miles to the south-west of Krasnyi. The 29th (Motorised) Infantry Division had reached the southern outskirts of Smolensk, the 18th Panzer Division, the Dnieper, north of Krasnyi. The Russians were withdrawing along the main road from Orsha to Smolensk in four or five columns abreast. On the east bank of the Dnieper 17th Panzer Division had captured the eastern and southern quarters of Orsha. At 17.00 hrs. I was with Nehring, whose 18th Panzer Division was engaged in heavy fighting about Grusino; he had just heard of heavy casualties to his supply units at Dobryn, 15 miles south-east of Orsha, where the encircled enemy was attempting to break through to the east. At 17.40 hrs. I drove off to-wards Smolensk. A bombing attack on my staff convoy produced no casualties. At 19.15 hrs. I had a conversation with the first general staff officer of the 29th (Motorised) Infantry Division, the excellent Major Franz, outside Smolensk; he reported that his division was making good progress in the Smolensk area but that they were suffering a perceptible number of casualties. Already justifiable requests for replacements, both in men and in equipment, were beginning to be heard.

At 23.00 hrs. I rejoined my advance headquarters, which had, meanwhile, arrived at Gorki.

On July 16th the 29th (Motorised) Infantry Division captured Smolensk. It was, therefore, the first of my divisions to reach its operational objective. It had given a splendid performance. Every member of the division, from the commander, General von Boltenstern, to the most humble private, had performed his duty as a brave soldier.

On July 16th my divisions were located as follows:

1st Cavalry Division, south-east of Starye Bychov; 4th Panzer Division, between Cherikov and Krichev; 3rd Panzer Division, between Chaussy and Moliatitchi; 10th (Motorised) Infantry Division, south of Mogilev.

10th Panzer Division, between Chislavitchi and Pochinok; *SS-Das Reich*, behind it; Infantry Regiment *Gross-Deutschland*, north of Mogilev.

29th (Motorised) Infantry Division, Smolensk; 18th Panzer Division, area Krasnyi–Gusino; 17th Panzer Division, area Liady–Dubrovno.

Advance units of the infantry reached the Dnieper. These consisted of the reconnaissance battalions and the few motorised units of which the infantry disposed. Their combat strength was accordingly weak.

Since July 13th the Russians had been launching heavy counterattacks. Some twenty enemy divisions moved from the direction of Gomel against the right flank of my Panzer Group, while the Russians encircled in Mogilev and Orsha attempted simultaneously to break out, the former garrison in a south and south-easterly direction, the latter towards the south. All these operations were controlled by Marshal Timoshenko, with the obvious objective of belatedly frustrating our successful crossing of the Dnieper.

On July 16th further Russian reinforcements were observed moving up from Gomel and Klinzy, as well as heavy traffic to the east of Smolensk. So we had to reckon on a continuation of the Russians' efforts. Despite the difficulties of the situation I held fast to my decision to reach the objectives assigned me as quickly as possible. The corps, therefore, continued to advance as before.

On July 17th I flew to XXIV Panzer Corps and visited 1st Cavalry Division which was engaged in bitter fighting against the Russians attacking on the east bank of the Dnieper.

On this day the following places were reached:

1st Cavalry Division, south of Starye Bychov; 10th (Motorised)

Sketch Map 12

Elnya

Situation 17.7.–20.7.1941

30 MILES

Situation on 17.7.
Developments up to 20.7.
Russian Counter-Attacks 20.7.

Leading Units of Infantry Corps

Elnya
Baltulin
10.Pz.
Pochinok
Srodolishtche
Roslavl
Desna →
Bryansk

Prudki
Monastirshtchina
XXXXVI.
Chistavitchi
I.R. "G.D."
Sosh
Oster

Smolensk
Hoth
29.m.
17.Pz.
Gusino
Krasnyi
Lady
18.Pz.
XXXXVII.
Mstislavl
47.R.
3.Pz.
Chaussy
Krichev
4.Pz.
Cherikov
Timoshenko

Dniepr
Dubrovna
17.Pz.
Gorki
Infantry
on 20.7.
I.R. "G.D."
XXIV.
10.m.
Propoisk

Usinger
Strauss
Orsha
Gleich
Mogilev
St.Bychov
1.K.D.

Infantry Division, west of Cherikov; 4th Panzer Division, Krichev; 3rd Panzer Division, Lobkovitchi.

10th Panzer Division, between Pochinok and Elnya; *SS-Das Reich*, Mstislavl; Infantry Regiment *Gross-Deutschland*, Rekotka.

29th (Motorised) Infantry Division, Smolensk; 18th Panzer Division, Katyn–Gusino.

17th Panzer Division, Liady–Dubrovno.

Strong enemy forces were committed around and to the east of Mogilev, east of Orsha, and north and south of Smolensk. The infantry following us spread out along the Dnieper.

Army Group South succeeded in establishing bridgeheads across the Dniester.

On this day I, together with Hoth and Richthofen, was decorated with the Oak Leaves to the Knight's Cross. I was the fifth man in the army, and the twenty-fourth in all the armed forces, to receive this decoration.

I spent July 18th with my XLVII Panzer Corps. 17th Panzer Division was withdrawn from its position as flank guard, east of Orsha, and was moved to the area south of Smolensk, where it was committed against the Russian forces attacking northwards towards that city. During the battle which developed in this area the brave commander of the division, General Ritter von Weber, received severe wounds from which he subsequently died.

During the course of the next two days the XLVI Panzer Corps captured Elnya and the surrounding country in the teeth of fierce Russian resistance from fortified positions. The battles on the right flank and in the rear of the corps went on.

By July 20th the following points had been reached:

1st Cavalry Division, south-east of Starye Bychov; 10th (Motorised) Infantry Division, west of Cherikov; 4th Panzer Division, Cherikov–Krichev; 3rd Panzer Division, Lobkovitchi.

10th Panzer Division, Elnya; *SS-Das Reich*, Kusino; Infantry Regiment *Gross-Deutschland*, west of Chislavitchi.

17th Panzer Division, south of Smolensk; 29th (Motorised) Infantry Division, Smolensk; 18th Panzer Division, Gusino.

The Russian counter-attacks against XXIV Panzer Corps and Smolensk went on; fresh counter-attacks were developing in the Elnya area. The infantry following behind us crossed the Dnieper. Hoth was engaged in encircling strong enemy forces to the north-east of Smolensk. To succeed in this he required Panzer Group 2 to assist him by advancing from the south, towards Dorogobush. I was very anxious to help him and on July 21st I went to XLVI Panzer Corps to give the necessary orders for a movement in that direction. The southern and western portions of Smolensk were under enemy artillery fire so that I had to make a cross-country detour around the town. Towards noon I passed a regiment of the 17th Panzer Division, at Sloboda, which was covering the south-east flank. Twenty-seven miles to the south-east of Smolensk I found the headquarters of XLVI Panzer Corps at Kisselievka, where I was briefed on the corps situation. I then went on to visit the positions of Infantry Regiment *Gross Deutschland*, south of Vaskovo station and some 21 miles north of Roslavl, where they were opposed by a rather weak enemy but one who had considerable artillery. All units of XLVI Panzer Corps were at that time engaged with the enemy and, for the moment at least, committed. However, in the course of the next few days the presence of the 18th Panzer Division would no longer be required in the Dnieper bend near Gusino; I resolved that as soon as this happened I should send it to replace Infantry Regiment *Gross-Deutschland*; XLVI Panzer Corps would then be in a position to support Hoth in strength. I gave the necessary orders over the wireless from XLVI Panzer Corps headquarters. This corps was to switch all available force in the direction of Dorogobush; the commander of the close support planes was to be responsible for breaking up the Russian counter-attacks which were in the process of being mounted from the area Spas-Demiansk north-westwards towards Elnya. During the drive back I had a number of wireless communications from my staff: higher headquarters were urgently desirous that *SS-Das Reich* be switched towards Dorogobush. However, at the moment I could do nothing more than what I had already arranged with XLVI Panzer Corps. Even from XLVII Panzer Corps, whom I visited once again on my way back, nothing further could be expected for the time being. It all depended on withdrawing 18th Panzer Division quickly from its flank guard duties at Gusino and thus making available the strength necessary for an advance northwards. But precisely on this point Field-Marshal von Kluge, in his anxiety for the left flank of my Panzer Group along the Dnieper, saw fit to intervene personally and ordered 18th Panzer Division to stay where it was. As at Bialystok he did not inform me of this direct action on his part. As a result of this the force needed for the attack on Dorogobush was unfortunately not available.

That evening I drove through enemy artillery fire near Smolensk. My valiant motor-cycle despatch rider, Höllriegel, was thrown from his machine at one point, but luckily sustained no injuries, and at last we reached my group headquarters at Chochlovo, west of Smolensk.

The town of Smolensk had suffered little from the battles that had been fought around it. After capturing the old town, situated on the south bank of the Dnieper, the division had crossed the river and captured the industrial areas on the north side on July 17th in order to facilitate the establishment of contact with Hoth. During these days, while visiting the positions, I took the opportunity to examine the cathedral. It was undamaged. But on entering it the visitor was surprised to find that the entrance and the left half of the place of worship had been fitted up as an Atheistic Museum. At the door stood the figure of a beggar, carved in wax, asking for alms. Inside were life-size wax figures of the bourgeoisie, in exaggerated poses showing them engaged in maltreating and plundering the proletariat. It was not pretty. The right half of the church had been kept open for religious services. An attempt had been made to bury the silver altar decorations and candles before our arrival, but there had apparently not been time. In any case this considerable treasure lay piled in the middle of the floor. I ordered a Russian found whom I could make responsible for the safeguarding of these valuable objects. The sacristan was brought to me, an old man with a full white beard. Through an interpreter I told him to take these precious objects under his care and to remove them. The valuable gilded woodcarvings on the iconostasis were undamaged. What later happened to the church I do not know. At that time we took trouble to see it came to no harm.

On July 23rd, at Talashkino, I met General Ritter von Thoma, who had been appointed to succeed General Ritter von Weber as commander of the 17th Panzer Division. He was one of our most senior and experienced panzer officers; he had been famous for his icy calm and exceptional bravery both in the First World War and in Spain, and was now to prove his ability once again. His division provided the link between the XLVI and XLVII Panzer Corps, and also covered the Dnieper against the attempted break-through which Fourth Army still expected the Russians to make southwards. The headquarters of XLVI Panzer Corps was in a wood 7 miles west of Elnya. General von Vietinghoff informed me about the Russian counter-attacks at Elnya: they were attacking from the south, east and north, with very heavy artillery support. On account of a shortage of ammunition, which was now making itself felt for the first time, the corps could only defend its most important positions. As soon as Infantry Regiment *Gross-Deutschland* was relieved by the 18th Panzer Division Vietinghoff wanted to attack towards Dorogobush in support of Hoth. Up to now all attempts to advance across the Usha, north-west of Elnya, towards Svirkolutchie had failed. The Glinka–Klimiatino road, which was marked 'good' on our maps, did not in fact exist. The roads that did lead north were swampy and impassable to motor vehicles. All movement had to be carried out on foot and was therefore both exhausting and time-consuming.

I then drove to 10th Panzer Division, where General Schaal gave me an impressive description of the fighting around Elnya. His troops had destroyed 50 enemy tanks in a single day but had then found themselves unable to capture the well-built Russian positions. He reckoned that he had lost one-third of his vehicles. Ammunition had to be fetched by road for a distance of 275 miles.

Finally, I went once again to *SS-Das Reich*, to the north of Elnya. On the previous day the division had taken 1,100 prisoners, but had been unable to move forward between Elnya and Dorogobush. Heavy bomber attacks had held up their advance. I visited the foremost unit, the motor-cyclists under command of the brave Hauptsturmführer (SS rank equivalent to captain) Klingenberg, as I wished to gain a personal impression of the terrain and the situation. This visit convinced me that the attack towards Dorogobush must be postponed until the arrival of Infantry Regiment *Gross-Deutschland*.

At 23.00 hrs. I reached my new command post, 1 mile south of Prudki.

During the next few days the heavy Russian attacks went on with undiminished violence. Nevertheless there was a certain progress made on the right wing, while 18th Panzer Division and the first of the infantry divisions provided welcome reinforcement to the centre. But all attempts to advance towards Dorogobush were a complete failure.

Intelligence reports during the last few days indicated that four new Russian armies were likely to appear eastward of the line Novgorod–Severski—west of Bryansk–Elnya–Rzhev–Ostashkov: the Russians were also believed to be fortifying this line.

By July 25th the following points had been reached:

1st Cavalry Division, the area south-east of Novye Bychov; 4th Panzer Division, Chernikov–Krichev; 10th (Motorised) Infantry Division, Chvikov; 3rd Panzer Division, Lobkovitchi.

263rd Infantry Division, Machine-gun Battalion 5, Infantry Regiment *Gross-Deutschland*, 18th Panzer Division and 292nd Infantry Division, the area south of Prudki and around the airfield of Shatalovka: this latter was now in use by our support planes, and must therefore be kept out of range of the enemy artillery.

10th Panzer Division, Elnya; *SS-Das Reich*, north of Elnya.

17th Panzer Division, Chenzovo and to the south; 29th (Motorised) Infantry Division, south of Smolensk.

137th Infantry Division, Smolensk.

Enemy cavalry cut the railway line near Bobruisk.

On July 26th the Russians continued to attack around Elnya. I requested that the 268th Infantry Division be sent up to strengthen the Elnya salient and to enable the panzer troops to be withdrawn; after all their marching and fighting they badly needed a period of rest and maintenance. At noon I went to 3rd Panzer Division to congratulate Model on a well-earned Knight's Cross and to learn the position on his division's front. Next I drove to 4th Panzer Division where I saw Generals Freiherr von Geyr and Freiherr von Langermann. Towards evening a message came in that the Russians had broken into our Smolensk bridgehead to the north of the Dnieper in the 137th Infantry Division's sector.

Wireless intelligence had informed us that there was a connection between the Russian 21st Army at Gomel, the 13th Army at Rodnia and the 4th Army to the south of Roslavl.

On this day Hoth succeeded in closing the pocket east of Smolensk from the north. The remnants of ten Russian divisions were thus at the mercy of 3rd Panzer Group. In our rear strong Russian forces which had been holding out around Mogilev were finally destroyed.

On returning to my headquarters I received a signal at 22.00 hrs. from Army Group, ordering me to be at Orsha airfield for a conference at 12.00 hrs. next day. Such a conference was necessary, since during the last few days divergences of opinion concerning the situation had appeared and these had to be cleared up. While Fourth Army had regarded the threat to the Smolensk area as very serious, we in the Panzer Group were of the opinion that our most dangerous enemy was now to the south of Roslavl and east of Elnya. As a result of units being retained on the Dnieper, west of Smolensk, crises and losses had occurred in the Roslavl area which could have been avoided. The relationship between the commander of the Fourth Army and myself had, in consequence, become strained to an undesirable degree.

On July 27th, accompanied by my chief of staff, Lieutenant-Colonel Freiherr von Liebenstein, I flew over Orsha to Borissov, the headquarters of the Army Group, in order to receive my instructions for future operations and to report on the condition of the troops under my command. I expected to be told to push on towards Moscow or at least Bryansk; to my surprise I learned that Hitler had ordered that my 2nd Panzer Group was to go for Gomel in collaboration with Second Army. This meant that my Panzer Group would be swung round and would be advancing in a south-westerly direction, that is to say towards Germany; but Hitler was anxious to encircle the eight to ten Russian divisions in the Gomel area. We were informed that Hitler was convinced that large-scale envelopments were not justified: the theory on which they were based was a false one put out by the General Staff Corps, and he believed that events in France had proved his point. He preferred an alternative plan by which small enemy forces were to be encircled and destroyed piecemeal and the enemy thus bled to death. All the officers who took part in this conference were of the opinion that this was incorrect: that these manœuvres on our part simply gave the Russians time to set up new formations and to use their inexhaustible man-power for the creation of fresh defensive lines in the rear area: even more important, we were sure that this strategy would not result in the urgently necessary, rapid conclusion of the campaign.

The *OKH*, too, had appreciated the situation quite differently a few days before. Proof of this lies in the following document, which reached me from a reliable Service source. Dated July 23rd, 1941, it runs as follows:

'Decisions concerning future operations are based on the belief that once the first operational objectives, as laid down in the orders for the campaign, have been reached, the bulk of the Russian Army capable of operational employment will have been beaten. On the other hand it must be reckoned that, by reason of his strong reserves of man-power and by further ruthless expenditure of his forces, the enemy will be able to continue to offer stubborn resistance to the German advance. In this connection, the point of main effort of the enemy's defence may be expected to be in the Ukraine, in front of Moscow and in front of Leningrad.

The intention of the OKH is to defeat the existing or newly created enemy forces, and by a speedy capture of the most important industrial areas in the Ukraine west of the Volga, in the area Tula–Gorki–Rybinsk–Moscow, and around Leningrad to deprive the enemy of the possibility of material rearmament. With these ends in view the individual tasks for the Army Groups and the major necessary redistribution of force will be worked out in greater detail and forwarded in writing in due course.'

Regardless of what decisions Hitler might now take, the immediate need of Panzer Group 2 was to dispose of the most dangerous enemy threat to its right flank. I therefore proposed to the Commander-in-Chief of the Army Group my plan for an attack on Roslavl; the capture of this important road centre would give us the mastery of the communications to the east, the south, and the south-west, and I asked that I be given the necessary additional forces to carry it out.

My plan was accepted and Panzer Group 2 was allotted:

(*a*) for the attack on Roslavl, VII Army Corps with the 7th, 23rd, 78th and 197th Infantry Divisions.

(*b*) for the relief of the panzer divisions in the Elnya bulge which were in need of rest and maintenance, the XX Army Corps with the 15th and 268th Infantry Divisions.

Meanwhile the 1st Cavalry Division was attached to Second Army.

The Panzer Group was no longer subordinate to Fourth Army. It was also renamed *Armeegruppe Guderian*.[1]

The attack for neutralising the threat to our flank from the Roslavl area was mounted as follows:

XXIV Panzer Corps, with two divisions (the 10th Motorised Infantry Division and the 7th Infantry Division from VII Army Corps), was to take over the defence of the deep flank in the area Klimovitchi-Miloslavitchi. Meanwhile with the 3rd and 4th Panzer Divisions it was to capture Roslavl and there make firm contact with the IX Army Corps which would be advancing from the north between the rivers Oster and Desna.

VII Army Corps, with the 23rd and 197th Infantry Divisions, was to advance in conjunction with the 3rd Panzer Division to the line of the road Roslavl-Stodolishtche-Smolensk by way of Petrovitchi-Chislavitchi. The 78th Infantry Division was to move forward behind these two divisions as second wave.

IX Army Corps was to advance southward with the 263rd Infantry Division between the highway and the River Oster and with the 292nd Infantry Division between the rivers Oster and Desna. Point of main effort was to be on the left flank, towards the Roslavl-Yekimovitchi-Moscow road. The 137th Infantry Division, brought down from Smolensk, was to be responsible for protecting the left flank. The corps was further strengthened by elements of the XLVII Panzer Corps, notably by that corps' artillery.

The attack was to be started by XXIV Panzer Corps and VII Army Corps on August 1st. The IX Army Corps did not believe that it could be ready by that date and was therefore to attack on August 2nd.

The next days were devoted to making the necessary preparations. In particular the newly subordinated infantry corps, which up to then had scarcely been in action against the Russians, had to be taught my methods of attacking. Since they had never worked in such close contact with tanks, problems arose which had to be cleared up. This was particularly the case with IX Army Corps, whose outstanding commander, General Geyer, was well known to me personally, since he had twice been my superior officer; first in the old days at the *Truppenamt* at the War Ministry and later when he was the commander of Army Area (*Wehrkreis*) V, in which Würzburg was located. General Geyer was famous for his 'razor-sharp intelligence,' on which Ludendorff had made a celebrated comment as far back as the First World

[1] A German *Armeegruppe* was an *ad hoc* formation of varying size but generally larger than a corps and smaller than an army. In this case, of course, the *Armeegruppe* had the combat strength at least of a large army. The German for an army group is a *Heeresgruppe*.

War. Now of course he was quick to detect the weaknesses in my plan
of attack and pointed them out at a corps commanders' conference.
I attempted to silence his criticism of my tactics by saying: 'This attack
is mathematical,' by which I meant that its success was certain. General
Geyer was by no means convinced that this was the case, and I had
to put up a stubborn self-defence against the remarks of my old
commander during that conference in the little Russian schoolroom.
It was only on the field of battle that he recognised the correctness of
the procedure that I had laid down; then he contributed greatly, by
means of his outstanding personal courage, to the success of the
enterprise.

On July 29th Colonel Schmundt, Hitler's chief adjutant, brought me
the Oak Leaves to the Knight's Cross and took the opportunity to
discuss my intentions with me. He explained that Hitler had three
objectives in view:

1. The north-east, that is to say Leningrad. This city must be
captured at all costs in order to free the Baltic for our shipping and
to ensure the supply route from Sweden and the provisioning of Army
Group North.

2. Moscow, whose industries were important, and

3. The south-east, that is the Ukraine.

According to what Schmundt told me, Hitler had not yet made up
his mind about an attack on the Ukraine. I therefore urged Schmundt
with all the force of which I was capable to advise Hitler in favour
of a direct push to capture Moscow, the heart of Russia, and against
the undertaking of any operations that must involve us in losses without
being decisive. Over and above that I begged him not to withhold the
new tanks and our replacements, since without them this campaign
could not be brought to a speedy and successful conclusion.

On July 30th thirteen enemy attacks on Elnya were repulsed.

On July 31st the *OKH* liaison officer, Major von Bredow, arrived
back at my headquarters with the following information: 'It is now
considered that the original objectives for October 1st, the line Lake
Onezhskoe–the Volga, cannot be reached by that date. On the other
hand it is believed with certainty that the line Leningrad–Moscow and
to the south can be reached. The *OKH* and the Chief of the General
Staff are engaged in a thankless undertaking, since the conduct of all
operations is being controlled from the very highest level. Final
decisions have not yet been taken concerning the future course of
events.'

But everything now depended on what these final decisions concerning the next stage of the campaign were to be, even down to such
details as to whether or not Elnya should be held; if there was to be

no further advance on Moscow the Elnya salient offered us only the danger of continuous, heavy casualties. Ammunition supply for the positional warfare which had developed on this sector was insufficient. This was hardly surprising when it is realised that Elnya was 450 miles from the nearest adequate railhead. It is true that the railway track had already been relaid as far as Orsha to conform to the German gauge, but it was still only capable of carrying very limited traffic. The stretches of track which had not been relaid were useless since there were but few Russian locomotives available.

All the same there was still hope that Hitler might change his mind and come to a decision other than that which had been outlined to us during the Army Group Centre conference at Borissov on July 27th.

On August 1st XXIV Panzer and VII Army Corps began their attack on Roslavl. Early in the morning of that day I went to VII Army Corps, but could find neither the corps' nor the 23rd Infantry Division's headquarters along the road of advance. While hunting for them I found myself among the leading horse cavalry of the 23rd Infantry Division's advance guard. Since there could be no headquarters ahead of them I stopped and let the cavalrymen give me their impressions of the enemy up to date. I then watched while the 67th Infantry Regiment marched past me; its commander was Lieutenant-Colonel Freiherr von Bissing, with whom I had for many years shared a house at Berlin-Schlachtensee. The comments of his soldiers, when they recognised me, betrayed pleasurable surprise. On my way to 3rd Panzer Division I became involved in a bombing attack by our own planes on the 23rd Infantry Division's march route which resulted in heavy casualties. The first bomb burst $5\frac{1}{2}$ yards from my car. Insufficient training and a lack of combat experience on the part of the young aviators were the cause of this unfortunate occurrence; and this despite clear recognition signals on the part of the troops on the ground and very plain orders to the fliers concerning the roads that we would be using. Apart from this the advance of the 23rd Infantry Division was completed without meeting serious opposition.

I spent the afternoon with the leading units of the 3rd Panzer Division in the area immediately to the west of the Oster and south of Choronievo. General Model informed me that he had taken the bridges over the stream intact and had thus been able to capture an enemy battery. I expressed my thanks for the performance of their troops to a number of battalion commanders on the spot.

In the evening I was at XXIV Panzer Corps headquarters in order to complete my picture of the day's events. I returned to my group headquarters at 02.00 hrs., after having been away from it for twenty-two hours.

Sketch Map 13

Roslavl

Situation 30.7.41.
Advances up to 3. 8. 41.

The main objective of our attack, Roslavl, had been captured.

In the morning of August 2nd I visited the IX Army Corps. From the command post of the 509th Infantry Regiment, of the 292nd Infantry Division, it was possible to watch the Russians as they withdrew. I then drove to Infantry Regiment 507, which was moving on Kosaki behind an advance guard. I finally visited the regiments and staff of the 137th Infantry Division and instructed them to continue their advance during the night so as to reach the highroad to Moscow as soon as possible. I arrived back at my headquarters at 22.30 hrs.

The performance of IX Army Corps during August 2nd had not been very impressive. I therefore decided to spend the next day, the 3rd, once again with this corps in order to hasten its advance and to ensure the success of the attack. I drove first to the headquarters of the 292nd Infantry Division, near Kovali, and from there to the 507th Infantry Regiment. On the road I met the corps commander with whom I had a detailed conversation concerning the control of the battle. When I arrived at Infantry Regiment 507 I advanced on foot with the leading rifle company and thus ensured that there were no needless delays without having to waste many words to do so. Three kilometres before the great Moscow highroad was reached I recognised, through my glasses, tanks to the north-east of Roslavl. Everything immediately halted. I therefore told the assault gun, which was accompanying the infantry vanguard, to fire white signal shells, the agreed recognition signal for our troops: 'Here I am!' Immediately I received a similar signal in answer from the Moscow road. They were my panzer troops from Panzer Regiment 35 of the 4th Panzer Division.

I now got into my car and drove over to the tanks. The last Russians threw away their guns and took to their heels. On the Moscow road where the bridge over the Ostrik was blown, the men of the 2nd Company of Panzer Regiment 35 scrambled over beams and planks to greet me. This was the company which my elder son had until recently commanded. He had won the hearts of his men and their confidence and affection for him were extended to his father. Lieutenant Krause, who was now the company commander, described his experiences to me and I congratulated the whole company on their performance.

The encirclement of the Russians around Roslavl was now complete. Between three and four divisions must be trapped. The task was now to hold them fast until they should surrender. Since a half-hour later General Geyer also appeared at this spot, I pointed out to him the great importance of holding the Moscow highway. The 292nd Infantry Division was to be responsible for containing the west side of the encirclement, the 137th Infantry Division the eastern side along the Desna.

Back at my headquarters I learned that VII Army Corps had already taken 3,700 prisoners, 60 guns, 90 tanks and an armoured train.

Meanwhile around Elnya heavy battles continued to rage, involving a great expenditure of ammunition. Our last reserve, the guard company of my Group headquarters, was sent to this sector.

On August 3rd the following points were reached:

7th Infantry Division and 3rd Panzer Division to the west of Klimovitchi; 10th (Motorised) Infantry Division, Chislavitchi; 78th Infantry Division, Ponetovka; 23rd Infantry Division, Roslavl; 197th Infantry Division and Machine-gun Battalion 5 to the north of Roslavl.

263rd Infantry Division to the south of Prudki; 292nd Infantry Division, Kosaki; 137th Infantry Division, the east flank on the Desna.

10th Panzer Division, 268th Infantry Division, *SS-Das Reich*, Infantry Regiment *Gross-Deutschland*, the area about Elnya; 17th Panzer Division to the north of Elnya; 29th (Motorised) Infantry Division to the south of Smolensk; 18th Panzer Division, Prudki.

XX Army Corps was in process of arriving.

I was ordered to Army Group headquarters early on the morning of August 4th in order to report to Hitler for the first time since the opening of the Russian Campaign. We had reached a decisive turning-point of the war.

Moscow or Kiev?

The conference with Hitler took place in Novy Borissov, at the head-quarters of Army Group Centre. Those present were Hitler and Schmundt, Field-Marshal von Bock, Hoth and myself, as well as a representative of the *OHK*, Colonel Heusinger, the Chief of the Operations Department. We were each given the opportunity to express our views and we did this alone so that no man knew what his pre-decessor might have said. But Field-Marshal von Bock, Hoth and I shared the opinion that a continuation of the offensive towards Moscow was of vital importance. Hoth reported that the earliest date by which his Panzer Group could resume its advance was August 20th; the date I gave for my Group was the 15th. Then Hitler assembled the whole company together and began himself to speak. He designated the industrial area about Leningrad as his primary objective. He had not yet decided whether Moscow or the Ukraine would come next. He seemed to incline towards the latter target for a number of reasons: first, Army Group South seemed to be laying the groundwork for a victory in that area: secondly, he believed that the raw materials and agricultural produce of the Ukraine were necessary to Germany for

the further prosecution of the war: and finally he thought it essential
that the Crimea, 'that Soviet aircraft carrier operating against the
Rumanian oilfields,' be neutralised. He hoped to be in possession of
Moscow and Kharkov by the time winter began. No decisions were
reached on this day concerning those problems of strategy which we
regarded as most important.

The conference then began to discuss more detailed questions. The important point for my Panzer Group was a decision not to evacuate the
Elnya salient, since it was not yet known whether this salient might not
still be needed as a jumping-off point for an attack towards Moscow.
I stressed the fact that our tank engines had become very worn as a
result of the appalling dust; in consequence they must be replaced with
all urgency if any more large-scale tank operations were to be carried
out during the current year. It was also essential that replacements
be provided for our tank casualties from current production. After
a certain amount of humming and hawing Hitler promised to supply
300 new tank engines for the whole Eastern Front, a figure which I
described as totally inadequate. As for new tanks, we were not to get
any, since Hitler intended to retain them all at home for the equipping
of newly set-up formations. In the ensuing argument I stated that we
could only cope with the Russians' great numerical superiority in tanks
if our tank losses were rapidly made good again. Hitler then said:
'If I had known that the figures for Russian tank strength which you
gave in your book were in fact the true ones, I would not—I believe—
ever have started this war.' He was referring to my book *Achtung!
Panzer!*, published in 1937, in which I had estimated Russian tank
strength at that time as 10,000; both the Chief of the Army General
Staff, Beck, and the censor had disagreed with this statement. It had
cost me a lot of trouble to get that figure printed; but I had been able
to show that intelligence reports at the time spoke of 17,000 Russian
tanks and that my estimate was therefore, if anything, a very conservative one. To imitate the ostrich in political matters has never been
a satisfactory method of avoiding danger; yet this is what Hitler, as
well as his more important political, economic and even military
advisers, chose to do over and over again. The consequences of this
deliberate blindness in the face of hard facts were devastating; and
it was we who now had to bear them.

While flying back I decided in any case to make the necessary
preparations for an attack towards Moscow.

Back at my headquarters I learned that IX Army Corps, worried
about a Russian break-through in the Yermolino area on the south-
eastern edge of the encirclement, had withdrawn from the Moscow

Sketch Map 14

Krichev – Miloslavitchi
Situation 9.8.41.

highway; in consequence the danger had arisen that the Russians encircled on August 3rd might now break out. Early on the 5th I therefore hurried to VII Army Corps and drove along the Moscow highway in order to plug any gaps in the southern flank of our encirclement. On my way I came across elements of the 15th Infantry Division, destined for Elnya, and was able to brief the divisional commander on conditions in that sector. I then went on to the 197th Infantry Division, whose commander, General Meier-Rabingen, informed me that the encirclement was no longer complete and that the Russians controlled the Moscow highway, at least by fire. At 4th Panzer Division I learned that the tanks of Panzer Regiment 35 had been relieved. I immediately got into wireless communication with XXIV Panzer Corps, which I made responsible for the security of the Moscow highway, and then drove back to VII Army Corps. This corps had already instructed the Reconnaissance Battalion of the 23rd Infantry Division to prevent any break-out by the Russians inside our encirclement. The measures so far taken seemed to me insufficient and I therefore set off, together with the chief of staff of the corps, Colonel Krebs, for Roslavl. (Krebs, an old friend from the days of the Goslar Jaeger Battalion, was to succeed me as Chief of Staff of the Army in the spring of 1945.) There I came upon Lieutenant Krause's company, the 2nd Company of Panzer Regiment 35, withdrawing to its rest area; the company commander was still engaged with the enemy. Until that morning the company had been beating off enemy attempts to break out, had destroyed a number of Russian guns and had taken several hundred prisoners. It had then withdrawn according to orders. I immediately turned the trusty company right about and told them to reoccupy their old positions in the line. I next sent off II Battalion of Infantry Regiment 332 to the Ostrik bridge, finally alerted such anti-aircraft troops as were available in Roslavl, and then set off for the front myself. I arrived at the Ostrik bridge exactly as a group of a hundred Russians appeared, moving towards it from the north. They were driven off. The bridge had been repaired in the course of the past few days and our tanks, driving across it, frustrated the enemy's attempts to break out. After the tanks had established contact with the 137th Infantry Division, I went once again to the headquarters of VII Army Corps; there I instructed General Martinek, a tried and true Austrian, who commanded VII Army Corp's artillery, to be responsible for keeping a careful watch on the danger spots along the Moscow highway. I then flew to my headquarters, where I signalled IX Army Corps to establish contact with Battle Group Martinek.

I now told my staff to prepare for an advance on Moscow, as follows: the Panzer Corps were to be committed on the right, along the Moscow

Fig. 10. Dawn, June 22, 1941

Fig. 11. Russia: The road forward

FIG. 12. Bridge building over the Dnieper near Kopys

FIG. 13. The Battle of Shklov

highway, while the infantry corps were to be brought forward in the centre and on the left wing. I intended my point of main effort to be on my right: by attacking the relatively weak Russian front on either side of the Moscow highway, and then rolling up that front from Spas Demiansk to Viasma, I hoped to facilitate Hoth's advance and bring our forward movement towards Moscow into the open. As a result of these ideas of mine I refused an *OKH* request, dated August 6th, that panzer divisions be detached from my command for an attack on Rogachev on the Dnieper, which lay far behind my front. My intelligence established that on this day there were hardly any enemy forces for a considerable distance around Roslavl. Towards Bryansk and the south there was no enemy for some 25 miles. This was confirmed on the following day.

By August 8th the battle of Roslavl was more or less over. We had captured 38,000 prisoners, 200 tanks and an equal number of guns. It was a considerable and highly satisfactory victory.

But before the attack on Moscow could be launched, or any other major operations undertaken, one condition must be fulfilled: our deep right flank in the Krichev area had to be secured. The clearing of this flank was also essential before Second Army would be in a position to attack Rogachev. Army Group (Bock) shared my opinion that the detachment of tank strength from my Panzer Group to Second Army would be a mistake in view of the long march involved (Roslavl-Rogachev 125 miles: there and back 250 miles) and the consequent inevitable wear and tear to the armoured equipment. Both staffs regarded the resumption of the advance on Moscow as the primary objective. Despite this clear recognition of the true facts, I continued to receive demands from Army Group—no doubt under pressure from the *OKH*—that I 'send a few tanks off to Propoisk.' A stop was finally put to this business by reason of a decision of General Freiherr von Geyr's: this involved the elimination of the constant threat to his right flank by attacking the enemy in the Miloslavitchi area to the south of Krichev. I approved this plan and persuaded Army Group to do likewise, so no more was heard about sending tanks to Propoisk.

On August 8th I visited the corps and divisions in and around Roslavl and to the south. On August 9th I joined the 4th Panzer Division for XXIV Panzer Corps' attack. The attack by Panzer Regiment 35 and Rifle Regiment 12 went in as though it were a model attack on the training-ground: Colonel Schneider's artillery gave valuable support.

A significant indication of the attitude of the civilian population is provided by the fact that women came out from their villages on to the very battlefield bringing wooden platters of bread and butter and eggs and, in my case at least, refused to let me move on before I had

eaten. Unfortunately this friendly attitude towards the Germans lasted
only so long as the more benevolent military administration was in
control. The so-called 'Reich commissars' soon managed to alienate
all sympathy from the Germans and thus to prepare the ground for
all the horrors of partisan warfare.

For some reason unknown to me the 2nd Panzer Division, which
had been kept in *OKH* reserve, was sent off to the West—that is to
say to France—on August 10th.

The advance of Second Army on Gomel during these few days was
made more difficult by the fact that the roads had no foundations;
this was a strong argument against attempting to follow the infantry
through that area.

By August 10th the following points had been reached:

7th Infantry Division area south of Chotovitchi; 3rd and 4th Panzer
Division attacking south-west of Miloslavitchi; 10th (Motorised)
Infantry Division, Miloslavitchi; 78th Infantry Division, Sloboda with
advance units Buchan; 197th Infantry Division, Ostrovaia with advance
units Aleshnia.

29th (Motorised) Infantry Division, Roslavl; 23rd Infantry Division
resting north of Roslavl; 137th and 263rd Infantry Divisions along the
Desna.

10th Panzer Division west of Elnya; 17th Panzer Division north-west
of Elnya; 18th Panzer Division east of Prudki; *SS-Das Reich* and
Infantry Regiment *Gross-Deutschland* in rest areas north-west of Elnya.

Up to this point all the steps taken by the Panzer Group had been
based on the belief that both the Army Group and the *OKH* regarded
the operations towards Moscow as the decisive move. Despite the
Novy Borissov conference of August 4th, I had not given up hope that
Hitler would agree with this point of view which—to me at least—
seemed the natural and obvious one. On August 11th I was disillusioned
on this score. My plan of attack, with point of main effort through
Roslavl towards Viasma, was turned down by the *OKH* and described
as 'unsatisfactory.' The *OKH*, however, did not produce a better plan
but contented themselves with deluging us during the next few days
with a positive stream of varying instructions; this made it quite
impossible for subordinate headquarters to work out any consistent
plan at all. Army Group had apparently agreed to the cancellation of
my plan, though they had unambiguously approved it as recently as
August 4th. Unfortunately I did not learn at the time that a few days
later Hitler was to change his mind and share my views on the Moscow
attack—though insisting that certain preliminary conditions be fulfilled
before it was launched. In any event, the *OKH* did not know how to

make use of the few moments of Hitler's approval. A few days later the whole picture was changed once again.

On August 13th I visited the Desna front, to the east of Roslavl, on either side of the Moscow highway. With a heavy heart I saw how my soldiers, confident that they would soon be advancing straight towards the Russian capital, had put up many signposts marked 'TO MOSCOW.' The soldiers of the 137th Infantry Division, with whom I spoke at the front, would talk only of a rapid resumption of the move to the east.

On August 14th XXIV Panzer Corps' battle in the Krichev area was brought to a successful conclusion. Three Russian divisions were smashed, 16,000 prisoners and a great many guns captured. Kostiukovitchi was taken.

When my plan of attack was turned down, I proposed that the Elnya salient, which now had no purpose and was a continual source of casualties, be abandoned. This proposal, too, was not acceptable either to Army Group or the *OKH*. With the feeble comment 'it is far more disadvantageous to the enemy than it is to us,' the whole point of my suggestion, that human lives be spared, was brushed aside.

On August 15th I was busy trying to persuade my superiors not to exploit the success of XXIV Panzer Corps by making them push on to Gomel. As I saw it such a march to the south-west would constitute a step backwards. Army Group attempted then to withdraw one panzer division from my command for this operation, being apparently uninterested in the fact that a single division cannot operate through the enemy's lines. The only possible course was to use the whole XXIV Panzer Corps, while covering its left flank with fresh forces. Since the beginning of the campaign on June 22nd XXIV Panzer Corps had, moreover, not passed a single day out of action and was urgently in need of a rest period for tank maintenance. When at last I had persuaded Army Group to give up this plan I received, half an hour later, an order from the *OKH* that one panzer division be sent to Gomel. XXIV Panzer Corps was therefore now ordered to advance, with 3rd and 4th Panzer Divisions leading and with the 10th (Motorised) Infantry Division moving behind, in a southerly direction towards Novosybkov and Starodub; when it had effected a break-through the right-hand division was to swing towards Gomel.

On August 16th the 3rd Panzer Division captured the road centre Mglin. Army Group Centre (Bock) had to surrender the XXXIX Panzer Corps, with the 12th Panzer Division and the 18th and 20th (Motorised) Infantry Divisions, to Army Group North (Leeb).

I shall pass over the fluctuations of opinion at Army Group Centre as expressed during the telephone conversations of the next few days. On August 17th the right wing of XXIV Panzer Corps was held up by strong enemy opposition, while the two left-hand divisions, the 10th (Motorised) Infantry Division and the 3rd Panzer Division, after capturing the rail centre of Unecha, were making good progress. The Gomel–Bryansk railway was cut and a deep penetration made. How could it best be exploited? It was to be assumed that Second Army's strong left wing, supported as it was by my right wing, would now launch an attack on Gomel. But curiously enough nothing of the sort happened. Instead, strong formations of Second Army marked off from that army's left flank in a north-easterly direction, passing far behind XXIV Panzer Corp's front, while leaving the Panzer Corps heavily engaged in the area Starodub–Unecha. I turned to Army Group and requested that units of Second Army be ordered finally to attack the enemy on my right flank. My request was granted, but when I inquired of Second Army whether they had received the relevant orders I was informed that on the contrary it was Army Group itself which had ordered the move of formations to the north-east. And this was at a time when a resolute plan of action was all the more desirable, since as early as August 17th there were indications that the enemy was evacuating Gomel. Indeed on that day XXIV Panzer Corps received orders to block the enemy's eastward escape route in the area of Unecha and Starodub.

On August 19th Panzer Group 1, fighting with Army Group South, captured a small bridgehead over the Dnieper near Zaporozhe. Second Army entered Gomel. My Panzer Group was ordered to advance through Klinzy–Starodub to Novosybkov, while XLVII Panzer Corps was entrusted with the task of covering XXIV Panzer Corps' eastern flank. The former corps ran into heavy enemy opposition at Pochep.

An appreciation on the future course of the war on the Eastern Front, dated August 18th, was submitted to Hitler by the Commander-in-Chief of the Army.

On August 20th the XXIV Panzer Corps repulsed enemy attacks along the line Surash–Klinzy–Starodub. Elements of the Russian forces succeeded in breaking through to the east in the area south of Unecha. Attacks on Elnya were beaten off.

On August 20th Field-Marshal von Bock ordered by telephone that attempts by the left wing of Panzer Group 2 to press on southwards towards Pochep were to be discontinued. He wanted the whole of the Panzer Group withdrawn to rest in the Roslavl area, so that he would have fresh troops at his disposal when the advance on Moscow for which he was hoping was resumed. He had no idea why Second Army

Sketch Map 15

Situation on 17.8.41.

Smolensk

Dnieper

10 5 0   10   20   30 MILES

Russian Concentrations
Prepared Positions
Movements
Fixed Defenses

Developments up to 20.8.

"G.D."
"SS R"
15. Elnya 292
XX   268.
18.Pz. 10.Pz.
132.
Covering

Spas-Demiansk

to Moscow 180 Miles

"G.D."
78.
263.
23.
197.

"SS R"
7.
18. Roslavl
Mass.
Pz.
29.m.

Sergeiev Skoie

Shumiatchi

Krichev

2. Army

7. Chotovitchi
Miloslavitchi
10.m. Klimovitchi

258.

258.
Kostiukovitchi
4.Pz.
Bielynkovit-
chi

34.

Covering Lines

Covering Lines

29.m.

Elmnts.
17.Pz. Elmnts. 29.m.

3.Pz. 4.Pz.

Mglin
17.Pz.

Pochep

167.

Surash
10.m.

3.Pz.

Klinzy

Unecha

Trubchevsk

1.K.D.

1.K.D.

Bomel

Novosybkov

3.Pz.
Starodub

Pogar

had not made better time in its advance; he had been continually
urging it to hurry.

On August 21st XXIV Panzer Corps took Kostobobr, and
XLVII Panzer Corps Pochep.

On August 22nd I handed over command of XX, IX and VII Army
Corps to Fourth Army. The Panzer Group's headquarters was moved
to Shumiatchi, to the west of Roslavl, in order to be nearer to the
mass of the divisions. On this day, at 19.00 hrs., a query came in from
Army Group: would it be possible to move armoured units capable
of fighting to the area Klinzy–Pochep for operations on the left flank
of Second Army? These operations were to be in a southerly direction
for the purpose of co-operation with Sixth Army of Army Group
South. It transpired that an order had arrived from the *OKH* or the
OKW which stated that a mobile formation was to participate in Second
Army's attack. I told Army Group that I regarded the employment
of the Panzer Group in this direction as a basically false idea: as for
splitting up the Panzer Group that, I said, would be criminal folly.

On August 23rd I was ordered to attend a conference at Army
Group headquarters, at which the Chief of the Army General Staff
was present. The latter informed us that Hitler had now decided that
neither the Leningrad nor the Moscow operations would be carried
out, but that the immediate objective should be the capture of the
Ukraine and the Crimea. The Chief of the General Staff, Colonel-
General Halder, seemed deeply upset at this shattering of his hopes,
which were based on a resumption of the Moscow offensive. We
discussed at length what could still be done to alter Hitler's 'unalterable
resolve.' We were all agreed that this new plan to move on Kiev must
result in a winter campaign: this in its turn would lead to all those
difficulties which the *OKH* had very good reasons for wishing to avoid.
I mentioned the road and supply problems which must arise if the
tanks were to be sent south; I also expressed doubts as to the ability
of our armoured equipment to perform these heavy new tasks as well
as the subsequent winter advance on Moscow. I went on to draw
attention to the condition of XXIV Panzer Corps, which had not had
one single day for rest and maintenance since the opening of the
Russian Campaign. These facts provided arguments which the Chief
of Staff could bring to Hitler's notice in still another attempt to make
him change his mind. Field-Marshal von Bock was in agreement with
me; after a great deal of chopping and changing he finally suggested
that I accompany Colonel-General Halder to the Führer's headquarters;
as a general from the front I could lay the relevant facts immediately
before Hitler and thus support a last attempt on the part of the *OKH*
to make him agree their plan. The suggestion was approved. We set

off later that afternoon and arrived at the Lötzen airfield, in East Prussia, just as it was getting dark.

I reported at once to the Commander-in-Chief of the Army, Field-Marshal von Brauchitsch, who greeted me with the following words: 'I forbid you to mention the question of Moscow to the Führer. The operation to the south has been ordered. The problem now is simply how it is to be carried out. Discussion is pointless.' I therefore asked permission to fly back to my Panzer Group, since in these circumstances any conversation I might have with Hitler would be simply a waste of time. But Field-Marshal von Brauchitsch would not agree to this. He ordered that I see Hitler and report to him on the state of my Panzer Group, 'but without mentioning Moscow!'

I went in to see Hitler. There were a great many people present, including Keitel, Jodl, Schmundt and others, but neither Brauchitsch nor Halder nor, indeed, any representative of the *OKH*. I described the state of my Panzer Group, its present condition and that of the terrain. When I had finished Hitler asked: 'In view of their past performance, do you consider that your troops are capable of making another great effort?'

I replied: 'If the troops are given a major objective, the importance of which is apparent to every soldier, yes.'

Hitler then said: 'You mean, of course, Moscow?'

I answered: 'Yes. Since you have broached the subject, let me give you the reasons for my opinions.'

Hitler agreed and I therefore explained basically and in detail all the points that favoured a continuation of the advance on Moscow and that spoke against the Kiev operation. I maintained that, from a military point of view, the only question was that of finally defeating the enemy forces which had suffered so heavily in the recent battles. I described to him the geographical significance of Moscow, which was quite different from that of, say, Paris. Moscow was the great Russian road, rail and communications centre: it was the political solar plexus; it was an important industrial area; and its capture would not only have an enormous psychological effect on the Russian people but on the whole of the rest of the world as well. I dwelt on the attitude of the soldiers; they expected nothing but an advance on Moscow and had already made the necessary preparations for such an advance with the greatest enthusiasm. I tried to show how a victory in this decisive direction, and the consequent destruction of the enemy's main forces, would make the capture of the Ukrainian industrial area an easier undertaking: once we had seized the communication hub of Moscow, the Russians would have extraordinary difficulty in moving troops from north to south.

I pointed out that the troops of Army Group Centre were now poised for an advance on Moscow; that before they could start on the alternative operation towards Kiev a great deal of time would be wasted in moving to the south-west; that such a move was towards Germany, i.e. in the wrong direction; and that for the subsequent attack on Moscow the troops would have to retrace their steps (from Lochvitsa to Roslavl, that is to say 275 miles), with consequent heavy wear to their strength and to their equipment. I described the condition of the roads over which my Group would have to move, giving as example the ones I knew as far as Unecha, and the unending supply problems which would become greater with every day's march towards the Ukraine. Finally, I touched on the enormous difficulties which must arise if the proposed operation were not terminated as fast as was now planned and were to be protracted into the period of bad weather. It would then be too late to strike the final blow for Moscow this year. I ended with the plea that all other considerations, no matter how important they might seem, be subordinated to the one vital necessity—the primary achievement of a military decision. Once that was secured, everything else would be ours for the taking.

Hitler let me speak to the end without once interrupting me. He then began to talk and described in detail the considerations which had led him to make a different decision. He said that the raw materials and agriculture of the Ukraine were vitally necessary for the future prosecution of the war. He spoke once again of the need of neutralising the Crimea, 'that Soviet aircraft carrier for attacking the Rumanian oilfields.' For the first time I heard him use the phrase: 'My generals know nothing about the economic aspects of war.' Hitler's words all led up to this: he had given strict orders that the attack on Kiev was to be the immediate strategic object and all actions were to be carried out with that in mind. I here saw for the first time a spectacle with which I was later to become very familiar: all those present nodded in agreement with every sentence that Hitler uttered, while I was left alone with my point of view. Undoubtedly he had already held forth many times on the subject of his reasons that had led him to take his strange decision. I was extremely sorry that neither Field-Marshal von Brauchitsch nor Colonel-General Halder had accompanied me to this conference, on the outcome of which, according to them, so very much depended, perhaps even the result of the war as a whole. In view of the *OKW's* unanimous opposition to my remarks, I avoided all further arguments on that occasion; I did not then think it would be right to make an angry scene with the head of the German State when he was surrounded by his advisers.

Since the decision to attack the Ukraine had now been confirmed,

Sketch Map 16

MILES
10 5 0   10   20   30   40

Smolensk

SS "R"

Dnieper

Elnya

Spas-Demiansk

to Moscow
180 Miles

10.Pz.

XXXXVI

6.D.R.

2/3.7.

1/3.7.

23.

19?.

Situation on 24.8.41.
(Conference with Hitler.)

→ Advances 22/23.8
  Situation 24.8.41.
  Enemy Positions 22.8.41.

Roslavl

18.
Pz.

Krichev

16?.

Miloslavitchi

258.

XXXXVII

29.
m.

Desna →

Elmnts
29.m.

Masse 4.Pz.

Bielynkovitchi

34.

31.

16?.

6.D.

10.m.

Surash

Elmnts
18.Pz.

to Bryansk

Elmnts
17.Pz.
Mglin

17.
Pz.

Pochep

Elmnts
4.Pz.

XXIV.

Unecha

Sudost →

112.

Klinzy

4.D.

Elm.

3.Pz.

Trubchevsk

1.K.D.

131.

7.Div.

3.Pz.D.

Starodub

Pogar

Desna →

Gomel

Novosybkov

to Kiev
210 Miles

260.

I did my best at least to ensure that it be carried out as well as possible. I therefore begged Hitler not to split my Panzer Group, as was intended, but to commit the whole Group to the operation; thus a rapid victory might be won before the autumn rains came. Those rains would turn the trackless countryside into a morass and the movement of motorised formations would be paralysed. This request of mine was granted.

It was long after midnight by the time I reached my quarters. On this same date, the 23rd of August, the *OKH* issued an order to Army Group Centre which contained the following: 'The object is to destroy as much of the strength of the Russian Fifth Army as possible, and to open the Dnieper crossings for Army Group South with maximum speed. For this purpose a strong force, preferably commanded by Colonel-General Guderian, is to move forward, with its right wing directed on Chernigov.' I was not informed of this order prior to my conversation with Hitler. Colonel-General Halder had not taken the opportunity to tell me about it during the course of the day. On the morning of the 24th I visited the Chief of the Army General Staff and told him of the failure of this last attempt to persuade Hitler to change his mind. I did not think that what I had to say would come as a surprise to Halder; yet to my amazement he suffered a complete nervous collapse, which led him to make accusations and imputations which were utterly unjustified. It is only the condition of Halder's nerves which can explain the telephone conversations he had about me with Army Group Centre and the resultant, quite untrue, portrait of myself that certain subordinates of that headquarters have seen fit to paint in their post-war publications. He was particularly angered by my attempts to ensure that the operation which was now ordered should, from the very beginning, be carried out in adequate strength. He showed absolutely no understanding of my point of view and, indeed, later on did his best to hinder me. We parted without having reached agreement. I flew back to my Panzer Group with orders to start the move towards the Ukraine on August 25th.

On August 24th XXIV Panzer Corps captured Novosybkov and threw the enemy back in the area Unecha–Starodub.

The Battle of Kiev

The most important part of Hitler's orders, dated August 21st, which laid the groundwork for the forthcoming operations, ran as follows:

I am not in agreement with the proposals submitted by the Army for the prosecution of the war in the East and dated August 18th.

I therefore order as follows:

1. Of primary importance before the outbreak of winter is not the capture of Moscow but rather the occupation of the Crimea, of the industrial and

coalmining area of the Donetz basin, the cutting of the Russian supply routes from the Caucasian oilfields, and, in the north, the investment of Leningrad and the establishment of contact with the Finns.

2. An unusually favourable operational situation has arisen as a result of our troops reaching the line Gomel–Pochep; this must be immediately exploited through a concentric operation by the inner wings of Army Groups South and Centre. The objective must be not merely to drive the Russian Fifth Army back across the Dnieper by means of a solitary attack by Sixth Army, but to destroy that enemy before he manages to withdraw behind the line the Desna–Konotop–the Sula. This will give Army Group South the necessary security for crossing the central Dnieper and for continuing to advance with its centre and left wing in the direction Rostov–Kharkov.

3. Without consideration of future operations Army Group Centre is therefore to employ as much force as is necessary for the achievement of its objective, the destruction of the Russian Fifth Army, while occupying such positions on the centre of its own front as will enable minimum forces to ensure the defeat of enemy attacks in that area.

4. The capture of the Crimean peninsula is of extreme importance for safeguarding our oil supplies from Rumania.

This order, whose existence was unknown to me when I talked to Hitler on the 23rd, provided the foundation for the instructions that my Panzer Group now received from the *OKH* and from Army Group Centre. My most grievous disappointment was the removal of XLVI Panzer Corps from my Panzer Group. Despite Hitler's promise to the contrary, Army Group withdrew this corps from my command and put it in reserve, behind Fourth Army, in the area Roslavl–Smolensk. I would thus have to embark on the new operations with only the XXIV and XLVII Panzer Corps, a force which had already been recognised and described as inadequate. My protests to Army Group fell on deaf ears.

I was given Konotop as my first objective. Further instructions for co-operation with Army Group South would be issued later.

The dispositions of my Panzer Group were now such that XXIV Panzer Corps in the area Unecha had not only to fight its way forward and break through the Russian forces once again, but also simultaneously to protect the Group's right flank against the enemy attempting to escape eastwards from the Gomel area. The task of XLVII Panzer Corps was as follows: with its only immediately available division, the 17th Panzer, it was to launch an attack to cover the Panzer Group's left flank against the considerable enemy forces on the east bank of the Sudost River to the south of Pochep. In this, the dry, season the Sudost did not provide a reliable obstacle.

Already the 29th (Motorised) Infantry Division was protecting an area of 50 miles along the Desna and the upper Sudost. To the east of Starodub the enemy still held positions to the west of the Sudost, in the flank of XXIV Panzer Corps. Even when the 29th (Motorised) Infantry Division had been relieved by infantry units, our left flank from Pochep to our first objective, Konotop, would still be some 110 miles long, and it was only then that the major operations would begin and the chief danger arise. Intelligence of the enemy's strength on our eastern flank was extremely fragmentary. In any case I had to reckon that the task of guarding that flank would necessitate the full employment there of XLVII Panzer Corps. The combat ability of our spearhead must further suffer from the fact that XXIV Panzer Corps was being committed to this new operation without having had any time for rest and maintenance; and this after a long and uninterrupted sequence of heavy battles and exhausting marches.

On August 25th the following advances were made:

XXIV Panzer Corps. 10th (Motorised) Infantry Division moved through Cholmy and Avdeievka; 3rd Panzer Division, through Kostobobr–Novgorod Severskie to the Desna; 4th Panzer Division, initially engaged in clearing the enemy from the west bank of the Sudost, was to be relieved by elements of XLVII Panzer Corps and then to advance behind 3rd Panzer Division.

XLVII Panzer Corps. 17th Panzer Division moved through Pochep to the southern bank of the Sudost and attacked towards Trubchevsk. Then, by crossing to the left bank of the Desna and pushing forward south-westward along the river, it was to facilitate XXIV Panzer Corps' crossing of that wide stream. The remaining units of the corps were on the march from the Roslavl area.

Early on the morning of the 25th I went to the 17th Panzer Division in order to take part in the division's attack across the Sudost and its tributary, the Rog, immediately to the south. I drove along a terrible sandy track, a very bad road, and a number of my vehicles broke down. As early as 12.30 hrs. I had to signal from Mglin for replacements of armoured command vehicles, personnel lorries, and motor-cycles. This was a grim omen for the future. At 14.30 hrs. I arrived at the headquarters of the 17th Panzer Division, 3 miles north of Pochep. It seemed to me that the calculation of the force necessary to carry out this difficult attack had been incorrect and that the force itself was therefore insufficient. As a result the advance was likely to be too slow in relationship to the speed of XXIV Panzer Corps. I informed the divisional commander, General Ritter von Thoma, and the corps commander, who arrived shortly afterwards, of my views in this matter of speed. In order to gain a personal impression of the enemy I went up to the front line, where Rifle Regiment 63 was attacking, and participated in a part of their attack on foot. I spent the night in Pochep.

Early on the 26th of August I visited an advanced artillery O.P. on the northern bank of the Rog, accompanied by my adjutant, Major Büsing: I wanted to see the effect of our dive-bomber attacks on the Russians' river defences. The bombs fell where they were supposed to, but their actual effect was negligible. On the other hand the psychological impact of the dive bombing on the Russians was considerable; they kept down in their fox-holes and as a result we crossed the river almost without casualties. Owing to careless behaviour on the part of an officer our presence in the O.P. became known to the Russians and we were subjected to well-aimed mortar fire. A shell landing very close to us wounded five officers, including Major Büsing, who was sitting close beside me. It was a wonder that I remained unhurt.

Opposite us were the Russian 269th and 282nd Divisions. After observing the crossing of the Rog and the completion of a bridge, I drove in the afternoon through Mglin to Unecha, where my head-quarters was now located. On my way there I received a surprising and most gratifying signal: by brilliant employment of his tanks Lieutenant Buchterkirch (of the 6th Panzer Regiment of 3rd Panzer Division) had managed to capture the 750-yard bridge over the Desna to the east of Novgorod Severskie intact. This stroke of good fortune should make our future operations considerably less difficult.

I did not reach my headquarters until nearly midnight. There I found General Paulus, who had arrived during the course of the afternoon in order to examine the situation: he was then *Oberquartiermeister I* at the *OKH*, or chief operational assistant to General Halder. He had not been empowered to make decisions. During my absence Paulus had discussed the position with Lieutenant-Colonel Freiherr von Lieben-stein, and had subsequently been in communication with the *OKH:* he had suggested that a unified command be set up to control the Panzer Group and the left wing of Second Army and that the 1st Cavalry Division be committed on the Panzer Group's left flank. He received the mystifying reply that there was no question for the time being of subordinating any elements of Second Army and that the movements of Second Army were 'to be regarded as simply tactical.' 1st Cavalry Division remained with Second Army, whose point of main effort was on its right. The Panzer Group was blamed for moving units in direc-tions other than that laid down by the operational order. But the enemy along the Desna on our deep left flank was too strong to be ignored, as the *OKH* apparently wished us to do. He had to be defeated there before we could pursue our southward advance. The next morning I had another conversation with Paulus in order to explain my train of thought to him. He faithfully repeated my remarks to the Chief of the Army General Staff, but they made no impression in view of the general animosity towards myself that reigned in those quarters.

By the evening of August 26th the left wing of Second Army was immediately to the south of Novosybkov. My boundary with Second Army was Klinzy–Cholmy–Sosniza (on the Desna, north-east of Makoshino), and with Fourth Army Surash–Unecha–Pochep–Brassovo.

Of XXIV Panzer Corps, the 10th (Motorised) Infantry Division was at Cholmy and Avdeievka; the 3rd Panzer Division at the Desna bridge, south of Novgorod Severskie; the 4th Panzer Division in action with the enemy south-east of Starodub.

Of XLVII Panzer Corps, 17th Panzer Division was fighting near Semzy, to the south of Pochep; 29th (Motorised) Infantry Division was guarding the Panzer Group's left flank from Pochep to Shukovka. With the arrival of the infantry divisions of the XII and LIII Army Corps it assembled its units towards its right wing. Meanwhile, the leading elements of the 18th Panzer Division, moving down from the north, had passed through Roslavl.

During this time infantry units were marching from west to east, at right angles to the line of advance of my Panzer Group, the 167th Infantry Division through Mglin, the 31st Infantry Division to the north of that town, the 34th Infantry Division through Kletnia, the 52nd Infantry Division through Perelasy, and the 267th and 252nd Infantry Divisions along the road Krichev–Cherikov–Propoisk. All these divisions belonged to Second Army. If only a fraction of this force had been sent southwards from the very beginning of the Kiev offensive, repeated crises on XXIV Panzer Corps' right flank would have been avoided.

On August 26th enemy resistance to Second Army stiffened along the Desna. In order to ensure a rapid victory I requested the despatch of XLVI Panzer Corps. My request was refused by the *OKH*.

On August 29th strong enemy forces, with air support, attacked XXIV Panzer Corps from the south and west. The corps was compelled to discontinue its own attacks by 3rd Panzer and 10th (Motorised) Infantry Divisions. Its task of clearing the enemy from the west bank of the Sudost completed, 4th Panzer Division was moved up through Novgorod Severskie to support 3rd Panzer Division. On this day I visited XXIV Panzer Corps as well as the 3rd and 4th Panzer Divisions, and after studying the situation I decided to order XXIV Panzer Corps as follows: the threat to the corps' right flank was to be neutralised on the 30th, and the southward advance resumed on the 31st. Meanwhile, XLVII Panzer Corps was to continue its attack along the eastern bank of the Sudost, and later of the Desna, in the direction of Novgorod Severskie. At 18.00 hrs. I flew back to my headquarters. This was the last time that I was accompanied by my first operations officer, Lieutenant-Colonel Bayerlein, who was to be transferred to Africa. His successor was Major Wolf.

By August 31st the bridgehead over the Desna had been considerably widened and the 4th Panzer Division was moved across the river. The 10th (Motorised) Infantry Division succeeded in crossing the Desna, to the north of Korop, but was thrown back again to the west bank by heavy Russian counter-attacks, besides being attacked on its right flank by strong enemy forces. By sending in the very last men of the division, in this case the Field Bakery Company, a catastrophe to the right flank was just avoided. The Russians attacked the XLVII Panzer Corps, moving the 108th and, from September 1st, the 110th Tank Brigades west and north-west from Trubchevsk for this purpose; the valiant 17th Panzer Division had a hard time. The 29th (Motorised) Infantry Division was sent across the Novgorod Severskie bridge and then swung north to protect the northern flank of XXIV Panzer Corps' bridgehead and to help 17th Panzer Division's advance. The 18th Panzer Division had relieved the 4th Panzer Division in the Sudost sector between the junction of that river with the Desna and Pochep. Since the beginning of the operation on August 25th XXIV Panzer Corps had so far taken 7,500 prisoners, XLVII Panzer Corps 12,000.

In view of the attacks on both flanks and heavy Russian pressure against the front, particularly against the 10th (Motorised) Infantry Division, it seemed to me doubtful whether the strength available was sufficient for a continuation of the attack. I therefore once again requested the Army Group to relinquish XLVI Panzer Corps. However, at first, only Infantry Regiment *Gross-Deutschland* was released, on August 30th; this was followed by the 1st Cavalry Division on September 1st and *SS-Das Reich*, from Smolensk, on the 2nd. A Russian penetration six miles deep, in the sector of the 23rd Infantry Division to the south of Elnya, had necessitated the employment there of 10th Panzer Division in a frontal counter attack. Infantry Regiment *Gross-Deutschland* was directed to Novgorod Severskie and *SS-Das Reich* to the right wing of XXIV Panzer Corps, where they arrived on the 2nd and 3rd of September, respectively.

This drop-by-drop method of reinforcement led me, on September 1st, to hold a wireless conversation with Army Group in which I requested that I be sent the whole XLVI Panzer Corps, and also the 7th and 11th Panzer Divisions and the 14th (Motorised) Infantry Division, which I knew were not committed at the time. With so adequate a mass of force I believed I could soon bring the Kiev offensive to a speedy and successful conclusion. The immediate consequence of the wireless conversation was the release of *SS-Das Reich*. But over and above that an intercept station of the *OKH* had listened in to what was said and this resulted in a positive uproar. The first echo came from the *OKH* liaison officer, Lieutenant-Colonel Nagel: a conference with Hitler ensued: and finally the *OKW* took steps which had most unfortunate results as far as I was concerned. But of all this, more later.

On September 2nd Field-Marshal Kesselring, who commanded an Air Fleet, appeared at my Panzer Group Headquarters. He brought the news that Army Group South was apparently making progress and had secured several bridgeheads across the Dnieper. As for future operations, obscurity reigned; opinions varied between Kharkov and Kiev.

On this day Generals Model and Ritter von Thoma were both slightly wounded.

On September 3rd I drove past the rear elements of the 10th (Motorised) Infantry Division and the fighting men of the field bakery to the motor-cyclists of *SS-Das Reich*, near Avdeievka. The enemy was to the west of this place and the SS Reconnaissance Battalion was advancing towards him. To begin with there was a certain amount of confusion, but the clear-headed divisional commander, General Hausser, soon put this to rights. I found this officer in Avdeievka and told him to be prepared to attack Sosnitza on the 4th. The 5th Machine-gun Battalion, which had just arrived from Roslavl, was placed under his command.

At noon I visited the 10th (Motorised) Infantry Division which had been heavily engaged during the last few days and had suffered tragically high casualties. The division enjoyed a certain relief from the arrival of the 4th Panzer Division along the southern bank of the Desna. As a result the Russians had discontinued their preparations, already referred to above, for a crossing of the river. During these last few days the 10th (Motorised) Infantry Division had been opposed by the 10th Russian Tank Brigade and the 293rd, 24th, 143rd, and 42nd Divisions, that is to say by an enormously superior enemy. I briefed the divisional commander, General von Loeper, on the situation and on the intentions of his neighbour, *SS-Das Reich*, and arranged that the right wing of his division should co-operate with the attack by the SS on the next day. I then visited a bridgehead to the south of the Desna held by the II Battalion of Infantry Regiment 20, whose troops made a good impression; I went on to see the I Battalion of the same regiment which had been forced back in its bridgehead a few days before but had soon made full amends for this misfortune. This battalion also made a good impression and I was able to express my conviction that in future it, too, would do its duty.

I learned from my staff by wireless that the 1st Cavalry Division was once again under command of the Panzer Group and was being brought up on the right of *SS-Das Reich*. I visited the commander of the SS division once again, to ensure that *SS-Das Reich* was covering the supply lines of the 10th (Motorised) Infantry Division, and then returned to my headquarters. I there learned that Borsna and Konotop, which lay in the lines of our advance, remained our next objectives. Corps headquarters of XLVI Panzer Corps, together with half the corps troops, were once again placed under the Panzer Group's command. Both the corps at the front reported the capture of 2,500 prisoners each, while an *ad hoc* formation, commanded by the Engineer-General Bacher and intended to protect our rear, had taken a further 1,200. XXIV Panzer Corps was insistent about the growing threat to its ever-lengthening southern flank and the increasing weakness of its spearhead. Krolevetz was captured.

On this day the liaison officer of the *OKH*, Lieutenant-Colonel Nagel, took part in a conference at Army Group headquarters, Borissov, at which the Commander-in-Chief of the Army was present. Nagel took this opportunity to express my views on the situation; he was, therefore, described as a 'loudspeaker and propagandist' and immediately relieved of his appointment. I was very sorry that this clear-sighted officer, who incidentally had a first-class knowledge of the Russian language, should have been punished for doing his duty, which was simply to express the views prevalent at the front.

But that was not all. That evening it began to rain and the roads were soon turned into mire. Two-thirds of *SS-Das Reich*, which was moving forward, was stuck fast.

I spent September 4th at the front with the 4th Panzer Division where I also found General von Geyr. It took me four and a half hours to cover 45 miles, so softened were the roads by the brief fall of rain. The 4th Panzer Division was engaged in attacking towards Korop–Krasnopolie. The enemy here had up to now resisted stubbornly, even against our tanks. But after the dive bombers had gone in his main resistance seemed to be broken. From captured documents General von Geyr had reached the conclusion that a continuation of the attack towards Sosnitza would be particularly profitable, since this would be along the boundary between the Russian Thirteenth and Twenty-first Armies. It was even possible that a gap might there be found. The 3rd Panzer Division reported progress. I looked for this division and found it advancing towards the River Seim, through Mutino and Spasskoie. General Model, too, had the impression that he had found a weak spot, if not an actual gap, in the enemy's defences. I told Model to push on

Sketch Map 18

The Battle of Kiev

| 10 | 0 | 10 | 20 | 30 | 40 | 50 | 60 | 70 MILES |

Situation 4.9.41.
" 6.9.41.
" 9.9.41.
" 11.9.41.
" 14.9.41.

to the Konotop–Bielopolie railway as soon as he was over the Seim, and to cut that line. While driving back I gave the orders for the next day to my staff by wireless. I learned in return that we might expect Hitler to interfere in the operations of the Panzer Group.

A telephone message from the Army Group had informed us that the *OKW* was dissatisfied with the operations of the Panzer Group and particularly with the employment of XLVII Panzer Corps on the eastern bank of the Desna. A report on my situation and intentions was demanded. That night an order came from the *OKH* in which it was stated that the attack by XLVII Panzer Corps was to be discontinued and the corps transferred back to the west bank of the Desna. These orders were cast in an uncouth language which offended me. The effect of the order on XLVII Panzer Corps was crushing. Both the corps headquarters and the divisions believed themselves to be on the brink of victory. The withdrawal of the corps and its re-deployment on the west bank would require more time than was needed for the completion of the attack. This corps alone had, since August 25th, captured 155 guns, 120 tanks, and 17,000 prisoners, while in the same period XXIV Panzer Corps had taken a further 13,000 prisoners, but for this no word of recognition was forthcoming.

On September 5th the 1st Cavalry Division was ordered to Pogar and placed under command of Fourth Army. We would have preferred to see the division used as a mobile flank guard to XLVII Panzer Corps on our left wing. Now its powers of mobility were to be wasted since it was to be employed as a static flank guard along the Sudost.

On this day *SS-Das Reich* captured Sosnitza.

Fourth Army was ordered to evacuate the Elnya salient. By now the casualties, which I had sought to avoid by a timely withdrawal in August, had been suffered to occur.

I spent September 6th again with *SS-Das Reich*. It was engaged in attacking the railway bridge over the Desna, near Makoshino. I went to some trouble to provide air support for this. As a result of the bad roads the whole division was not yet assembled. On the way there I passed a number of its units, some on the march, others resting in the woods. The excellent discipline of the troops made a first-class impression and they loudly expressed their satisfaction at once again forming part of the Panzer Group. The bridge was captured during the afternoon and a further crossing-place over the Desna thus secured. My staff convoy was compelled on several occasions to drive through hostile artillery fire, but suffered no casualties or damage. On the way back we met elements of the 1st Cavalry Division and SS units moving up on foot because of the bad condition of the road. At the divisional head-quarters I gave orders that the Desna bridgehead be sufficiently en-larged so that the division might attack from the bridgehead towards the west bank of the Seim and thus help XXIV Panzer Corps to cross that river.

On September 7th the 3rd and 4th Panzer Divisions succeeded in establishing bridgeheads on the south bank of the Seim. On this day the Army Group ordered an advance to the line Neshin–Monastir-shtchino, with point of main effort towards Neshin. The order was modified at 05.25 hrs. on the 8th by the signal: 'New direction of advance Borsna–Romny, point of main effort right.' On the same day I had a conversation at Second Army, in Gomel, with the Commander-in-Chief of the Army concerning the operations planned for early October with objective Moscow. Apart from this Field-Marshal von Brauchitsch referred again to XLVII Panzer Corps' battles towards Trubchevsk; he objected to my request for reinforcement which I had made by radio on the 1st of September, on the grounds that it might have been overheard by the *OKW*; and he expressed his opinion that at that period the Panzer Group had unnecessarily widened its operational front. l justified my actions by pointing out that the strong enemy forces on my left flank could not simply be ignored and had to be defeated. Up to now we had taken 40,000 prisoners and captured 250 guns. Our spearheads were nearing the Bachmach–Konotop railroad.

On this day Second Army took Chernigov. It was ordered to advance Neshin–Borsna.

Also on this day Lieutenant-Colonel Nagel left us and his successor, Major von Kahlden, arrived to take his place. He performed his mission with the same tact and understanding as Nagel and, in his time, Below before him.

In Army Group North, Panzer Group 4 and the Eighteenth Army were preparing for an assault on the outer defences of Leningrad. This attack was to be launched on September 9th.

On September 9th XXIV Panzer Corps crossed the Seim. I was with the 4th Panzer Division during this battle and watched units of Rifle Regiments 33 and 12 advance on Gorodishtche. Dive bombers gave effective support to the spearheads of the rifle regiments and of Panzer Regiment 35. But the limited combat strength of all units showed how badly they needed rest and recuperation after two and a half months of exhausting fighting and heavy casualties. Unfortunately there could be no question of that for the time being. In the late afternoon, at the headquarters of XXIV Panzer Corps, General Freiherr von Geyr told me that the SS were also attacking and the 3rd Panzer Division intended to push on towards Konotop. Prisoners had stated that the Fortieth

Russian Army had been put in between the Thirteenth and Twenty-first. The ammunition situation was tolerable but fuel supplies were running low.

In the evening I flew back to my headquarters at Krolevetz. There I found that Army Group had sent us a message during the day: the 1st Cavalry Division was not to remain along the Sudost, but was to be moved farther north. As a result the 18th Panzer Division could not now be moved up behind the Panzer Group and fresh troops were needed to exploit our success on the Seim. In the evening we received heartening news: XXIV Panzer Corps had in fact found the enemy's weak spot, between Baturin and Konotop, and advance elements of 3rd Panzer Division were driving on Romny, our objective. The division was thus behind the enemy's lines. The problem now was how to make the most of this success as quickly as possible; in view of our limited strength, the bad roads and, above all, our 145 miles long south-east flank, this was no easy task. Since I had no reserves available, all I could do to add the necessary punch to 3rd Panzer Division's advance was to go with the division myself. I therefore decided to drive to the front again on the 10th of September.

When I arrived at Ksendovka General Freiherr von Geyr informed me that the 3rd Panzer Division had captured Romny and seized a bridgehead across the River Romen. The 3rd Panzer Division had by-passed Konotop without capturing the town. The 4th Panzer Division was advancing on Bachmach, and *SS-Das Reich* on Borsna. Prisoners' statements revealed that the Russian forces fighting in the Ukraine were still strong enough to defend themselves but were no longer capable of launching an attack. General Freiherr von Geyr was instructed to ensure the rapid occupation of the important railway station at Konotop, through which our supplies would have to come; 4th Panzer Division was to continue southward from Bachmach and *SS-Das Reich* was to move on to Kustovzy from Borsna. This last division was to be responsible for maintaining contact with Second Army. I then drove on to the 3rd Panzer Division.

On the Seim bridge we were attacked by Russian bombers, on the road we were shelled by Russian artillery. As a result of rain the condition of the road had still further deteriorated and it was dotted with vehicles hopelessly stuck in the mud. It was impossible for the columns to observe their customary march discipline and they were badly straggled out. The machines for towing the guns had, moreover, to tow the lorries.

At Chmeliov I arranged for accommodation for the night with 3rd Panzer Division's headquarters, since there could be no question of my driving back to my headquarters that day. I then went on to Romny. To the north of that town the Romen provided a strong defensive line, which the Russians had further improved by means of anti-tank ditches and wire entanglements. The fact that the Russians had been unable to hold this strong position was proof that the 3rd Panzer Division had taken them completely by surprise and that with one more push our break-through would be complete. Immediately outside Romny I found General Model, who briefed me on the details of his operation. The town was in his hands, but enemy stragglers were still at large in the gardens and it was therefore impossible to drive through except in armoured vehicles. The mopping up was to start at 17.00 hrs. In the northern part of the town I came upon a group of staff officers receiving orders from Colonel Kleemann. They were particularly worried by Russian air attacks, since our air force was incapable of offering adequate fighter cover; the reason for this was that the Russian airfields were located in a fair-weather zone, while our fields were in a bad-weather zone and the rain had made them unusable. We were at that moment attacked by three Russian machines firing their machine-guns; the bombs fell elsewhere.

From Romny I sent a wireless signal to my staff, giving my instructions for the next day. XLVI Panzer Corps, with the 17th Panzer Division and Infantry Regiment *Gross-Deutschland*, was to advance on Putivl and Shilovka (ten miles to the south of Putivl). I requested strong fighter cover for Model.

On this day Bachmach was captured. Infantry Regiment *Gross-Deutschland* reached Putivl. Army Group instructed us to make preparations to attack towards the River Udai on either side of Priluki.

Army Group South was preparing a crossing of the Dnieper, near Kremenchug. From here they were to advance north and meet us near Romny.

During the whole night it poured with rain. My drive back on the 11th, therefore, proved very difficult. The first to fall out were the motor-cyclists. It was heavy going even for my cross-country vehicle with a four-wheel drive. Our command tanks and a towing vehicle borrowed from the artillery finally got us going again. At an average speed of 6 miles per hour we drove through the mud to Girovka, where I found the regimental headquarters of Lieutenant-Colonel Audörsch; the telephone lines were broken and it was in vain that I attempted to find out what the situation was. I finally learned from the motor-cyclists of 3rd Panzer Division that we had captured Konotop. 4 miles to the north of Girovka I came across the Reconnaissance Battalion of the 10th (Motorised) Infantry Division. At 14.00 hrs. I found General von Loeper in Konotop and told him what had happened at Romny, and at 15.30 hrs. I arrived at XXIV Panzer Corps' headquarters. I there heard that *SS-Das Reich* had taken Borsna. The corps was ordered to advance with its right wing through Monastirishtche and with its left through Piriatin to Romny. The XLVI Panzer Corps was told to push on southwards through Putivl.

At 18.30 hrs. I arrived back at my headquarters. On the 10th I had covered 100 miles in 10 hours, on the 11th 80 miles in 10½ hours. The boggy roads made any faster progress impossible. These time-wasting drives gave me sufficient insight into the difficulties that lay ahead of us. Only a man who has personally experienced what life on those canals of mud we called roads was like can form any picture of what the troops and their equipment had to put up with and can truly judge the situation at the front and the consequent effect on our operations. The fact that our military leaders made no attempt to see these conditions for themselves and, initially at least, refused to believe the reports of those who did, was to lead to bitter results, unspeakable suffering and many avoidable misfortunes.

Army Group informed us that evening that Colonel-General von Kleist's Panzer Group 1 had been unable to reach its objective on account of the mud. This was hardly surprising to anyone who knew the condition of the roads as described above.

17th Panzer Division reached Voronesh–Gluchov, and on the 11th of September Gluchov.

During the course of September 12th Panzer Group 1 advanced through Semenovko to Lubny; the 3rd Panzer Division was pushed forward to Lochvitsa and captured the bridge over the Ssula to the north of that town. The Second Army, held up by bad weather, was approaching Neshin.

Army Group North believed that they had made a decisive penetration of the defensive front before Leningrad.

On September 13th we requested Army Group Centre that the 18th Panzer Division, which was still guarding the Sudost sector of our deep left flank, be relieved by infantry; this request was refused, with the comment that it came too late to make any difference to the ultimate decision. No consideration was given to the confused situation on our eastern flank or to the potential dangers that threatened from that quarter and which made the creation of at least a weak reserve a matter of urgency.

Panzer Group 1 took Lubny.

On September 14th my Panzer Group headquarters was moved to Konotop. The bad weather continued. Air reconnaissance was im-

Sketch Map 19

Crisis at Romny – Putivl.
Situation 18.9.41.

possible. Ground reconnaissance was stuck in the mud. The units of
the XLVI and XLVII Panzer Corps detailed to protect the flank were
almost immobilised. The uncertainty along the protracted south-
eastern flank increased from day to day. In order at least to ensure
contact with Panzer Group Kleist I decided to drive to XXIV Panzer
Corps despite the existing difficulties. My road ran through Krolovetz–
Baturin–Konotop–Romny to Lochvitsa. I met General Freiherr von
Geyr in Michenki (4 miles to the south of Baturin) and he informed me
that there appeared to be enemy forces in the Lochvitsa area and that
it was therefore important that the gap between our forces and Kleist's
be filled. He had, in consequence, ordered his divisions to advance to
the Ssula and close it. A strong Russian concentration was known to
exist near Ssencha, 7 miles to the south of Lochvitsa. I drove on
through Romny, where I saw crowds of people in their Sunday best
going peaceably about their business. After Pochep and Konotop,
Romny was the best-preserved Russian town that we had yet seen. I
reached Model's headquarters, at Lochvitsa, just as darkness was
falling. Up to then he had only managed to bring one of his regiments
this far forward; the rest of his men were struggling along in the mud
far to the rear. He informed me that the strong Russian concentration
consisted primarily of supply troops. Only some of the units in question
were equipped for combat. The Russian tanks that had been seen had
probably been withdrawn from maintenance depots to cover the
retreat. Inside the vast Kiev pocket there were presumably elements of
five Russian armies, the Twenty-first, Fifth, Thirty-seventh, Twenty-
sixth, and Thirty-eighth.

Enemy attacks on our south-eastern flank, in the area of Yampol, to
the south of Putivl, were beaten off.

Büsing, Kahlden, and I spent the night in the Lochvitsa schoolhouse.
I spoke to Liebenstein by wireless and ordered that the 10th (Motorised)
Infantry Division be brought up with all speed to Romny and the rear
elements of 3rd Panzer Division be freed to move to Lochvitsa. The
schoolhouse was a solid building and well appointed for its purpose;
indeed, almost all the schools in Soviet Russia were in good condition.
A great deal was done there in the way of schools, hospitals, nurseries,
and sports buildings. Institutions of this sort were in general kept clean
and neat; the occasional exception—as in other matters—proved the
rule.

Early on the 15th of September I visited the advance guard of the
3rd Panzer Division, which was commanded by Major Frank; during
the previous day it had advanced southwards from Lochvitsa and
thrown back the Russians to the west; and in the night it had overrun
fifteen Russian lorries full of riflemen, some of whom had been killed

and the rest made prisoner. From Frank's O.P., near Lubny, a fine view could be obtained over the countryside and Russian supply columns were to be seen marching from west to east. These movements were stopped. I found Model with the II Battalion of Rifle Regiment 3 and he gave me his opinion of the situation. I next visited a number of units of the 3rd Panzer Division and spoke with Lieutenant-Colonel Munzel, the commander of Panzer Regiment 6. On this day Munzel had at his disposal only one Panzer IV, three Panzer III's and six Panzer II's, that it to say ten tanks were all that was left of a whole regiment. These figures give a vivid picture of how badly the troops needed a rest and a period for maintenance. They show that these brave men had given of their last in order to reach the objectives assigned them.

I radioed Liebenstein to instruct XXIV Panzer Corps that *SS-Das Reich* be sent south to the River Udai, between Kustovzy and Pere-volochnoie, and thence be directed on Ssrebnoie–Beresovka in conjunction with 4th Panzer Division. 10th (Motorised) Infantry Division was to advance on Glinsk, to the west of Romny. I then boarded a plane to the south of Romny and flew back to my Panzer Group headquarters.

On this day 17th Panzer Division began to move towards Putivl.

In the evening I found Liebenstein in Konotop. He had flown to Army Group during the day and had there been given our instructions for the next phase of the campaign, the advance on Moscow. The purpose of these new operations was to be 'the destruction of the final remnants of Army Group Timoshenko.' Three-quarters of the German Army was to be committed for this purpose. Liebenstein's renewed request for the release of 18th Panzer Division had been turned down; Field-Marshal von Bock had remarked that he had asked Colonel-General Halder which were the more important, the business in the south or the preparations for the new undertaking, and Halder had replied 'the latter.'

On September 16th we moved our advanced headquarters to Romny. The encirclement of the Russians was progressing. On this day we made contact with Panzer Group Kleist (which formed the southern arm of the pincer-move). *SS-Das Reich* took Priluki. Second Army was withdrawn from the front for the new operation. Before the Battle of Poltava, in December 1708, Romny had been for a few days the headquarters of King Charles XII of Sweden.

I spent September 17th visiting the 4th Panzer Division in Ssrebnoie. Since no firm contact had been established between this division and *SS-Das Reich*, to its right, I decided to go on to the latter. The road led through no-man's-land. In the woods to either side there was ample evidence of recent Russian encampments. Immediately outside Perevolochnoie I saw two gun barrels pointed ominously in our direction; we passed a few anxious moments before I established that the gun crews had fled, leaving their horses behind a nearby haystack. In the middle of the village I came upon the motor-cyclists of the SS division who were engaged in fighting for the Udai crossing. From here I went on to Kustovzy, also on the Udai, where other SS troops were engaged. Colonel Bittrich briefed me on the course of the battle. I then drove back for 60 miles through no-man's-land, Ivaniza and Yaroshevka to Romny. The road was so appalling that I only arrived back at my Group headquarters towards dawn.

On the 17th of September we arranged with Panzer Group Kleist that the 25th (Motorised) Infantry Division relieve the 3rd Panzer Division. Thus this brave division would at last have a chance to repair its vehicles.

On this day the Russians made appreciable efforts to take the offensive against our eastern flank. The 10th (Motorised) Infantry Division and Infantry Regiment *Gross-Deutschland* had to fight fiercely in the area of Konotop. There was an increase of enemy strength opposite our Desna bridgehead near Novgorod Severskie. It is true that the Russian railroads from the east towards Kiev had been repeatedly cut by our bombers; but the Russians displayed great skill in repairing them again, so that the appearance of fresh forces along our excessively protracted flank must be anticipated in the near future.

In the area of Army Group North, Dietskoie Selo, the former Tsarkoie Selo, had been captured and the attack against Leningrad itself was begun. The mass of the panzer divisions which had been employed here were placed at the disposal of Army Group Centre and began to move south: these were the staff of Panzer Group 4, the staffs of XLI, LVI, and LVII Corps, the 3rd (Motorised) Infantry Division, and the 6th, 20th and, later, 1st Panzer Divisions.

On September 18th we found ourselves in the midst of a crisis in the Romny area. Since early morning the sounds of fighting were audible from the left flank and these increased in intensity as the morning went on. A fresh enemy—the 9th Russian Cavalry Division and another division with tanks—was driving on Romny from the east in three columns, and managed to penetrate to within half a mile of the edge of the town. From one of the high watchtowers of the prison, on the outskirts of Romny, I had an uninterrupted view of the enemy attack. XXIV Panzer Corps was made responsible for the defence. Available were two battalions of the 10th (Motorised) Infantry

Sketch Map 20

Pochep   Sudost

Desna

10 5 10   20   30   MILES
                              40

1. Cav.

18. Pz.   Pogar

Trubchevsk

18.
Pz.

Developments from 19.9.-
                    22.9.41.

XXXXVII.

Situation 19.9

"   "   20.9.

"   "   21.9.

"   "   22.9.

29. m.

Novgorod
Severskie

18.Pz. Yampol

Gluchov

Elmnts.
17.Pz.

Rylsk

XXXXVI.

Makoshino

Seim

Desna

Baturin

Seim

2

G.D.

Elmnts

17.

Voroshba

Konotop

½ 10. m.   Pz.

Bielopolie

10. m.

½ R

½   R

XXIV.   10
         m.

Priluki

Romny

3.
Pz.

4. Pz.

4.
Pz.

3. Pz.

3. Pz.

Division and a few anti-aircraft batteries. Our air reconnaissance was suffering from enemy local air superiority. Lieutenant-Colonel von Barsewisch flew a sortie himself, in the course of which he only just escaped being shot down by Russian fighters. There was a heavy bomber raid on Romny. Finally, however, we succeeded in holding the town and our advanced headquarters. All the same Russian reinforcements were moving up on the line Kharkov–Sumy and were being unloaded at Sumy and Shuravka. As defence against this new threat XXIV Panzer Corps was instructed to withdraw part of *SS-Das Reich* and of the 4th Panzer Division from the encirclement front and send them off towards Konotop and Putivl. The threat to Romny led us, on September 19th, to move the Group headquarters back to Konotop. General von Geyr did his best to make this move easier by sending a wireless signal: 'The troops will not regard it as cowardice if the Panzer Group withdraws its headquarters from Romny.' In any case we were better located in Konotop in view of the operations towards Orel and Bryansk that lay ahead. XXIV Panzer Corps wanted to postpone the attack on this fresh enemy from the east until the corps was in a position to strike with all its force. I sympathised with this view, but could not approve the plan since the availability of *SS-Das Reich* for this operation might not last for more than a few days; it was destined to form part of XLVI Panzer Corps, together with Infantry Regiment *Gross-Deutschland*, and to return to the Roslavl area. Besides, recent unloadings near Seredina Buda and more transports moving through Sumy to the north were strong incentives to hurry.

On this day Kiev fell. XLVIII Panzer Corps, of Panzer Group 1, captured Gorodishtche and Belusovka.

September 20th was a day of limited successes against the enemy to the east, but fighting went on against the encircled Russians, both in the sector of 3rd Panzer Division, which found itself opposed by the staff of the Russian Fifth Army, and farther to the south, in the sector of the 25th (Motorised) Infantry Division, where part of the enemy's forces seemed to have broken out.

Since the 13th of September we had taken 30,000 prisoners.

On the 20th I visited XLVI Panzer Corps. General von Vietinghoff described the difficulties his corps had had while fighting their way southwards from Gluchov during the past few days. The students from the Russian War School at Kharkov had put up a particularly brave fight under the command of their instructors. Mine fields and bad weather had held up the advance. Heavy battles were still going on in the neighbourhood of Putivl, Shilovka, and Bielopolie. I went to find Infantry Regiment *Gross-Deutschland*, which was doing well under the

Sketch Map 21
Situation on 23.9.1941

command of Colonel Hörnlein, to the east of Shilovka. Bielopolie was taken.

On September 21st enemy pressure in the Gluchov area increased. Russian concentrations were reported to the north of that town. We launched an attack towards Nedrigailov.

Panzer Group 1 reported 43,000 prisoners, and Sixth Army 63,000 captured since the beginning of the Battle of Kiev.

On September 22nd I once again drove to the front, through Putivl towards Rylsk, in order to inspect the defensive measures that were being taken in this threatened sector. In Viasenka I found the staff of the 17th Panzer Division, now led once again by General von Arnim who had recovered from the wound received at Stolpce and had relieved General Ritter von Thoma a few days earlier. The enemy was attacking Gluchov and Cholopkovo from the north and north-east and had partially encircled the defending troops. Two new Russian divisions had been identified on the 17th Panzer Division's front. While driving back to XLVI Panzer Corps' headquarters we had to pass through a belt of concentrated Russian fire, but luckily we did so without suffering any harm. I there said good-bye with heartfelt thanks to General von Vietinghoff who was departing for his new assignment with Panzer Group 4. I placed 17th Panzer Division under direct command of my Panzer Group and subordinated Infantry Regiment *Gross-Deutschland* to that division. 17th Panzer Division received orders to defeat the enemy in the Gluchov area. These orders were carried out.

The number of prisoners captured around Kiev reached the total of 290,000.

As from September 23rd regrouping for the new operation began. For this purpose the main concentration area of Panzer Group 2 was around and to the north of Gluchov.

Attacks by the 4th Panzer Division and *SS-Das Reich* drove the enemy back eastwards from Kamlicha. Heavy traffic along the Bryansk–Lgov railway pointed to the bringing up of fresh Russian reinforcements.

On September 24th I flew to the headquarters of Army Group Centre at Smolensk, for a final conference on the new offensive. The Commander-in-Chief of the Army and the Chief of the Army General Staff were both present. At this conference it was decided that the main offensive by the Army Group would be launched on October 2nd, but that my Panzer Group 2 on the extreme right wing would start its attack on September 30th. This was done at my request. In the area across which Panzer Group 2 would now be attacking there were no metalled roads available and I wished to make full use of the limited

Fig. 14. Crossing the Dnieper near Kopys

Fig. 15.   With General Marras on the banks of the Dnieper near Kopys

period of fine weather which we might still expect in order to reach the good roads around Orel before the mud set in and to secure the transverse Orel–Bryansk road so that I might have a decent supply route. Another consideration that influenced my decision was the fact that I could only expect strong air support if I could arrange for the bomber missions to be flown two days before the attacks by the other armies of Army Group Centre were due to start.

The next few days were devoted to eliminating the enemy pocket near Kiev and re-deploying my corps for their new task; equally important was arranging that they rest after their exhausting marches and battles of the past months and that their equipment receive the necessary maintenance. However, only three days could be allotted to the gallant troops for this purpose and even this short period for rehabilitation was not vouchsafed to all units.

What were clearly fresh enemy formations[1] were now heavily attacking to the east of Gluchov and against the Novgorod Severskie bridgehead. These kept us occupied during the next few days. On September 25th the enemy attacked Bielopolie, Gluchov and Yampol, but was beaten off. Great numbers of prisoners fell into our hands.

On this day Army Group North reported to the *OKH* that it could not continue the assault on Leningrad with the forces at its disposal.

On September 26th the Battle of Kiev was brought to a successful conclusion. The Russians surrendered. 665,000 men were taken prisoner. The Commander-in-Chief South-west Front and his chief of staff fell in the last phase of the battle while attempting to break out. The Commander of the Fifth Army was among the prisoners captured. I had an interesting conversation with this officer, to whom I put a number of questions:

1. When did you learn that my tanks had penetrated behind you? *Answer:* 'About the 8th of September.'

2. Why did you not evacuate Kiev at once? *Answer:* 'We had received orders from the Army Group to evacuate the area and withdraw eastwards and had already begun to do so, when we received contrary orders to turn about and to defend Kiev in all circumstances.'

The carrying out of this second order resulted in the destruction of the Kiev Army Group. The enemy was never to make the same mistake again. Unfortunately, though, we were to suffer the direst calamities as a result of just such interference from higher levels.

The Battle of Kiev was undoubtedly a great tactical victory. But whether great strategic advantages were to be garnered from this tactical

[1] The strength of a Russian division was considerably less than that of the normal European division. The Germans therefore referred to them as *Verbaende*: this has been translated as 'formations' throughout.—*Tr.*

success remained questionable. It all depended on this: would the German Army, before the onset of winter and, indeed, before the autumnal mud set in, still be capable of achieving decisive results? It is true that the planned assault on Leningrad had already had to be abandoned in favour of a tight investment. But the *OKH* believed that the enemy was no longer capable of creating a firm defensive front or of offering serious resistance in the area of Army Group South. The *OKH* wanted this Army Group to capture the Donetz Basin and reach the River Don before winter.

But the main blow was to be dealt by the reinforced Army Group Centre, with objective Moscow. Was there still sufficient time for this to succeed?

The Battles of Orel and Bryansk

For the offensive towards Orel and Bryansk—a necessary preliminary to the attack on Moscow—Panzer Group 2 was reorganised as follows:

XLVI Panzer Corps, with *SS-Das Reich* and Infantry Regiment *Gross-Deutschland*, was handed over to Panzer Group 4 in the Roslavl area.

The 1st Cavalry Division was once more subordinated to Panzer Group 2. In addition, Panzer Group 2 was given command of:

XLVIII Panzer Corps, under General of Panzer Troops Kempff, with the 9th Panzer Division and the 16th and 25th (Motorised) Infantry Divisions.

XXXIV Army Corps, under General Metz, with the 45th and 134th Infantry Divisions, and

XXXV Army Corps, under General Kempfe, with the 293rd, 262nd, 296th, and 95th Infantry Divisions.

I decided to attack with point of main effort through Gluchov towards Orel and therefore put the XXIV Panzer Corps in the centre of my line. On XXIV Panzer Corps' right I placed the XLVIII Panzer Corps at Putivl, and on its left the XLVII Panzer Corps at Shostka. XXXIV Army Corps was to guard the right flank and XXV Army Corps and the 1st Cavalry Division the left; the infantry corps were to advance echeloned in depth on both wings of the panzer corps.

Before assembling at Putivl the XLVIII Panzer Corps was to advance through Sumy and Nedrigailov and attack the enemy in those areas. By this manœuvre I intended to secure my right flank before the major operation began. It was a bold scheme, but I had underestimated the powers of resistance of the Russians who had not been engaged in the Kiev battle XLVIII Panzer Corps—as will be shown—did not succeed in throwing back the enemy opposite it, but had to break off the battle and march to its assembly area behind Infantry Regiment *Gross-Deutschland's* front. The 25th (Motorised) Infantry Division had a hard time in shaking off the enemy and unfortunately lost a number of its vehicles in the process. I should have done better to have followed Liebenstein's advice and have marched them up from the beginning behind the front. In any event this was a case where the early arrival of XXXIV Army Corps' infantry would have been welcome. But this could not be expected for another five days.

We had at last been given 100 tanks as replacements for our panzer divisions. Unfortunately 50 of these were misdirected to Orsha and therefore arrived too late. Nor did we receive adequate supplies of fuel.

The heaviest concentration of strength for the operation took place in the Roslavl area. At the start of the offensive the 1st Panzer Division, *SS-Das Reich*, 3rd (Motorised) Infantry Division and Infantry Regiment *Gross-Deutschland* were assembled behind the front line in that sector. There, too, the 2nd and 5th Panzer Divisions, previously held in reserve, were also committed. It is questionable whether this massing of armoured strength at the centre of the attack was correct. My opinion was that it would have been wiser to leave the XLVI Panzer Corps with Panzer Group 2. The two well-rested panzer divisions would also have been better employed in a flanking movement than in a frontal assault.

On September 27th I visited XLVIII Panzer Corps in order to form a personal impression of its condition. After a short conversation at the corps headquarters in Romny I went to the 9th Panzer Division, at Krasnaia, six miles to the south of Nedrigailov. This division was commanded by General Hubitzki. I then drove back through Nedrigailov.

On September 28th and 29th it became clear to me that XLVIII Panzer Corps' attempt to advance straight to Putivl had failed. The attack in this area was, therefore, broken off. As deception, this operation in the Shtepovka area was probably successful, for the enemy seems to have been uncertain where our main thrust was going to come in. Under cover of the Infantry Regiment *Gross-Deutschland*, which was still holding its old sector, XLVIII Panzer Corps was moved across to the north.

Our attack began on the 30th as follows:

XLVIII Panzer Corps from the area Gadiach–Shtepovka through Nedrigailov towards Putivl, with 9th Panzer Division leading. 25th and 16th (Motorised) Infantry Divisions were to follow as soon as they had been relieved by the infantry of XXXIV Army Corps.

XXIV Panzer Corps, with the 3rd and 4th Panzer Divisions leading and the 10th (Motorised) Infantry Division following behind, from

Gluchov along the line of, and to the south-east of, the road to Sevsk and Orel.

XLVII Panzer Corps, with the 18th and 17th Panzer Divisions in front, from Yampol with its right wing directed on Sevsk. The 29th (Motorised) Infantry Division, on the left and to the rear, was to make for Seredina Buda.

The infantry corps which were to provide flank protection were marching up, partially through Kostobobr and partially through Romny. The 1st Cavalry Division was on the west bank of the Sudost, on either side of Pogar.

Our attack took the enemy by surprise. The XXIV Panzer Corps made particularly good progress, reaching the Chinel heights. The XLVII Panzer Corps took Shuravka and pushed on in a north-easterly direction.

Early on the morning of the 30th I went to Gluchov where we set up our new headquarters. From there I informed General Kempff of the need to have forces ready very soon in the Putivl area for the protection of XXIV Panzer Corps' east flank. Kempff reported in reply that in the fighting around Shtepovka the Russians had taken two battalions of Infantry Regiment 119 by surprise and captured their vehicles. It seems that the enemy had attacked with heavy tanks. This was an unpleasant loss. Elements of the 9th Panzer Division had now to be turned about in order to put the situation to rights again. General Freiherr von Geyr informed me that owing to bad weather the dive bombers had been unable to take off. Furthermore, he imagined that he was being opposed only by the enemy's rearguards, while General Lemelsen reported that the enemy had been completely taken by surprise.

Army Group was informed that the withdrawal of Infantry Regiment *Gross-Deutschland* must be postponed since Kempff's corps was under attack from strong enemy forces and advance units of XXXIV Army Corps would not be available to relieve him until the evening of October 1st. It would be another four days before the mass of the infantry could be expected to arrive.

The population of Gluchov asked our permission to use their church as a place of worship once again. We willingly handed it over to them.

On October 1st XXIV Panzer Corps took Sevsk. We had succeeded in breaking through the enemy front. The advance was energetically pursued, so far as the fuel situation would permit. I drove from Gluchov, through Essman, to 4th Panzer Division at Sevsk. On the side of the road lay shot-up Russian vehicles of all sorts, a further proof that the enemy had been surprised by our attack. On a hill surmounted by a windmill, just off the road of the advance, I saw Generals Freiherr von

Geyr and Freiherr von Langermann. Considerable elements of the
4th Panzer Division had already reached Sevsk. The countryside
showed traces of fierce fighting. There were dead and wounded Russians
to be seen, and during the short walk to the windmill I and my companions found fourteen unwounded Russians hiding in the long grass,
whom we made prisoners; among them was an officer who was still
engaged in talking to someone in Sevsk on a telephone. Two miles to
the north of Sevsk, which we had already captured, I found Colonel
Eberbach, the gallant commander of the panzer brigade of 4th Panzer
Division. When I asked him whether the advance could be pursued as
far as Dmitrovsk, he replied that it could. In consequence I ordered
that the divisions go on, even though the generals had previously
informed me, incorrectly as it turned out, that the advance could not
be continued owing to lack of fuel. While I was talking to Eberbach a
number of Russian bombs fell on the road of our advance and in Sevsk.
I then drove on to the foremost of the victorious tanks and thanked
the men and their commander, Major von Jungenfeldt, for their brave
performance. On my way back I told the corps commander of my
order that the advance be continued. On this day the spearhead of
XXIV Panzer Corps covered a distance of 85 miles.

The advance units of our right-hand neighbour, Sixth Army, went
over to the attack in the Gadiach area. Other units advanced on
Mirgorod, in order to close the gap between us and the Seventeenth
Army.

On October 2nd the attack was resumed with violence. A complete
break-through was achieved and the Russian Thirteenth Army was
thrown back to the north-east. I visited the 10th (Motorised) Infantry
Division and its Infantry Regiment 41, commanded by Colonel Traut.
Our casualties during these days were happily light. But if the figures
for total casualties since the start of the campaign were examined it
was a grave and tragic total. The troops had received a number of
replacements, but although these were keen and eager men they yet
lacked the combat experience and toughness of the older men.

4th Panzer Division took Kromy and thus reached the metalled road
that led to Orel.

The whole of Army Group Centre had been attacking successfully
along its entire front since early morning and was much helped by the
good weather. Our left-hand neighbour, Second Army, broke through
the Sudost–Desna position despite stubborn enemy resistance.

On October 3rd the 4th Panzer Division arrived at Orel. We had thus
reached a good road and captured an important rail and road centre
which would serve as a base for our future operations. Our seizure

Sketch Map 23

Orel

Situation 5.10.41

of the town took the enemy so completely by surprise that the electric trams were still running as our tanks drove in. The evacuation of industrial installations, carefully prepared by the Russians, could not be carried out. Along the streets leading from the factories to the station lay dismantled machines and crates filled with tools and raw materials.

XLVII Panzer Corps was instructed to head for Bryansk.

To our south Sixth Army was set in motion, with its right wing towards Kharkov and its left through Sumy towards Bielgorod. This move was important for the safety of our right flank. Panzer Group 4 had broken through the enemy and was advancing on Mosalsk–Spas Demiansk in order to surround the enemy forces to the west of Viasma. Panzer Group 3 captured a bridgehead over the Dnieper near Cholm.

On October 4th advance elements of XXIV Panzer Corps took Moin on the road to Tula. The 3rd and 18th Panzer Divisions were driving on Karachev. The 17th Panzer Division was engaged in building a bridgehead across the Nerussa and thus making possible a further advance northwards.

Our left-hand neighbour crossed the Bolva. The railway Suchinitchi–Elnya was reached. Panzer Group 3 took Bieloi. In the rear area of the Army Group partisan activity now became noticeable for the first time.

Since on the next day I intended visiting XLVII Panzer Corps I sent my command vehicles forward to Dmitrovsk with instructions to await me at the landing strip outside that town. I was thus spared a long drive over bad roads and I reached General Lemelsen's headquarters at 10.30 hrs. on October 5th. The 18th Panzer Division was sent across the Orel–Bryansk road in a northerly direction while 17th Panzer Division was ordered to capture Bryansk by a *coup de main*. From Lemelsen's headquarters at Lobanovo I flew back in my little liaison plane to the headquarters of XXIV Panzer Corps at Dmitrovsk. General Freiherr von Geyr complained about the poor state of our fuel supply; the future extent of our movements was ultimately dependent on this. Unfortunately captured stocks were small. But as we had occupied Orel airfield I sent an urgent request to the commander of Air Fleet 2 that he fly us in the needed quantity, approximately 100,000 gallons, to that field. On this day, as it happened, I gained a vivid impression of the liveliness of the Russian air force. Immediately after I had landed on Sevsk airfield, where twenty German fighters had also just come in, the Russians bombed it; this was followed by an air attack on the corps headquarters which sent the glass in the windows flying about our ears. I drove at once along the road of advance of 3rd Panzer Division. Here too we were subjected to a series of bombing attacks by small groups of from three to six Russian bombers; but they flew high and their aim was consequently pretty inaccurate. The Air Fleet promised us stronger fighter cover for the 6th, so we could reckon on an improvement of the situation.

On this day my Panzer Group 2 was renamed Second Panzer Army.

The 25th (Motorised) Infantry Division was moved forward to Sevsk and placed at the disposal of my Army. XLVIII Panzer Corps took Rylsk; XXIV Panzer Corps enlarged its bridgeheads over the Susha to the north of Orel; XLVII Panzer Corps captured Karachev.

Our right-hand neighbour hoped to reach Psiol and a line that would secure our right flank during the course of October 6th. To our left the XXXIII and XIII Army Corps were advancing on Suchinitchi. Yuchnov was captured.

On October 6th our headquarters was moved forward to Sevsk. 4th Panzer Division was attacked by Russian tanks to the south of Mzensk and went through some bad hours. This was the first occasion on which the vast superiority of the Russian T34 to our tanks became plainly apparent. The division suffered grievous casualties. The rapid advance on Tula which we had planned had therefore to be abandoned for the moment.

On the other hand we had good news from the 17th Panzer Division which had succeeded in capturing Bryansk and its bridges over the Desna, and had thereby ensured our maintaining good contact with Second Army which was advancing to the west of the Desna. Our supply arrangements were to a great extent dependent on the establishment of the road and rail connections Orel–Bryansk. The encirclement of the enemy forces fighting in the area between the Desna and the Sudost was drawing closer. A bridgehead was established across the Navlia, to the north of Borshtchev.

Another encouraging factor was the quietness up to date on our open flank, where Kempff's corps was struggling through the mud towards Dmitriev, while General Metz's XXXIV Army Corps was moving up to Rylsk.

First Panzer Army (Kleist), of Army Group South, was directed to move on the Sea of Azov. Our right-hand neighbour intended to advance towards Shtepovka. Elements of the 25th (Motorised) Infantry Division, which had been held down in this area, were thus freed to follow Kempff's Corps to Putivl. Our left-hand neighbour took Shisdra and was ordered to move towards Bryansk and to co-operate with Second Panzer Army.

During the night of October 6th–7th the first snow of the winter fell. It did not lie for long and, as usual, the roads rapidly became nothing

H*

but canals of bottomless mud, along which our vehicles could only advance at snail's pace and with great wear to the engines. We asked for winter clothing—we had already done this once before—but were informed that we would receive it in due course and were instructed not to make further unnecessary requests of this type. Nevertheless I repeated my demands on several occasions, but the clothing did not reach the front during the course of that year.

XLVIII Panzer Corps was advancing on foot through the mire towards Dmitriev. Russian counter-attacks against Bryansk were repulsed. The 29th (Motorised) Infantry Division reached the mouth of the Revna.

Our right-hand neighbour was approaching Shtepovka, and on our left LIII Army Corps was nearing Bryansk from the west. We hoped thus to ease the situation of XLVII Panzer Corps and free the supply route Roslavl–Bryansk–Orel. Farther to the north Second Army captured Suchinitchi and Meshtchevsk. In the Viasma area Fourth and Ninth Armies succeeded in enveloping some forty-five Russian formations.

The *OKH* was of the opinion that these satisfactory developments now made possible the further prosecution of the offensive for Moscow. The intention was to prevent the Russians from establishing fresh defensive positions to the west of Moscow. The *OKH* proposed that Second Panzer Army should continue to advance through Tula and seize the Oka crossings between Kolomna and Serpuchov—undoubtedly a very large objective. This was to correspond to a similar move by Panzer Group 3 to the north of Moscow. The Commander-in-Chief of the Army found Army Group Centre to be in full agreement with this plan of his.

On October 8th I flew along the line of our 'road' from Sevsk over Dmitrovsk to Orel, where I found my command vehicles which I had previously sent on ahead. The state of the traffic along the 'road' as far as Kromy was appalling; from there on we had a metalled road as far as Orel, though already this consisted largely of one bomb crater after the next. General Freiherr von Geyr informed me that the enemy opposite 4th Panzer Division had been reinforced; a tank brigade and an infantry division had been recently identified. The 3rd Panzer Division was marching northwards, with orders to capture Bolchov. The 4th Panzer Division's task for the 9th of October was to take Mzensk. Descriptions of the quality and, above all, of the new tactical handling of the Russian tanks were very worrying. Our defensive weapons available at that period were only successful against the T34 when the conditions were unusually favourable. The short-barrelled 75 mm. gun of the Panzer IV was only effective if the T34 were attacked

from the rear; even then a hit had to be scored on the grating above
the engine to knock it out. It required very great skill to manœuvre
into a position from which such a shot was possible. The Russians
attacked us frontally with infantry, while they sent their tanks in, in
mass formation, against our flanks. They were learning. The bitterness
of the fighting was gradually telling on both our officers and our men.
General Freiherr von Geyr brought up once again the urgent need for
winter clothing of all sorts. In particular there was a serious shortage
of boots, shirts and socks. This was obviously a very serious business.
I decided to visit the 4th Panzer Division at once and find out for
myself what the situation was. On the battlefields that had been fought
over during the 6th and 7th of October the commander of the battle-
group that had been there engaged himself described the course of the
fighting to me. The tanks knocked out on either side were still in
position. The damage suffered by the Russians was considerably less
than that to our own tanks.

Back in Orel I found Colonel Eberbach, who also told me the story
of the recent battles, and then I talked again to General Freiherr von
Geyr and to the commander of the 4th Panzer Division, Freiherr von
Langermann. For the first time during this exacting campaign Colonel
Eberbach gave the impression of being exhausted, and the exhaustion
that was now noticeable was less physical than spiritual. It was indeed
startling to see how deeply our best officers had been affected by the
latest battles.

What a contrast to the high spirits in evidence at the *OKH* and at
Army Group Centre! Here was a radical difference of attitude which
as time went on grew wider until it could scarcely be bridged; though
at this time Second Panzer Army was unaware that its superiors were
drunk with the scent of victory.

That evening XXXV Army Corps signalled increased enemy pressure
in the area north of Sisemka and west of Sevsk. From this it could
be assumed that the Russian forces trapped to the south of Bryansk
were attempting to break out to the east. I got into communication
with the 1st Cavalry Division, which was still stationed along the west
bank of the Sudost, and asked whether any change had been noticed
in the behaviour of the enemy along that sector. The reply was negative,
but nonetheless I ordered the division to launch an attack against the
east bank of the river. This would show whether the enemy was still
holding his positions or was withdrawing. 1st Cavalry Division
immediately secured a bridgehead.

In the evening Army Group telephoned me and suggested that it
would make the problems of our left flank much simpler if XXXV Army
Corps were subordinated to Second Army. I replied that it would be

better if the sector along the southern flank of the Trubchevsk encirclement were controlled from a single headquarters. Army Group next
pointed out that our worries about our right flank would be decreased
if XXXIV Army Corps were placed under command of Sixth Army
which could then use the corps for the capture of Kursk. This idea,
which seems to have emanated from the *OKH* or the *OKW*, was not
practicable at the time, since it would have deprived us of our flank
protection to the right. It is true that Dmitriev was captured on this
day, but the bad weather was holding up the rear elements of
XLVIII Panzer Corps and the crisis continued.

On October 9th the Russian attempt to break out near Sisemka,
which had threatened on the previous day, succeeded. The right wing
of the 293rd Infantry Division was heavily attacked and forced back
through Sisemka and Shilinka. Since the 25th (Motorised) Infantry
Division, the Panzer Army's reserve, had not yet arrived in position,
Infantry Regiment 41 of the 10th (Motorised) Infantry Division had
to be put in at once to close the gap between the 29th (Motorised)
Infantry Division and the 293rd Infantry Division. The XLVIII Panzer
Corps, which had been instructed by Army Group Centre to advance
on Kursk and Livny, was now ordered to withdraw all available forces
to Sevsk. At 12.00 hrs. the commander of the 25th (Motorised) Infantry
Division arrived in Sevsk and took over command of all troops fighting
between the 29th (Motorised) Infantry Division and the 293rd Infantry
Division. While a violent battle raged here, 1st Cavalry Division had
moved the bulk of its forces across the Sudost without meeting serious
opposition and was advancing on Trubchevsk. The division had allowed
itself to be deceived by the enemy and was now eager to make good
its mistake. There was heavy enemy pressure throughout the day along
the line of the roads Trubchevsk–Sevsk, Trubchevsk–Orel and
Trubchevsk–Karachev, but only a small number of Russians succeeded
in breaking free across the Seredina Buda–Sevsk road. Those who did
unfortunately seem to have included the staff of the Russian Thirteenth
Army.

The headquarters of the Panzer Army was moved to Dmitrovsk
during a heavy snowstorm. Owing to the weather the roads grew
consistently worse. Countless vehicles were stuck.

Despite all this, Bolchov was captured. The 18th Panzer Division,
working closely with XLIII Army Corps of the Second Army, managed
to encircle the Russians in the area to the north of Bryansk.

While these events were taking place, the southern wing of our
Eastern Front was preparing to advance on Taganrog and Rostov.
Advanced elements of our neighbour, Sixth Army, were approaching
Achtyrka and Sumy.

To our left the Urga was crossed in the direction of Moscow and Gshatsk taken.

On October 10th fresh instructions arrived from the Army Group. These included: the capture of Kursk, the elimination of the Trubchevsk pocket, the complete sealing of the encirclement that was taking place north-west of Bryansk, and the advance on Tula—all, of course, to be carried out immediately. Liebenstein naturally inquired what priority was to be assigned to these various orders which, apparently, emanated from some higher headquarters. We received no answer.

The next few weeks were dominated by the mud. Wheeled vehicles could only advance with the help of tracked vehicles. These latter, having to perform tasks for which they were not intended, rapidly wore out. Since chains and couplings for the towing of vehicles were lacking, bundles of rope were dropped from aeroplanes to the immobilised vehicles. The supplying of hundreds of such vehicles and their crews had now to be done by the air force, and that for weeks on end. Preparations made for the winter were utterly inadequate. For weeks we had been requesting anti-freeze for the water coolers of our engines; we saw as little of this as we did of winter clothing for the troops. This lack of warm clothes, was, in the difficult months ahead, to provide the greatest problem and cause the greatest suffering to our soldiers—and it would have been the easiest to avoid of all our difficulties.

The enemy continued his attempts to break out through the 29th (Motorised) Infantry Division and the 293rd Infantry Division. The 4th Panzer Division managed to fight its way into Mzensk.

To our right Sixth Army took Sumy; to our left XIII Army Corps crossed the Ugra to the west of Kaluga. Here too a deterioration of the weather began to make itself felt.

On October 11th the Russians attempted to break out of the Trubchevsk encirclement along either bank of the Navlia. Between the 29th and 25th (Motorised) Infantry Divisions there was severe fighting and the enemy succeeded in creating a gap in our defences which was only sealed by the timely arrival of the 5th Machine-gun Battalion. At the same time heavy street fighting took place in XXIV Panzer Corps' area in Mzensk, to the north-east of Orel, into which town the 4th Panzer Division had fought its way; the division could not receive support quickly enough on account of the mud. Numerous Russian T34's went into action and inflicted heavy losses on the German tanks. Up to this time we had enjoyed tank superiority, but from now on the situation was reversed. The prospect of rapid, decisive victories was fading in consequence. I made a report on this situation, which for us was a new one, and sent it to the Army Group; in this report I described in plain terms the marked superiority of the T34 to our Panzer IV and drew the relevant conclusions as they must affect our future tank production. I concluded by urging that a commission be sent immediately to my sector of the front, and that it consist of representatives of the Army Ordnance Office, the Armaments Ministry, the tank designers and the firms which built the tanks. If this commission were on the spot it could not only examine the destroyed tanks on the battlefield but could also be advised by the men who had to use them what should be included in the designs for our new tanks. I also requested the rapid production of a heavy anti-tank gun with sufficient penetrating power to knock out the T34. The commission appeared at Second Panzer Army's front on November 20th.

On October 11th my Army was informed that on Hitler's orders Infantry Regiment *Gross-Deutschland* was being placed under command and that it was to be used to strengthen the relatively weak line now held by the 18th Panzer Division to the north-east of Bryansk along the Karachev–Chvastovitchi road. We were further informed that a reorganisation was envisaged whereby Second Army would be moved to our right flank and would assume command of the XXXIV and XXXV Army Corps while we, in return, would take over some of the units which at present formed part of Second Army. From this it was clear that a further advance in a north-easterly direction was contemplated.

The battles for the reduction of the pockets continued.

At the southern end of the front the battle for the Sea of Azov was brought to a victorious conclusion; 100,000 prisoners were taken and 212 tanks and 672 guns captured. The Supreme Command reckoned that the Sixth, Twelfth, Ninth and Eighteenth Russian Armies had been destroyed and believed that conditions were now suitable for a continuation of the advance to the Lower Don. The *SS-Leibstandarte 'Adolf Hitler'* was 12 miles to the north-west of Taganrog. The progress of the Seventeenth Army, south of Kharkov, and the Sixth Army, in the Sumy area, was slower. Here fresh Russian forces with tanks occasionally forced our people to go over to the defensive. This had a disadvantageous effect on the operations of my right wing. Since Eleventh Army had now been turned south to capture the Crimea the thrust by Army Group South was fanning out.

In the northern area of Army Group Centre all movement was slowed up by falls of snow. Panzer Group 3 reached the Upper Volga near Pogoreloie.

The snow continued on October 12th. We were still sitting tight in our little town of Dmitrovsk, with the appalling mud swamps outside the door, awaiting instructions from the *OKH* concerning reorganisation. The large encirclement south of Bryansk and the smaller one to the north of the town had both been completed, but our troops were stuck in the mud and immobilised, including the XLVIII Panzer Corps which at the beginning of the operation would so willingly have driven along hard roads through Sumy and which was now struggling forward through the mire towards Fatesh. In the Mzensk area the battles against the freshly arrived enemy went on. The infantry of XXXV Army Corps were needed to mop up in the forests of the Trubchevsk pocket and were therefore moved across to that area.

Not only we but also Army Group South, with the exception of First Panzer Army, were now bogged down. Sixth Army succeeded in capturing Bogoduchov, to the north-west of Kharkov. To our north XIII Army Corps took Kaluga. Panzer Group 3 seized Stariza and went on towards Kalinin.

The *OKH* issued instructions for the encirclement of Moscow but these never reached us.

On October 13th the Russians continued their attempts to break out between the Navlia and Borchevo. The XLVII Panzer Corps had to be reinforced by elements of the 3rd Panzer and 10th (Motorised) Infantry Divisions of the XXIV Panzer Corps. Despite this, and thanks to the immobility of our units, a group of about 5,000 Russians succeeded in fighting their way through our lines as far as Dmitrovsk, where they were finally checked.

Panzer Group 3 fought its way into Kalinin. Ninth Army reached the western edge of Rzhev.

On October 14th we moved our headquarters to Orel where we found good quarters in the House of the Soviets. During the next few days activity on either side was limited. With great difficulty XXIV Panzer Corps moved the 4th and 3rd Panzer Divisions to the area north-west of Mzensk and prepared them for an attack across the Susha; meanwhile XLVII Panzer Corps, the encirclement battle completed, was being assembled and deployed along the Orel–Karachev–Bryansk road. Infantry Regiment *Gross-Deutschland* was placed under command of XXIV Panzer Corps and brought forward to Mzensk. XLVIII Panzer Corps attacked towards Fatesh and prepared to attack Kursk from the north-west, while XXXIV Army Corps was to advance on that city from due west; the intention was to defeat the strong Russian forces, under General Yefremov, which were in the Kursk area and thus get rid of the continual threat to our right flank.

Despite fierce Russian resistance Sixth Army succeeded in

capturing Achtyrka. The rest of Army Group South was bogged down.

Army Group Centre's attack was also held up by the weather. Borovsk, 50 miles west of Moscow, was occupied by LVII Army Corps.

On October 15th Sixth Army took Krasnopolie, to the east of Sumy.

In preparation for the advance through Mzensk I visited the 4th Panzer Division on October 16th.

On this day the Rumanians captured Odessa. XLVI Panzer Corps was nearing Moshaisk.

On October 17th the Russians encircled to the north of Bryansk surrendered. Together with Second Army we captured 50,000 prisoners and 400 guns, thus destroying the bulk of the Fiftieth Russian Army. There were enemy counter-attacks in the Fatesh area.

On October 18th Eleventh Army began its attack on the Crimea. First Panzer Army, after capturing Taganrog, drove towards Stalino. Sixth Army took Graivoron.

To the north of Second Panzer Army the 19th Panzer Division occupied Maloyaroslavets. Moshaisk was captured.

On October 19th First Panzer Army began to prepare for its advance on Rostov. It fought its way into Stalino. Seventeenth and Sixth Armies continued to move successfully towards Kharkov and Bielgorod. Bad weather, however, held up their advance. This applied also to Army Group Centre. XLIII Army Corps took Lichvin. For twenty-four hours this corps was subordinated to Second Panzer Army.

On October 20th the Russians encircled near Trubchevsk surrendered. The whole Army Group was bogged down.

First Panzer Army was fighting in Stalino. Sixth Army was approaching Kharkov. By the 21st it had fought its way through the mud to the western outskirts of that city.

On October 22nd the attack by XXIV Panzer Corps through Mzensk failed owing to insufficiently close co-operation between the artillery and the tanks. A second attempt was made in the area of the 3rd Panzer Division to the north-west of Mzensk, with all the available armour, and on this occasion succeeded. In pursuit of the beaten enemy Chern was captured on the 24th of October. I had taken part in both these attacks and was fully conscious of the difficulties imposed on our troops by the damp ground and by the extensive Russian minefields.

On October 22nd the 18th Panzer Division, which had moved down along the good road through Kromy, had taken Fatesh.

Sketch Map 24

10 5 0   10   20   30   MILES
                                              40

Situation on 14.10.41

Arsenievo

Bielev

Chern

A r m y

Desna →

2./

Bryansk

Chvastovitchi

52.
112.
18.Pz.
XXXXIII.
I.R.G.D.

Bolchov
3.Pz.

Mzensk
4.Pz.

XXIV

Oka

Orel

Karachev

17.
Pz.

XXXXVII.

← Revna

29.
m.   ← Navlia

1./
K.

10. m.

25. m.

Kromy

Susha

293.

Dmitrovsk

to Livny →

262.
XXXV.   Sisemka

Seredina Buda

Swapa

Sevsk

9.Pz.
XXXXVIII.

Dmitriev
16. m.

Fatesh

Jefremov (?)

Gluchov

Lgov

Kursk

Rylsk   ← Seim

45.

XXXIV.

134.

On October 24th Sixth Army occupied Kharkov and Bielgorod, both of which the enemy had previously evacuated. On our left XLIII Army Corps captured Bielev on the Oka.

On October 25th I watched the advance of Infantry Regiment *Gross-Deutschland* on Chern and also the battle fought by Battle Group Eberbach to the north of that village.

By October the 25th the battles around Bryansk might be regarded as over. On this day the reorganisation of the armies on the right wing of Army Group Centre, already mentioned above, took effect. The XXXIV and XXXV Army Corps, together with the XLVIII Panzer Corps less the 25th (Motorised) Infantry Division, were surrendered by Second Panzer Army to Second Army. The 1st Cavalry Division returned to its home station in East Prussia where it was to be re-equipped and retrained as the 24th Panzer Division. In exchange Second Panzer Army received General Heinrici's XLIII Army Corps, with the 31st and 131st Infantry Divisions, and General Weisenberger's LIII Army Corps, with the 112th and 167th Infantry Divisions. Later the 296th Infantry Division was also placed under my Army's command. The 25th (Motorised) Infantry Division remained with Second Panzer Army.

The task of Second Panzer Army was now to advance on Tula, while the new Second Army was to head eastwards: that is to say we were once again going in divergent directions.

With the victorious end of the twin battles of Bryansk and Viasma Army Group Centre had undoubtedly won a great tactical success. Whether it still possessed sufficient strength to launch a further attack and thus operationally to exploit its tactical victory was the most serious question which had so far confronted the Supreme Command in this war.

The Advance to Tula and Moscow

Second Panzer Army was now ready to advance on Tula. The single road that was available for this purpose, the one from Orel to Tula, was certainly not intended to carry heavy vehicles and tanks and began to disintegrate after a few days' use. Furthermore the Russians, experts at demolition, had blown all the bridges along the line of their withdrawal and had laid extensive minefields on either side of the road in all suitable localities. Corduroy roads had to be laboriously laid for miles on end in order to ensure that the troops received even the limited supplies available. The strength of the advancing units was dependent less on the number of men than on the amount of petrol on hand to keep them going. As a result of this the bulk of the tanks still at the disposal of XXIV Panzer Corps was massed together under command of Colonel Eberbach and, together with Infantry Regiment

Sketch Map 25.

MILES
10 5 0   10   20   30

Advance to Tula.

Situation 27.10. – 14.11. 41.

Situation
27.10.41

Developments
up to 14.11.41

Serpuchov   Oka →
Kashira
17.
52.
4. Army
XIII.
260.   Aleksin
Kaluga
131.   31.
XXXXIII.
131.
XXXXIII.
Tula
I.R.
G.D.
Yasnaya
Polyana   3.Pz.   Uslovaia
Dedilovo
Bielev   31.   ←Upa   4.Pz.
Odoievo   Krapivna   112.
LIII.   Plava   Bogorodisk   161.
112.   Plavskoie   LIII.
167.   3.
Pz.   Teploie   Volovo
I.R.   X
6.D.   3.-13.11.
4.   29.m.
Pz.
XXIV.   Chern   10.m.
Mzensk   Spaskoie   18.Pz.
XXXXVII.
Oka   Susha   yefremov
Orel   Novosil
10.
m.
XXXXVII.
(Assembling)
XXXV.   2. Army
XXXXVIII.   2. Army

Gross-Deutschland, formed the advance guard which was now set in motion towards Tula. On October 26th LIII Army Corps reached the Oka and XLIII Army Corps widened the 31st Infantry Division's bridgehead over that river near Bielev. Our right-hand neighbour swung his XLVIII Panzer Corps on Kursk. To our left Fourth Army was forced on to the defensive by Russian counter-attacks.

On the 27th and 28th of October I accompanied Eberbach in his advance. On the 27th the *OKW* was playing with the idea of switching us towards Voronezh, where Russian forces were reported to be arriving from the east. But no roads led there. In any case an essential preliminary to any such operation must be the capture of Tula. I asked Liebenstein to explain this to our superiors. I spent the night of the 27th–28th October in Chern, in a small, abandoned, bug-infested hospital for children. Our van had reached the neighbourhood of Plavskoie. LIII and XLIII Army Corps were enlarging their bridgeheads across the Oka. Fourth Army repelled fierce Russian attacks.

On October 28th I learned from Liebenstein that the *OKW* had given up the idea of the switch to Voronezh. The advance towards Tula continued. Owing to a lack of fuel, Eberbach allowed one battalion of Infantry Regiment *Gross-Deutschland* to ride on the tanks. We reached Pissarevo, 20 miles to the south of Tula. Reconnaissance troops of XLIII Army Corps penetrated to Odoievo. I again spent the night in Chern and in the morning flew back to my Army headquarters.

On October 28th we were informed of Hitler's instructions that 'fast-moving units should seize the Oka bridges to the east of Serpuchov.' We could only advance as fast as our supply situation would allow. Travelling along the now completely disintegrated Orel–Tula road our vehicles could occasionally achieve a maximum speed of 12 miles per hour. There were no 'fast-moving units' any more. Hitler was living in a world of fantasy.

On this day First Panzer Army crossed the Mius and Seventeenth Army the Donetz.

On October 29th our leading tanks reached a point some 2 miles from Tula. An attempt to capture the town by a *coup de main* failed owing to the enemy's strong anti-tank and anti-aircraft defences; we lost many tanks and officers.

General Heinrici, always a practical and sensible man, who commanded XLIII Army Corps, now came to see me and described the bad condition of his troops' supplies: among other things, there had been no issue of bread since October 20th.

By October 30th the LIII Army Corps was advancing from the west along the Orel–Tula road. After the final destruction of the Bryansk pocket, on October 19th, the corps, commanded by General Weisenberger, had moved east, the 167th Infantry Division through Bolchov–Gorbachevo and the 112th Infantry Division through Bielev–Arsenievo–Zarevo. During this march it had suffered much from the prevailing mud and had been unable to take all its motorised vehicles, in particular its heavy artillery, with it. The motorised parts of the corps had to make a detour by following the 'good' road from Orel to Mzensk. In view of the Russians reported to be arriving from the east since October 27th, I felt compelled to commit LIII Army Corps as flank guard on our right against the line Yepifan–Stalinogorsk.

The condition of the Orel–Tula road had meanwhile grown so bad that arrangements had to be made for 3rd Panzer Division, which was following behind Battle Group Eberbach, to be supplied by air.

In view of the impossibility of launching a frontal attack on Tula General Freiherr von Geyr suggested that in order to continue our advance we by-pass the town to the east. I agreed with this and ordered that the attack go on towards Dedilovo and the crossing-places over the Shat. General Freiherr von Geyr was also of the opinion that there was now no possibility of using motorised troops until the frosts set in. In this he was undoubtedly correct. It was only possible to gain ground very slowly and at the cost of great wear and tear to the motorised equipment. As a result of this the reopening of the Mzensk–Tula railroad assumed very great importance. Despite consistent exhortations to hurry, the repair work was making only slow progress. The lack of locomotives made me look around for alternative transport and I suggested the use of railway lorries, but none were sent me.

On November 1st XXIV Panzer Corps reached a point to the west of Dedilovo.

As the leading elements of LIII Army Corps were nearing Teploie, on November 2nd, they were surprised to run into the enemy. This turned out to be a very strong Russian force, consisting of two cavalry divisions, five rifle divisions and a tank brigade, which was advancing along the Yefremov–Tula road with the apparent intention of attacking the flank and rear of the formations of XXIV Panzer Corps that were immobilised outside Tula. The Russians were plainly as surprised by the appearance of LIII Army Corps as LIII Army Corps was by theirs. A long-drawn-out battle developed in the Teploie area which lasted from November 3rd to November 13th; after being reinforced by the tanks of Eberbach's brigade, LIII Army Corps finally succeeded in defeating the enemy and throwing him back on Yefremov. The Russians lost 3,000 men taken prisoner in addition to a great number of guns.

During the night of November 3rd–4th there had been a frost and this made it easier for the troops to move; on the other hand we were now confronted with the constant problem of the cold, from which

our soldiers were already beginning to suffer. To defend the deep flank
of the Panzer Army in the Mzensk–Chern area and farther east I
employed the unarmoured elements of the 17th Panzer Division which
had recently arrived from Karachev. Engineers, construction battalions
and units of the Reich labour service were working without pause in
an attempt to improve the Orel–Tula road.

It was at this time that XLVIII Panzer Corps took Kurst.

On November 5th I received a brief visit from Field-Marshal
von Bock. Army Group had reached the conclusion, on November 4th,
that the Russians were systematically withdrawing from the territory
west of the Don between Voronezh and Stalinogorsk. This view had
been forwarded to the *OKH*. Events in Second Panzer Army's area
proved it to be quite incorrect. On the contrary, the enemy was
attacking in the Teploie area.

On November 6th I flew to the front. The impressions I gained
during this flight may best be given by quoting the following passage
from a letter which I wrote at the time:

It is miserable for the troops and a great pity for our cause that the enemy
should thus gain time while our plans are postponed until the winter is more
and more advanced. It all makes me very sad. With the best will in the world
there is nothing you can do about the elements. The unique chance to strike
a single great blow is fading more and more, and I do not know if it will ever
recur. How things will turn out, God alone knows. We can only go on hoping
and keep our courage up, but this is a hard time that we are passing
through . . .

I hope that I'll soon be able to strike a more cheerful note. I don't enjoy
complaining. But for the moment it is difficult to keep one's spirits up.

On November 7th we suffered our first severe cases of frost bite.
We heard that First Panzer Army had been attacking Rostov-on-Don
since November 5th.

On November 8th LIII Army Corps made progress in the Teploie
area. XXIV Panzer Corps repulsed enemy attacks from Tula.

On November 9th it was plain that the enemy was planning to attack
both to the east and the west of Tula. As a result XXIV Panzer Corps,
after having sent Panzer Brigade Eberbach to the support of LIII Army
Corps, had itself gone over to the defensive. 17th Panzer Division, less
its tanks, was attached to XXIV Panzer Corps and moved forward to
Plavskoie. Since fresh enemy formations were appearing to the east of
Chern the division responsible for protecting our flank in the Mzensk–
Chern area was strengthened by further elements of XLVII Panzer

Corps. As an example of how critical the situation in the Tula area was at this time, four weak rifle battalions of the 4th Panzer Division were responsible for a front of 20 miles to the west of Dedilovo with the additional task of maintaining contact between LIII Army Corps and the 3rd Panzer Division fighting outside Tula.

On November 12th the temperature dropped to + 5° (Fahr.) and on the 13th to − 8. On this date a conference took place at Army Group Centre at which the chiefs of staff of the various armies were present: the Chief of the Army General Staff presided. This was the occasion on which the 'Orders for the Autumn Offensive, 1941' were issued. The objective assigned to Second Panzer Army was the city of Gorki (formerly Nijni-Novgorod) which was approximately 400 miles from Orel, and 250 miles *east* of Moscow—with the intention of cutting off the Russian capital from its rearward communications. Liebenstein immediately protested that our Army in present circumstances could not advance beyond Venev. This was not the month of May and we were not fighting in France! I completely agreed with my chief of staff and I immediately informed the commander of Army Group Centre in writing that the Panzer Army was no longer capable of carrying out the orders that had been issued it. While writing my report I had in mind the impression I had gained during a visit to the front on November 13th and 14th when I had visited LIII Army Corps and XXIV Panzer Corps.

On November 13th I set off in my little Fieseler-Storch from Orel, but soon flew into a snowstorm to the north of Chern and was compelled to land on Chern airfield. I drove from there by car, in 40 degrees of frost, to General Weisenberger's headquarters at Plavskoie. This was the last day of the Teploie battle and General Weisenberger described his experiences to me. He was told to push on towards Volovo-Stalinogorsk, and I promised him that he might keep Panzer Brigade Eberbach until such time as 18th Panzer Division was in a position to cover his left flank against the Russians who had been thrown back on Yefremov. The combat strength of the infantry had sunk to an average of 50 men per company. The lack of winter clothing was become increasingly felt.

In XXIV Panzer Corps the frost was unpleasantly in evidence, since the tanks could not move up the ice-covered slopes for lack of the requisite calks for the tanks. General Freiherr von Geyr did not believe that he would be able to mount an attack before November 19th. To do so at all he would need the return of Panzer Brigade Eberbach and fuel for four days; at present all that he had was one day's supply. My opinion was that he should attack on the 17th of November, since

he would thus keep in accord with the movements of LIII Army Corps
and would stop the enemy from forming a new defensive front in the
area Volovo–Dedilovo. Apart from that, XLIII Army Corps was being
attacked west of Tula and needed relief. The right flank was to be
protected by XLVII Panzer Corps with the 18th Panzer Division and
the 10th and 29th (Motorised) Infantry Divisions.

I spent the night at Plavskoie.

In the morning of November 14th I visited the 167th Infantry
Division and talked to a number of officers and men. The supply
situation was bad. Snow shirts, boot grease, underclothes and above
all woollen trousers were not available. A high proportion of the men
were still wearing denim trousers, and the temperature was 8 below
zero! At noon I visited the 112th Infantry Division, where I heard the
same story. Our troops had got hold of Russian overcoats and fur
caps and only the national emblem showed that they were Germans.
All the stocks of clothing that the Panzer Army held were immediately
sent to the front, but the shortages were so great that these provided
a mere drop in the ocean.

Eberbach's fine brigade had only some fifty tanks left, and that was
all we had available. The establishment for the three divisions should
have been 600. Ice was causing a lot of trouble, since the calks for the
tracks had not yet arrived. The cold made the telescopic sights useless;
the salve which was supposed to prevent this had also not arrived. In
order to start the engines of the tanks fires had to be lit beneath them.
Fuel was freezing on occasions and the oil became viscous. This unit,
too, lacked winter clothing and anti-freeze mixture.

XLIII Army Corps reported heavy casualties.

I again spent the night at Plavskoie.

On November 15th the Russians resumed their attacks on XLIII Army
Corps.

On November 17th we learned that Siberian troops had appeared
in the Uslovaia sector and that more were arriving by rail in the area
Riasan–Kolomna. The 112th Infantry Division made contact with
these new Siberian troops. Since enemy tanks were simultaneously
attacking the division from the Dedilova area, the weakened troops
could not manage this fresh enemy. Before judging their performance
it should be borne in mind that each regiment had already lost some
500 men from frostbite, that as a result of the cold the machine-guns
were no longer able to fire and that our 37 mm. anti-tank gun had
proved ineffective against the T34. The result of all this was a panic,
which reached back as far as Bogorodisk. This was the first time that

such a thing had occurred during the Russian campaign, and it was a warning that the combat ability of our infantry was at an end and that they should no longer be expected to perform difficult tasks. By switching the 167th Infantry Division to Uslovaia LIII Army Corps was able to rectify the situation in the 112th Infantry Division's sector without having to ask for outside support.

Meanwhile the deep right flank of the Panzer Army had been secured by the arrival of units of XLVII Panzer Corps. In a letter dated the 17th of November, 1941, I wrote:

We are only nearing our final objective step by step in this icy cold and with all the troops suffering from the appalling supply situation. The difficulties of supplying us by railroad are constantly increasing—that is the main cause of our shortages, since without fuel the trucks can't move. If it had not been for this we should by now be much nearer our objectives. Yet the brave troops are seizing all their advantages and are fighting with wonderful endurance despite all their handicaps. Over and over again I am thankful that our men are such good soldiers. . . .

While these winter battles went on, we had to deal with the problem of supplying the homeland, the Army and the Russian civilian population with food. The 1941 harvest had been a rich one throughout the country and there was ample grain for bread. Nor was there any shortage of cattle. As a result of our wretched rail communications only a small amount of this food could be sent to Germany from the area of Second Panzer Army. But the needs of the troops were assured as were those of the Russian civilians in the towns, of which Orel was our most important; indeed stock sufficient to last until March 31st, 1942, was issued now and the Russian administration was entrusted with its distribution. Posters were stuck up on the walls in order to inform the civilians of this provision that had been made for them and to calm any anxiety they might otherwise have felt. In the rich and fruitful black earth country the Russians had built huge grain silos in which the golden harvest was stored. Though the Russians had destroyed some of these during their retreat, a number were unscathed, and even when a silo was burning when we arrived it was possible to rescue a portion of its contents which could at least be given to the populace.

In Orel a number of factories, whose machines the Russians had not had time to take away with them, were started working again. This provided some of the needs of the Army and also meant employment and bread for the workers. Among these was a factory producing tin goods and a shoe factory where leather and felt boots were made.

As an indication of the attitude of the Russian population, I should like to quote a remark that was made to me by an old Czarist general whom I met in Orel at this time. He said: 'If only you had come twenty years ago we should have welcomed you with open arms. But now it's too late. We were just beginning to get on our feet and now you arrive and throw us back twenty years so that we will have to start from the beginning all over again. Now we are fighting for Russia and in that cause we are all united.'

On November 18th Second Panzer Army launched the attack which had been ordered in Orel on the 13th. The following units were involved:

XLVII Panzer Corps.

18th Panzer Division attacked the industrial town of Yefremov which was captured after violent street fighting on the 20th and was held against heavy counter-attacks.

10th (Motorised) Infantry Division attacked through Yepifan to Michailov.

29th (Motorised) Infantry Division attacked towards Spaskoie-Gremiatchi with the task of guarding the Army's eastern flank against the Russian forces which had recently arrived in the area Riasan-Kolomna.

25th (Motorised) Infantry Division had been ordered to stay where it was by the *OKW* in order to harvest the corn. As soon as it was freed it was to follow the other divisions as corps reserve.

LIII Army Corps.

167th Infantry Division attacked through Stalinogorsk towards Venev.

112th Infantry Division was in the Stalinogorsk area where it was to remain on account of its lack of strength until relieved by the 56th Infantry Division, which was being brought up from Army Group reserve in the Karachev area and which was to capture a bridgehead across the Don.

XXIV Panzer Corps.

With the 17th, 3rd and 4th Panzer Divisions, Infantry Regiment *Gross-Deutschland* and the 296th Infantry Division moving up from the south, this corps was to take Tula by an attack on that town from both east and west. A battle group of the 17th Panzer Division was to advance ahead of this corps and of LIII Army Corps to Kashira, with the purpose of capturing the Oka bridges and thus preventing the arrival on the battlefield of any reinforcements that might be sent down from Moscow.

XLIII Army Corps.

This corps, with the 31st and 131st Infantry Division, was to advance through Lichvin and Kaluga, between the Upa and the Oka, with the task of mopping up any enemy forces in that area and of ensuring contact between Second Panzer Army and Fourth Army.

Second Army, which was on our deep right flank, was ordered to advance eastward from Orel. So we could expect no support from this army. In any case it was almost immediately held up by Russian entrenchments to the west of the Yeletz–Yefremov road and was forced to conclude that it had been mistaken in maintaining that the Russians had withdrawn to the east bank of the Don.

To the left of Second Panzer Army Fourth Army was to attack across the Oka, to the north of Aleksin, in the direction of Serpuchov. This army contained some thirty-six divisions.

Second Panzer Army, on the other hand, controlled only twelve-and-a-half divisions. The infantry was still without winter clothing and was almost incapable of movement. The distance it was capable of covering per day was 3, or at the most 6, miles. It seemed to me questionable whether my Army was capable of carrying out the task assigned it.

With the help of effective air support XLVII Panzer Corps succeeded in capturing Yepifan and XXIV Panzer Corps Dedilovo on the 18th of November; the next day the latter corps reached Bolochovo. On the 21st of November LIII Army Corps secured Uslovaia and on the 24th XXIV Panzer Corps took Venev, destroying 50 Russian tanks while doing so. XLIII Army Corps was marching slowly towards the Upa. While these movements were being completed a strong new enemy force appeared: this was the Fiftieth Russian Army with the 108th Tank Brigade, the 299th Rifle Division, the 31st Cavalry Division and other units under command, and it proceeded to attack the leading troops of XLVII Panzer Corps. The situation became critical once more.

After a hard struggle through mud and ice First Panzer Army on November 19th reached the northern edge of Rostov on Don where a fierce battle developed. Rostov was finally captured on November 21st. The Russians had blown the bridges across the Don. The Panzer Army reckoned on early counter-attacks and went over to the defensive. On November 20th the XLVIII Panzer Corps of Second Army took Tim where it was counter-attacked on the 23rd.

On the 21st of November I wrote as follows:

The icy cold, the lack of shelter, the shortage of clothing, the heavy losses of men and equipment, the wretched state of our fuel supplies, all this makes the duties of a commander a misery and the longer it goes on the more I am crushed by the enormous responsibility which I have to bear, a responsibility which no one, even with the best will in the world, can share.

I have been at the front three days running in order to form a clear picture of the conditions there. If the state of the battle allows I intend to go to Army Group on Sunday in order to find out what are the intentions for the immediate future, concerning which we have so far heard nothing. What those people are planning I cannot guess, nor how we shall succeed in getting straight again before next spring. . . .

During the afternoon of November 23rd I decided personally to visit the commander of Army Group Centre and to request that the orders I had received be changed since I could see no way of carrying them out. I explained to Field-Marshal von Bock the gravity of Second Panzer Army's situation, described the exhausted condition of the troops and above all of the infantry, the lack of winter clothing, the breakdown of the supply system, the shortage of tanks and guns, and spoke of the threat to our long and insufficiently guarded right flank that had arisen from the arrival of new, Far Eastern units in the Riasan–Kolomna area. Field-Marshal von Bock replied that he had already informed the *OKH* verbally of the contents of my earlier reports and that the *OKH* were thoroughly aware of the true nature of the conditions at the front. He then spoke on the telephone to the Commander-in-Chief of the Army and handed me an ear-piece so that I might listen in to the conversation. After repeating what I had said concerning the situation he requested the Commander-in-Chief of the Army to change my task, to cancel the order for the attack and to allow my Army to go over to the defensive in suitable winter positions.

The Commander-in-Chief of the Army was, plainly, not allowed to make a decision. In his answer he ignored the actual difficulties, refused to agree to my proposals and ordered that the attack continue. After repeated requests that at least I be assigned an objective that I could hope to reach and that I could transform into a defensible line, he finally gave me the line Michailov–Zaraisk and declared that the thorough destruction of the railroad Riasan–Kolomna was essential.

The results of my flying visit to Army Group headquarters were unsatisfactory. On the same day I had sent the *OKH's* liaison officer at my headquarters, Lieutenant-Colonel von Kahlden, to tell the Chief of the Army General Staff about our situation. He was at the same time to attempt to arrange that the attack be cancelled. His visit also achieved nothing. In view of the manner in which the Commander-in-Chief of the Army and the Chief of the Army General Staff refused my requests, it must be assumed that not only Hitler but also they were in favour of a continuation of the offensive. In any case the military persons in authority now knew of the highly insecure situation in which my Army was placed, and at that time I had to assume that Hitler, too, was being kept fully informed.

Sketch Map 26

The Battle for Moscow.
Situation 1.12.41.
Developments up to 5.12.41.

On November 24th the 10th (Motorised) Infantry Division took
Michailov. The 29th (Motorised) Infantry Division, moving through
Yepifan to the north, covered over 25 miles. On November 25th the
advanced battle group of the 17th Panzer Division was approaching
Kashira. Our right-hand neighbour captured Livny.

On November 26th LIII Army Corps reached the Don, crossed it
with the 167th Infantry Division near Ivanozero, and driving to the
north-east of that town attacked the Siberians near Danskoie. The brave
division captured 42 guns and a number of vehicles besides taking
4,000 prisoners. The 29th (Motorised) Infantry Division of XLVII
Panzer Corps attacked the same enemy from the east and succeeded
in encircling him.

I spent this day with LIII Army Corps and decided to go on the
27th of November to XLVII Panzer Corps and the 29th (Motorised)
Infantry Division. In the morning I learned from General Lemelsen,
in Yepifan, that a crisis had arisen in the 29th (Motorised) Infantry
Division during the course of the night. The mass of the 239th Siberian
Rifle Division, abandoning their guns and vehicles, had succeeded in
breaking out eastwards. The thinly spread 29th (Motorised) Infantry
Division had failed to prevent this and had suffered heavy casualties
while attempting to do so. I went by way of the divisional headquarters
to the hardest hit of the regiments, Infantry Regiment 71. At first I
was of the opinion that a failure of reconnaissance and security arrangements had been the cause of the misfortune. Reports by the battalion
and company commanders, however, made it quite clear that the troops
had done their duty and had been simply overwhelmed by numerical
superiority. The great number of dead, all in full uniform and with
their weapons in their hand, were grim proof of the truth of what I
had heard. I did my best to encourage the badly shaken soldiers and
to help them get over their misfortune. The Siberians—though without
their heavy weapons and vehicles—had slipped away because we had
just not had the strength to stop them. This was the most disturbing
single factor of the day. The motor-cyclists of the 29th (Motorised)
Infantry Division set off at once in their pursuit, but in vain.

I drove on to the Reconnaissance Battalion and then to Rifle
Regiment 33 of the 4th Panzer Division and spent the night at
XXIV Panzer Corps headquarters. Only he who saw the endless expanse
of Russian snow during this winter of our misery and felt the icy wind
that blew across it, burying in snow every object in its path: who
drove for hour after hour through that no-man's-land only at last to
find too thin shelter with insufficiently clothed, half-starved men:
and who also saw by contrast the well-fed, warmly clad and fresh

Siberians, fully equipped for winter fighting: only a man who knew all that can truly judge the events which now occurred.

Colonel Balck, who was then with the department of the *OKH* that handled Panzer Troops, accompanied me on this drive. I asked him to describe what he had seen to the Commander-in-Chief of the Army.

Our most urgent task was now the capture of Tula. Until we were in possession of this communications centre and its airfield we had no hope of continuing to advance either northwards or eastwards. I had visited the corps commanders in order to help in preparing for the assault, an operation concerning the difficulties of which I cherished no illusions. We wished to capture the town by a double envelopment, by XXIV Panzer Corps from the north and east and XLIII Army Corps from the west. During the course of the operation LIII Army Corps was to cover the northern flank against Moscow and XLVII Panzer Corps the extended eastern one against the troops arriving from Siberia. The 10th (Motorised) Infantry Division, after reaching Michailov on the 27th of November, had, as ordered, sent demolition parties to blow up the Riasan–Kolomna railway, but these had unfortunately been unable to reach their objective; the Russian defences were too strong for them. Due to the cold the greater part of the 18th Panzer Division's artillery fell out during the march to Yefremov. Already on November 29th overwhelming enemy pressure was beginning to be felt against the 10th (Motorised) Infantry Division. Skopin had to be evacuated.

The ability of the troops, even of XXIV Panzer Corps, to attack had suffered heavily as a result of the months of fighting. The corps artillery could now muster only eleven pieces.

At the southern end of the Eastern Front Russians in superior strength began to attack Rostov on November 27th. The enemy opposite Second Army, to our right, had been reinforced. On the left wing of my Army XLIII Army Corps reached the Tula–Aleksin road. There it met strong enemy forces which immediately counter-attacked.

In Fourth Army the 2nd Panzer Division reached Krasnaya Polyana, 14 miles north-west of Moscow.

On November 28th the Russians began to re-enter Rostov. First Panzer Army was faced with the problem of evacuating the town.

Our progress in XLIII Army Corps' sector remained slight. On this day Army Group gave up all idea of the long-range objectives laid down by the *OKH* and *OKW* and simply ordered: 'Successful completion of the battle of Tula.'

On November 30th the *OKW* expressed its doubts as to whether my forces were sufficiently concentrated for the attack on Tula. They could only have been strengthened by the withdrawal of troops from XLVII Panzer Corps, which would have lessened the protection to our flank. In view of the ever-growing threat from the east this seemed to me too dangerous a step to take. On the same day, however, an event occurred on the extreme southern flank of our front which suddenly cast a brilliantly clear light on our whole situation: Army Group South evacuated Rostov. On the next day the Army Group commander, Field-Marshal von Rundstedt, was relieved of his command and replaced by Field-Marshal von Reichenau. This was the first ominous sign. But neither Hitler and the *OKW*, nor the *OKH*, heeded the warning.

Total casualties on the Eastern Front since June 22nd, 1941, had now reached the total of 743,000 men; this was 23 per cent of our average total strength of three-and-a-half million men.

On this same 30th of November the enemy opposite my northern flank, near Kashira, was reinforced. It seemed that he had withdrawn troops from the centre of his front, to the west of Moscow, and moved them to what he regarded as his threatened flank.

I heard of the death of Colonel Mölders, my comrade-in-arms of the previous summer, and was deeply grieved by this sad loss of one of our finest soldiers.

An intensification of guerilla warfare in the Balkans necessitated the commitment of ever-stronger forces in that area.

The evacuation of Rostov and the withdrawal of First Panzer Army behind the line of the Mius was unavoidable according to the new commander of Army Group South, Field-Marshal von Reichenau. The dismissal of Rundstedt was thus shown to have been pointless within twenty-four hours after it had occurred.

Meanwhile preparations for the attack by my Army were made in such a way that it might be synchronised with the advance that Fourth Army had planned for December 2nd. But on December 1st we learned that Fourth Army would not be ready until December 4th. I should willingly have postponed my attack to wait for theirs, particularly as this would have allowed time for the 296th Infantry Division to arrive. But XXIV Panzer Corps did not believe that it could remain any longer in its narrowly constricted assault area. I therefore decided to launch my attack with this corps on December 2nd.

We had set up our advanced headquarters at Yasnaya Polyana, the estate of Count Tolstoi, and I visited it on December 2nd. Yasnaya Polyano was located immediately behind the headquarters of Infantry

Fig. 16. Before the attack

Fig. 17. An anti-tank ditch in the Stalin line

FIG. 18.   Near Roslavl, August 5, 1941

FIG. 19.   Panzer Regiment 35 advancing before the Battle of Gorodishtche

Regiment *Gross-Deutschland*, 4 miles to the south of Tula. There were two dwelling-houses on the estate, the 'Castle' and the 'Museum,' both preserved in the style of late nineteenth-century country houses; there was also a number of farm buildings. I ordered that the 'Castle' be left for the exclusive use of the Tolstoi family. We took up our quarters in the 'Museum.' All furniture and books belonging to the Tolstois were collected in two rooms, the doors of which were then locked. We contented ourselves with simple furniture which we built ourselves from rough planks. The house was heated by means of wood which we obtained from the nearby woods. No stick of furniture was burned, no book or manuscript touched. Any post-war statements by the Russians to the contrary belong in the realm of fantasy. I myself visited Tolstoi's grave. It had been well looked after. No German soldier disturbed it. It remained in that condition until we evacuated the estate. Unfortunately the Russian propagandists, in the years of hatred since the war, have not hesitated to tell the grossest lies in order to prove our alleged barbarity. But there are still enough witnesses alive to prove the truth of what I here have said. It is, however, true that the Russians had laid mines about the grave of their greatest writer.

On December 2nd the 3rd and 4th Panzer Divisions and Infantry Regiment *Gross-Deutschland* succeeded in breaking through the most advanced enemy positions. The attack took the Russians by surprise. It was continued on December 3rd in a blizzard. The roads became icy and movement was more difficult than ever. 4th Panzer Division crossed the Moscow–Tula railroad and captured six guns: the division finally reached the Tula–Serpuchov road. By then the strength of the troops was exhausted, as was their supply of fuel. The enemy withdrew to the north and the situation remained critical.

Reconnaissance on December 4th reported enemy spearheads preparing to attack in strength both north and south of the Tula–Serpuchov road. In the 3rd Panzer Division's area heavy battles were developing in the wooded country to the east of Tula. Only limited progress was made on this day.

But the decisive factors affecting the whole Tula operation were, first, whether XLIII Army Corps still possessed sufficient attacking strength to close the ring about the city and establish contact with 4th Panzer Division to the north of the town, and secondly, whether Fourth Army's attack could exert sufficient pressure on the enemy to prevent him from reinforcing the Tula front with troops withdrawn from his central sector.

On December 3rd I had visited XLIII Army Corps at Griasnovo in order to form a personal impression of the combat ability of the troops. Early on December 4th I drove to the headquarters of the

I

31st Infantry Division and thence to its 17th Infantry Regiment and
to that regiment's III (Jaeger) Battalion; this was my old Goslar Jaeger
unit, where I had started my military career and whose 11th Company
I had commanded in 1920–22. In lengthy conversation with the company commanders I raised the serious question of whether the troops
still possessed enough offensive strength for the task that lay ahead
of them. The officers did not attempt to hide their anxieties, but in
answer to my question whether the troops could attack successfully
they replied that they could. 'We can knock the enemy out of his
positions once more.' Whether the other units of XLIII Army Corps
were as energetic as my old Goslar Jaegers remained unknown. But
in any event the impressions I gained from this battalion decided me
to try the attack once again.

The drive back was endless and, on account of the drifting snow and
icy inclines, dangerous as well. Finally, my armoured command tank
drove into an abyss, one of those well-known chasms that the autumn
rains cut deep into the clay soil. There was no hope of extricating the
vehicle in the darkness. Luckily, on the far side of the gorge I came upon
a signals truck from my headquarters which took me to Yasnaya
Polyana, where I arrived during the course of the night.

During December 4th XLIII Army Corps had made its preparations
to attack and the 296th Infantry Division, under General Stemmermann,
had continued its difficult march towards Tula. But there was no attack
by these units on that day. Meanwhile the thermometer dropped to
− 31 degrees Fahrenheit. Air reconnaissance reported strong enemy
forces moving south from Kashira. Intensive Russian fighter activity
prevented more detailed observation.

On December 5th XLIII Army Corps attempted to attack but could
make no progress beyond certain initial successes by the 31st Infantry
Division. The 296th Infantry Division only reached Upa after dark
and in a state of exhaustion. I had myself personally visited one of
its regiments. On the 29th (Motorised) Infantry Division's sector the
Russians attacked with tanks to the north-east of Venev. The threat
to our flanks and rear in the area north of Tula, together with the fact
that XXIV Panzer Corps had been almost immobilised by the frost,
which was now − 68 degrees, raised the question of whether it would
be right to continue the attack. It could only be so if Fourth Army
were attacking at the same time—and successfully. But unfortunately
this was not the case. Rather, the contrary happened. Co-operation
by Fourth Army was limited to an action by a fighting patrol two
companies strong which, after completion of its mission, returned to

its previous position. This episode had no effect on the enemy opposite XLIII Army Corps. Fourth Army had gone over to the defensive.

On account of the threats to our flanks and rear and of the immobility of our troops due to the abnormal cold, I made the decision during the night of the 5th-6th December to break off this unsupported attack, and to withdraw my foremost units into defensive positions along the general line Upper Don-Shat-Upa. This was the first time during the war that I had had to take a decision of this sort, and none was more difficult. The fact that my chief of staff, Liebenstein, and my senior corps commander, General Freiherr von Geyr, were in complete agreement did not make it any easier for me.

During the course of the night I informed Field-Marshal von Bock of what I had decided. His first question was: 'Where actually is your headquarters?' He imagined that I was in Orel and too far away from the fighting front. But that was one mistake which no panzer general ever made. I was close enough to the battle and to my soldiers to be able to form a clear judgment of both.

It was not only my Second Panzer Army which was in so grave a situation. In this same night of December 5th-6th, Hoeppner's Fourth Panzer Army and Reinhardt's Third, which had reached a point only 20 miles north of the Kremlin, were forced to abandon their attacks because they lacked the necessary strength to seize the great prize that now lay so near. In Ninth Army's sector the Russians even went over to the offensive on either side of Kalinin.

Our attack on Moscow had broken down. All the sacrifices and endurance of our brave troops had been in vain. We had suffered a grievous defeat which was to be seriously aggravated during the next few weeks thanks to the rigidity of our Supreme Command: despite all our reports those men, far away in East Prussia, could form no true concept of the real conditions of the winter war in which their soldiers were now engaged. This ignorance led to repeatedly exorbitant demands being made on the fighting troops.

A prompt and extensive withdrawal to a line where the terrain was suitable to the defence, and where there were already prepared positions, seemed the best and most economical way of rectifying the situation; once there we could have remained where we were until spring came. For Second Panzer Army the obvious choice was the Susha-Oka position, which had been partially fortified in October. But this was exactly what Hitler refused to allow. I have no way of knowing whether the international situation, as well as Hitler's obstinacy, was exerting a decisive influence during these days; but I assume this to be the case since Japan joined in the war on December 8th and this was followed by Hitler's declaration of war on the United States on December 11th.

The soldiers wondered at the time why, when Hitler declared war on America, Japan did not do likewise against the Soviet Union. A direct consequence of this was that the Russian forces in the Far East remained available for use against the Germans. These forces were being moved at an unprecedented speed and in great numbers to our front. The result of this policy of Hitler's was not an alleviation of our difficulties but an additional burden of almost incalculable weight. It was the soldiers who had to carry it.

The war was now really 'total' enough for anyone. The economic and military potential of the greater part of the globe was united against Germany and Germany's feeble allies.

But to return to Tula. In the next few days the withdrawal of XXIV Panzer Corps proceeded according to plan, while heavy enemy pressure continued to be exerted against LIII Army Corps from the Kashira area; during the night of the 7th–8th December Michailov, in the XLVII Panzer Area, fell to the Russians and heavy casualties were inflicted on the 10th (Motorised) Infantry Division. To our right Second Army lost Yeletz at this time; the enemy was driving on Livny while building up his strength before Yefremov.

My point of view at that time can be seen from a letter which I wrote on December 8th:

We are faced with the sad fact that the Supreme Command has overreached itself by refusing to believe our reports of the increasing weakness of the troops and by making ever new demands on them, by having made no preparations for the cruel winter weather and by being surprised when the Russian cold reached −32°. The troops were no longer strong enough to capture Moscow and I therefore decided with a heavy heart, on the evening of December 5th, to break off our fruitless attack and to withdraw to a previously selected and relatively short line which I hope that I shall be able to hold with what is left of my forces. The Russians are pursuing us closely and we must expect misfortunes to occur. Our casualties, particularly from sickness and frostbite, have been bad, and though it is to be hoped that at least a proportion will be able to rejoin their units after rest and treatment, for the moment there is nothing that can be done. The loss of vehicles and guns owing to frost has been far greater than was feared. We are making what use we can of sleds, but these are naturally not very much help. Fortunately we have so far been able to keep our fine tanks in running order. The gods alone can tell how much longer we shall be able to use them in this cold.

Our misfortunes began with Rostov; that was the writing on the wall. When I flew to Army Group on November 23rd I neither found comprehension nor managed to achieve any results; the same old business went on as before. Then my northern neighbour broke down; my southern one was already very weak, and so I was left no alternative but to break off my attack, since I could hardly roll up the whole Eastern front by myself, let alone at a temperature of $-32°$.

I asked Balck to give the Commander-in-Chief of the Army my views on the situation, but I do not know if he managed to do so.

Yesterday Richthofen visited me. [Field-Marshal Richthofen of the Luftwaffe.] We had a long conversation alone together and discovered that we agree on the general situation. I also talked to General Schmidt, who is in the same position as myself and who commands the army on my right. He too shares my views. So I am not alone in my opinions, but that makes no difference since nobody is interested . . .

I would never have believed that a really brilliant military position could be so b . . . . d up in two months. If a decision had been taken at the proper time to break off and settle down for the winter in a habitable line suitable for the defence, we would have been in no danger. For months past now it has all been one great question mark. . . . I am not thinking about myself but rather about our Germany, and that is why I am frightened.

On December 9th the enemy exploited his success in the Livny area and succeeded in encircling part of the 95th Infantry Division. On my front I ordered XLVII Panzer Corps to begin to withdraw south-west; XXIV Panzer Corps beat off Russian attacks from Tula.

On December 10th I sent written reports to Schmundt, Hitler's chief adjutant, and to the younger Keitel, head of the Army Personnel Office, in which I described our situation; I wished that there be no more illusions cherished in those quarters. On the same day I wrote to my wife:

I hope that these letters of mine [the two referred to above] will reach their proper destination since even now, with clear thinking and firm determination, a great deal can still be saved. The enemy, the size of the country and the foulness of the weather were all grossly underestimated, and we are suffering for that now . . . The only good thing is the fact that at least I decided on my own responsiblity to break off the attack on the 5th of December; had I not done so a catastrophe could not have been avoided.

On December 10th Russian troops were observed unloading in the Kastornaia and Yeletz area. On Second Army's front the enemy widened his penetration and crossed the Livny–Chernova road. On my front the 10th (Motorised) Infantry Division was defending Yepifan. LIII Army Corps and XXIV Panzer Corps reached the Don–Shat–Upa line.

During the course of the day an uncomfortable gap occurred between the 296th and the 31st Infantry Divisions.

On December 11th the corps of our-right hand neighbour continued to withdraw westwards. Yefremov was threatened and had to be evacuated on December 12th.

In order to close the gap in XLIII Army Corps sector Fourth Army was told to send me the 137th Infantry Division. But in view of the great distance that it had to cover and the bad weather, this division could not be expected to arrive for some time. On December 12th all the available mobile forces of my Army had to be sent to the support of my right-hand neighbour, who was in trouble.

On December 13th Second Army continued to withdraw. In these circumstances Second Panzer Army's intention to hold a line Stalinogorsk–Shat–Upa became impracticable, particularly as the 112th Infantry Division was no longer strong enough to resist the attack of fresh Russian forces. The withdrawal had to be resumed to a line behind the River Plava. Neither the Fourth Army on our left nor the Fourth and Third Panzer Groups could hold their positions.

On December 14th I met the Commander-in-Chief of the Army, Field-Marshal von Brauchitsch, in Roslavl. Field-Marshal von Kluge was also present. To attend this meeting I had had to drive for twenty-two hours through a blizzard. I described in detail to the Commander-in-Chief of the Army the condition of my troops, and I asked for and received his permission to withdraw my Army to the line of the Susha and Oka; during the battles of the previous October this had constituted our front line at one period and consequently had been fortified to a certain extent. The question was also raised of how the gap between XXIV Panzer Corps and XLIII Army Corps, now some 25 miles wide, might best be closed. Fourth Army was supposed to hand over the 137th Infantry Division to Second Panzer Army for this purpose. But Field-Marshal von Kluge had so far sent off only four battalions and the divisional commander. I described this force as totally inadequate and asked that the remaining half of the division be sent me at once. While fighting to re-establish contact the brave divisional commander, General Bergmann, lost his life. The vital gap could not be closed.

The result of the Roslavl conference was the following order: 'Second Army is placed under command of the commander, Second Panzer Army. Both armies will hold a line in front of Kursk—in front of Orel–Plavskoie–Aleksin, withdrawing in case of necessity to the Oka.' I could rightly assume that the Commander-in-Chief of the Army would inform Hitler of this decision; but subsequent events make it at least doubtful whether he did, in fact, ever do so.

On this day a Russian penetration in Second Army's front, which had begun on December 13th, was deepened through Livny towards Orel; as a result the 45th Infantry Division was encircled and partially destroyed. Icy surfaces made all movement difficult. Frostbite was costing us more casualties than was the enemy. XLVII Panzer Corps had to be pulled back since its right-hand neighbour, the 293rd Infantry Division of Second Army, was withdrawing from Yefremov.

On December 16th, at my urgent request, Schmundt, who was in our neighbourhood, came to meet me at Orel airfield, where we had half an hour's conversation. I described the situation to him in the gravest terms and asked him to repeat what I had said to the Führer. I expected Hitler to telephone me during the night and to answer the proposals that I had made via Schmundt. It was during this conversation that I learned of the approaching changes in the Army High Command and the imminent departure of Field-Marshal von Brauchitsch. During that night I wrote:

I frequently cannot sleep at night and my brain goes round and round while I try to think what more I can do to help my poor soldiers who are out there without shelter in this abominable cold. It is frightful, unimaginable. The people at the *OKH* and *OKW*, who have never seen the front, have no idea what the conditions here are like. They keep on sending us orders which we cannot possibly carry out and they ignore all our requests and suggestions.

During that night I received the telephone call from Hitler that I had been expecting. He commanded that we hold fast, forbade further withdrawals and promised that we should receive replacements—to the number, I think, of 500 men—by air. It was a very bad line and Hitler repeated his orders. As for our withdrawals, these had already begun as a result of my conversation with Field-Marshal von Brauchitsch in Roslavl and could not now be halted.

On December 17th I visited the commanders of the XXIV and XLVII Panzer Corps and of the LIII Army Corps in order to learn once again what the state of our troops was like and to discuss the situation. The three generals were all agreed that it was impossible, with the strength at our disposal, to organise a defensive line east of the Oka. The problem was how to keep up the combat strength of the troops until the arrival of fresh formations should permit the construction of a defence which could hold fast. They reported that the troops were beginning to doubt the ability of a Supreme Headquarters which had ordered the last, desperate attack against an enemy whom they had so grossly underestimated. 'If only we were mobile and had our old combat strength, then it would be child's play. The Russian is trained and equipped for winter warfare and we are not.'

On this day Second Army became nervous lest the enemy break through to Novosil.

In view of the general situation I decided, with Army Group's approval, to fly to the Führer's headquarters and personally to describe to Hitler what the position was in my Army, since neither telephonic nor written communications had produced any results. The conference was arranged for December 20th. By that date Field-Marshal von Bock had reported himself sick and had been replaced as Commander of Army Group Centre by Field-Marshal von Kluge.

On December 18th Second Army was ordered to hold a line Tim–Livny–Verchoie and to withdraw in the course of the next few days, in conjunction with the right wing of Second Panzer Army, to the line Bolshaia Reka–Susha. Second Panzer Army was to occupy the line Mogilki–Vershoie Plavy–Ssorochenka–Chunina–Kosmina.

XLIII Army Corps was placed under command of Fourth Army.

On December 19th XLVII Panzer Corps and LIII Army Corps withdrew to the line of the Plava. I decided to bring XLVII Panzer Corps back to a line from Oserki to the north-west of Podissiniovke and to assemble XXIV Panzer Corps in the Orel area as army reserve so as to give the units of that corps a short rest and to create an operational, mobile force at my disposal.

Fourth Army was strongly attacked on its right wing and partially thrown back.

My First Dismissal

'Little monk, little monk, you are taking a hard road!' These words of Frundsberg to Dr. Martin Luther before the Diet of Worms of 1521, were quoted to me by my comrades when they learned of my decision to fly to Hitler's headquarters. They were applicable enough. I was perfectly well aware that it would not be easy for me to bring Hitler over to my way of thinking. At that time, however, I still believed that our Supreme Command would listen to sensible propositions when they were laid before it by a general who knew the front. This belief I retained while making the long flight from the ice-bound battle area north of Orel to the well-appointed and well-heated Supreme Headquarters far away in East Prussia.

At 15.30 hrs. on December 20th I landed at Rastenburg airfield. I was to confer with Hitler for five hours, with only two breaks of half an hour each, one for the evening meal and one for the general weekly briefing which Hitler always attended personally.

I was received by Hitler at about 18.00 hrs. Keitel, Schmundt and other officers of Hitler's entourage were also there. Neither the Chief of Army General Staff nor any other representative of the *OKH* was present, though Hitler had appointed himself Commander-in-Chief of the Army after the dismissal of Field-Marshal von Brauchitsch. And so, as on the 23rd of August, 1941, I stood in lonely opposition to the ranks of the *OKW*. As Hitler came forward to greet me I saw to my surprise, for the first time, a hard unfriendly expression in his eyes, and this convinced me that some opponent of mine must have turned him against me. The dim lighting of the room served to increase this unpleasant impression.

The conference began with my description of the state of Second Panzer Army and Second Army. I then spoke of my intention of withdrawing both armies bit by bit to the Susha–Oka position, an intention which, as already stated, I had expressed to Field-Marshal von Brauchitsch on December 14th, in Roslavl, and which he had approved. I was convinced that Hitler must have been informed of this. I was, therefore, all the more taken aback when he shouted: 'No! I forbid that!' I informed him that the withdrawal was already in progress and that there was no intermediate line at which it could be halted for any length of time before the rivers were reached. If he regarded it as important to preserve the lives of the troops and to hold a position throughout the winter he had no choice but to permit the withdrawal to be completed.

HITLER: 'If that is the case they must dig into the ground where they are and hold every square yard of land!'

I: 'Digging into the ground is no longer feasible in most places, since it is frozen to a depth of five feet and our wretched entrenching tools won't go through it.'

HITLER: 'In that case they must blast craters with the heavy howitzers. We had to do that in the First World War in Flanders.'

I: 'In the First World War our divisions in Flanders held, on the average, sectors 2 to 3 miles wide and were supported in the defence by two or three battalions of heavy howitzers per division with proportionately abundant supplies of ammunition. My divisions have to defend fronts of 25 to 35 miles and in each of my divisions there are 4 heavy howitzers with approximately 50 shells per gun. If I use those shells to make craters I shall have 50 hollows in the ground, each about the width and depth of a wash tub with a large black circle around it. I shall not have a crater position. In Flanders there was never such cold as we are now experiencing. And apart from that I need my ammunition to fire at the Russians. We can't even drive stakes into the ground for carrying our telephone wires; to make a hole for the stake we have to use high explosives. When are we to get sufficient explosives to blast out defensive positions on the scale you have in mind?'

But Hitler insisted on his order, that we remain where we were, being carried out.

I*

I: 'Then this means taking up positional warfare in an unsuitable terrain, as happened on the Western Front during the First World War. In this case we shall have the same battles of material and the same enormous casualties as then without any hope of winning a decisive victory. If such tactics are adopted we shall, during the course of this coming winter, sacrifice the lives of our officers, our non-commissioned officers and of the men suitable to replace them, and this sacrifice will have been not only useless but also irreparable.'

HITLER: 'Do you think Frederick the Great's grenadiers were anxious to die? They wanted to live, too, but the king was right in asking them to sacrifice themselves. I believe that I, too, am entitled to ask any German soldier to lay down his life.'

I: 'Every German soldier knows that in war-time he must risk his life for his country and our soldiers have certainly proved up to now that they are prepared to do so. But such a sacrifice may only be asked of a man if the results to be obtained from it are worth having. The intentions I have heard expressed will lead to losses that are utterly disproportionate to the results that will be achieved. My soldiers will not have protection against the weather and the Russians until they reach the Susha–Oka line and the fortified positions that were built there during the autumn. I beg you to remember that it is not the enemy who is causing us our bloody losses: we are suffering twice as many casualties from the cold as from the fire of the Russians. Any man who has seen the hospitals filled with frost-bite cases must realise what that means.'

HITLER: 'I know that you have not spared yourself and that you have spent a great deal of time with the troops. I grant you that. But you are seeing events at too close a range. You have been too deeply impressed by the suffering of the soldiers. You feel too much pity for them. You should stand back more. Believe me, things appear clearer when examined at longer range.'

I: 'Naturally it is my duty to lessen the suffering of my soldiers so far as that lies within my power. But it is hard when the men have even now not yet received their winter clothing and the greater part of the infantry are still going about in denim uniforms. Boots, vests, gloves, woollen helmets are either non-existent or else are hopelessly worn out.'

HITLER shouted: 'That is not true. The Quartermaster-General informed me that the winter clothing had been issued.'

I: 'I dare say it has been issued but it has never arrived. I have made it my business to find out what has happened to it. At present it is in Warsaw station, where it has been for the last several weeks, since it cannot be sent on owing to a lack of locomotives and obstructions to the lines. Our requests that it be forwarded in September and October were bluntly refused. Now it's too late.'

The Quartermaster-General was sent for and had to admit that what I had said was correct. Goebbels' campaign that Christmas for clothes for the soldiers was a result of this conversation. The clothes thus collected did not actually reach the soldiers during the winter of 1941–42.

The question of fighting strength and ration strength was next raised. As a result of the heavy vehicle losses, during the mud period and from the great cold, the transport available was insufficient both for the fighting troops and for the supply troops. Since we had received no replacements for the transports lost, the troops were having to supplement their insufficient vehicles by using whatever they could find in the country. This consisted mostly of sleds and sledges, which had a very limited load capacity. A great number of such vehicles was required to replace the lorries we had not got. Thus we needed a proportionately higher number of men to move the supplies. Hitler now insisted that the number of supply troops and of soldiers in the units' supply columns, which he considered far too great, be drastically cut down to provide more rifles for the front. Needless to say this had been done to the greatest possible extent that was consistent with not endangering our supply services. Further reduction was only feasible if the condition of other supply means, and particularly of the railroads, was improved. It was difficult to make Hitler grasp this simple fact.

Then came the question of shelter. A few weeks before there had been an exhibition in Berlin of the arrangements which had been made by the *OKH* for the care of the troops during the coming winter. Field-Marshal von Brauchitsch had insisted upon personally showing Hitler around the exhibition. It was all most handsomely presented and was featured in the newsreels. Unfortunately, however, the troops possessed none of these beautiful things. As a result of the continual movement it had been impossible to do any building and the countryside had little to offer. Our living conditions were utterly wretched. And of this, too, Hitler was ignorant. The Armaments Minister, Dr. Todt, was present during this part of the discussion; he was a man of understanding and of normal, human sensibility. He was deeply moved by my description of life at the front, and he presented me with two trench stoves which he had just had made; these stoves, constructed to be shown to Hitler, were to serve as models for the troops who could then build them themselves with materials available in the countryside. This was at least one positive result of the lengthy discussion.

During the evening meal I sat next to Hitler and I took the opportunity to describe incidents of life at the front to him. But the effect of my anecdotes was not what I had expected. Both Hitler and his entourage were plainly convinced that I was exaggerating.

After dinner, when our discussion was resumed, I proposed that

general staff officers who had had actual experience of front-line
fighting during this war be transferred to the *OKW* and the *OKH*. I
said: 'Judging by the reactions of the gentlemen of the *OKW* I have
reached the conclusion that our messages and reports are not being
correctly understood and, as a result, are not being properly inter-
preted to you. It seems to me, therefore, necessary that officers with
front-line experience be transferred to fill general staff positions at the
OKH and *OKW*. It's time the guard was changed. In both these headquarters officers have been sitting miles away from the fighting since the
beginning of the war, that is to say for over two years, without even
once seeing the front. This war is so different from the First World
War that service at the front in that war is no help in understanding this
one.'

I had stirred up a hornet's nest with this suggestion. Hitler replied
angrily: 'I cannot now be separated from my personal staff.'

I: 'There is no need for you to change your adjutants. That's not the
point. What does matter is that the important general staff positions be
occupied by officers who have had recent experience of the front, and
particularly of the front during the winter war.'

This request, too, was gruffly refused. My conversation with Hitler
was thus a complete failure. As I left the conference room I heard
Hitler say to Keitel: 'I haven't convinced that man!' The breach was
now complete and could no longer be closed.

The next morning before starting the flight back I telephoned General
Jodl, the chief of the Armed Forces Command Staff, and repeated to
him that present methods must lead to intolerable sacrifices of life for
which there could be no possible justification. Reserves were needed
urgently to occupy positions behind the front and out of contact with
the enemy. This call of mine had no recognisable effect.

After my telephone conversation with Jodl, on December 21st, I
flew back to Orel. By Hitler's orders the left-hand boundary of my Army
was changed to the junction of the rivers Shisdra and Oka. This
alteration increased the responsibilities of my Panzer Army to an
undesirable extent. I spent the rest of the day working out and issuing
orders in accordance with Hitler's intentions.

With the object of ensuring that these orders were carried out I
drove, on December 22nd, to the divisions of XLVII Panzer Corps.
After a brief conversation at corps headquarters I went to Chern, where
the 10th (Motorised) Infantry Division was located, and explained to
General von Loeper the purpose of the orders issued and the reasons
that led Hitler to make his decision. In the afternoon I visited the 18th
and 17th Panzer Divisions for the same reason. I arrived back in Orel
after a freezing drive at about midnight. The commanders of the

western end of my front were at least now fully informed, by me personally, of the change in the situation resultant on Hitler's orders; I thought, therefore, that I could face the coming events of the next few days with a clear conscience.

I spent December 23rd instructing the other corps commanders. LIII Army Corps reported that the 167th Infantry Division was also being heavily attacked now. The 296th Infantry Division fell back on Bielev. The defensive power of the corps could by this time only be rated as poor. Between its left wing and the XLIII Army Corps a great gap still existed which could not be closed on account of the almost total immobility of the troops once they were off the roads; the country-side was, in fact, impassable. I therefore decided to withdraw the 3rd and 4th Panzer Divisions to Orel by way of the Tula–Orel road, to give them a short period of rest for three days to recuperate, and then to move them north under command of XXIV Panzer Corps through Karachev and Bryansk with the object of attacking the flank of the enemy forces that were pressing towards the Oka. But deep enemy penetrations of Second Panzer Army's front necessitated the switch of part of this force to the new danger-points and delayed their assembly in the Lichvin area. The immobile elements of XXIV Panzer Corps were collected together at Orel for the protection of that town.

I spent December 24th visiting a number of hospitals to see the Christmas festivities. I was able to bring a little good cheer to many a brave soldier. But it was a heart-rending business. I spent most of the evening working alone; later Liebenstein, Büsing, and Kahlden came to see me and we spent a short time together in comradely fashion.

On December 24th Second Army lost Livny. To the north of that place the enemy crossed the Oka. By order of the *OKH* the 4th Panzer Division was sent off to Bielev to check the enemy advance. The unified counter-attack by XXIV Panzer Corps which I had planned thus seemed likely to become impossible on account of the dispersal of the corps' forces.

During the night of December 24th–25th the 10th (Motorised) Infantry Division lost Chern as a result of a Russian enveloping attack. The Russian success became unexpectedly great, because the elements of LIII Army Corps fighting on the left of the 10th (Motorised) Infantry Division were unable to hold and the enemy thus achieved a break-through. Parts of the 10th (Motorised) Infantry Division were encircled in Chern. I immediately reported this misfortune to Army Group. Field-Marshal von Kluge accused me in violent terms, saying that I must have ordered the evacuation of Chern and, what is more, must have done so at least twenty-four hours before. The exact contrary was the case. I had, as already mentioned, personally given Hitler's orders according to which the town was to be held. I therefore angrily denied the unjust accusations that Field-Marshal von Kluge made against me.

On December 25th the elements of the 10th (Motorised) Infantry Division which had been encircled succeeded in breaking out and reaching our lines with several hundred prisoners. I ordered a withdrawal to the Susha–Oka position. In the evening I had another sharp argument with Field-Marshal von Kluge, who accused me of having sent him an incorrect official report. He hung up with the words: 'I shall inform the Führer about you.' This was going too far. I told the Chief of Staff of the Army Group that if I was to be treated in this fashion I had no wish to continue to command my Army and that I would request that I be relieved of my command. I immediately sent off a telegram to this effect. But Field-Marshal von Kluge was ahead of me. He had requested the *OKH* that I be removed, and on the morning of December 26th I was informed that Hitler had transferred me to the *OKH* officers' reserve pool. My successor was to be the commander of Second Army, General Rudolf Schmidt.

On December 26th I said farewell to my staff and issued a short order of the day to my troops.

On December 27th I left the front, spending the night in Roslavl; the night of the 28th–29th I passed in Minsk; the 29th–30th in Warsaw, the 30th–31st in Posen, and on New Year's Eve I arrived in Berlin.

Further disagreement arose between Field-Marshal von Kluge and my staff concerning my final order of the day to my soldiers. Army Group wished to prevent publication of the order, since Field-Marshal von Kluge was afraid that it might contain criticisms of higher commanders. Needless to say the order was quite unobjectionable. Liebenstein ensured that my men at least received a parting greeting from me.

My final order ran as follows:

The Commander of Second Panzer Army. Army headquarters 26.12.1941.
                              Daily Army Order.
Soldiers of the Second Panzer Army!
The Führer and Supreme Commander of the Armed Forces has today relieved me of my command.

At this time when I am leaving you I remember our six months of battle together for the greatness of our land and the victory of our arms, and I recall with honour and respect all those who have bled and died for Germany. From the bottom of my heart I thank you, my comrades-in-arms, for the trusty devotion and true comradeship which you have at all times shown during these long months. We have been together in success and in adversity and my greatest joy has lain in my chances to help you and to protect you.

Good luck to you!

I know that you will continue to fight as bravely as ever and that despite the hardships of winter and the numerical superiority of the enemy you will conquer. My thoughts will be with you in your hard struggle.

You are waging it for Germany!

Heil Hitler!

signed, GUDERIAN.

7. ON INACTIVE SERVICE

The unfair treatment that I had received began by making me feel, understandably I think, very embittered. I therefore requested, during the early days of January, 1942, in Berlin, that a military court of inquiry be set up to examine my past conduct; this would have led to the refutation of the charges that Field-Marshal von Kluge had made against me and would have made clear the reasons underlying my past behaviour. My request was turned down by Hitler. I was not informed on what grounds he did this. It was, however, plain that a clarification of the business was regarded as undesirable. It was fully recognised that I had been unjustly treated. Immediately before my departure from Orel, Colonel Schmundt had appeared; he had been sent by Hitler to discover what was the truth. Liebenstein and a number of the front-line generals had told him the whole story, which he had passed on to his colleagues at Supreme Headquarters with the following comment: 'The man has been treated unjustly. His whole army is on his side and believes in him. We must see what we can do to put this business to rights.' There can be no doubt concerning the goodwill of Schmundt, who was a high-minded and honourable man. He did not, however, succeed in having his good intentions realised. The reason for his failure was the attitude of various other personages involved.

So now I sat in Berlin with nothing whatever to do, while my soldiers continued their hard struggle. I knew that I was being watched, that every step I took and every remark I made was being observed. As a result, for the first few months I lived in complete retirement and hardly ever left my home. I received only a few guests. One of the first was Sepp Dietrich, the commander of the *Leibstandarte*, who telephoned me from the Chancellery to say he was coming to see me. He explained to me that he had done this deliberately in order to show 'the people at the top' that they had treated me unjustly and to make it plain to them that he did not wish to be identified with such behaviour. Nor did Dietrich make any bones about telling Hitler how he felt about my case.

The changes in the higher levels of command in the Army were by no means limited to the dismissal of Field-Marshal von Rundstedt and of myself. Many generals of hitherto high repute were deprived of their office either for no reason at all or on some very slender excuse. Among these were Generals Geyer, Förster, and Hoeppner. Field-Marshal Ritter von Leeb and General Kübler went at their own request. Colonel-General Strauss reported that his health had broken down.

This 'house-cleaning' was not carried out without arousing considerable protest. Most noticeable was the case of Colonel-General Hoeppner; when Hitler dismissed him he simultaneously denied him the right to wear his uniform or decorations, cancelled his pension and deprived him of the use of the house previously allotted to him. Hoeppner refused to recognise these illegal orders and the lawyers of the *OKH* and the *OKW* showed sufficient courage on this occasion to stand up to Hitler; they pointed out to him that he was not entitled to give such orders without first arranging for a disciplinary investigation of Hoeppner's conduct, the findings of which would undoubtedly be in Hoeppner's favour. In the course of a telephone conversation with his immediate superior, Field-Marshal von Kluge, Hoeppner had referred in terms of irritation to the 'civilian leadership'; Kluge had believed that the reference was to Hitler and had repeated the remark. Hitler became extremely angry when he heard of this. The result of the ill-feeling thus engendered was the law passed by the Reichstag on April 26th, 1942, which removed the last checks to totalitarian authority in the legislative, executive, and judicial spheres.[1] This law marked the culmination of a long process which had begun with the unfortunate Authorisation Act of March 23rd, 1933; the German dictator was now given complete despotic power. Germany had thus ceased to be a modern state whose structure was based on the rule of law. The soldiers had played no part in the passing of either of these two Acts. They had simply to bear their evil consequences.

The unpleasantness of the past few months had increased the weakness of my heart, which was already beginning to show sign of strain; on the advice of my doctor I therefore decided to go with my wife to Badenweiler for a four weeks' cure at the end of March, 1942. The peacefulness of the beautiful countryside in spring and the medicinal baths of the little spa combined to soothe both heart and soul after the strain of events in Russia. But when we returned to Berlin my dear wife caused me great anxiety; as a result of a most malignant blood-poisoning she was confined to her bed for many months. Apart from this, my personal situation in Berlin had become so unpleasant as a result of the endless stream of visitors with their tiresome questions that we decided to spend a small inheritance on buying a little house near Lake Constance or in the Salzkammergut; thus we would escape from the atmosphere of the capital. At the end of September I asked General Fromm, the Commander of the Training Army, to arrange that I be given the necessary leave to do this; in reply he asked that I come to see him. A few days before Rommel had sent me a telegram from Africa in which he said that he had to return to Germany on

[1] It granted Hitler the right to change laws by decree without discussion by the Reichstag.

account of ill health and that he had proposed to Hitler that I deputise
for him during his absence. This proposal had been turned down by
Hitler. Fromm now asked me whether I was anticipating renewed
employment. I said that I was not. On the day of my return from the
Salzkammergut Fromm telephoned me again and requested that I go
to see him. He informed me that he had had a conversation with
Schmundt on the previous day and had learned from him that there
could be no question of my being re-employed. But the Führer had
heard that I was contemplating buying a property in southern Germany.
He knew that I came from the Warthegau, or West Prussia, and he
therefore desired that I settle there and not in South Germany. It was
his intention to make a national donation to all men who had been
decorated with the Oak Leaves to the Knight's Cross, and such
donations were to consist primarily of land. It was suggested that I
look for a suitable property in the country of my origin. When I heard
this I realised that I could now put my grey uniform away and settle
down once and for all to civilian life.

But at first there was no question of this. My bad heart took a turn
for the worse during the autumn of 1942. At the end of November I
suffered a complete collapse, was almost totally unconscious for
several days and could take no nourishment; I only recovered slowly,
thanks to the excellent medical treatment I received from Professor von
Domarus, one of Berlin's leading specialists. By Christmas I was able
to leave my bed for a few hours at a time; during January I continued
to make slow progress; and by the end of February I was well enough
to set off in search of a house in the Warthegau where I might start my
new civilian career as a landowner. But this was not to be.

During 1942 the German Army had once again launched an offensive
—from June 28th to the end of August—which had been successful in
that the southern wing (Kleist) had reached the Caucasian mountains
while Paulus' Sixth Army to the north had advanced as far as Stalingrad
on the Volga. Those operations were once again based on an eccentric
plan. The objectives assigned were beyond the power of the troops,
weakened as they were by the hardships of the 1941–42 winter campaign. As in August of 1941, Hitler was driving for objectives of
economic and ideological significance without first ensuring that the
enemy's military strength was broken. The capture of the Caspian
oilfields, the cutting of the Volga as a maritime artery, and the neutralisation of the industrial centre of Stalingrad, such were the motives
that led him to undertake operations which, from a military point of
view, were nonsensical.

I could only follow these developments through the Press and wireless, though occasionally a friend would supply me with more detailed information. But this was enough to make me realise how markedly our situation had deteriorated; after the disaster of Stalingrad, in January 1943, and even before the intervention by the Western powers, we were already in grave peril. And the English trial landing at Dieppe, on August 19th, 1942, foreshadowed the opening of a second front in France.

In November 1942 the Allies landed in North Africa. The situation of our troops fighting in that theatre thus became perilous.

On September 25th Hitler had dismissed the Chief of the Army General Staff, Colonel-General Halder, and had appointed General Zeitzler to succeed him. At the same time responsibility for the employment of General Staff Corps personnel was taken away from the Chief of the General Staff and was given to the Army Personnel Office, which was directly subordinate to Hitler. By this act the Chief of the General Staff was deprived of one of his last means of controlling the General Staff Corps. Zeitzler protested in vain. With the dismissal of Halder, Hitler had completed the re-allocation of military power which he had not felt strong enough to carry out during the autumn of 1939, though even then he had nursed a deep and irreconcilable distrust for the leading figures of the Army. For three years now men had been working together along lines that went against their deepest convictions, men whose opinions were at variance and who felt a profound lack of trust in one another. Would this now all be changed? Would Hitler display more confidence in Zeitzler than he had shown for Brauchitsch and Halder? Would he now pay attention to the advice of his specialists? The destiny of Germany was dependent on the answer to these questions.

In any case, the new man set to work with the greatest energy. He did not hesitate to give Hitler his opinions and he fought hard for his point of view. Five times he offered to resign his post and five times his offer was refused, until at last Hitler's distrust of him grew so great that he finally let him go. He did not succeed in persuading Hitler to change his attitude.

The course of events on the Eastern Front during Zeitzler's tenure of office is shown on maps 27 and 28.

8. THE DEVELOPMENT OF THE ARMOURED FORCE, JANUARY 1942 TO FEBRUARY 1943

After assuming the functions of Commander-in-Chief of the Army, in December 1941, Hitler began to be increasingly preoccupied with the technical development of military weapons. He devoted his attention especially to the armoured force. The data given below comes mainly from the records of the former Chief Assistant (*Hauptdienstleiter*) Saur, who worked with Albert Speer, the Minister for Armaments and War Production. Those records show Hitler's eagerness to promote progress in weapon development; they also cast a light on his erratic character and are thus interesting documents.

As already stated, a group of responsible designers, industrialists, and officers of the Army Ordnance Office visited my Panzer Army in November 1941, with the object of studying at first hand our recent combat experience when fighting the superior Russian tank, the T34, and of deciding what measures should be taken to help us regain technical supremacy over the Russians. The officers at the front were of the opinion that the T34 should simply be copied, since this would be the quickest way of putting to rights the most unhappy situation of the German panzer troops: but the designers could not agree to this. This was not primarily because of the designers' natural pride in their own inventions, but rather because it would not be possible to mass-produce essential elements of the T34—in particular the aluminium diesel engines—with the necessary speed. Also, so far as steel alloys went, we were at a disadvantage compared to the Russians owing to our shortage of raw materials. It was, therefore, decided that the following solution be adopted: the construction of the *Tiger* Tank, a tank of some 60 tons, which had recently been started would continue: meanwhile, a light tank, called the *Panther*, weighing between 35 and 45 tons, was to be designed. On January 23rd, 1942, the design for this tank was submitted to Hitler. It was at this conference that Hitler ordered that German tank production be increased to a capacity of 600 units per month. In May of 1940 our capacity, inclusive of all types, had been 125 units. So it can be seen that the increase in productivity of an industry making one of the most vital weapons of war had been extraordinarily small during this period of almost two years of war; this surely provides proof that neither Hitler nor the General Staff correctly estimated the importance of the tank to our war effort. Even the great tank victories of 1939–41 had not sufficed to change this.

During this conference, on January 23rd, 1942, Hitler expressed an opinion which was to be a continual source of confusion to him in his understanding both of the technical development and of the tactical and operational employment of tanks. He believed that the hollow-charge shell, which was about to be issued to the artillery, and which showed increased power of armour penetration, would lead to a considerable decrease in the future effectiveness of tanks. He believed that if this new development should, in fact, fulfil its promise, the answer was to have much more self-propelled artillery and he therefore wished to divert tank chassis to the artillery for this purpose. On this 23rd of January, 1942, he requested that measures be taken along the lines indicated.

On February 8th, 1942, the Minister for Armaments and War Production, Dr. Todt, was killed in an aeroplane accident. He was succeeded by Speer.

In March the Krupp Company and Professor Porsche were instructed to prepare designs for a tank that was to weigh 100 tons. Work on this tank was to be so hastened that the experimental model could be produced by the spring of 1943. In order to hurry the development of tanks more designers were required: to acquire them the peacetime activity of the automobile factories was discontinued. On March 19th, 1942, Speer informed the Führer that by October, 1942, there would be 60 Porsche Tigers and 25 Henschel Tigers available, and that by March, 1943, a further 135 would be produced, bringing the total by that time to 220—assuming that they were all employable.

In April Hitler ordered the design of tank shells for the 80 mm. and 75 mm. guns that were to be installed in the Tiger and Panther tanks. The first experimental Tigers were produced by the Henschel and Porsche companies.

In this same month Hitler was talking about an expedition against Malta, for which he required 12 Panzer IV's with 80 mm. of frontal armour in order to attack the island fortress. But nothing more was heard about this very necessary operation.

In May 1942 Hitler approved the design of the Panther that was submitted by the MAN Company and also ordered the construction of flats capable of transporting super-heavy tanks. The production of assault guns was to be increased to 100, that of Panzer III's to 190 per month.

In June of 1942 Hitler was concerned as to whether the armour of the tanks was sufficiently thick. He ordered that the frontal armour of the Panzer IV and of the assault guns be increased to 80 mm., and

he expressed doubts whether 80 mm. would be enough frontal armour
for the Panthers by the spring of 1943. He therefore ordered that an
investigation be carried out to determine whether it was possible to
increase the armour of that tank to 100 mm. At the same time he
ordered that in any event all the vertical surfaces of the tank were to
be at least 100 mm. thick. He also ordered that attempts be made to
increase the frontal armour of the Tiger to 120 mm.

At a conference held on June 23rd, 1942, the following production
figures for May, 1943, were estimated:

Armoured Reconnaissance Vehicles, built on the chassis
   of the old Panzer II 131
Panther Tanks 250
Tiger Tanks 285

Hitler was entirely satisfied with this programme. He wanted the
rapid development of an air-cooled diesel engine for tanks, a desire
that General Lutz had expressed as early as 1932, but that had only
been fulfilled in the case of the little Panzer I which the Krupp Company
had built. Hitler examined in detail the basic problems of tank construction and agreed to the fundamental priorities on which the experts
had decided: these were, first, the strongest possible armament, secondly,
great speed, and thirdly, heavy armour. But he was a paradoxical man
and he continued to insist that heavy armour was also a primary
requirement. Then his fantasy led him into the realms of the gigantic.
The engineers Grote and Hacker were ordered to design a monster
tank weighing 1,000 tons. 100 mm. belly armour was ordered for the
Porsche Tiger that was in process of construction and the armament
was to consist either of a 150 mm. L37 cannon or a 100 mm. L70.
Professor Porsche promised delivery of the first model by May 12th,
1943. On July 8th, 1942, he ordered that the first Tiger Companies
were to be made ready with all speed for operations against Leningrad.
By July 23rd, that is to say fifteen days later, Hitler had changed his
mind; he now demanded that the Tigers be ready for operations in
France by September at the latest. It would thus appear that he was
already expecting a large-scale Allied landing.

In order to improve the old Panzer III, Hitler ordered that it be
re-equipped with the 75 mm. L24 cannon. He was very anxious that
there should be a great increase in tank production. But at the same
conference the question of mounting self-propelled guns on tank chassis
was again seriously discussed, even though the production of such
weapons must inevitably result in a decrease in the number of tanks
produced.

In August, 1942, Hitler ordered an inquiry to be made as to how quickly the 88 mm. cannon could be installed in the Tiger tank. This gun was constructed to be capable of firing a shell that would penetrate 200 mm. of armour. He also ordered that all Panzer IV's sent to the factories for repair be re-equipped with long-barrelled guns, so that the power of those tanks' armament might be increased.

In September of 1942 a new construction programme was introduced, according to which the production figures for the spring of 1944 were to be as follows:

Leopard (light reconnaissance tank)	150
Panther	600
Tiger	50
Total tank production	800

Assault guns	300
Light self-propelled guns	150
Heavy self-propelled guns	130
Super-heavy self-propelled guns	20
Total artillery pieces on tank chassis .	600

In order to do as little damage as possible to tank production, it was ordered that the self-propelled guns be armoured with un-hardened steel. All the same it was plain to see that the principal pre-occupation now was the production of guns rather than of tanks, that is to say of defensive and not offensive weapons; furthermore these defensive weapons were unsatisfactory, for the troops were already beginning to complain that a self-propelled gun on a Panzer II or Czech T38 chassis was not a sufficiently effective weapon.

During the discussion on the subject of the Porsche Tiger, Hitler expressed his opinion that this tank, being electrically powered and air cooled, would be particularly suitable for employment in the African theatre, but that its operational range of only 30 miles was quite unsatisfactory and must be increased to 90 miles. This was undoubtedly correct; only it should have been stated when the first designs were submitted.

The discussions that took place in September already show the influence of the heavy fighting in and around Stalingrad. Among other matters, it was decided that the assault guns must be improved. They were to be equipped with the long 75 mm. L70 gun and given 100 mm. of frontal armour. Heavy infantry guns were to be mounted on assault gun chassis or built into Panzer IV's. Some of the Porsche Tigers then in construction were to be changed into assault guns by having the revolving turret removed and being equipped with a long

88 mm. cannon and 200 mm. of frontal armour. The installation of
a 210 mm. mortar in this tank was discussed. There can be no doubt
that the tanks available to us at that time were not suitable for street
fighting; on the other hand the correct solution for the problem was
not this constant modification to the design of tanks actually in production, with the resultant creation of countless variations to the
original type, each of which would need innumerable different spare
parts. The repair of tanks in the field was being made almost impossible.

In September of 1942 the first Tigers went into action. A lesson
learned from the First World War had taught us that it is necessary
to be patient about committing new weapons and that they must be
held back until they are being produced in such quantities as to allow
their employment in mass. In the First World War the French and
British used their tanks prematurely, in small numbers, and thereby
failed to win the great victory which they were entitled to expect.
Military experts had long ago established this criticism as valid. I
myself had often spoken and written on the subject. Hitler was well
aware of the facts. But he was consumed by his desire to try his new
weapon. He therefore ordered that the Tigers be committed in a quite
secondary operation, in a limited attack carried out in terrain that was
utterly unsuitable; for in the swampy forests near Leningrad heavy
tanks could only move in single file along the forest tracks, which,
of course, was exactly where the enemy anti-tank guns were posted,
waiting for them. The results were not only heavy, unnecessary
casualties, but also the loss of secrecy and of the element of surprise
for future operations. Disappointment was all the greater since the
attack bogged down in the unsuitable terrain.

In October tank production suffered further in favour of the production of assault guns: Panzer IV's were diverted to carrying the 75 mm.
L70 cannon and Panthers the long 88 mm. L71. Furthermore, 40 to 60
heavy infantry guns were to be built on to Panzer IV bodies. Hitler
also talked of mounting mortars on Panzer IV's; these were to have
extra short barrels and be used as mine-throwers. Interesting as all
these new designs were, the actual result was simply a decrease in
the production of the only useful combat tank available to us at that
time, the Panzer IV; and furthermore it was only in this month that
the production figures for that tank reached the really very modest
total of 100. Nor was that all. The Armament Ministry proposed that
reconnaissance Panthers be produced in addition to the Leopards which
had already been planned. Luckily nothing came of this project.

In the field of tank production the wrong line was thus taken. On
the other hand Hitler insisted quite correctly that the Tiger be armed
with the long 88 mm. flat trajectory gun, preferring this weapon to

one of heavier calibre but lesser muzzle-velocity. The primary purpose of the tank gun must be to fight enemy tanks, and to this all other considerations must be made subordinate.

In November Hitler successfully demanded that the production of Tigers be increased from 13 to 25 per month. This figure was attained during the course of that same month. The production of assault guns now reached 100.

At the beginning of December there were renewed discussions concerning the correct employment of tanks. It was then pointed out to Hitler that the commitment of the Tigers piecemeal was highly disadvantageous. He now expressed the opinion that commitment in detail was suitable to the requirements of the Eastern theatre, but that in Africa employment in mass would be more rewarding. Unfortunately I do not know on what grounds this incomprehensible statement was based.

The construction of the Panzer III was now entirely discontinued, the industrial capacity thus freed being given over to the building of assault guns. The production figure for assault guns was to reach 220 per month by June 1943, of which 24 were to be armed with light field howitzers. This gun, with its low muzzle velocity and its very high trajectory, was undoubtedly well suited to the requirements of the infantry, but its production resulted in a fresh weakening of our defensive power against hostile tanks.

During a conference with the engineers Porsche and Dr. Müller (from Krupps) Hitler said that he expected a specimen model of the *Mäuschen* or *Mouse*, the 100-ton tank, to be ready by the summer of 1943: he would then require the Krupp Company to produce 5 of these tanks per month.

Reports began to come in of difficulties that were arising in the replacement of spare parts as a result of the multiplication of the many types caused by the constant alterations to the designs.

In January 1943 there were further discussions concerning armour, tank guns and the mammoth tank. It was ordered that the vertical surfaces of the old Panzer IV be 100 mm. armour plate, and the frontal armour of the Panther was also to be 100 mm. Production of the light reconnaissance tank, the Leopard, was cancelled before it was ever started, since 'neither the armour nor the armament envisaged for this model is suitable for the conditions that are anticipated to prevail in 1944.'

It was ordered that the Tiger be equipped with a long 88 mm. gun, with frontal armour of 150 mm. and side armour of 80 mm. Porsche's Mouse was to go into production and the figure raised to 10 per month. This gigantic offspring of the fantasy of Hitler and his advisers did not at the time even exist in the form of a wooden model. All the same it was decided that mass production was to begin at the end of 1943, that it was to be armed with a 128 mm. gun and the eventual installation of a 150 mm. gun was to be studied.

For street fighting Hitler ordered the construction of three Ram-Tigers,[1] to be constructed on Porsche's chassis. This 'knightly' weapon seems to have been based on the tactical fantasies of armchair strategists. In order that this street-fighting monster might be supplied with the necessary petrol, the construction of fuel-carrying auxiliary vehicles and of reserve containers was ordered. Hitler also ordered the construction of multiple smoke mortars for tanks and declared that the helicopter was the ideal aircraft for artillery observation and for co-operation with tanks.

Hitler's appeal, 'To all those engaged in Tank Production,' on January 22nd, 1943, and his delegation of full powers to Minister Speer for increasing such production, indicate the growing anxiety concerning the declining power of the German armoured forces in relationship to that of the enemy, who was steadily continuing the mass production of his outstanding model, the T34.

Despite the recognition of this fact, early in February Hitler ordered the construction of the so-called *Hummel* or *Lobster* (a heavy field howitzer) and of the *Hornisse* or *Hornet* (an 88 mm. gun) as self-propelled guns on a Panzer IV chassis. He ordered that the total productive capacity of the old Panzer II and of the Czech T38 tank be devoted to making carriages for self-propelled guns—the former to mount a light field howitzer, the latter a 1940 model, 75 mm. anti-tank gun. He ordered that 90 Porsche Tiger *Ferdinands* be made ready with all speed. To protect the Panzer IV, the Panther and the assault guns against the effect of the Russian infantry's tank-destroying weapon, the equipment of these models with a so-called *Schürze* or 'apron' was ordered: this consisted of sheets of armour plating to be hung on the outside of tanks to cover vertical surfaces and the wheels and tracks.

Finally, the General Staff took a hand in the tank situation which was becoming ever more confused and unsatisfactory; the General Staff requested the abandonment of all tank construction programmes with the exception of the Tiger and of the Panther, which latter was not yet in mass-production. Hitler readily accepted this proposal, and the Armaments Ministry was also pleased by the greater simplicity in production which would result. This new plan contained only one major weakness; with the abandonment of the Panzer IV Germany would, until further notice, be limited to the production of 25 Tigers

---

[1] This tank, a product of Hitler's imagination, was designed with the purpose of ramming enemy tanks or of breaking the walls of houses and other vertical obstacles.

per month. This would certainly have led to the defeat of the German Army in the very near future. The Russians would have won the war even without the help of their Western allies and would have occupied the whole of Europe. No power on earth could have stopped them. The problems of Europe would thus have been greatly simplified and we should all have learned what real 'democracy' is like!

The dangers that now threatened us were so enormous that officers of the armoured force itself and the few men of insight in Hitler's military entourage began to look around for someone who might be capable, even at this late hour, of staving off the chaos that threatened us all. My pre-war writings were placed on Hitler's desk and they managed to persuade him to read them. It was then proposed to him that he send for me. Finally, they succeeded in overcoming Hitler's distrust of my person to the extent that he agreed to listen to me at least once. And so on February 17th, 1943, to my very great surprise, I was telephoned by the Army Personnel Office and ordered to report at Supreme Headquarters in Vinnitsa for a conference with Hitler.

9. INSPECTOR-GENERAL OF ARMOURED TROOPS

Appointment and First Actions

When I was called to the telephone on February 17th, 1943, to speak to the Army Personnel Office I had no idea of what lay ahead of me. Only a week before, having recovered from my heart complaint, I had been to see General Bodewin Keitel,[1] the head of the Personnel Office, to find out about the general situation and one or two individuals. Judging by what he had then said to me there could be no question of my re-employment: rather, the contrary. Now General Linnarz, Keitel's assistant, informed me that I was to report directly to the Führer at Vinnitsa. He could not give me a reason for this summons. But it was plain to me that only the direst necessity would have driven Hitler to take such a step. Stalingrad, the unheard-of surrender of a whole army on the field of battle, the heavy casualties that resulted from this national catastrophe, the cruel defeats suffered by our allies who had not proved capable of holding their fronts on either side of the destroyed Sixth Army with the limited means at their disposal, all this had led to a grave crisis. Morale had reached a low point both in the Army and the country.

External and internal political blows now aggravated the situation.

After landing in North Africa the Western Powers had made rapid progress. The growing importance of this theatre of war was underlined by the meeting of Roosevelt and Churchill at Casablanca from January 14th–23rd, 1943; for us the most important result of this conference was the insistence that the Axis Powers surrender unconditionally. The effect of this brutal formula on the German nation and, above all, on the Army was great. The soldiers, at least, were convinced from now on that our enemies had decided on the utter destruction of Germany, that they were no longer fighting—as Allied propaganda at the time alleged—against Hitler and so-called Nazism, but against their efficient, and therefore dangerous, rivals for the trade of the world.

For some time the architects of the destructive dogma of Casablanca boasted of what they had done. On February 11th, 1943, Winston Churchill said in the House of Commons:

'It was only after full and cold, sober and mature consideration of these facts, on which our lives and liberties certainly depend, that the President,

[1] Brother of the Chief of the *OKW*.

with my full concurrence as agent of the War Cabinet, decided that the note of the Casablanca Conference should be the unconditional surrender of all our foes. Our inflexible insistence upon unconditional surrender does not mean that we shall stain our victorious arms by any cruel treatment of whole populations.'

Less than two years after making this speech—on December 15th, 1944, to be exact—Winston Churchill promised the Poles East Prussia (with the exception of Königsberg, which was to go to the Russians), Danzig and 200 miles of the Baltic coast, adding that they were free 'to extend their territory at the expense of Germany to the west.' He then declared:

'The transference of several millions of people would have to be effected from the east to the west or north, and the expulsion of the Germans, because that is what is proposed—the total expulsion of the Germans— from the area to be acquired by Poland in the west or north. . . . There will be no mixture of populations. . . .'

Was it not atrocious so to treat the population of Eastern Germany? Was it not unjust? The House of Commons was obviously not unanimous in its approval of Churchill's policy, for he felt compelled to justify himself once again on February 24th, 1945, saying:

'What, for instance, should be our attitude towards the terrible foe with whom we are grappling? Should it be unconditional surrender, or should we make some accommodation with them for a negotiated peace, leaving them free to regather their strength for a renewal of the struggle after a few uneasy years? The principle of unconditional surrender was proclaimed by the President of the United States at Casablanca and I endorsed it there and then on behalf of this country. I am sure it was right at the time it was used, when many things hung in the balance against us which are decided in our favour now. Should we then modify this declaration, which was made in the days of our comparative weakness and lack of success, now that we have reached a period of mastery and power? I am clear that nothing should induce us to abandon the principle of unconditional surrender and enter into any form of negotiation with Germany or Japan, under whatever guise such suggestions may present themselves, until the act of unconditional surrender has been formally executed. . . .'

Winston Churchill is no longer so certain that his actions at that time were wise. Both he and Bevin have clearly modified the policy then adopted. Today many British statesmen no doubt wish that the decisions taken at the Yalta conference of February, 1945, had been other than what they were. It was there stated:

'It is not our purpose to destroy the people of Germany, but only when Nazism and militarism have been extirpated will there be hope for a decent life for Germans and a place for them in the comity of nations.'

Does such a hope now exist?

It cannot be denied that in neutral countries the probable future development of European affairs was better understood at the time of which I am writing—February 1943—than it was in the Cabinet offices of the Western Powers. On February 21st, 1943, the Spanish Foreign Minister, Jordana, handed a note to the British ambassador, Sir Samuel Hoare, in which it was stated:

'If events develop in the future as they have up to now, it would be Russia which will penetrate deeply into German territory. And we ask the question: if this should occur, which is the greater danger not only for the Continent but for England herself, a Germany not totally defeated but with sufficient strength to serve as a rampart against Communism, a Germany hated by all her neighbours, which would deprive her of authority though sne remained intact, or a Sovietized Germany which would certainly furnish Russia with the added strength of her war preparations, her engineers, her specialised workmen and technicians, which would enable Russia to extend herself with an empire without precedent from the Atlantic to the Pacific? . . .

'And we ask a second question: is there anybody in the centre of Europe, in that mosaic of countries without consistency or unity, bled moreover by war and foreign domination, who could contain the ambitions of Stalin? There is certainly no one. . . . We may be sure that after the German domination, the only domination which could live in the countries is Communism. For this reason we consider the situation as extremely grave and think that people in England should reflect calmly on the matter, since should Russia succeed in conquering Germany, there will be no one who can contain her. . . .

'If Germany did not exist Europeans would have to invent her and it would be ridiculous to think that her place could be taken by a confederation of Lithuanians, Poles, Czechs and Rumanians which would rapidly be converted into so many more states of the Soviet confederation. . . .'[1]

Sir Samuel Hoare replied on February 25th, 1943, presumably on the authority and with the approval of his Government, in the following terms:

'The Minister says that the great danger to Europe is Communism and that a Russian victory will make all Europe Communist. . . . The British view is very different. . . . Will any single country be able to dominate Europe at the end of this war? Russia, at least, will need a long period of reconstruction and recovery in which she will depend greatly upon the British Empire and the United States of America for economic help. . . . Whilst giving full credit and admiration to the Russian army, we are convinced that the final victory will not be the victory of any single Ally but of all the Allies. . . . There will then (after the war) undoubtedly be great British and American armies on the Continent. . . . They will be composed of fresh, front-line troops, whose

---

1 *Ambassador on Special Mission*, by the Rt. Hon. Sir Samuel Hoare, Viscount Templewood, pp. 190 and 191, Collins, London, 1946.

ranks will not have been previously decimated by years of exhausting war on the Russian front. . . .

'As for ourselves, I make the confident prophecy that at that moment Great Britain will be the strongest European power. . . . British influence, it seems to me, will be stronger in Europe than at any time since the fall of Napoleon. . . . We shall not shirk our responsibilities to European civilisation or throw away our great strength by premature or unilateral disarmament. Having, with our Allies, won the war, we intend to maintain our full influence in Europe, and to take our full share in its reconstruction. . . .'[1]

Such are the words of Sir Samuel, England's spokesman in Franco's neutral Spain. They sound very self-assured. Hitler, refusing instinctively to attempt diplomatic negotiations, was well aware that he could not possibly reach any agreement with the Western Powers. His fate— which, however, was also the fate of the German nation—was balanced on the edge of the sword.

The dismissal of Raeder and Schacht had caused a noticeable increase in Germany's internal tension. The creaking of the timbers was becoming audible.

It was under the shadow of these events that, accompanied by Lieutenant Becke, I set off by train for Rastenburg in East Prussia, whence I was to go on by aeroplane. In the train I found General Kempff, my old comrade-in-arms, from whom I learned a great deal about the course of operations during the previous year. At Rastenburg I was met by Keitel's adjutant, Major Weiss, but he could give me no precise information concerning the reasons for my journey. Accompanied by Kempff and my old colleague from the Inspectorate of Motorised Troops and the peacetime 2nd Panzer Division, Chales de Beaulieu, I flew on to Vinnitsa. We arrived there in the afternoon of the 19th and were assigned quarters in the army hostel called the *Jagerhöhe*.

During the morning of the 20th General Schmundt, Hitler's principal adjutant, came to see me. We had a detailed conversation concerning Hitler's intentions and the prospects of translating them into facts. Schmundt explained to me how the German armoured force, as a result of the increasing supremacy of the Russians, had reached a state in which the need for its renovation could no longer be ignored. The General Staff and the Armaments Ministry were at loggerheads; more important than this, the panzer troops themselves had lost confidence in the High Command and were asking with insistence that control of their arm of the Service be vested in someone who had practical know-

---

[1] *Ambassador on Special Mission*, by the Rt. Hon. Sir Samuel Hoare, Viscount Templewood, pp. 194 and 195, Collins, London, 1946.

ledge and experience of the armoured forces. Hitler had therefore decided to entrust me with this responsibility. Schmundt asked me if I had any suggestions to make concerning the carrying out of this request. I replied that in view of the needs of my country and of my arm of the Service, I was prepared to accept Hitler's offer. But I could only be of use in this position if certain prior conditions were fulfilled, all the more so since I had only just recovered from a serious illness and did not wish to waste my strength in such fruitless struggles for authority as those in which I had always previously been involved when holding similar appointments. I must therefore insist that I be subordinated neither to the Chief of the Army General Staff nor to the Commander of the Training Army but directly to Hitler. Furthermore, I must be in a position to influence the development of our armoured equipment both with the Army Ordnance Office and with the Armaments Ministry, for otherwise the re-establishment of the combat effectiveness of this arm of the Service would be impossible. Finally, I must be able to exert the same influence over the organisation and training of tank units in the Waffen-SS and the Luftwaffe as in the Army. It went without saying that I must also control the tank units of the Training Army and of the schools.

I requested Schmundt that these conditions of acceptance be submitted to Hitler and that I only be summoned to see him in the event of his agreeing to them. If he did not, then it would be better to let me return to Berlin and to give up all idea of re-employing me. This conversation with Schmundt lasted for two hours.

Shortly after Schmundt's return to Supreme Headquarters I was sent a message summoning me to a conference with Hitler at 15.15 hrs. that afternoon. I was received punctually at that hour; to begin with Schmundt was present, but later Hitler and I withdrew to his study where we were alone together. I had not seen Hitler since the black day of December 20th, 1941. In the intervening fourteen months he had aged greatly. His manner was less assured than it had been and his speech was hesitant; his left hand trembled. On his desk lay my books. He began the conversation with the words: 'Since 1941 our ways have parted: there were numerous misunderstandings at that time which I much regret. I need you.' I replied that I was willing, provided he could ensure me the necessary circumstances in which to do useful work. Hitler now told me that it was his intention to appoint me Inspector-General of Armoured Troops. Schmundt had explained to him my attitude towards the problem. He agreed with it and asked me accordingly to prepare a draft of the assignment of duties for that post and to submit this to him. He mentioned that he had re-read my pre-war writings on armoured troops and had noticed that I had even

FIG. 20.   The outskirts of Orel on the Oka: a typical Russian town

FIG. 21. Dmitrovsk: early winter

FIG. 22. Night battle before Moscow, 1941

then correctly prophesied the course of future developments. I was now to put my theories into practice.

Hitler then turned to the actual military situation. He was well aware of the grave deterioration to our position, both military, political and moral, that had resulted from Stalingrad and our consequent retreats on the Eastern front; and he expressed his determination—inevitable, from his point of view—to hold fast and to put the war situation to rights. This first meeting with Hitler lasted some 45 minutes; the conversation was on a professional level throughout and ended at about 16.00 hrs.

I next went to see the Chief of the Army General Staff, General Zeitzler, in order that I might study the military situation. I spent the evening in the company of Generals Köstring, formerly military attaché in Moscow, von Prien, field commandant of Vinnitsa, and Buschenhagen, the commander of the 15th Infantry Division. I knew all these officers well and much was explained to me concerning developments during my long absence on inactive service. What Prien told me about the German administration was highly distasteful. German methods, particularly those of the Reich Commissar Koch, had turned the Ukrainians from being friends of Germany into our enemies. Unfortunately our military authorities were powerless against this policy. It was carried out through Party and administrative channels, without the collaboration of the military and usually without the Army's knowledge and against its will. Only rumours of the various clashes reached our ears.

I spent February 21st discussing with Jodl, Zeitzler, Schmundt, and Colonel Engel, one of Hitler's adjutants, the major features of the assignment of duties which I was drawing up.

On February 22nd I flew to Rastenburg in order to prepare the draft of the assignment of duties with Field-Marshal Keitel, who was not located with the advanced echelon of Supreme Headquarters at Vinnitsa. The Commander of the Training Army, General Fromm, was also summoned here on February 23rd. The document was completed during the course of the next few days and approved and signed by Hitler on February 28th. Since it formed the basis for my activities during the coming years I shall quote it in full.

ASSIGNMENT OF DUTIES
TO THE INSPECTOR-GENERAL OF ARMOURED TROOPS

1. The Inspector-General of Armoured Troops is responsible to me for the future development of armoured troops along lines that will make that arm of the Service into a decisive weapon for winning the war.

The Inspector-General of Armoured Troops is directly subordinated to

K

myself. He has the command powers of an army commander and is the senior officer of armoured troops.[1]

2. The Inspector-General of Armoured Troops is responsible, in consultation with the Chief of the Army General Staff, for the organisation and training of armoured troops and of the large mobile formations of the Army.

He is further entitled, by my orders, to direct the armoured troops of the *Waffen-SS* and the *Luftwaffe* in matters of organisation and training.

I reserve to myself the right of making basic decisions.

His requirements for the technical development of his weapons and for *production plans* are to be drawn up in conjunction with the Minister of Armaments and Munitions and submitted to me for approval.

3. In his capacity as senior officer of his arm of the Service, he is also in command of the training troops of his arm. It is *his responsibility* to ensure that *a constant stream of fully employable reserves both in men and in armoured vehicles* be available to the field army; this includes equally individual vehicles, drafts of replacements and newly formed units.

It is *his responsibility* to decide, under my direction, *what proportion of tanks and of armoured vehicles is to be allotted* to the army in the field and what to the training army.

4. The Inspector-General of Armoured Troops will ensure that the *new units of, and replacements for, armoured and mobile troops are made ready punctually as ordered and according to plan.* In this connection he will decide, in conjunction with the Army General Staff, on the best employment for such tank crews of the field army as no longer have tanks.

5. The Inspector-General of Armoured Troops will evaluate reports of combat experience in relationship to the command, armament, training and organisation of armoured troops.

In this connection he is entitled to visit and inspect all armoured units of the armed forces and of the *Waffen-SS*.

The Inspector-General of Armoured Troops is entitled to communicate directly with the armoured troops of the field army on all subjects.

His opinions and conclusions are also to be brought to the attention of all interested branches of the Services, as well as of the Ministry of Armaments and Munitions.

The Inspector-General of Armoured Troops will control the preparation of all documents, regulations, etc., intended for the armoured troops. Documents dealing with the command of units and of collaboration with other arms of the Service are to be published in conjunction with the Chief of the Army General Staff.

6. The Inspector-General of Armoured Troops, as senior officer of his arm of the Service, is permanently in command of:

(a) All reserve and training units of mobile troops (excepting reserve units of the cavalry and of motor-cyclists) which are grouped together in special commands.

---

[1] In this assignment of duties 'armoured troops' includes: tank troops, rifle components of panzer divisions (*Panzergrenadiere*), motorised infantry, armoured reconnaissance troops, anti-tank troops and heavy assault gun units.

(*b*) All schools for mobile troops (excepting cavalry and motor-cyclist schools), both of the field and of the training army, together with all instructional troops attached to such schools.

7. The Inspector-General of Armoured Troops is empowered to give instructions on matters with which he is concerned to all branches of the staffs of the Army. All branches are ordered to supply the Inspector-General of Armoured Troops with any assistance that he may require.

Supreme Headquarters, 28th February, 1943.

The Führer.
Signed: ADOLF HITLER.

This assignment of duties bestowed upon me a great deal of authority which was not granted to the senior officers of other arms of the Service attached to the *OKH*; these colleagues of mine were subordinated to the Chief of the Army General Staff, whose permission they had to obtain before being allowed to visit the troops, exercised no influence over the Training Army and the schools, and were not permitted to publish any written material. The results achieved by these unfortunate men were therefore, inevitably, very limited. This is the explanation of why previous senior officers of the armoured force had never succeeded in accomplishing any basic improvements. Experienced officers from the front had no desire to hold such a position and when they received a direct order to do so they attempted as best they could to be returned with all speed to duty with troops, where at least something could be achieved. For the panzer troops, at any rate, my appointment as Inspector-General changed all this. I was not surprised that the General Staff, particularly its Chief, and the *OKH* were so markedly unenthusiastic about this assignment of duties, which they regarded as an encroachment upon their own hallowed rights. One result of this was that I became involved in difficulties and held up by lack of co-operation from certain quarters over and over again; indeed, this attitude has persisted even after the war, and in some cases my opponents have not hesitated to misrepresent facts. Be that as it may, the new regulations did no damage to our cause as a whole and enabled the armoured force to remain, up to the bitter end, a strong weapon, equipped according to the needs of the time and of its task.

Only one important mistake crept into this assignment of duties while the document was on its way from Rastenburg to Hitler's desk in Vinnitsa: in the footnote to paragraph 1, defining the term 'armoured troops,' I had included the assault gun units though these had previously been regarded as forming part of the artillery. I had good reasons for this, since the production of assault guns was absorbing a high proportion of our tank production, while the performance of assault guns in an anti-tank role was limited by the fact that they were equipped with insufficiently powerful pieces. Even less effective were the old anti-tank battalions. These latter were still using guns towed by half-tracked vehicles with insufficient penetrative force to pierce the armour of the enemy's tanks, so that they were for all intents and purposes useless. It was my intention to change all this. But somebody smuggled in the word 'heavy' while I was not looking, so that the Inspector-General's control was limited to the heavy assault guns only, which latter were just coming into existence and were to be equipped as tank destroyers on a Tiger or Panther basis. At my very first interview I therefore had to complain about this trick that had been played on me, or rather not on me personally but on the anti-tank defences of the Army and therefore on the Army as a whole.

While the assignment of duties was circulating through normal bureaucratic channels, I set off for Berlin in order to collect my staff and to prepare for the work ahead. I secured my old office building in the Bendlerstrasse, where I had been housed in pre-war days when I was Chief of Mobile Troops. As chief of staff I chose an officer with great experience at the front, an ardent tank man, Colonel Thomale; he set to his new task with the same energy and devotion to duty which he was to show right up to the final collapse. I was pleased for personal as well as for professional reasons to have him occupying this most important position on my staff. I also had two General Staff Corps officers working with me, one handling organisation and the other employment: these were Lieutenant-Colonel Freyer who, as a result of severe wounds, was no longer fit for service at the front: the other was the fresh and youthful Major Kauffmann. The latter was subsequently replaced by Major Freiherr von Wöllwarth. My adjutant was Lieutenant-Colonel Prince Max zu Waldeck, who had also been severely wounded. I was given an assistant for each branch of the armoured force: these were all officers with experience of their particular branch at the front and were generally older men who had been badly wounded and were in need of a period of less active service. They were changed from time to time when they had regained their health and could exchange the dusty atmosphere of an office for the fresh air at the front. By means of this system of replacements, the Inspectorate-General remained in close and living contact with the troops in action. For the training units an Inspector of Armoured Troops in the Home Territories was appointed, with office in Berlin: General Eberbach held this position for a time. His chief of staff, Colonel Bolbrinker, was simultaneously head of *In 6*, the department dealing with armoured troops in the General Army Office that was controlled by the Commander of the Training Army. This was done by arrangement between Fromm and myself, with the intention of ensuring the closest possible co-ordination between my actions and those of the Training Army in this sphere; the system proved satisfactory up to the very end of the war. The armoured troops' schools were placed under a Commander of Schools, and for a long time this was General von Hauenschild, an officer who had been severely wounded. Finally, I arranged for a limited number of officers to be attached to my staff to act as a sort of liaison officers between my staff and the fighting troops; these were in general convalescent officers not yet fit enough to rejoin their units, but capable of service at home. These I used principally for studying and evaluating events at the front and for investigating any unusual occurrences in the battles that were being fought.

Service manuals were the responsibility of Colonel Theiss, whom I had first met in 1938 when he was commanding the Tank Battalion of the old Austrian Army. He held the post until the collapse and also was of great service in collecting material for a history of the war.

In Berlin I visited the various Service organisations with which I would have to collaborate in future. Among others I went to see Field-Marshal Milch at the Air Ministry, an old and valued friend from pre-war days. Milch gave me detailed and enlightening character studies of the influential personalities of the time. Of the great number of National-Socialist dignitaries he regarded only a very few as having any true importance and any real influence on Hitler, and these he suggested that I visit. They were Goebbels, Himmler, and Speer; the latter I would in any case have to see, as he was Munitions Minister.

Acting on Milch's suggestion, I called on Dr. Goebbels on March 3rd, announcing myself to him in my new capacity as Inspector-General of Armoured Troops. He received me in a most friendly fashion and immediately engaged me in a lengthy conversation about the political and military situation. Dr. Goebbels was undoubtedly one of the cleverest members of Hitler's intimate circle. It was, perhaps, to be hoped that he might be willing to help improve our position. It therefore seemed to me important to make him understand the needs of the troops and of the higher command. Since in this, our first, conversation together he showed himself open to reason, I pointed out to him the bad organisation and even worse clash of personalities that existed within our Supreme Command. I explained to him how the multiplication of overlapping staffs—*OKW*, Armed Forces Command Staff, *OKH*, Air Force, Navy, *Waffen-SS*, Armaments Ministry—had produced a confusion of leadership; that the Führer, who was becoming increasingly prone to intervene in matters of subordinate importance, was bound eventually to be overwhelmed by the chaotic situation; that

Hitler was not trained as a General Staff Corps officer and would be
well advised to appoint some Chief of the Armed Forces General Staff
as his assistant; and that the man chosen should be one who understood how to function as an operational commander and who was more
qualified to fill this difficult office than was Field-Marshal Keitel. I
requested Dr. Goebbels that he undertake to lay all this before Hitler
in some suitable form, since I thought it would have more effect coming
from a civilian of Hitler's most intimate and trusted circle than it would
from a general in whom, as I knew from previous experience, the
Führer did not feel unlimited confidence. It was Dr. Goebbels' opinion
that this was a very thorny problem, but he promised to do his best
when a suitable occasion arose to lead the conversation along the lines
I had suggested and to urge Hitler that he reorganise the supreme
command in a more practical form.

During this period I also went to see Speer, who greeted me in his
friendly, open fashion. In the months to come I always found working
with this sensible, natural man both easy and pleasant. Speer's ideas and
decisions were the product of a healthy intellect and were not influenced
by sickly, personal ambition or by pride of office. It is true that at that
time he was still a most enthusiastic follower of Hitler's; but he possessed, nonetheless, so independent a brain that he could see the
mistakes and weaknesses of the system and therefore did his best to
rectify them.

In order to form an idea of the state of the tank industry I immediately visited the Alkett Company at Spandau and the Daimler-Benz
Company at Berlin-Marienfelde.

Finally I drew up new war establishment tables for Panzer and
Panzergrenadier[1] Divisions for the year 1943 and—so far as it was
possible to anticipate—for 1944 as well. I intended to economise on men
and equipment while increasing the combat strength of the divisions by
the introduction of new weapons and fresh tactics. This undertaking led
to my first conference with Hitler, which I requested for March 9th. I
flew to Vinnitsa, accompanied by Colonel Thomale, where, at 16.00 hrs.,
I found a large gathering collected together all anxious to observe my
début. I was very annoyed to see this crowd of people walk in since I
had hoped to be able to state my case to the smallest possible audience.
But I had made the mistake of previously sending a résumé of what I
intended to say to Hitler's adjutants' office. Now all those officers who
were at all interested in my plans appeared one by one: the whole *OKW*,
the Chief of the Army General Staff together with a number of his

---

[1] The previous (Motorised) Infantry Divisions had been partially re-equipped and
renamed Panzergrenadier Divisions: they did not, however, normally contain a tank
component, save when they were *Waffen-SS* Divisions.—*Tr.*

departmental heads, my two opposite numbers, the senior officers of Infantry and Artillery, and finally Schmundt, the chief adjutant. All these gentlemen had some criticism to make of my plans, in particular of my expressed wish that the assault guns be placed under my General-Inspectorate and that the anti-tank battalions of the infantry divisions be re-equipped with assault guns in place of their present ineffective weapons drawn by half-tracks. As a result of the lively opposition that these gentlemen put up, and which I had certainly not anticipated, the conference lasted for some four hours. I was so exhausted by the time it was over that when I left the conference room I fell to the ground in a faint. Luckily I was only unconscious for a moment and nobody was aware of what had happened.

The notes for this conference, which I had previously prepared as an *aide-mémoire* for myself and which I took to Vinnitsa with me, have, owing to a lucky accident, been preserved. I include them here since they are an indication of what the many conferences which I was to hold with Hitler, and of which this was the first, were like:

Conference Notes

1. *The task for* 1943 is to provide a certain number of panzer divisions *with complete combat efficiency* capable of making limited objective attacks.

For 1944 *we must* prepare to launch large-scale attacks. A panzer division only possesses complete combat efficiency when the number of its tanks is in correct proportion to its other weapons and vehicles. German panzer divisions were designed to contain 4 tank battalions, with a total strength of roughly 400 tanks per division. If the number of tanks falls appreciably below the 400 mark, then the whole organisation (its manpower and vehicle strength) is no longer in true proportion to its offensive power. At the moment we unfortunately have no panzer division which, in this sense, can be said to possess complete combat efficiency.

Our success in battle this year, and even more so next year, depends on the re-creation of that efficiency. If this can be achieved, then, together with the U-boats and the air force, we shall win this war. If we fail to achieve this, then the land battles will be long drawn out and will cause us heavy casualties. (Read out article by Liddell Hart—on the organisation of armoured forces, past and future.)

So the problem is this: without delay, and regardless of all special interests, to re-create panzer divisions with complete combat efficiency. In this connection it is better to have a few strong divisions than many partially equipped ones. The latter type need a large quantity of wheeled vehicles, fuel, and personnel, which is quite disproportionate to their effectiveness; they are a burden, both to command and to supply; and they block the roads.

2. In order to achieve these aims so far as organisation is concerned, I propose the following war establishments for 1943. (Diagram 1—unfortunately no longer available.)

In this connection the following points apply to tank equipment:

The mainstay of our tank equipment is at present the Panzer IV. In view of the current need of replacements for the African and Eastern theatres, as well as the need for training tanks, present production only permits the new establishment or full re-equipment of *one* tank battalion per month. Apart from this, we can reckon on equipping a limited number of battalions with Panthers and Tigers during 1943; but the Panther battalions at any rate will not be ready for action before July or August.

In order, somehow, to re-equip the panzer divisions so that they may have complete combat efficiency, I therefore propose that use be made of the relatively large number of light assault guns that are now being produced.

I believe that it is essential that each month *one* tank battalion be equipped with light assault guns and incorporated into the panzer divisions, and that this continue until such time as the factories are producing enough tanks to meet the full requirements of the panzer divisions.

Further, the production of the Panzer IV must be increased during the year 1944–45, so far as this can be done without damaging the production of Panthers and Tigers.

3. For 1944 I propose war establishments in accordance with Diagram 2 (unfortunately no longer available). So far as tanks are concerned it embodies the following major modification: the expansion of the tank regiment to a brigade of four battalions.

4. *The tank figures* envisaged in this diagram are to be achieved by means of increased production of Panzer IV's, Panthers and Tigers, and—until such time as this figure is reached—by appropriation of light assault guns built on a Panzer IV chassis and armed with a 75 mm. L48 cannon.

Another essential for achieving these figures is that each tank must be given a longer life. For this, the following are necessary:

(*a*) A thorough testing and perfecting of new models (Panther!).

(*b*) Thorough training of the crews (participation in final assembly, individual and unit training).

(*c*) Allotment of sufficient demonstration equipment to the training units. (See annex—no longer available.) General Hube's letter concerning his experiences at the front. (No longer available.)

(*d*) Continuity of training and the necessary time for training (no moving of new formations in training away from their stations and the nearby factories).

5. *The essential success on the battlefield* can only be achieved by a drastic concentration of armoured strength at the decisive spot in suitable terrain; surprise both as to numbers and equipment is also indispensable.

For this, the following are required:

(*a*) Secondary war theatres must not be supplied with tanks of new design: armour for such theatres should be limited to captured tanks.

(*b*) Concentration of all tank units (including Tigers, Panthers, Panzer IV's, and for the time being a proportion of the light assault guns) in the panzer divisions and corps under commanders who are experts in the use of armour.

(*c*) The state of the terrain must be taken into consideration before an attack is ordered.

(*d*) New equipment must be held back (that is to say, for the time being, Tigers, Panthers, and heavy assault guns) until the new weapon is available in sufficient quantity to ensure a decisive surprise success.

Premature commitment of new equipment simply invites the enemy to produce an effective defence against it by next year, which we shall not be able to cope with in the short time then available.

(*e*) The avoidance of the setting up of new formations: the cadres of the old panzer and motorised divisions consist of trained men with a sound knowledge of their equipment and are an incalculable asset in re-forming their divisions. New formations can never be of equivalent value.

The present system of committing panzer divisions for long periods of time in a purely defensive role is wasteful. It postpones the rehabilitation of those divisions and thus delays their being made ready for the attacking role.

The problem, therefore, is the immediate withdrawal of numerous panzer division cadres from the front for rehabilitation.

6. *Anti-tank defence* will devolve more and more on the assault guns, since all our other anti-tank weapons are becoming increasingly ineffective against the new enemy equipment or else are too expensive in terms of casualties sustained.

All divisions on the main battle fronts, therefore, need to be supplied with a certain complement of these weapons; the secondary fronts will have to make do with a higher command reserve of assault guns, while the divisions are for the time being equipped with self-propelled anti-tank guns. In order to economise on personnel and material, a gradual amalgamation of the assault-gun battalions and the anti-tank battalions is necessary.

The new heavy assault guns are only to be committed on the major battle fronts and for special tasks. They are primarily tank-destroyers.

The value of the new 75 mm. L70 assault gun is as yet untried.

7. *The armoured reconnaissance battalions* have become the step-child of the panzer divisions. Their value in Africa is easy to see, though on the Eastern front at the moment this is not the case. But we must not allow ourselves to be deceived by this fact. If, as we hope, we are once again to launch a great offensive in 1944 we shall need competent ground reconnaissance units.

The following are required:

(*a*) A sufficient number of light 1-ton armoured troop-carrying vehicles (at the moment in process of construction, and beginning to be available).[1]

(*b*) An armoured reconnaissance car capable of great speed (35–45 m.p.h.) with adequate armour and armament.

At the time being no such vehicle is being built. I request that I be authorised to go into this problem with Minister Speer and to make the necessary proposals.

8. *For the panzergrenadiers* the main problem is the continued mass-

[1] These were half-tracked.

production in sufficient volume of the 3-ton armoured troop-carrying vehicle
without any further alteration to its design.

The armoured engineers and the armoured signal troops will also have to
make do with this vehicle.

9. *The artillery* of the panzer and motorised divisions will from now on be
receiving the adequate number of self-propelled gun-carriages which has
been requested for the past 10 years. For organisation see annex. (No longer
available.) Tanks of latest design must be supplied for artillery observers.

10. As matters of basic importance I request:

(*a*) Approval of the Inspector-General's staff organisation with station
Supreme Headquarters, and that of the Inspector of Troops, Home Territories, with station Berlin.

(*b*) Approval of the war establishments.

(*c*) Subordination of all assault artillery to the Inspector-General.

(*d*) The abandonment of plans for the formation of new armoured or
motorised divisions, both in the Army and in the *Waffen-SS*. The assimi-
lation of these divisions, and of the Hermann Goering Division[1] to the new
war establishment.

(*e*) Approval for the continued production of the Panzer IV in 1944–45.

(*f*) The design of a new armoured reconnaissance vehicle, though this
design will be based so far as possible on parts already available for
production.

(*g*) Further research into the need for building a light assault gun mounting
a 75 mm. L70 cannon. The possibility of abandoning this model in favour
of the light assault gun with a 75 mm. L48 cannon and armoured troop-
carrying vehicles.

Every one of the points in the above document gave rise to a lively
discussion. Finally they were all agreed to, at least in theory, with the
exception of my request that the assault artillery be placed under
command of the Inspector-General. At this suggestion the whole conference became incensed. All those present, with the single exception
of Speer, disapproved, in particular of course the gunners; Hitler's
chief adjutant also spoke up against me, remarking that the assault
artillery was the only weapon which nowadays enabled gunners to win
the Knight's Cross. Hitler gazed at me with an expression of pity on his
face, and finally said: 'You see, they're all against you. So I can't approve
either.' The results of this decision were far-reaching: the assault
artillery remained an independent weapon; the anti-tank battalions
continued to be equipped with ineffective, tractor-drawn guns, and the
infantry divisions remained without adequate anti-tank defence. It was
nine months before Hitler was convinced that a mistake had been made,

---

[1] The *Hermann Goering Panzer Parachute Division* was a very large armoured division
formed of Luftwaffe personnel and controlled, except operationally, by the Luftwaffe.
The *Waffen-SS* panzer divisions were also generally larger and more lavishly equipped than
their army equivalents.—*Tr.*

and even by the end of the war it had not proved feasible to supply all the divisions with the urgently needed defensive weapons. For the rest, even the proposals that had been approved were continually questioned and their execution impeded: this applied principally to my urgent and repeated requests for the withdrawal and timely rehabilitation of the panzer divisions, so that the Supreme Command might have a mobile reserve available. The fact that up to the bitter end our highest *military* leaders were themselves incapable of grasping the decisive need of possessing a mobile and powerful strategic reserve played an important part in our defeat. Hitler must share the blame for this with his military advisers, since these not only failed to support me, but actually hindered me in my attempts to create such a reserve.

On March the 10th I flew back to Berlin and settled down to work. On March the 12th I visited the Tank School at Wünsdorf: on March 17th the Henschel works at Cassel which were producing our Tigers, a considerable proportion of our Panthers, and the 88 mm. anti-tank gun model 43: on March 18th Panzer Battalion 300 at Eisenach, which was responsible for experiments with remote-controlled tanks, and also the armoured force N.C.O. school at Eisenach: and on March 19th I was present in Rügenwalde for a demonstration before Hitler of the railway gun 'Gustav,' the 'Ferdinand' tank and of the Panzer IV equipped with the armoured 'apron.'

The Ferdinand tank was a Tiger of Professor Porsche's design, electrically driven, with an 88 mm. L70 cannon in a fixed turret, as in an assault gun. Apart from this single, long-barrelled gun it possessed no other armament and so was valueless for fighting at close range. This was its great weakness, despite its thick armour-plating and its good gun. But since it had now been built, to the number of 90 units, I had to find some use for it, even though I could not, on tactical grounds, share Hitler's enthusiasm for this product of his beloved Porsche. A panzer regiment of two battalions, each with 45 tanks, was set up with the 90 Ferdinand-Tigers.

The 'aprons' were sheets of armour plating which were hung loose about the flanks and rear end of the Panzer III, the Panzer IV and the assault guns; they were intended to deflect or nullify the effect of the Russian infantry's anti-tank weapons, which could otherwise penetrate the relatively thin, vertical body-armour of those types of vehicle. This innovation was to prove useful.

The 'Gustav' was a powerful 800 mm. railway gun which required a double-track line to move along. It had nothing to do with me and after the demonstration of loading and firing the weapon I was about to leave when Hitler suddenly called out to me: 'Listen to this! Dr. Müller (of Krupp's) has just told me that "Gustav" could also be fired

at tanks. What do you think of that?' For a moment I was dumbfounded
as I envisaged the mass-production of 'Gustavs,' but I soon pulled myself
together and replied: 'It could be fired at them, I dare say, but it could
certainly never hit one.' Dr. Müller protested violently. But how would
it be possible to fight tanks with a gun which required forty-five
minutes to reload between shots? When I questioned Dr. Müller on
the minimum practical range of his weapon even he had to admit that
his statement was nonsense.

On March 22nd I discussed with the commander of the *Hermann
Goering* Parachute Division how his formation might best be reorganised; at that time this formation, which could produce only a
single division for actual combat, was 34,000 men strong. The majority
of this large number of men were leading a pleasant life in Holland. In
view of our replacement problem this was intolerable, even in 1943.

Finally, towards the end of March, the new organisation for our
Panzergrenadiers was decided upon in accordance with our latest
experience.

Dr. Goerdeler's Visits

It was during this time, when I was so extremely busy with my work,
that my old friend, General von Rabenau, brought Dr. Goerdeler to
see me, as the latter was anxious to talk to me. Dr. Goerdeler explained
to me that since Hitler was incapable of performing his duties as
Chancellor of the Reich and Supreme Commander of the Armed
Forces, it was desirable that his activities as such be curtailed. He
described to me in detail his programme of government and of reform;
this programme showed high idealism and the social adjustments
envisaged would undoubtedly have been most desirable, although Dr.
Goerdeler's doctrinaire manner might not have facilitated the solution
of the problems he posed. Dr. Goerdeler could not guarantee foreign
support in the event of his plans succeeding. It was apparent that during
his long-drawn-out attempts to establish contacts abroad he had been
given a somewhat cold shoulder. Our enemies had refused to abandon
the 'unconditional surrender' slogan, even in the event of Dr. Goerdeler
being successful.

I asked Dr. Goerdeler how he envisaged setting limitations to Hitler's
powers. He replied that Hitler would be retained as nominal head of
the state but would actually be interned on the Obersalzberg or in some
other safe place. When I asked how the leading National Socialists
were to be removed—since without doing so the proposed change of
system was doomed from the beginning—I was informed that this was
a matter for the armed forces to decide. But Dr. Goerdeler had not
succeeded in winning over to his way of thinking a single commander
of troops on active service. He asked me, when visiting the front, to

promote his ideas and to let him know whether, and which of, the commanding generals were inclined to join with him. To my question as to who was actually in control of this undertaking, he replied Colonel-General Beck. I was very surprised that a man like Beck, the hesitancy of whose character was well known to me, should be involved in such a business. A man of his type was the very last person suited to take part in a *coup d'état*, since he was incapable of taking a decision, and also had no popularity with the troops, to whom he was indeed more or less unknown; he was a philosopher but no revolutionary.

The weaknesses and mistakes of the National-Socialist system and the personal errors that Hitler made were by then plain to see—even to me; attempts must therefore be made to remedy them. In view of Germany's dangerous situation as a result of the Stalingrad catastrophe and of the demands made for unconditional surrender to all its enemies (including the Soviet Union) a way would have to be found that did not lead to a disaster for the country and the people. Hence the vast responsibility and the enormous difficulties that confronted anyone who tried to think quietly how he might best hope still to save Germany. I came to the conclusion that Dr. Goerdeler's plan would be harmful to our general interest and was furthermore incapable of being put into practice; I therefore declined to take any part in it. Like the rest of the Army, I also felt myself bound by the oath of allegiance that I had taken. I therefore asked Dr. Goerdeler to give up his proposed plan.

Disregarding my doubts, Dr. Goerdeler asked me, nevertheless, to procure him the information he had requested. This I agreed to do, since I hoped thereby to show Dr. Goerdeler that my attitude was not unique but that other generals thought as I did; by this means I trusted that I might persuade this undoubtedly idealistic man to abandon a course of action which I regarded as unsound. As a result I met Dr. Goerdeler again in April and was able to assure him that I had not found a single general who was prepared to join in his plan. The individuals I had sounded had all refused to take any part in the proposed action, not only on account of their oath of allegiance but also because of the grave situation at the front. I once again urged Dr. Goerdeler to give up the whole project.

Dr. Goerdeler, who incidentally during our talks together expressly denied that there was any question of assassination, finally asked me not to speak of our conversations. I kept my word until 1947, when I read a book by the barrister Fabian von Schlabrendorff, entitled, *Offiziere gegen Hitler* ('Officers against Hitler'); this book made it plain that either Dr. Goerdeler or General von Rabenau had not kept his word to be silent about me. Incidentally, the assertions concerning myself in the above-mentioned book of Schlabrendorff's are not true.

I did not speak to Dr. Goerdeler again after April 1943, and I heard
no more about his projects.

But let us return to my military activities.

"*Operation Citadel*"

On March 29th I flew to the headquarters of Army Group South, at
Zaporozhe, to see Field-Marshal von Manstein. Here a considerable
victory had recently been won; by using armoured formations in the
correct operational way Kharkov had been recaptured. The lessons to
be learned from this, in particular concerning the way the Tiger
battalions of the *Gross-Deutschland* and *SS-Leibstandarte 'Adolf Hitler'*
Divisions had been employed, provided the reason for my flight to see
Manstein. At his headquarters I found my old friend Hoth, the commander of the Fourth Panzer Army, who also told me of his experiences.
I once again realised what a pity it was that Hitler could not tolerate the
presence of so capable and soldierly a person as Manstein in his environ-
ment. Their characters were too opposed: on the one hand Hitler,
with his great will-power and his fertile imagination: on the other
Manstein, a man of most distinguished military talents, a product of
the German General Staff Corps, with a sensible, cool understanding,
who was our finest operational brain. Later, when I was entrusted with
the duties of Chief of the Army General Staff, I frequently proposed to
Hitler that Manstein be appointed chief of the *OKW* in place of Keitel,
but always in vain. It is true that Keitel made life easy for Hitler; he
sought to anticipate and fulfil Hitler's every wish before it had even
been uttered. Manstein was not so comfortable a man to deal with; he
formed his own opinions and spoke them aloud. Hitler finally answered
my repeated proposal with the words: 'Manstein is perhaps the best
brain that the General Staff Corps has produced. But he can only
operate with fresh, good divisions and not with the remnants of divisions
which are all that is now available to us. Since I can't find him any
fresh, operationally capable formations, there's no point in giving him
the job.' But the truth is that he did not wish to do so and was trying
to justify his refusal by such circuitous excuses.

I then flew on to Poltava, where General Kempff's army command
(*Armee-Abteilung*) was located, and from there went to visit the *Gross-
Deutschland* Division on March 30th and the SS Panzer Division
Leibstandarte 'Adolf Hitler' and General von Knobelsdorff's corps
headquarters on the 31st. At all these headquarters my primary purpose
was to study our recent experience with the Tigers, so that I might form
a clear picture of that tank's tactical and technical capabilities and thus
be able to deduce how best Tiger units might be organised for the

future. A final visit to Manstein at Zaporozhe ended my first trip to the front as Inspector-General.

These journeys resulted in a conference with Speer concerning an increase in the production of Tigers and Panthers; in the same connection I went to see Hitler on April 11th at Berchtesgaden, on the Obersalzberg, my first visit to this place. A remarkable feature of the Führer's villa, the *Berghof*, was that—at least in the part accessible to us—there were no connecting doors between any of the rooms. Only the great conference hall was impressive: it had large windows commanding a magnificent view, a number of valuable hangings and pictures, including a wonderful Feuerbach, and a raised area by the fireplace, where Hitler, after the so-called evening briefing, was in the habit of spending a few hours in the company of his more intimate circle, his military and party adjutants and his female secretaries. I was never included in this circle.

On the same date I called on Himmler, with the purpose of arranging that the armoured formations of the *Waffen-SS* be organised in accordance with the establishments laid down for the Army. My efforts met with only partial success. In particular Himmler would not agree to my urgent request that the setting up of new units be abandoned. It is true that Hitler had approved my views on this subject during our conference of March 9th, when I pointed out the disadvantages of new formations; but so far as the *Waffen-SS* was concerned, he and Himmler had reached certain conclusions which they did not impart to any of the soldiers. Hitler's idea was to make himself independent of the Army, whose leaders he never trusted, by forming this private army in which he believed that he could place implicit confidence; it would thus be a Praetorian guard that would be ready for anything, should the Army ever refuse to follow him on account of its Prussian-German traditions. This policy of Hitler's and Himmler's was to put the *Waffen-SS* in a very unpleasant position after the war, since the *Waffen-SS* was blamed for the misdeeds of the rest of the SS and particularly of the operational commanders of the *SD* or *Sicherheitsdienst*.[1] But even during the war the preferential treatment received by the *Waffen-SS* in the quality and quantity of its replacements, as well as of arms and equipment, led to a certain amount of understandable ill-feeling on the part of the less-favoured army formations. If such ill-feeling disappeared in the comradeship of the front, this is simply an indication of the German soldier's selfless nature, regardless of the colour of the uniform he wore.

I spent April 12th visiting the Chief of the *Luftwaffe* General Staff, Colonel-General Jeschonnek. I found a tired man whose mood was one of outspoken discouragement. I did not manage to have a frank

[1] The 'Security Service' with many an atrocity to its discredit.—*Tr.*

discussion with him about matters of concern to both our arms—the air and the armoured forces—nor, indeed, did I succeed in establishing any human contact with him. Shortly afterwards, in August 1943, grieved by Hitler's and Goering's reproaches concerning the failure of the air force, Jeschonnek took his own life. In so doing he was following in the footsteps of his comrade, Udet; the latter had felt himself forced to make the same desperate decision in November 1941, since he could see no other way out of his dilemma—a dilemma consisting, on the one hand, of what he recognised as the needs of the war and, on the other, of Goering's incompetence and idleness. My request that I might be received by the Commander-in-Chief of the Air Force came to nothing; that gentleman was too preoccupied with his non-military activities to spare me the necessary time.

Back in Berlin I had a long conversation with Schmundt on April 13th. The situation in Africa had become hopeless, and I asked Schmundt to help me arrange that the many superfluous tank crews—particularly the irreplaceable commanders and technicians with years of experience behind them—be now flown out. Either I failed to convince Schmundt or else he did not press my arguments with sufficient energy to Hitler, for when I next saw the Führer and personally mentioned the matter I met with no success. The question of prestige—as so often—proved more powerful than common sense. A great number of machines which were returning empty to Italy could have carried out those valuable men; this would have made the reforming and rehabilitation of units both at home and at the front an easier undertaking. This conference, again on the Obersalzberg, took place on April 29th; on the same day I discussed questions of organisation and equipment with Buhle, Keitel, and Speer.

Units were still being sent over to Africa and there 'committed to the flames,' among others our newest Tiger battalion. All argument against such a policy was quite ineffective; later the same thing was to happen in the defence of Sicily. On this occasion, when I urged that the Tigers be withdrawn to the mainland, Goering joined in the argument with the remark: 'But Tigers can't pole-vault across the Straits of Messina. You must realise that, Colonel-General Guderian!' I replied: 'If you have really won air supremacy over the Straits of Messina the Tigers can come back from Sicily the same way they went out.' The air expert then fell silent; the Tigers remained in Sicily.

On April 30th I flew from Berchtesgaden to Paris in order to introduce myself in my new capacity to the Commander-in-Chief West, Field-Marshal von Rundstedt, and to visit the armoured units in his area; I also wished to examine the potentialities of the Atlantic Wall as a

Sketch Map 27.

Developments of Situation on the
Eastern Front, from 22.2.43 to 4.3.1944

Situation 22.3.43
14.6.43
22.7.43
9.11.43
19.12.43
10.2.44
4.3.44

defence against tank landings. At Rouen, the headquarters of LXXXI
Army Corps, I had a discussion with my old colleague from the French
campaign of '40, General Kuntzen, concerning coast defence, and at
Yvetot I visited Panzer Regiment 100, which was equipped with
captured French tanks. I got no farther, for a telegram arrived from
Hitler summoning me to a conference at Munich.

I arrived there on May 2nd. The first session was on May 3rd, and a
second took place on May 4th, by which time my chief of staff, General
Thomale, had come down from Berlin with new material. Those present
included the *OKW*, the Chief of the Army General Staff with his
principal advisers, the commanders of Army Groups South, von
Manstein, and Centre, von Kluge, the commander of the Ninth Army,
Model, Minister Speer, and others; the problem under discussion was
the extremely important one of whether Army Groups Centre and
South would be in a position to launch an offensive on the Eastern
Front in the foreseeable future—that is to say, during the coming
summer of 1943. This had arisen as a result of a proposed operation
by the Chief of the Army General Staff, General Zeitzler, which envisaged a double enveloping attack against the big Russian salient
west of Kursk; such an operation, if successful, would destroy a large
number of Russian divisions, would decisively weaken the offensive
strength of the Russian Army, and would place the German High
Command in a more favourable position for continuing the war in the
east. This question had already been eagerly discussed in April; but in
view of the heavy blow suffered so recently at Stalingrad and of the
consequent defeat to the whole southern flank of the German front in
the East, large-scale offensive operations seemed scarcely possible at
this time. But now the Chief of the General Staff believed that by
employing the new Tigers and Panthers, from which he expected decisive
successes, he could regain the initiative.

Hitler opened the conference with a speech lasting three-quarters of
an hour; he described factually the situation on the Eastern Front and
then went on to outline the Chief of the General Staff's proposals and
the arguments that General Model had raised against them. Model had
produced information, based largely on air photography, which showed
that the Russians were preparing deep and very strong defensive
positions in exactly those areas where the attack by the two army
groups was to go in. The Russians had already withdrawn the mass of
their mobile formations from the forward area of their salient; in
anticipation of a pincer attack, as proposed in this plan of ours, they
had strengthened the localities of our possible break-throughs with
unusually strong artillery and anti-tank forces. Model drew the correct
deduction from this, namely, that the enemy was counting on our launch-

ing this attack and that in order to achieve success we must adopt a fresh tactical approach; the alternative was to abandon the whole idea. The manner in which Hitler expressed these opinions of Model's made it plain that he was impressed by them, and that he had by no means decided to order an attack on the lines proposed by Zeitzler. He now asked Field-Marshal von Manstein to be the first to express his opinion on Zeitzler's plan. Manstein, as often when face to face with Hitler, was not at his best. His opinion was that the attack would have had a good chance of succeeding if it had been launched in April; now its success was doubtful and he would need a further two full-strength infantry divisions in order to be in a position to carry it out. Hitler replied that two such divisions were not available and that Manstein must make do with what he already had; he then repeated his question, but unfortunately received no very clear answer. He next turned to Field-Marshal von Kluge, who spoke unambiguously in favour of Zeitzler's plan. I asked permission to express my views and declared that the attack was pointless; we had only just completed the reorganisation and re-equipment of our Eastern Front; if we attacked according to the plan of the Chief of the General Staff we were certain to suffer heavy tank casualties, which we would not be in a position to replace in 1943; on the contrary, we ought to be devoting our new tank production to the Western Front so as to have mobile reserves available for use against the Allied landing which could be expected with certainty to take place in 1944. Furthermore, I pointed out that the Panthers, on whose performance the Chief of the Army General Staff was relying so heavily, were still suffering from the many teething troubles inherent in all new equipment and it seemed unlikely that these could all be put right in time for the launching of the attack. Speer supported these arguments of mine from the standpoint of arms production. But we were the only men present at this session who were prepared bluntly to oppose Zeitzler's plan. Hitler, still not fully convinced by the arguments advanced in its favour, did not reach any definite decision on this day.

Apart from the military matters that were discussed, I had an important personal experience that day in Munich in that this was the first occasion on which I had seen Field-Marshal von Kluge since the events of December 1941. The unfriendly way in which he greeted me re-opened all the old wounds. I was very cool towards him. After the conference Herr von Kluge invited me to have a word with him in another room and asked me to explain my distant manner. I had no choice but to tell him what I felt very deeply, in particular the fact that he had never given me satisfaction for his behaviour in December 1941, despite the subsequent clarification of the real situation as it had been at that time. We parted without anything having been achieved.

Some time later Schmundt came to see me in Berlin and showed me a letter which Field-Marshal von Kluge had addressed to Hitler and in which he challenged me to a duel. Herr von Kluge knew perfectly well that duelling was prohibited and that Hitler would never have countenanced two of his generals fighting one another in war-time. All the same he requested Hitler to act as his second.

Schmundt informed me on behalf of Hitler that the Führer did not wish a duel to take place; he further desired that the whole affair be suitably cleared up once and for all. In obedience to Hitler's wish I wrote a letter to Field-Marshal von Kluge in which I said that I was sorry if my behaviour at Munich had offended him, but that in view of the grave and so far unrighted injury that he had done me in 1941 I had no alternative but to behave the way I did.

In the tank production field it was decided during April, in accordance with my suggestion, that the Panzer IV should continue to be built until such time as a high-level of mass-production was absolutely assured for the Panthers. The monthly figure for new tanks was raised to 1,955. A strengthening of the anti-aircraft defences around the principal tank-production centres—Cassel, Friedrichshafen and Schweinfurt— was ordered. During the course of the conference at Munich on May 4th, I had also requested that alternative accommodation be assigned to the tank factories, but this suggestion was opposed by Speer's principal assistant, Herr Saur; he maintained that the enemy was concentrating on the destruction of the *Luftwaffe's* production centres: he did not believe that they would attack the tank factories even if, at some future date, they should regard the destruction of the aircraft industry as completed.

Hitler was in Berlin on May 10th and I was summoned to the Chancellery for a discussion on Panther production, since the industry did not think that it could complete its programme according to the original schedule. By way of compensation, the industry promised that instead of 250 tanks it would deliver the handsome total of 324 by May 31st. After the conference I seized Hitler's hand and asked him if I might be allowed to speak frankly to him. He said I might and I urged him earnestly to give up the plan for an attack on the Eastern Front; he could already see the difficulties that confronted us; the great commitment would certainly not bring us equivalent gains; our defensive preparations in the West were sure to suffer considerably. I ended with the question: 'Why do you want to attack in the East at all this year?' Here Keitel joined in, with the words: 'We must attack for political reasons.' I replied: 'How many people do you think even know where Kursk is? It's a matter of profound indifference to the world whether we hold Kursk or not. I repeat my question: Why do we want to attack in the East at all this year?' Hitler's reply was: 'You're quite right. Whenever I think of this attack my stomach turns over.' I answered: 'In that case your reaction to the problem is the correct one. Leave it alone!' Hitler assured me that he had as yet by no means committed himself and with that the conversation was over. Apart from Field-Marshal Keitel, who is no longer among the living, my chief of staff, Thomale, and Herr Saur of the Armaments Ministry were witnesses to this scene.

On the next day I took the train to Lötzen, where my staff was temporarily located, and had a look at our accommodation there. On the 13th of May I saw Speer once more and in the afternoon attended a further conference with Hitler. On May 1st Hitler had inspected the wooden model of a 'Mouse,' a tank designed by Professor Porsche and the Krupp Company which was to be armed with a 150 mm. cannon. It's total weight was supposed to be 175 tons; it must therefore be assumed that, after Hitler had ordered his usual supplementary changes to the initial design, it would weigh nearer 200 tons. But the model displayed carried no machine-guns for close-range fighting. For this reason I had to turn it down. This was the same mistake that Porsche had made in designing his Ferdinand Tiger and which had rendered the Ferdinand useless at close quarters; ultimately no tank can avoid fighting at close range, particularly if it is to co-operate with infantry. Our discussion grew heated, since everyone present except me regarded the Mouse as a very handsome tank. It did, indeed, promise to be 'gigantic.'

After this demonstration I flew to Berlin.

I spent May 24th and 25th visiting Panzer Battalion 654 at Bruck an der Leitha. This battalion was equipped with the Porsche Tigers already mentioned above. I also visited the Nibelungen works at Linz which were producing Panthers and anti-tank guns and flew from there to Paris on May 26th in order to visit the armoured force battalion commander's school. On May 27th I visited Panzer Battalion 216 at Amiens, and on the 28th a company commanders' course at Versailles as well as the commanders of the 14th and 16th Panzer Divisions at Nantes. Finally, I visited the fortress of St. Nazaire on the 29th in order to form an idea of the defensive capabilities of the Atlantic Wall. The impressions I gained of the fortifications in no way corresponded to my expectations which were based on the vociferous propaganda I had read and heard. Then I flew on the 30th to Berlin and on the 31st to Innsbruck to meet Speer. On June 1st I went to Grafenwöhr and inspected both Panther Battalions 51 and 52 and on the same day returned to Berlin.

Meanwhile the *OKW* had had the bizarre idea of sending the 1st Panzer Division to Greece, where it was to guard against possible English landings in the Peloponnese. This division had just been brought up to full strength and equipped with the first completed Panther battalion. It provided our strongest reserve. Now it was to be wasted in this extraordinary fashion. When I protested irritably I became involved in an utterly grotesque argument with General Keitel. I maintained that a mountain division would be far more suitable for Greece; he replied that it would be impossible to supply such a division with the necessary amount of fodder as this would require too much transport. Against such arguments there was nothing more that I could say: but I did, on my own initiative, prevent the Panthers being sent down there. One of the tank officers who had been sent to Greece by air to reconnoitre reported to me at once that the narrow mountain tracks and bridges were not wide enough to take Panthers. This argument won me Hitler's belated approval for my action. We were soon bitterly to miss the 1st Panzer Division in Russia.

I spent June 15th worrying about our problem child, the Panther; the track suspension and drive were not right and the optics were also not yet satisfactory. On the next day I told Hitler of my reasons for not wishing to see the Panthers sent into action in the East. They were simply not yet ready to go to the front.

In Munich I met Field-Marshal Rommel at the Vier Jahreszeiten Hotel in order to discuss with him the lessons he had learned in the African theatre. That evening I returned by air to Berlin. On the 18th I inspected artillery weapons at Jüterbog and flew the same day to Berchtesgaden for a conference with Hitler. On the way there we landed at Grafenwöhr, which enabled me once again to investigate the troubles of the 51st and 52nd Panther Battalions so that I was able to report on them at first hand to Hitler. Apart from the technical weaknesses of the not yet perfected tanks, neither the crews nor the commanders were by then sufficiently experienced in their handling, while some of them even lacked adequate battle experience. Unfortunately not even these considerations sufficed to persuade Hitler or his Chief of the Army General Staff to abandon the ill-starred offensive in the East, which was now begun under the code name *Citadel*.

We had lost the African theatre on May 12th with the capitulation of Tunis. On July 10th the Allies landed in Sicily. On the 25th Mussolini was deposed and imprisoned. Marshal Badoglio was entrusted with the task of forming a new government. The defection of Italy had therefore to be reckoned with in the near future.

While these events in the South were bringing the war ever closer to Germany, in the East Hitler launched an offensive which was both inadequately planned and carried out. From the area of Bielgorod in the south ten panzer, one panzergrenadier, and seven infantry divisions attacked, while in the north seven panzer, two panzergrenadier, and nine infantry divisions went in from the area west of Orel. Everything that the German Army could muster in the way of attacking strength was committed in this offensive; Hitler had himself correctly said in Munich that it must not fail, since even a return to our original positions would spell defeat. It is not yet clear how Hitler was eventually persuaded to launch this attack. It seems likely that pressure by the Chief of the Army General Staff was the deciding factor.

The attack began on July 5th. Our tactics were those that had been used many times before against the Russians, who as a result knew exactly what to expect. Hitler had had two alternative plans: one to attack through Sevsk against the most advanced part of the Russian salient, the other to break through and roll up the Russian front southeast of Kharkov. He had scrapped both these plans in favour of the Zeitzler plan which involved a double envelopment of the Russian salient in the Tim area with the purpose of regaining the initiative on the Eastern Front.

I visited both the attacking fronts during the time between the 10th and the 15th of July; I went first to the southern and then to the northern area, and talked to the tank commanders on the spot. I there gained an insight into the course that events were taking, the lack of our men's experience in the attack and the weaknesses of our equipment. My fears concerning the premature commitment of the Panthers were justified. Also the ninety Porsche Tigers, which were operating with Model's army, were incapable of close-range fighting since they lacked sufficient ammunition for their guns, and this defect was aggravated by the fact that they possessed no machine-gun. Once they had broken into the enemy's infantry zone they literally had to go quail shooting with cannons. They did not manage to neutralise, let alone destroy, the enemy rifles and machine-guns, so that the infantry was unable to follow up behind them. By the time they reached the Russian artillery they were on their own. Despite showing extreme bravery and suffering unheard-of casualties, the infantry of Weidling's division did not manage to exploit the tanks' success. Model's attack bogged down after some 6 miles. In the south our successes were somewhat greater but not enough to seal off the salient or to force the Russians to withdraw.

The Russian counter-attack began on July 15th towards Orel, the defence of which weakened our own offensive. The town had to be evacuated on August 4th. On the same day Bielgorod fell.

Up to this time the Susha–Oka position to the north-east of Orel had weathered every storm. This was the defensive line that I had chosen in December 1941 for my Second Panzer Army and into which I had withdrawn that army. This had been the reason for my quarrel with Hitler which Field-Marshal von Kluge had made use of in order to bring about my dismissal.

By the failure of *Citadel* we had suffered a decisive defeat. The armoured formations, reformed and re-equipped with so much effort, had lost heavily both in men and in equipment and would now be unemployable for a long time to come. It was problematical whether they could be rehabilitated in time to defend the Eastern Front; as for being able to use them in defence of the Western Front against the Allied landings that threatened for next spring, this was even more questionable. Needless to say the Russians exploited their victory to the full. There were to be no more periods of quiet on the Eastern Front. From now on the enemy was in undisputed possession of the initiative.

Disagreements during the Second Half of 1943

On July 15th I had gone to France in order to inspect the armoured units located there. At the end of July I was visiting Tiger units at the troop-training area of Senne, near Paderborn, when I received a telegram from Hitler summoning me to East Prussia. During the conference there I fell sick. I had become infected with dysentry during my visit to Russia, had originally taken no notice of this and undergone no treatment and now, as a result, I was confined to a sick-bed. As soon as I was able to travel I flew back to Berlin for proper treatment; however, I had to undergo an operation in early August which kept me laid up until the end of that month.

Immediately before being operated on I was visited by General von Treskow, who had formerly been Field-Marshal von Kluge's first operations officer. He informed me that he came on behalf of the Field-Marshal. The latter wished me to know that he was prepared to accept a reconciliation between us if I was ready to take the first step. He proposed that he and I should then work together with the object of diminishing Hitler's powers as Supreme Commander of the Armed Force. My very exact knowledge of Field-Marshal von Kluge's unstable character prevented me from accepting this suggestion. I was therefore bound to decline General von Treskow's offer.[1]

My condition improved slowly. The heavier enemy air-raids on

---

[1] For my own efforts along these lines see p. 293.

Berlin, which began in August 1943, did not, however, permit the rest that a convalescent requires. So my wife and I accepted an invitation of Speer's to go to a government-controlled inn, located among the beautiful Alpine scenery of Upper Austria, which had been converted into a convalescent home. We arrived there on September 3rd and on the very next day heard that our Berlin home had been largely destroyed by a direct hit and was certainly uninhabitable. What remained of our possessions was stored in a barrack's cellar at Wünsdorff. This was a severe blow. We were debating whether we should not migrate permanently to Upper Austria, when I received a telegram informing me that the donation which had been first mentioned in the autumn of 1942 had now been made. Schmundt had arranged this when he heard about the destruction of our home. In view of our position we had no choice but to accept the gift in the spirit in which it was made. In October 1943 I took my wife to Deipenhof, in the Hohensalza district, which was to be her home until the arrival of the Russians on January 20th, 1945.

Meanwhile during my absence an attempt had been made to stop producing Panzer IV's and to build assault guns in their place. The Todt Organisation, which was building the Atlantic Wall and other fortifications, proposed that tank turrets be built into pill-boxes; in view of our limited production this would undoubtedly be a serious blow to our mobile tank forces and showed a complete lack of comprehension of the real situation.

Immediately I had returned from convalescent leave I tackled the problem of anti-aircraft tanks. Hitler approved the construction of twin 37 mm. guns. On the other hand he did not approve of the installation of the quadruple 20 mm. gun, which was already available, on a Panzer IV chassis, so the production of this important defensive weapon was once more postponed.

On October 20th, 1943, Hitler inspected a quantity of new equipment at the troop-training area Arys. This included wooden models of the Tiger II—which our enemies were later to christen the 'King Tiger' and which was an exceptionally successful new model—of the Vomag tank-destroyer, and of the *Jagd-Panzer* ('the hunting panzer'), an iron model of the *Jagd-Tiger* with a 128 mm. gun, the 380 mm. armoured mortar on a Tiger chassis, together with the special Panzer III and other light and heavy armoured equipment designed to run on railway lines.

A severe bombing attack on October 22nd hit the Henschel works at Cassel and temporarily stopped all production there. It now became plain that I had been right earlier in the year when I had anticipated air attacks on our tank-producing centres in the near future. I went at once to Cassel to express my sympathy to the factory workers, most of whom had lost their homes and counted many dead and wounded among their dependants. In the great bombed assembly shed I was given the opportunity of addressing the workers; I avoided using the clichés that were current at the time and that would have been doubly unacceptable on so grave an occasion as this. What I said was warmly listened to by the workers; we understood one another. I was frequently to receive evidence of their attitude towards me through friendly messages that the workers sent me and which gave me great pleasure.

This bombing attack was followed by another on November 26th directed against the Berlin works of Alkett, Rheinmetall-Borsig, Wimag, and the Deutsche Waffen-und Munitionsfabriken.

On December 7th it was decided that the full production capacity of the old Czech 38-ton tank be switched to tank destroyers; these, to be built on the Czech tank chassis, and protected by sloping armour plate, were to mount a recoilless gun and a machine-gun with a curved barrel. They passed their tests very satisfactorily. This tank destroyer was intended to be the basic weapon for the anti-tank battalions of the infantry divisions, and was thus the belated answer to my proposals made on March the 9th.

The defensive weakness of the infantry against the ever-growing masses of Russian tanks had resulted in increased casualty figures. One evening during his briefing Hitler burst out in a long and violent diatribe against the senselessness of sending infantry divisions into action with insufficient anti-tank weapons. I happened to be present at the time. I was standing opposite Hitler while he let himself go on this subject, and doubtless he noticed the somewhat sarcastic expression on my face, for he suddenly broke off, gazed at me in silence for a moment or two, and then said: 'You were right. You told me all this nine months ago. Unfortunately I didn't listen to you.' I was now at last in a position to carry out my ideas on this score, but it was too late. Only one-third of our anti-tank companies could be equipped with the new weapon by the time the Russians launched their 1945 winter offensive.

So much for technical tank development up to the end of 1943. The operational situation had changed greatly during the second half of that year, very much to our disadvantage.

When our unfortunate Kursk offensive was broken off, the Eastern Front ran as follows: Taganrog, on the Sea of Azov—along the Donetz to a point immediately west of Voroshilovgrad—along the Donetz again to the bend in that river south of Kharkov—inclusive Bielgorod–Ssumy–Rylsk–Ssevsk–Dimitrovsk–Trossna–Mzensk (east of Orel)–Shisdra–

Spas-Demiansk–Dorogobush–Velish (west of Velikie-Luki)—through Lake Ilmen—along the Volchov to the north-east of Chudova—a line running south of Schlüsselburg, Leningrad and Oranienbaum—the coast of the Gulf of Finland.

The Russians now proceeded to attack this front, first of all in the sectors of Army Groups A, South and Centre. A Russian attack towards Stalino was repulsed during the period 16th–24th July. On the other hand fifty-two rifle formations[1] and ten tank corps attacked towards Kharkov and Poltava and succeeded in establishing a deep penetration of our front. A break-through was prevented, but on the 20th of August Kharkov was lost. A fresh offensive was launched on the 24th of August from the Taganrog–Voroshilovgrad line, and here the Russians did manage to break through. By the 8th of September the German line had had to be withdrawn to a line Mariupol–west of Stalino–west of Sslaviansk. By mid-September the Donetz line had been abandoned; at the end of September the Russians were outside Melitopol and Zaporozhe and had reached the line of the Dnieper all the way from the latter town to the Pripet Marshes.

The Russian counter-attack against Army Group Centre came in on July 11th. By August 5th Orel had fallen. Between August 26th and September 4th the enemy succeeded in making a deep penetration towards Konotop–Neshin and this he managed to enlarge during the next few days. By the end of September the point where the Dnieper emerges from the Pripet Marshes had been reached; from here the front ran northwards, through Gomel on the east of the Dnieper to Velish.

During the second half of October the Russians crossed the Dnieper between Dniepropetrovsk and Kremenchug. By the end of that month the German front south of Zaporozhe had collapsed and by the middle of November had been thrown back across the Dnieper. We retained two bridgeheads, a large one near Nikopol and a smaller one to the south in the Cherson area. Farther north the Russians captured Kiev between the 3rd and 13th of November and pushed on to Zhitomir.

Hitler decided to counter-attack. In accordance with his usual bad habit this attack was to be launched with inadequate forces. After discussing the matter with the Chief of the Army General Staff, I took advantage of a conference on tank questions, held on November 9th, 1943, to propose to Hitler that he give up the idea of numerous small-scale counter-attacks and that he concentrate all our panzer divisions available south of Kiev for the proposed operation through Berdichev towards Kiev. In this connection I proposed that the panzer division

See footnote, p. 224.

which was taking part in Schörner's defence of the Nikopol bridgehead
be withdrawn, together with the panzer divisions of Kleist's army group
which were holding the Dnieper in the Cherson area. I used my
favourite old expression, *Klotzen, nicht Kleckern* (roughly: 'boot 'em,
don't spatter 'em'). Hitler paid attention to what I said but did not
make his arrangements accordingly. A short memorandum I composed
on the subject was taken into consideration, but the reactions of the
responsible commanders in the field stopped Hitler from acting on it.
The Berdichev counter-offensive was launched in insufficient strength
and after heavy winter fighting broke down in December. The attempt
to recapture Kiev and re-establish the Dnieper line failed. On the 24th
of December, 1943, the Russians went over to the attack again and
threw the German front line back through Berdichev to a point outside
Vinnitsa.

The operations of 25th Panzer Division are a good example of
Hitler's tactics in the attack. But before describing these I must go
back somewhat in time.

After the Stalingrad disaster a number of the panzer divisions which
had been there destroyed were reconstituted; for this purpose the very
slender cadres that remained were employed, these being men who
through sickness or wounds or for some other reason had avoided
capture. After the loss of Africa I undertook a similar programme
for the divisions destroyed in that theatre. The 21st Panzer Division
was reformed in France with occupation troops and captured equipment. The 25th Panzer Division was set up in the same fashion in
Norway. This division was commanded by General von Schell. Schell
had been a colleague of mine at the Defence Ministry in 1927–30,
when I was working on the problem of troop transportation by
motorised vehicles. He had then been sent on detached service to
America where for a long time he had studied the problems of
motorisation in Henry Ford's country, whence he returned with many
stimulating ideas. Shortly before the war he became Chief of Department *In* 6 (*k*) at the General Army Office, and thus the Army's leading
adviser on motorisation. In view of Hitler's great interest in this
problem it was inevitable that the two men should see a considerable
amount of one another. Schell was a clever, determined and eloquent
man. He succeeded in making Hitler accept his views on simplification
of types, mass production and other such matters, and as a result—an
unusual occurrence in Germany—was appointed Under-Secretary of
State in the Ministry of Transport and made responsible for the future
development of the country's transportation stock. In this capacity he
soon ran up against opposition on the part of the industry—and of

those elements of the Party which were connected with the industry—since the industrialists were unwilling to give up their old methods of production. These people undermined Hitler's trust in Schell, with the result that he was dropped. He was sent to Norway, a very quiet theatre where there were no laurels to be won. The energetic and indefatigable man, however, soon managed to form a useful force from the scattered occupation troops. I supported his efforts that this force be expanded into a panzer division and requested that the unit be moved to France; as a result of the *Citadel* disaster large-scale transfers from France to the Eastern Front had become necessary and replacements for the West were badly needed. Of course the newly formed unit had to be supplied with new equipment in place of the captured material which it was now using. Even more urgently it needed instruction in the use of this equipment and unit training. It had to be taught the lessons that others had learned on the Eastern Front; after that it might well be employed in some operation that was not beyond its initial capabilities.

But what happened? In October 1943 the division was ordered by Hitler to surrender 600 of its new vehicles to the 14th Panzer Division, another recently formed unit destined for the Eastern theatre; the reason for this was that the *OKW* and the *OKH* believed that the 25th Panzer Division would be remaining in France for a long time and could therefore make do with inferior French vehicles. The principal effect of this loss of equipment was felt by the division's supply services, which were thereby only capable of functioning in the conditions then prevailing in the West. At this time the division's armoured reconnaissance battalion was in the process of being re-equipped with armoured troop-carrying vehicles. The divisional engineers had received new transport. The I Battalion of Panzer-grenadier Regiment 146 had been issued with new armoured troop-carrying vehicles. Panzer Regiment 9 was not yet fully equipped. Artillery Regiment 91 had to switch from captured Polish guns to German light field howitzers and 100 mm. guns. The anti-aircraft battalion lacked one battery and the anti-tank battalion a company of assault guns. All these deficiencies were well known. They were to be made up gradually in France.

Nevertheless in mid-October the transfer of the division to the Eastern Front was ordered. I immediately complained personally to Hitler, asking him at least to postpone his order until I had had an opportunity of inspecting the division once again, as I wished to form an impartial opinion of its efficiency and ensure that it was not sent into the heavy battles on the Eastern Front before it was ready. I went to France at once. After inspecting the troops and talking at length with the

commanders I sent a message back stating that the division needed
a minimum of four weeks for the issuing of new equipment and
essential training. This message went in the form of a telegram. It
crossed another telegram ordering the division's immediate departure.
Hitler, the *OKW* and the *OKH* simply ignored the reports of the unit
commanders and of the responsible Inspector-General. Its departure
was definitely fixed for October 29th.

This lack of preparedness on the part of the division was not all.
The movement plan for its transport eastwards was in accordance
neither with the wishes of the division nor with the tactical situation
at the front. It was also changed several times while the division was
in transit. The anti-tank battalion was split up into its individual guns
which travelled with various units. In order to increase the division's
striking power I had assigned to it the newly formed Tiger Battalion 509.
Incidentally, this battalion had also not completed its equipment;
furthermore, at this moment a change of battalion commander was
ordered. When the battalion set off the old commander had already
left while the new one had not yet arrived.

The division was thus hurriedly shipped to Army Group South. The
Army Group ordered that the wheeled elements of the division unload
in the Berdichev–Kosatin, the tracked elements in the Kirovograd–
Novo Ukrainka area. The division was thereby left in doubt as to
where the gun tractors and the armoured troop-carrying vehicles were
to be unloaded. The two unloading areas were some three days' march
apart. The division's first general staff officer went with the advance
party through Berdichev to Novo Ukrainka, while the divisional
commander reported at Army Group headquarters at Vinnitsa. At
Berdichev an unloading officer was supposed to arrange for the
unloading and assembly of the wheeled elements—that is to say of
those units equipped with wheeled transport. The march to the
assembly area was then to start on November 6th. Telephonic communication did not exist between units. In order to receive their orders
the responsible commanders had to drive for long distances by car.

On November 5th the enemy made a deep penetration near Kiev.
On November 6th Army Group South issued orders in the following
vein: '25th Panzer Division is placed under command of Fourth Panzer
Army. Available wheeled elements will move off in the course of this
day to the Biala Zerkov–Fastov area. The division will be responsible
for its own protection while assembling. Tracked elements of the
division will be moved up from the Kirovograd area to rejoin the rest
of the division.'

Army Group was well aware of the state of the division.

At 16.00 hrs. the divisional commander assembled the unit commanders who had so far arrived and gave them their orders. Each regimental and battalion commander was issued a 1: 300,000 map.

At this time the divisional commander disposed of the following units:

Panzergrenadier Regiment 146	Regimental staff, two battalion staffs, each battalion two companies strong.
Panzergrenadier Regiment 147	Ditto.
Panzer Regiment 9	Regimental staff, staff of 2nd Battalion, elements of various companies: total tank strength, 30 Panzer IV, 15 Tigers.
Panzer Artillery Regiment 91	Regimental Staff, staff of 1st Battalion with 1 and 2 Batteries, personnel of 3rd Battalion without their guns.
Anti-tank Battalion	Staff and one *ad hoc* company.
Signals Battalion	More or less complete, but without its commander who was with the advance party.
Engineer Battalion	Complete, less light engineering column and bridging column.
Anti-aircraft Battalion	Staff and one battery.

With the divisional commander there were only his adjutant and second orderly officer, together with a few vehicles and motor-cyclists.

In view of the urgency of the situation the divisional commander decided to organise a number of march groups, to which units would be assigned according to their readiness to move off and their distance from the division's starting-point. These groups would move through Kasatin and Skvira to the sector west of Biala Zerkov. There he intended to await the arrival of the remainder of his division and arrange for its assembly. He did not believe that it would be possible to move off before 22.00 hrs. on the 6th of November since the issuing of orders by car would require a considerable amount of time. He still lacked wireless communication; not that this made any difference, since wireless silence had been imposed for the immediate future.

After the subordinate commanders had left to return to their units, Fourth Panzer Army, with whom 25th Panzer Division's commander had at last managed to establish telephonic communication, issued the following order: '25th Panzer Division is to proceed with all speed to Fastov which will be held in all circumstances. The commander of the 25th Panzer Division will assume the responsibilities of battle commandant, Fastov. He will be in command of two *Landesschütz* (Home Defence) Battalions, a Leave Battalion (i.e. a battalion rapidly thrown together of men returning from leave) and a regiment of the SS-Panzergrenadier Division *Das Reich* which will arrive in the course of the evening.' His route was given him as Kosatin–Skvira–Popelnia–Fastov, but owing to partisans having blown a bridge he was compelled to follow a country track eastwards of Skvira instead.

The divisional commander decided to travel at the head of the first march group. The march started punctually and began smoothly enough. During the second half of the night retreating columns, consisting almost entirely of Luftwaffe personnel, caused considerable confusion which was only cleared up by energetic action on the part of the divisional commander. Up to this point the weather had been good, but now it deteriorated; heavy rain began to fall and went on falling throughout the following day, turning the roads into quagmires. The wheeled vehicles were compelled to make large detours, though the tracked vehicles managed to go on. There was no contact now between the various march groups.

At about 12.00 hrs. on November 7th the divisional commander learned from retreating soldiers that the enemy had already entered Fastov. Together with his orderly officer, he hurried forward to arrange the attack on that place. Since he had already been several times the target for enemy rifle fire during this advance, he now travelled in an armoured troop-carrying vehicle: with his orderly officer in another such vehicle, he led the vanguard. He thus ran into Russian T34 tanks. The 9th Company of Panzergrenadier Regiment 146, following immediately behind with its four heavy infantry guns, was fired on and panicked. The divisional commander then drove back to find the II Battalion of Panzergrenadier Regiment 146, which was supposed to be marching up. He discovered that they too were retreating but managed to turn them around, got them in some sort of order again and brought them forward to Trilissy. He remained with the troops lest they panic once again and ordered them to dig in as darkness was falling. During the night Russian tanks managed to make their way among the battalion's transport, which they partially destroyed. The divisional commander now decided that he would break through the Russian tanks that were swarming about him in the darkness and head for Fastov that night, so as to reach the elements of his division that had gone on ahead. His little battle group consisted of one company in front and one behind, with the vehicles and heavy weapons in the middle. General von Schell went at the head of the leading company. After heavy fighting he succeeded in breaking through the encircling enemy tanks at 04.00 hrs. in the morning of the 8th of November; at about 14.00 hrs. he reached the headquarters of XLVII Panzer Corps at Biala Zerkov. His division was now placed under command of this corps.

Sketch Map 27a

Operations by 25 Panzer Division, November 1943

to Kiev

Grebenki

Slavia

Fastovelz

Fastovetz

Fastov

Trilissy

Biala-Zerkov

Krassnelessy

koie

Mal. Polovez

Koshanka

Stavishtchi

Mal. Polovez

Skvira

25 miles

Popelnia

30 miles

From Kasatin

Meanwhile other elements of the division, commanded by Colonel Freiherr von Wechmar, were moving towards Fastov by way of Grebenki and Slavia. Early on the 9th of November General von Schell joined them. The village of Fastovetz, to the east of Fastov, was held by a strong enemy force which had to be attacked. With the divisional commander leading the assault himself it was captured at noon and an attack on Fastov immediately ordered. The enemy suffered heavy casualties. On the 10th of November the attacking force succeeded in reaching the eastern outskirts of Fastov, but when trying to advance further came up against overwhelming enemy strength both in the town and to the south of it, so that they had to be satisfied with mopping up Slavia. All the same this operation had succeeded in holding up the enemy's advance.

The division had been committed, when not yet ready and piecemeal, in an extremely difficult operation; despite the personal exertions of General von Schell it could not be said to have achieved a great deal. It is true that it caused the enemy heavy casualties, but while so doing it had itself suffered severely. A lack of battle experience caused the green troops to show a tendency to panic before they became accustomed to the difficulties of winter fighting on the Eastern Front. The responsible local higher commands (Army Group, Army and Panzer Corps) were compelled by the urgency of the moment to commit the division in the manner described above. But the Supreme Command must bear the blame for failing to realise that these young troops needed more careful handling.

In later battles, from the 24th to the 30th of December, 1943, this unfortunate division found itself once again in a most difficult situation; while holding a 25-mile front it was attacked and thrown back by the enemy in overwhelming strength. It suffered such severe casualties that it would have to be reformed almost from scratch. Hitler and the *OKH* wanted to dissolve it. I prevented this at the time, since the division was in no way responsible for its fate. General von Schell became seriously ill and had to leave the front. He suffered greatly from the unmerited failure of this division which he had spent so many months of loving work and great skill in building up. Hitler's distrust of him was such that he never again held a command. So his capacity for hard work and his great talent for organisation and training remained unused.

In order to have at least something ready for the Western Front I ordered the collection of all the demonstration units from the schools into one division to be trained together in France. This was called the *Panzer-Lehr* Division (the Panzer Demonstration Division). It was

given new equipment and assigned specially selected officers. Its commander was General Bayerlein, who, it will be recalled, had at one
time been my first operations officer in Russia. Hitler approved the
formation of this division in December with the remark: 'An unexpected
help on which I had not reckoned.'

Meanwhile severe fighting continued almost without a pause. The
Russians succeeded in breaking through Army Group Centre's line
in the Rechitsa area, between the Pripet and the Beresina. There were
fierce battles for Vitebsk and Nevel. Gomel and Propoisk were lost,
but our troops maintained a bridgehead on the far bank of the Dnieper
to the east of Mogilev and Orsha.

It may well be asked whether the retention of these bridgeheads
over the Dnieper in present circumstances—when a resumption of our
offensive eastwards was clearly and permanently out of the question—
was still a sensible proposition. At Nikopol Hitler wished to exploit
the supplies of manganese there available. This was an economic reason
for retaining that bridgehead, though a weak one and, as already seen,
the bridgehead was operationally harmful to us. So far as all the others
were concerned it would have been better to give them up and retire
behind the broad river line. Thus reserves could have been built up
—primarily in the form of panzer divisions—and with such reserves
it would have become possible to fight a mobile war and to pursue
an operational plan. But if Hitler heard the word 'operational' he lost
his temper. He believed that whenever his generals spoke of operations
they meant withdrawals; and consequently Hitler insisted with fanatical
obstinacy that ground must be held, all ground, even when it was to our
disadvantage to do so.

The severe casualties suffered during the heavy winter fighting had
utterly confounded the *OKH*. They produced no programme for the
building up of our forces in the West against the invasion that could
be anticipated with certainty for the spring of 1944. I therefore regarded
it as my duty to bring up repeatedly the need for withdrawing panzer
divisions from the front and restoring their strength in time. The *OKW*
might have been expected to show the greatest interest in what promised
soon to be its most vital theatre, yet here too I failed to find any support.
So the freeing of forces for the West continued to be postponed until
one day, in Zeitzler's presence, I spoke once again to Hitler on the
subject. The question immediately under discussion was the withdrawal
of one particular panzer division. Zeitzler said that the withdrawal
had been ordered in the clearest terms. I had to contradict him, pointing
out that the relevant *OKH* orders contained many loopholes of which
the generals at the front could avail themselves in their own interests.

My remarks on this subject brought a heated denial from the Chief
of the Army General Staff. But the most recent *OKH* order concerning
the withdrawal of a division had run somewhat as follows: 'The
X Panzer Division is to be withdrawn from the front as soon as the
battle situation makes this possible. Battle groups will, however, remain
in contact with the enemy until further notice. The *OKH* is to be
notified when the withdrawal begins.' The phrase 'until further notice'
was standard in orders of this sort. The immediate reaction of the
army group or army commander who was to release the division was
almost equally standard; he would reply that the battle situation did
not permit the immediate withdrawal of the division in question. Weeks
often went by before it did do so. The battle groups which even then had
to be left behind constituted, needless to say, those elements of the
division with the greatest fighting strength, particularly the tanks and
the panzergrenadiers: it was just these that it was most necessary to
rest and re-equip. The normal procedure was that, first of all, the
complete divisional supply services would appear, followed by the staff
and a fair proportion of the divisional artillery; with the result that I
was still unable to carry out my work since the most important units
remained behind. Zeitzler was very angry with me, but the interests
of the Western theatre could not be ignored.

By the beginning of the invasion on June 6th, 1944, we had succeeded
with difficulty in making ten panzer and panzergrenadier divisions
ready for operations in the West and, to a certain extent, in replenishing
and training them. I shall revert to this matter later on. I entrusted
the training of these formations, which included, moreover, three reserve
panzer divisions formed from replacement units and transferred from
Germany to France, to my old and trusted comrade-in-arms, General
Freiherr von Geyr; after repeated arguments on the subject Hitler still
refused to give General von Geyr a command at the front. Geyr's
official position was 'General of Panzer Troops West.' Territorially and
operationally he was subordinate to the Commander-in-Chief West,
Field-Marshal von Rundstedt; so far as his activities within the
armoured force were concerned he received his orders from me. Our
work together was based on mutual confidence and was, I think, of
help to the troops.

There were a few more noteworthy incidents during that eventful
year of 1943. I have already mentioned how, during my visit to Goebbels,
I brought up the question of the mismanagement of affairs by the
Supreme Command and how I asked the minister to urge Hitler that
it be reorganised; I had hoped that the appointment of a Chief of the
Armed Forces General Staff with the necessary authority would

lessen Hitler's direct influence on military operations. Goebbels had pronounced the problem a thorny one, but had nevertheless promised to do what he could at an appropriate time. At the end of July, 1943, the minister happened to be in East Prussia and I took advantage of this to visit him and to remind him of our former important converation. He immediately began to discuss the matter, admitting the increasing deterioration of our military situation, and adding thoughtfully: 'When I think of the Russians reaching Berlin and us having to poison our wives and children so that they should not fall into the hands of that atrocious enemy, your question oppresses me like a mountain weighing on my soul.' Goebbels perfectly understood what the result of the war would be if it were to continue to be run as heretofore, but unfortunately he did not act accordingly. He never had sufficient courage to speak to Hitler on the lines that I have indicated and thus to attempt to influence him.

I therefore tried next to sound out Himmler, but received an impression of such impenetrable obliquity that I gave up any idea of discussing a limitation of Hitler's power with him.

In November I went to see Jodl, to whom I submitted my proposals for a reorganisation of the Supreme Command: the Chief of the Armed Forces General Staff would control the actual conduct of operations, while Hitler would be limited to his proper field of activities, supreme control of the political situation and of the highest war strategy. After I had expounded my ideas at length and in detail Jodl replied laconically: 'Do you know of a better supreme commander than Adolf Hitler?' His expression had remained impassive as he said this, and his whole manner was one of icy disapproval. In view of his attitude I put my papers back in my brief-case and left the room.

In January, 1944, Hitler invited me to breakfast, with the words: 'Somebody's sent me a teal. You know I'm a vegetarian. Would you like to have breakfast with me and eat the teal?' We were alone together at a small round table in a rather dark room, since the only light came from one window. Only his sheepdog bitch, Blondi, was there. Hitler fed her from time to time with pieces of dry bread. Linge, the servant who waited on us, came and went silently. The rare occasion had arisen on which it would be possible to tackle and perhaps to solve thorny problems. After a few opening remarks the conversation turned on the military situation. I brought up the matter of the Allied landings in the West which were to be expected for the coming spring, and remarked that our reserves at present available to meet them were insufficient. In order to free more forces it was essential that a stronger defence be established on the Eastern Front. I expressed my astonish-

ment that apparently no thought had been given to providing our
front there with a backbone in the form of field fortifications and a
defensive zone in our rear. Specifically it seemed to me that the reconstruction of the old German and Russian frontier fortifications would
offer us better defensive possibilities than did the system of declaring
open towns as 'strong points'—which declarations, incidentally, usually
came at the last moment when it was too late to take measures which
would justify the phrase. With these remarks I soon saw that I had
stirred up a hornet's nest.

'Believe me! I am the greatest builder of fortifications of all time.
I built the West Wall; I built the Atlantic Wall. I have used so and so
many tons of concrete. I know what the building of fortifications
involves. On the Eastern Front we are short of labour, materials and
transport. Even now the railways cannot carry enough supplies to
satisfy the demands of the front. Therefore I cannot send trains to
the East full of building materials.' He had the figures at his fingertips
and, as usual, bluffed by reeling off exact statistics which his listener
was not for the moment in a position to contradict. All the same, I
disagreed strongly. I knew that the railway bottle-neck only began
beyond Brest-Litovsk and I tried to make clear to him that the building
I had in mind would not affect transports travelling to the front, but
only those going to the line of the Bug and the Niemen: that the
railways were quite capable of shouldering this burden: that there could
scarcely be a shortage of local building materials and local labour:
and finally that it was only possible to wage war on two fronts with
success if at least temporary inactivity could be assured on one front
while the other was being stabilised. Since he had made such excellent
preparations for the West there was no reason why he should not do
likewise for the East. Thus cornered Hitler proceeded to bring out his
much-repeated thesis, namely, that our generals in the East would
think of nothing save withdrawal if he permitted the building of
defensive positions or fortifications in their rear. He had made up his
mind on this point and nothing could bring him to change it.

The conversation then turned on the generals and the Supreme
Command. Since my indirect attempts to effect a concentration of the
military command and a limitation to Hitler's immediate influence had
failed, I now felt it my duty to propose directly to him that a general
he trusted be appointed Chief of the Armed Services General Staff;
by this act he could get rid of the obscure confusion of command
functions that now reigned among the Armed Forces Command Staff,
the *OKH*, the *Luftwaffe*, the Navy and the *Waffen-SS*, and could
ensure a more successful control of our combined forces than had
existed up to date. But this attempt on my part was a total failure.

Hitler refused to part with Field-Marshal Keitel. So distrustful was he that he immediately recognised my suggestion as an attempt to limit his powers. I achieved nothing. Besides, was there any general whom Hitler trusted? After this conversation I was bound to admit to myself that there was none.

So nothing was altered. Every square yard of ground continued to be fought for. Never once was a situation which had become hopeless put right by a timely withdrawal. But many, many times Hitler was to say to me, dully: 'I can't understand why everything has gone wrong for the past two years.' My reply was always the same and was always ignored: 'Change your methods.'

The Year of Decision

Nineteen forty-four began on the Eastern Front with fierce Russian attacks in mid-January. In the Kirovgorod area these were initially held. On January 24th and 26th a pincer attack was launched against the German salient west of Cherkassy, and on January 30th another salient east of Krivoirog was also attacked. Both these operations were successful. Russian superiority in strength was considerable. The following forces were employed:

Against Army Group South Ukraine . 34 rifle formations,
11 tank formations.
Against Army Group North Ukraine . 67 rifle formations,
52 tank formations.

During the second half of February the front was relatively quiet, but on March 3rd, 4th and 5th the Russians attacked again and threw the Germans back to, and over, the line of the Bug.

Army Group Centre managed generally to retain control along their sector of the front until the end of March.

In April the Crimean peninsula, exclusive of Sebastopol, was lost. The enemy crossed the Bug as well as the upper reaches of the rivers Pruth and Sereth. The Russians entered Czernowitz. A final Russian large-scale attack was held and after the loss of Sebastopol the front became settled until August.

The enemy had also attacked on Army Group North's front in January. At first he only achieved limited successes in the areas north of Lake Ilmen and south-west of Leningrad. But beginning on January 21st he threw in powerful forces which forced the German front back across the Luga and, in February, across the Narva. By

March the Germans had withdrawn behind the Velikaia and Lakes Pleskau and Peipus. Here they managed to hold.

The Eastern Front was given only a short breathing-space, until June 22nd. Our expenditure of force during the winter campaign had been heavy. There were no reserves available. Everything that could be spared had to be stationed behind the Atlantic Wall, which was not in fact a wall at all, but a system of fortifications intended to frighten the enemy.

I was at this time entrusted by Hitler with a distasteful special assignment. As usual, he was asking for scapegoats to carry the blame for the various withdrawals and surrenders of the previous winter. One of these was Colonel-General Jänicke, whom he made responsible for the loss of the Crimea. Remarks by high Party functionaries served to increase his suspicions. I was instructed to investigate the case of Jänicke, and was simultaneously informed that somebody would have to be punished for what had happened in the Crimea. In view of Hitler's frame of mind at the time, only delaying tactics offered the possibility of a successful outcome to the inquiry. I therefore went very thoroughly to work, interviewing all persons in any way connected with the events and in particular the Party functionaries. Jänicke finally complained about the slowness of my methods. But I am certain that I did more for him by thus ensuring his ultimate acquittal than could have been achieved by a rapid inquiry and a report submitted at an unfavourable time.

As already mentioned, I had begun to study the problem of defending the Western Front in 1943. With the new year this problem assumed increasing importance. In February I went to France for a tour of inspection and for conversations with Field-Marshal von Rundstedt and General von Geyr. We were in complete agreement that enemy sea and air superiority made our task more difficult. Allied air supremacy must in particular affect our ability to move our forces. It seemed likely that in order to achieve sufficient speed and concentration we should have to move only by night. Our opinion was that it all depended on our making ready adequate reserves of panzer and panzergrenadier divisions: these must be stationed far enough inland from the so-called Atlantic Wall, so that they could be switched easily to the main invasion front once it had been recognised: these moves must be facilitated by repairs to the French road network and by the construction of alternative river-crossings, underwater bridges or bridges of boats.

When visiting the troops I realised how great the enemy's air superiority already was. Whole formations of hostile aircraft manœuvred above our troops in training, and there was no telling when the bomb bays might open to discharge their loads on the training area beneath.

Back at Supreme Headquarters I studied the instructions issued by the *OKW* for the forthcoming battle on the Western Front, together with the reserves that were being made available. I thus discovered that the panzer divisions, which were the principal reserve, were to be stationed very near the coast. Disposed thus, they could not be withdrawn and committed elsewhere with sufficient rapidity should the enemy land at any other point than that at which he was expected. I pointed out this error during a conference with Hitler and proposed a different arrangement of our motorised forces. Hitler replied: 'The present arrangement is the one suggested by Field-Marshal Rommel. I don't like to give contrary orders over the head of the responsible field-marshal on the spot without having first heard his opinion. Go to France again and discuss the matter once more with Rommel.'

In April I paid another visit to France. The enemy air forces were becoming ever more active and were already beginning to attack operational targets. Thus our tank depot at Camp de Mailly was completely destroyed a few days after I had visited it. It was thanks to General von Geyr's foresight that the troops and their equipment —much against the men's will—had been scattered throughout neighbouring villages and woods and thus suffered no damage worth mentioning.

After fresh conversations with Field-Marshal von Rundstedt and the General Staff Corps officers of his staff concerning the disposition of reserves, I went as instructed, and accompanied by General von Geyr, to see Rommel at La Roche Guyon. I had known Rommel since before the war. He had at one time commanded the Goslar Jaeger Battalion which had been my original unit and with which I had always maintained friendly contact. Then we had met during the Polish Campaign —on the occasion of Hitler's visit to my corps in September 1939, after the Battle of the Corridor. Rommel was then military commander of the Führer's headquarters. He had later transferred to the armoured force, and had proved an outstanding commander, first of the 7th Panzer Division in France in 1940 and later of the Africa Corps and of Panzer Army Africa, where he had established his reputation as a general. Rommel was not only an open, upright man and a brave soldier; he was also a highly gifted commander. He possessed energy and subtlety of appreciation; he always found an answer to the most difficult problems; he had great understanding of his men and, in fact, thoroughly deserved the reputation that he had won for himself. In September 1942, when sickness had compelled Rommel to leave Africa, he had asked Hitler to appoint me his deputy during his absence, although he knew that I was on bad terms with Hitler. This request had been curtly refused. No doubt this was a piece of luck for me, since the defeat at El Alamein took place shortly afterwards, and I should probably have been as unable to avoid it as was Stumme and Stumme's successor, Rommel himself.

Rommel's sad experiences in Africa had so convinced him of the overwhelming nature of Allied air supremacy that he believed there could be no question of ever moving large formations of troops again. He did not even think that it would be possible to transfer panzer or panzergrenadier divisions by night. His views on this subject had been further strengthened by his experiences in Italy in 1943. So when General von Geyr had proposed the grouping of our motorised reserves back from the Atlantic defensive front he had immediately come up against opposition on Rommel's part, since what Geyr wanted was that these reserves be employed in a mobile role and organised accordingly. I had been informed of the negative results of this conversation. I was therefore not surprised by Rommel's highly temperamental and strongly expressed refusal when I suggested that our armour be withdrawn from the coastal areas. He turned down my suggestion at once, pointing out that as a man from the Eastern Front I lacked his experiences of Africa and Italy; that he knew, in fact, far more about the matter in hand than I did and that he was fully convinced that his system was right. In view of this attitude of his, an argument with Rommel concerning the distribution of our motorised reserves promised to be quite fruitless. I therefore decided not to make any further attempts to alter his opinions and made up my mind once more to submit my contrary views to Rundstedt and to Hitler. Also it was quite plain that no more panzer and panzergrenadier divisions could be sent to the Western Front beyond those already there. Only two SS divisions, the 9th and 10th, which had been 'lent' to the Eastern Front during the spring, were to come back to the West as soon as the invasion began. So I could make Rommel no promises on this score. General command in the Western theatre as exercised by the Commander-in-Chief West could only be made easier if the *OKW* reserves were freed for this theatre and if the Commander-in-Chief were given complete command authority over Army Group Rommel. Neither happened.

Since taking over command of Army Group B in France Rommel had done a great deal to increase the defensive strength of the Atlantic Wall in his area. In accordance with his theory that the coast must be the main line of defence he had arranged for forward defences in front of the coast in the form of underwater obstacles. Behind the coastal fortifications he had built obstacles to airborne landings in all the terrain that seemed to him suitable for such operations. These were generally stakes, the so-called 'Rommel's asparagus.' Extensive mine-fields were laid. All troops of his command had to devote any time not actually spent in training to the digging of defences. Army Group B was kept very busy indeed. No matter how one may admire the great exertions made, it is nevertheless a matter of considerable regret that Rommel failed to understand the need for possessing mobile reserves. A large-scale land operation—which in view of our hopeless inferiority on the sea and in the air offered us the only chance of success—he held to be impossible and he therefore neither wanted nor tried to organise one. Furthermore, at least at the time of my visit, Rommel had made up his mind where the Allies would land. He assured me several times that the English and American landings would take place in the coastal area north of the mouth of the Somme; he ruled out all alternative landing-places with the argument that for such a difficult and large-scale sea crossing the enemy, for supply reasons alone, must seize a beachhead as close as possible to his principal ports of embarkation. A further reason was the greater air-support that the enemy could give to a landing north of the Somme. On this subject, too, he was at that time quite impervious to argument.

On all these points Rommel's views coincided with those of Hitler, though based on different grounds. Hitler had remained a man of the 1914–1918 trench-warfare epoch and had never understood the principles of mobile operations. Rommel believed such operations to be no longer possible as a result of the enemy's air supremacy. So it is little wonder that both the Commander-in-Chief West and I found that Hitler turned down our proposals for the re-distribution of our motorised formations, on the grounds that Rommel possessed more recent experiences of battle than did either of us.

On June 6th, 1944, the following forces were stationed in France:

48 infantry divisions, of which 38 were located along, and 10 behind, the coast: of these latter, 5 were between the Scheldt and the Somme, 2 between the Somme and the Seine and 3 in Brittany.

10 panzer and panzergrenadier divisions, located as follows:

1st SS Panzer Division *Leibstandarte 'Adolf Hitler,'* at Beverloo, Belgium;

2nd Panzer Division in the area Amiens–Abbéville;

116th Panzer Division to the east of Rouen (north of the Seine);

12th SS Panzer Division *Hitler Jugend* in the Lisieux area (south of the Seine);

21st Panzer Division in the Caen area;

Panzer-Lehr Division in the area Le Mans–Orléans–Chartres;

17th SS Panzergrenadier Division in the area Saumur–Niort–Poitiers;

11th Panzer Division in the Bordeaux area;

2nd SS Panzer Division *Das Reich* in the area Montauban–Tolouse;

9th Panzer Division in the area Avignon–Nîmes–Arles.

All hopes of successful defence were based on these ten panzer and panzergrenadier divisions. With considerable effort it had proved possible to rest them and, to a certain extent, to build up their strength.

Four of these divisions were under Rommel's command, the 2nd, 116th, 21st and 12th SS. The 1st SS, *Panzer-Lehr* and 17th SS Panzergrenadier were in *OKW* reserve. The 9th, 11th and 2nd SS were located in Southern France to be used against a landing that was anticipated on the Mediterranean coast.

This dispersal of strength ruled out all possibility of a great defensive victory. But apart from that, events took the most unsatisfactory course imaginable. To begin with, on the day of the landings Rommel was in Germany, on his way to a conference with Hitler. The latter, as was his custom, had gone late to bed and could not be disturbed when the first reports of the invasion began to arrive early on June 6th. Jodl, who was responsible for controlling operations in Hitler's absence, could not make up his mind to free the *OKW* reserve at once—a reserve, after all, of three panzer divisions—since he was by no means certain that the landings in Normandy constituted the main operation and were not merely a feint. Since the *OKW* was also incapable of making up its collective mind on the question of a Mediterranean landing, neither were the panzer divisions in Southern France immediately switched north. The 21st Panzer Division, which was on the spot, had received orders, contrary to General Freiherr von Geyr's training instructions, which forbade it to launch its counter-attack before receiving Rommel's permission to do so: thus the best opportunity for attacking the British airborne forces was lost. Then Rommel moved the 116th Panzer Division to a point even nearer the coast at Dieppe and left it there until mid-July.

Many higher commanders displayed ignorance in the employment of armoured forces. Divisions, in particular the *Panzer-Lehr* Division, received direct orders to move up in daylight despite the enemy's air supremacy: frontal counter-attacks were ordered in the area controlled by the enemy's naval guns: and thus Germany's sole possible military force for defeating the invasion was prematurely ground down. The panzer units suffered enormous casualties. And these could not now be made good, since after June 22nd the whole Eastern Front threatened to collapse and all available replacements had to go there instead of to the previously favoured Western Front.

Defence against the invasion would have proved far easier if Hitler and the *OKW* had approved the proposals of General Freiherr von Geyr and of the Inspector-General of Armoured Troops, by which *all* the panzer and panzer grenadierdivisions would have been concentrated ready in two groups, one north and the other south of Paris, while thorough preparations would have been made for moving these forces to the actual invasion front.

But even the dispositions that were in fact made would have yielded better results if the High Command had been quite clear as to its intentions. On June 16th, that is to say nearly two weeks after the landing, the 116th Panzer Division was still on the coast between Abbéville and Dieppe, the 11th Panzer Division was in the Bordeaux area, the 9th Panzer Division was around Avignon, and the SS Panzer Division *Das Reich* was fighting guerrillas in Southern France, while the other panzer divisions, reinforced by the 9th and 10th SS brought across from the Eastern Front, were wasting their strength in heavy frontal battles in an area within range of the enemy's naval guns. But apart from the panzer divisions, at this date there were still seven infantry divisions doing nothing in their coastal sectors north of the Seine, waiting for a landing that never materialised.

The following details are worth mentioning:

On June 7th General Freiherr von Geyr assumed command of the Caen sector, first of all under Seventh Army, then under Army Group B. The 12th SS and *Panzer-Lehr* Divisions were committed on the left of the 21st Panzer Division, which was already engaged. On the 10th of June General Freiherr von Geyr intended to launch his counter-attack, but a successful enemy bombing raid put the staff of his Panzer Group West out of action. I SS Panzer Corps took over command. After several days' delay the SS *Leibstandarte* '*Adolf Hitler*' and the 2nd Panzer Division began to arrive and were committed piecemeal. On June 28th Panzer Group West having been reconstituted took over command of the I and II SS Panzer Corps and LXXXVI and XLVII Panzer Corps. General von Geyr's proposal for a concentrated attack with all available strength was turned down by Rommel, who had lost his faith in the possibility of mounting a successful attack. Whether other, political considerations played a part in this overdue and piecemeal commitment of the reserves is an open question.[1]

[1] Compare Hans Speidel, *Invasion, 1944*, Rainer Wunderlich Verlag, Hermann Leins, Tübingen and Stuttgart, p. 71. 'Also political considerations made it seem desirable to the Field-Marshal that reliable armoured units remain readily available against future events.' Compare also Freiherr von Geyr, *Invasion Without Laurels*, in the Irish publication *An Cosantoir*, No. 1, 1950: 'The 2nd Panzer Division (an Army, not an SS Unit) was held back by Rommel for some time, because in expectation of the "20th July Plot" to assassinate Hitler, he wished to have a "reliable" Army division available for any emergency. Although the situation at the front obliged him to commit the 2nd Panzers on the western sector of the battlefield, where it opposed the 1st U.S. Division, Rommel did manage to keep his 116th Panzer Division in reserve until the middle of July.' And later: 'His (Rommel's) refusal may have had a political reason.'

The commander of Seventh Army, General Dollmann, died on June 28th. Colonel-General Hausser was appointed in his stead.

On June 29th a conference attended by the senior commanders from the Western Front took place at Hitler's residence on the Obersalzberg. Field-Marshals von Rundstedt, Sperrle and Rommel were present. This was the last occasion on which I saw Rommel. I again received the impression that I had gained at his headquarters at La Roche Guyon the previous April: namely, that as a result of the enemy's air supremacy Rommel no longer believed mobile defence to be possible. At this conference the principal matter under discussion was the strengthening of fighter formations. Goering promised to supply 800 fighter planes if Sperrle could provide the crews. This the latter could not do. He said, so far as I can recall, that he had only 500 crews available, thereby arousing Hitler's anger. The evil result of this day was the dismissal, shortly afterwards, of Rundstedt, Geyr and Sperrle. Field-Marshal von Kluge succeeded Rundstedt; he had spent the last few weeks at Supreme Headquarters for the purpose of studying the general situation and of being available in any eventuality. Herr von Kluge was at that time *persona gratissima* with Hitler.

The new High Command West that took over on July 6th did not succeed in altering the course of events. Field-Marshal von Kluge arrived in France still filled with the optimism that prevailed at Supreme Headquarters. In consequence he had an immediate disagreement with Rommel, but soon had to accept the latter's more sensible appreciation of the situation.

Herr von Kluge was a hard-working soldier, his knowledge of small-scale tactics was good, but he was totally ignorant concerning the employment of armoured formations in mobile operations. His influence on the command of armour was invariably, so far as I ever came across it, restrictive. He was an expert at breaking up units. It is therefore hardly surprising that the command in the West continued to try to cure each symptom that appeared instead of attacking the root of the disease, and going over to mobile warfare with what still remained of its armoured strength. What did remain was in fact squandered in further frontal attacks with limited objectives made under fire of the enemy's naval guns.

On July 11th Caen fell. On July 17th, while driving back from the front, Rommel's car was attacked by an English fighter-bomber; the driver was severely wounded, the Field-Marshal being thrown from the car and suffering a cracked skull and other wounds which necessitated his going to hospital. With his departure, the strongest personality in the Western theatre was gone.

Sketch Map 28

The Destruction of Army Group Centre

Situation 22.6. to 1. 8. 44.

Libau
Riga
Mitau
Memel
Schaulen
2. Balt. Front
Dünaburg
Dvina
Idriza
1. Balt. Front
Memel
Königsberg
Insterburg
Kovno
Polotsk
Vitebsk
Mariampol
Neris
Sudauen
Vilna
Berezina
3 White Rus. Front
Dnieper
Ortelsburg
Lyck
Molodeczno
Borissov
Orsha
Smolensk
Johannisburg
Grodno
Lida
Kolno
Mogilev
Ostenburg
Volkovisk
Chaussy
Warsaw
Biala Podl
2 White Rus. Front
Pruzana
Bobruisk
Deblin
Brest
Litowsk
Ragachev
Dnieper-Bug-Canal
Pinsk
Pripet
Lublin
Masyr
Gomel
Sangomir
1 White Rus. Front
Luzk
Sarny
Rovno
Karosten

Situation 22.6 44
3. 7. 44
13. 7. 44
1. 8. 44

On this day the invasion front ran from the mouth of the Orne, through the southern outskirts of Caen–Caumont–St. Lo—to Lessay on the coast.

In Normandy the Western Allies were assembling their assaulting forces in order to break out of the bridgeheads that they had won, and the situation there could only be described as extremely tense. Meanwhile on the Eastern Front events had happened which threatened us with a gigantic catastrophe in the immediate future.

On June 22nd the Russians, using 146 rifle and 43 tank formations, went over to the attack along the whole of the front of Army Group Centre, which was commanded by Field-Marshal Busch. This attack was completely successful. By July 3rd the Russians had reached the northern edge of the Pripet Marshes and a line Baranowicze–Molodeczno–Koziany. They continued to advance without pause, extending their attacks to the front of Army Group North, and by mid-July had reached a line running, approximately, Pinsk–Pruzana–Volkovisk–Grodno–Kovno–Dünaburg–Pleskau. At their points of main effort, which were directed towards the Vistula at Warsaw and towards Riga, they poured forwards and it seemed as though nothing could ever stop them. Since July 13th they had also been attacking Army Group A and had won ground towards Przemysl—the San line—Pulavy on the Vistula. The result of this attack was the destruction of Army Group Centre. We suffered the total loss of some twenty-five divisions.

In view of these shattering events Hitler moved his headquarters in mid-July from the Obersalzberg to East Prussia. All units that could be scraped together were rushed to the disintegrating front. In place of Field-Marshal Busch, Field-Marshal Model, who already commanded Army Group A, was also given command of Army Group Centre—or to be more precise of the gap where that army group had been. Since he could not perform both functions for any length of time, Colonel-General Harpe was appointed to command Army Group A. I knew Model well from the days when he commanded the 3rd Panzer Division in 1941. During my description of the 1941 Russian campaign I have portrayed his character enough; he was a bold, inexhaustible soldier, who knew the front well and who won the confidence of his men by his habitual disregard for his personal safety. He had no time for lazy or incompetent subordinates. He carried out his intentions in a most determined fashion. He was the best possible man to perform the fantastically difficult task of reconstructing a line in the centre of the Eastern Front. Harpe was a former panzer officer of Westphalian origin, calm, reliable, brave and determined. A man of cool understanding and with a clear brain. He too was the right man for the job he had now been given. The outstanding performance and leadership of these two generals were primarily responsible for the re-establishment of an Eastern Front. Of course this required a certain amount of time. Meanwhile an unexpected event occurred which threatened to make all attempts to defend the homeland illusory.

10. JULY 20TH AND ITS SEQUEL

There was a very real danger of the Russians breaking through into East Prussia as a result of their victory and of our absence of reserves. I therefore had ordered on July 17th, in my capacity as commander of the armoured force training schools, that the demonstration units at Wünsdorf and Krampnitz which were capable of fighting should be sent from Berlin to the fortified area around Lötzen in East Prussia.

During the afternoon of July 18th a Luftwaffe general whom I had known in the old days asked if he might come to see me. He informed me that the new Commander-in-Chief West, Field-Marshal von Kluge, intended to arrange an armistice with the Western Powers without Hitler's knowledge, and that with this object in view was proposing shortly to establish contact with the enemy. I was utterly horrified by this piece of information. I saw what the immediate effect of Kluge's act would be on our tottering Eastern Front and on the whole future of Germany. Our defences, both in the East and in the West, would collapse at once and the Russians would surge irresistibly forwards. Up to this moment I had never imagined that any German general, in command of troops actually in contact with the enemy, could possibly envisage taking such a step in direct opposition to the Head of the State. Since I could not believe the information he gave me, I asked the man with whom I was talking to tell me what his sources were. He proved reluctant to do so. Nor would he inform me why he had made this startling disclosure to me or what results he expected to achieve by so doing. When I asked whether this proposed action was to take place in the immediate future he replied that this was not the case. So I had time to think over what I should do about the extraordinary piece of information that I had received. At my headquarters, however, I was busied with a constant series of conferences and visits, which made it difficult to think such a matter out clearly; I therefore decided, on July 19th, to drive to Allenstein, Thorn and Hohensalza, ostensibly to inspect the troops in those places, but actually to work out during the drive what decisions I should take. If I were to inform Hitler of what I had heard without being able to state the source from which it came, I might be doing Field-Marshal von Kluge a grave injustice by arousing such very serious and unconfirmed suspicions against him. Should I keep the information to myself, and it turned out to be true, then I must share the guilt for the evil consequences that were bound to ensue. It was extremely difficult to decide what was the correct line of action for me to follow.

On July 19th I visited the anti-tank troops at Allenstein. While there I was summoned to the telephone; my chief of staff, General Thomale, asked me to postpone for three days the transfer of the panzer demonstration units from Berlin to East Prussia already ordered. General Olbricht, the head of the General Army Office, had telephoned him and requested this postponement; on the next day, July 20th, 1944, there was to be an *Exercise Valkyrie* for reserve and demonstration units in the Berlin area which could not take place without the participation of the panzer demonstration troops. *Exercise Valkyrie* was the cover name for training exercises against the possibility of enemy air landings or of internal unrest. That, at least, is the meaning which I had always attached to it. When Thomale assured me that the situation in East Prussia was not for the moment critical and that the departure of the units in question might well be postponed for two or three days, I gave my reluctant approval that the troops take part in the exercise.

On the afternoon of this day I inspected reserve units at Thorn and on the morning of July 20th I drove to Hohensalza to inspect the anti-tank troops stationed there. I spent the evening of that day at my home at Deipenhof. I went for a walk in the late afternoon from which I was summoned back by a motor-cycle despatch rider, who told me that a telephone call was expected from Supreme Headquarters. When I reached the house I was told of the announcement that had been made on the wireless concerning the attempt to assassinate Hitler. It was midnight before I spoke to General Thomale on the telephone; he described briefly the facts of the attempt on Hitler's life, told me the name of the assassin, and informed me that Hitler had ordered that I report at Supreme Headquarters next day since he intended to dismiss Zeitzler and to appoint me in his place. An aeroplane would be at Hohensalza at 08.00 hrs. on the 21st to take me back to East Prussia.

All other stories about my activities on July 20th are pure invention. I knew nothing about the assassination attempt, I talked to nobody about it, and the only telephone conversation I had during that day was the one described above with General Thomale at midnight.

The incidents that led up to my appointment as Chief of the Army General Staff were written down by General Thomale in a document composed under oath and now in my possession. They were as follows:

At 18.00 hrs. on July 20th, 1944, General Thomale was in his office when he was telephoned by an officer of the General Staff Corps, Lieutenant-Colonel Weizenegger of Colonel-General Jodl's Armed

Forces Command Staff, who asked where I was. Thomale told him.
He was then ordered to report at once in person to Hitler at Supreme
Headquarters. He arrived there at about 19.00 hrs. Hitler, who was
accompanied by his adjutant, Colonel von Below, received him. Hitler
began by asking again where I was and whether I was in good health.
Thomale answered this latter question in the affirmative. Hitler then
stated that he had decided to appoint General Buhle Chief of the
Army General Staff. But since Buhle had been wounded in the assassination attempt, and since it was not yet known how long it would take
him to recover, he had decided that for the meantime Colonel-General
Guderian would be entrusted with performing the duties of Chief of
the Army General Staff. Thomale was ordered to arrange that I report
to Hitler the following morning.

From these facts it may be seen that Hitler did not originally intend
to appoint me successor to Zeitzler, with whom he had been on bad
terms for some time. He only picked me for this not very enviable
post when the man for whom it was destined was incapacitated by
the assassination attempt. All the conclusions that Hitler's enemies
have drawn since the war from my appointment as acting Chief of
Staff are therefore invalid. They either belong in the realms of fantasy
or are simply malicious slanders. Actually even the rumour-mongers
must admit that voluntarily to tackle the situation on the Eastern Front
in July 1944, was no very enticing proposition—and this was then the
principal task of the man who filled that high-sounding, historic
appointment.

Needless to say I have been frequently asked why I agreed to accept
the difficult position at all. It would be simple to reply: because I was
ordered to do so. As a description of future events will show, the
Eastern Front was tottering on the edge of an abyss from which it was
necessary to save millions of German soldiers and civilians. I should
have regarded myself as a shabby coward if I had refused to attempt
to save the eastern armies and my homeland, eastern Germany. That
my attempt to do so was ultimately a failure will remain, until the day
I die, the distress and grief of my life. There can be scarcely anyone
who feels more painfully than I do for the fate of our eastern territories
and for their innocent, valiant, true and brave inhabitants. After all,
I am myself a Prussian.

On July 21st, 1944, I flew from Hohensalza to Lötzen. As soon as
I arrived I had a short talk with Thomale, who told me of his con-
versation with Hitler and who described the attempted assassination.
I next saw Field-Marshal Keitel, Colonel-General Jodl and General
Burgdorf, who had succeeded Schmundt, severely wounded by the

bomb, as Hitler's chief adjutant and as head of the Army Personnel Office; they briefed me on the matters connected with the new appointment as Chief of the Army General Staff. The principal problem would be the almost complete replacement of all officers occupying General Staff Corps positions in the *OKH*. Of the officers previously with the *OKH*, some had been wounded in the assassination attempt, some were suspected of complicity in the plot and had already been arrested, while others were already known to me and their future collaboration undesired; others again had never seen. the front and must for this reason be reassigned. Before this meeting I arranged that I would take over my new duties in the *OKH* building at 16.00 hrs.

After this conversation with the officers of the *OKH* I reported to Hitler at about noon. He seemed to be in rather poor shape; one ear was bleeding; his right arm, which had been badly bruised and was almost unuseable, hung in a sling. But his manner was one of astonishing calm as he received me. He appointed me responsible for carrying out the duties of the chief of the Army General Staff, and informed me that for some time he had been unable to agree with my predecessor, Zeitzler. Zeitzler had on five occasions offered to resign his appointment; such behaviour was wrong in wartime, and should be no more permissible to generals in authoritative positions than it was to soldiers in the field. The latter could not give notice or resign if something displeased them. He therefore forbade me most strictly ever to tender a resignation.

The conversation then turned on individuals. My requests concerning the *OKH* appointments were approved. In this connection I remarked that the new Commander-in-Chief West did not have a lucky touch in commanding large armoured formations and I therefore proposed he be given another assignment. Hitler interrupted me with the words: 'And furthermore he had foreknowledge of the assassination attempt.' Keitel, Jodl and Burgdorf all three now stated that Field-Marshal von Kluge was the best horse in the stable and that he could not therefore be spared, despite his knowledge of the plot. Thus any attempt to remove Herr von Kluge quietly from the Western Front failed. Since Hitler was undoubtedly far better informed about Field-Marshal von Kluge's attitude than I was, I decided to take no further steps in this matter.

After our military discussions were over Hitler added one or two personal remarks. He informed me that my life was in danger and that he had therefore arranged that I be guarded by men of the Secret Field Police. These latter made a thorough search of my quarters and my vehicles, but found nothing suspicious. All the same I decided, for the first time since being a soldier, that I needed a bodyguard. I therefore appointed a number of reliable panzer troops to guard my quarters and my office building, and they did this faithfully until my dismissal. From time to time the men assigned to this duty were replaced by others.

Hitler then advised me to consult his personal physician, Morell, about the weak heart which he knew I had, and to let Morell give me injections. The consultation took place, but after talking to my Berlin doctor I refused the proposed injections. The example of Hitler was hardly an inducement to place oneself in the hands of Herr Morell.

The assassination attempt had resulted in a serious contusion to Hitler's right arm; both his ear-drums were destroyed and the Eustachian tube in his right ear was damaged. He quickly recovered from these physical effects. His already existing malady, plain for all to see in the trembling of his left hand and left leg, had no connection with the attempt on his life. But more important than the physical were the moral effects. In accordance with his character, the deep distrust he already felt for mankind in general, and for General Staff Corps officers and generals in particular, now became profound hatred. A by-product of the sickness from which he suffered is that it imperceptibly destroys the powers of moral judgment; in his case what had been hardness became cruelty, while a tendency to bluff became plain dishonesty. He often lied without hesitation, and assumed that others lied to him. He believed no one any more. It had already been difficult enough dealing with him; it now became a torture that grew steadily worse from month to month. He frequently lost all self-control and his language grew increasingly violent. In his intimate circle he now found no restraining influence, since the polite and gentlemanly Schmundt had been replaced by the oafish Burgdorf.

After reporting to Hitler I paid a brief visit to the so-called 'Briefing Room,' the scene of the assassination attempt, the condition of which has been frequently described, and then made my way to the *OKH* and the office block assigned to the Chief of the Army General Staff, which was to be my place of work from now on. I found the office block empty. There was nobody to meet me. After looking through various rooms I eventually came upon a private soldier by the name of Riehl, sound asleep. I sent this splendid fellow off to find me an officer. After some time had elapsed he reappeared with Major Baron Freytag von Loringhoven, whom I knew from my days with the armoured force and who had been my orderly officer when I commanded a panzer army in 1941. I asked Freytag to undertake the duties of my adjutant. I then attempted to telephone the army groups in order to find out the situation at the front. There were three telephones in the Chief of Staff's office, and no way of telling what purpose each one served. I picked up the nearest one. A female voice answered. When I said my name she screamed and hung up on me. It took some time before I managed to calm down the switchboard operators sufficiently to secure the connections I wanted.

The development of the military situation up to July 20th, 1944, has been described in the previous chapter. It was now appalling. Before being able to be of any assistance the *OKH* had first to be put back in working order again. This control centre for the whole Eastern Front was in a desperate state. My predecessor had intended to move the *OKH* back to the Maybach Camp, at Zossen near Berlin. Considerable portions of the staff had indeed already gone there, including the Quartermaster-General and all his people, the chief of the Armed Forces and Army Transport Services and numerous other important departments. Most of our signals network had also been moved. It was only with considerable difficulty that contact with the army groups could be maintained and the supply services to the whole Army, which was the *OKH's* responsibility, controlled from East Prussia. The first decision I must make was where the *OKH* was to be located in future. I decided on East Prussia, since Hitler and the *OKW* were to remain there. Those elements which had already moved to Zossen were recalled.

The next step to take in order to make the *OKH* operational again was to appoint the necessary officers. I sent for General Wenck, who was then Schörner's chief of staff, and made him chief of the Operations Department. I soon increased his responsibilities, making him Chief of the *OKH* Command Staff, which controlled not only the Operations and Organisation Departments, but also that part of the army intelligence service called 'Foreign Armies East'; thus the whole apparatus for controlling the battle in the East was concentrated in one place. Colonel von Bonin was now put in charge of the Operations Department and Lieutenant-Colonel Wendland of the Organisation Department, while the reliable Colonel Gehlen had 'Foreign Armies East.' The Quartermaster-General, General Wagner, had committed suicide and was succeeded by Colonel Toppe. General Berlin, who had been my artillery adviser both in France and in Russia, was appointed General of Artillery with the *OKH*; General Praun, who had been my chief signals officer during the 1940–41 campaign, became Chief Signals Officer for the Army and the Armed Forces. It was a few days before all these men could reach East Prussia and even longer before they were fully broken in to their new work. Of the more important officers of the old *OKH* only the Chief Transport Officer of the Armed Forces and the Army, the excellent General Gercke, retained his post.

During the first few weeks I was fully occupied in getting the machine

in running order again. I had no time to spare for the contemplation
of other problems. Matters which today seem important to the men
involved in them, I hardly noticed. I was so busy that I was quite
unaware of day-to-day happenings other than those at the front. My
new colleagues and I worked late into the night in our efforts to save
the front.

What were the actual results of the attempt made to assassinate
Hitler on July 20th?

The man who was to be killed was in fact slightly wounded. His
physical condition, not of the best beforehand, was further weakened.
His spiritual equipoise was destroyed for ever. All the forces of evil
that had lurked within him were aroused and came into their own. He
recognised no limits any more.

If the assassination was intended seriously to affect Germany's
governmental machine, then the most important officials of the
National-Socialist regime should also have been eliminated. But not
one of these was present when the bomb exploded. No plans had
been made for the removal of Himmler, Goering, Goebbels or Bormann,
to name only the most important. The conspirators made no attempt
to ensure that they would be able to carry out their political plans
in the event of the assassination succeeding. The man who actually
did it, Graf Stauffenberg, was indeed well aware of this, as is proved
by the fact that he did not carry out his intentions some days earlier on
the Obersalzberg, giving as his reason the absence of Himmler and
Goering whom he had expected to be present in the room. I do not
know what made Graf Stauffenberg decide to make his attempt on
July 20th even though the conditions for complete, political success
were not then fulfilled. Perhaps the issue of an order for the arrest
of Dr. Goerdeler had driven him to act at once.

Even if Hitler had been killed and the conspirators had succeeded
in seizing power, they would still have required an adequate body of
reliable troops. But they had not one single company at their disposal.
As a result they could not even gain control of Berlin when Graf
Stauffenberg landed with the false news that the assassination in East
Prussia had succeeded. The officers and men of the units assembled
for *Exercise Valkyrie* had not the slightest idea of what was going on.
This explains what the conspirators have called their 'refusal to act.'
Even my agreement, on quite different grounds, to postpone the transfer
of the armoured force demonstration units was of no use to the con-
spirators since they did not dare reveal their plans to the troops and
their commanders.

So far as foreign policy was concerned the conditions necessary for success of the undertaking did not exist. The links between the leaders of the conspiracy and important figures in the enemy countries were very slender. Not one leading political figure among the enemy had shown the slightest inclination to make any agreement with the conspirators. It is no exaggeration to say that if the assassination had succeeded Germany's condition would be not one jot better than it is today. Our enemies were not solely interested in destroying Hitler and Nazism.

The immediate victims of the assassination attempt were Colonel Brandt of the Operations Department of the *OKH;* General Korten, Chief of the Air Force General Staff, General Schmundt, Hitler's chief adjutant, and a stenographer named Berger. Apart from these men, many members of the *OKH* and the *OKW* were wounded. These victims were unnecessary.

The next victims were those who took part in, or knew of, the conspiracy, together with their families. Only a small proportion of those condemned were in fact actively involved in the conspiracy. The great majority merely knew something about it and out of loyalty to their friends kept silent concerning the rumours and fragments of gossip that they had heard; the price they paid for their loyalty was a bitter death. The first to die were those leaders who had not—like Colonel-General Beck, Quartermaster-General Wagner, General von Treskow, Colonel Baron Freytag von Loringhoven and others—already taken their own lives or—like Graf Stauffenberg, Olbricht, Merz von Quirnheim and von Haeften—been summarily executed by Fromm.

Hitler ordered that all the accused be tried by one tribunal, the so-called People's Court (*Volksgerichtshof*). For the soldiers this meant that they would not be tried by court-martial but according to a special court of civilian judges; they would thus be liable not to the usual military sentences and military executions, but would be subjected to special laws dictated by Hitler and based on hatred and a thirst for revenge. Under the dictatorship there was no legal method of appealing against such laws.

In order that the soldiers accused of complicity or of foreknowledge might be tried by the People's Court it was necessary that they first be dismissed from the Armed Forces. These dismissals were to be carried out after an investigation by a military court which Hitler ordered to be set up and which was called the 'Court of Honour'; this was presided over by Field-Marshal von Rundstedt, and those ordered to attend were Keitel, Schroth, Kriebel, Kirchheim and myself. I requested, in view of the very heavy duties entailed by my new appointment and by my position as Inspector-General of Armoured

Troops which I also retained, that I might be excused this unpleasant task. My request was ignored. All I managed to achieve was permission that General Kirchheim be my standing deputy at those sessions of the court which my military duties made it impossible for me to attend. At first I took no part whatever in the proceedings: then Keitel came to see me, on instructions from Hitler, and told me that I must appear at least occasionally. So for better or for worse I had to attend two or three of these repulsive sessions. What I heard was extremely sad and upsetting.

The preliminary examinations had been made by Kaltenbrunner and SS-Group-Leader Müller of the Gestapo. The former was an Austrian lawyer, the latter a Bavarian official. Neither had any understanding of the officers' corps; Müller's attitude towards that corps may be described as compounded of hatred and of a feeling of inferiority; for the rest his was a coldly calculating and ambitious nature. Apart from these two the Chief of the Army Personnel Office, General Burgdorf, and his assistant, General Meisel, were present at the sessions; they were responsible for procedure and also acted as Hitler's observers. The reports of the preliminary investigations consisted principally of statements made by the accused; these were in general of an almost incredible frankness, such as officers are accustomed to make to a Court of Honour consisting of their peers with a concept of honour identical to their own. It had apparently never occurred to these unfortunate men that when they were being investigated by the Gestapo they were up against people with quite a different code. Their statements not only contained matters relating to the man who made it, but also gave the names of others together with what they had done or not done. Every person whose name thus came up was arrested and interrogated. In this way the Gestapo quickly succeeded in building up an almost complete picture of the whole scope of the conspiracy and of the whole circle that had been involved in it. And that was not all. In view of the statements they had made it was often impossible to declare these officers innocent of participation in the plot. On the rare occasions when I was present I did my best to save any man who could be saved. Only in sadly few cases was this labour of love successful. Of the other members of the court, Kirchheim, Schroth and Kriebel acted as I did. Field-Marshal von Rundstedt gave us his constant support.

The Court of Honour had only one function: this was to decide whether or not the accused, according to the results of the preliminary investigation, was to be tried by the People's Court, either on the accusation of complicity or of foreknowledge. If the court decided he should be tried, the branch of the *Wehrmacht* concerned discharged the man in question from the Armed Forces. He was thereby no longer subject to military law. These investigations might only be based on the documents already available. Examination of the accused was not allowed.

During these melancholy sessions one was constantly beset by the most difficult problems of judgment and of conscience. Every word uttered had to be most carefully weighed, and in setting one man free there was always the danger that this would bring misfortune to others whether unsuspected or not yet arrested.

The sentences of death pronounced by the People's Court were to be carried out by hanging, a form of execution hitherto unknown to German law and particularly to German military law. Up to then a soldier condemned to death was shot. Execution by hanging was an Austrian importation. Unfortunately it is still performed today.

Any man who attempts a *coup d'état* should reckon on the fact that if he fails he is liable to be condemned to death for high treason. But how many of those condemned as a result of 20th July had realised what was actually happening? Surely only very few. In any case this argument carried no weight with Hitler. So it came about that officers were condemned who had heard of the intended *coup d'état* only immediately before July 20th and who had failed to report their knowledge to the proper authorities simply because they had not immediately recognised the importance of what they had heard. Men who were in no way accomplices were sent to their death merely for the crime of having helped a friend who was wanted by the police. Perhaps the most shocking example of this was the case of General Heisterman von Ziehlberg, the son-in-law of the greatly respected General von Tschischwitz, my former Inspector and divisional commander. On the 20th of July, 1944, Ziehlberg was in command of a division on the Eastern Front. His first general staff officer, Major Kuhn, who had previously worked in the Organisation Department of the *OKH*, knew of the conspiracy. Ziehlberg received a telegram ordering him to arrest Kuhn at once and to send him under close supervision to Berlin. He gave Kuhn permission to drive forward alone, to a new command post. He wanted thus to give him a chance. Kuhn, however, did not take this opportunity to shoot himself but instead deserted to the enemy. Ziehlberg was arrested and tried by court-martial. He received a mild sentence. A little later Hitler learned of this. He ordered a fresh investigation with the object of enforcing the death penalty on the grounds that Kuhn, as a former member of Organisation Department of the *OKH*, had knowledge of most secret matters and his desertion to the enemy was therefore extremely harmful to the German war effort. Ziehlberg was shot in February 1945. My unfortunate old commander lost his other son-in-law in the same way, though for a different reason; this was that most amiable man, General Gothsche, and he was executed for saying that we were no longer capable of winning the war.

Sad as was the fate of those condemned to death, the condition of those whom they left behind was almost worse. The crime of consanguinity for which they had to suffer caused them great hardship and spiritual anguish. There was little that could be done to help them or to mitigate their sufferings.

From every point of view the results of the attempted assassination were frightful. For myself I refuse to accept murder in any form. Our Christian religion forbids it in the clearest possible terms. I cannot therefore approve of the plan of assassination. Apart from this religious reason, I must also say that neither the internal nor the external political situation was conducive to a successful *coup d'état*. The preparations made were utterly inadequate, the choice of personalities to fill the principal roles incomprehensible. The driving force had originally been Dr. Goerdeler, an idealist who believed that the *coup d'état* could be performed without the assassination. Both he and his fellow conspirators were undoubtedly convinced that what they were doing was in the higher interests of their nation. Dr. Goerdeler had also decided on the choice of the majority of the people destined by the conspirators to hold office in the new government. He had drawn up lists of names in this connection which, through his own carelessness, fell into the hands of the Gestapo. The character of Colonel-General Beck, who was to have been Head of the State, I have already described at sufficient lengths. His behaviour on 20th July proved that my previous opinion of him was correct. Field-Marshal von Witzleben was a sick man. He hated Hitler with a burning hatred, but lacked the determination necessary to carry out a military *putsch* in such critical and difficult circumstances. Colonel-General Hoeppner was a brave fighting man; I doubt, however, if he was fully aware of the extent of the responsibilities that he incurred by his actions on 20th July. General Olbricht was a first-class officer and very good at his job; but he had no command and no troops with which to carry out a *coup d'état*. By July 20th, 1944, the plan had been under discussion and debate for years on end. The number of people in the know increased constantly. It is hardly surprising that the Gestapo finally got wind of one or other of the groups of conspirators and that a wave of imprisonments threatened them all. This threat doubtless persuaded the impulsive Graf Stauffenberg to turn to assassination, a decision that the other conspirators were hardly likely to have reached on their own. The assassination was a failure. But the assassin was completely deceived as to the effect of his bomb and behaved with more than foolhardiness. The part played in the business by Colonel-General Fromm, the commander of the Training Army, is still obscure. He, too, eventually lost his life in consequence. General Heinrich von Stülpnagel, the military commander in France, a man of high principles whom I knew well and always visited when passing through Paris, had to die a dreadful death. But the worst of all was Field-Marshal Rommel's end, of which I did not learn until I was in prison after the war. It was only when I heard of this that I realised the full extent of the tragedy through which we had passed.

Of course one question will always be asked: what would have happened had the assassination succeeded? Nobody can answer this. Only one fact seems beyond dispute: at that time the great proportion of the German people still believed in Adolf Hitler and would have been convinced that with his death the assassin had removed the only man who might still have been able to bring the war to a favourable conclusion. The odium thus created by his death would have been attached primarily to the corps of officers, the generals and the general staff, and would have lasted not only during but also after the war. The people's hatred and contempt would have turned against the soldiers who, in the midst of a national struggle for existence, had broken their oath, murdered the head of the government and left the storm-wracked ship of state without a captain at the helm. It also seems unlikely that our enemies would have treated us any better in consequence than they actually did after the collapse.

The next question is: what should have happened? To this I can only reply: a very great deal has been spoken and written about resistance to the Hitler regime. But of those men who are still alive, the speakers and the writers, who had access to Hitler, which of them did, in fact, even once, offer any resistance to his will? Which of them dared, even once, to express opinions in Hitler's presence that were contrary to the dictator's and to argue with him to his face? That is what should have happened. During the months in which I attended Hitler's briefings and the countless conferences on military, technical and political subjects at which he was present, only very few men ever dared to contradict him, and of those few even fewer are still alive today. For I cannot call those men 'resistance fighters' who only whispered their disapproval in corridors and only urged others on to act. This is a matter of profoundly differing attitudes. If a man disagreed with Hitler, then it was his duty to tell him so whenever he had an opportunity to do so. This was true particularly and primarily during the period when such expressed disagreement might have had an effect, that is to say in the period before the outbreak of war. Any man who was quite sure that Hitler's policy was bound to lead to war, that war must be prevented, and that a war would inevitably bring our nation to disaster, such a man was duty bound to seek and find occasions, before the war started, to say so without ambiguity both to Hitler and to the German people; if he could not do this from inside Germany, then he should have done so from abroad. Did the responsible men at the time in fact do this?

11. CHIEF OF THE GENERAL STAFF

Let us return to the grave military situation.

After the General Staff of the *OKH* had been put in working order once again, we could still only function in a very cumbersome and slow fashion, since Hitler insisted on approving every detail and refused to allow the Chief of the General Staff the most limited powers of decision. I therefore requested that I be given the right to issue instructions to the Eastern army groups on all matters that were not of fundamental importance. I also asked that I be permitted to give directions to all General Staff Corps officers of the Army on such subjects as concerned the General Staff as a whole. Both requests were refused by Hitler. Keitel and Jodl were in agreement with him. Keitel approved Hitler's decision in his own handwriting, while Jodl countered my remonstrances with the remark: 'The General Staff Corps ought actually to be disbanded!' If the most prominent members of that corps were prepared themselves to saw through the bough on which they sat, obviously there was no hope for the institution as a whole. The first results of Hitler's refusal to agree to my request were soon apparent in a number of gross breaches of discipline; these necessitated my transferring the officers responsible to the staff of the *OKH*, since there at least I did retain certain limited disciplinary powers. There I allowed the very self-confident young gentlemen in question to cool their heels for several weeks and to consider their manners. I had occasion to inform Hitler of this expedient of mine. He gazed at me in astonishment, but said nothing.

During the early days of my new appointment I asked Hitler if I might have a private conversation with him. He asked: 'Do you wish to discuss Service matters or is it something personal?' Of course it was a Service matter and one that could only be discussed between himself and myself alone if the necessary degree of frankness were to be achieved. Any third party would have been a hindrance to the conversation I had in mind. Hitler was perfectly well aware of this. That was why he refused my request, adding that on the occasions when he discussed Service matters with me Field-Marshal Keitel and two stenographers were always to be present. As a result of this regulation I only rarely had the opportunity of talking to the Supreme Commander with that bluntness which, without damaging his authority, was only possible in private conversations. Keitel was also partly responsible for this very disadvantageous regulation; he was afraid that he might not learn about important facts quickly enough and might thus be gradually pushed aside. I was compelled to carry out my duties in the same restrictive circumstances from which my predecessors had suffered. This did not make it easy to improve the general atmosphere or settle disagreements more calmly.

When I was compelled to assume the duties of Chief of the General Staff, on July 21st, 1944, the situation on the Eastern Front was far from satisfactory.

Our strongest force seemed to be Army Group South Ukraine, which consisted of the Sixth and Eighth Armies as well as Rumanian troops and a portion of the Hungarian Army. Its front ran from the mouth of the Dnieper on the Black Sea coast—along that river to a point south of Kichinev—north of Jassy—south of Falticeni—across the rivers Pruth and Sereth—and finally north-west to the Sereth's catchment area. During the spring battles in March and April, this army group had succeeded in defeating enemy attacks north of Jassy and had finally managed to withdraw a number of divisions into reserve. It was at this time commanded by General Schörner, who enjoyed Hitler's special confidence.

To the north of Army Group South Ukraine was Army Group North Ukraine. Up to July 12th, 1944, this army group had been conducting a fairly successful defence along a front that ran from the area of Radautz on the upper Sereth—east through Buczacz to Delatyn—Tarnopol—Jezierna—to Beresteczko in the area south of Kovel. On July 13th the Russians had attacked, had broken through the army group's front at three points, and by July 21st had captured Lvov, the San bend north of Przemysl, Tomaszov, Cholm and Lublin, while their spearheads had reached a line running roughly from Pulavy on the Vistula to Brest-Litovsk on the Bug.

If the picture here was bad, the situation on Army Group Centre's front had become catastrophic since June 22nd and, indeed, could scarcely have been worse. The Russians attacking between the Beresina and the Pripet had succeeded, during the period June 22nd to July 3rd, in breaking through the German front in the areas Rogachev, Chaussy, north of Orsha and on both sides of Vitebsk; after totally destroying twenty-five German divisions they had forced the army group back to a line Davidgrodek–Baranowicze–Molodeczno–Koziany–the Dvina north of Polotsk. During the course of the next few days the Russians forcefully exploited their surprisingly great success, captured Pinsk and reached a line Pruzana–Volkovisk–the Niemen east of Grodno–Kovno–the Dvina east of Dünaburg–Idriza. Thus not only Army Group Centre but also Army Group North was involved in the general collapse. By

Sketch Map 29.

Developments in the Baltic States.

Situation from 23.7. to 4.10.44.

Gulf of Finland

Baltischport

2/10 Hapsal

Dagö

26/9.

Ösel

Pernau

Gulf of Riga

Haynasch

Narva

Lake Peipus

Lake-Würz

Dor-pal

Lake Pleskau

Pleskau

N

Windau

Riga

Tuckum

Mitau

Schwanenburg

Own Attacks 16 – 26.9.44.

Autz

Doblen

Stockmannshof

Kreutzbg.

Schaulen

Dvina

Dünaburg

M

Heydekrug

Raseinen

Tilsit

Kovno

Situation	23.7.44	▆▆▆	◄▨▨▨
"	4.8.44	●●●●●	◄▨▨▨
"	1.9.44	▬▬▬	◁▭
"	4.10.44	▬▬▬	◁▭

July 21st the Russians had advanced in what seemed irresistible strength
to the line of the Vistula, from Sandomir to Warsaw–Siedlce–Bielsk
Podlaski–Bialystock–Grodno–Kovno and, what was particularly unpleasant, through Ponievisch to Schaulen and Mitau. North of Mitau
they reached the coast of the Gulf of Riga and thus cut off Army Group
North from the rest of the front.

Army Group North, whose right wing had been north of Polotsk,
held a front running from there–Idriza–Ostroff–Pleskau–Lake Peipus–
Narva–the coast of the Gulf of Finland. As a result of the disaster to
Army Group Centre, by July 21st its right wing had had to be withdrawn to a line Mitau–Dünaburg–Pleskau. But this was obviously not
the end of its withdrawals.

My predecessor left me not only a disorganised staff but also a completely disintegrating front. There were no reserves available to the
OKH. The only forces immediately to hand were those in Rumania
behind Army Group South Ukraine. A glance at a railway map will
show that it was bound to take a considerable time to move them up.
The limited forces that could be produced by the Training Army were
already on their way to the generally beaten Army Group Centre.

In agreement with the commander of Army Group South Ukraine,
whose chief of staff, General Wenck, now became my principal operational assistant and who knew the situation in Rumania well, I proposed
to Hitler that all divisions that could be made available in Rumania be
moved away from there and be used to plug the gap between Army
Groups Centre and North. This was agreed at once. Hitler also ordered
that the commanders of Army Groups South Ukraine (Schörner) and
North (Friessner) exchange posts. Instructions were issued to the new
commander of Army Group South Ukraine which, for Hitler, allowed
that officer unusual latitude of decision. These energetic measures
succeeded in bringing the Russian offensive to a halt in the area
Doblen–Tuckum–Mitau. My intention was not only to re-establish
contact between the two army groups but also, by means of evacuating
the Baltic States, radically to shorten the whole front. Such an evacuation was essential in order to avoid risking the total destruction of
Army Group North in its present precarious position. General
Schörner was ordered to draw up a plan for the evacuation. He
reported that it could be completed in three to four weeks. This was too
slow. We would have to act more quickly if we were to anticipate the
enemy and have the formations in position and in a fit state to defend
East Prussia. I therefore ordered that the evacuation of Esthonia and
Latvia be completed within seven days, that a bridgehead be captured
in the Riga area, and that all panzer and motorised formations be
assembled at once in the area west of Schaulen. It was there that I

expected the Russians to launch their next attack. This would have to be defeated if contact were to be re-established between Army Group North in Courland and Army Group Centre.

The German attack, which lasted from September 16th to September 26th, 1944, succeeded in re-establishing contact between the two army groups. That it was successful is due to the brave actions of Colonel Graf Strachwitz and his improvised panzer division. The essential was now immediately to make the most of the favourable situation. This Army Group North refused to do. Schörner believed that the Russians would not attack again west of Schaulen but at Mitau. He therefore retained his armour—in disobedience to his instructions signed by Hitler—in the Mitau area. My requests that he carry out his orders were ignored. I do not know whether Schörner had received approval for this behind my back. He was in direct communication with Hitler. In any case, as a result the thin German front west of Schaulen was once again broken through in October. The Russians reached the Baltic between Memel and Libau. A fresh attempt to re-establish contact with Army Group North by attacking along the coast failed; it remained cut off from the rest of the front and from now on could only be supplied by sea.

I now became involved in a long and bitter argument with Hitler concerning the withdrawal of those valuable troops which were essential for the defence of Germany. The sole result of this argument was further to poison the atmosphere.

While these important developments and heavy battles were taking place on the left wing of the long front, and while Field-Marshal Model by means of his own courageous example was re-establishing Army Group Centre's front east of Warsaw, the Poles inside Warsaw revolted; this uprising, led by General Bor-Komorowski, took place immediately behind our front line and constituted a major danger to that front. Communications with General von Vormann's Ninth Army were broken. The possibility of immediate co-operation between the Poles who had risen and the Russians could not be ignored. I requested that Warsaw be included forthwith in the military zone of operations; but the ambitions of Governor-General Frank and the SS national leader Himmler prevailed with Hitler, with the result that Warsaw—though lying immediately behind, and later actually in, the front line—was not incorporated in the Army's zone of operations but remained under the jurisdiction of the Governor-General. The national leader of the SS was made responsible for crushing the uprising, and for this purpose he employed the SS Group-Leader von dem Bach-Zelewski with a number of SS and police formations under his command. The battle, which lasted for weeks, was fought with great brutality. Some of the SS units involved—which, incidentally, were not drawn from the *Waffen-SS*—failed to preserve their discipline. The Kaminski Brigade was composed of former prisoners of war, mostly Russians who were ill-disposed towards the Poles; the Dirlewanger Brigade was formed from German convicts on probation. These doubtful units were now committed to desperate street battles where each house had to be captured and where the defendants were fighting for their lives; as a result they abandoned all moral standards. Von dem Bach himself told me, during the course of a conversation on equipment problems, of the atrocities committed by his men whom he was no longer able to control. What I learned from him was so appalling that I felt myself bound to inform Hitler about it that same evening and to demand the removal of the two brigades from the Eastern Front. To begin with Hitler was not inclined to listen to this demand of mine. But Himmler's liaison officer, the SS Brigade-Leader Fegelein, was himself forced to admit: 'It is true, my Führer, those men are real scoundrels!' As a result he had no choice but to do as I wished. Von dem Bach took the precaution of having Kaminski shot and thus disposed of a possibly dangerous witness.

The uprising did not finally collapse until October 2nd. When the Poles began to show an inclination to surrender I urged Hitler to announce that they would be granted the full rights of prisoners of war as guaranteed by international law. This I hoped would shorten the senseless struggle. Hitler accepted my advice. Colonel-General Reinhardt, who had succeeded Model as commander of Army Group Centre on August 15th, received instructions accordingly. It was on these instructions that the army based its conduct.

It is always difficult in an uprising to distinguish the organised fighting man from innocent civilians. General Bor-Komorowski has himself written on this subject:[1]

During the battles our commanders could hardly tell the soldiers from the civilians. Our people had no uniforms and we could not prevent the civilians from wearing white and red arm-bands. They, like the soldiers of the home army, used German weapons, which increased the problems of our scarce ammunition. For the civilians would waste a hail of bullets and hand grenades on a single German soldier. Every one of the early reports I received complained about the great waste of ammunition.

Since the Poles were also wearing German uniforms from captured stores, the feeling of insecurity among the Germans increased and with it a tendency towards greater brutality. It is little wonder that Hitler,

[1] In *The Unconquerables*, by General Bor-Komorowski, published by *The Reader's Digest*, February, 1946.

Sketch Map 30
The Cutting-off of
Army Group North.
5.–25.10.1944

Dagö

Hapsal

Leningrad Front

6 Rifle Units
2 Tnk Units

Ösel

Swortbe

Pernau

Gulf of Riga

Windau

Tuckum

N

Frauenburg

Mitau

12 Rifle Units
5 Tnk Units

Riga

12 Rifle Units
4 Tnk Units

Stockmannshof

Kreutzburg

Libau

Weinoden

Autz

Moschaiken

11 Rifle Units
4 Tnk Units

29 Rifle Units
1 Tnk Corps
8 Tnk Units

Schaulen

2. Balt. Front

Memel

15 Rifle Units
2 Tnk Corps
2 Tnk Units

Dünaburg

Dvina

11 Rifle Units
1 Tnk Corps
1 Tnk Unit

1. Balt. Front

Heydekrug

Tauroggen

Georgenburg

5 Rifle Units
2 Tnk Units

Memel

Tilsit

Kovno

Insterburg

M

Eydkau

Gumbinnen

who was regularly briefed on the events in Warsaw by Fegelein or by Himmler himself, lost his temper and issued very harsh orders for the prosecution of the fighting and for the treatment of Warsaw. His anger found expression in a directive, dated the 11th of October, 1944, and sent from the 'Signal office of the Higher SS and Police Commander East' to Governor-General Frank at Cracow, and which ran as follows:

Subject: New policy with regards to Poles.

Senior-Group-Leader von dem Bach has been entrusted with the task of pacifying Warsaw, that is to say he will raze Warsaw to the ground while the war is still going on and in so far as this is not contrary to military plans for the construction of strongpoints. Before it is destroyed, all raw materials, all textiles, and all furniture will be removed from Warsaw. The responsibility for this is assigned to the civil administration.[1]

Of this order, which went through SS channels, I had at the time no knowledge. I first read it when I was in prison in Nuremberg in 1946. Nevertheless I had heard rumours that were circulating at headquarters concerning the intended total destruction of Warsaw, and I had also been present when Hitler had had an outburst of rage on the subject. I therefore felt it my duty to speak of the need for preserving that city, which Hitler had declared a fortress and which as a result was needed to shelter German soldiers. The preservation of the buildings was all the more important since the Vistula was now our front line, and the Vistula ran through the centre of the city.

The repeated uprisings of 1943 and 1944 had in any case led to great destruction, and the battles from the autumn of 1944 until the Russians attacked in January 1945 gave the tragic city its death-blow.

When the men who had revolted surrendered they were handed over to the SS. Bor-Komorowski was an old acquaintance of Fegelein's whom he had frequently met at international sporting events before the war. Fegelein took charge of him.

The question has frequently been asked why the Russians, who knew all about the Warsaw uprising, did not do more to help it and indeed stopped their offensive along the line of the Vistula. There can be no doubt that the Poles who had risen regarded themselves as owing allegiance to their Government in Exile, which was located in London, and it was from there that they received their instructions. They exemplified those elements in Poland which were conservative and which looked towards the West. It may be assumed that the Soviet Union had no interest in seeing these elements strengthened by a successful uprising and by the capture of their capital. The Soviets doubtless wanted the credit for such actions to go to their dependent Poles in the Lublin

[1] From the *Isar-Post*, Nuremberg, 23rd February, 1946. (Dana.)

camp. But this is a matter for the former Allies to sort out among themselves. All that concerned us was that the Russians did not then advance beyond the Vistula and we were consequently granted a short breathing spell.

Be that as it may, an attempt by the Russian XVI Tank Corps to cross the railway bridge over the Vistula at Deblin on July 25th, 1944, had failed with the loss of thirty tanks. The bridge could be blown in time. Further Russian tank forces were stopped to the north of Warsaw. We Germans had the impression that it was our defence which halted the enemy rather than a Russian desire to sabotage the Warsaw uprising.

On August 2nd the First Polish Army, belonging to the 'Free Democratic Army of Poland,' attacked across the Vistula with three divisions in the Pulavy–Deblin sector. It suffered heavy casualties but secured a bridgehead which it managed to hold until the arrival of Russian reinforcements.

At Magnuszev the enemy succeeded in establishing a second bridgehead over the Vistula. The forces that crossed here were ordered to advance along the road that ran parallel with the Vistula to Warsaw, but they were stopped at the Pilica.

The German Ninth Army had the impression, on August 8th, that the Russian attempt to seize Warsaw by a *coup de main* (which in view of their hitherto uninterrupted successes they might well have believed possible) had been defeated by our defence despite the Polish uprising, and that the latter, from the enemy's point of view, had been begun too soon. During the period from July 26th to August 8th, 1944, Ninth Army reported the capture of 603 prisoners and 41 deserters, the destruction of 337 tanks and the capture of 70 guns, 80 anti-tank guns, 27 mortars and 116 machine-guns. Such figures are considerable, particularly when it is remembered that during the period in question Ninth Army had been constantly withdrawing.

Neither in the West nor in the East had any attempt been made to prepare fortified positions; in the former theatre Hitler had believed that he could rely on the Atlantic Wall, in the latter he was obsessed with the idea that if a fortified line existed the generals would conduct a less energetic defence and would be inclined to withdraw prematurely. As a result of the defeats we had suffered we had now lost most of the space formerly available for manœuvre in the East and the front line was dangerously close to the German border; if each local misfortune was not to entail a withdrawal of the whole front, it was now essential that something be done. As I had already said to Hitler in January, it seemed to me of primary importance that the former German fortifications along the eastern frontier be reconditioned. Then the vital links between those fortifications and the principal river lines must themselves be fortified. In conjunction with the General of Engineers at the *OKH*, General Jakob, I worked out a construction programme.

For the study of fortification problems I ordered that the old Fortifications Department of the General Staff, dissolved by my predecessor, be set up once again under Lieutenant-Colonel Thilo. The construction plan that we drew up was issued by me, on my own responsibility, as an order to all the competent authorities before I submitted it to Hitler; when I did this I attached a note in which I explained that the matter seemed to me one of such importance and urgency that I had been forced to ask for his *post facto* approval. Hitler only accepted this reasoning reluctantly; it was a method to which I could obviously not resort frequently. In any case the building of fortifications now got under way. The earthworks were generally built by volunteers, women, children and old men, the only remaining untapped labour source in the country. The Hitler Youth proved of particularly great value in helping with this work. All these trusty Germans worked with energy and intelligence, despite the worsening weather, in the hope of providing some protection for the land they loved so much and some support for the soldiers fighting the bitter defensive battles. That later the work done did not in all cases fulfil our expectations was neither their fault nor was the principle to blame; it was due simply to the impossibility of supplying the garrisons and the weapons required to man the fortifications. All such troops and equipment, whether originally destined for the Eastern Front or not, had had to be rushed to the Western, which was in a critical state. Only such remnants as the West could not use were left for the East. But I should like to take this opportunity of thanking from the bottom of my heart the men and women who gave us such devoted and faithful help. Furthermore, a number of the fortified positions then constructed performed their function for a long time. In time to come it will be possible to evaluate correctly the defence of Koenigsberg and Danzig, of Glogau and Breslau; it is impossible now to say how fast the Russians' advance would have been, and how much more of Germany would as a result have been scorched at their hand, had these German fortifications not then been built.

I was well aware that in order to withstand the enemy these fortifications would have to be manned, armed and provisioned. I therefore ordered the setting up of fortress units, to be formed from personnel not fully fit for service in the field but quite capable of manning fortified positions if properly handled. The first to be formed were one hundred fortress infantry battalions and one hundred artillery batteries. Fortress machine-gun, engineer and signal units were to follow. But even before the first of these formations were fit for active service 80 per cent of them had to be sent to the Western Front. My most energetic protests were of no avail; I only learned too late what had been ordered and by then there was nothing I could do about it. The ill-prepared units were thrown into the mill-race of our collapse in the West and were destroyed before they could achieve any results worth mentioning. In the East the handsome fortifications and strong points remained ungarrisoned. They were therefore unable, when the time came, to give the withdrawing formations of the field army the requisite support.

It was the same story with the arms as with the men. My first request that the stores of captured weapons be put at my disposal was turned down by Keitel and Jodl with something approaching scorn; I was informed that there were no captured guns in store in Germany. However, the chief of the Army Department at the *OKW*, General Buhle, informed me that there were thousands of guns and other heavy weapons stored in the ordnance depots; for years they had been cleaned and greased once a month but never used. I ordered that they be installed in the most important points of the eastern fortifications and that the training of crews to man them be undertaken. Jodl, however, succeeded in having this order of mine countermanded and another one issued by which every gun of more than 50 mm. calibre and with more than 50 rounds available be sent to the Western Front. But these guns also arrived there too late, while they would have been of incalculable value on the Eastern Front. Furthermore, since as long ago as 1941 our 50 mm. and 37 mm. anti-tank guns had been useless against the Russian T34 and it was therefore precisely the larger calibre weapons that the Eastern Front needed to fight the enemy's tanks.

As for supplies, it was ordered that the fortifications be provisioned for three months. Wireless signal centres were installed, fuel depots prepared. Whenever my travels took me to the zone of fortifications I made use of the opportunity to supervise personally the work that was being done. My efforts received the most unselfish support from countless colleagues, in particular from Colonel-General Strauss. They immediately and unreservedly placed themselves at my disposal, quite forgetting that sickness or an arbitrary decree of Hitler's had deprived them of their former positions. A few district Party leaders (*Gauleiter*) were also helpful; if their excessive zeal led on occasion to friction, their desire to make themselves useful must be acknowledged nevertheless.

Having been largely deprived of control over the fortress troops I now turned to an idea that had been suggested long before by General Heusinger's Operations Department of the *OKH* and turned down by Hitler: this was for the formation of a *Landsturm*, or home defence

M*

force, in the threatened eastern provinces. I was interested in this idea of setting up units, led by officers and consisting of men in the eastern territories capable of active service but hitherto exempted from the Army because of being employed in reserved occupations; these units would only be called out in the event of a Russian break-through. I took my proposal to Hitler and suggested that the SA,[1] so far as it could produce reliable men, be entrusted with the task of setting up this force. I had already ensured the collaboration of Schepman, the chief of staff of the SA, a sensible man and one who was well disposed towards the armed forces. Hitler began by approving this proposal of mine but on the next day he informed me that he had reconsidered the matter and intended now to entrust the formation of these units to the Party, that is to say to *Reichsleiter* (National Director) Bormann; he also wished it to be called the *Volkssturm*. Bormann did nothing to begin with; after repeated urgings on my part he did finally instruct the *Gauleiters*, or district party leaders—not only of the frontier districts but of all Germany—to proceed with the undertaking. As a result the *Volkssturm* was expanded to an undesirable extent, since there were neither sufficient trained commanders nor an adequate supply of weapons available for so large a force—quite apart from the fact that the Party was less interested in the military qualifications than in the political fanaticism of the men it appointed to fill the responsible posts. My old comrade-in-arms, General von Wietersheim, was a member of the rank and file of a company commanded by some worthless Party functionary. As a result, the brave men of the *Volkssturm*, prepared to make any sacrifice, were in many cases drilled busily in the proper way of giving the Hitler salute instead of being trained in the use of weapons of which they had had no previous experience. Here too great idealism and self-sacrifice went unappreciated and unthanked. I shall refer to this again later on.

All these apparently desperate measures were necessary because the last drafts of combat troops that the Training Army at home had managed to produce were destined, not for the defence of the East, but for an offensive in the West. In August and September the Western Front had been broken, and since there were no fortified lines or prepared positions on which the troops could immediately fall back they had had to be withdrawn all the way to the West Wall.[2] But the West Wall was no longer a fully equipped defensive line, since its armaments had largely been moved to the Atlantic Wall where they had in most cases been lost. The retreat had been so precipitate, and the

---

[1] The *Sturmabteilungen*, or Storm Troopers. Originally the Party's para-military organisation, it had been superseded in this role by the SS after the murder of Roehm, on June 30th, 1934.—*Tr.*

[2] The so-called Siegfried Line along Germany's western frontier.—*Tr.*

Sketch Map 31.
The Loss of Rumania
Situation 16.3.44. — 4.10.44.

Situation 16.3.44
Russ. attacks up to 16.4.44
Situation 20.8.44
Russ. attacks up to 29.8.44
Russ. attacks up to 4.10.44

Kremenchug
Dniepropetrovsk
Zaporozhe
Dnieper
Cherson
Nikolaiev
Odessa
Peromojsk
Vinnitsa
Bug
Dniester
Proskuroff
Bu...
Kishinev
Jas...
Pruth
Botosani
Seroth
Galatz
Costanza
Danube
Buchorest
Ploesti
Focsani
Bukau...
Kronstadt
Piresti
Klausenburg
Marmarossziget
Debrecen
Turnu Severin
Theiss
Belgrade
Sava
Morava
Zajezar
Nish
Sofia
Crimea
Sebastopol

pursuit by the Allies so determined, that many positions were lost which might have offered the chance of successful counter-actions if only there had been reserves available to hold them. Hitler lost his temper each time this occurred, and invariably ordered that such positions be held, but there were no troops to carry out these orders. He therefore determined, in September, to mobilise all the remaining strength of Germany for a final, determined effort. Since the assassination attempt of July 20th, 1944, the national leader of the SS, Himmler, had been placed in command of the Training Army. He had assumed the title of Commander-in-Chief of that army and was now engaged in creating those 'political soldiers' and particularly the 'political officers' of which he and Hitler had long dreamed. The new formations were called *Volks Grenadier* (People's Grenadier) Divisions, *Volks Artillerie* (People's Artillery) Corps, etc. The officers were specially selected by the Army Personnel Office, now headed by the idealist Schmundt's most unidealistic successor, General Burgdorf, and might not be transferred to other, less ecstatic formations of the Army. 'National Socialist Control Officers'[1] were appointed. However, when a number of these gentry on the Eastern Front felt obliged to make reports direct to Bormann, who had a deep hatred of the Army and who hurried with the information thus received to Hitler, I decided that things were going too far and I put a stop to interference of this sort. I also saw to it that the guilty men were punished. Needless to say the row that ensued, and the simultaneous mismanagement of the plans for the *Volkssturm*, did nothing to improve the general atmosphere at Supreme Headquarters.

It was Hitler's intention to resume the offensive with the final levy of active troops during the month of November, his objective being to defeat the Western Powers and to throw them back into the Atlantic. The new formations, the final harvest of our country's strength, were to be devoted to this ambitious plan. I shall have occasion to refer to this again later.

On August 5th, 1944, while we were preoccupied by the events connected with the assassination attempt and by the collapse of the Eastern Front, Marshal Antonescu, the Head of the Rumanian State, had appeared at Hitler's headquarters in East Prussia. I was instructed to brief the Marshal on the state of the Eastern Front. Hitler, Keitel and the others who usually attended such briefings were present, as well as Ribbentrop and his assistants from the Ministry for Foreign Affairs. My words were to be translated into French by the chief

---

[1] These men fulfilled a function very similar to that of the political commissars previously attached to units and formations of the Soviet Army.—*Tr*.

interpreter attached to the Foreign Ministry, Ambassador Schmidt. Ambassador Schmidt was not only an extremely pleasant man, whose company I much enjoyed, but also the best interpreter I have ever come across; he had a quite remarkable ability for translating exact shades of meaning from one language into another. For several decades he had taken part in countless, extremely difficult conferences on almost all imaginable subjects. However, he had never before had to interpret when military matters were under discussion. After only a few sentences it became apparent that he lacked the requisite technical military phraseology. It therefore seemed to me easier to speak in French myself, and I had the satisfaction of being well understood by Marshal Antonescu.

During the conference Antonescu showed that he fully grasped the difficulties of our situation and the need for reforming, first of all, Army Group Centre's front and then for re-establishing contact between Army Groups Centre and North. He proposed himself that Moldavia be evacuated and that we withdraw to a line Galatz–Focsani–the Carpathian Mountains, if the common interests of the allied powers should make such a withdrawal desirable. I immediately translated this magnanimous offer to Hitler and reminded him of it again later. Hitler gratefully accepted Antonescu's offer and—as will be seen—drew certain conclusions from it.

The next morning Antonescu invited me to his quarters in the *Wolfsschanze* for a private conversation alone with him. I found this talk most instructive. The Rumanian Marshal showed that he was not only a good soldier but also displayed an exact knowledge of his country, its communications and economic condition, as well as of the political necessities. Everything he said was based on solid common sense and was expressed with amiability and courtesy, qualities to which at that time we in Germany were not exactly accustomed. He soon began to speak of the attempted assassination and did not try to disguise how deeply it had shocked him. 'Believe me, I can have implicit faith in every one of my generals. The idea of officers taking part in such a *coup d'état* is unthinkable to us!' At the time I could not reply to these serious reproaches. But fourteen days later Antonescu was to be faced with a very different situation, and we with him.

Among those who had accompanied the Marshal on this visit was the Rumanian Foreign Minister, Michai Antonescu. This man gave the impression of slyness and was not an attractive character. His friendliness seemed to have a rather slimy quality. With them they had brought the German Ambassador to Rumania, Killinger, and the head of the German military mission in that country, General Hansen. I had lengthy conversations with both these men concerning their opinions.

Neither of them thought a great deal of Antonescu, but believed that the Germans should support the young king as the figurehead of the Rumanian state. In this they were making a serious mistake which was to involve the German military authorities in a quite false sense of security, as a result of which the scattered reports we received of intended treachery were not evaluated correctly.

At the end of July Colonel-General Friessner had succeeded Schörner as commander of Army Group South Ukraine; he now agreed with Antonescu's suggestions and shortly after the latter's visit to Supreme Headquarters he proposed to Hitler that our front be withdrawn to the line Galatz–Focsani–the Carpathian Mountains. Hitler, with certain reservations, agreed, but insisted that he must receive clear proof of the enemy's intentions to attack before he would issue the necessary orders for the withdrawal and before any such movement be begun. Until that time the present front must continue to be held. Intelligence received at Supreme Headquarters concerning the situation in Rumania during the next few days was highly confused and contradictory; in general—owing to the attitude of the responsible German authorities in that country—it was favourable. All the same the Foreign Minister, von Ribbentrop, had such a deep lack of confidence in the reports sent him by his ambassador that he believed it necessary to transfer a panzer division to Bucharest and requested Hitler that this be done. I was present when this matter was discussed and I decided Ribbentrop's attitude was the correct one. But I could not make a division available from among those that were engaged on the Eastern Front, for the situation there was far too critical already. I therefore proposed that the 4th SS *Polizei* Division be withdrawn from fighting the guerrillas in Serbia and used for this more urgent task in Rumania. This was a motorised division and could therefore reach the Rumanian capital with the requisite speed. But Jodl declared that the division was not available, even though Wallachia at that time was one of the so-called *OKW* theatres of war and, as it did not count as part of the Eastern Front, was therefore directly under Jodl's authority. Hitler could not make up his mind. Nothing was done.

Trouble was brewing in Bulgaria as well as in Rumania. I received reports from Colonel von Jungenfeldt, who was engaged in training Bulgarian tank units in the use of German equipment. These reports painted a gloomy but unfortunately true picture of the situation; the morale of the Bulgarian troops was poor and their general behaviour made their reliability suspect. I submitted these reports to Hitler, but he would not believe them; on the contrary he expressed his complete conviction that the Bulgarians had so profound a hatred of Bolshevism as to make it certain that they would never willingly fight on the side of the Russians. My request that no more German armoured equipment be sent to the Bulgarians, and that what had already been sent be returned, was refused; an attempt to withdraw it on my own initiative was frustrated by Jodl.

On August 20th, 1944, the Russians launched their attack against Army Group South Ukraine. This was successful against those sectors that were held by Rumanian troops. But that was not all; the Rumanians deserted in large numbers to the enemy and turned their guns against their allies of yesterday. Neither the German troops nor their leaders had reckoned on such treachery. Although Hitler immediately authorised the withdrawal of the Army Group's front, the troops attempted to hold out in places and to carry out a fighting retreat step by step. In order to avoid a complete collapse and consequent annihilation an immediate withdrawal and rapid seizure of the bridges over the Danube were essential. As this was not done the Rumanians reached that river before the Germans, closed the crossing-places, and thus left their former allies at the mercy of the Russians. Sixteen German divisions were completely destroyed, an irreplaceable loss in view of our already very difficult situation. These German soldiers fought valiantly to the bitter end; their military honour was unsullied. They were in no way responsible for their sad fate. The misfortune could only have been avoided if the decision to withdraw to the line Galatz–Focsani–the Carpathian Mountains had been implemented before ever the Russians launched their attack; the whole Russian plan would thus have been forestalled and we should have been in possession of a line so shortened that we could have held it even without the assistance of the Rumanians. But to take such a decision required a clear grasp of the political situation and of the morals of the Rumanian leaders. Antonescu himself had been grossly deceived concerning the nature of his organisation and he paid for his mistake with his life. The reliance he placed on his generals and officers was unfortunately unjustified; but it had made a certain impression on the German leaders, with the result that they too were deceived. Within a few weeks Rumania was lost. On September 1st the Russians fought their way into Bucharest. Bulgaria, whose king had died in mysterious circumstances on August 28th, 1943, broke its alliance and went over to the enemy on September 8th. We lost the 88 Panzer IV's and the 50 assault guns that we had delivered to the Bulgars. Hitler's hopes of forming at least two anti-bolshevist Bulgarian divisions proved to be illusory. The German soldiers in Bulgaria were disarmed and imprisoned. The Bulgars, too, went over to the Russians and from then on fought against us.

It was now plain to Hitler that the Balkans could no longer be defended. He ordered a gradual withdrawal with delaying actions. In order to make available forces for the defence of Germany this withdrawal was far too slow.

On September 19th, 1944, Finland signed an armistice with Great Britain and Russia. The immediate consequence of this was that the Finns broke off diplomatic relations with Germany. Field-Marshal Keitel's visit to Field-Marshal Mannerheim on August 20th, 1944, had availed nothing; the Finns were already suing for peace on September 3rd.

It is little wonder that these events began to have their effect on Hungary's loyalty to its ally. The Regent, Admiral Horthy, had indeed never deeply believed in collaboration with Hitler and had only done so under the compulsion of political necessity. His attitude, compounded of caution and restraint, had already been in evidence on the occasion of his visit to Berlin in 1938. During the war Hitler had had repeatedly to exert heavy pressure in order to make Horthy carry out those measures which Germany considered desirable. Now, at the end of August 1944, Hitler sent me to Budapest with a letter for the Regent and instructions that I form my own impression of his attitude. I was received, in the castle at Budapest, with the customary honours and courtesy. The first words that the Regent uttered, after we had sat down, were: 'Look, my friend, in politics you must always have several irons in the fire.' I knew enough. The clever and experienced politician had, or at least thought he had, more than one iron in the fire. Admiral Horthy and I had a long, pleasant conversation on the subject of the problems of nationality in Hungary, a country in which for hundreds of years racial groups of many sorts had lived in close proximity to one another. He emphasised the close and friendly relations which had long bound his country to Poland and which Hitler had, in his opinion, not sufficiently considered. He asked that the Hungarian cavalry division, at present fighting in the Warsaw area, be sent home in the near future; this I was in a position to say would be done; we were engaged in sending home all the Hungarians still on Polish soil. But I could not form a favourable picture of the situation in Hungary, and this I had to tell Hitler. All the fair words of the Chief of the Hungarian General Staff, Vörös, could not change the impression I gained.

By the end of August the Russians had reached the gates of Bucharest and had entered Transylvania. The war was knocking at the portals of Hungary. It was under the shadow of these events that my visit to Budapest took place.

While these grave events were taking place in Eastern Europe, on the Western Front our forces were engaged in bloody and costly defensive battles. On July 17th Field-Marshal Rommel had been the victim of a British fighter-bomber attack. Field-Marshal von Kluge had taken over his command as well as the task of controlling all operations in the West. On this date the German front still ran from the mouth of the Orne—the southern edge of Caen–Caumont–St. Lô– Lessay, on the coast. On July 30th the Americans broke through this front at Avranches. A few weeks later, on August 15th, the mass of the German Army in the West, thirty-one divisions, was fighting for its very existence. Twenty divisions, two-thirds of this force, were in the process of being encircled near Falaise. The enemy's armoured and motorised formations were advancing through Orléans and Chartres towards Paris. Normandy and Brittany had been lost, with the exception of a part of the Atlantic Wall defences inside which five divisions were cut off. Weak American forces had landed on the Mediterranean coast between Toulon and Cannes. The 11th Panzer Division, which was supposed to operate against these forces, found itself unfortunately on the wrong side of the Rhône, on the west bank near Narbonne. The rest of the German divisions were located as follows:

$2\frac{1}{2}$ divisions in Holland.
7 divisions on the Channel between the Scheldt and the Seine.
1 division on the Channel Islands.
2 divisions on the coast between the Loire and the Pyrenees.
$7\frac{1}{2}$ divisions on the Mediterranean coast.
1 division on the Franco–Italian Alpine frontier.

Only two and a half divisions could be made available to parry the Allied thrust for Paris. Two new SS divisions were sent as reinforcements to Belgium, while three infantry divisions were moved into France by way of Cologne and Koblenz.

Now the Armed Forces Command Staff began to appreciate the value of rearward prepared positions. Their maps of the time show a Seine position and a Somme–Marne position. These existed solely on the maps.

Hitler now decided that Model should replace Field-Marshal von Kluge. In order that Model might devote attention to the main invasion front, Field-Marshal von Rundstedt was once again made responsible for controlling all operations in the West.

That day, the 15th of August, was one of violent scenes at Supreme Headquarters. I had briefed Hitler on the situation of our armoured forces in the West as I saw it from the reports I had received and I said: 'The bravery of the panzer troops is not enough to make up for the failure of the other two Services—the air force and the navy.' This

put Hitler in a raving temper. He requested that I follow him into
another room. There the argument continued and our voices must have
grown louder and louder, for eventually an adjutant, Major von
Amsberg, entered with the remark: 'The gentlemen are talking so
loudly that every word is clearly audible outside. May I close the
window?'

Hitler was desperate when he learned that Field-Marshal von Kluge
had failed to return from a visit to the front. He imagined that the
Field-Marshal had established contact with the enemy. He therefore
ordered that he report to Supreme Headquarters. But Field-Marshal
von Kluge killed himself by taking poison while on the way there.

On August 25th, 1944, Paris fell.

Hitler and the Armed Forces Command Staff were now confronted
with the need for making a vital decision concerning the future
prosecution of operations. This involved deciding clearly where the
point of main effort was to be made in the defence of Fortress
Germany.

That the defence must be continued was a matter beyond doubt
both to Hitler and to his military advisers. All thought of negotiation,
either collectively with all our enemies or singly with those in the West
or those in the East, had been rendered fruitless in advance by their
unanimous requirement that we surrender unconditionally. If we were
to go over completely to the defensive we could reckon on a long
resistance but hardly on a favourable outcome to the war.

If it were decided to make our main defensive effort in the East,
this would lead to a solidification of the front which might well halt
any further Russian advance. Upper Silesia and large areas of Poland,
essential to Germany for the production of war materials and of food
supplies, would remain under our control. On the other hand this
solution would leave our Western Front to its own resources, and
within the foreseeable future it must collapse beneath the overwhelming
superiority of the Western Powers. Since Hitler had no reason to
believe that the Western Allies would be willing to make a separate
peace for the purpose of discomforting the Russians, he refused to
follow this course.

It was Hitler's opinion that if our main effort were concentrated
in the West and all our available forces gathered together there, we
should be in a position to strike a powerful blow against the Western
Allies before they reached, or at any rate crossed, the Rhine.

Prerequisites for this course of action were:

1. Stabilisation of the Eastern Front and the holding of that front
until the offensive with limited objectives in the West had been com-

pleted and the forces there employed could be freed for transfer to the East.

2. The carrying out of this offensive to be completed in the shortest possible time, and certainly before the frosts set in, since this would presumably be the signal for a renewed Russian attack and therefore the necessary forces must be available for transfer eastwards by that time.

3. Rapid preparation of the attacking force, in order that the plan might be practicable.

4. A successful battle to gain time on the Western Front preparatory to the launching of the attack.

Hitler and the *OKW* believed that the attack could certainly be launched by mid-November and that there would be strong reserves available for transfer to the Eastern Front by mid-December. The prospect of a mild autumn and a delayed frost in the East made it seem probable that the Russian winter offensive would not start before the new year. In view of these considerations it was decided that my views concerning the Eastern Front must take second place.

It is obvious that I, being responsible for the Eastern Front, could only regard these plans with the gravest misgivings. Once the decision had been taken, I regarded it as my duty to ensure that the first pre-requisite of the proposed operation, the stabilisation of the Eastern Front, be carried out.

Apart from the building of rearward lines and positions, already mentioned above, attempts were now made to construct strong points at the front with all the means at our disposal. By mid-December all the panzer and panzergrenadier divisions had gradually been with-drawn from the front; they were now assembled in four groups as a mobile reserve and were brought up to strength so far as this was possible. The Eastern Front's weakness in infantry made it only possible to withdraw a single infantry division from the front; it was assembled as a reserve in the Cracow area.

The bridgeheads over the Vistula which the Russians had captured during the previous summer had to be eliminated or at least reduced in size so as to delay the enemy's attack and to increase his difficulties in launching it.

Finally, in order to shorten the front and to create a reserve it was necessary to evacuate our forces still in the Baltic States by sea, since the attempt to re-establish land communications with them had failed.

Unfortunately we did not manage to carry out the whole of our eastern programme successfully. It is true that we did succeed in building the necessary fortified lines and positions, but the indispensable gar-risons and weapons were not forthcoming as a result of the catastrophic and rapid sequence of events on the invasion front in the West. The value of the fortifications built therefore remained limited. They further suffered as a result of an order by Hitler that the 'Great Defensive Line,' to which the troops were to withdraw immediately before the enemy launched its attack, was not—as the army groups and I desired— to be some 12 miles behind the normal main defensive line, but was to be built at an insufficient depth of only 1 to 3 miles back.

On the Vistula the elimination of one Russian bridgehead was successfully completed while the others were reduced in size. But when a number of the divisions were withdrawn and the very active commander of Fourth Panzer Army, General Balck, was transferred to the Western Front, I regret to say that no further successes were achieved in these important operations. The bridgeheads, and particularly the important one at Baranov, remained a serious threat.

Also highly disadvantageous to us was the failure to shorten our front which resulted from the retention of Army Group North in Courland. Although I insisted over and over again that Courland must be evacuated and a strong reserve set up from the formations of Army Group North, Hitler continued to refuse to sanction the withdrawal, partly for reasons of prestige and partly because of the arguments advanced by Grand-Admiral Dönitz which supported his own attitude. Hitler was afraid that this evacuation might have an undesirable effect on Swedish neutrality and evil consequences for the U-boat training area in the Gulf of Danzig. Also he believed that by retaining an area on the Baltic to the north of the Eastern Front he was tying up a disproportionately large number of Russian divisions which would otherwise be committed against more vital sectors of our front. The repeated offensives launched by the Russians in Courland strengthened him in this conviction.

With the same or similar arguments Hitler and the Armed Forces Command Staff turned down all proposals for a timely evacuation of the Balkans and of Norway and for a shortening of the front in Italy.

But it was not only the programme in the East that remained largely unfulfilled. The situation in the West developed far more unfortunately.

The neglect of our western defences, including the West Wall, since 1940 and the confining of all our constructional activities exclusively to the Atlantic Wall now began to exact a very heavy toll. It was not only from the Eastern Front that the new units formed with such trouble in the autumn of 1944 had now to be withdrawn. These units, insufficient as they were and consisting of soldiers who could scarcely be described as even third-class military material, were not enough to breach the gap in the West. Furthermore, the rear echelon soldiers of the armies in France had collapsed. As a result the ungarrisoned and unarmed fortifications were quite valueless. Their rapid loss compelled us to fight a mobile war with almost immobile units, a bombed communications network in our rear and enemy air superiority above us. While our panzer units still existed, our leaders had chosen to fight a static battle in Normandy. Now that our motorised forces had been squandered and destroyed they were compelled to fight the mobile battle that they had hitherto refused to face. Favourable chances that the boldness of the American command occasionally offered us we were no longer in a position to exploit. The original intention—to counter-attack the southern wing of the advancing American armies— had to be given up. But the worst was yet to come: the time schedule by which the offensive was to be launched in mid-November could no longer be kept and the attack was postponed until mid-December. This worsened the prospects for the timely release and transfer of our reserves to the East, and indeed decreased our chances of holding the now weakened Eastern Front at all.

The preparations of our offensive forces for the attack in the West were not completed in time. The battle for time that was fought on the Western Front was not successful. But despite these unfavourable circumstances Hitler and the *OKW* stuck to their determination that an attack be launched in the West. They succeeded in keeping their intentions secret. The enemy was taken completely by surprise. Security measures, so far as our own staffs and units went, were indeed carried to such lengths that the distribution of supplies for the attacking force, in particular the fuel supplies, suffered in consequence.

Operations on the Eastern Front

While the Western Front was being thrown back from the Atlantic to the West Wall, in the East heavy fighting continued without pause. At the southern end of this front all attempts to stop the Russian advance failed. Within a short time they had occupied all of Rumania, all of Bulgaria and finally large parts of Hungary. In the latter country Colonel-General Friessner's Army Group South Ukraine was fighting; on September 25th its now inappropriate name was changed to Army Group South. In October all of Transylvania was lost to the Russians, though not without heavy fighting in the Debrecen area where German counter-attacks succeeded in temporarily halting the enemy. In the area controlled by the Commander-in-Chief South-East, Field-Marshal Freiherr von Weichs, Belgrade was lost during the course of the month. This area was still an *OKW* theatre of operations and was not controlled by the *OKH*, even though the Balkan Front was now certainly part of the Eastern Front. The boundary between the areas controlled by the *OKW* and the *OKH* ran through a village on the Danube near the mouths of the Drava and the Baja. This was utterly senseless. The Russians crossed the Danube at a point immediately south of this boundary between the two Supreme Command staffs' areas, and therefore in the territory controlled by the Commander-in-Chief South-East, who was concentrating his attention on his scattered fronts many miles away to the south. On October 29th the Russians reached the outskirts of Budapest, and on November 24th they won a bridgehead over the Danube at Mohacs. At this date there were still German troops in Salonica and Durazzo while the Morava valley was already held by the enemy. The intensification of guerrilla warfare in the Balkans made the evacuation of these areas increasingly difficult. On November 30th the Russians broke the Commander-in-Chief South-East's front at Pecs, north of the Drava, pushed on to Lake Balaton and rolled up Army Group South's line along the Danube. By December 5th they had reached the southern outskirts of Budapest. On the same day they also crossed the river to the north of that city, pushed on to Vac, and could only be held with difficulty to the east of the Gran. Farther to the north-east they took Miskolc and reached a point south of Kosice. Our forces had withdrawn from the Balkans as far as a line Podgorica-Uzice and were continuing northward.

The Russians attacked again on December 21st and by Christmas Eve had succeeded in encircling Budapest. They reached a line Lake Balaton-Stuhlweissenburg-west of Komarno-north of the Danube to the Gran. From there the front more or less followed the line of the Hungarian frontier. The battles were fought with great ferocity by both sides. Our casualties were heavy.

In the area of Colonel-General Harpe's Army Group North Ukraine (renamed Army Group A in September) the Russians had reached the line of the Vistula as far as Warsaw during the course of their summer offensive. Farther south there was fighting between the rivers San and Visloka. This army group consisted of First Panzer Army, under Colonel-General Heinrici, in the Carpathians, Seventeenth Army, under General Schultz, between those mountains and the Vistula, and Fourth Panzer Army, under General Balck and later under General Gräser, along the Vistula. About August 1st the Russians secured a number of bridgeheads across the Vistula, of which the most important was at Baranov, while there were smaller ones at Pulavy, Magnuszev, and a fourth point. The Russians' advances through the mountains were of course slower and smaller. The situation at Baranov was particularly critical during the period of August 5th–9th. Here for days on end the Russians were on the point of breaking through. It was thanks to the inexhaustible energy and skill of General Balck that a major disaster was finally avoided. After launching fierce attacks that lasted

for weeks on end, Balck succeeded in considerably reducing the size of the Baranov bridgehead, eliminating another minor one, and also winning back some of the ground lost at Pulavy. The Russians thereupon switched their point of main effort to the mountains. In the Sanok and Jaslo areas they managed to break into, but not through, our positions. The eastern Beskidy range could be held until events in Hungary compelled First Panzer Army to withdraw to the line Kosice–Jaslo. At the beginning of the new year the line held by this army group ran along the Slovak frontier to a point east of Kosice–west of Debica–west of Staszov–south of Opatov–the Vistula north of its junction with the San–Warsaw. Also there were the various bridgeheads mentioned above.

Army Group Centre consisted of Ninth Army, under General von Vormann, Second Army, under Colonel-General Weiss, Fourth Army, under General Hossbach, and Third Panzer Army, under Colonel-General Reinhardt until August 15th and then under Colonel-General Rauss. After Field-Marshal Model was transferred to the Western Front, on August 15th, Colonel-General Reinhardt was appointed to command this army group. In August the enemy had reached a point immediately before Warsaw, and from there the army group's front line then ran Ostrov–Sudauen–the frontier of East Prussia–west of Schaulen–west of Mitau. In September the enemy advanced north-east of Warsaw as far as the Narev, establishing bridgeheads across that river in October on either side of Ostenburg. In the period October 5th–19th the Russians, as already described above, broke through the German front west of Schaulen and thus finally cut off Army Group Centre from Army Group North. On October 19th Army Group Centre withdrew its left wing on Memel, and on October 22nd evacuated the two bridgeheads it had been holding on the northern bank of the river, at Tilsit and Ragnit. During the period October 16th–26th the Russians attacked East Prussia in the area Wolfsburg–Gumbinnen–Goldap. After heavy fighting this attack was held and even, on occasion, thrown back a short distance. What happened in East Prussia was an indication to the inhabitants of the rest of Germany of their fate in the event of a Russian victory.

As already described, Army Group North had been withdrawn, during the period 14th–26th September, into a bridgehead in the Riga area, from where it was to join Army Group Centre with all speed. This intention was frustrated by the divergent views of the army group commander, Colonel-General Schörner. He kept his armoured strength around Riga and Mitau instead of moving it to the area west of Schaulen and he thus contributed to the success of the Russians' breakthrough at Schaulen and the final severance of contact between his army group and the rest of the army. Army Group North consisted of the Sixteenth and Eighteenth Armies with an initial total strength of twenty-six divisions; even after the evacuation by sea of a portion of this force, there were still sixteen divisions with the army group, all urgently needed for the defence of Germany. After the evacuation of Riga during the period October 7th–16th, the army group's front remained almost static until the end of the year, running from the coast south of Libau–Prekuln–south of Frauenburg–east of Tuckum–the coast of the Gulf of Riga.

In general the long front from the Carpathians to the Baltic was relatively quiet so that the building of fortifications and the withdrawal of panzer and panzergrenadier divisions to form a mobile reserve was successfully carried out. All the same, twelve weak divisions could provide only a very inadequate reserve for such an enormous front, approximately 725 miles long, and against such vast superiority of strength as the Russians now possessed.

The fortifications built on the Eastern Front had meanwhile made our line, long and far too thin as it was, yet sufficiently strong for quiet periods. We did our best to make use of the experience we had gained during the recent battles, but in so doing came up against Hitler's opposition. One essential requirement at the front was that the ordinary main line of defence (*Hauptkampflinie*)—to be defended on normal occasions—must be separated from the major line of defence (*Grosskampflinie*), which was intended to be held in the event of the Russians launching a large-scale attack against any one sector. The officers at the front wished to build this major defensive line some 12 miles behind the main line of defence, to camouflage it carefully and to install a holding garrison inside it. They further wanted a standing authority to withdraw the bulk of their forces into this major defensive line as soon as the Russian artillery preparation that heralded a forthcoming attack should begin, leaving only rearguards in the old main line of defence; the Russian's barrage would thus be wasted, his assault, so laboriously prepared, would be fruitless and by the time he came up against our well-prepared defensive positions he could in consequence be repulsed. There can be no doubt that this theory was absolutely correct. I approved it and submitted it to Hitler. He lost his temper, saying that he refused to accept the sacrifice of 12 miles without a fight and ordered that the major defensive line be built from 1 to 2 miles behind the main line of defence. He was basing his ideas on the conditions prevailing in the First World War when he gave those nonsensical orders, and no arguments could bring him to see reason. This mistake of his was to cost us dear when the Russians broke through in January of 1945 and our reserves—again on a direct

order of Hitler's and against my judgment—were once again too close
to the front. Main line of defence, major defensive positions, reserves,
all were buried beneath the tidal wave of the initial Russian break-
through and lost to us. Hitler's rage was turned against the men who
had built the defences and—since I stood up to him—against me. He
ordered that the minutes of the conferences held in the autumn of 1944
on the subject of a major defensive line be sent for, maintaining now
that he had always wanted a 12-mile gap. 'Who was the half-wit who
gave such idiotic orders?' I pointed out to him that it was he himself
who had done so. The minutes were brought and read aloud. After
a few sentences Hitler broke off the reading. He was convinced at last.
Unfortunately it was by then too late, for the Russian break-through
was an accomplished fact.

I shall have occasion to refer again to Hitler's tactics when describing
the great Russian offensive. Since he continued to believe that he was
the only real front-line soldier at Supreme Headquarters—and indeed
so far as the majority of his military advisers were concerned he did
know far more about active service than they—and since the grotesque
flattery of his Party comrades, led by Ribbentrop and Goering, had
given him the illusion that he was a great military leader, he absolutely
refused to learn from others. 'There's no need for you to try to teach
me. I've been commanding the German Army in the field for five years
and during that time I've had more practical experience than any
gentlemen of the General Staff could ever hope to have. I've studied
Clausewitz and Moltke and read all the Schlieffen papers. I'm more
in the picture than you are!' That was one of the many reprimands
that I was vouchsafed when attempting to give him a slightly clearer
idea of the requirements of the time.

Apart from our own troubles we were also most anxious about the
fighting ability and the loyalty of our Hungarian allies. I have already
mentioned the attitude which the Regent, Horthy, had assumed
towards Hitler. Understandable as this attitude may be from the
Hungarian point of view, for the Germans it seemed unreliable. The
Head of the Hungarian State was hoping for a *rapprochement* with
the Anglo-Saxon powers. He wished to establish contact with them
by air. Whether he did in fact attempt to do so, and whether the
Western Powers were agreeable to his propositions, I do not know.[1]
But I do know that a number of senior Hungarian officers were
deserting to the common enemy, among them, on October 15th,
General Miklos whose acquaintance I had made when he was military
attaché in Berlin, and the Chief of the Hungarian General Staff, Vörös,
who had recently visited me in East Prussia, had assured me of his

[1] I am aware of Erich Kordt's opinion, as given in his book *Wahn und Wirklichkeit*.

loyalty to the alliance, and had accepted a motor-car as a present from me. In this car, my own Mercedes, he drove off a few days later to the Russians. No reliance could be placed on the Hungarians any more. Hitler therefore overthrew Horthy's government and put Salaszy in his place; this latter was a Hungarian Fascist of little ability and less tact. This happened on October 16th, 1944. Conditions in Hungary were in no wise improved as a result, and what remained of mutual trust and sympathy was destroyed.

In Slovakia, which had originally been entirely on the German side, partisans had now been very active for a long time. Travel by railway became increasingly perilous. Through trains were compelled to stop, the passengers searched and German soldiers, and particularly German officers, murdered. This led to severe counter-measures. Hatred and murder stalked the country, as was to be more and more the case in other lands. The Great Powers had deliberately called out the partisans, who fought without regard for international law; this led inevitably to defensive counter-measures being taken; the prosecutors and judges at Nuremberg later said that these defensive counter-measures were contrary to international law and criminal, despite the fact that when the Allies entered Germany they drew up a far harsher penal code than ever did the Germans in occupied territories. That a disarmed and exhausted Germany did not give them occasion to pass sentences according to that code is beside the point.

In order to complete the picture it is necessary to glance at the situation in Italy. On July 4th, 1944, the Allies had entered Rome. The Commander-in-Chief South, Field-Marshal Kesselring, was holding a line in the Apennines to the north of the eternal city, and his army group was fighting fiercely against superior enemy forces. More than twenty divisions were tied down in these defensive battles. The Italians who had remained true to Mussolini were of little assistance owing to their limited combat ability and could only be used on the Riviera. Behind the German front there was bitter partisan fighting, begun with Italian cruelty, that compelled energetic counter-measures if the effort of supplying the army group was not to be totally abandoned. The military tribunals of the victor nations who later judged the events that there took place did not assume the cloak of impartial justice, but preferred to act simply according to their own prejudices.

The Ardennes Offensive

Early in December Hitler moved his headquarters from East Prussia to Ziegenberg, near Giessen, so that he might be closer to the Western Front where the crucial and final German attack was now about to be delivered.

The entire strength of the German Army that could be collected together during the last few months was to attack from the Eifel towards the Meuse south of Liége, with the object of breaking through the relatively thinly held Allied front in this sector; this force was then to cross the Meuse towards Brussels and Antwerp, thus achieving a strategic break-through; the enemy forces to the north of the break-through were finally to be encircled and destroyed. Hitler believed that such an operation—if successful—would severely weaken the Western Allies and would give him time to move strong forces eastward so that he would be in a position to defeat the anticipated Russian winter offensive. He thus expected to gain time, to shatter the enemy's hopes of total victory, so that he would drop his insistence on unconditional surrender, and to make him willing to accept a negotiated peace.

The weather and delays in making ready the new formations forced him repeatedly to postpone the date of the attack, originally intended for mid-November. It was eventually launched on December 16th.

Two panzer armies had been formed for this attack, Fifth Panzer Army, under General von Manteuffel, and Sixth Panzer Army, under the SS Colonel-General (*Oberstgruppenführer*) Sepp Dietrich. The point of main effort was to be on the right wing, in Sixth Panzer Army's sector, which contained the best-equipped units of the *Waffen-SS*. Fifth Panzer Army was in the centre. General Brandenberger's Seventh Army was responsible for protecting the left flank of the two attacking armies; but this army lacked the mobile strength necessary for carrying out its difficult assignment.

Both the Commander-in-Chief West, Field-Marshal von Rundstedt, and the commander of Army Group B, Field-Marshal Model, had proposed that the attack be made with a limited objective, since they did not regard the forces available as sufficiently strong to achieve the long-range operational results envisaged in the Hitler plan. They wished the attack to be limited to the area east of the Meuse with the purpose of defeating the enemy forces located along the east bank between Aachen and Liége. But Hitler turned down this proposal and insisted on his more grandiose plan.

The attack therefore began on December 16th and General von Manteuffel's Fifth Panzer Army immediately succeeded in making a deep penetration of the enemy's positions. The foremost armoured units of this army, the 116th and 2nd Panzer Divisions, reached points very close to the Meuse. Elements of the 2nd Panzer Division actually reached the river bank. Sixth Panzer Army was less successful. Heavy congestion on the narrow, ice-bound roads, belated switching of the rearward, blocked units to Fifth Panzer Army's sector, and insufficiently rapid exploitation of initial success caused this army to loose mobility, that prime requisite for all large-scale operations. Since Seventh Army also ran into difficulties, parts of Manteuffel's armour had soon to be moved south to strengthen the threatened left flank. From that point on a break-through in the grand manner was no longer possible. Even by December 22nd it was plain that a less ambitious objective would have to be chosen. A sensible commander would on this day have remembered the looming dangers on the Eastern Front which could only be countered by a timely breaking-off of the operation in the West that was already, from the long view, a failure. However, not only Hitler, but also the *OKW* and particularly the Armed Forces Command Staff could, during these fateful days, think of nothing save their own Western Front. The whole tragedy of our military leadership was revealed once again towards the end of the war in this unsuccessful Ardennes Offensive.

On December 24th it was plain to any perceptive soldier that the offensive had finally broken down. It was necessary immediately to change direction and to face east once again before it was too late.

Defensive Preparations in the East

From my headquarters, now moved to the Maybach camp near Zossen, I observed with a heavy heart the progress of our offensive in the West. For the sake of my country I had hoped that it would lead to a complete victory. But since, on December 23rd, it was clear that it could no longer result in a great success, I decided to drive to Supreme Headquarters and to request that the battle, which was causing us heavy casualties, be broken off and that all forces that could be spared be immediately transferred to the Eastern Front.

Intelligence of the imminent Russian offensive had meanwhile increased. The assembly areas of the major enemy forces were confirmed. Three main attacking groups had been identified:

1. In the Baranov bridgehead a Russian force consisting of 60 rifle formations, 8 tank corps, 1 cavalry corps and 6 other tank formations was ready to attack.

2. To the north of Warsaw 54 rifle formations, 6 tank corps, 1 cavalry corps and 9 other tank formations were assembled.

3. On the East Prussian border there was a force of 54 rifle formations, 2 tank corps and 9 other tank formations.

Apart from these the following forces had been identified:

Fifteen rifle and 2 tank formations south of Jaslo,

Eleven rifle formations, 1 cavalry corps and 1 tank corps in the Pulavy area,

Thirty-one rifle formations, 5 tank corps and 3 other tank units south of Warsaw.

We calculated that the attack would begin on January 12th. The Russians' superiority to us was 11: 1 in infantry, 7: 1 in tanks, 20: 1 in guns. An evaluation of the enemy's total strength gave him a superiority of approximately 15: 1 on the ground and 20: 1 in the air, and this estimate did not err on the side of exaggeration. I am certainly not inclined to underestimate the German soldier. He was outstanding and he repeatedly attacked and defeated enemy forces with a superiority of five to one. The individual qualities of the German soldier, when well led, more than compensated for such numerical inferiority. But now, after five years of intensive fighting, with ever-diminishing supplies, weapons, and above all with decreasing hope of victory, the burden put upon him was indescribably heavy. The Supreme Command, and above all Hitler himself, should have done everything in their power to lighten this stupendous burden or at least to ensure that the soldiers were capable of bearing it.

I was faced with the problem of whether in fact what was now demanded of our soldiers was humanly feasible. It is true that I had been preoccupied with this question since the start of the Russian campaign, and indeed ever since Molotov's visit to Berlin in 1940. But now it had assumed enormous significance: for us the question was, simply, 'to be or not to be.'

And no alternative existed unless and until the impending Russian offensive was somehow, somewhere, brought to a standstill. To do this it was necessary immediately to transfer forces from the West to the East, to build up a strong reserve army in the Lodz–Hohensalza area, and to force the Russian armies which broke through to fight a war of movement, for this was a type of battle in which the German commanders and soldiers, despite the long war and their consequent exhaustion, were still superior to the enemy.

It was on these principles that I wished to fight the battle in the East, but first I had to win a battle against Hitler for the release of the necessary forces. On December 24th I drove to Giessen and from there to a conference at Supreme Headquarters.

Those present—apart, of course, from Hitler—included Field-Marshal Keitel, Colonel-General Jodl, General Burgdorf and a number of junior officers. I outlined the enemy's dispositions and strength as given above. The work of my department, 'Foreign Armies East,' was first class and absolutely reliable. I had known its head, General Gehlen, and his colleagues' methods and results for long enough to be able to judge their efficacy. General Gehlen's estimates of the enemy were, in due course, proved correct. That is an established historical fact. But now Hitler saw these matters from another point of view. He declared that the reports prepared by 'Foreign Armies East' were based on an enemy bluff. He maintained that a Russian rifle formation had a maximum strength of 7,000 men, that the tank formations had no tanks. 'It's the greatest imposture since Ghengis Khan,' he shouted. 'Who's responsible for producing all this rubbish?' Since the attempt on his life Hitler had himself attempted to bluff on the grand scale. He ordered the formation of artillery corps which in fact were no stronger than brigades. Panzer brigades were two battalions, that is to say with the strength of regiments. Tank-destroyer brigades consisted of only one battalion. In my opinion these methods served rather to confuse our own military organisation than to conceal our real weakness from the enemy. His mentality, becoming ever more extraordinary, led him now to believe that the enemy were attempting similar impostures on him, villages *à la Potemkin*, and that in fact the Russians would not launch a serious attack in the foreseeable future. I received proof of this during the course of the evening meal, when I was seated next to Himmler. At that time Himmler was simultaneously Commander-in-Chief of the Training Army, commander of Army Group Upper Rhine (an organisation for defending that river and for catching fugitives and deserters), Minister of the Interior, Chief of the German Police and National Leader of the SS; he harboured no doubts about his own importance. He believed that he possessed powers of military judgment every bit as good as Hitler's and needless to say far better than those of the generals. 'You know, my dear Colonel-General, I don't really believe the Russians will attack at all. It's all an enormous bluff. The figures given by your department "Foreign Armies East" are grossly exaggerated. They're far too worried. I'm convinced there's nothing going on in the East.' There was no arguing against such naïveté.

Far more dangerous was Jodl's opposition to moving our main defensive effort eastward. Jodl did not wish to lose the allegedly recaptured initiative in the West. He saw that the Ardennes Offensive had bogged down, but he believed that that attack had damaged the enemy's operational time-table. He believed that by launching further attacks, at places where the enemy least expected them, it would be possible to achieve further limited successes and that a series of such successes would eventually cripple the enemy. With this object in view he had ordered a fresh attack in northern Alsace-Lorraine. German troops were to advance southwards towards Saverne from either side of Bitche. This attack, launched on January 1st, also had a certain initial success. But its objectives, Saverne and even Strasbourg, were still far away. Jodl, entranced by his own ideas, strongly opposed my request for the transfer of troops from the Ardennes and the Upper Rhine. 'We must not lose the initiative that we have just regained,' he repeated over and over again as an argument against my proposal. I pointed out that the Ruhr had been already paralysed by the Western Allies' bombing attacks, that means of transport had been destroyed by the enemy's air supremacy and that this state of affairs must become worse and not better: on the other hand, I said, the industrial area of Upper Silesia could still work at full pressure, the centre of the German armament industry was already in the east, and the loss of Upper Silesia must lead to our defeat within a very few weeks. All this was of no avail. I was rebuffed and I spent a grim and tragic Christmas Eve in those most unchristian surroundings. The news of Budapest's encirclement, which reached us that evening, did not tend to raise anyone's spirits. I was dismissed with instructions that the Eastern Front must take care of itself. When I requested once again that Courland be evacuated, when I asked that at least the units previously engaged in Finland and now coming back through Norway be sent to the East, I was again disappointed. It was precisely those troops coming from Norway that were to be used in the Vosges battle; they were mountain troops and therefore particularly suited to that terrain. As a matter of fact I knew that part of the Vosges between Bitche and Saverne well from the days of my youth. Bitche had been my first station when I was an ensign-cadet and a second lieutenant. But a single mountain division committed there was not enough to make any fundamental difference to the course of the battle.

On December 25th, Christmas Day, I went by train back to Zossen. While I was travelling, and without having previously informed me, Hitler ordered the transfer of Gille's SS Corps with its two SS divisions from the area north of Warsaw, where it had been assembled behind the front as the reserve of Army Group Reinhardt, to Budapest, with the task of lifting the siege of that city. This irresponsible weakening of an already greatly over-extended front was a matter of despair to Reinhardt as it was to me. All protests remained fruitless. In Hitler's opinion the relief of Budapest was more important than the defence of Eastern Germany. He advanced reasons of external politics when I asked him to reverse this ill-starred order, and turned down my request. Thus two of the fourteen and a half panzer or panzer-grenadier divisions assembled as a reserve against the impending Russian attack were sent to a secondary front. Only twelve and a half remained for a front of approximately 750 miles.

Back at my headquarters I again studied the enemy situation with Gehlen and discussed with him and Wenck what steps we might still take to improve our own. We came to the conclusion that only the discontinuation of offensive operations in the West and the immediate transfer of our main defensive effort to the East still offered us a slender chance of holding the major Russian attack. I therefore decided, on New Year's Eve, once again to request Hitler that he make the only possible decision, and so I set off once more for Ziegenberg. I had decided that this time I must act with greater circumspection than before. Therefore when I arrived at Ziegenberg I first visited Field-Marshal von Rundstedt and his chief of staff, General Westphal, explained the position on the Eastern Front to those two gentlemen, told them what I proposed should be done, and asked for their help. Both Field-Marshal von Rundstedt and his chief of staff showed, as so often before, complete understanding for the needs of the other front. They gave me the numbers of three divisions on the Western Front and one on the Italian Front which were immediately available, were located near a railway and which could be transferred east as soon as Hitler gave his approval. A warning order was immediately despatched to the units in question. I informed the Chief of Field Transport and told him to arrange for the necessary trains to be made ready. Armed with these achievements I next went in to see Hitler. Here it was the same rigmarole as on Christmas Eve. Jodl declared that he had no available forces as the Western Front must keep what it had in order to retain the initiative. But this time I could contradict him by producing the statements of the Commander-in-Chief West. He was plainly put out of countenance by this. When I gave Hitler the numbers of the divisions available, Jodl asked me angrily where I had got them from; when I told him—from the Commander-in-Chief of his own front—he relapsed into sulky silence. There was really no argument he could now advance. I therefore got the four divisions, but no more. These four, of course, were only to be the beginning, but as it turned out they were all that the *OKW* and the Armed Forces Command Staff surrendered to the Eastern Front. And even this wretched pittance was to go, by Hitler's orders, to Hungary.

On the morning of New Year's Day I went to see Hitler and informed him that that afternoon Gille's SS Corps, under command of Balck's Sixth Army, would launch an attack with the object of relieving Budapest. Hitler expected great results from this attack. I was sceptical since very little time had been allowed for its preparation and neither the troops nor their commanders possessed the same drive as in the old days. Despite initial success the attacking force did not succeed in breaking through to the encircled city.

The results of my visit to Supreme Headquarters were thus again slight. At Zossen I held further discussions and once more examined the situation. I then decided to visit Hungary and Galicia personally so that I might talk to the various commanders-in-chief on the spot, see if they could give me any assistance, and form a clear opinion of our future prospects. During the period January 5th–8th, 1945, I visited General Wöhler, who had succeeded Friessner in command of Army Group South, and then General Balck and the SS General Gille; I discussed with them the future prosecution of operations in Hungary and found out why the attack to relieve Budapest had failed. The principal reason seemed to be that the initial success won during the night attack of January 1st had not been exploited with sufficient boldness to constitute a break-through on the following night. We had neither commanders nor troops of the 1940 quality any more; otherwise this attack might well have been successful, troops might then have been available for transfer elsewhere, and the Danube front might have been stabilised for a time.

From Hungary I went to Cracow to see Harpe. He and his reliable chief of staff, General von Xylander, gave me their clear and logical views on the problems of defence against the Russians. Harpe proposed that immediately before the attack anticipated for January 12th should materialise we evacuate such parts of the bank of the Vistula as we still held and withdraw some 12 miles to the next defensible position which was considerably shorter. This would enable us to withdraw a few divisions from the front and build up a reserve. This idea was both sound and correct, but had little prospect of gaining the approval of Hitler. Harpe was an upright man and he requested that his opinion be submitted to Hitler nevertheless, even though this might well have unpleasant consequences for him personally. The defensive preparations that had been carried out by his army group were thorough and as complete as they could be with the means at our disposal.

Finally, I had a telephonic conversation with Reinhardt. He made a similar proposal to Harpe's, which in his case involved giving up the Narev line, withdrawing to the shorter line of the East Prussian border, and thus being in a position to pull back a few divisions to constitute a reserve. But here again I could hold out little hope that I should succeed in persuading Hitler to approve this plan.

I now knew what was most critical so far as the army groups were concerned and I therefore decided once again to visit Hitler at the eleventh hour. My intention was to try to persuade him that he make the Eastern Front the point of our main defensive effort, that he free forces for this purpose from the Western Front, and that he agree to the wishes of the army group commanders concerning the withdrawal of the front line, since there was no other way of creating a reserve in time.

On January 9th I was once again at Ziegenberg, determined this time not to give in and to make it quite clear to Hitler where his duty lay. The conference took the usual form. Only this time the chief of staff of my Inspectorate of Armoured Troops, General Thomale, was also present.

Gehlen had made a most careful report on the enemy situation with maps and diagrams showing the relative distributions of strength. Hitler completely lost his temper when these were shown to him, declaring them to be 'completely idiotic' and ordering that I have the man who had made them shut up in a lunatic asylum. I then lost my temper and said to Hitler: 'The man who made these is General Gehlen, one of my very best general staff officers. I should not have shown them to you were I in disagreement with them. If you want General Gehlen sent to a lunatic asylum then you had better have me certified as well.' Hitler's demand that I relieve General Gehlen of his post I brusquely refused. And with that the hurricane was over. But nevertheless the conference was from a military point of view unsuccessful. Harpe's and Reinhardt's proposals were turned down, with the now customary and odious remarks about generals for whom operations meant nothing but a retreat to the next rearward position. It was altogether most unsatisfactory.

All attempts to assemble reserves behind the most immediately threatened sectors of the very tense Eastern Front foundered on the rocks of Hitler's and Jodl's incomprehension. The attitude of the *OKW* was based principally on a vague hope that our very precise intelligence of the great forthcoming Russian attack might be based on nothing but bluff. The men at that headquarters were only too anxious to believe what they wanted to believe, and they closed their eyes when confronted by the ominous truth. Ostrich politics were here combined with ostrich strategy. To console me Hitler said, at the end of the conference: 'The Eastern Front has never before possessed such a strong reserve as now. That is your doing. I thank you for it.' I replied: 'The Eastern Front is like a house of cards. If the front is broken through at one point all the rest will collapse, for twelve and a half divisions are far too small a reserve for so extended a front.'

Reserves at this time were located as follows:
17th Panzer Division, Pinczow area,
16th Panzer Division, south of Kielce,
20th Panzergrenadier Division, between Vierzonik and Ostrowicz,
10th Panzergrenadier Division (battle group only), Kamienna area,
19th Panzer Division, Radom area,
25th Panzer Division, Mogielnica area,
7th Panzer Division, Zichenau area,

Panzergrenadier Division *Gross-Deutschland*, Chorzele area,
18th Panzergrenadier Division, east of Johannisburg,
23rd Infantry Division (not ready for operations), Nikolaiken area,
10th Bicycle Brigade, Sensburg area,
Elements of Panzergrenadier Division *Brandenburg* (a new formation), south of Drengfurt,
Panzer Corps *Hermann Goering*, with
1st Panzer Parachute Division *Hermann Goering*, west of Gumbinnen,
2nd Panzer Parachute Division *Hermann Goering*, at the front in East Prussia, south-east of Gumbinnen.
5th Panzer Division, Breitenstein area,
24th Panzer Division, in transit from Hungary to Rastenburg.

With Hitler's parting remark—'The Eastern Front must help itself and make do with what it's got'—I returned, in a very grave frame of mind, to my headquarters at Zossen. Hitler and Jodl knew perfectly well that if the attack we expected should materialise the Eastern Front was quite incapable of holding it with the resources available; they also knew that if they waited until the attack started before ordering the transfer of available reserves from west to east such forces, thanks to the enemy's air supremacy and the consequent slowing up of all means of transport, must inevitably arrive too late. I do not know how much their incomprehension was due to the fact that they both came originally from parts of Germany far from the threatened area. At my last conference I came to the conclusion this fact played a not unimportant part in the decisions they were taking. For us Prussians it was our immediate homeland that was at stake, that homeland which had been won at such cost and which had remained attached to the ideals of Christian, Western culture through so many centuries of effort, land where lay the bones of our ancestors, land that we loved. We knew that if the assault from the East succeeded our homes were lost. After the examples of Goldap and Nemmersdorf we feared the worst for the inhabitants. But even these fears of ours fell on deaf ears. A request from the generals at the front that civilians be evacuated from the most immediately threatened areas was turned down by Hitler; he said it was just another manifestation of the generals' alleged defeatism and he was afraid that such evacuation would have a bad effect on public opinion. In this attitude he was supported by the Gauleiters, and particularly by Gauleiter Koch of East Prussia. The latter could not do enough to bring the generals into disrepute. The army groups' operational zones remained limited to narrow strips of territory extending to a depth of 6 miles behind the front. The heavy artillery batteries were actually stationed in the so-called 'Home Area,' which was subordinate to the Gauleiters and where no strong point might be built, no tree felled, without such action causing an immediate quarrel with the civil administration—that is to say with the Party.

The Russian Offensive

On January 12th, 1945, the Russian assaulting force in the Baranov bridgehead launched its well-prepared attack. Already on the 11th we had had direct evidence that the opening of the offensive was imminent. Prisoners stated that during the night of the 10th–11th billets had had to be handed over to tank crews. An intercepted wireless message read: 'Everything ready. Reinforcements arrived.' Since December 17th, 1944, the number of guns in the Baranov bridgehead had increased by 719, of mortars by 268. Prisoners captured from the Pulavy bridgehead stated: 'Attack imminent. First wave to be composed of punishment units. Attack to be supported by 40 tanks. Thirty to forty tanks located in a wood 1–2 miles behind the main line of defence. Minefields cleared during the night of January 8th.' Air reconnaissance reported enemy movements towards the Vistula bridgeheads. In the Magnuszev bridgehead 60 new gun positions were established.

Intelligence from the Narev front, in the areas north of Warsaw, around Ostenburg and in East Prussia was similar in content. It seemed here that the enemy's point of main effort would be in the sector Ebenrode–Lake Willuhn and east of Schlossberg.

Only in Hungary—on account of our New Year attack—and in Courland did our intelligence indicate that there would not be an attack within the next few days. But this meant only a breathing-space for those fronts.

So on January 12th the first blow fell at Baranov. Fourteen rifle divisions, two independent tank corps and elements of another army were committed. The mass of the Russian tanks assembled in this area was apparently held back during the first day, since the enemy wished to decide, according to the results of the initial attack, in which direction he could best advance. The Russians had a superabundance of equipment and could afford such tactics.

The enemy's attack succeeded and he penetrated far into the German defences.

On this day a great convergence of Russian offensive force was observed moving into the bridgeheads over the Vistula farther to the north at Pulavy and Magnuszev. Thousands of vehicles were counted. Here, too, the attack was obviously about to start. It was the same story to the north of Warsaw and in East Prussia. Here it was established that the Russians had cleared paths through the minefields and tanks were observed immediately behind the enemy's front.

Army Group A had sent in its reserves for a counter-thrust. A direct order from Hitler had resulted in these forces being stationed closer to the front than Colonel-General Harpe had originally intended. The result of this interference was that they were shelled by the strong Russian artillery and suffered heavy casualties before ever they reached the battle area. The Russians succeeded in partially encircling these armoured forces. Now, under command of General Nehring, they had to be withdrawn westwards, fighting their way back and out of the Russian's mobile encirclement as they did so; this most difficult manœuvre was successfully carried out thanks to the stalwart behaviour of the troops, a highly creditable performance. A number of infantry formations became involved in this mobile encirclement battle and slowed down our armoured forces. But despite this hindrance, and thanks to the comradely assistance that was so freely given by all involved, the battle reached a successful conclusion.

On January 13th the Russian forces that had broken through west of Baranov advanced towards Kielce and from there swung northwards. The Russian Third and Fourth Guards Tank Armies now made their appearance. The total enemy force committed in this sector amounted by this time to 32 rifle divisions and 8 tank corps. This was the greatest concentration of force in the narrowest area that had been seen since the beginning of the war.

South of the Vistula there were indications that an attack would soon be launched in the Jaslo area. At Pulavy and Magnuszev the enemy's preparations were complete and the mine-fields were being lifted.

In East Prussia the major attack began, as expected, in the sector Ebenrode–Schlossberg. From twelve to fifteen rifle divisions with a proportionate number of tank units moved forward. Here too the enemy succeeded in penetrating our defences.

On this day Hitler's offensive in Alsace finally broke down.

On January 14th it became clear that the Russian intention was to thrust forward into the industrial area of Upper Silesia: this did not surprise us. Further strong forces were moving out of the Baranov bridgehead in a north-westerly or northerly direction, with the obvious purpose of establishing contact with other enemy columns pushing out from the Pulavy and Magnuszev bridgeheads. The German defence had indeed succeeded in throwing back the first Russian attacks from these

Sketch Map 3.3
The Catastrophe
in January 1945.

Heydekrug
5 Inf. Divs.
Memel
Tilsit
Kovno
Stolp
Gdynia
Danzig
Königsberg
Insterburg
54 Inf. Divs.
2 Tank Corps
9 Tank Units
Dirschau
Bartenstein
Sudauen
Elbing
Lötzen
Grodno
Konitz
Allenstein
Lyck
Augustov
Osterode
Disengagements
Bobr.
Dr. Eylau
Ortelsburg
Graudenz
Kulm
Helze
Bromberg
Thorn
Narero
Hohensalza
Leslau
Schröttersburg
Vistula
54 Inf. Divs.
6 Tank Corps
1 Cav. C.
9 Tank Units
Bug
Gnesen
Warsaw
Praga
Brest Litovsk
Posen
Kutno
31 Inf. Divs.
5 Tank Corps
3 Tank Units
Kalisz
Lodz
Magnuszev
Piotrkow
Radom
Pulavy
Warthe
Lublin
11 Inf. Divs.
1 Tank Corps
1 Cav. C.
Breslau
Kielce
Opatov
Situation 12.1.45
Oder
Brieg
Baranov
42 Inf. Divs.
6 Tank Corps
4 Tank Units
25.1.45
Oppeln
Neisse
18 Inf. Units
2 Tank Corps
1 Cav. C.
2 Tank Units
Beuthen
Ratibor
Cracow
Vistula
Plesso
Jaslo
SAN
Mahrisch-
Ostrau
Neu-
Sandec
Carpathian Mountains
Neumarkt
Disengagements
High Tatra

bridgeheads; nevertheless the general situation made it unlikely that this sector of the front could be held.

Russian preparations on the Rominten Heath and near Goldap pointed to a probable extension of the attack in East Prussia.

On January 15th it became clear that the enemy forces in the Cracow area were making their main thrust towards a line Czestochowa–Kattowice. Another strong force was heading for Kielce. It was to be assumed that from there they would continue towards Piotrkow–Tomaszow in order to join with the forces coming from the Pulavy bridgehead. These latter seemed to consist of two rifle armies and one tank army. The attack from the Magnuszev bridgehead was clearly aimed at Warsaw.

South of Cracow the Russian attack in the Jaslo area began.

In Army Group Centre's sector the enemy made deep penetrations in the Vistula–Bug triangle and on either side of Ostenburg. These attacks were aimed at Nasielsk and, westwards, towards Zichenau–Praschnitz. The situation opposite the Russians' Narev bridgeheads and in East Prussia grew more critical.

In Army Group South-East's sector it was confirmed that the Thirty-seventh Russian Army, south of the Danube, had been relieved by Bulgarian forces. The transfer of these Russian troops to Army Group South's front with an offensive purpose must now be reckoned on.

Needless to say, from the beginning of the great Russian offensive I had kept Hitler fully and frankly informed by telephone of the grave developments taking place, and had urgently requested that he return at once to Berlin and thus at least demonstrate that our main defensive effort was now in the East. His replies during the first few days consisted merely of a constant repetition of the instructions he had given me on January 9th: 'The Eastern Front must make do with what it's got. What's more, you must yourself see that the troops transferred from the West arrived too late.' The roundabout channel of communication and command from Zossen to Ziegenberg repeatedly held up the taking of necessary measures at a time when the greatest possible expedition was vitally necessary. On January 15th Hitler interfered for the first time in the defensive battle, by issuing an order, despite my protests, for the transfer of the *Gross-Deutschland* Corps from East Prussia to Kielce where it was to block the break-through that the Russians were threatening to make towards Posen. It is obvious that this move could not have been made in time to stop the Russians and would have involved a weakening of East Prussia at the very moment when the enemy's attack there was about to become highly dangerous. If the corps was taken away the same disastrous situation must develop in East Prussia that already existed along the Vistula. So this powerful striking force—consisting of the Panzergrenadier Division *Gross-Deutschland* and the Luftwaffe Panzer Parachute Division *Hermann Goering*, commanded by the Panzer Corps *Gross-Deutschland*, and led by the trusted General von Saucken—sat in railway sidings while its destination was the subject of argument. My refusal to carry out this order infuriated Hitler. He would not rescind it and now finally decided to leave his camp in the forests of Hesse and his skirmishes in the Vosges and to return to Berlin and the decisive front. Now at least I should be face to face with him and should be able to tell him those things which he had to be told but which could only partially be said over the telephone. And this was clearly not a question of a pleasant conversation. Hitler was well aware of this, which was why he postponed seeing me for as long as he possibly could.

Saucken's Corps had to unload in an area that was being shelled by the Russians. It fought a hard battle and finally succeeded in establishing contact with General Nehring's XXIV Panzer Corps.

Hitler appeared in Berlin on January 16th. On that same day I had a conference with him in the already partly bombed Chancellery, which was where he now established his Supreme Headquarters.

Hitler had finally decided that the Western Front must go over to the defensive so that forces could be made available for transfer to the East. As soon as I entered I learned of this apparently highly satisfactory, if very belated, decision. I had prepared a plan for the use of the forces that would thus become available; this involved their immediate transfer to, or if time allowed across, the Oder with the purpose of attacking the flanks of the Russian spearhead and thus decreasing its offensive momentum. When I now asked Jodl what Hitler had ordered he informed me that the Führer had issued instructions for the transfer of the mass of the forces being made available, that is to say the Sixth Panzer Army, to Hungary. On hearing this I lost my self-control and expressed my disgust to Jodl in very plain terms, but could get no reaction from him whatever beyond a shrug of the shoulders. I have never discovered whether he had advised or otherwise encouraged Hitler to take this decision. During the ensuing conference with Hitler I expressed my views and my disagreement with the proposed course of action. Hitler could not accept my opinions and reaffirmed his intention to attack in Hungary, to throw the Russians back across the Danube and to relieve Budapest. An argument that was to last for several days now began on the subject of this ill-begotten plan. After I had disposed of the military reasons that he advanced he produced economic ones: since the bombing of the German synthetic oil plants, our retention of the Hungarian oilfields and refineries became essential to us and

assumed a decisive importance for the outcome of the war. 'If you don't
get any more fuel your tanks won't be able to move and the aeroplanes
won't be able to fly. You must see that. But my generals know nothing
about the economic aspects of the war.' He was completely infatuated
with this idea and it was impossible to persuade him that it was
incorrect.

So the troops we were to receive from the West were to be split up
into two groups. When I tried to revert to this point at the conference
that now took place, he interrupted me: 'I know what you're going to
say about how I should strike one hard blow and not fiddle around, but
you must understand that . . .' and so on and so forth as above.

The transport of the troops to Hungary took far longer, on account
of the limited capacity of the railways to the south-east, than did the
transports to the Berlin area, where many stretches of double track
road were available and where in case of the unavoidable destruction
caused by the enemy air forces numerous alternative by-passes had
been built.

Once this stormy scene was over other problems arose. Disagreement
was violent. First of all there was the matter of the major defensive line
and its idiotic siting; it was now that he was forced to admit, by the
stenographer's record, that he was himself to blame for this. Next came
the question of the location of reserves, which he thought to have been
too far back from the front, while the generals held exactly contrary
views and blamed Hitler for having insisted that they be too far forward.
We then discussed Harpe's leadership, which in my opinion could not
have been better. But, since a scapegoat had to be found, Hitler insisted,
despite my liveliest remonstrances, on Harpe's dismissal and his replacement by Colonel-General Schörner, who was therefore summoned from
Courland where there were no more laurels to be won. Schörner began
his new job by dismissing the brave, capable, and upright commander
of the Ninth Army, General Freiherr Smilo von Lüttwitz. This command was now given to General Busse. Schörner also had a violent
argument with the outstanding General von Saucken which necessitated
the latter's rapid transfer to another sector. Saucken was given command of an army. I also arranged matters so that Harpe was given
command of an army in the West a few weeks later: I had similarly
arranged for the re-employment of Balck when that officer had been
the victim of an intrigue by Himmler in the West.

This argumentative day did produce one positive result in that my
opinions concerning operations in the West were finally, if very
belatedly, accepted: the pointless offensives were to be discontinued
and all forces that could possibly be spared transferred to the East.
The matter of Courland and the evacuation of the troops there engaged

was discussed yet again, but once more no clear decision was taken. It was, however, agreed that the 4th Panzer Division be withdrawn.

The military situation called more than ever for immediate energetic action. To the south-east of Sarajevo the Yugoslav partisan divisions were exercising increased pressure on Army Group E. The enemy was being reinforced between Lake Balaton and the Danube. The Russian bridgehead across the Gran was growing stronger. They were pursuing the retiring Army Group A with uncommon speed. The Russians had crossed a line Slomniki–Miechow in a westerly direction and part of this force was turning towards Cracow. Farther north they were attacking towards Czestochowa–Radomsko–Piotrokow–Tomaszow. A continuation of their attack towards Lodz–Lowicz–Sochaczew must be reckoned on. Strong reserve forces were following up behind the groups that had broken through; part of these reserves had come from the Carelian and Finnish fronts. We were now reaping the disadvantages of our allies' defections. In Army Group Centre's sector the threatened deterioration of the situation took place. Some thirty to forty Russian rifle divisions attacked towards Przasnysz–Szczytno–Plonen, while other forces were moving up behind them through Bialystock and Ostrov. It was the same story in the Rominten Heath sector and in the areas of Schlossberg and Gumbinnen.

Despite all these ominous portents Hitler refused to allow the transfer of troops from the Western Front to northern Germany or the evacuation of Courland.

By January 17th fifteen Russian tank corps had been identified opposite Army Group A and their intended main axis of advance established beyond a doubt. A further eight tank corps were engaged against Army Group South and three more against Army Group Centre. The main Russian forces were now advancing westwards towards a line running Cracow–Wartenau–Czestochowa–Radomsko. In the Kielce area they were still being resisted by General Nehring's XXIV Panzer Corps. Strong enemy forces were advancing on Warsaw, while others were pouring through Lowicz and Sochaczew towards the Vistula with the intention of preventing XLVI Panzer Corps, which was withdrawing from the Warsaw area, from crossing that river. This corps was supposed to move to a position south of the Vistula where it could block an immediate Russian break-through to Posen by way of Hohensalza–Gnesen; such a break-through would mean the cutting off of East and West Prussia from the rest of Germany. Unfortunately the corps, in spite of its orders, allowed itself to be thrown across to the north bank by heavy enemy pressure. The enemy forces now poured westwards against no opposition, towards the German frontier.

On Army Group Centre's front the speed and weight of the Russian attack towards Szczytno–Przasnysz was intensified while there was evidence that the battle was about to be joined along the hitherto quiet Narev front.

In the late afternoon officers of the Operations Department informed me of the constantly deteriorating situation on the Warsaw front and proposed the establishment of a new defensive line on the premise that Warsaw was already in enemy hands. When I asked the reason for this, the head of that department, Colonel von Bonin, told me that according to the latest information received the loss of Warsaw was inevitable if it had not, indeed, already taken place. Signal communications with the fortress were broken. In view of this I approved the suggestion made and, since the rapid issue of the necessary orders was of prime importance, gave instructions that the army group be immediately informed accordingly. I then went to confer with Hitler at the Chancellery in Berlin. While briefing him on the situation and the orders that I had given for its stabilisation, a wireless message was brought in. This was from the commandant of the Warsaw fortress and stated that the city was still in German hands but would have to be evacuated in the course of the coming night. I informed Hitler of these facts, and he at once lost his temper and ordered that Warsaw be held at all costs. He insisted on the immediate despatch of orders to that effect and angrily refused to listen to my belief that they would come too late. The garrison of Warsaw, which according to my original intentions should have been a fortress division, now consisted—owing to the previously mentioned transfers to the Western Front—of only four fortress infantry battalions, of limited combat ability, and a few artillery and engineer units. They could not possibly have held the city and would certainly have been taken prisoner if the commandant had obeyed Hitler's orders. He therefore decided to withdraw his weak garrison, even though he received those orders before beginning to do so. Now Hitler's rage knew no bounds. He completely lost all comprehension of, and interest in, the frightful general situation and thought of nothing save the misfortune of losing Warsaw, which after all was in fact only of comparatively minor importance. The next few days he devoted to studying the loss of Warsaw and to punishing the General Staff for what he regarded as its failure.

On January 18th the German troops in Hungary attacked between Lake Balaton and the Bakony forest, the wooded and mountainous terrain west of Budapest, in a renewed attempt to relieve that city. They were initially successful and reached the bank of the Danube. But on the same day the Russians fought their way into the unfortunate town, whose fate was therefore now sealed. The efforts made in Hungary would have proved considerably more effective if carried out on Polish territory or in East Prussia, but this Hitler refused to see. In Poland the Russians were fighting in the Czestochowa–Radomsk area, and at Piotrkow, Lodz and Kutno. A weaker force was attacking the German bridgehead over the Vistula at Hohenburg. North of the Vistula the enemy was advancing on Leslau–Soldau and attacking towards Ortelsburg–Neidenburg. On the Narev front there were increased indications that a major offensive was about to be launched. As usual Hitler refused to permit the withdrawal of the troops now isolated in this sector, even though the Russian attack farther north had by this time reached the Inster west of Schlossberg.

The whole of our briefing conference on this day was devoted to the Warsaw business mentioned above, despite the fact that the violent developments at the front had made this of merely academic interest. During our afternoon meeting Hitler told me to arrange that the General Staff Corps officers responsible for issuing the reports and signals connected with the withdrawal from Warsaw be held for interrogation. I made it quite clear to him that I alone was responsible for the events of the previous day and therefore it was I whom he must arrest and have interrogated, and not my subordinates. He replied: 'No. It's not you I'm after but the General Staff. It is intolerable to me that a group of intellectuals should presume to press their views on their superiors. But such is the General Staff system and that system I intend to smash.' A long and angry argument ensued between us in which I was all the more outspoken since for once I was alone with him. It was useless. That night I sent General Wenck to the 'evening briefing,' with instructions to point out to Hitler once again that he was about to commit an injustice, that I was prepared to be arrested myself, but that I would not allow my subordinates to be interfered with. Wenck did as I asked him. However, that same night Colonel von Bonin and Lieutenant-Colonels von dem Knesebeck and von Christen were arrested. General Meisel, of the Army Personnel Office, performed this task under cover of machine pistols. I was not even informed and therefore unfortunately could not intervene. The next day I was simply confronted with a *fait accompli*. I therefore went alone to see Hitler and in the strongest words at my disposal protested against the arrest of my utterly guiltless colleagues; I also pointed out that in consequence of this action the work of the most vital section of the *OKH* must be interrupted at a highly critical stage of the war. Completely inexperienced young officers must now suddenly be put in to replace the arrested men and must be entrusted with preparing the groundwork for the most important decisions, and with drawing up the most complicated orders that had perhaps ever fallen to the lot of German officers. I requested than an inquiry into my own behaviour be ordered, and this request was granted. During these tense and fateful days I was interrogated for hours on end by Messrs. Kaltenbrunner and Müller, who have already been mentioned in connection with the trials after July 20th: these interrogations squandered not only my time but also my nervous energy and my ability to work, and meanwhile on the Eastern Front a battle for life or death was being fought involving our very homeland and the existence of our German nation. The interrogation by Kaltenbrunner had at least one positive result in that it involved the release, after a few weeks, of Knesebeck and Christen, though not of Bonin. But they were not to return to General Staff duties, being instead given the command of regiments at the front. On the third day of his new assignment the brave, clever, and amiable Knesebeck was killed at his headquarters—after having attempted once again to intervene on behalf of his friend and superior, Bonin. Christen luckily did not lose his life. Bonin, for no reason and for no offence, was shipped from one concentration camp to another until at last, in the general collapse, he was privileged to exchange Hitlerian for American captivity. We met again in prison.

While I was both angered and hurt by the insults offered me on January 19th, and while my time was being wasted in interrogations by Kaltenbrunner and Müller, the bitter battles for Eastern Germany went on without pause. The Russians in Hungary were rapidly assembling mobile troops for the purpose of counter-attacking our force that was attempting to relieve Budapest. An intercepted Russian wireless signal from that front read: 'With such means he will achieve nothing. A mass of all arms and a wall of troops is waiting for him.' So we must be ready for strong enemy counter-measures. North of the Carpathians the Russians continued to push forward towards Breslau and the industrial area of Upper Silesia. In view of the weakness of our defence developments were likely to be very rapid there. Farther to the north the enemy was moving on Kalisz, Posen and Bromberg. Lodz fell. The enemy was now faced with almost no opposition. Only the XXIV Panzer Corps and the Panzer Corps *Gross-Deutschland*, engaged in mobile encirclement battles, continued steadfastly and valiantly to fight their way westwards, picking up numerous smaller units on the way. Generals Nehring and von Saucken performed feats of military virtuosity during these days that only the pen of a new Xenophon could adequately describe.

In the Mielau–Soldau district the Russians began to advance on Deutsch-Eylau. Farther south they were approaching Thorn–Graudenz. To the north-east they were attacking the Neidenburg–Willenberg line. South of Memel yet another critical situation was developing. Army

Group North, in Courland, reported enemy movements; this report did not give any clear indication of what the Russians' intentions in this sector were likely to be. The only certainty was that our forces in Courland would not be available for the defence of the homeland against the coming assault, and that the enemy formations which were tied up in the north in no way compensated for the absence of our own troops from the principal front. Hardly a conference went by without my urging Hitler that he at last agree to a speedy withdrawal of Army Group North: it was always in vain.

On January 20th the enemy set foot on German soil. This was the beginning of the last act. Early that morning I learned that the Russians had reached the German frontier at a point east of Hohensalza. My wife left Deipenhof in the Warthegau a half-hour before the first shells began to fall. She had had to stay until the last possible moment since her earlier departure would have been the signal for the civilian population to flee. She was under constant supervision by the Party. She had finally to leave behind such of our possessions as had escaped destruction when our Berlin home was bombed in September 1943. Now, like so many millions of other Germans, we were exiles, banished from our homes, and we are proud to have shared their fate. We shall know how to bear our lot. As she left Deipenhof the workers on the estate stood in tears beside her car and many would willingly have accompanied her. My wife had won the affections of those people and for her, too, the departure was hard. On January 21st she arrived at Zossen, where for lack of other accommodation she shared my quarters; henceforth she was also to share my difficult destiny, and to be at all times my help and my support.

On January 20th the battles west of Budapest had continued indecisively. Vörös, the former Chief of the Hungarian General Staff, was with the Russians. In Silesia the enemy crossed the frontier and continued his rapid advance towards Breslau. In the Posen area, as already stated, the frontier was also crossed. North of the Vistula powerful enemy forces were attacking the Thorn–Graudenz line. Very strong reserves were moving up behind the enemy troops along the main line of advance; these were dispositions of which we had never again been capable since the French campaign of 1940. South of Memel the enemy reached a line Wehlau–Labiau and continued in the general direction of Koenigsberg. Army Group Centre was in danger of being doubly encircled by two huge pincers, of which the southern one was moving north towards Koenigsberg, while the other, following the course of the Memel, was approaching the East Prussian capital from the east. On the Narev, opposite Fourth Army, the Russians were prepared to wait quietly, in the certainty of success on the fronts where they had broken through.

January 21st was marked by extensive enemy penetrations into the industrial area of Upper Silesia, advances towards Gnesen–Posen and Bromberg–Thorn, while forward elements reached Schneidemühl, and others attacked towards Riesenburg–Allenstein. When Hitler once again refused Reinhardt's urgent request that Fourth Army be withdrawn from the Narev salient, both Reinhardt and Fourth Army's commander, General Hossbach, were understandably in despair. The latter general, in view of the threatening encirclement of his whole army, took a correspondingly desperate decision on January 22nd. He ordered his army to turn about and to attack in a westerly direction, with the intention of breaking through to West Prussia and the Vistula. There he hoped to establish contact with Colonel-General Weiss's Second Army.

Hossbach did not inform his army group of this independent decision of his until the initial moves had begun on January 23rd. The *OKH* and Hitler were simply not told at all. The first we heard was that the fortress of Lötzen, the strongest of the bulwarks covering East Prussia, had been lost without a fight. It is little wonder that this news of the loss of our best armed, best built and best garrisoned fortress was like a bombshell to us and that Hitler completely lost all self-control. This happened on January 24th. Simultaneously the Russians broke through on the Masuren Canal, farther to the north, and attacked the north flank of Hossbach's army with the result that his disengaging movement could not now be carried out according to plan. On January 26th Hitler realised that in Army Group Centre's area something was going on of which he not only did not approve but of which he had not even been informed. He decided that he had been deceived and he reacted accordingly. He burst out in uncontrollable rage against Reinhardt and Hossbach: 'They're both in the same racket with Seydlitz! This is treason! They deserve to be court-martialled. They are to be dismissed immediately, along with their staffs, because the staff officers knew what was going on and failed to report it.' I attempted to calm the infuriated man, who had lost all pretence at self-control, saying: 'As far as Colonel-General Reinhardt is concerned I'm prepared to offer my right arm as surety for him. He has frequently enough told you personally what the situation of his army group was. I also regard it as unthinkable that Hossbach should have any contact with the enemy. The contrary is clearly the case.' But at that time any attempt to excuse or to explain was merely pouring oil on the flames. The fire continued to rage and was not damped down until Hitler and Burgdorf had decided who were to succeed the two generals. Colonel-General

Rendulic was appointed to command the army group; he had only recently been sent to Courland as Schörner's successor there, and was an Austrian, clever and subtle, who knew how to handle Hitler. Hitler had such faith in him that he now entrusted him with the desperate task of defending East Prussia. General Friedrich-Wilhelm Müller was appointed to succeed Hossbach; he had proved himself a most capable officer at the front but had never previously held a higher command.

Reinhardt himself had been seriously wounded in the head on January 25th. On January 29th we met and discussed recent events. I did not at that time receive a clear explanation of Hossbach's actions.

So events continued to run their tragic course in East Prussia where our defensive forces were facing total collapse, while Hitler's distrust of his generals, already profound, was further deepened. Meanwhile on the rest of the Eastern Front the retreat continued amidst heavy fighting.

On the Budapest front the Germans recaptured Stuhlweissenburg, but we knew that our forces were insufficient to win a decisive victory there, and unfortunately the Russians knew this too. In Upper Silesia the enemy was advancing on Tarnowitz. He was pressing on towards the line Cosel–Oppeln–Brieg, with the intention of cutting off the industrial area and winning bridgeheads over the Oder. Strong forces were moving on Breslau and on the Oder between that town and Glogau. He made further progress towards Posen and in East Prussia; his pincer movements to cut off that province continued. The Russians were making their main effort through the line Deutsch-Eylau–Allenstein, in the direction of Koenigsberg. In Courland all was still quiet.

On January 23rd there was fighting between Peiskretscham and Grossstrehlitz; the enemy's intention to cross the Oder between Oppeln and Ohlau now became plain. There were attacks on Ostrow and Krotoszyn and hostile tanks reached Ravica. The area Gnesen–Posen–Nakel was in enemy hands. There was fighting around Posen. In East Prussia the Russians continued to advance towards Bartenstein. By order of Reinhardt the Tannenberg Memorial was blown up after the removal of the sarcophagi containing the remains of Hindenburg and of his wife.

In Courland the Russians attacked Libau.

On January 23rd the new liaison man from the Foreign Ministry, Ambassador Dr. Paul Barandon, came to see me. Despite repeated requests on my part, his predecessor had never once called on me since I had taken up my post in July 1944. He apparently had not thought it necessary that the Foreign Ministry be kept informed of the situation

at the front. I described that situation now to Dr. Barandon in undisguised terms. We discussed together the possibility of the Foreign
Ministry coming somehow to our assistance, for we were agreed that
the time was ripe for such a move. We wished that the very limited
diplomatic relations still possessed by the Foreign Ministry be employed
to arrange an armistice, at least on one front. We hoped that our
Western adversaries might perhaps realise the dangers inherent in a
rapid Russian advance into, or even through, Germany, and might
therefore be willing either to sign an armistice or at least to make an
unofficial agreement which would enable us to defend Eastern Germany
with what remained of our forces in exchange for our surrender of
Western Germany. It is true that this was a very slender hope. But a
drowning man will clutch at any straw. We wished to leave no course
untried which might stop the bloodshed and save Germany and all
Western Europe from the terrible fate which threatened us all. We
therefore agreed that Dr. Barandon should arrange that I have a
private interview with the Foreign Minister, von Ribbentrop. He was
the Führer's principal political adviser and I therefore wished to
describe the situation to him as frankly and as fully as I had just done
to Barandon; I intended then to propose to him that we approach
Hitler together for the purpose of arranging the complete employment
of the slender diplomatic resources still available to a now isolated
Germany. That these resources were neither promising nor likely to be
particularly effective we well knew, but that did not lessen our determination to do our duty, and our duty was to take all possible steps to
bring the war to an end. Dr. Barandon immediately went to see Herr
von Ribbentrop and arranged that I should meet him on January 25th.

The disasters on the Eastern Front continued to spread. In Hungary
the enemy's measures for attacking our penetration began to be felt.
In Silesia he reached Gleiwitz. Between Cosel and Brieg, as between
Dyherrnfurth and Glogau, he was clearly making ready to cross the
Oder. Breslau was attacked frontally, but the fortress held out, as did
Glogau and Posen. In East Prussia the Russians were striving to break
through to Elbing.

On January 25th Russian preparations for a counter-attack south of
Lake Velencze became increasingly evident. North of the Danube as
well, it was plain that they were about to launch an attack against
General Kreysing's Eighth Army in the Leva–Ipolysac–Blauenstein
area. In Upper Silesia preparations for an assault on the industrial area
continued. The enemy reached the Oder.
After encircling Posen the Russians by-passed that fortress and

headed for the Oder–Warthe bend, which was supposed to be covered by a defensive line; but this line, carefully built before the war, had been robbed of its installations, which had been sent west to the Atlantic Wall, so that now it was only the shell of a fortified line. The Russians were massing in the area Schneidemühl–Bromberg, with the intention of advancing north along the west bank of the Vistula and thus rolling up the troops defending that river line from the rear.

In order to anticipate this danger I had requested Hitler that a new army group be formed to control the area between the old Army Group A (which had been re-designated Army Group Centre on January 25th) and the old Army Group Centre (now called Army Group North). This new army group would take control and reorganise the defence on this sector of the front. I spoke to Colonel-General Jodl concerning the choice of a general and staff to command this new army group, which would be occupying the most vital sector of all. I proposed that one of the two army group staffs in the Balkans be given this assignment and expressed my preference for that of Field-Marshal Freiherr von Weichs. I knew that gentleman very well, and had a high opinion of him both as a man and as a soldier. He was as clever as he was upstanding and valiant and he was the man to master so difficult a situation if anyone could still do so. Jodl agreed to support my proposal during the conference with Hitler. So I felt that the matter was decided. When, on January 24th, I made the suggestion to Hitler, he replied: 'Field-Marshal von Weichs seems to me to be a tired man. I doubt if he's still capable of performing such a task.' I defended my choice in a most lively manner, adding that Jodl was of my opinion. But I was to be disappointed, for Jodl unfortunately dropped a sneering remark about the Field-Marshal's deep and genuine religious sense, with the result that Hitler immediately refused to sanction his appointment. Instead, he ordered that Himmler be given command of the new army group. This preposterous suggestion appalled me and I used such argumentative powers as I possessed in an attempt to stop such an idiocy being perpetrated on the unfortunate Eastern Front. It was all in vain. Hitler maintained that Himmler had given a very good account of himself on the Upper Rhine. He also controlled the Training Army and therefore had a source of reinforcements immediately to hand, so that he, more than anyone else, was in a position to find both men and material for recreating a front. Even my modest attempt at least to provide the National SS Leader with the experienced staff of Army Group von Weichs was a failure. On the contrary, Hitler ordered that Himmler assemble his own staff. He chose the very brave SS Brigade-Leader Lammerding as his chief of staff; this man, who had previously commanded a panzer division, was totally ignorant of the very considerable general staff duties that his post as chief of an unformed army group staff involved. The limited help I was able to give, by assigning General Staff Corps officers to the new headquarters, was far from sufficient to compensate for the basic lack of knowledge of the commander and his chief. For organising the defence Himmler now picked a number of SS leaders who for the most part were uniformly incapable of performing their allotted tasks. Only after very bitter experiences, damaging to our cause as a whole, did the arrogant Himmler finally agree to listen to me.

On January 25th I met the German Foreign Minister in his newly built and splendid official residence on the Wilhelmstrasse. I did not mince my words with Herr von Ribbentrop. Apparently he had not realised the gravity of the situation and he asked, anxiously, if what I had told him was the exact truth: 'The General Staff seems to me to be losing its nerve.' As a matter of fact a man needed an almost cast-iron nervous system to carry out these exploratory conversations with the requisite calm and clear consideration. After my detailed exposition I asked the 'architect of Germany's foreign policy' if he was ready to accompany me to see Hitler and to propose to him that we attempt to secure an armistice at least on one front. I was thinking primarily of an armistice in the West. Herr von Ribbentrop replied in these words: 'I can't do it. I am a loyal follower of the Führer. I know for a fact that he does not wish to open any diplomatic negotiations with the enemy, and I therefore cannot address him in the manner you propose.' I then asked: 'How would you feel if in three or four weeks time the Russians were to be at the gates of Berlin?' With every mark of horror Ribbentrop cried: 'Do you believe that that is even possible?' When I assured him that it was not only possible but, as a result of our actual leadership, certain, for a moment he lost his composure. Yet when I repeated my request that he accompany me to see Hitler he did not dare agree. All I managed to get out of him was a remark made just as I was leaving: 'Listen, we will keep this conversation to ourselves, won't we?' I assured him that I should do so.

When I appeared at Hitler's briefing that night, I found him in a state of great agitation. I must have been a little late, for as I entered the conference room I could already hear him talking in a loud and excited voice. He was insisting that his *Basic Order No. 1*—by which no one was allowed to discuss his work with any man who did not need such knowledge for his own official duties—be exactly obeyed. When he saw me he went on in an even louder voice: 'So when the Chief of the General Staff goes to see the Foreign Minister and informs him of the situation in the East with the object of securing an armistice in the West, he is doing neither more nor less than committing high treason!' Thus I knew that Ribbentrop had not kept silence. So much the better. Now Hitler at least knew what the real picture was. As it happened he refused adamantly to discuss the proposal I had made to Ribbentrop. He ranted on for a while until he realised that his words were making not the slightest impression on me. It was only when I was in prison that I learned what had happened: immediately after my departure the Foreign Minister had prepared a report on the conversation we had had, which he forwarded to Hitler. He did this, it is true, without mentioning my name, but then that was scarcely necessary.

So my attempt to work with the Foreign Minister in an attempt to arrange an armistice on at least one front was a failure. It may be argued against such an attempt that at that time the Western Powers were hardly in a mood to take part in any such negotiations, particularly since they had bound themselves by an agreement with the Russians only to deal with Germany collectively. All the same my opinion was that an attempt must be made to induce Hitler to take such a step. I was therefore determined not to be discouraged by Herr von Ribbentrop's refusal to act, but to try the same plan through other channels. During the first week of February I approached one of the most important men in Germany with this end in view, but my proposal was turned down in exactly the same words as those which Ribbentrop had used. A third attempt I made in March will be described later.

By January 27th the Russian tidal wave was rapidly assuming, for us, the proportions of a complete disaster. South-west of Budapest they had gone over to the offensive once again. In the Hungarian capital street-battles against what was left of the German garrison continued. In the Upper Silesian industrial area the situation was growing more critical. Russian forces were advancing on the Moravian Gates, on Troppau, Moravska-Ostrava and Teschen. Developments in the Warthegau and East Prussia were particularly grim. Posen was encircled and one of its forts already lost. The enemy was moving on Schönlanke, Schloppe, Filehne, Schneidemühl and Usch. Nakel and Bromberg had been captured. He was moving forward west of the Vistula towards Schwetz. At Mewe he also crossed that river. In Marienburg a battle was fought for the beautiful old Ordensburg. Himmler had moved his headquarters to the Ordensburg Croessinsee. From there, and without the approval of the *OKH*, he ordered the evacuation of Thorn, Kulm, and Marienwerder. Hitler this time made no comment. By reason of this independent decision of Himmler's the Vistula line was lost without a fight. It was only a matter of days before the troops still east of that river must inevitably be cut off.

In East Prussia there was heavy fighting around Frauenburg, Elbing,

Karwinden, and Liebemühl. There was strong enemy pressure on
Friedland. There were attacks north of Koenigsberg. A crisis arose in
Samland. In Courland, on the other hand, the German troops achieved
defensive successes, but these were hardly sufficient reason for rejoicing.

On this day I ordered the transport of all recruits of the 1928 class
from the eastern to the western army areas, in order to prevent the commitment of these untrained young men in the battles then raging. I am
glad to say that this action of mine was successful. As early as the
autumn of 1944 I had protested, both verbally and in writing, against
the mobilisation of boys of sixteen.

At Himmler's headquarters the lack of organisation soon began to
make itself felt in that its signals service failed to function. I told Hitler
of this unsatisfactory state of affairs. But he took no interest in what I
had to say since he had just been informed by the chief of the Army
Personnel Office of the measures taken by Kings Frederick William I and
Frederick the Great when faced with insubordination. General Burgdorf
had consulted historical sources and now produced some crude examples
of legal sentences delivered two hundred years ago. When Hitler heard of
them he replied with deep satisfaction: 'And people are always imagining that I am brutal! It would be desirable if all the prominent men in
Germany were to be informed of these sentences.' This at least showed
that he was aware of his own brutality by now and was trying to justify
it by means of historical parallels. The appalling state in which we all
found ourselves was, to him, unimportant in comparison.

On the same day the transfer of Sixth Panzer Army to the East began.
As already stated, as soon as Hitler returned to Berlin he had ordered
that the Western Front go back on the defensive. He had brought with
him his own plan for the employment in the East of the forces that would
thus be freed. I now proposed to him that all available forces be
assembled in two groups east of Berlin, one in the Glogau–Kottbus
area, the other in Pomerania east of the Oder; these groups would thus
be in a position to attack the very advanced Russian spearheads at a time
when they were still weak and were receiving no supplies, as the Eastern
fortifications were still holding out behind them. But Hitler clung to his
original plan, which was not to use these forces to defend Germany and,
in particular, the German capital, but to employ them in an offensive
in Hungary. Jodl reckoned that the transfer of the first corps would
take fourteen days. Many weeks must pass before the whole movement
was completed. There could be no question of launching the proposed
offensive before early March. And how was Berlin to manage until
then?

The greater part of the industrial area of Upper Silesia was now in enemy hands. Further prolongation of the war could thus be only a matter of months. Speer, as long ago as December, had pointed out to Hitler in a written report how important was the preservation of this, our last, industrial area in view of the destruction of the Ruhr, but his advice was originally ignored in favour of offensive operations on the Western Front. Now this source of strength was lost to us as well. Speer composed a new memorandum which began unambiguously enough: 'The war is lost.' He gave it to me to read before submitting it to Hitler. Unfortunately there was no contradicting it. Hitler read the first sentence and then locked it away in his safe along with all the other warnings he had received. During these tragic days I was present on one occasion when, after the evening briefing, Speer requested that Hitler receive him. Hitler refused to see him, remarking: 'All he wants is to tell me again that the war is lost and that I should bring it to an end.' Speer refused to be fobbed off in this way and once again sent the adjutant in to Hitler with the memorandum. Hitler said to the young SS officer: 'Put the document in my safe.' Then he turned to me and said: 'Now you can understand why it is that I refuse to see anyone alone any more. Any man who asks to talk to me alone always does so because he has something unpleasant to say to me. I can't bear that.'

On January 28th the Russians crossed the Oder near Lüben and established a bridgehead. We were expecting them to continue their advance towards Sagan. Farther to the north they were pouring westwards from the Kreuz–Schneidemühl area towards the Oder between Frankfurt and Stettin, apparently to prepare a base for their later attack on Berlin. As he became increasingly aware of Germany's weakness the plans of the Russian who commanded the operation, Marshal Zhukov, grew ever bolder. The attack towards the Oder was carried out by the First and Second Guards Tank Armies and the Eighth Guards, Fifth Assault and Sixty-first Armies. Apart from this force the enemy still disposed of ample troops to attack in a northerly direction from the Nakel–Bromberg area behind the Germans defending the Vistula line. In East Prussia he was pushing along the coast north-east-wards, with the intention of severing Army Group North's sea communications. Farther east the encirclement of Koenigsberg was being gradually completed.

During the nightly briefings on January 29th Hitler referred once again to his frequently expressed desire that officers who, in his opinion, had not done their duty should be degraded. Tried and trusted officers at the front were, in the heat of the moment and without any proper inquiry being made, demoted by one or more ranks. I saw this happen to the commander of an anti-tank battalion, a man who had been

wounded seven times, who had won the Golden Decoration for
Wounds, and who had hurried back to the front after having barely
recovered from his last severe wound. His battalion had been put into
trains and moved along behind the Western Front, its destination being
frequently changed while it was repeatedly attacked by hostile aircraft.
The unit thus became split up and the battalion was as a result sent
into action piecemeal. Hitler ordered that the commander, a reserve
officer who had only been recently promoted from Major to Lieutenant-
Colonel as a reward for gallantry in the face of the enemy, be reduced
to Second Lieutenant. My chief of staff at the Inspectorate-General of
Armoured Troops, Thomale, was present on this occasion and both he
and I protested strongly. An important personage, who during the
whole course of the war had never once seen the front, thereupon
remarked drily: 'The Golden Decoration for Wounds means absolutely
nothing.' Thus nothing could be done. On the same day I brought up
the case of my former supply officer during the Russian campaign of
1941. This was an elderly lieutenant-colonel of the reserve, by the name
of Heckel. He had been denounced in his home town—he came from
the Linz area—and as a result had been transferred to a mortar battalion
with the rank of private and ordered to carry mortar shells about. In
the Nuremberg records I found some fragmentary remarks that I had
made at this time and which the stenographer had noted down and thus
preserved; I should like to quote them here as they are revelatory. 'In
this mortar battalion there is a lieutenant-colonel who was my supply
officer in Poland, France, and Russia, who was decorated and to whom
I myself gave the Iron Cross First Class. This man was denounced by
his compatriots in the Upper Danube area because of alleged remarks
which in fact he never made and which are anyhow supposed to date
from the period before the *anschluss*. As a result this upright, blameless
lieutenant-colonel, who had previously proved himself to be first class
at his job and without a stain on his character, was shipped off to a
mortar battalion at Wildflecken, where he has to lug mortar bombs
about and from where he has written me the most appalling letters I
have ever read. He writes: "I have lost my reputation without guilt,
without any proper investigation or inquiry, simply because some
filthy scoundrel saw fit to denounce me, and now I don't know what I
can do to help myself." So far as I know that man's character has not
yet been cleared.' The result of my intervention on his behalf was
unsatisfactory. I only quote the stenographer's record in order to show
the tone that a man then had to adopt in order to produce the slightest
effect on the calloused and brutalised mentalities at Supreme Headquarters. I often intervened on behalf of unfortunate individuals who
for some reason or other—usually a ridiculous one involving them in

disagreement with the Party functionaries—had suddenly found themselves incarcerated in a concentration camp or sent to a penal unit. Unfortunately it was only rarely that one even heard of such cases.

Apart from that, anxiety to be of help to individuals was often smothered by the appalling general situation and by an excess of worry and work. Even then a day was only twenty-four hours long. If I had to go twice a day to Supreme Headquarters—which was usually the case during this tense period—this involved two trips from Zossen to Berlin and back, that is to say a drive of forty-five minutes each way or three hours on the road per day. The conferences with Hitler never lasted less than two, and usually more than three, hours—a further six hours. Thus the briefings alone took up at this time eight or nine hours of my day, hours during which absolutely no useful work could be done. These briefings were simply chatter and a waste of time. Furthermore, since the assassination attempt Hitler had insisted that I be present throughout the whole of the meetings of the Armed Forces Command Staff and of the other staffs of the Armed Forces. In normal times this would have been a justifiable demand. My predecessor, towards the end of his time, had been in the habit of opening such conferences by discussing his business and then withdrawing from the room, and this had annoyed Hitler. This was why he ordered me to be present throughout. But at this period of overwork and overstrain it was a physical and spiritual agony to have to sit for hours on end listening to quite unimportant speeches—as for example those made by the representatives of the air force or the navy, two Services which by now scarcely functioned at all any more. Hitler's addiction to lengthy monologues did not decrease as the military situation became more and more acute. On the contrary, by means of interminable talk, he attempted to explain the reasons for the failure of the German Command, both to himself and to others, ascribing the guilt, of course, to innumerable circumstances and individuals though never, even remotely, to himself. On the days when I had to attend two conferences I would only arrive back at Zossen early on the following morning. It was often five a.m. before I could retire to my quarters for a short rest. At eight o'clock the day's work began with a conference of officers at the *OKH* and the reading of the day reports from the army groups. With brief intervals for the most essential meals, work went on without interruption until the car was ready to take me to the Chancellery. My return was often delayed by an air-raid warning, which always resulted in Hitler saying that he was frightened lest we be killed and therefore forbidding our departure. I therefore frequently sent my principal assistant, General Wenck, to deputise for me at the evening briefings so that I might win a little time for quiet thought or for catching up on my work at Zossen. Often, too, I attempted by my absence to show Hitler my disapproval of his violent outbursts against the corps of officers or even against the army as a whole. He invariably noticed this and for a day or two he would show better manners; but such improvements never lasted for long.

On January 30th the Russians launched a heavy attack against Second Panzer Army in the area south of Lake Balaton, in Hungary. On the Oder the Russians were assembling their forces in the Ohlau area, presumably with the intention of enlarging their bridgehead there. An increase in enemy strength was also reported from the Lüben bridgehead. South of the Warthe the enemy had made a successful operational break-through. North of the Warthe he was advancing westward and had captured the area Soldin–Arnswalde, so that he was directly threatening Stettin. He also attacked strongly south of Braunsberg, in the Wormditt area, north of Allenstein and south of Bartenstein; these attacks were doubtless intended to frustrate our own attack westward and to hit it in the rear. The fortress of Koenigsberg was cut off to the south and west.

On January 31st the Russians in Hungary attacked our front between the Danube and Lake Balaton. Preparations were evident for further attacks north of the Danube. In their bridgehead across the Oder they were obviously making ready for an advance on Sagan and Kottbus. They were continuing their advance on either side of the Warthe. Our defensive positions in the Oder–Warthe bend had scarcely been occupied and were hardly capable of being defended; the Russians broke through them. In Pomerania the German defence succeeded for the time being in denying the line Schloppe–Deutsch-Krone–Konitz to the enemy. In East Prussia he was exerting pressure on Heilsberg. In Courland he threatened to resume his attacks.

The appalling month of January had justified all our fears of what this new great Russian offensive would bring. The enemy's advance had been disproportionately fast as a result, first, of the incomprehensible conduct of operations on the Western Front by Hitler and the Armed Forces Command Staff, secondly, because of the resultant delay in troop movements from the Western to the Eastern Front, and thirdly, because of the appointment of a military ignoramus to command in the most difficult of all sectors, that of Army Group Vistula. The enemy had, for all intents and purposes, severed East and West Prussia from the rest of Germany and thus created two new isolated defensive localities which could only be supplied by sea or air and whose continued resistance was therefore only a matter of time. In order to supply the isolated parts of the army, the air force and the navy had largely to abandon combat operations. And their fighting ability was already sufficiently low without the imposition of this further burden. The Russians were gaining increased momentum as they became aware of our growing weakness. Their tank forces assumed bolder tactics. Hitler therefore ordered, on January 26th, 1945, the setting up of a tank-destroyer division. The very name of this new formation was remarkable and extraordinarily significant. But that was not the end of it. This division was to consist of bicycle companies, commanded by brave lieutenants; they were to be equipped with anti-tank grenades and were in this fashion to stop the T34's and the heavier Russian tanks. The division was to be committed company by company. It was too bad about the brave men involved.

During the early days of February the situation, both on the Eastern and on the Western Fronts, deteriorated.

In the East, despite all my plans for an immediate evacuation, Army Group Courland was still holding the northern tip of Courland with twenty infantry and two panzer divisions. These divisions consisted of good troops with considerable combat ability. Up to this time Hitler had only agreed to the withdrawal of four infantry divisions and one panzer division.

Army Group North had by this time been forced back into the narrow strip of Samland, into Koenigsberg, and into the territory south of the East Prussian capital called Ermland. Like Army Group Courland, this army group, too, had to be supplied by sea or air. Its nineteen infantry and five panzer divisions had suffered very heavy casualties. The army group also contained remnants of further divisions.

Army Group Vistula held a thin line running from the Vistula, between Graudenz and Elbing, through Deutsch-Krone to the Oder between Schwedt and Grünberg. It consisted of twenty-five infantry and eight panzer divisions.

Army Group Centre held a sector adjoining that of Army Group Vistula in Silesia and reaching to the Carpathian Mountains. The Russians had already secured bridgeheads over the Oder at points both north and south of Breslau. The industrial area of Upper Silesia was lost to us. This army group consisted of some twenty infantry and some eight and a half panzer divisions.

Finally Army Group South, between the Carpathians and the Drava, consisted of nineteen infantry and nine panzer divisions. It had the task, after the arrival of reinforcements from the West, of attacking on either side of Lake Balaton, with the objective of recapturing the right bank of the Danube. This would ensure the southern flank of the

Eastern Front and would enable Germany to retain the Hungarian oilfields.

In the West, since the failure of the Ardennes Offensive, the front had been pushed back to a line running along the Maas from Driel–the Waal–Arnhem–the Rhine–Cleves–the Maas again to Roermond–the Roer to Düren–the Schnee-Eifel–Our–Sauer–the Moselle from Piesport to Remich–the Saar to Saarguemines–Bitche–Haguenau–the Upper Rhine.

The SS divisions intended for the attack in Hungary were assembling in two rest areas, one around Bonn and Ahrweiler, the other centred on Wittlich and Traben–Trarbach; elements of certain divisions had not yet been withdrawn to these areas. All movement was very difficult and extremely slow. The enemy's air superiority held up transport and discouraged the commanders.

The Eastern Front now counted some one hundred and three weak infantry divisions and some thirty-two and a half equally weakened panzer and panzergrenadier divisions. Along the Western Front there were approximately sixty-five infantry and twelve panzer divisions, though of the latter four were being made ready for transfer to the East.

In view of this general situation I decided once again to urge Hitler that he postpone the offensive in Hungary and that instead he attack the Russian spearhead which had reached the Oder at a point between Frankfurt and Küstrin; the flanks of this spearhead were still vulnerable if attacked from a line Glogau–Guben in the south and Pyritz–Arnswalde in the north. I hoped by such an action to give increased protection to the capital and interior of Germany and to win time for armistice negotiations with the Western Powers.

The necessary preconditions for this operation were prompt evacuation of the Balkans, Italy, Norway, and particularly of Courland. In the early days of February, I visited the Japanese ambassador, Oshima, and then went on to see Hitler, to whom I explained my plan. He immediately turned down all my proposals concerning the evacuations mentioned above. I became more insistent and finally said to the stubborn man: 'You must believe me when I say it is not just pigheadedness on my part that makes me keep on proposing the evacuation of Courland. I can see no other way left to us of accumulating reserves, and without reserves we cannot hope to defend the capital. I assure you I am acting solely in Germany's interests.' Trembling all down the left side of his body, he jumped to his feet at this and shouted: 'How dare you speak to me like that? Don't you think I'm fighting for Germany? My whole life has been one long struggle for Germany.' And he proceeded to treat me to an outburst of unusual frenzy until Goering finally took me by the arm and led me into another room, where we soothed our nerves by drinking a cup of coffee together.

I next saw Grand-Admiral Dönitz and asked him, or rather begged him, to give me his support in this matter of evacuations when next I should raise it. Enough shipping space was available if the decision to abandon the heavy equipment was taken. But that Hitler had refused to sanction.

Hitler then summoned me back into the conference room, where I once again spoke up in favour of the evacuation of Courland. This caused a new outburst of rage on Hitler's part. He stood in front of me shaking his fists, so that my good chief of staff, Thomale, felt constrained to seize me by the skirt of my uniform jacket and pull me backwards lest I be the victim of a physical assault.

The result of this dramatic scene was not the withdrawal of the Courland troops to form a reserve, as I desired. My plan was abandoned save for a limited attack from the Arnswalde area with the object of defeating the Russians north of the Warthe, and of retaining Pomerania and our link with West Prussia. I had a hard struggle to ensure that even this limited operation was properly carried out. According to my calculations, which were supported by General Gehlen's intelligence of the enemy, the Russians could increase their forces on the Oder by about four divisions per day. If our attack was therefore to make any sense at all it must be launched with lightning speed, before further Russian troops had arrived and before they became aware of our intentions. The deciding conference on this operation took place at the Chancellery on February 13th. Apart from those who usually attended these conferences, there were also present the National Leader of the SS, Himmler, in his capacity of commander of Army Group Vistula, the SS Colonel-General Sepp Dietrich, commander of the Sixth Panzer Army, and my principal assistant, General Wenck. I had decided that for the duration of the operation Wenck should be attached to Himmler's headquarters and be in charge of the actual carrying out of the attack. I had also decided that it must be launched on February 15th, since if it were postponed beyond that date it would no longer be practicable. I was well aware that both Hitler and Himmler would oppose these decisions of mine, since they were both subconsciously frightened of undertaking an operation which must make plain Himmler's incompetence. Himmler expressed his belief to Hitler that the attack should be postponed, since a small portion of the ammunition and fuel had not yet been unloaded and issued to the troops. I, arguing against this, produced my reasons as given above. Hitler immediately, and strongly, disagreed with me.

I: 'We can't wait until the last can of petrol and the last shell have been issued. By that time the Russians will be too strong.'

HITLER: 'I don't permit you to accuse me of wanting to wait.'

I: 'I'm not accusing you of anything. I'm simply saying that there's no sense in waiting until the last lot of supplies have been issued and thus losing the favourable moment to attack.'

HITLER:'I just told you that I don't permit you to accuse me of wanting to wait.'

I: 'General Wenck must be attached to the National Leader's Staff, since otherwise there can be no prospect of the attack succeeding.'

HITLER: 'The National Leader is man enough to carry out the attack on his own.'

I: 'The National Leader has neither the requisite experience nor a sufficiently competent staff to control the attack single-handed. The presence of General Wenck is therefore essential.'

HITLER: 'I don't permit you to tell me that the National Leader is incapable of performing his duties.'

I: 'I must insist on the attachment of General Wenck to the army group staff so that he may ensure that the operations are competently carried out.'

And so it went on for two hours. His fists raised, his cheeks flushed with rage, his whole body trembling, the man stood there in front of me, beside himself with fury and having lost all self-control. After each outburst of rage Hitler would stride up and down the carpet edge, then suddenly stop immediately before me and hurl his next accusation in my face. He was almost screaming, his eyes seemed about to pop out of his head and the veins stood out on his temples. I had made up my mind that I should let nothing destroy my equanimity and that I would simply repeat my essential demands over and over again. This I did with icy consistency.

When Hitler turned his back on me and marched towards the fireplace, I glanced at Lenbach's portrait of Bismarck that hung above the mantel. The eyes of that mighty statesman, the Iron Chancellor, seemed to be grimly watching the performance taking place beneath him. From that dimly lit end of the conference hall a glint of steel from his cuirassier's helmet seemed to reach across to me, and his expression was of one who asks: 'What are you doing with my country?' And at my back I could almost feel the weight of Hindenburg's gaze, whose bronze bust stood at the opposite side of the room. His eyes, too, seemed to ask a question: 'What are you doing to Germany? What will become of my Prussians?' It was a frightening hallucination, and yet it served to fortify my resolve. I remained cold and immovable. No outburst of Hitler's remained unanswered. I wanted him to realise that I was in no way impressed by his ravings. He realised it.

Suddenly Hitler stopped short in front of Himmler and said: 'Well, Himmler, General Wenck will arrive at your headquarters tonight and will take charge of the attack.' He walked over to Wenck and told him that he was to report to the army group staff forthwith. Then he sat down in his usual place, called me over to him and said: 'Now please continue with the conference. The General Staff has won a battle this day.' And as he said this he smiled his most charming smile. This was the last battle that I was to win, and it came too late. I had never before taken part in such a scene. I had never seen Hitler rave so violently.

After this gloomy incident in the gigantic drama of our destruction was over I retired to the ante-room and seated myself at a small table. There Keitel found me and said: 'How could you contradict the Führer that way? Didn't you see how excited he was getting? What would happen if as the result of such a scene he were to have a stroke?' But I remained equally cold in my manner towards Keitel, and simply replied: 'A statesman must be prepared to be contradicted and to listen to the truth, for otherwise he is unworthy of the name.' Other persons of Hitler's entourage now took Keitel's side in the discussion and I had a further hard passage before those anxious and timorous spirits were calmed. I then arranged for my assistants to issue the necessary orders for the attack by telephone. There was no time to be lost. At any moment the authority I had so hardly won might be taken from me by a reversal of the newly made decisions. Later, men who had been present at this scene were to tell me that during years at Supreme Headquarters they had never known Hitler to erupt so violently; this outburst had put all his other ones in the shade by comparison.

On February 15th the Third Panzer Army, under Colonel-General Rauss, was ready to attack. Early on the 16th, under the personal supervision of General Wenck who knew exactly what my intentions were, the attack began. During the 16th and 17th good progress was made and we were already beginning to hope that it might succeed despite all our troubles and doubts and might win us the necessary time for taking further steps. But after Hitler's evening briefing on the 17th, Wenck, seeing that his driver was tired, himself took the wheel of his car; he was over-exhausted, fell asleep, and drove into the parapet of a bridge on the Berlin–Stettin highway. He was badly hurt and had to go to hospital. With his departure the attack bogged down and could never regain its initial momentum. Wenck was incapacitated for several weeks. He was replaced by General Krebs, who had recently been relieved of his appointment as chief of staff to Model in order that he might be given a command at the front.

I knew Krebs well from my old days with the Goslar Jaegers. He was a clever officer, with a good military education behind him, but he lacked experience as a commander since he had spent the whole war in various staff appointments. During his long career as a staff officer he had proved himself highly capable at staff work and had also shown a

great talent for being adaptable and accommodating, qualities which
hardly fitted him to stand up to a man like Hitler. Furthermore, he had
been a close friend of General Burgdorf, the head of the Army Personnel
Office, since the days when they had been at the War Academy together.
Burgdorf soon drew Krebs into the inner circle at Supreme Headquarters, the circle that revolved about Bormann and Fegelein, and
with them, too, Krebs soon struck up an intimate friendship. These
personal relationships finally deprived him of his freedom of action and
independence of thought in the grisly drama that was being played out
in the Chancellery. So long as we worked together these influences were
not apparent, since I usually represented the *OKH* personally. But after
my dismissal they became evident.

On the first occasion when he reported to Hitler, Krebs was awarded
the Oak Leaves to the Knight's Cross; this was an early indication of
Burgdorf's influence. A few days later Krebs and I went together to see
Hitler. We arrived there ahead of time and the other officers were not
yet present. Hitler therefore invited us into his small private study. He
pointed to Graff's portrait of Frederick the Great that hung above his
desk and said: 'When bad news threatens to crush my spirit I derive
fresh courage from the contemplation of this picture. Look at those
strong, blue eyes, that wide brow. What a head!' We then discussed
the great king's qualities as a statesman and a military leader. Hitler
admired him more than he did any other man and was only too eager to
emulate him. Unfortunately his abilities did not correspond to his desires.

At this time fell the seventieth birthday of the leader of the National
Labour Service, Hierl. He was an outstanding man, an ex-officer, who
had performed his duties in the Party with great conscientiousness and
in a thoroughly upright and honourable manner. Hitler decorated Hierl
with the German Order. He spent the evening of February 24th with
Dr. Goebbels. I was also invited to partake of the simple meal. Since I
was very fond of the leader of the National Labour Service, I accepted
the invitation. After dinner, as was by now habitual, the air-raid warning
sounded. We went down to the shelter where we found Frau Magda
Goebbels and her well-brought up and pleasant children, whose acquaintance I now made. While we waited there for the raid to be over I could
not help recalling the conversations I had had with Dr. Goebbels in
1943. Now here I was, in the midst of this little family, the happiness or
destruction of which was bound up with Hitler's fate. The thought
that their days were numbered was saddening and I did not feel like
talking. Dr. Goebbels' presentiment which he had expressed to me two
years before was to be exactly fulfilled in April. Poor woman, poor
innocent children!

At this period, too, the Head of the Hungarian State, Salaszy, paid us a visit. I was present when Hitler received him in the gloomy hall of the Chancellery, now stripped of all its decorations. The conversation was awkward. The new man did not give the impression of one from whom much might be expected. He seemed to have risen in the world almost against his will. We had no allies any more.

The Allied air offensive had brought ever-increasing devastation to Germany during the last few months. The armament industry had suffered heavily. The destruction of the synthetic oil plants was a particularly severe blow, since our fuel supplies were mainly based on those installations. On January 13th the synthetic oil plant at Pölitz, near Stettin, was bombed. On the next day the oil installations at Magdeburg, Derben, Ehmen, and Brunswick were bombed, together with the Leuna works·and the fuel plant at Mannheim, and on the 15th the benzol plants at Bochum and Recklinghausen. Also on the 14th the Heide oil plant in Schleswig-Holstein was destroyed. According to German figures this cost the Allies fifty-seven aircraft, but at the same time the Germans lost two hundred and thirty-six. The destruction of the greater part of our synthetic fuel industry meant that the German Command now had to make do with such supplies as came from the wells at Zistersdorf in Austria, and from around Lake Balaton in Hungary. This fact partially explains Hitler's otherwise incomprehensible decision to send the mass of the forces freed in the West to Hungary; he wanted to keep control of the remaining oil wells and refineries which were of vital importance both to the armoured force and to the air force.

On January 20th the Hungarians had signed an armistice with the Russians. One of the conditions of this document was that the Hungarians must make eight divisions available to the Russians for operations against Germany. In consequence the situation in that country was not only militarily but also politically extremely tense.

By the end of January the two corps of Generals Nehring and von Saucken had fought their way back through Kalisz. On February 1st the Russians reached the Oder near Küstrin; they had already penetrated into an area west of Kulm and of Elbing. On February 2nd Thorn fell. On February 3rd the enemy by-passed Schneidemühl, which was being bravely defended, and entered Outer Pomerania. On February 5th the Kurische Nehrung, a long and narrow tongue of land between the Baltic and the Bay of Courland, was lost. There was fighting around Posen, Frankfurt on Oder, and Küstrin. In Pomerania the Russians pushed forward between Pyritz and Deutsch-Krone.

On February 6th fighting began inside the town of Posen. Near

Küstrin the Russians won a bridgehead over the Oder. On February 8th their attacks at Pyritz and Arnswalde were repulsed but the battles in those areas continued for several days.

From February 10th the enemy began to attack west of the Vistula in the Schwetz and Graudenz areas. On February 12th Elbing was lost.

The Allies continued to attack the German oil plants as well as numerous towns. Berlin in particular now experienced the full fury of the air raids.

On February 13th we lost Schwetz on the Vistula, a great deal of territory in Pomerania and—on our extreme right wing in Hungary—the castle at Budapest. On February 15th Konitz, Schneidemühl and Tuchel fell, on the 16th Grünberg, Sommerfeld and Sorau. Breslau was encircled. On the 18th the same happened to Graudenz. On February 21st Dirschau fell.

On the other hand between February 17th and 22nd Army Group South managed to eliminate a Russian bridgehead across the Gran. This success was due to the intelligent leadership of the army group commander, General Wöhler, of whom Hitler remarked at the conference when his plan of attack was discussed: 'Wöhler is no National-Socialist, it's true, but at least he's a man!'

On February 24th we lost Posen and Arnswalde, on the 28th Schlochau, Hammerstein, Bublitz, and Baldenburg in Outer Pomerania, on the 1st of March Neustettin.

Finland declared war on Germany on the 3rd of March.

On this day German troops attacked in the area of Lauban, in Silesia, in order to recapture the sole rail-link east of the Riesengebirge between Berlin and Silesia. The attack was successful until March 8th but had only local significance.

On March 4th the Russians reached the Baltic between Köslin and Kolberg. All Outer Pomerania was now lost to us.

The behaviour of the Russians in the occupied German provinces was indescribably atrocious. I myself saw fleeing columns of refugees. Numerous accounts by eye-witnesses reached the *OKH* as well as the Propaganda Ministry. State-Secretary Naumann, of the Propaganda Ministry, asked me on behalf of Dr. Goebbels if I would address both the domestic and the foreign Press and protest against the atrocities that the Russians were committing. I agreed to do so on March 6th, since I wished at least to try to ameliorate the sufferings of the German people by means of an appeal to the chivalry of our adversaries. In the course of this appeal I referred to the Anglo-American air terror. I regret to say that this desperate plea of mine was without success. Humanity and chivalry had both disappeared during those months. The war of revenge pursued its unutterably ferocious course, and when ten days later Naumann asked me to speak on the wireless I declined to make a second futile appeal. I could no longer offer my poor nation any hope.

On this 6th of March the Western Allies penetrated deep into the centre of Cologne. In the East the Russians were pressing on to Stettin.

On March 7th the Western Powers broke through the German front towards Koblenz. In the East Graudenz fell. The Russians continued irresistibly to occupy Pomerania.

On March 8th the enemy in the West succeeded in capturing the bridge over the Rhine at Remagen intact. The destruction of this vital crossing-place was impossible owing to a lack of explosives. Hitler raved and demanded victims. Five officers were summarily executed.

On March 9th the Russians reached the eastern bank of the Oder on either side of Stettin. We managed to retain a bridgehead on that bank.

In Hungary our attack was launched at last and achieved initial success. But spring had begun down there and the ground was soft in consequence, which made it difficult for our tanks to advance. No great results could therefore be anticipated for the offensive. North of Lake Balaton a certain amount of territory was recaptured, but south of that lake the attack soon bogged down.

On March 12th there was street fighting inside Breslau.

The air war went on with undiminished fury. Berlin was bombed for the twentieth successive night.

On March 13th the Russians fought their way into Küstriner Neustadt. They reached the Gulf of Danzig and Putzig. Our own attack in Hungary made progress. But in view of the catastrophic development of the situation as a whole this limited success was quite unimportant.

Finally all prospect of a decisive success failed here too. Up to this time the morale of the SS divisions had been good but now it cracked. The panzer troops continued to fight bravely but whole SS units, taking advantage of the cover thus offered, proceeded to retreat against orders. There could be no more reliance placed on such divisions. When Hitler heard of this he almost went out of his mind. He flew into a towering rage and ordered that the divisions—which included his own body-guard, the *Leibstandarte*—have their armbands taken away from them. He wanted to send me to Hungary to see that this order was carried out. I refused to do so, pointing out that the National Leader of the SS, who was present at the time, was the direct commander of the *Waffen-SS* and was also responsible for its discipline; I therefore proposed that he be entrusted with this assignment and that he go to Hungary to ensure that justice be done. Up to now Himmler had always refused to allow the Army any influence on his SS units; he now tried to change this policy, but it did him no good, since I had far more important matters to attend to. This mission of his to Hungary did not win him much affection from his *Waffen-SS*.

During this period of acute anxiety the leader of the Party's national organisation (*Reichsorganisationsleiter*), Dr. Ley, appeared one night at Hitler's headquarters with a new proposal. He suggested that a volunteer corps be formed from the National Socialist Party officials who no longer had any employment in Western Germany. 'I can promise you at least forty thousand fanatical fighters, my Führer. They can hold the Upper Rhine and the passes through the Black Forest. You can rely on that. Approve, my Führer, that this élite corps of volunteers be given the proud title of the *Freikorps Adolf Hitler*. The chief of the General Staff must hand over eighty thousand sub-machine-guns at once.' I was somewhat less enthusiastic than Dr. Ley about the value of this new formation and proposed to him that he first of all submit to me the actual figures for the number of volunteers enrolled, after which I should see to it that they were all armed. I never heard another word from him about it. Hitler had remained silent throughout. He probably no longer had much confidence in his organisation leader.

Breslau, Glogau, Kolberg, Danzig and Koenigsberg continued to hold out. A heavy battle was raging outside Stettin. Hitler now sent for Colonel-General Rauss, the commander of the Third Panzer Army, in order to find out from him what the position was and what was the combat ability of his army. Rauss began by outlining the general situation. Hitler interrupted him: 'I'm already in the picture so far as the general situation goes. What I want from you is a detailed exposition of the combat ability of your divisions.' Rauss now gave him an exact description which showed that he knew every yard of his front and was capable of judging the value of every unit under his command. I was present while he spoke and found his exposition outstandingly lucid. When he had finished Hitler dismissed him without comment. Rauss had scarcely left the Chancellery shelter, where this conference had taken place, before Hitler turned to Keitel, Jodl and myself and shouted: 'What a miserable speech! The man talked of nothing but details. Judging by the way he speaks he must be a Berliner or an East Prussian. He must be relieved of his appointment at once!' I replied: 'Colonel-General Rauss is one of our most capable panzer generals. You, my Führer, interrupted him yourself when he was trying to tell you about the general situation and you ordered him to give you a detailed exposition of the state of his divisions. And as for his origin, Rauss is an Austrian and therefore a compatriot of yours, my Führer.'

HITLER: 'Absolutely impossible. He can't be an Austrian.'

JODL: 'Oh yes he can, my Führer. He talks exactly like Moser, the actor.'

I: 'Please let me urge you, before you make any decisions, to remember that Colonel-General Rauss showed an exact knowledge of all his front, that he was able to give a personal evaluation of every division under his command, that throughout a long war he has consistently fought with great distinction, and that finally—as I already said—he is one of our best panzer generals.'

Hitler's opinion of him remained unfavourable. When I pointed out that we had no surfeit of good generals my remark was ignored. Rauss was relieved of his command. I walked out of the room in a rage and went to see Rauss in order to prepare him for the injustice that he was about to suffer at the hands of his compatriot, Hitler, and which I was incapable of preventing. Rauss was replaced by General von Manteuffel whom the failure of the Ardennes Offensive and the transfer of numerous panzer units away from the West to the East had now made available for fresh employment.

Meanwhile the Foreign Ministry had apparently decided—though too late—to open negotiations with the Western Allies through the intermediary of a neutral power. A certain Dr. Hesse, whom Ribbentrop trusted, appeared in Stockholm but had no success. Nevertheless the rumours concerning this mission brought me into contact with my adviser on foreign policy, Dr. Barandon, once again. We decided that I should go to see the National Leader of the SS, Himmler, and should propose to him that he use such international channels as were available to him—in particular the Red Cross and similar organisations—in an attempt to bring the increasingly senseless slaughter to an end.

After the disappearance from the scene of General Wenck, Himmler had proved a complete failure so far as the offensive in the Arnswalde area went. Conditions at his headquarters grew steadily more chaotic. I received no reports from his sector of the front and never had the impression that orders issued by the *OKH* were being carried out there. I therefore drove, in mid-March, to his headquarters near Prenzlau in order to find out what the situation was. Himmler's chief of staff, Lammerding, greeted me at the entrance with the words: 'Can't you rid us of our commander?' I told Lammerding that this was purely a matter for the SS. When I asked for the National Leader I was told that he was suffering from influenza and was being treated by his personal physician, Professor Gebhardt, in the Hohenlychen sanatorium. I immediately drove there, where I found Himmler in apparently robust health, and decided that I, at least, would never have permitted a slight cold in the head to take me away from my troops when they

were involved in so critical a situation. I then pointed out to this
SS potentate that he held, on his own, a whole series of the highest
appointments in the state: he was National Leader of the SS, Chief
of the German Police, Minister of the Interior, Commander-in-Chief
of the Training Army, and finally he commanded Army Group Vistula.
Each of these posts required the full-time activity of one man, or at
least such had been the case during the early stages of the war; and
no matter what respect I might have for his ability, such a plethora
of offices was bound to be beyond the strength of any one individual.
Meanwhile he must have realised by now that a command of troops
at the front is no easy matter. I therefore proposed to him that he give
up his command of the army group and concentrate on his other offices.

Himmler was no longer so self-confident as in the old days. He
hesitated: 'I can't go and say that to the Führer. He wouldn't approve
of my making such a suggestion.' I saw my chance and took it: 'Then
will you authorise me to say it for you?' Himmler now had to agree.
That same evening I proposed to Hitler that the overburdened Himmler
be relieved of his command of Army Group Vistula and that in his
stead Colonel-General Heinrici, at present in charge of First Panzer
Army in the Carpathians, be appointed to succeed him. Hitler disliked
the idea, but after a certain amount of grumbling finally agreed. Heinrici
was appointed on March 20th.

What could have induced a civilian like Himmler to insist on holding
a military command? That he was totally ignorant of military matters
was a fact of which he, and indeed all of us, Hitler included, were well
aware. So why did he do it? Apparently one of his motives was his
measureless ambition. Above all he wanted to win a Knight's Cross.
Then too, like Hitler, he completely underestimated the qualities that
are necessary for a man to be a successful commander of troops. On
the very first occasion when he had to undertake a task before the eyes
of all the world—one that could not be carried out by means of back-
stairs intrigue and fishing in troubled waters—the man inevitably
proved a failure. It was complete irresponsibility on his part to wish
to hold such an appointment; it was equally irresponsible of Hitler
to entrust him with it.

At this time Speer, whose attitude towards the course of events was
becoming one of increasing scepticism, came to see me. He brought
me the information that Hitler intended to arrange for the destruction
of all factories, water and electrical installations, railways and bridges
before they should fall into enemy hands. Speer rightly pointed out
that such a crazy deed must result in mass misery and death to the
population of Germany on a scale never before seen in history. He
asked for my help in ensuring that no such order be carried out. I

readily agreed to give it him and I immediately set to work drafting an order in which I laid down the defensive lines that were to be held throughout Germany and specifically ordered that only immediately in front of these few lines might demolitions be carried out. Nothing else whatever in Germany was to be destroyed. All installations that served to feed the populace and to provide it with work were to remain untouched. On the next day I took my draft to Jodl, who had to be informed of its contents since it dealt with a matter which concerned all parts of the Armed Forces. Jodl submitted my draft to Hitler, but unfortunately not when I was present. When I saw him again on the following day, and asked him what Hitler's reaction had been, he gave me an order of Hitler's to read which was the exact contrary of Speer's and my intentions.

In order to give an example of Speer's forthright manner of speech, I should like to quote an extract from a memorandum which he submitted to Hitler on March 18th, 1945, when he and I were trying to prevent the destruction of bridges and factories:

It must be established that, in the event of the battles moving further into German territory, nobody is entitled to destroy industrial installations, mining installations, electrical and other utility works, communication facilities, or inland waterways. A destruction of bridges on the scale at present envisaged would do more damage to our communications network than all the air raids of the past years. Their destruction implies the elimination of all chance of survival for the German people. . . .

We have no right, at this stage of the war, to order demolitions which would affect the future existence of the German people. If the enemy has decided to destroy this nation, which has fought with unparalleled bravery, then the enemy must bear the guilt before history for such a deed. It is our duty to leave the German nation all possible facilities which will enable that nation to re-arise at some time in the distant future.[1]

Hitler's reaction to this memorandum of Speer's, with the conclusions of which I too had identified myself, culminated in these words:

If the war should be lost, then the nation, too, will be lost. That would be the nation's unalterable fate. There is no need to consider the basic requirements that a people needs in order to continue to live a primitive life. On the contrary, it is better ourselves to destroy such things, for this nation will have proved itself the weaker and the future will belong exclusively to the stronger Eastern nation. Those who remain alive after the battles are over are in any case only inferior persons, since the best have fallen.[2]

He frequently produced shocking remarks of this sort. I have myself heard him talk in this way, and I replied to him that the German

---

[1] Quoted during the Nuremberg process, 20th June, 1946.
[2] Quoted in the Nuremberg process, 20th June, 1946.

nation would live on: that, according to the laws of nature, it would live on even if the contemplated destructions were carried out: and that such destruction would simply burden that nation with new and avoidable miseries if his intentions were carried out.

Despite all this the order for destruction was issued on March 19th and this was followed, on March 23rd, by instructions from Bormann for its implementation. The demolitions were to be the responsibility of the Gauleiters in their capacity as commissars for the defence of the Reich. The armed forces had refused to undertake this duty. Bormann had ordered that the populace of the threatened territories be transported to the interior of Germany or, if this proved impossible, be made to march there on foot. The carrying out of this order would have resulted in a catastrophe on a gigantic scale, since no measures to ensure a food supply were taken.

The military authorities therefore combined with Speer to frustrate the implementation of this insane order. Buhle prevented the issue of explosives so that the demolitions could not be carried out. Speer visited one command post after another explaining what the consequences must be if the order were obeyed. We could not prevent all destruction, but we succeeded in considerably reducing the amount that was carried out.

12. THE FINAL COLLAPSE

On March 15th the headquarters of the *OKH* was heavily attacked from the air. The raid lasted for forty-five minutes and the whole bomb load of an air fleet—enough high explosive to pulverise a large town—was unloaded on our little camp. We were undoubtedly a military objective and we could therefore hardly object at the enemy's attempt to eliminate us. When the air-raid siren sounded at about noon I was working, as usual, in my office. My wife, it will be recalled, was a refugee from the Warthegau and since she had nowhere else to go Hitler had permitted her to stay with me. She was watching the non-commissioned officer who was engaged in tracing the bombers' path on the map, and she noticed that when the planes reached Brandenburg they did not, as was customary, continue to Berlin, but turned directly towards Zossen. She had the presence of mind to inform me of this immediately. I at once ordered all departments to repair to the air-raid shelters and had just reached the one assigned to myself when the first bombs began to fall. As a result of this last-minute warning our casualties were happily light. Only the Operations Department had failed to take my advice. In consequence General Krebs and a number of his colleagues were more or less seriously wounded. Krebs had received a blow on the temple; when I went to see him a few minutes after the explosions were over he collapsed unconscious before my eyes. He had to go to hospital and was not able to return to work for several days.

Such was our situation when Heinrici arrived on a visit to Zossen preparatory to taking up his new appointment as commander of Army Group Vistula. His first task was to be the relief of the little fortress of Küstrin which the Russians had encircled. Hitler wished him to do this by making an attack with five divisions from the small bridgehead we still held across the Oder near Frankfurt-on-Oder. I felt that such an attack was pointless and proposed that our first step must be the elimination of the Russian bridgehead near Küstrin and the re-establishment of direct contact with the besieged garrison. This difference of opinion had led to repeated arguments between Hitler and myself. The commandant of the fortress, the construction of which dated from the time of Frederick the Great, was the police general Reinefarth, who had made a name for himself at Warsaw; he was a good policeman but no general.

But before describing this counter-attack I must revert to the

o*

Chancellery and an event of a political nature that now took place there. On March 21st, in accordance with the decision taken by Dr. Barandon and myself, I went to see Himmler with the purpose of urging him that he use his official contacts in neutral countries to arrange for an armistice. I found him in the Chancellery garden, taking a stroll with Hitler among the rubble. Hitler saw me and called out, asking what it was I wanted. I replied that I was desirous of talking with Himmler. So Hitler walked away and I had the National SS Leader to myself. I told him bluntly what he had already known for a long time: 'The war can no longer be won. The only problem now is how most quickly to put an end to the senseless slaughter and bombing. Apart from Ribbentrop you are the only man who still possesses contacts in neutral countries. Since the Foreign Minister has proved reluctant to propose to Hitler that negotiations be begun, I must ask you to make use of your contacts and to go with me to Hitler and urge him that he arrange an armistice.' Himmler replied: 'My dear Colonel-General, it is still too early for that.' I said: 'I don't understand you. It is not now five minutes to twelve but five minutes past twelve. If we don't negotiate now we shall never be able to do so at all. Don't you realise how pitiful our situation has become?' Our conversation continued in this inconclusive vein for some time, but without result. There was nothing to be done with the man. He was afraid of Hitler.

That evening, after the briefing, Hitler signalled me to stay behind. He said to me: 'I notice that your heart trouble has taken a turn for the worse. You must immediately take four weeks' convalescent leave.' This would have provided a very welcome solution to my personal problems, but on account of the state of my staff I could not accept the offer. I therefore replied: 'At the moment I cannot leave my post because I have no deputy. Wenck has not recovered from his injuries. Krebs was severely wounded in the enemy air raid of March 15th and is not capable of returning to work. The Operations Department, as a result of the imprisonments that you ordered after the Warsaw affair, is even now not yet fully competent. I shall attempt to find a deputy as quickly as I can and shall then go on leave.' While we were talking a man came in and informed Hitler that Speer wished to see him. Hitler replied that he could not receive him that night. And once again I had to listen to his now almost stereotyped outburst, 'Always when any man asks to see me alone it is because he has something unpleasant to say to me. I cannot stand any more of these Job's comforters. His memoranda begin with the words: "The war is lost!" And that's what he wants to tell me again now. I always just lock his memoranda away in the safe, unread.' Speer was instructed to return in three days' time.

During this difficult month of March many conversations took place which are sufficiently interesting to be worth preserving. Thus one evening Hitler lost his temper at the high prisoner-of-war claims that were being issued by the Western Allies. He said: 'The soldiers on the Eastern Front fight far better. The reason they give in so easily in the West is simply the fault of that stupid Geneva convention which promises them good treatment as prisoners. We must scrap the idiotic thing.' Jodl contradicted this wild and senseless proposal with great energy and, with my support, succeeded in persuading Hitler to post- pone taking any such step. Jodl also prevented Hitler from appointing as commander of an army group a general who had recently been punished for gross irregularity of conduct and dismissed the Service. By this time Jodl had come to agree that the General Staff Corps must be under unified control and had recognised that his former attitude towards this problem was incorrect. Now that the end was approaching he seemed to possess greater clarity of vision than before and even appeared to shake off the lethargy in which he had been sunk since the Stalingrad disaster.

On March 23rd the Western Powers reached the upper and central Rhine along its whole length, and north of the mouth of the Ruhr crossed the lower Rhine on a broad front. On the same day the Russians broke through near Oppeln in Upper Silesia.

On the 24th the Americans crossed the upper Rhine and advanced towards Darmstadt and Frankfurt. In the East the heavy fighting around Danzig continued. The Russians attacked at Küstrin.

On March 26th the Russians launched a fresh offensive in Hungary. Our attempt to re-establish contact with the defenders of Küstrin failed.

On March 27th Patton's tanks entered the outskirts of Frankfurt-on- Main. Heavy fighting developed around Aschaffenburg.

On this day, during the noon conference, Hitler became very excited about the failure of our counter-attack at Küstrin. His accusations were directed principally at the commander of the Ninth Army, General Busse. He had expended too little ammunition in the artillery prepara- tion preceding the attack. In the First World War, in Flanders, it was customary to fire off ten times as many shells before an operation of this sort. I pointed out to him that Busse had had no more ammunition to hand and therefore was not in a position to fire more shells than he had in fact done. 'Then you should have arranged for him to have more!' he shouted at me. I showed him the figures for the total quantity that had been allotted me and proved to him that this had all been given to Busse. 'In that case the troops let us down!' I gave him the figures of the very heavy casualties suffered by the divisions involved, which only sufficed to prove that the troops had performed their duty with the greatest self-sacrifice. The conference ended in an atmosphere of profound ill-feeling. Back at Zossen I checked up once again on the figures for the ammunition employed, the casualties suffered and the performance of the troops engaged and wrote a straightforward report for Hitler, which I asked General Krebs to submit to him during the evening briefing, since I was in no mood for further futile arguments. Krebs was also told to arrange that I be allowed to visit the front at the Frankfurt bridgehead on the following day. I wanted personally to decide whether Hitler's intention to launch a five-division attack east of the Oder from this narrow bridgehead for the purpose of relieving Küstrin was, in fact, a practical proposition. Up to now my arguments against this plan of Hitler's had availed nothing.

Late that night Krebs returned to Zossen from Berlin. He informed me that Hitler had forbidden my visit to the front and had ordered that both General Busse and I appear at his noon briefing on March 28th. Hitler had been annoyed by my report which he had regarded as an attempt to correct him. The conference promised to be a stormy one.

On March 28th, 1945, at 14.00 hrs., the usual group met in the constricted shelter at the Chancellery. General Busse was also present. Hitler appeared and Busse was told to make his report. After a few sentences Hitler interrupted the general and made the same accusations of negligence which I had thought to quash on the previous day. After listening to two or three sentences I became angry. It was my turn now to interrupt Hitler and I drew his attention to my spoken and written reports of March 27th. I said: Permit me to interrupt you. I explained to you yesterday thoroughly—both verbally and in writing—that General Busse is not to blame for the failure of the Küstrin attack. Ninth Army used the ammunition that had been allotted it. The troops did their duty. The unusually high casualty figures prove that. I therefore ask you not to make any accusations against General Busse.' Hitler then said: 'I must ask all you gentlemen to leave the room with the exception of the Field-Marshal and the Colonel-General.' As soon as the large gathering had withdrawn into the ante-room Hitler said to me, briefly: 'Colonel-General Guderian, your physical health requires that you immediately take six weeks' convalescent leave.' I raised my right hand. 'I shall go,' I said, and I turned toward the door. I had the door-knob in my hand when Hitler called me back, saying: 'Please remain here until the end of the conference.' I sat down again in silence. The others taking part in the conference were summoned back into the room and the meeting went on as though nothing had occurred. All the same, Hitler did refrain from levelling any further accusations at Busse. Two or three times I was briefly asked for my opinion, and then—after several interminable hours—the conference was over. Those who attended it left the shelter. Keitel, Jodl, Burgdorf and I were summoned to remain behind. Hitler said to me: 'Please do your best to get your health back. In six weeks the situation will be very critical. Then I shall need you urgently. Where do you think you will go?' Keitel advised me to visit Bad Liebenstein. It was very beautiful there. I replied that it was already occupied by the Americans. 'Well then, what about Bad Sachsa in the Harz?' asked the solicitous Field-Marshal. I thanked him for his kindly interest and remarked that I intended to choose my place of residence for myself and that I planned to pick a locality which would not be overrun by the enemy within the next forty-eight hours. Once again I raised my right hand and then, accompanied by Keitel, left the Chancellery shelter for ever. On the way to the car park Keitel assured me that I had been right not to oppose Hitler's wishes again. Besides, what else could I have said at this stage? Any word of opposition would have been excessive.

That evening I arrived back at Zossen. My wife greeted me with the words: 'It lasted a terribly long time today.' I replied: 'Yes, and that is the last one. I have been dismissed.' We fell into each other's arms. It was a relief for both of us.

On March 29th I said farewell to my colleagues, handed over my duties to Krebs and packed up my few possessions. On March 30th my wife and I left Zossen by train and headed south. I had originally intended to go to a hunting lodge near Oberhof in the Thuringian Mountains, but the rapid advance of the Americans made this impossible. We therefore decided to visit the Ebenhausen sanatorium near Munich where I could undergo a course of treatment for my heart. There, on April 1st, I found accommodation and excellent treatment from that outstanding heart specialist, Dr. Zimmermann. A friendly warning that I was likely to be supervised by the Gestapo enabled me to prevent this by arranging that I be guarded by two members of the Field Police.

On May 1st I took my wife to Dietramszell, where Frau von Schilcher offered her most friendly hospitality. I myself went to the Tyrol, where the staff of the Inspectorate-General of Armoured Troops had been transferred, and there I sat down and waited for the end of the war. After the unconditional surrender of May 10th I accompanied this staff into American captivity.

The only information I received concerning events subsequent to March 28th came from the wireless. I shall therefore not attempt to discuss them here.

13. LEADING PERSONALITIES OF THE THIRD REICH

My career brought me into contact with a number of people who exerted a greater or lesser degree of influence on the course of my country's history. I therefore regard it as my duty to describe the impressions I formed of these men at first hand. I am, of course, aware that such impressions can only be subjective in nature; but they are those of a soldier and not of a politician, and must in consequence be in many respects different from those that political men will have formed from their particular point of view; their value is that they are based on the military correctitude and concept of honour which have always been traditional in the German Army; they will require amplification by the observations and judgments of other men, so that finally from the comparison of many sources a more or less definitive picture may be made of the characters of those people on whose activities or whose negligence the course of that historical period depended. It was an unfortunate time for us and one that culminated in an unparalleled collapse.

Up to now I have attempted to describe my own experiences and impressions as they occurred at the time and without making use of the hindsight derived from subsequent knowledge. From now on, in these closing pages, I shall follow a different method and shall avail myself of what I have learned since our defeat, whether from conversations or from published material.

Hitler

At the central point of that circle of personalities which ruled our fate stood the figure of Adolf Hitler.

Of humble origin, limited schooling, and with insufficient training in the home, coarse in speech and in manner, he stands before us as a man of the people who was most at ease among an intimate group from his own part of the country. To begin with, he did not feel awkward in the company of persons of a higher cultural background, particularly when the conversation dealt with art or music or similar matters. Later on, certain elements of his closest entourage, persons themselves of low culture, deliberately awakened in him a strong dislike for those people of a more spiritual nature and with a socially superior background with whom he had previously been able to get on; they did this with the conscious purpose of bringing him into conflict with those classes and thus of destroying what influence they still possessed. In this attempt they were very successful, and for two reasons: first, because in Hitler resentment still slumbered as a relic of his difficult and humble early years; secondly, because he believed himself to be a great revolutionary and thought that the representatives of older traditions would hinder him in, and perhaps even deflect him from, the fulfilment of his destiny.

This provides one key to Hitler's psychology. From this complex of emotions sprang his increasing dislike of princes and noblemen, scholars and aristocrats, officials and officers. Shortly after his seizure of power he certainly tried hard to behave in a manner acceptable to good company and in international society; once war had broken out he finally abandoned any such attempt.

He had an unusually clever brain and was equipped with remarkable powers of memory, particularly for historical data, technical figures and economic statistics; he read everything that was put before him and thus filled in the gaps in his education. He was continually amazing people by his ability to quote relevant passages from what he had read or had heard at conferences. 'Six weeks ago you said something quite different,' was a favourite and much-dreaded remark of the man who became Chancellor and Supreme Commander of the Armed Forces. And there was no arguing with him about this, for he would have the stenographer's record of the conversation in question immediately available.

He possessed a talent for casting his ideas into an easily assimilated form, which he would then hammer into his listeners' minds by means of endless repetition. Almost all his speeches and expositions, whether for audiences of thousands or to a small group of individuals, began with the words: 'When in the year 1919 I decided to become a politician . . .' and his political talks and exhortations ended invariably with: 'I shall not give in and I shall never surrender.'

He possessed natural oratorical talents of an unusually high order, the effects of which never failed so far as the masses were concerned and which also worked on educated people. He understood brilliantly how to adjust his manner of speech according to the mentality of his audience. His style varied according to whether he was addressing industrialists or soldiers, devout Party comrades or sceptics, Gauleiters, or minor functionaries.

His most outstanding quality was his will power. By the exercise of his will he compelled men to follow him. This power of his worked by means of suggestion and, indeed, its effect on many men was almost hypnotic. I have frequently observed such cases. At the *OKW* almost nobody contradicted him; the men there were either in a state of permanent hypnosis, like Keitel, or of resigned acquiescence, like Jodl.

Even self-confident individuals, men who had proved their bravery in the face of the enemy, would surrender to Hitler's oratory and would fall silent when confronted by his logic, which it was so hard to refute. When speaking in a small circle he would observe his listeners one by one and would see exactly what effect his words were having on each man present. If he noticed that one or the other was not giving in to his powers of suggestion, that he was not a 'medium,' then he would address his words directly to this resisting spirit until such time as he believed he had achieved his aim. But if the anticipated reaction was even then not manifested the independence thus shown vexed the hypnotist: 'I haven't convinced that man!' His immediate reaction was to get rid of such persons. The more successful he was the less tolerant he became.

It has been deduced from Hitler's great power over the masses that the Germans are an unusually suggestible race. But in all countries and at all times men have succumbed to the suggestive powers of unusual personalities, even if the wielders of those powers were not always good men in the Christian sense. A fine example from recent history is offered by the leading men of the French revolutionary period, followed immediately by the personality of Napoleon. The French followed the great Corsican into complete disaster, even though they must long have been aware that the course he was pursuing could only lead to defeat. In both the World Wars, and despite their love of peace, the people of the United States proved suggestible to the influence of the two presidents who were leading them to war. The Italians followed their Mussolini. To say nothing of Russia, where a gigantic nation, contrary to its original convictions, turned bolshevist through the force of Lenin's ideas. But in this case we, as contemporaries, know that Lenin sowed his revolutionary seed on fertile ground, for the economic incompetence of the Czarist regime, with the resultant widespread dissatisfaction and impoverishment of the mass of the people, had made that nation eager to listen to any promise of improvement.

The reasons for the Germans' submission to Hitler's powers of suggestion must first be sought in the failure of policy as manifested by the victor nations after the First World War. This policy prepared the ground in which the seeds of National-Socialism were to take root; it gave us unemployment, heavy reparations, oppressive annexation of territory, lack of freedom, lack of equality, lack of military strength. When the victorious nations, in drafting the Versailles Treaty, failed to observe President Wilson's Fourteen Points the Germans lost their trust in the good faith of the Great Powers. As a result, the man who now promised to free them from the bondage of Versailles had a relatively easy task, particularly since the formal democracy of the Weimar Republic, try though it might, could achieve no significant successes in the diplomatic field and at home proved incapable of mastering Germany's internal difficulties. So when Hitler promised both internal and external political improvement he soon had many followers, until at last a point was reached where he controlled the largest party in the land and thus, according to democratic procedure, assumed power. The soil had truly been well tilled. In consequence the Germans cannot rightly be accused of being any more suggestible than other nations.

Hitler promised the Germans that abroad he could free them from the injustices of Versailles and that at home he would abolish unemployment and party strife. These were aims which were entirely desirable and with which any good German must agree. Who would not have approved of them? At the beginning of his career this programme, to which all decent Germans heartily subscribed, brought him the support of those millions of men who were beginning to doubt the ability of their politicians and the good will of their former enemies. As one futile conference succeeded the last, as reparations grew more intolerable, as our inequality was increasingly protracted, so more and more men turned to the swastika. It is necessary to remember the almost desperate condition of Germany as 1932 became 1933. More than six millions of unemployed, that is to say, with their dependants, twenty-five millions of hungry human beings; the demoralisation of the younger working men, who now simply lounged about at the street corners in Berlin and the other big cities; the increase in crime—all this gave the Communists six million votes. And these millions would doubtless have increased if Hitler had not drawn them to him and given them fresh ideals and a new faith.

It must also be remembered that shortly before this France and Great Britain had refused to allow an economic union between Germany and Austria, although such a union would have brought about a limited improvement to the economies of both countries concerned and could in no way have been politically dangerous to the two Western Powers. Austria at the time stood on the very brink of economic catastrophe as a result of the Treaty of St. Germains, the counterpart of the Treaty of Versailles; it cannot exist without economic co-ordination with some large industrial area; now it is to be hoped that a European economic union will solve this problem. At that time the prohibition of any sort of Austro-German economic union served to embitter even the most clear-headed and 'westward-looking' Germans, since it was a sign of senselessness and of undisguised ill-will on the part of the victor nations—and that, twelve years after the end of the

war and six years after the admission of Germany to the League of
Nations. Men in a position to judge the situation as it then was have
claimed that this played an important part in Hitler's electoral successes
during the years 1931 and 1932.

In any event the time came at last when Hitler had collected together
so strong a party that it could no longer be ignored. The Field-Marshal
President von Hindenburg, after long struggling with his conscience,
finally appointed him Chancellor; this was certainly an extremely
difficult decision for the old President to make and, like him, many
Germans disapproved both of Hitler personally and of the manner in
which he behaved.

Once in power Hitler soon eliminated the opposition. The violent
way in which this was done showed a new side to the nascent dictator's
nature. He need make no attempt to disguise this aspect of his character,
since the opposition was weak and divided and collapsed almost
without a blow being struck as soon as it was strongly attacked. As a
result Hitler was able to pass those laws by which he broke the safe-
guards that the Weimar Republic had thought to erect against the
dictatorship of any individual man.

This ruthless elimination of all internal opposition culminated in
the brutal murder of Roehm. A number of further assassinations of
men who had nothing whatever to do with Roehm was simultaneously
carried out for quite other reasons and without Hitler's approval; but
these crimes went unpunished. The Field-Marshal President, standing
as he was in the shadow of death, was no longer able to intervene.
But at that time Hitler still felt that he must apologise to the Officer
Corps for the murder of General von Schleicher, and he promised the
Corps that such an event would never occur again.

That no retribution could be demanded for the crimes of June 30th,
1934, was already a clear indication of the dangers that threatened
Germany. But that was not all; it also increased greatly Hitler's consciousness of his own power. A law had been cleverly passed which
settled the problem of the succession after Hindenburg's death, and an
equally cleverly organised plebiscite made him legally the Head of the
State.

Hitler was asked whether he intended to establish and legalise his
position by the re-introduction of the monarchy. Later on, when discussing this question with officers in Berlin, he said that he had given
it a great deal of consideration. He had, however, found only one case
in all history of a wise monarch tolerating the presence of an outstanding chancellor, recognising his achievements, and being prepared
to keep him in office and to collaborate with him as his partner in
political matters until the end: he was referring to Kaiser William I

and Bismarck. In all history he could find no other example of so magnanimous and wise a monarch. He had discussed the question with his friend Mussolini, but what the latter had told him of his difficulties with the Italian King had made him reluctant to saddle himself with the burden of a reinstated monarchy.

Hitler chose dictatorship.

And his dictatorship achieved a number of outstanding successes: the disappearance of unemployment, the raising of the workers' morale, the re-creation of national feeling, the elimination of party strife. It would be wrong not to grant him the credit for these achievements.

Once his internal power was affirmed, Hitler turned to his external political programme. The return of the Saar, the re-introduction of military self-determination, the occupation of the Rhineland, the incorporation of Austria—all these were completed to the delight of the German nation and with the toleration, and even the approval, of foreign powers. Indeed, the foreign nations now showed a profound understanding for the rightful claims of the German people, and the Western countries in particular, with a true feeling for justice, recognised the tragic errors of the Versailles Treaty. Hitler's task was more difficult when he undertook the liberation of the Sudetenland, a territory that had suffered for twenty years from the undeniably overbearing nationalism of the Czechs. The Czech State was bound by alliance to the French Republic. Its creation in 1918 was the result of a mis-application of the principle concerning the self-determination of nationalities, but to attempt to rectify that mistake now was to run the risk of war with France. Hitler judged the statesmen of the Western Powers according to the impressions they had so far made on him. His highly developed political instinct told him that the majority of Frenchmen, and the more important French politicians, would not regard the rectification of this palpable injustice as a proper cause for war. His judgment of the probable reaction of the British, with whom he was anxious to live in peace, was similar. He was not wrong. The British Prime Minister, Chamberlain, and the French Premier, Daladier, came to Munich, as did Hitler's friend Mussolini, and the four states-men signed an agreement authorising the Germans to move against Czechoslovakia. This agreement was based principally upon the opinion of the politically far-sighted British observer, Lord Runciman. The immediate result of the Munich pact was the preservation of peace, but it all served to increase Hitler's self-confidence and his consciousness of power *vis-à-vis* the West. No matter how worthily the Western statesmen may have represented their countries' true interests, so far as Hitler was concerned their ultimate willingness to compromise was valueless since it had only been exacted from them under the threatening pressure of his own personality. The warnings of those Germans who knew the British people fell on deaf ears, and indeed only served to reinforce Hitler in his preconceived ideas.

By the beginning of 1938 Hitler had gained control of all the machinery of government of Germany, and only one organisation was left which might still offer serious resistance to his regime, the Army. Therefore, shortly before the incorporation of Austria, the Army was cleverly and irresponsibly deprived of its leaders in the Blomberg–Fritsch crisis. The pill was immediately sugar-coated with the success of the *anschluss*. The representatives of the Army at the time, clear-sighted though powerless, did not protest. The true significance of what had happened remained unknown to the majority of the generals and even more so to the Army as a whole. Any intentions towards rebellion on the part of those few who were aware of what was going on remained purely theoretical or, at most, never got beyond the form of memoranda. Externally these men preserved the appearance of loyalty. Not so much as a murmur of a threat, let alone of actual resistance, reached the ears of any wider group, even within the Armed Forces. Furthermore, as one year succeeded the next, the opposition within the Army was continually weakened, since the new age groups that were now called to the colours had already served in the Hitler Youth, and in the National Labour Service or the Party, and had thus already sworn allegiance to Hitler. The Corps of Officers, too, became year by year more impregnated with young National-Socialists.

Thus Hitler's self-confidence grew, and, as his power became more firmly established in both external and internal matters, so he developed an over-bearing arrogance which made everything and everybody appear to him quite unimportant in comparison to himself. This attitude of his assumed unhealthy proportions owing to the mediocrity and, indeed, insignificance of the men he had summoned to fill the most important appointments in the Third Reich. Up to this time Hitler had been receptive to practical considerations, and had at least listened to advice and been prepared to discuss matters with others; now, however, he became increasingly autocratic. One example of this change in his behaviour is furnished by the fact that after 1938 the Cabinet never again met. The Ministers did their work in accordance with the instructions issued by Hitler to each of them singly. There was no longer any collective examination of major policy. Many Ministers from then on never, or only very seldom, saw Hitler at all. While the Ministers were attempting to carry out their duties through the normal channels of authority a new bureaucracy of the Party came into existence, parallel to that of the State. Hitler's slogan: 'The State does not control the Party: the Party controls the State,' had created an entirely novel situation. Administrative power passed into the hands of the Party, that is to say of the Gauleiters. These men were appointed, not on account of their qualifications for high administrative office, but because of their achievements within the Party; and in such appointments sufficient attention was by no means always paid to the suitability of the man's character.

Since many Party functionaries attempted to copy Hitler's ruthlessness in achieving their aims, political morals soon tumbled. The national administration was emasculated.

It was the same story with the judiciary. The fateful Authorisation Act entitled the dictator to give his regulations the force of law without the approval of parliament being necessary. But even if the regulations had required the seal of parliament, this would have made no difference to the course of events, since after 1934 the parliament was only theoretically elected by universal suffrage and secret ballot. The same state of affairs exists today in the Soviet Union.

By the spring of 1939 Hitler's *hubris* had reached the point where he decided to incorporate Czechoslovakia into the Reich as a Protectorate. This step, it is true, was carried out without provoking actual war, but the grave warnings that now emanated from London should have caused him to stop and think. After the occupation of Czechoslovakia Memel was re-incorporated into the Reich. The position of Germany was now so powerful that there seemed no reason why the remaining outstanding national aspirations could not be left to solve themselves gradually and peacefully. But such a policy was quite foreign to Hitler. The reasons for this may be asked. And one of the first answers must be Hitler's extraordinary premonition that he was to die an early death. 'I know that I shall not live to be old. I have not much time to lose. My successors will possess less energy than I. They will be too weak to take the fateful decisions that must be taken. I, therefore, have to do it all myself during my own lifetime.' And so he drove himself, his colleagues, his whole nation forward at a breathless pace along the road that he had chosen. 'When Fortuna, the lucky goddess, flashes past in her golden chariot, that is the time to leap forward and to grasp the tip of her wand. If the opportunity is not then seized she will disappear for ever.' And he leaped.

For the autumn of 1939 Hitler had determined on the elimination of the Polish Corridor as his objective. The proposals which he made to the Poles seem, in retrospect, to have been not too outrageous. But the Poles, and in particular the Polish Foreign Minister, Beck, were not interested in reaching a peaceful settlement. They preferred to rely on the British guarantee, which was offered them at a moment when they had not yet made up their minds what course they would pursue; the immediate consequence was that they chose war.[1] When the die was cast Britain, and under Britain's influence France, also, declared war on Germany. The Second World War had begun. Hitler's intention that the war be limited to Poland had been frustrated.

Before starting the Polish war, Hitler had the foresight to secure his rear by means of an agreement with the Soviet Union. Thus to begin with the bogey of a war on two fronts seemed to be banished. In making this agreement, however, Hitler had been acting against the dictates of his own anti-bolshevik ideology in the interests of his national policy. His uncertainty concerning the nation's reaction to this step was expressed to me during the luncheon in October 1939, at which I sat next to him.[2] But the nation, and particularly the Army, were pleased to have their rear thus made secure, since a state of war on the wrong front—that is to say against the Western Powers—now existed. It is of course also certain that the German nation did not regard war against the Soviet Union as either necessary or desirable. They would have liked to see a fair peace made after the completion of the Western Campaign of 1940.

After that campaign Hitler was on the very pinnacle of success. There was, however, one fly in the ointment; the greater part of the British Expeditionary Force had escaped through Dunkirk. Winston Churchill was simply stating a fact when he said that, despite the casualties, Dunkirk was a victory, and in particular a victory of the British over the German air force.[3] For in the skies above Dunkirk, and later over England, the Luftwaffe suffered such heavy casualties owing to its mistaken employment that it lost for ever its initial, if always limited, superiority.

The blame for the faulty use of the air force must be apportioned equally to Hitler and to Goering. Neither the bravery nor the military and technical ability of the Luftwaffe sufficed to compensate for the vanity of its Commander-in-Chief and for the indulgence that Hitler showed towards the ambitions of his principal disciple. Only much later did Hitler form a true picture of Goering's worth—or rather worthlessness—but it is significant that on 'grounds of policy' he always refused to replace him in an appointment that was, for better or for worse, decisive to the outcome of the war.

It has often been maintained that Hitler showed unshakable loyalty to his 'old comrades.' So far as Goering is concerned this was unfortunately true. It is also true that he frequently complained about him, but he never drew the correct conclusions from his own observations.

[1] Compare Marshal Smigly-Rydz's statements at Danzig in the spring of 1939.
[2] See page 84.
[3] See Vol. II of Winston Churchill's *The Second World War*.

The Western Campaign showed another facet of Hitler's character. Hitler made his plans with great boldness. Norway was a courageous undertaking, as was the armoured break-through at Sedan. In both these cases he gave his approval to the boldest proposals. But when, in the execution of these plans, he was confronted by the first difficulty —in contrast to his unshakable pertinacity when faced by political trouble—he would give in, perhaps because he was instinctively aware of his lack of talent in the field of military science.

This happened in Norway, when the situation at Narvik grew serious and it became essential to keep one's nerves under control and not to give in. In this particular case it was Lieutenant-Colonel von Lossberg and General Jodl who saved the day. It happened again at Sedan when it was a question of exploiting powerfully and rapidly a surprising, large-scale initial success which neither he nor his advisers anticipated. I was held up first on May 15th and then on May 17th, 1940, by Hitler's orders. The fact that I did not stop was not thanks to Hitler. But the worst of all was the order not to advance across the Aa, outside Dunkirk,[1] since it was solely on account of this that the British were able to withdraw into the fortress ahead of us and embark in their ships. If our panzer forces had been allowed a free hand we would, so far as it is possible to tell, certainly have reached Dunkirk before the Englishmen, who would, as a result, have been cut off. The resultant blow to English morale would have made an appreciable difference to the prospects of a successful German landing in England and might even have led to our enemies being willing to discuss peace terms despite Churchill.

But yet another blunder was to follow. The lame armistice with France, the ending of the Western Campaign before the Mediterranean coast had been reached, the postponement of the African landing and of the immediate continuation of the French campaign by means of an attack on Gibraltar and the Suez Canal, all this proves the justice of the assertion that Hitler, bold and even rash as he was in the drafting of plans, became timid in the execution of his military intentions. He would have served Germany better if he had shown more care and foresight in his planning and more speed and determination in the execution. 'First weigh the considerations, then take the risks,' is a German adage originally coined by Field-Marshal Moltke.

The question of the African undertaking was affected by two facts: first, Hitler believed that he must consider Mussolini's point of view; secondly, his attitude was conditioned by his purely continental approach to military matters. His personal knowledge of the world was very limited and he had absolutely no understanding of the

[1] See page 117.

meaning of sea power and all that it implies. I do not recall whether or not he had ever read the book by the American Admiral Mahan, *The Influence of Sea Power upon History*; in any case, he never acted according to the precepts there laid down.

As a result of this lack of knowledge he was, in the summer of 1940, unsure how he might lead his country back to peace. He did not know how to deal with the English. His armed forces were ready. They could not remain mobilised and inactive for an indefinite length of time. He felt an itch to act. What was to happen? The old ideological enemy, against whom he had struggled throughout his career and which, by opposing it, had brought him the mass of his supporters' votes, stood intact on the eastern frontier. He was tempted to make use of the time allowed him by the temporary lull on the Western Front in order to complete the reckoning with the Soviets. He was clearly aware of the threat that the Soviet Union and the communist urge to world hegemony offered both to Europe and to the whole of Western civilisation. He knew that in this matter he was in agreement with the majority of his fellow-countrymen and, indeed, with many good Europeans in other lands. The question of whether these ideas of his could in fact be militarily executed was, of course, quite another matter.

To begin with perhaps he only toyed with these ideas, but as time went on he began to take them more and more seriously. His unusually vivid powers of imagination led him to under-estimate the known strength of the Soviet Union. He maintained that mechanisation on land and in the air offered fresh chances of success, so that comparison with the campaigns of Charles XII of Sweden or Napoleon was no longer relevant. He maintained that he could rely with certainty upon the collapse of the Soviet system as soon as his first blows reached their mark. He believed the Russian populace would embrace his National-Socialist ideology. But as soon as the campaign began almost everything was done to prevent any such thing from taking place. By ill-treating the native populations in the occupied Russian territories that were administered by high Party functionaries, and by reason of his decision to dissolve the Russian state and to incorporate considerable areas into Germany, Hitler succeeded in uniting all Russians under the banner of Stalin. They were now fighting for Holy Mother Russia and against a foreign invader.

In part responsible for this blunder was his habit of under-estimating other races and nations. This had become evident before the war, within Germany, in his significantly short-sighted and irresponsibly harsh treatment of the Jews. It now assumed an even more sinister aspect. If any single fact played a predominant part in the collapse of

National-Socialism and of Germany it was the folly of this racial policy.

Hitler wished to unite Europe. His failure to understand the characteristic differences of the various nations, combined with his methods of centralised control, doomed this intention from the start.

The Russian war soon showed the limitations of Germany's strength. But Hitler did not conclude from this that he must either break off the undertaking or at least choose more modest objectives; on the contrary, he plunged into the unlimited. He was determined, by means of reckless violence, to force defeat upon the Russians. With incomprehensible blindness he was simultaneously courting war with the United States. It is true that Roosevelt's order to his ships that they might open fire on Germany's naval vessels had produced a state of affairs that was close to war. But between that and actual, open warfare there might have lain a very long road had Hitler's overweening arrogance not closed it.

This frightening gesture on his part coincided with our first decisive defeat on the battlefields before Moscow. Hitler's strategy, lacking in consistency, and subject to continual vacillation in its execution, had crashed. From now on ruthlessly harsh treatment of his own troops was to make up for a failure of capability on the part of the controlling mind. For a time this proved successful. But in the long run it was not enough simply to remind his soldiers of the sacrifices made by Frederick the Great's grenadiers on the orders of that powerful king and commander. It was not enough that he should identify himself with the German people and thus, because he was prepared for privation, that he should simply ignore the population's basic requirements.

I must now turn to Hitler's personal characteristics as they impressed me. What sort of a man was he? He was a vegetarian, a teetotaler and a non-smoker. These were, taken independently, very admirable qualities which derived from his personal convictions and from his ascetic way of life. But, connected with this, was his isolation as a human being. He had no real friend. His oldest Party comrades were, it is true, disciples, but they could hardly be described as friends. So far as I could see there was nobody who was really close to him. There was nobody in whom he would really confide his deepest feelings. There was nobody with whom he could talk freely and openly. As he never found a true friend, so he was denied the ability deeply to love a woman. He remained unmarried. He had no children. Everything on this earth that casts a glow of warmth over our life as mortals, friendship with fine men, the pure love for a wife, affection for one's own children, all this was and remained for ever unknown to him. His path through the world was a solitary one and he followed it

alone, with only his gigantic plans for company. His relationship with
Eva Braun may be cited as a contradiction of what I have here written.
I can only say that I knew nothing of this and that so far as I am
aware I never once saw Eva Braun, though for months on end I was
with Hitler and his entourage almost every day. It was only when I
was in prison that I first learned of that liaison. It is obvious that this
woman cannot have had any influence over Hitler, and the more's the
pity, for it could only have been a softening one.

Such was Germany's dictator, a man lacking the wisdom and
moderation of his great examples, Frederick the Great and Bismarck,
a man going in solitary haste from success to success and then pressing
on from failure to failure, his head full of his stupendous plans, clinging
ever more frantically to the last vanishing prospects of victory, identi-
fying himself ever more with his country.

He turned night into day. Until far into the early hours one conference would succeed another. His meals, which, until the Stalingrad
disaster, had provided him with brief periods of rest in company with
the men of the *OKW*, were thereafter brought to him separately. Only
very rarely would he invite one or two guests to eat with him. He
would hastily swallow his dish of vegetables or of farinaceous food.
He drank with it either cold water or malt beer. After the last conference of the night was over he would sit for hours on end with his
adjutants and his female secretaries, discussing his plans until after
dawn had broken. Then he would retire for a short rest, from which
he was usually awakened by the brooms of the charwoman banging
against his bedroom door at nine o'clock at the latest. An over-hot
bath was then supposed to reawaken his still drowsy mind. So long
as all was going well this irregular way of life did not appear to do
him any harm. But as one blow followed another and his nerves began
to give way he turned increasingly to drugs; he had injections to make
him sleep, to wake him up again, to calm his heart, to stimulate it
once more; his personal physician, Morell, gave him whatever he
asked, but all the same the patient still frequently took far more than
the prescribed quantity, particularly of a heart medicine that contained
strychnine. Thus, in due course, he ruined both his body and his mind.

When, after the Stalingrad disaster, I first saw him again following
an interval of fourteen months I noticed the change in his condition.
His right hand trembled, he stooped, he stared fixedly, his eyes had a
tendency to bulge and were dull and lustreless, there were hectic red
spots on his cheeks. He was more excitable than ever. When angered
he lost all self-control and then both what he would say and do became
unpredictable. The external symptoms of his malady grew ever more
pronounced, though the change was barely perceptible to his closer

circle who saw him every day. Finally, after the assassination attempt of July 20th, 1944, it was no longer simply his left hand but the whole left side of his body that trembled. He would place his right hand on his left and cross his right leg over the left one so that, when he was seated, this trembling might be less noticeable. He now walked awkwardly, he stooped more than ever, and his gestures were both jerky and slow. He had to have a chair pushed beneath him when he wished to sit down. His mind, it is true, remained active; but this very activity was itself unhealthy, since its mainsprings were his distrust of humanity and his anxiety to conceal his physical, spiritual, political and military bankruptcy. Thus he attempted continually to deceive both himself and others in his efforts to keep his edifice standing, for he really knew what was the true state of himself as well as of his cause.

With a fanatic's intensity he grasped at every straw which he imagined might save himself and his work from destruction. His entire and very great will-power was devoted to this one idea which was now all that preoccupied him—"never to give in, never to surrender."

Thus within the man whom the German nation had raised from obscurity to be its leader, because it hoped that he would give it a new social order, a resurrection from the defeat of the First World War, and true peace both internally and externally, the demon conquered the genius. Abandoned by his good fairies, he ended in utterly destroying his own handiwork, and with him a fine, upstanding, hard-working and loyal nation was cast down into the depths.

The doctors with whom I talked in prison, and who knew Hitler and his maladies, told me that he suffered from *Paralysis Agitans*, which is also called Parkinson's disease. The layman, though quite well able to observe the more superficial symptoms of this illness, would not be able to diagnose it for what it was. The first doctor correctly to name Hitler's malady—so far as I now recall, at the beginning of 1945—was Professor de Crinis of Berlin, who committed suicide shortly after. His diagnosis remained secret. The personal physicians said nothing. The German Cabinet was thus unable to form any clear picture of Hitler's physical condition; but even had it been in a position to do so it remains doubtful whether it would have been able to take the steps that were, in consequence, necessary. It may be assumed that the root of the appalling disease did not, in his case, lie in some earlier venereal infection, but rather that it derived from a severe chill suffered at some time in the past; for example, from a cold in the head. It is for the doctors to make their estimates on this subject. All the German people needs to know is that the man at their head, in whom they had an implicit trust such as few nations have ever

given a leader, was a sick man. This sickness was his misfortune and
his fate. It was also the misfortune and the fate of his country.

The Party

Apart from Hitler's deputy, Rudolf Hess, the most outstanding
personality of the National-Socialist German Workers' Party was
Hermann Goering, who was appointed as Hitler's eventual successor.
An officer on the active list during the First World War, a fighter ace
who had taken over from Richthofen, a knight of the order *Pour le
Mérite*, after that war was over he had been one of the founders of
the SA.[1]

A ruthless and very informal man, he began by showing considerable
activity, and he laid the foundations for the construction of a modern
German air force. Whether without his driving energy and his insistence
on the creation of a third and independent branch of the armed forces
a really up-to-date and operationally efficient air force could in fact
have been formed is doubtful in view of the limited understanding for
this development that was shown by the senior branches of the armed
forces, even despite the outstanding qualities of the first Chief of the
Air Force General Staff, General Wever.

Once, however, Goering had seen the young German air force
through its teething troubles, he surrendered more and more to the
charms of newly won power. He adopted a feudal manner of life,
collecting decorations, precious stones and antiques, building his
famous country seat, Karin Hall, concentrating with visible results on
the joys of the table. On one occasion, while sunk in contemplation
of old pictures in an East Prussian castle, he suddenly cried out:
'Magnificent! I, too, am a man of the Renaissance. I adore splendour!'
His style of dress grew ever more eccentric; at Karin Hall or while
hunting he adopted the costume of the ancient Teutons, and when
on duty his uniform was always unorthodox; he either wore red boots
of Russian leather with golden spurs—an item of dress scarcely essential
to an aviator—or else he would appear at Hitler's conferences in long
trousers and black patent-leather pumps. He was strongly scented and
he painted his face. His fingers were covered with heavy rings in which
were set the many large gems that he loved to display. From a medical
point of view these distressing manifestations are accounted for by
disturbances to his hormones.

As plenipotentiary responsible for the Four-Year Plan he exercised
great influence on Germany's economy.

In political matters he proved himself considerably more far-

[1] The *Sturmabteilungen*, or Nazi Party storm troopers.—*Tr.*

sighted than his Party comrades, in that he attempted at the last moment to prevent the outbreak of war. For this purpose he made use of a Swedish acquaintance, Birger Dalerus, but unfortunately without success.

During the war his influence was uncommonly disastrous. He overvalued the Luftwaffe and he was responsible for halting the Army outside Dunkirk, for the failure of the attack on Great Britain, for making a promise he could not keep to supply the Sixth Army in Stalingrad by air and thus for Hitler's order that the town be held, and for many another disaster.

From what I saw of him after 1943 I can only conclude that at that time he knew little or nothing about the state of the Luftwaffe. When he attempted to interfere with the actions of the Army such interference was either motivated by crass ignorance or by strong dislike.

His role as Hitler's heir presumptive led him to adopt a very conceited and self-satisfied manner.

By August 1944 at the latest Hitler recognised the incompetence of the Commander-in-Chief of the Luftwaffe. In Jodl's and my presence he addressed him in very blunt terms: 'Goering! The Luftwaffe's doing nothing. It is no longer worthy to be an independent Service. And that's your fault. You're lazy.' When the portly *Reichsmarschall* heard these words great tears trickled down his cheeks. He had no reply. The scene was altogether so unpleasant that I suggested to Jodl that he and I go into another room and leave the two of them together. As a result of this conversation I urged Hitler to act according to what he now realised and to appoint some competent air force general to succeed the *Reichsmarschall*. I told him that we dare not risk losing the whole war on account of the incompetence of one man like Goering. But Hitler replied: 'For political reasons I cannot do as you suggest. The Party would never understand my motives.' When I said that in my opinion political considerations urgently demanded the appointment of a new Commander-in-Chief of the Air Force, since if that were not soon done there would be no policy left to consider, I failed to make any impression. Until the very end Goering retained his offices and his titles, even though in the final months he joined Galland in sending back his decorations and his gold braid as a protest against Hitler's criticisms of the Luftwaffe. It is true that he continued to obey Hitler's order that he attend conferences, but now he dressed with extreme simplicity, without decorations or orders and wearing an ordinary soldier's forage cap, which for him was not a very becoming style.

He seldom dared speak the truth to Hitler.

Only in prison and by the manner of his death did Goering do something to atone for his past negligence. By taking his own life he escaped from his terrestrial judges, after having openly defended his own past actions.

The most impenetrable of all Hitler's disciples was the National Leader of the SS, Heinrich Himmler. An inconspicuous man with all the marks of racial inferiority, the impression he made was one of simplicity. He went out of his way to be polite. In contrast to that of Goering his private life might be described as positively Spartan in its austerity.

His imagination was all the more vivid, and even fantastic. He seemed like a man from some other planet. His racial doctrine was fallacious and led him to commit terrible crimes. His attempt to educate the German people in National-Socialism resulted only in concentration camps. As late as 1943, long after Stalingrad, he still believed that Russia should be colonised by Germans as far as the Urals. On one occasion, when I said to him that it was already impossible to find volunteer colonists for the east, he insisted that the land as far as the Urals must be Germanised by compulsory colonisation if necessary and by planting the land with German peasants conscripted for that purpose.

As for the consequences of Himmler's racial theories, I have, from personal observation and experience, nothing to say. Hitler and Himmler succeeded in keeping this part of their programme strictly secret.

Himmler's 'methods of education,' as practised in the concentration camps, have meanwhile become sufficiently well known. During his lifetime the general public knew only a little about this. The atrocities carried out in those camps were made known to most people, as to myself, only after the collapse. The way the concentration camp methods were kept secret can only be described as masterly.

After 20th July Himmler became filled with military ambition: this led him to have himself appointed commander of the Training Army and even commander of an army group. In military matters Himmler proved an immediate and total failure. His appreciation of our enemies was positively childish. His decisions when in command of Army Group Vistula, in 1945, were dictated by fear. Despite this he retained Hitler's confidence almost up to the end. All the same even this paladin bowed down before the dictator. I was in a position on several occasions to observe his lack of self-assurance and of civil courage in Hitler's presence. The most spectacular example of this I have already described when dealing with the events of February 13th, 1945.[1]

Himmler's most notable creation was the SS. After the collapse this

[1] See p. 413.

organisation was accused and condemned in root and branch. And that was unjust.

The SS originated as Hitler's bodyguard. A desire to supervise not only the uninitiated mass of the populace but also the Party organisation led to its increase in strength. After the concentration camps were set up Himmler made the SS responsible for their control. This marks the point at which the SS was subdivided into two main groups: the *Waffen-SS*, or Armed SS, a primarily military organisation, and the *Allgemeine-SS*, or General SS. The man entrusted with the task of training future leaders for the *Waffen-SS* was the former army general, Hausser, formerly chief of staff of my old division at Stettin. General Hausser was a first-class officer, a brave and clever soldier and a man of outstandingly upright and honourable character. The *Waffen-SS* had every reason to feel gratitude towards this remarkable man—not least of all for the fact that it was spared the general obloquy that at Nuremberg, after the collapse, was heaped on the SS as a whole.

During the war, owing to Hitler's insistence, the *Waffen-SS* was continually expanded. From 1942 on it no longer received sufficient volunteers to fill the ranks of its many formations so that from that period replacements were drafted to the SS in exactly the same way that they were conscripted into the Army. The *Waffen-SS* thus lost its political character of being a volunteer Party guard. However, Himmler continued to exert his influence in order to make sure that it received the highest standard of recruits and the best available equipment. But this favouritism was unimportant in comparison to the feeling of comradeship which existed on the battlefield between *Waffen-SS* and army formations. I fought with the *SS-Leibstandarte 'Adolf Hitler'* and with the SS Division *Das Reich*: later, as Inspector-General of Armoured Troops, I visited numerous SS divisions. I can therefore assert that to my knowledge the SS divisions were always remarkable for a high standard of discipline, of *esprit de corps*, and of conduct in the face of the enemy. They fought shoulder to shoulder with the panzer divisions of the Army, and the longer the war went on the less distinguishable they became from the Army.

There can, of course, be no doubt that Himmler had quite other ends in view when he arranged for the expansion of the *Waffen-SS*. Both Hitler and he distrusted the Army, for their intentions were dark and there always existed the danger for them that if the Army recognised them in time it might resist. Therefore, despite the disadvantages involved, they increased the number of *Waffen-SS* divisions to thirty-five. A large number of units were formed consisting of foreign personnel, whose reliability was on occasion very good, on occasion doubtful. Finally, however, Hitler began to distrust even those allegedly most loyal of his adherents. The fact that in March 1945 he ordered them to surrender their armbands is indicative of the degree of estrangement that by then existed between Hitler and the *Waffen-SS*.

A far different judgment must be passed on the *Allgemeine-SS*. Here, too, there were doubtless idealists to be found, who originally believed that they had joined an order with special responsibilities and therefore entitled to special privileges. There were also many men of good character and spirit, men drawn from the most varied professions and careers, who had simply been appointed members of the SS by Himmler without any questions being asked. But as time went on the picture changed; the SS took over numerous police functions of a most dubious sort. Then units of the *Allgemeine-SS* were also armed. The number of foreign formations was here also constantly on the increase; these were markedly worse than the units of the *Waffen-SS*, as, for example, was shown by the behaviour of the Kaminski and Dirlewanger Brigades in the crushing of the Warsaw uprising.[1]

I never had anything to do with the *SD* and its *Einsatzkommandos* (Operational commandos) and am therefore not able to give any first-hand information concerning them.

Himmler ended his life by committing suicide though he had previously consistently condemned such an action, which he claimed to regard as contemptible and which he had forbidden the SS. He therefore escaped his judges here below and left behind less responsible men to carry the burden of his great guilt.

One of the cleverest men in Hitler's close circle was Dr. Joseph Goebbels, the Gauleiter of Berlin and also Minister for People's Enlightenment and Propaganda. He was a skilled orator and in the struggle against the Communists for Berlin's vote he had demonstrated great personal courage. But he was also a dangerous demagogue, quite unscrupulous in his agitations against the churches and the Jews, or against parents and school teachers; and he was largely responsible for the notorious pogrom, the so-called 'Crystal Night,' of November 1938.

He was certainly in a position to recognise the errors and weaknesses of the National-Socialist system, but he lacked the courage necessary to lay his knowledge before Hitler. In Hitler's presence he—like Goering and Himmler—was a little man. He both feared and idolised him. Hitler's powers of suggestion were seldom so apparent as in his relationship with Goebbels. The highly skilled demagogue fell silent in Hitler's presence. He did his best to unravel his master's wishes, and in his propaganda—at which he might almost be called a genius—he seldom, if ever, displeased the dictator.

[1] See page 355.

I was particularly disappointed by his lack of courage in 1943, when he refused to grasp what he called 'the thorny problem' of the supreme leadership of the armed forces and the State.[1] As a result of this failure of will, he was forced to end his own life and those of his dependants in the frightful way that he even then already foresaw.

Next to Himmler the most sinister member of Hitler's entourage was Martin Bormann. He was a thick-set, heavy jowled, disagreeable, conceited and bad-mannered man. He hated the army, which he regarded as the eternal barrier to the limitless supremacy of the Party, and he attempted, with success, to do it harm whenever he could, to sow distrust, to prevent necessary measures being taken, to drive all decent persons away from Hitler's entourage and from positions of authority and to replace them with his creatures.

Bormann saw to it that Hitler was not kept informed of the real internal political situation. He prevented even the Gauleiters from seeing Hitler. Thus a grotesque state of affairs arose by which the Gauleiters—in particular Forster of West Prussia and Greiser of the Warthegau—came to me, the representative of the military they so distrusted, and asked for my help in arranging that they be allowed to see Hitler since Bormann consistently prevented them from obtaining interviews through normal Party channels.

The sicker that Hitler grew and the worse the military situation became, the fewer were the number of people who could reach the dictator. Everything had to be done through this sinister guttersnipe, Bormann, and thus his methods became increasingly successful.

I had repeated angry altercations with him, because over and over again he would sabotage the taking of necessary military measures for the sake of the obscure political game that he was playing. He would also attempt to interfere in matters that purely concerned the Army, always with unfortunate results.

Bormann was the *éminence grise* of the Third Reich.

National and District Controllers

The National-Socialist Party was led by the National Controllers (*Reichsleiter*) and District Controllers (*Gauleiter*). Every side of German life was embraced by the Party's system and controlled by the Party's schematic organisation. The first step was the Hitler Youth and the League of German Maidens. After leaving the Hitler Youth the young males joined the National Labour Service whose leader was Hierl. This organisation, originally volunteer in nature, had a good influence thanks to the decency of its leader and his assistants, though nowadays

[1] See pp. 293 and 324.

it might be reproached for its rigidly military system and training methods.

German workers were controlled by Dr. Ley in his capacity as *Reichsorganisationsleiter* (National Controller of Organisation). Arrangements were made for the holidays of the working class by the *Kraft durch Freude* (Strength through Joy) organisation, while the Winter Aid and National-Socialist Assistance groups took care of the unfortunate. Private and religious charities were looked on with disfavour and their activities curtailed.

There was a National Health Controller, a National Peasant Controller and so on.

The legal system was under Reichsleiter Frank and was to be developed according to National-Socialist ideals. But in this field National-Socialism showed a particular lack of creative ability.

In foreign affairs Reichsleiter Alfred Rosenberg's organisation paralleled that of the Foreign Minister. Rosenberg's ideological enthusiasm led him frequently to act in opposition to the official policy with, of course, unfortunate results.

Even sport was regimented. The National Sport Leader, von Tschammer und Osten, performed his duties well. On the occasion of the Olympic Games he was able to increase the esteem in which the Third Reich was held.

A woman, the National Women's Leaderess, completed the picture.

The above list is by no means exhaustive; I give it simply in order to show what the principle was. There were many mutually antagonistic forces at work. Yet as a group all these individuals did jobs that were equivalent to those of the normal apparatus of the State and in consequence friction inevitably and frequently arose.

This duplication and contradiction of effort becomes even more apparent when we turn to the next level of National-Socialist officials, the District Controllers, or Gauleiter.

The National-Socialists wished to give the German Reich a new form and therefore replaced the old provincial administration with *Gaue*, or Districts. This reformatory intention was to be realised by means of the appointment of Gauleiters. After the Austrian *anschluss*, the establishment of the Protectorate of Bohemia–Moravia and the seizure of Posen and West Prussia, so-called National Districts (*Reichsgaue*) were created for these territories, which, though considered to be outside the national frontiers, yet gave an indication of what the future organisation was intended to be. But this organisation remained a hybrid thing, like so many other plans that were initiated with the greatest enthusiasm but never completed.

The Gauleiters were in fact Hitler's deputies, and in the Reichsgaue they were actually called *Reichsstatthalter*.[1] They were appointed on the basis of their services to the Party and not for any administrative talents or distinction of character. That is why, among other highly admirable men, there were to be found a number of disreputable persons who did no honour either to the name of Germany or to the reputation of the Nationalist-Socialist Party.

Only occasionally were the offices of the Gauleiters combined with those of the highest local administrators, as for example in Mainfranken, where the Gauleiter was likewise President of the Council (*Regierungspresident*). In general the Gauleiters were additional and superior to the *Regierungspresidenten*, the *Oberpresidenten* of the Provinces and the *Ministerpresidenten* of the *Länder* or States.

As a result the pyramidal state, the *Führerstaat*, which Hitler wished to create and which had formed part of his political programme, did not in fact exist. On the contrary, the condition of the national administration became ever more chaotic and even anarchic, and this tendency was increased by the appointment of numerous National Commissars, Generals Plenipotentiary, Special Commissioners and the rest. As time went by the whole system grew increasingly out of hand.

It was the same story in many different fields. The huge building programme remained uncompleted, neither the national highroads nor the Party buildings being ever finished: the re-erection of Berlin, Münich and other great towns did not take place. Similarly the great national reforms bogged down at an early stage. The reform of the schools by the incompetent Minister of Education, Rust, came to nothing. The reorganisation of the Evangelical Church by the State Bishop, Müller, was a failure. It was the same story over and over again of grandiose plans and feeble execution, because both wisdom and moderation were lacking, because arrogance took its toll in these fields too, and finally because the outbreak of war put an end to all such endeavours.

Hitler's Intimate Circle

A picture of the leading personalities of the Party contains more darkness than light. Hitler's knowledge of mankind had proved defective when it came to choosing the leaders for his own Party. This makes it appear all the more curious that he should have kept a number of young men around him who were most carefully selected and who preserved their decency of character despite the temptations to which they were exposed. Both the military and the Party adjutants were upright men and, indeed, almost everyone employed in those positions was notable for politeness, good manners and discretion.

[1] Roughly, lieutenant-governors.—*Tr.*

Next to Bormann, Fegelein at the end made the most displeasing impression. He was an SS-Brigade Leader, Himmler's permanent representative, and by his marriage to Eva Braun's sister, became as it were Hitler's brother-in-law, a position which he abused in a particularly tactless fashion. Other unpleasant individuals were his personal physician, Morell, who was guilty of questionable professional practices, and, I am sorry to say, General Burgdorf, who succeeded Schmundt as head of the Army Personnel Office after the latter's death. These persons were a clique, constantly intriguing and forming a barrier between Hitler and the rest of the world which prevented him from learning the truth. They all drank far too heavily and thus—at the end, at least, when the collapse was imminent—offered a very sad example to others.

The Government

Beside the unique Party machine there stood the government of the country. The Cabinet, as originally nominated by Hindenburg, had consisted of a majority of bourgeois ministers and a minority of National-Socialists. Apart from Hitler the Party members to start with were the Minister of the Interior, Frick, and the Minister of Aviation, Goering. But very soon other Party members were appointed to the Cabinet, including the Minister for People's Enlightenment and Propaganda, Dr. Goebbels; the Minister of Education, Rust; the Minister of Food, Darré; the Postmaster, Ohnesorge, and two Ministers without Portfolio, Hess and Roehm.

Nevertheless von Papen continued to be Vice-Chancellor; Freiherr von Neurath, Foreign Minister; Graf Schwerin von Krosigk, Minister of Finance; Seldte, Minister of Labour; von Blomberg, Minister of War; Hugenberg, Minister of Economics—succeeded by Schmitt and, later, by Schacht—Gürtner, Minister of Justice; Baron Eltz von Rübenach and later Dorpmüller, Minister of Transport. They were all good, competent executives and, in some cases, outstanding men. Their influence on Hitler was slight.

As the National-Socialist Party became more and more firmly established through the greater concentration of power in Hitler's hands, the Ministers were increasingly pushed aside. After 1938 there were, for all intents and purposes, no more meetings of the Cabinet and each Minister simply administered his own department. From that time on they no longer exercised the slightest influence in major political matters. In foreign affairs this change became evident when the Foreign Minister, Freiherr von Neurath, left and was replaced by Herr von Ribbentrop. On the same day Hitler personally assumed the dual role of Minister of War and Commander-in-Chief of the Armed

Forces. Papen was kicked out after June 30th, 1934. Later Funk replaced Schacht. In 1941 Hess flew to England.

The men of this group whom I knew personally to a greater or lesser extent were the Finance Minister, Graf Schwerin von Krosigk, the Minister of Labour, Seldte, and the two Ministers for Armaments and War Production appointed successively during the war, Todt and Speer. I also knew the Minister of Food, Darré.

Graf Schwerin von Krosigk is a typical outstanding high German official. He was partially educated in England, a remarkable and modest man.

Seldte, who had at one time been head of the *Stahlhelm*, the ex-service men's organisation, was a decent man, but possessed no power.

Todt, an intelligent individual and a believer in moderation, did his best to exert a humanising influence.

Speer preserved a sensitive heart through all the horrors of the closing years of the Third Reich. He was a good comrade, with an open character and an intelligent, natural manner. Originally an independent architect, he became Minister after Todt's early death. He disliked bureaucratic methods and attempted to act according to a healthy understanding of human nature. We worked together without friction and always did our best to give one another such assistance as lay within our power, which is surely the obvious and sensible way to behave. But of how many prominent men in the Third Reich could it be said that they pursued this obvious and sensible course? Speer always retained his objectivity. I never saw him become exaggeratedly excited. He managed to calm down his occasionally highly temperamental colleagues, and when inter-departmental strife arose he always did his best to pacify both parties.

Speer possessed sufficient courage to speak his mind to Hitler. At an early stage he explained to him clearly and fully why the war could no longer be won and why it must therefore be ended. This brought down Hitler's anger upon him.

Even before the war Darré had opposed Hitler. He was eliminated, no doubt due to machinations by some competitor within the Party.

But taken all in all it must be regretfully admitted that the Cabinet was not in a position to exert any influence worth mentioning on events during the period of the Third Reich.

14. THE GERMAN GENERAL STAFF

The General Staff was Scharnhorst's and Gneisenau's progeny. Its godparents were the spirit of Frederick the Great and the national desire for freedom from the yoke of Germany's oppressor, Napoleon. After the war of liberation against the French Emperor had been successfully concluded, Europe settled down to a long period of peace. The national economies, weakened by years of war, had to be built up anew; the states were therefore compelled to limit their military expenditure. In this peaceful Europe the continued existence of the Prussian General Staff was hardly noticeable. It was during the period of calm that one of the most important works of military science was composed, *Vom Kriege* ('On War'), by the director of the Prussian War Academy, Carl von Clausewitz.

This little-read but much-criticised book contains the first attempt to create a philosophy of war and to analyse its characteristics from a detached standpoint. It played a great part in forming the attitude of mind of several generations of German General Staff Corps officers. From it derives that striving to observe both men and affairs coolly and sensibly which has been the foremost quality of all outstanding members of the German General Staff. It served also to strengthen the patriotism and the idealism which inspired such officers.

If Scharnhorst, Gneisenau and Clausewitz are to be regarded as the spiritual parents of the Prusso-German General Staff, Field-Marshal Graf von Moltke must be regarded as its greatest and most finished son. It was Schlieffen who coined the apothegm: 'Great achievements, small display: more reality than appearance,' and this was a recognition of the qualities of Moltke and of his school. As a result of Bismarck's outstanding statesmanship he was enabled to fight and win three wars and thus to assist in the unification of the German nation and people. By so doing he simultaneously enhanced the authority of his organisation, the General Staff.

After Moltke's death the German General Staff did not, perhaps, avoid being influenced by the conditions prevailing at the turn of the century. The growing prosperity of Germany after the successful completion of the struggle for unity affected both the Officer Corps and the General Staff. At last Germany had achieved its position as a first-class power in the comity of European nations, and this created a state of military self-confidence which was most highly developed among the officers of the General Staff Corps, the intellectual élite of the Army. It was with this attitude that the General Staff went to war in 1914. During that war it performed its duty. If in those four years it was, in relationship to the generals, more in evidence than heretofore, this was less the responsibility of the General Staff Corps than of the generals themselves who, partly through age and partly through a failure to grasp military technique and a correspondingly one-sided preoccupation with troop service, allowed themselves to become increasingly over-shadowed.

It has been maintained that the General Staff under Ludendorff assumed an entirely disproportionate importance, that it suffered from hypertrophy. But without Ludendorff's powerful creative energy it is doubtful if the General Staff, and indeed the German Army, would ever have been capable of the great efforts that it made. Ludendorff can hardly be blamed for the fact that in that war Germany finally went down before the enemy's vast preponderance of strength, since he only assumed a position of authority in 1916; indeed, had it not been for the emergence of himself and of Hindenburg the war would surely have been already lost that year. Those two great soldiers undertook an almost superhuman and utterly thankless task. It would be unjust to blame them for what later happened. Despite the unfortunate outcome of the war and the post-war dissensions that followed the defeat, Hindenburg and Ludendorff remained the two outstanding representatives of all that was best in the German General Staff Corps. The difficulties of the war we had to wage often, it is true, forced Ludendorff to make harsh and even ruthless decisions. Many of his pupils were later to believe that this attitude of his, dictated in his case by necessity, was in fact an essential element in the character of a good General Staff Corps officer; it was specifically this least amiable quality in his waging of war that they chose to copy; thus there arose a type of officer distinguished for his ruthless determination and pushing energy, which was not attractive and which did the General Staff Corps' reputation no good either among the general public or among the troops. But when considering the long sequence of individuals who were typical of the Prusso-German General Staff, this last type plays a very insignificant and unimportant part.

Scharnhorst was the son of a peasant. Born in Lower Saxony he was taciturn, deliberate, selfless, brave, unassuming, incorruptible, and un-selfish. He organised the Prussian Army during the War of Liberation, founded the General Staff and died as a result of severe wounds received on the field of battle.

Gneisenau, Blücher's chief of staff, defended Kolberg in 1806. By nature he was vivid, fiery, and extremely brilliant and he advised his commander during many battles, some successful, some unsuccessful. After the defeat at Ligny on June 16th, 1815, he urged Blücher to march towards the allied English Army; it was this action that led to the victory of Waterloo on June 18th, 1815, and the defeat of Napoleon by the allied armies.

Clausewitz was never privileged to hold high office in wartime. He wrote *Vom Kriege*. He was the type of quiet, retiring, scholarly man, often to be found in the German General Staff Corps. Little known during his lifetime, he was to exercise a great influence on future generations.

Moltke was the most important Chief of the German Army General Staff. He was world-famous as a thinker and planner and proved himself to be a genius at command in war. Distinguished in manner and reticent by nature, his deliberate and very thorough intellect was his most marked characteristic. He had a great influence. He was not only a great soldier but a noble man, a fine writer and an attentive observer of foreign nations and customs.

Schlieffen was distinguished, clever, cool, and inclined to sarcasm. He was forced to draw up plans during a period of vacillating policy and inferior chancellors. He attempted, by means of the clarity and determination of his military planning, to compensate for the aimlessness and irresolution of the politicians. Like Moltke, he possessed a comprehension for the technical requirements of the age. The clarity and convincing strength of his ideas so impressed his successor, the younger Moltke, that his plan of campaign remained, except for minor details, unaltered after his death and was indeed put into practice, in conditions different from those that he had envisaged, in 1914. The failure of the so-called Schlieffen Plan cannot therefore be blamed on him but only on his less competent successors. He never had the opportunity to prove himself in battle.

Hindenburg was a straightforward man, clear, resolute and chivalrous. To those he trusted he allowed a very free hand. He also had a clear appreciation of events and a profound knowledge of human nature. 'If the Battle of Tannenberg had been lost, there can be no question as to who would have been held responsible for the defeat.'

Ludendorff was a strong-willed man with an enormous capacity for work and an outstanding talent for organisation. He was filled with

burning patriotism and he fought a titanic struggle to stave off the
defeat that threatened to engulf his country. His achievements, at a
most difficult period, were very considerable.

Seeckt was clear-headed, deliberate, and cool. The impression he
made in public was almost one of shyness. He was as gifted a strategist
as he was an organiser, though he possessed less comprehension for
technical matters than had Moltke or Schlieffen. After the collapse of
1918 he created the Weimar Republic's 100,000-man army. By the
terms of the Versailles Treaty this army was not allowed a General
Staff. Seeckt had to submit to this order. But he found ways, during
the period of disarmament, to maintain among the officers of the staff
the old General Staff Corps spirit. His struggle to keep the army free
from the influence of party politics was undoubtedly correct from his
point of view; it had, however, in the long run an unfortunate result in
that the Officer Corps in general, and the future General Staff Corps
officers in particular, were in consequence largely uneducated in matters
of internal and external politics. That was the principal weakness of his
system.

Beck was highly educated, calm and distinguished. When our right
to military self-determination had been re-established, he devoted himself to reconstructing the General Staff in the spirit of Moltke. He had
little understanding for the technical requirements of the age. He stood
aloof from the problems of aviation, motorisation, and radio. He found
the revolutionary developments brought about in warfare by technical
progress disagreeable, and he attempted to hinder them; similarly, he
would have no part in the political revolution represented by National-
Socialism. He was by nature a conservative and a procrastinator, and it
was this aspect of his character that was his undoing.

From the above brief characterisations of a few prominent representatives of the German General Staff it is possible to draw certain
deductions concerning its spirit as a whole. During its long existence
the object of the General Staff Corps was to select those officers with
the finest brains and characters and so to train and educate them
that they could lead the German armed forces in any circumstances, no
matter how difficult, in which those forces might be called upon to fight.
Prerequisites for appointment to the General Staff were integrity of
character and unimpeachable behaviour and way of life both on and
off duty. Next came military competence; a man had to have proved
himself at the front, had to have an understanding for tactical and
technical matters, a talent for organisation and powers of endurance

P*

both physical and mental; he had also to be industrious, of a sober temperament and determined.

In selecting officers from this point of view it is possible that intellectual ability was sometimes overvalued in comparison to strength of character and particularly to warmth of personality; but these last two qualities are much less easily estimated, particularly since they do not by their very nature tend to be spectacular.

The great majority of the General Staff Corps officers, especially the older ones, were well aware of those traditions of their corps. But that does not mean that it was always these officers who found themselves in a position to select their successors. Even if that had been the case, it still does not follow that they would necessarily have possessed sufficient knowledge of human nature to enable them to find men with the requisite qualities.

There can be no doubt that old traditions are in theory of great value to any army. The characters of the more eminent General Staff officers of the past, as outlined above, should have provided a younger generation with good models without, at the same time, hindering or perhaps even preventing contemporary development. But in practice tradition is not always regarded as simply supplying ideals of behaviour, but rather as a source of practical example, as though an imitation of what was done before could reproduce identical results despite the fact that meanwhile circumstances and methods have completely altered. Hardly any mature institution can avoid this fallacious aspect of tradition. The Prusso-German Army and its General Staff were not immune from making this mistake in a number of ways. In consequence there was inevitably a certain internal stress between misunderstood tradition and the new tasks that had to be performed. In my time such stress was aggravated by a number of different causes: by the new political condition of Germany, by the altered balance of power in Europe and the world, by the growing importance of technical matters, with the consequent expansion of war into 'total war' and also the resultant widening of the field of political action until a point was reached where it embraced the whole globe.

It is certain that by no means all General Staff officers grasped this new state of affairs. Such lack of comprehension was particularly the case with the older officers, that is to say with those who occupied the more important positions. Modern developments required reorganisation along the lines of a combined armed forces and, in particular, a unified Supreme Command for all those forces. And this most essential requirement, necessitated by political, military, and technical developments, was not initiated before the Second World War by the Army

General Staff. On the contrary, the leaders of the pre-war General Staff consistently opposed and hindered the timely creation of a comprehensive and effective Supreme Command of the armed forces.

As in the question of an Armed Forces Supreme Command, so when it was a matter of setting up an independent, operational air force or of developing the newly conceived armoured force within the Army, the Army General Staff opposed these innovations. The importance of these two technical achievements in so far as they affected the operations of the combined armed forces was neither sufficiently studied nor appreciated, because it was feared that they might result, in the one case, in a decrease of the importance of the Army as a whole and, in the other, in a lessening to the prestige of the older arms of that Service.

Any attempt to widen the General Staff Corps officers' appreciation of the political situation was prevented, first, by the traditional limitation of their interests to purely military matters and, secondly, by Hitler's principle according to which every fragment of the machinery which controlled the State was kept in a sort of specialised, water-tight compartment and no man might know more than was essential for the performance of his own particular job. He regarded it as his unique privilege to be in a position where he might form a comprehensive picture; this, of course, was highly disadvantageous to the German cause as a whole.

The younger generation of staff officers felt this state of tension and stress more acutely than did the older and did their best to resolve it. Their efforts along these lines were not looked on with sympathy by their seniors. The younger men, in opposition to the older, believed that there was no time to be lost; the representatives of tradition wanted, and so far as they were able to do insisted, on a slow and gradual evolution.

It was this clinging to a faulty concept of tradition that primarily brought the General Staff into opposition to Hitler, that awakened his distrust for its competence and reliability and that in the long run created a state of conflict between him and it which had very grave effects on the conduct of the war.

An ideal General Staff Corps officer might be described as possessing the following qualities: sincerity of conviction, cleverness, modesty, self-effacement in favour of the common cause, and strong personal convictions combined with the ability tactfully to present these convictions to his commanding general. If his opinions were not accepted he must be sufficiently master of himself loyally to carry out his commander's decisions and to act at all times in accordance with his wishes. He must fully understand and feel for the needs of the troops and he must be inexhaustible in his efforts to help them. He must have operational, tactical, and technical understanding; in technical matters he must not allow himself to become swamped in details, but yet must know enough to be able to correlate technical innovations with the command of troops in war.

It goes without saying that the General Staff Corps officer must also possess all the virtues required of every officer and soldier and must possess them in a highly developed form: courage, determination, willingness to assume responsibility, a gift for improvisation, physical endurance, as well as considerable industriousness.

Every General Staff Corps officer should do regular tours of duty with troops, both of his original arm of the Service and of other arms, in all sorts of conditions, so that he may collect practical knowledge of various types of fighting and of actual command. In this matter practice, in the years immediately preceding the war, was far divorced from the ideal. The chief reason for this was the shortage of General Staff Corps officers due to the Army's strict adherence to the Versailles Treaty's prohibition of the Great General Staff. This bad state of affairs became worse during the war, in this case because of the reluctance of the higher staffs to suffer the inevitable inconvenience resulting from the departure for the front of their experienced staff officers. In this, the worst example of all was that set by the *OKW* and the *OKH*. There were members of those staffs who, during a war of almost six years' duration, never once saw the front.

Perhaps the most important aspect of the General Staff Corps lay in the fact that its members were trained to judge events and make appreciations, both operational and tactical, according to a definite and uniform system. From this basic uniformity of reaction it was hoped to create a wide uniformity of decision. The French describe this as *l'unité de doctrine*. The Chief of the General Staff, in whom were vested no command powers by which he could exert his will, hoped by means of this similarity of thought-process on the part of all General Staff Corps officers to pervade all formations down to and including divisions with his influence and thus to ensure unity of tactical and operational procedure throughout the whole Army. In order that he might make his ideas known to his officers he created the so-called *Generalstabsdienstweg* (General Staff channel of communication), an institution which led to a certain amount of misunderstanding and which therefore was opposed by Hitler.

The strategic concepts of the General Staff should not crystallise around definite, rigid principles, but must fit the changing political situation and the tasks arising therefrom. Germany's geographical position in Central Europe, surrounded by strongly armed neighbours, compelled the study of a war on several fronts. Since the possibility of such a war invariably involved the prospect of fighting against superior force, this problem, too, had to be carefully examined. The operational thinking of the old General Staff was primarily continental in nature. But the introduction of operational air forces meant that the intervention by powers across the seas would have to be taken far more into consideration. In many cases this fact was not grasped with sufficient clarity.

In view of the possibility of a war against several enemies simultaneously, there was a strategic choice between defending secondary fronts and attacking the principal enemy. There was also the problem of switching the attack from one front to another.

The strict limitations of our resources compelled the General Staff to study how a war could most quickly be concluded. From this there followed the concept of using motors in every form. As a result of the success of our rapid campaigns at the beginning of the Second World War our enemies coined the word *Blitzkrieg* or 'lightning war.'

On account of its geographical position Germany has always been compelled to fight 'on interior lines,' and in that sort of fighting attack alternates with defence. 'Europe now is one family and when discord breaks out in the home it is hard for any member of the family to stand aloof, particularly if he lives in the middle of the house.'[1] In this very apt phrase Schlieffen described our eternal situation which has involved us—very often unwillingly—in every European conflict. The German nation is no more warlike than the other nations of Europe but it lives 'in the middle of the house' and therefore in its long and varied history has seldom managed to avoid involvement in its neighbours' conflicts. As a result of this both its statesmen and its military leaders have repeatedly been confronted with difficult, if not actually insoluble, problems. In view of its limited resources Germany has always striven for a rapid end to any conflict and has of necessity done its best to avoid long wars of attrition and the danger of intervention by third parties. The solving of this problem was the supreme achievement of Bismarck's statecraft and Moltke's strategy.

After the defeat of 1918 the Army was entirely led by officers drawn from the old Imperial Army. There were no others. These officers were prepared to serve the Weimar Republic, even though they did not approve of everything involved in the change from monarchy to republic. They had to sacrifice many a privilege and many a well-loved tradition and this they did in order to prevent their country being at that time overwhelmed by the Asiatic Bolshevik flood that threatened Germany from the East. The Weimar Republic never succeeded in transforming this *mariage de convenance* into a true union of love.

[1] Schlieffen *Gesammelte Schriften*, Vol. II, p. 390; *Gneisenau:* Verlag E. S. Mittler u. S.

There was never any real feeling of mutual affection between the new State and the Officer Corps, even though individuals such as Dr. Gessler, for many years Defence Minister, tried intelligently, skilfully and with genuine feeling to bring this about. This fact was to be significant later on in the attitude adopted by the Officer Corps towards National-Socialism. It is true that the various governments of the Weimar period did do their best to give the armed forces whatever they could in view of the external political situation and the bad state of Germany's economy. But they did not succeed in achieving any close contact with the Officer Corps or in giving that corps any enthusiasm for their political ideals. The armed forces always, basically, remained estranged from the new regime. The cool and sensible attitude of Seeckt increased the already existing tendency of the Officer Corps to stand aloof from politics. The General Staff, or the *Truppenamt* as it was then called, contributed markedly to this attitude of mind.

When National-Socialism, with its new, nationalistic slogans, appeared upon the scene the younger elements of the Officer Corps were soon inflamed by the patriotic theories propounded by Hitler and his followers. The completely inadequate state of the country's armaments had lain like a leaden weight on the Officer Corps for many long years. It is no wonder that the first steps towards rearmament inclined them to favour the man who promised to breathe fresh life into the armed forces after fifteen years' stagnation. The National-Socialist Party further increased its popularity in military circles since to begin with Hitler showed himself to be well disposed towards the Army and refrained from interfering in its private affairs. The previous gap in the Army's political life was now filled, and interest was aroused in political questions, though hardly in the manner that the democrats seem to have expected. Be that as it may, once the National-Socialists had seized power, the leaders of the armed forces could hardly remain aloof from National-Socialist politics, even had they wished to do so. The General Staff certainly played no leading role in this new development; if anything, the contrary was true. The prime example of the sceptical attitude of the General Staff was that of General Beck. He had a number of adherents at the centre, but no influence over the Army as a whole and even less in the other services. Beck and his successor, Halder, might try to put the brake on the swing towards National-Socialism at the hub of military authority; their effect on policy in general was nil and it simply followed its course without the support of, and in opposition to, the General Staff. Once again—as before the First World War—Germany found itself in a political situation from which there seemed to be no way out and which made the war look difficult, if not hopeless, before ever it began. Once again the soldiers, led by the generals and the General Staff Corps officers, had to find a way out of an impasse for which they were not responsible.

All the reproaches that have been levelled against the leaders of the armed forces by their countrymen and by the international courts have failed to take into consideration one very simple fact: that policy is not laid down by soldiers but by politicians. This has always been the case and is so today. When war starts the soldiers can only act according to the political and military situation as it then exists. Unfortunately it is not the habit of politicians to appear in conspicuous places when the bullets begin to fly. They prefer to remain in some safe retreat and to let the soldiers carry out 'the continuation of policy by other means.'

National policy conditions the theories of the soldiers in the preparations for war during the period of so-called 'mental warfare.' The international legal tribunals of the last few years have proved that up to 1938 the plans of the German General Staff were exclusively defensive in nature. The military and political condition of Germany permitted no other. Despite the re-armament that had been in progress since 1935, the specialists of the General Staff had no illusions concerning the long period of time that must elapse before the armed forces, and in particular the new weapons—the air force and the armoured force—would be fit for active service. It was only a direct order from Hitler, the political Head of the State, that forced another course of action on the unwilling soldiers.

Until the autumn of 1938 there existed within the Army a system by which the chiefs of staff, down to and including the chief of staff of an army corps, shared the responsibility for the decisions taken by their respective commanding generals. This system, which involved the forwarding of a report by the chief of staff should he disagree with his commander, was discontinued on Hitler's orders. This resulted in a basic change to the positions of the chiefs of staff in general and to that of the Chief of the Army General Staff in particular. The system of joint responsibility by commanders and chiefs of staff was one inherited from the old Prussian Army and preserved in the 100,000-man army and which had simply been taken over by the armed forces of the Third Reich when re-armament began. During the First World War it had often led to chiefs of staff of strong personality dominating their respective commanders. In accordance with the leader principle (*Führerprinzip*) which he propagated, Hitler now logically ordered that the man who was in command must bear the entire and undivided responsibility; by this decree he automatically abolished the joint responsibility of the Chief of the Army General Staff in relationship to himself in his capacity as Supreme Commander of the Armed Forces.

As already indicated, the Army General Staff was reluctant to accept the concept of a combined armed forces command. Had this not been so we should, before the outbreak of the Second World War, have possessed an Armed Forces General Staff and an Armed Forces Supreme Command existing as effective bodies instead of the caricatures of them that we actually had. The fact that a few individuals in the General Staff favoured the concept of an armed forces command made no difference to the general situation, particularly since the air force and the navy also opposed it. Indeed, in their attitude towards an Armed Forces Supreme Command the commanders-in-chief of the three Services behaved like true republicans. The logical result of all this was the attitude of the General Staff towards the actual *OKW* that was in fact formed—a brain child of General Reichenau's, who did his best to make his good and great idea attractive to Hitler and Blomberg—and which, in view of the firmly unco-operative attitude of all three Services, was inevitably a failure. So long as Reichenau remained head of the Armed Forces Staff he managed to continue to develop his ideas. Once he was replaced by Keitel the driving-force was no longer there. Keitel was not the man to prevail against the opposition of the three Service heads.

At this point I should like to say a few words about the *OKW*. Field-Marshal Keitel was basically a decent individual who did his best to perform the task allotted him. He soon fell under the sway of Hitler's personality and, as time went on, became less and less able to shake off the hypnosis of which he was a victim. He preserved his Lower Saxon loyalty until the day of his death. Hitler knew that he could place unlimited confidence in the man; for that reason he allowed him to retain his position even when he no longer had any illusion about his talents as a strategist. The Field-Marshal exerted no influence on the course of operations. His chief activities were in the administrative field, which had previously been the domain of the War Ministry. It was Keitel's misfortune that he lacked the strength necessary to resist Hitler's orders when such orders ran contrary to international law and to accepted morality. It was only this weakness on his part that permitted the issuing to the troops of the so-called 'Commissar Order' and other notorious decrees. He paid for this with his life at Nuremberg. His family were not permitted to mourn at his grave.

Colonel-General Jodl, the chief of the Armed Forces Command Staff, had in fact controlled the operations of the combined armed forces ever since the Norwegian Campaign of April, 1940. He like Keitel, was a decent man; originally he too had fallen under Hitler's spell, but he had never been so hypnotised as was Keitel and therefore

never became so uncritical. After his quarrel with Hitler during the
Stalingrad period he withdrew completely into his work, most of which
he did with his own hands and without the customary office and clerical
assistance. He was silent and resigned on the question of reforming the
military and political command, and adopted the same attitude towards
the reorganisation and unified leadership of the General Staff. Only in
the last few weeks of the war did he rise to fresh heights. He was to
share Keitel's bitter fate.

If these two officers had assumed a different point of view in their
dealings with Hitler they could have prevented much evil from taking
place. Hitler only tended to give in when confronted by a unified
opposition. But such unity in military matters scarcely ever existed, and
this enabled him to make the *OKH* increasingly powerless and to ignore
any objections that it might raise.

For all that—they were my comrades.

So far as the *OKH* was concerned, during the Polish Campaign its
authority was more or less complete. But even then differences of
opinion must have arisen, and this led Hitler to entrust the operations
in Norway entirely and directly to the Armed Forces Command Staff.
The *OKH* played no part in this campaign whatever. The discussions
concerning the operational plan to be employed against the Western
Powers in 1940 served only to sharpen mutual opposition. In Russia
profound divergences of opinion soon came to light, culminating in
December, 1941, in Hitler's quarrel with Field-Marshal von Brauchitsch.
This latter was a well-trained General Staff officer. Unfortunately he
was not the man to stand up to an opponent of Hitler's calibre. From
the very beginning he was never in a position of complete independence
in his relationship to Hitler. In consequence his behaviour was always
influenced by his consciousness of lack of freedom, and this in turn
decreased his power to act.

After Brauchitsch's departure there was never again a Commander-
in-Chief of the Army. In this command—as the name implies—there
were vested command powers. Such powers must be either unlimited or
non-existent. And after December 19th, 1941, they were exercised
exclusively by Hitler. That date marks the practical decease of the
General Staff of the old Prusso-German stamp.

For myself, I wore the uniform of the General Staff Corps proudly
for fifteen years. Among my teachers and my superiors I met a whole
series of exemplary characters for whom I have emotions of eternal
gratitude. Among my comrades I found many good and loyal friends

and among my subordinates the best possible assistants and advisers. I thank them all from the bottom of my heart.

Twice, after the loss of a World War, the General Staff has been dissolved on the orders of the victors. Both these actions show the unwilling respect in which our former enemies hold that most excellent organisation.

'The rest is silence.'

'To Be, or Not to Be, That is the Question!'

My story is ended. It has been very difficult for me to show what it was that led to our second defeat and to describe what I myself experienced. I am only too well aware of the inadequacy of all human endeavour not to recognise the mistakes we made and my own shortcomings.

At a difficult time a prince of my royal family once sent me a small portrait of Frederick the Great on which he had inscribed these words that the great king addressed to his friend, the Marquis d'Argens, when his own defeat seemed imminent. 'Nothing can alter my inner soul: I shall pursue my own straight course and shall do what I believe to be right and honourable.' The little picture I have lost, but the king's words remain engraved on my memory and are for me a model. If, despite everything, I could not prevent the defeat of my country, I must ask my readers to believe that this was not for lack of a will to do so.

This book is intended as a token of gratitude to the dead and to my old soldiers, and as a monument to preserve their fame from oblivion.

APPENDIX I

My Career

17 June, 1888	Born at Kulm on the Vistula.
1894	School at Colmar in Alsace.
1901–3	Cadet School, Karlsruhe.
1903–7	Chief Cadet School, Gross-Lichterfelde, Berlin.
28 February, 1907	Ensign in 10th Hanoverian Jaeger Battalion, Bitche.
April–December, 1907	War School, Metz.
27 January, 1908	Second lieutenant, with seniority 22 June, 1906.
1 October, 1909	Transferred with my battalion to Goslar in the Harz.
1 October, 1912–30 September, 1913	Attached 3rd Telegraph Battalion, Koblenz.
1 October, 1913–outbreak of war	Attached War Academy, Berlin.

First World War

2 August, 1914–April, 1915	Commanding a wireless station, originally with 5th Cavalry Division in the West, then with Fourth Army in Flanders.
October, 1914	Promoted lieutenant.
April, 1915–January, 1916	Assistant Signals Officer with Fourth Army.
December, 1915	Promoted captain.
January, 1916–August, 1916	Assistant Signals Officer with Fifth Army and with various headquarters subordinate to this army.
August, 1916–April, 1917	Signals Officer with Fourth Army.
April, 1917	Transferred to a General Staff position with 4th Infantry Division.
May, 1917	Attached temporarily to 52nd Reserve Division as an acting General Staff Officer during the Battle of the Aisne.
June, 1917	Similar attachment to the headquarters of the Guards Corps.
July, 1917	Similar attachment to the headquarters of the X Reserve Corps.
August, 1917	Return to 4th Infantry Division.
September, 1917	Commander of IInd Battalion, 14th Infantry Regiment.
October, 1917	A General Staff position with Army Command C.

January–February, 1918	General Staff Officers' Course, Sedan.
28 February, 1918	Transferred to the Army General Staff.
May, 1918	Transferred to the staff of XXXVIII Reserve Corps as quartermaster.
October, 1918	Transferred to the General Staff of the German military administration in occupied Italy as Ia (operations officer).

Freikorps and Frontier Defence

November, 1918	Central Office for Eastern Frontier Defence in the Prussian War Ministry, Berlin.
January, 1919	Frontier Defence Command South, Breslau.
March, 1919	Frontier Defence Command North, Bartenstein.
May, 1919	General Staff of the 'Iron Division,' Riga (later Mitau).
October, 1919	Reichswehr Brigade 10, Hanover.
January, 1920	Commanding 3rd Company, 10th Jaeger Battalion, Goslar.
March, 1920	Disturbances in the Hildesheim and Ruhr areas.
Autumn, 1920	Occupation of the neutral zone at Friedrichsfeld, near Wesel.
March–May, 1921	Disturbances in Central Germany, Dessau and Bitterfeld.

Between the Wars

16 January–31 March, 1922	Attached 7th (Bavarian) Motorised Transport Battalion, Munich.
1 April, 1922	Transferred to Defence Ministry, Motorised Troops Department.
1 October, 1924	Transferred to the staff of the 2nd Division, Stettin.
1 February, 1927	Promoted major.
1 October, 1927	Transferred to the Defence Ministry, Army Transport Department of the *Truppenamt*.
1 October, 1928	Simultaneously tactical instructor at the Motor Transport Instructional Staff, Berlin.
1 February, 1930	Commander of the 3rd (Prussian) Motor Transport Battalion, Berlin–Lankwitz.
1 February, 1931	Promoted lieutenant-colonel.
1 October, 1931	Transferred to the Defence Ministry as chief of staff to the Inspectorate of Motorised Troops.
1 April, 1933	Promoted colonel.
1 July, 1934	Chief of staff to the Armoured Troops Command.

15 October, 1935	Commander of 2nd Panzer Division, Würzburg.
1 August, 1936	Promoted major-general.
4 February, 1938	Commander of XVI Army Corps, Berlin, and simultaneously promoted lieutenant-general.
10 March, 1938	Occupation of Austria.
2 October, 1938	Occupation of the Sudetenland.
20 November, 1938	Chief of Mobile Troops and promoted general of panzer troops.

Second World War

August, 1939	Commander XIX Army Corps.
September, 1939	Polish campaign.
May–June, 1940	Western campaign.
1 June, 1940	Commander Panzer Group Guderian.
19 July, 1940	Promoted colonel-general.
16 November, 1940	Commander Panzer Group 2.
5 October, 1941	Commander Second Panzer Army.
26 December, 1941	Transferred to the commanders' reserve pool of the OKH.
1 March, 1943	Inspector-General of Armoured Troops.
21 July, 1944	Also entrusted with the duties of Chief of the Army General Staff.
28 March, 1945	Sent on leave.

Decorations Received in Second World War

5 September, 1939	Clasp to Iron Cross Second Class.
13 September, 1939	Clasp to Iron Cross First Class.
27 October, 1939	Knight's Cross to the Iron Cross.
17 July, 1941	Oak Leaves to the Knight's Cross.

APPENDIX II

The Supreme Commander   *Berlin,* 31.8.39
of the Armed Forces
OKW/WFA Nr. 170/39 g.K. Chefs. L1
Top Secret

Directive No. 1
for the prosecution of the war

1. Having exhausted all political possibilities of rectifying the intolerable situation on Germany's eastern frontier by peaceful means, I have decided to solve the problem *by force*.

2. The attack *on Poland* is to be carried out in accordance with the plans laid down for *Case White*, as modified by the fact that meanwhile the army has almost completed its deployment.

Allotment of tasks and operational objectives remain unchanged.

Date of the attack .   .   .   .   .   .   1 September, 1939.

Hour of the attack .   .   .   .   .   04.45 hrs.

This hour applies equally to the launching of the operations Gdynia–Gulf of Danzig and Dirschau Bridge.

3. *In the West* the problem is unambiguously to saddle England and France with the responsibility for opening hostilities. Any insignificant violation of the frontier is for the time being only to be dealt with purely by means of local counter-measures.

We have guaranteed the neutrality of Holland, Belgium, Luxembourg and Switzerland and their neutrality is to be strictly observed.

At no point is the western land frontier of Germany to be crossed without my explicit approval.

At sea this also applies to all warlike actions, or actions that might be construed as warlike.

The defensive measures of the air force are for the time being to consist solely in repelling enemy air attacks within the borders of Germany; so far as possible the frontiers of neutral states are not to be crossed when repelling attacks by single aircraft or by small formations. Only in the event of large formations of French and English aircraft flying across neutral states towards German territory and thus endangering our western air defences will our defensive forces be free also to fly over neutral soil.

It is particularly important that the OKW be informed with all speed in the event of our Western enemies violating the neutrality of any other country.

If England and France open hostilities against Germany it is the task of those elements of the armed forces operating in the West by the employment of minimum forces to ensure the maintenance of conditions which will permit a victorious conclusion to the operations against Poland. As part of this task maximum damage is to be inflicted on the enemy forces and on his sources of economic strength. I retain in all cases the right to decide when *offensive* operations may be initiated.

The Army will hold the West Wall and will take the necessary steps to prevent it from being outflanked to the north by means of a violation of Belgian or Dutch territory on the part of the Western Powers. Should French forces move into Luxembourg the army is authorised to blow the frontier bridges.

The Navy will start warfare against commercial shipping, with main effort directed against the shipping of England. To increase the effectiveness of this warfare it may be assumed that certain zones will be declared danger zones. The Naval High Command (OKM) will report what sea areas may usefully be designated danger zones and to what extent. The text of such declarations will be prepared in conjunction with the Foreign Ministry and will be submitted to me, through the OKW, for approval.

The Baltic is to be made safe against enemy penetration. The OKM will decide whether for this purpose the entrances to the Baltic should be closed by minefields.

The Air Force has the primary task of preventing any operations by the French or English air forces against the German army or German territory.

In connection with the war against England, the Air Force is to prepare to interrupt England's seaborne supplies, armament industries and troop transports to France. Favourable opportunities for effective attack on massed units of the English fleet, in particular on battleships and aircraft carriers, are to be exploited. I retain the right of decision concerning attacks on London.

Attacks against the English home territories are to be prepared with this in mind: inadequate success with limited force is in all circumstances to be avoided.

signed: A. HITLER

Distribution:

OKH	1st copy
OKM	2nd copy
OKL	3rd copy
OKW:	
Chief Armed Forces Command	
Staff	4th copy
Spare	5th–8th copies

APPENDIX III

Inspector General of Armoured Troops   *H.Q., O.K.H.*
Nr. 3940/44. g. Kdos.   7.11.1944

The Military Adjutant with the Führer.

1. During the Western Campaign Panzer Divisions Nos. 1–10 were engaged.
2. Panzergrenadier Divisions did not then exist in their present form. The three Light Divisions which had taken part in the Polish Campaign had been transformed into Panzer Divisions before the beginning of the Western Campaign.
3. The organisation of the Panzer Divisions was as follows:

   (a) Nos. 1–5 and 10th Panzer Division: two Panzer Regiments, each of two Battalions. German equipment.
   (b) 9th Panzer Division: one Panzer Regiment of two battalions. German equipment.
   (c) 6th, 7th and 8th Panzer Divisions (formerly Light Divisions): one Panzer Regiment of three battalions. Czech equipment.

Total: 35 battalions.

4. Within the above divisions the following tanks moved against the enemy on 10.5.40:

> 523 Panzer I
> 955 Panzer II
> 349 Panzer III
> 278 Panzer IV
> 106 Czech 35 tanks
> 228 Czech 38 tanks
> 96 small armoured command vehicles, chassis I
> 39 large armoured command vehicles, chassis III
>
> ———
>
> 2,574 tanks

These 2,574 tanks carried the following weapons:

> 4,407 Machine-guns 13 or 34 (Czech)
> 955 20 mm. guns
> 349 37 mm. guns
> 334 37 mm. guns [sic. *Tr.*]
> 278 75 mm. guns

The Panzer II, equipped with a 50 mm. gun, was not available in May, but during the course of the Western Campaign 40 were committed. Since the first assault guns of the production programme initiated in February 1940 were only delivered in April, there was no quantity of assault guns worth mentioning employed in the Western Campaign.

5. For other weapons and strength in personnel of the Panzer Divisions see annex attached [*unfortunately not available*].

APPENDIX IV

Headquarters, XIX Army Corps   *Corps H.Q., Neufchâteau*
Operations Department   11.5.40

Corps Orders for 12.5.40

1. During the course of today's successful attack the corps has thrown back a brave and skilfully fighting enemy towards the Semois.

2. *The task of the divisions* for 12.5.40 is to cross the Semois and to mop up the enemy forces along the northern bank of the Meuse.

10*th Panzer Division* will place Infantry Regiment *Gross-Deutschland* at the disposal of corps in the direction of St. Médard.

2*nd and* 10*th Panzer Divisions* will clear their routes of advance so as to ensure than the divisions in the second line of the advance are able to take over the task of guarding the flanks.

2*nd Panzer Division* will therefore turn through Membre and Alle towards Sugny and the crossroads ¾ of a mile south-west of Poupehan. In this connection the road through Membre is to be cleared. The division is then to advance along the road through Alle that later leads through Rochehaut to the road junction 5 miles north-east of Bouillon (the corps supply route).

10*th Panzer Division*, as ordered already on the evening of May 10th, is to turn with the mass of its forces towards the Semois crossing at Cugnon and is no longer to occupy panzer roads 3 and 4. Line of further advance from Cugnon, through Quatre Chemins towards Sedan. It will be in contact with the corps supply route through Léglise.

3. *Boundaries:*

Between 2*nd and* 1*st Panzer Divisions:* Grandvoir–Chaumont–Nolleveaux (1st)–Cornimont–Rochehaut (1st)–crossroads 2½ miles south of Alle (2nd)–Bosseval et Briancourt (2nd)–the western edge of the Meuse bend–Frénois–the Frénois–Chéméry road–the Ardennes Canal as far as the bridge 2 miles east of le Chesne (villages, roads and canal all inclusive to 1st).

Between 1*st and* 10*th Panzer Divisions:* Grapefontaine–Orgeon (10th)–Noinforetaine–Bouillon–Bellevaux–road fork 2 miles south of Bouillon (10th)–Illy–the central Meuse bridge in Sedan (1st)–the southern road bridge in Sedan–Noyers Pont Maugis (10th)–Bulson (1st)–Villers Maisoncelle (1st)–Stone–Oche (1st).

4. *Corps headquarters* originally Neufchâteau, later moving along the Bertrix–Bouillon road.

5. The divisions will carry out their preparations for crossing the Meuse on 13.5.40 in accordance with the instructions already issued by corps.

6. *The Luftwaffe* will continue to support the corps on 12.5.40 as follows: until 09.00 hrs. on this side of the Meuse, thereafter on the far side.

signed: GUDERIAN.

Distribution:
  Divisions under command
  General
  Operations
  Intelligence
  Artillery Commander

APPENDIX V

Headquarters, XIX Army Corps *Corps H.Q.,*
Operations Department *12.5.40, 17.50 hrs.*

Preliminary Order for the attack across the Meuse

1. An Anglo-French motorised army of some twenty divisions advancing with its left wing moving through Antwerp has been attacked in all parts by the German Air Force and has been smashed. The Albert Canal has been crossed at all points. Liége has fallen.

2. *Group von Kleist* will attack across the Meuse tomorrow, 13.5.40, in the sector Charleville–Sedan. The group will receive exceptionally strong air support from the air force which is for this purpose freed from its tasks in Belgium. The group will in all circumstances seize crossings over the Meuse.

3. *This corps' task* will be in accordance with the intention given above. Orders for the units involved in the attack will follow during the course of the evening.

4. In preparation for the success of this *decisive* attack it is essential that the divisions reach the Meuse today. *Artillery and engineers are to be brought forward* so that the launching of the attack can be assured to the best of the corps' ability.

5. *I am relying on the energy of the gentlemen in command of the divisions.*

signed: GUDERIAN.

Distribution:
1st Panzer Division
2nd Panzer Division
10th Panzer Division
Corps H.Q. Operations
Intelligence
File

At 18.35 hrs. Corps H.Q. ordered:

For the attack on 13.5.40 the heavy artillery battalions of the 2nd and 10th Panzer Divisions are placed under command of Artillery Commander 101. They are to be employed in 1st Panzer Division's sector, etc.[1]

[1] In connection with the Corps Order for the attack across the Meuse it is to be noted that very careful training of the divisions prior to the opening of the Western Campaign greatly facilitated the issuing of the order. During the night 12th–13th May, 1940, the divisions issued orders to their unit commanders which began: "Attack in accordance with map exercise carried out on..............." It was only thanks to these very thorough preliminary studies that it proved possible to carry out the preparations for the attack in the very limited time available. Only minor alterations to the plan as laid down during the map exercise proved necessary.

1st Panzer Division   *Div. H.Q.,*
Operations Department   12.5.40, 18.45 *hrs.*

1. *For the attack across the Meuse* on 13.5.40 the orders contained in the annex attached will apply. It is, however, unlikely that all the engineer and artillery support envisaged will in fact be available.

2. Commanders are to make maximum effort to ensure that the division reaches its attacking positions. Despite the attached orders, these positions will be advanced to the Meuse. Villages will not be occupied. All vehicles not needed for the immediate attack are to be left behind in the area north of the Semois; in the case of units already south of the Semois such vehicles will be parked clear of the roads in the Ardennes.

3. *Infantry Regiment Gross-Deutschland* will move to its jumping-off position by way of the road network 1 mile north-west of Bellevaux and through Bouillon.

4. *Prisoner-of-war assembly points:* North of the Meuse, Illy; south of the Meuse, Bulson. Guard duties at each point to be the responsibility of one section of Rifle Regiment 1.

5. *Casualty clearing point:* Bouillon.
Main dressing station: Bertrix.
Field hospital: Neuenburg.

6. *Commander of Armoured Engineer Battalion* 37 takes over the duties of the Commander of Engineer Regiment 102.

7. *Divisional H.Q.* will be first of all in the wood north of Fleigneux.

10th Panzer Division   *Div. H.Q.,*
Operations Department   12.5.40, 19.30 *hrs.*

Preliminary Order[1] for the attack across the Meuse.

1. An Anglo-French motorised army of some twenty divisions has been smashed by the air force. The Albert Canal has been crossed at all points. Liége has fallen.

2. Tomorrow 10th Panzer Division will attack across the Meuse.

3. In preparation for the success of this decisive attack it is essential that the Rifle Brigade throw the enemy, still on this side of the Meuse in the division's sector, back across the river. For the purpose of this attack the 1st Battalion of Artillery Regiment 90 is placed under the command of the Rifle Brigade. Division is to be informed when the objectives have been reached.

signed: SCHAAL.

[1] These two preliminary orders were based on the orders for the map exercise carried out in Koblenz. They served as directive until the final orders for the attack across the Meuse were issued.

APPENDIX VI

Headquarters, XIX Army Corps   *Corps H.Q., Bellevaux*
Operations Department   13.5.40, 08.15 *hrs*.

Corps Order No. 3
for the attack across the Meuse

1. As a result of sharp fighting on May 12th, the XIX Army Corps has thrown the enemy across the Meuse along almost all the corps front. Strong enemy resistance is to be expected on the Meuse.

2. On the 13th of May the *point of main effort* of our Western Offensive lies in the sector of Group von Kleist.

The Group's *objective* is the seizure of crossings over the Meuse between Monthermé and Sedan. Almost the whole of the German air force will support this operation. By means of uninterrupted attacks lasting for eight hours the French defences along the Meuse will be smashed. This will be followed by an assault across the river by Group von Kleist at 16.00 hrs. and the establishment of bridgeheads. XLI Army Corps, on the right of this corps, will cross the river at 16.00 hrs. on May 13th in the Monthermé and Nouzonville areas and will form a bridgehead in the area southern edge of Daville–Sorel–northern edge of Charleville.

XIV Army Corps will be assembled behind XIX Army Corps and will be ready to move forward either through Neufchâteau or through Florenville according to the development of the situation.

3. XIX Army Corps will make the necessary preparations in its previously assigned sector during the course of the morning so as to be in a position to seize crossings over the Meuse between the mouth of the Bar and Bazeilles at 16.00 hrs. As soon as the crossings have been carried out a bridgehead will be established running Boutancourt–Sapogne–Chéhéry–Noyers Pont Maugis.

Boundary with XLI Army Corps: Martelange–Nanoussart–Longliers–Grandvoir–Assenois–north-west of Bertrix–Carlsbourg–Gross Fays–Mouzaive–Sugny–Lumes–Hannogne 9 miles south-west of Montcornet. All localities inclusive to XLI Army Corps.

4. *The attack will be launched as follows:*

    (*a*) *Right attacking group:* between the Ardennes Canal and the Meuse bend (exclusive). *Troops:* 2nd Panzer Division.

    (*b*) *Central attacking group:* between the Meuse bend (inclusive) and Torcy (inclusive)
        Troops: 1st Panzer Division, with Infantry Regiment *Gross-Deutschland* and Assault Engineer Battalion 43.

    (*c*) *Left attacking group:* between Sedan and Bazeilles.
        Troops: 10th Panzer Division, less Infantry Regiment *Gross-Deutschland*.

Boundaries:

Between Right and Central attacking groups:

Mogimont–Rochehaut–cross roads 3 miles south of Alle–Bosseval et Briancourt (localities to Right attacking group)–the western bank of the Meuse bend–Frénois–the Frénois–Chémery road–Singly–Poix Terron (localities to Central attacking group).

Between Central and Left attacking groups:

Bellevaux–Noirefontaine–Bouillon (localities to Central group)–road fork 2 miles south of Bouillon (Left)–Illy–central Meuse bridge in Sedan (Central)–southern Meuse bridge in Sedan–Noyers Pont Maugis (Left)–Bulson (Central)–Stonne (Central).

5. *Tasks:*

(a) *2nd Panzer Division* will move forward from its jumping-off position on either side of Donchéry at 16.00 hrs., will attack across the Meuse and will seize the high ground south of Donchéry. The division will then swing immediately westward, will cross the Ardennes Canal to the Bar bend inclusive, and will roll up the enemy defences along the Meuse, with right wing advancing to Boutancourt and left wing to Sapogne and Feuchères.

(b) *1st Panzer Division*, with Infantry Regiment *Gross-Deutschland* under command, will be ready to attack across the Meuse between Glaire and Torcy at 16.00 hrs. After mopping up inside the Meuse bend it will push forward to the Bellevue–Torcy road. The division will proceed to attack the Bois de la Marfée heights and will push on to a line Chéhéry–Chaumont.

(c) *10th Panzer Division*, in conjunction with 1st Panzer Division, will by 16.00 hrs. have captured the strong points on the eastern edge of Sedan and will also by this hour have secured its jumping-off positions in the Sedan–Bazeilles sector.

The division will attack across the Meuse at 16.00 hrs. and will capture the high ground running from Noyers Pont Maugis–Pont Maugis.

6. *Co-operation with the Air Force.* The scheme of co-operation with the air force, both in space and time, is given in the attached time schedule and on the 1 : 300,000 map showing bomb target areas.

XIX Army Corps will co-operate directing with Close Support Leader II as heretofore.

7. *Anti-aircraft Regiment 102* will first protect the corps in its preparations for the crossing, will then cover the crossing (for which purpose it is to commit its guns very far forward) and will finally give protection to the bridgehead.

8. *Reconnaissance:*

(a) *Air Reconnaissance:* by the squadrons in the areas Charleville–Tournes–St. Rémy–Le Chesne–Sommauthe–Pouilly–Tétaigne–Francheval.

(b) *Ground Reconnaissance:* by the divisions as ordered for their respective sectors.

9. *Signal Communications:* Signal Battalion 90 will maintain line and wireless links with 1st, 2nd and 10th Panzer Divisions and wireless links with Group von Kleist and XLI Army Corps. It will maintain contact between corps headquarters and the divisional headquarters at Vrigne aux Bois (2nd Panzer Division), Flaigneux (1st Panzer Division) and Givonne (10th Panzer Division).

10. *Corps Headquarters:* Bellevaux: after 12.00 hrs., La Chapelle.

signed: GUDERIAN.

1st Panzer Division   *Div. H.Q.,*
Operations Department   13.5.40, 12.00 *hrs.*

Divisional Order No. 5
for the attack across the Meuse on 13.5.40

1. As a result of sharp fighting on May 12th the XIX Army Corps has thrown the enemy across the Meuse along almost all the corps front. Strong enemy resistance is to be expected along the Meuse.

2. On the 13th of May the point of main effort of our Western offensive lies in the sector of Group von Kleist.

The Group's objective is the seizure of crossings over the Meuse between Monthermé and Sedan. Almost the whole of the German air force will support this operation. By means of uninterrupted attacks lasting for eight hours the French defences along the Meuse will be smashed. XIX Army Corps will then proceed to cross the Meuse at 16.00 hrs.

3. XIX Army Corps will make the necessary preparations in its previously assigned sector during the course of the morning and of midday so as to be in a position to seize crossings over the Meuse between the mouth of the Bar and Bazeilles at 16.00 hrs.

4. *The attack will be launched as follows:*

(a) *Right attacking group:* 2nd Panzer Division between the Ardennes Canal and the Meuse bend (exclusive).

(b) *Central attacking group:* reinforced 1st Panzer Division between the Meuse bend (inclusive) and Torcy (inclusive).

(c) *Left attacking group:* 10th Panzer Division between Sedan and Bazeilles.

5. *Boundaries:*

unchanged, except:

Right-hand boundary with 2nd Panzer Division: from Chéhéry to Singly (7 miles west of Chéhéry)–Poix Terron (localities inclusive to 1st Panzer Division).

Left-hand boundary with 10th Panzer Division: unchanged.

6. *Task:*

2nd Panzer Division will move forward from its jumping-off position at 16.00 hrs., will attack across the Meuse, and will seize the high ground south of Donchéry. The division will then swing immediately westwards, will cross the Ardennes Canal to the Bar bend inclusive, and will roll up the enemy defences along the Meuse, with right wing advancing to Boutancourt and left wing to Sapogne and Feuchères.

1st Panzer Division, with Infantry Regiment *Gross-Deutschland* under command, will be ready to attack at 16.00 hrs. After mopping up inside the Meuse bend it will push forward to the Bellevue–Torcy road. The division will proceed to attack the Bois de la Marfée heights and will push on to a line Chéhéry–Chaumont.

Unit tasks remain as previously ordered, but *x*-hour and *y*-hour may now be ignored. Surprise attack by K.1 begins at 16.00 hrs.

10th Panzer Division, in conjunction with 1st Panzer Division, will by 16.00 hrs. have captured the strongpoints on the eastern edge of Sedan and will also by this hour have secured its jumping-off positions in the Sedan–Bazeilles sector. The division will attack across the Meuse at 16.00 hrs. and will capture the high ground running from Noyers Pont Maugis–Pont Maugis.

7. *Artillery Commander 101* (for table of subordinate battalions, see Annex) will prepare the Meuse crossing and will support the division's attack in accordance with the fire plan.

8. *Co-operation with the air force:* The scheme of co-operation with the air force, both in space and time, is given in the attached time schedule and sketch map showing bomb target areas.

Flak Regiment 102 is for the time being under command of the corps to cover the crossing of the river.

9. *The schedule for crossing* remains unchanged in accordance with the divisional order attached.

10. *Reconnaissance and Signal Communications:* unchanged.

Cover Names, Series C, are increased as follows:

Infantry Regiment *Gross-Deutschland*	Scheusal
Artillery Commander 101	Neubau
Artillery Regiment 49	Taschenspieler
Observation Battalion 1	Ziegelstein
I Battalion, Infantry Regiment *Gross-Deutschland*	Eschenholz
II Battalion, Infantry Regiment *Gross-Deutschland*	Andenken
III Battalion, Infantry Regiment *Gross-Deutschland*	Miesmuschel
IV Battalion, Infantry Regiment *Gross-Deutschland*	Ofenrohr
Assault Engineer Battalion 43	Monokel

11. *Supply:*

(*a*) *Ammunition supply point:* 1 mile east of Fays les Veneurs, will remain ready to issue.

(*b*) *Fuel issuing point:* In the northern part of the wood north of Noirefontaine, will be ready to issue by approximately 17.00 hrs. on 13.5.40. Reception approximately ½ of consumption.

(*c*) *Main dressing station:* Corbion.

(*d*) *Vehicle Repairs:* from P.M. on 13.5 one Workshop Company will be ready to work at Bertrix.

Q

One Tank Parts Replacement Staff of Group von Kleist has moved forward to Redingen (Luxembourg).

(*e*) *Prisoner Assembly Point:* remains Illy and, south of the Meuse, Frénois. Guard duties are the responsibility of the Rifle Brigade.

12. *Divisional headquarters:* Until the start of the attack, point 360, 2 miles north of St. Menges. As the attack proceeds divisional headquarters will move forward along the line already indicated.

Annex to Divisional Order No. 5 for the 13*th May,* 1940.

Special Artillery Order for the Meuse Crossing on 13.5.40

1. Artillery Commander 101 will be responsible for making the necessary artillery preparations for the Meuse crossing.

2. *Allotment* of the artillery for the preparatory bombardment and for the carrying out of the attack.

(*a*) *With* 2*nd Panzer Division:* Artillery Regiment 74, less III (Heavy) Battalion.

(*b*) *With* 1*st Panzer Division:* Artillery Commander 101. Anti-infantry units: Artillery Regiment 73 with Battalions I–III. Anti-artillery and point of main effort units: Artillery Regiment 49, with II Battalion Artillery Regiment 45, II Battalion Artillery Regiment 69, III Battalion Artillery Regiment 74, III Battalion Artillery Regiment 90 (I/10), Heavy Artillery Battalion 616.

At the disposal of the Artillery Commander: Observation Battalion 1, Mortar Battalion.

(*c*) *With* 10*th Panzer Division:* Artillery Regiment 90 less III (Heavy) Battalion.

3. *Artillery Observation:*

(*a*) The observation points of the artillery with 2nd and 10th Panzer Division are to be so chosen that at least one battalion with each of those divisions will be able to observe the sector of 1st Panzer Division.

(*b*) *Observation by Observation Battalion* 1.

Observation Battalion 1 is to be so disposed that it can carry out artillery observation in the target areas G, H, L, M and D.

(*c*) *Observation by the Air Force.*

The division's artillery flyers will be allotted their tasks by the air force but will also report directly to Artillery Commander 101 (with 1st Panzer Division).

Two artillery flyers of 4/Army Recce 31 will be placed under command of Artillery Regiment 49 from 10.00 hrs.

4. *Tasks of the Artillery:*

For support of the attack by the artillery see fire plan.

Control of the artillery throughout the corps will be by Artillery Commander 101 until the divisions have crossed a line running: high ground south of Donchéry–Bois de la Marfée–high ground in the Noyers Pont Maugis area. *Targets:* as per the target areas already allotted (see target area map).

Annex to Divisional Order No. 5

Fire Plan for the attack on 13 May, 1940

1ST PANZER DIVISION

Stage of the battle	Time period	Infantry	Weapons for anti-strongpoint fire	Artillery	Air Force
Preparations for crossing the Meuse	08.00 to 15.00 hrs.	Targets in Target Area K	Pillboxes and strong points along the Meuse in Glaire and Torcy	(a) Support to the preceding operations by shooting at targets in Target Areas K and L. (b) Harassing fire along the Meuse. (c) Anti-pillbox fire. (d) Anti-artillery and anti-flak fire in Target Areas G, H, L, M, O.	See Time Schedule. Close support Group II: (a) Destruction of inhabited localities in Target Areas G, H, L, M, O. (b) Bombing of artillery positions.
Preparations for crossing the Meuse	15.00 to 15.50 hrs.	As above	Anti-pillbox fire along the Meuse	(a) Concentrated fire on crossing-places. (b) Shooting at targets in Target Areas K and L. (c) Anti-artillery and anti-flak fire	
Immediately before the crossing.	15.50 to 16.00 hrs.	Concentrated fire on the crossing-places	As above	Concentrated fire on the crossing places.	See Time Schedule. Close support Group will destroy villages of Glaire and Torcy. Attacks on Target Area L 1–7
Beginning of the crossing and first assault	from 16.00 hrs.	Support of the riflemen	Anti-pillbox fire before and after the crossing	Support of the infantry in the division's sector	See Time Schedule.

Note: From 16.00 to 16.30 hrs. the Mortar Battalion will drop smoke along the Glaire–Torcy road, from 17.30 to 18.30 hrs. along the Bellevue–Torcy road.

Annex to Divisional Order No. 5

Time Schedule for the Attack across the Meuse on 13.5.40

Time	Air Force	Ground Troops
08.00		Preparations for Meuse crossing so far as this can be done. Artillery activity according to Fire Plan.
08.00–12.00	Harassing attacks on sectors BI and CI.	Preparations for the crossing under cover of the harassing attacks. Artillery activity according to Fire Plan.
12.00–16.00	Concentrated annihilation bombing of sectors AI, BI and CI	Continuation and conclusion of preparations. Artillery activity according to Fire Plan.
16.00–17.30	Switch of harassing attacks to sectors AII, BII and CII and works in the Mouzon area. Dive bombing attacks on sectors BI and CI	Surprise crossings
17.30 until dusk	Attacks on targets of opportunity in the areas on the enemy side of sectors AII, BII, CII	Seizure of the bridgehead
Night	Harassing attacks on roads running north and east from Hirson, Laon, Rethel, Vouziers, Stenay and attacks on any traffic observed on those roads.	Bridge building. Move across the river of tanks and artillery

10th Panzer Division   *Div. H.Q., Pré St. Rémy*
Operations Department, No. 5   13.5.40

Divisional Order for the attack across the Meuse, 13.5.40

1. As a result of sharp fighting on May 12th the XIX Army Corps has thrown the enemy across the Meuse on almost all the corps front. Strong enemy resistance is to be expected along the Meuse.

2. *The point of main effort* of the battle in the West lies in the area of Group von Kleist on May 13th.

Its objective is the seizure of crossings over the Meuse between Monthermé and Sedan. Almost the whole of the German air force will support this operation. By means of uninterrupted attacks lasting for eight hours the French defences along the Meuse will be smashed.

3. *XIX Army Corps* will make the necessary preparations in its previously assigned sector during the course of the morning and of midday so as to be in a position to seize crossings over the Meuse between the mouth of the

Bar and Bazeilles at 16.00 hrs. After the crossing has been achieved a bridge-head will be established running Boutancourt–Sapogne–Chéhéry–Noyers Pont Maugis.

10*th Panzer Division* will attack at 16.00 hrs. on May 13th, across the Meuse in the sector Sedan south–Bazeilles (inclusive) and will capture the heights of Noyers Pont Maugis.

Boundary with 1st Panzer Division the road fork 2 miles south of Bouillon –Illy–the central Meuse bridge at Sedan (all inclusive to 1st Panzer Division) –the southern Meuse bridge at Sedan–Noyers Pont Maugis (both inclusive to 10th Panzer Division)–Bulson–Stonne (both inclusive to 1st Panzer Division).

4. *The attack will be launched as follows:*

Right: Attacking Group 10th Rifle Brigade.
  Commander: Commander of 10th Rifle Brigade.
  Troops: Rifle Regiment 86.
    1st Company of Engineer Battalion 41 with 90 small and 45 large kapok rafts.
    2nd Company of Engineer Battalion 49 (less one platoon) as engineer assault troops.
    90th Anti-tank Demonstration Battalion (less one company).
    1 Battery of Heavy Anti-Aircraft Battalion 36 (less one gun).
    1 and 2 Heavy Infantry Gun Companies.
Left: Attacking Group Rifle Regiment 69.
  Commander: Commander of Rifle Regiment 69
  Troops: Rifle Regiment 69.
    1st Company of Engineer Battalion 49 with 65 small and 30 large kapok rafts.
    One platoon of the 2nd Company of Engineer Battalion 49 as engineer assault troops.
    One company of the 90th Anti-tank Demonstration Battalion.
    One gun of Heavy Anti-aircraft Battalion 36.

Boundary: between the right and left attacking groups: Givonne east–Balan east–Pont Maugis west–Noyers Pont Maugis east–Beau Menil farm east

5. *Tasks:*

The right and left attacking groups will make ready for the assault in their respective sectors by the afternoon of May 13th; they will bring up their supporting troops and will engage pillboxes and strongpoints on the Meuse as well as targets in the sector of the attack. The attacking groups will arrange to move their assaulting spearheads up to the Meuse in such a way as to be able to attack across the Meuse at 16.00 hrs. For this purpose the period of our air attacks is to be particularly fully exploited by every man engaged.

The *right* attacking group will take as its first objective the strongpoints west of Wadelincourt, will then turn south, will mop up the strongpoints south of Wadelincourt and will capture Noyers Pont Maugis and the heights immediately to the west.

The *left* attacking group will capture Pont Maugis and the strongpoints to the east with point of main effort on its right wing and co-operating with the right attacking group it will then take as its objective the road Noyers Pont Maugis–Pont Maugis.

6. The commanders of the attacking groups will arrange for start lines, under officer supervision, for the assaulting troops and, in the case of the right attacking group, for the units that will follow on the military bridge.

7. *Artillery Regiment 90* (less I Battery of Artillery Battalion 105) will support the attack in accordance with the Fire Plan. One battalion will be assigned to the support of each attacking group.

8. Those elements of Engineer Battalions 41 and 49 not assigned to an attacking group will assemble at 16.00 hrs. in the area north of La Chapelle whence they move up to the Meuse as ordered by the commander of Engineer Battalion 41 and will build ferries and, later, a bridge.

It is intended that a bridge be built at Sedan south.

9. *The 1st Battery of Anti-aircraft Battalion 71* will cover the preparations for the assault and the attack across the Meuse, with point of main effort in the sector of the right attacking group. The 3rd Battery of Anti-aircraft Battalion 55 will cover the move up of the Panzer Brigade.

10. *Reconnaissance:*

    (a) *Air:* 3/Army Recce 14 will reconnoitre in the area of the roads Donchéry–Chéméry–Tannay–Brieulles–Vaux–Pouilly–Tétaigne–Francheval.

        Individual assignments according to special orders.

    (b) *Ground:* Armoured Reconnaissance Battalion 90 is holding two reconnaissance groups ready and at the disposal of the division in the area north of La Chapelle.

11. *Signal Communications:*

Armoured Signal Battalion 90 will maintain wireless communications as heretofore as well as to the attacking groups and to the commander of the bridge-building operation. It will arrange with the officers responsible for the crossings to have three links with the three crossing-places. The operators with the attacking groups are to cross the Meuse with the foremost infantry.

12. *Traffic Control:* The road Mortehan–La Chapelle exclusive is assigned to Road Commandant III and the Panzer Brigade; the road La Chapelle–Sedan (later Wadelincourt) to Road Commandant IV and Armoured Reconnaissance Battalion 90.

13. *Divisional Reserve:* 4th Panzer Brigade will be held ready in reserve in the wood Belle Virée from 17.00 hrs., later in the area east of La Chapelle. The brigade commander will be with divisional headquarters.

14. *Main Dressing Station:* La Virée farm ($\frac{1}{2}$ mile south of La Chapelle).

15. *Divisional Headquarters:* Prés St. Rémy.

    Advanced Divisional H.Q.: High ground south-west of Givonne.

signed: SCHAAL.

APPENDIX VII

Headquarters, XIX Army Corps　　　　　　　　*Corps H.Q., wood near La*
Operations Department　　　　　　　　　　*Chapelle*, 13.5.40, 22.30 *hrs.*

1. Only one French Fortress Brigade and artillery are engaged in the defence of the Meuse. They have been severely shaken.

2. Of this corps the following have crossed the Meuse and reached the areas indicated:

2nd Panzer Division, the area south-west of Donchéry.

1st Panzer Division, the northern edge of the Bois de la Marfée.

10th Panzer Division, Wadelincourt.

3. The divisions will continue to attack with maximum energy and will reinforce their elements already across the river with all available troops. The divisions on either wing will make their point of main effort on their interior wings and will thus ensure close mutual co-operation.

4. The divisions will capture their objectives according to the map exercise, with the exception of the 10th Panzer Division, which will advance only as far as the area east of Bulson and will then swing west.

2nd Panzer Division will advance through Boutancourt to Poix Terron.

1st Panzer Division will advance through Vendresse–La Chesne, and with its left wing along the Aisne to Rethel.

10th Panzer Division will for the time being cover the corps left flank along the line assigned to it.

5. Corps headquarters will remain for the time being at La Chapelle.

signed: GUDERIAN

APPENDIX VIII

Headquarters, XIX Army Corps   *Corps H.Q., wood near La Chapelle*
Operations Department   14.5.40, 21.00 *hrs.*

Corps Order No. 5 for May 15th, 1940

1. The corps has today defeated and smashed two French divisions with tanks and other strong army troops. Thousands of prisoners have been captured.

2. The attack will be continued on May 15th, 1940. The mass of our troops will advance from the area already captured in a westerly direction and will reach as primary objective the line Wasigny–Rethel.

3. *Tasks:*

    (*a*) *2nd Panzer Division* will send a strong left wing through Boulzi-court and Poix Terron, will move south of the Petit Forêt de Signy, and will reach the line Wasigny–Séry.

    (*b*) *1st Panzer Division* will advance across a line Singly–Omont and will reach the line Séry–Rethel.

        Boundaries: Chéhéry–Singly–La Horgne–Mazerny (to 1st) Faissault (to 2nd)–Drovizy (to 1st)–Séry (to 2nd).

        Move off of these two divisions to be at a time which I shall order.

    (*c*) *10th Panzer Division*, with Infantry Regiment *Gross-Deutschland* which is henceforth under command, will protect the left flank of the corps along the line of the Ardennes Canal–the Stonne heights –the Meuse bend south of Villemontry. This line will be captured and prepared for defence.

4. Artillery Commander 101, with the II Battalion Artillery Regiment 45, Heavy Artillery Battalion 616, II Battalion Artillery Regiment 69 and II Battalion 1, remains under command of 1st Panzer Division. Likewise the Mortar Battalion, though for the time being it will remain in its present lodgement area.

5. *Reconnaissance:*

Reconnaissance Area for XIX Army Corps:
    Charleville–Rozoi–Montcornet–the Montcornet–Neufchâtel road–the railway line Neufchâtel–Pont Faverger–Grandpré–Dun–Mouzon.
Boundary:
    Between the armoured squadron and 4/Army Recce 31: Le Chesne–Attigny–Blanzy–Neufchâtel.
    Between 4/Army Recce 31 and 3/Army Recce 31: Le Chesne–Grandpré.
Task of 4/Army Recce 31:
    To establish whether the enemy is moving up forces along the roads

within the reconnaissance area against the front and flanks of 1st Panzer Division. Report drops: Corps H.Q. and 1st Panzer Division.

The divisions will reconnoitre in their respective sectors of advance:
(*a*) forward as far as a line Montcornet–Neufchâtel,
(*b*) on the right flank as far as a line Charleville–Hirson,
(*c*) on the left flank as far as a line Vouziers–Rheims.

10th Panzer Division will reconnoitre as far as a line Clairmont–Verdun.

In view of the limited reconnaissance forces available only the main roads of advance will be reconnoitred.

signed: GUDERIAN.

APPENDIX IX

Headquarters, XIX Army Corps   *Corps H.Q., Soize*
Operations Department   16.5.40

Corps Order No. 7 for May 17th, 1940

1. *The enemy* opposing 1st and 2nd Panzer Divisions has once again been decisively defeated and is withdrawing westward along the whole front.

XIX Army Corps has reached the area west of Montcornet with the mass of its forces. Advance units are moving towards the Oise between Origny and Hamégicourt.

XIV Army Corps, following behind and to the left of XIX Army Corps, is covering the left flank along the Aisne.

2. XIX Army Corps will continue to advance in a north-westerly direction on May 17th, by-passing St. Quentin and Péronne. Move off 09.00 hrs.

3. The advance will be as follows (for march routes see Annex 1):

   (*a*) *Right:* 2nd Panzer Division across the line Origny–Ribémont along march routes 1 and 2.

   (*b*) *Left:* 1st Panzer Division across the line Mézières sur Oise–Hamégicourt along march routes 3 and 4.

4. *10th Panzer Division* is once again under command. It will follow behind the left wing along the march routes previously numbered (on 16th May) 2 and 3, as far as Noircourt. Then it will send its *left wing column* through Dizy-le-Gros, Clermont Pierrepont, Hamégicourt. Then march route 4 in accordance with Annex 1.

A road will be freed for the right wing column.

5. *The 2nd (Motorised) Infantry Division* is placed under command of XIV Army Corps.

6. *Reconnaissance:* see Annex 2.

7. *Corps Headquarters:* originally Soize (3 miles east of Montcornet), then moving along march routes 2 and 3.

signed: GUDERIAN.

APPENDIX X

Headquarters, XIX Army Corps   *Corps H.Q., Soize*
Operations Department   18.5.40, 00.45 *hrs.*

Corps Order No. 8 for 18 May, 1940

1. The enemy has today continued to withdraw, south-westwards. He is apparently holding the crossing-places over the Somme. He has launched isolated tank attacks from the direction of Laon towards Montcornet through Clairmont and La Ville aux Bois.

2. *XLI Army Corps* is advancing on Cambrai.

Boundary with XLI Army Corps: St. Gobert–Neuvillette–Nauroy–Gouzeaucourt (all to XLI Army Corps)–Bapaume (to XIX Army Corps).

3. *XIX Army Corps* will attack from the Oise bridgeheads at 05.30 hrs. on 18.5.40 towards Bapaume. Its first objective will be the securing of a bridgehead running: the heights north-west of Bellicourt–east of Villeret-le Vergier–Vendelle–Fléchin–Poeuilly–Tertry–Monchy–Falvy.

4. *Tasks of the divisions:*

(a) *2nd Panzer Division* will attack from the Origny and Ribémont bridgeheads, will seize the Somme crossings on either side of Morcourt, and will capture without delay the high ground between Villeret and Le Vergier. The bridge of St. Quentin is to be captured by a surprise attack and the rest of the town to be taken by means of weak forces entering it from the rear. Care is to be taken to avoid a battle inside the town.

(b) *1st Panzer Division:* will attack from the Bézières and Hamégicourt bridgeheads, will seize the Somme crossings on either side of Castres and will push on at once to the high ground on either side of Poeuilly.

Notes to (a) and (b): The divisions will carry out the attack in the same manner as the attack across the Meuse. Strong artillery support is to be used from the very beginning with the purpose of smashing all enemy attempts to organise the defence. All chances of seizing the crossing-places by means of surprise attacks are to be exploited. With this in view reinforced reconnaissance forces are to be thrown across the Oise at the beginning of the attack.

(c) *10th Panzer Division* will follow behind the left wing of the corps along the roads designated below. It will cover the left flank of the corps, first of all in the Laon direction, then along the Serre, the Crozat Canal, and the Somme. It will mop up along the right banks of the Canal and of the Somme, will occupy the bridges and will prepare them for demolition.

Boundary between 2nd and 1st Panzer Divisions: Marey (2nd)–Châtillon (1st)–Faucouzy (2nd)–Parpeville–Ribémont–St. Quentin–Fayet–Maissemy (all 2nd)–Vendelle–Marquaix–Temploix–Moislains–Rancourt–Combles–Flers –Warlencourt (all 1st).

5. *Reconnaisance:* see Annex.

In order to avoid any confusion of units in front of the anticipated defended localities along the Somme, the ground reconnaissance troops will move off at least half an hour ahead of the main bodies.

Point of main effort for reconnaissance by 1st and 10th Panzer Divisions, the left flank.

6. *Anti-aircraft Regiment 102* will cover the jumping-off areas and crossing-places over the Oise from 05.30 hrs. and will later move forward to the Somme.

7. *Corps Headquarters*, as at the beginning of the attack, 05.30 hrs., Villers-le-Sec.

signed: GUDERIAN.

Roads for 10*th Panzer Division:*

(*a*) Erlon–La Ferté–Chevresis–Hamégicourt–Seraucourt–Tertry–Péronne–Cléry–Longeuval.

(*b*) Dersy – Crécy – Achéry – Vendeuil – Artemps – Sancourt – Péronne and thence as (*a*).

Postscript to Corps Order No. 8 *for* 18.5.40.

Bomb line:

Arras–Bapaume–the Somme to Ham–the railway line La Fère–Laon–Rethel (all towns exclusive).

APPENDIX XI

Headquarters, XIX Army Corps   *Corps H.Q., Villers-le-Sec*
Operations Department   18.5.40.

Corps Order No. 9 for 19th May, 1940

1. *The enemy* is withdrawing from the north in a south-westerly direction. Serious fighting continues in the area of our right wing and of XLI Army Corps' right flank. English troops identified near St. Christ on the Somme, also north of Péronne and on the Bouchavesnes heights. In the areas Ham, Jussy, Remigny and Quesy the enemy withdrew across the Somme during the evening of May 18th.

2. *Group von Kleist* is continuing to advance towards Bapaume and leading units have reached the general line Cambrai–Péronne.

XLI Army Corps' advance units have reached the line Cambrai–Metz en Couture.

Boundary with XLI Army Corps: St. Gobert–Neuvillette–Levergies–Gouzeaucourt (XLI)–Bapaume–Berles-au-Bois–Sombrien (XLI)–Magnicourt (XLI).

The Commander-in-Chief of the Army has explicitly approved further advances by Group von Kleist.

3. *XIX Army Corps* will move forward on May 19th, 1940, and will first of all reach the line Fins–Péronne with 1st and 2nd Panzer Divisions. From here it will capture a bridgehead over the Canal du Nord and advance towards the line Le Mesnil–Cléry.

The Canal will be crossed at 14.00 hrs.

The corps will also, during the night 18th–19th May, establish bridgeheads over the Somme in the Péronne and Ham areas in order to give the Supreme Command the opportunity to swing south-west when the time comes.

4. *Tasks of the divisions:*

(a) *2nd Panzer Division* will cross the Canal between Équancourt and Manancourt. It will capture the high ground around Le Mesnil and then will turn sharply south at a point west of the Péronne road and will thus assist the advance of 1st Panzer Division.

(b) *1st Panzer Division* will force a crossing of the Canal to either side of Moislains, point of main effort being with the northern wing. It will then push on to the high ground south of Rancourt and will swing in against the flank and rear of the enemy holding the high ground north of Péronne.

Notes to (a) and (b):

Artillery preparation for both divisions will be arranged by Artillery

Commander 101 to conform to the bombing plan. After the enemy has been
destroyed a bridgehead will be established running: Équancourt–Le Mesnil–
Sailly Saillisel–Rancourt–Cléry. Steps to prepare the defences of this bridgehead will be taken.

Boundary between 2nd and 1st Panzer Divisions: the western edge of
St. Quentin–Payet–Maissémy–Montigny–Roisel–Aizécourt–Bois de Vaux–
southern edge of Bois St. Pierre Vast (all places to 2nd Panzer Division)–
Combles–Flers–Warlencourt (all places to 1st Panzer Division).

1st Panzer Division, as already told verbally, will, during the evening of
the 18th, capture and hold the bridgehead west of Péronne running roughly:
Biaches–La Maisonette–Bellevue Ferme.

(c) *10th Panzer Division* will be responsible for protecting the left flank
by sending units to block the crossings of the Somme and the Serre.
The division will probably be engaged on this task until the evening of
May 19th. The enemy who crossed in the areas Ham, Jussy, Remigny
and Quessy is to be thrown back across to the south bank of the Canal
de Quentin early on the morning of the 19th. The bridges are to be
blocked off or alternatively destroyed according to instructions already
issued verbally.

In the Ham area a bridgehead running roughly from the bridge
west of Eppeville–Maille Villette Galant will be established and held.

The mass of the division will also be moved across the Oise in the
Essigny-le-Grand area so that a crossing of the Somme in a north-
westerly direction along two roads will be possible.

5. *The Air Force* will support the attack of 1st Panzer Division by bombing
the installations and wooded areas around Bouchavesnes as well as Moislains
and Rancourt during the period 13.45–14.00 hrs. The Canal is to be crossed
immediately the bombing ceases.

The bomb line is laid down as:

(a) Arras–Albert–Roye–Boyon–Berry au Bac.

(b) The line of the Canal du Nord.

6. *Reconnaissance:*

(a) *Air reconnaissance* in the areas Le Cateau–Cambrai–Arras–Doullens
–Amiens–Montdidier.
Direct instructions will divide the area between 4/(Army) 31 and
the armoured squadrons.

(b) *Ground reconnaissance* by 2nd and 1st Panzer Divisions as far as
the bomb line in the sector Haucourt–crossroads 4 miles north-east
of Nesle–Roye–Noyon–Chauny.

7. *Anti-aircraft:* Anti-aircraft Regiment 102 will use the mass of its force
to cover the advance of the two divisions to their jumping-off areas, the
crossing of the Canal and the establishment of the bridgeheads. Elements
will be detached to cover the move of 10th Panzer Division and to protect it
in its new lodgement area.

8. *Reports:* Reports will be submitted as soon as the jumping-off area has been successfully reached and as soon as the assault has been successfully launched.

9. *Signal Battalion 80* will arrange for wireless links with the divisions and for the laying of cable between corps headquarters and the divisional headquarters.

10. *Corps Headquarters* from 13.00 hrs., 19th May, 1940, Holnon Wood.

signed: GUDERIAN.

APPENDIX XII

Headquarters, XIX Army Corps   *Corps H.Q., Villers-le-Sec*
Operations Department   *18.5.40, 13.00 hrs.*

1. With reference to Corps Order No. 8 concerning flank protection of the corps by 10th Panzer Division along the Serre and the Somme Canal between Falvy and Mortiers, for this purpose the following units will be placed under command of 10th Panzer Division as of 16.00 hrs., 18 May:

Staff, Engineer Regiment 511, with
Engineer Battalion 666
Engineer Battalion 49
Engineer Battalion 37
Engineer Battalion 41 (will later relieve Engineer Battalion 37).
Anti-tank Demonstration Battalion of 10th Panzer Division.

Commanders of these Battalions will report to divisional headquarters, 10th Panzer Division, Renansart.

2. *10th Panzer Division* will arrange, in agreement with the commander of Engineer Regiment 511, which bridges shall be destroyed and which shall only be prepared for demolition.

These decisions shall be based on the following principle: bridges that are unimportant and that simply require a waste of guard personnel will be blown; bridges that are necessary for operational movement (advances) will not be blown.

Commander of Engineer Regiment 511 will forward to corps headquarters, through 10th Panzer Division, his plan for blocking and demolition, with sketchmaps.

3. *10th Panzer Division* will retain the mass of the division this side of the Canal west of the Oise. Only weak forces will be moved to the far side and will reconnoitre as far as a line Noyon–Coucy le Château–Laon.

4. The area south of the railway line Nesle–Ham–La Fère–Laon–Neufchâtel is a bomb target area. Any troops that are therefore in this area must give *ample* recognition and identification signals to the flyers.

signed: GUDERIAN.

APPENDIX XIII

Headquarters, XIX Army Corps   *Corps H.Q., St. Marleville*
Operations Department   19.5.40, 24.00 *hrs.*

Corps Order No. 10 for 20th May, 1940

1. *The enemy* opposite the corps front has been defeated. He is attempting to break through from Belgium towards the south-west.

2. *XIX Army Corps* is pressing on without pause towards the north-west, the mouth of the Somme and the Channel Coast.

On the corps right XLI Army Corps is advancing.

Boundaries: Between 2nd Panzer Division and 1st Panzer Division: Combles–Longueval–Pozières–Varennes–Puchevillers–Canaples–Flixécourt –the Somme (all localities to 1st Panzer Division)–Dreuil–Oisemont (localities to 2nd Panzer Division)–the mouth of the Ligar.

Left-hand boundary of 1st Panzer Division: the Somme.

3. At 06.00 hrs. the divisions will advance from the line so far achieved and will reach the Somme.

2nd Panzer Division a line north of the Somme–Flixécourt (exclusive). Point of main effort, Abbéville.

1st Panzer Division: Flixécourt (inclusive)–the mouth of the Avre (east of Amiens). Point of main effort, Amiens.

4. *10th Panzer Division* will move all available forces to the Péronne area and relieve 1st Panzer Division. The division will itself be relieved of its protective duties along the left flank by the 29th (Motorised) Infantry Division. When this has been done, 10th Panzer Division will cover the Somme sector, mouth of the Avre–Péronne, until relieved once again by the 29th (Motorised) Infantry Division.

5. *Command:*

   (a) Infantry Regiment *Gross-Deutschland* is once again under command of the corps. It is subordinated to 10th Panzer Division. The regiment will reach the St. Quentin area during the course of the afternoon and will then be moved up by order of the division.

   (b) The Armoured Reconnaissance Demonstration Battalion is once again under XIX Army Corps. It is intended that it be employed on the left flank.

   (c) 1st Company of Heavy Anti-tank Battalion 8 reached Attigny at 06.00 hrs. on its way to Combles.

6. The divisions will carry out demolitions to the rail network as follows:

The railway lines running across the right-hand corps boundary will be destroyed by 2nd Panzer Division.

The railway lines running across the left-hand corps boundary will be destroyed by 1st Panzer Division.

7. *Reconnaissance* will be carried out by the divisions far forward within their respective sectors; 10th Panzer Division will reconnoitre south of the Somme as far as Amiens and then south of the Amiens–Molliens–Horsoy –Aumale road.

Forward limit of reconnaissance: Le Tréport–Aumale–Poix–Conty– Moreuil–Nesle.

8. *Corps Headquarters* will follow behind 1st Panzer Division along the road Vermand–Roisel–Tincourt–Temploix–Moislains, as far as Combles. Later it will move on to Albert.

signed: GUDERIAN.

Headquarters, XIX Army Corps
Operations Department

Annex to Corps Order No. 10, for the 20th May, 1940

1. *Special Instructions for Air Reconnaissance*

Air reconnaissance in the area Cambrai–Arras–Avesnes–Hesdin–Étaples– Channel Coast–Dieppe–Neufchâtel–Grandvilliers–Ailly–Nesle.

Each squadron will send 1 officer to corps headquarters at 06.00 hrs. on May 20th (squadrons already informed by wireless).

All serviceable He 126s of 4/(Army) 31 will, as of 06.00 hrs. of 20 May, be placed under command of 2/(Army) 23. Two Fi 156s will report to corps headquarters to be at disposal of the headquarters at 06.00 hrs., May 20th.

2. *Special Instructions for Anti-aircraft Defence*

Anti-aircraft Regiment 102 *will give protection against:*

    (*a*) high- and low-level attacks on the Ancre crossings. For this purpose, one mixed battalion per divisional sector.

    (*b*) tanks at the Somme crossings between Péronne and Amiens. For this purpose, one mixed battalion plus one battery of Light Anti-aircraft Battalion 91.

    (*c*) low-level attacks and tanks at Combles and Amiens by Light Anti-aircraft Battalion 91.

APPENDIX XIV

Headquarters, XIX Army Corps
Operations Department

Corps H.Q., Albert
20.5.40, 16.30 hrs.

1. On reaching the Somme the divisions will go over to the *defensive* in the following sectors:

2nd Panzer Division, between Abbéville and the mouth of the Nièvre.

1st Panzer Division, between the mouths of the Nièvre and of the Ancre.

10th Panzer Division, between the mouth of the Ancre and Péronne (inclusive).

2. The divisions will establish bridgeheads in their respective sectors at the following points: Abbéville, Condé Folie, Corbie, Bray and Péronne. Bridges are to be prepared for demolition.

3. All other *crossing-places* are also to be prepared for demolition and vehicles withdrawn to the north bank.

The *railway lines* near Abbéville, south of L'Étoile, at Flixécourt and near Amiens are to be broken.

The *bridges* at which no bridgehead is to be established in accordance with para. 2 will be blocked.

Demolition of the bridges will only be carried out in the event of enemy attacks.

4. *The carrying out of the instructions* laid down in para. 3 within the Corps area is entrusted to the commander of Engineer Regiment 511, Colonel Müller, who is directly subordinated to corps headquarters and who will carry out the task in co-operation with the divisions.

5. *Equipment* will be brought to Péronne and will be distributed by Colonel Müller. ·

6. *Corps Headquarters* as of 18.00 hrs. 20th May, either Allonville, 4 miles north-east of Albert, or Querrieu. Quartermaster department: Pont Noyelles.

For the Corps Command
The Chief of Staff

signed: NEHRING.

APPENDIX XV

Headquarters, XIX Army Corps   *Corps H.Q., Querrieu*
Operations Department   *20.5.40, ? hrs.*

Corps Order No. 11 for 21st May, 1940

1. Today's battles have brought us complete success. Along the whole front the enemy is in retreat in a manner that at times approaches rout.

By 18.00 hrs. the corps had reached the line St. Riquier–Mouflers–Amiens –Péronne.

Location of the *6th Panzer Division* unknown.

8th Panzer Division at 16.45 hrs. north of Doullens.

2. *The corps* will hold the line reached along the Somme (see Order of 20.5.40, 16.30 hrs.).

In addition the divisions will mop up in their areas between the Somme and the Authie and beyond to Bapaume.

The mass of the divisions is to be so deployed north of the Somme that the divisions will all be in a position to defeat an enemy breaking through from the north.

The divisions will have carried out the necessary regrouping by midday, May 21st, and will report their new locations.

Further Points:

(a) In this connection the mass of *10th Panzer Division* will be moved to points around and west of Albert.

(b) *Infantry Regiment Gross-Deutschland* has already received orders, via 10th Panzer Division, to move this night (20–21 May) to the area south of a line Thièvres–Ham and to secure the crossing over the Authie in this sector.

Regimental Headquarters: Beauval.

The regiment will be placed under command of 1st Panzer Division as of 09.00 hrs., 21st May.

3. The divisions and the Armoured Reconnaissance Demonstration Battalion (now once again under command) are assigned the following areas between the Somme and the River Authie–Bapaume for mopping up and defence.

(a) *The Armoured Reconnaissance Demonstration Battalion:* north-west of the Abbéville–Hesdin road (exclusive) to the coast. The battalion will arrive during the 21st May. *Headquarters:* Hautvillers.

(b) *2nd Panzer Division* from there to a line mouth of the Nièvres–Doullens (exclusive).

(c) *1st Panzer Division* from there to a line Amiens–Coigneux (both inclusive).

(*d*) *10th Panzer Division* from there to a line Péronne–Bapaume (inclusive). The covering line will be only thinly manned.

4. *Air Reconnaissance* as ordered directly by corps headquarters.

Ground Reconnaissance from the bridgeheads to the line Le Tréport–Aumale–Conty–Noreuil–Chaulnes.

5. *Anti-aircraft Regiment* 102 will be responsible for anti-aircraft protection.

6. *Signal Battalion* 8 will lay lines to the divisions.

7. *Corps Headquarters:* Querrieu Château.

signed: GUDERIAN.

APPENDIX XVI

Headquarters, XIX Army Corps　　　　　　　*Corps H.Q., St. Querrieu*
Operations Department　　　　　　　　　　　*21.5.40, 21.00 hrs.*

Corps Warning Order No. 12 for 22nd May, 1940

(This order only becomes effective on the issuing of codeword *Abmarsch Nord*)

1. *The enemy*, encircled in Belgium and Northern France, is offering desperate resistance and is attempting to break through to the south. Elements of his forces are being evacuated by sea.

2. *XIX Army Corps* will turn north from the Abbéville–Amiens–Péronne –Doullens–river Authie area on 22nd May, 1940 and will advance across the line Hesdin–Étaples with right wing directed on St. Omer, left wing moving along the coast to Boulogne.

3. Forward elements will *cross* the Authie at 08.00 hrs., as follows:

> Right: 10th Panzer Division,
> Centre: 1st Panzer Division with Artillery Commander 101 and Infantry Regiment *Gross-Deutschland* under command,
> Left: 2nd Panzer Division.

4. *Allotment of roads*, see Annex 2.

5. *Guarding of bridges* along the corps sector of the Somme, between St. Valéry and Corbie (exclusive) will be taken over by the 2nd (Motorised) Infantry Division. The relief of the elements of the Panzer Divisions at present engaged on this task will begin at 22.00 hrs., 21 May, 1940, in accordance with arrangements to be made directly between the Panzer Divisions and the 2nd (Motorised) Infantry Division. Reliefs must be completed by 05.00 hrs., 22nd May, 1940.

> (*a*) The following units will be placed under temporary command of the 2nd (Motorised) Infantry Division:
>
> > (i) The Armoured Reconnaissance Demonstration Battalion for the sector St. Valéry–Abbéville (exclusive). The Battalion will later be relieved by elements of the 2nd (Motorised) Infantry Division and will be once again under corps command.
> >
> > (ii) The Staff of Engineer Regiment 511 (Colonel Müller) with Engineer Battalions 41 and 666. These will be relieved during the course of 22nd May, 1940, and will be then once again under corps command.
> >
> > Engineer Battalion 37 (at present engaged between Condé Folie and Amiens) will be relieved by Engineer Battalion 32. 3 Company of Armoured Engineer Battalion 37 is placed under command of 1st Panzer Division forthwith.

(*b*) The 2nd (Motorised) Infantry Division will ensure that all roads are cleared for the move of the Panzer Divisions by 05.00 hrs., 22nd May, 1940.

(*c*) The *Somme bridges* are *prepared* for demolition and may only be blown if there is a danger of their being lost as a result of enemy attacks. The bridges in the bridgeheads Abbéville, Condé Folie, Picquigny and Amiens are only to be blown in cases of absolute necessity.

(*d*) *Ground Reconnaissance* will be carried out by the 2nd (Motorised) Infantry Division as far as the line the River La Bresle–Aumale–Conty.

(*e*) 10*th Panzer Division* in the sector Péronne–Corbie will be progressively relieved by the 13th (Motorised) Infantry Division, reliefs to start 17.00 hrs., 21st May, 1940. The division will then assemble in the area north-west and west of Albert.

By 13.00 hrs., 22nd May, 1940, it will be completely clear of the Albert–Amiens road and will inform XIV Army Corps by wireless when this has been done.

6. *Reconnaissance:* See Annex 2.

7. *Anti-aircraft Protection:* see Annex 2.

8. *Corps Headquarters* will be moving as follows: the road Querrieu–Amiens Nord–St. Quen–Ochpierre sur Authie–then north-west along the valley of the Authie–Argoulles, where it will halt–then on through Bois Jean–Montreuil–the wood at La Vallé Glorian. Further moves will be notified.

signed: GUDERIAN.

Group von Kleist   *Havrincourt,*
Operations Department   21.5.40, 22.30 *hrs.*

Group Order No. 12 for 22nd May, 1940

1. *From thirty to forty enemy divisions* are cut off in Northern France and Belgium. Strong attempts to break through southwards may be anticipated.

2. *Group von Kleist* will defeat all enemy attacks against the line Tinques–St. Pol–Hesdin–Étaples.

In the event of receiving special orders the Group will attack and finally destroy the enemy.

3. *Boundaries:* Between Corps Hoth and Group von Kleist: as already given until Avesnes le Comte–Tinques–Dieval–Wametz–St. Omer (all localities inclusive to Group von Kleist).

Boundary between XLI and XIX Army Corps: Hesdin–Desvres–Marquise (all localities and roads inclusive to XIX Army Corps).

4. *Task:*

XLI Army Corps will attack in its sector. Strength to be massed on its right wing. The *SS-Verfügungs-Division* is placed under command. This division is to be employed as flank protection towards the east.

XIX Army Corps will attack in its sector.

10th Panzer Division is to be immediately placed at the disposal of the Group, west of Doullens. (An officer will report at Group Headquarters to receive orders.)

Both corps will ensure that the harbours of Calais and Boulogne are under artillery bombardment as soon as possible.

XIV Army Corps will take over all rearward protective duties along the Somme from Péronne to the mouth of the river. The line of the Somme is to be held, the bridgeheads already seized to be expanded. The Somme bridges are to be prepared for demolition but will only be blown if they can no longer be held in the face of heavy enemy attack.

V Army Corps will arrange that the 29th (Motorised) Infantry Division along the Somme between Péronne–St. Simon be relieved by the 62nd and 87th Infantry Divisions. The Somme will be held. Any enemy forces still on the north bank after the arrival of the Infantry Divisions will be thrown across the river.

5. *Bomb lines:* Within the sectors of attack, bombs will only be dropped in accordance with direct, timed requests from the corps, or on fleeing enemy columns which have been indentified with certainty as such. Bomb line south of the Somme, 6 miles south of that river.

6. *Signal Regiment*, etc.

7. *Command:* 9th Panzer Division is placed under direct command of Group von Kleist and will be moved to the Doullens area.

8. *Group Headquarters:* as of 10.00 hrs., Lucheux, 4 miles north-east of Doullens.

                                                      signed: (illegible).

APPENDIX XVII

Group von Kleist
Operations Department

Lucheux
22.5.40, 22.50 *hrs.*

Group Order No. 13 for 23 May, 1940

1. On May 22nd great successes were achieved in the sectors of XIX Army Corps and XLI Army Corps. The enemy resisted Group Hoth strongly and attacked in that sector several times.

Further attempts to break out on the part of the enemy forces encircled in Northern France and Belgium must be anticipated.

2. Group von Kleist will occupy Boulogne and Calais on 23rd May, will establish bridgeheads in the sector Aire–St. Omer–Gravelines and will thus make it possible to turn east and completely destroy the enemy.

3. *Tasks:*

XLI Army Corps will advance north, will establish bridgeheads with all speed near Aire and St. Omer and will then re-group so as to be in a position by noon on 23rd May to advance eastwards from the bridgeheads.

XIX Army Corps will occupy Boulogne and Calais, will establish bridgeheads between Momelin (2½ miles north of St. Omer) and Gravelines and will them re-group so as to be in a position by the afternoon of 23rd May to advance eastwards from the bridgeheads.

XIV Army Corps will continue to carry out the tasks assigned in Group Order No. 12.

4. *Boundaries:* The exact boundary between XLI Army Corps and Group Hoth is not yet fixed. It will be notified by wireless.

Boundary between XLI and XIX Army Corps from Hesdin to the Boulogne –St. Omer road unchanged: from the Boulogne–St. Omer road–Colombert –St. Momelin (2½ miles north of St. Omer). All localities inclusive to XIX Army Corps.

5. *Command:*

(a) *The SS-Verfügungs-Division* is placed under command of Group Hoth from 23rd May.

(b) 9th Panzer Division is withdrawn into Fourth Army reserve.

6. *Bomb line until noon, 23rd May:* The area east of the line Béthune–Cassel–Bergues (localities inclusive) is free for bombing.

7. *Signal Regiment* will lay an axial line through XLI Army Corps to St. Omer.

8. *Group Headquarters* remains Lucheux.

signed: VON KLEIST.

APPENDIX XVIII

Headquarters, XIX Army Corps
Operations Department

Corps H.Q., *Château St. Colembert*
25.5.40, 11.00 *hrs.*

Corps Order No. 13 for 25 May, 1940

1. *Boulogne* is captured, while fighting continues in Calais. On the Canal front St. Omer–Gravelines weaker enemy forces are resisting stubbornly.

Group von Kleist is holding the line of the Canal, Aire–Gravelines, XLI Army Corps the St. Omer bridgehead.

2. *XIX Army Corps* is holding the line reached on the 25th May. The corps will defend the Canal sector St. Momelin–Gravelines, including the bridgeheads already established, and will guard against and prevent enemy landings along the Channel coast.

Calais will be captured on 25th May.

Divisions and corps troops will rest all elements not engaged in operations and will make use of the halt to the advance in order to carry out replacements and maintenance of all sorts, with the purpose of becoming once again fully operationally effective in the shortest possible time.

3. *Tasks:*

   (*a*) *The Canal Front:* 1*st Panzer Division* will defend the line of the Canal between St. Momelin and the mouth of the Canal and will guard the coast between the mouth of the Canal and Pte. Walde.

      For this purpose Infantry Regiment *Gross-Deutschland* and the *SS-Leibstandarte 'Adolf Hitler,'* already committed between St. Momelin and Holque, are placed under command.

   (*b*) *Coastal Front:* between Pte. Walde and the mouth of the Authie the coast is to be guarded and enemy landings prevented.

      The coastal defence installations already in existence are to be made ready for repelling attacks from seawards.

      The following will be employed for this purpose:

      Right: 10th Panzer Division between Pte. Walde and Audresselles (both inclusive).

      Left: 2nd Panzer Division between Audresselles (exclusive) and the mouth of the Authie.

      The Armoured Reconnaissance Demonstration Battalion is placed under command for this purpose. It is to be given the sector between the mouths of the Canche and the Authie and by the morning of 26th May will have reached Merlimont, 3 miles south of Étaples.

4. *Boundaries:*

   (*a*) With XLI Army Corps, Coulomby–Journy–Tilques–St. Momelin–Vimecelle (all inclusive to XIX Army Corps).

(b) *Between 1st and 10th Panzer Divisions*, Desvres–Nabrinhen (both to 1st)–Guines (to 10th)–Pte. Walde (to 1st).

(c) *Between 10th and 2nd Panzer Divisions*, Samer–Bainethun–Audresselles (all to 10th).

(d) With XIV Army Corps, the line of the River Authie.

5. *Rifle Brigade 11*, under command of the corps as of 18.00 hrs., 24th May, will reach the wooded area north of Desvres on May 25th where it will be at the disposal of the corps.

Tasks for 25th May:

Disarming of enemy forces in the Paris–Plage area. Attack on Cap Gris Nez and capture of this strongpoint.

6. *Corps Artillery:*

After the capture of Calais Artillery Commander 101 and the Corps Artillery (II Battalion, Artillery Regiment 45, Heavy Battalion 616) will once again be directly subordinate to corps. They will be located in the area Licques–Herbinghen–Bainghen–Hoecqunighen.

7. *Security Regiment 1* will be placed under command of 1st Panzer Division as of 16.00 hrs., 25th May.

8. *Reconnaissance* as far as the Belgian frontier.

9. All crossing-places over the Canal between Momelin and Gravelines are to be prepared for demolition. Demolitions will only be carried out on the orders of corps headquarters or in cases of extreme necessity.

10. *Anti-aircraft Protection:* in accordance with special order.

11. *Corps Headquarters:* Château Colembert.

Quartermaster's Department: Le Vast.

signed: GUDERIAN.

APPENDIX XIX

Order for the Relief of 1st Panzer Division by 20th (Motorised) Infantry Division

1. *20th (Motorised) Infantry Division* has once again been assigned to the corps and is being brought up from the south. Beginning today, this division will relieve 1st Panzer Division (including Infantry Regiment *Gross-Deutschland*) in the sector Holque–Gravelines–the coastal sector to a point north of Pte. Walde.

Leibstandarte 'Adolf Hitler' will remain in its present location and will be placed under command of 20th (Motorised) Infantry Division.

Group von Kleist regards it as important that the hand-over of command functions take place during the course of the coming night.

2. *1st Panzer Division*, when it has been relieved, will assemble in the area to either side of the Samer–Montreuil road (both villages inclusive) so that it will be in a position rapidly to move off either north or south.

Billeting staff to precede! Location of divisional headquarters to be notified!

It is important that 1st Panzer Division reach its new lodgement area rapidly so that the troops may be given sufficient rest, and equipment and vehicle maintenance be carried out.

3. *Corps Headquarters:* Le Fresnoy, ½ mile south-east of Almethun.

Quartermaster Department: Le Vast.

> For the Corps Command
> The Chief of Staff.
>
> signed: NEHRING.

APPENDIX XX

Headquarters, XIX Army Corps   *Corps H.Q., Château le Fresnoy*
Operations Department   26.5.40, 20.00 *hrs.*

Corps Order No. 14 for 27th May, 1940

1. *The enemy* is holding the Aa Canal sector.

2. *Group von Kleist* will attack in the morning of 27th May, with the left wing of XLI Army Corps (6th or 3rd Panzer Division) from the St. Omer area through Cassel towards Poperinghe.

3. *XIX Army Corps* will attack with the 20th (Motorised) Infantry Division through the sector held by the *Leibstandarte 'Adolf Hitler*,' axis of advance Watten–Wormhoudt.

4. *Tasks:*

The following units are placed under command of the 20th (Motorised) Infantry Division:

Artillery Commander 101	
Leibstandarte 'Adolf Hitler'	Move up as already
Infantry Regiment *Gross-Deutschland*, with under	ordered.
command II Battalion Artillery Regiment 56	Commanders to
Heavy Artillery Battalion 616	H. Q. *Leibstandarte*
III (Heavy) Battalion Artillery Regiment 74	*A. H.* Eperlecques,
III Battalion Artillery Regiment 677 (11 Rifle	20.00 hrs., 26th
Brigade)	May.
Light Anti-aircraft Battalion 91 (*only* for the attack)	

The division will attack from the Watten–St. Pierre bridgehead and will capture the dominating heights east of Watten. It will send a strong right wing through Arncke–Ledringhem to Hezeele.

Reinforced Infantry Regiment Gross-Deutschland will cover the left flank of the attack by advancing on Drincham and capturing the high ground in the Crochte–Pitgam area. It will then face north.

II Battalion, Artillery Regiment 56 of 1st Panzer Division is instructed to collaborate with the Regiment and will receive more precise orders on this subject through Artillery Commander 101.

The advance of Infantry Regiment *Gross-Deutschland* from its jumping-off area is to be further supported by Artillery Regiment 73.

III Battalion Artillery Regiment 677 will only take part in the preparatory bombardment. It will then be left behind on the east bank at the disposal of Rifle Brigade 11.

The bringing up of long-barrelled artillery for the bombardment of Dunkirk is envisaged.

Divisional Headquarters: First of all Eperlecques.

Time of attack: x-hour.

5. *Air Reconnaissance:* Combined squadrons of 4/(Army) 31 and 2/(Army) 23 in the area St. Omer–Poperingen–Veurne–the coast as far as Gravelines. East of the Franco–Belgian frontier reconnaissance by 3/(Long Range) 31.

6. *Anti-aircraft Regiment 102* will be responsible for protecting the assembly area for the attack west of Watten. It will protect the attacking troops during the attack.

7. *Signal Regiment 80* will lay a main line to Eperlecques.

8. *Corps Reserve.* Rifle Brigade 11 will be in readiness to move off from its lodgement area at *x* plus 1. Roads to be examined towards the Canal. Commander to report to corps headquarters.

9. On receipt of this order 20th (Motorised) Infantry Division will detach two officers, with vehicles, to report to corps headquarters.

10. *Corps Headquarters:* Château le Fresnoy. At the beginning of the attack the *Corps Commander* will be at Eperlecques.

signed: GUDERIAN.

Addition to Corps Order No. 14

As of 16.00 hrs., 27th May, the following chain of command becomes effective:

The attack will be as follows:

Right: 20th (Motorised) Infantry Division, with under command, *Leibstandarte 'Adolf Hitler.'*

Left: 2nd Panzer Division with under command, Infantry Regiment *Gross-Deutschland.*
Rifle Brigade 11.
4th Panzer Brigade.

Boundary: Between 20th (Motorised) Infantry Division and 2nd Panzer Division (Rifle Brigade 11): Merkeghen–Zegerscappel–Rexpoede (all inclusive to Rifle Brigade 11).

For the Corps Command
The Chief of Staff.

signed: NEHRING.

APPENDIX XXI

Corps Order No. 15

1. *XIX Army Corps* will be relieved by XIV Army Corps on 29th May, 1940. Time of command hand over, 10.00 hrs.

2. *2nd and 1st Panzer Divisions* will during the course of the day be relieved by 9th Panzer Division. Reliefs will take place in accordance with instructions issued by XIV Army Corps.

The following units will remain in position and will be placed under command of XIV Army Corps:

11th Rifle Brigade.
Infantry Regiment *Gross-Deutschland.*
Leibstandarte 'Adolf Hitler.'
Heavy Artillery Battalion 740.
Heavy Battery 607.
(Temporarily) Army Recce Squadrons of XIX Army Corps.

3. When the relief has been satisfactorily completed all steps are to be taken to make the divisions *fully operationally effective* once again.

4. The divisions will be lodged in the following areas:

1st Panzer Division: Audruicq (inclusive)–Ardres (exclusive)–Licques–Alquines–Coulomby–Vaudringhem–Lumbres (all inclusive).

10th Panzer Division: Ardres (exclusive)–Guines–Rinxens–the northern edge of the wood east of Bainethun (all inclusive)–Le Vast–Colembert–Licques (all exclusive).

2nd Panzer Division: Licques–Colembert (both exclusive)–the wood east of Alquines (villages exclusive)–the road through Jeury to Licques (exclusive).

The divisions will occupy their lodgement areas in such a way as to be able either to make a counter-attack eastwards or to march off southwards.

5. Besides arranging billeting areas for their light anti-aircraft battalions the divisions will also allow for billeting in each divisional area one heavy anti-aircraft battalion. Arrangements will be made with the commander of Anti-aircraft Regiment 102.

6. *The Panzer Brigades* can move off to their new areas on the morning of 29th May, 1940, provided that the divisional commanders regard the situation on their respective fronts as tactically sufficiently secure.

7. The location of divisional headquarters will be notified to Corps Headquarters by 12.00 hrs., 29th May, 1940, by telephone so that Signal Battalion 80 can make the necessary arrangements.

There is no objection to the headquarters of 10th Panzer Division remaining in its present location.

8. *Corps Headquarters* will for the time being be at Louches Chau.,
Quartermaster Department, Landresthun.

For the Corps Command
The Chief of Staff.

signed: NEHRING.

APPENDIX XXII

The Führer and Supreme Commander of the
Armed Forces   18 *December*, 1940
OKW/WFSt./Abt.L (I) Nr. 33 408/40 g.Kdos.
Chefsache.
Top Secret.

Directive No. 21
OPERATION BARBAROSSA

The armed forces of Germany must be prepared, even before the con-clusion of the war with England, *to defeat Soviet Russia* in *one rapid campaign* ('Operation Barbarossa.')

The Army must in this case be prepared to commit all available formations, with the proviso that the occupied territories must be secured against surprise attacks.

The Air Force will have to make available for the support of the army in the Eastern Campaign forces of adequate strength to ensure a rapid ter-mination to the land action and to give the East German territories maximum protection against enemy air raids. This making of the main effort in the East must not be carried to a point at which we can no longer adequately protect the totality of our battle and our armament zones against enemy air attacks, nor must the offensive against England, and in particular against England's supply routes, suffer in consequence.

For *the Navy* the point of main effort will remain consistently against *England*, even while the Eastern Campaign is in progress.

I shall give the order for the *assembly* of troops, etc., for the proposed operation against Soviet Russia, should the occasion arise, eight weeks before the operation is due to begin.

Preparations that require more time than this shall—so far as they have not already been made—be begun at once and are to be completed by the 15th May, 1941.

Great stress, however, must be laid on disguising any offensive intentions.

Preparations by the high commands are to be based on the following considerations:

1. *General Intention*

The mass of the army stationed in Western Russia is to be destroyed in bold operations involving deep penetrations by armoured spearheads, and the withdrawal of elements capable of combat into the extensive Russian land spaces is to be prevented.

By means of a rapid pursuit a line is then to be reached from beyond which the Russian air force will no longer be capable of attacking the German home territories. The final objective of the operation is to be the attainment

of a line sealing off Asiatic Russia and running, in general, the Volga–
Archangel. From such a line the one remaining Russian industrial area in
the Urals can be eliminated by the air force should the need arise.

In the course of this operation the Russian *Baltic Fleet* will rapidly be
deprived of its bases and thus will no longer be capable of combat.

Effective intervention by the Russian *air force* is to be prevented from
the very beginning of the operation by means of powerful attacks against it.

2. *Anticipated Allies and their Tasks*

1. On the wings of our operation we can count on active co-operation in
the war against Soviet Russia by *Rumania* and *Finland*.

How exactly the combat forces of those two countries will be under
German control when they go into action is a matter that the Armed Forces
High Command will arrange and lay down at the proper time.

2. *Rumania's* task will be to pin down the enemy's forces opposite that
sector and to give assistance in rearward areas.

3. *Finland* will cover the movement of the Northern German Group
coming from Norway (elements of Group XXI) and will then operate in
conjunction with this group. The elimination of Hangö will also be Finland's
responsibility.

4. It may be anticipated that the *Swedish* railways and roads will be made
available for the movement of the Northern German Group, at the latest
when the operation has begun.

3. *The Conduct of the Operations*

(*A*) *Army* (in approbation of the intentions submitted to me):

The area of operations is divided into southern and northern halves by
the Pripet Marshes. The point of main effort will be made in the *northern*
half. Here two army groups are to be committed.

The southern of these two army groups—in the centre of the whole front—
will have the task of breaking out of the area around and to the north of
Warsaw with exceptionally strong armoured and motorised formations and
of destroying the enemy forces in White Russia. This will create a situation
which will enable strong formations of mobile troops to swing north; such
formations will then co-operate with the northern army group—advancing
from East Prussia in the general direction of Leningrad—in destroying the
enemy forces in the area of the Baltic states. Only after the accomplishment
of these offensive operations, which must be followed by the capture of
Leningrad and Kronstadt, are further offensive operations to be initiated
with the objective of occupying the important centre of communications and
of armaments manufacture, Moscow.

Only a surprisingly rapid collapse of the Russian ability to resist could
justify an attempt to achieve both objectives simultaneously.

The primary task of Group XXI, even during the Eastern operations,
remains *the protection of Norway*. Forces available other than those needed
for this task (Mountain Corps) will first of all be used to protect the Petsamo

area and its mines together with the Arctic road, and will then advance, in conjunction with Finnish forces, against the Murmansk railway and will cut the Murmansk area's land supply route.

Whether an operation of this nature can be carried out by *stronger* German forces (two to three divisions) coming from the area Rovaniemi and to the south is dependent on Sweden's willingness to make the Swedish railways available for such a move.

The mass of the Finnish army will have the task, in accordance with the advance made by the northern wing of the German armies, of tying up maximum Russian strength by attacking to the west, or on both sides, of Lake Ladoga. The Finns will also capture Hangö.

The army group *south of the Pripet Marshes* will make its point of main effort from the Lublin area in the general direction of Kiev, with the object of driving into the deep flank and rear of the Russian forces with strong armoured formations and of then rolling up the enemy along the Dnieper.

The German-Rumanian group on the right flank will have the task of

(a) protecting Rumanian territory and thus of covering the southern flank of the whole operation;

(b) in co-ordination with the attack by the northern wing of Army Group South of tying up the enemy forces on its sector of the front; then, as the situation develops, of launching a second thrust and thus, in conjunction with the air force, of preventing an orderly enemy withdrawal beyond the Dniester.

Once the battles south or north of the Pripet Marshes have been fought, the pursuit is to be undertaken with the following objectives:

In the south the rapid occupation of the economically important Donetz Basin,

In the north the speedy capture of Moscow.

The capture of this city would be a decisive victory both from the political and from the economic point of view; it would involve, moreover, the neutralisation of the most vital Russian rail centre.

(B) *Air Force:*

It will be the task of the air force, so far as possible, to damage and destroy the effectiveness of the Russian air force, and to support the operations by the army at the points of main effort, that is to say in the sectors of the central army group and in the area where the southern army group will be making its main effort. The Russian railways will either be destroyed, or, in the case of more important objectives close to hand (i.e. railway bridges), will be captured by the bold use of parachute and air-borne troops. In order that maximum forces may be available for operations against the enemy air force and for direct support of the army, the munitions industry will not be attacked while the major operation is in progress. Only after the conclusion of the mobile operations will such attacks, and in particular attacks against the industrial area of the Urals, be considered.

(C) Navy:

During the war with Soviet Russia it will be the task of the navy to protect the German coast line and to prevent any hostile naval force from breaking out of the Baltic. Since once Leningrad has been reached the Russian Baltic fleet will have lost its last base and will thus be in a hopeless position, major naval operations are to be previously avoided. After the destruction of the Russian fleet it will be the responsibility of the navy to make the Baltic fully available for carrying sea traffic, including supplies by sea to the northern wing of the army. (The sweeping of minefields!)

4.

It is important that all the Commanders-in-Chief make it plain that the taking of the necessary measures in connection with this directive is being done as a *precaution* against the possibility of the Russians adopting an attitude towards us other than what it has been up to now. The number of officers engaged in the early stages on these preparations is to be kept as small as possible, and each officer is only to be given such information as is directly essential to him in the performance of his task. Otherwise the danger will arise of our preparations becoming known, when a time for the carrying out of the proposed operation has not even been decided upon. This would cause us the gravest political and military disadvantages.

5.

I anticipate further conferences with the Commanders-in-Chief concerning their intentions as based on this directive.

Reports on the progress made in the proposed preparations by all services of the armed forces will be forwarded to me through the Armed Forces High Command.

signed: ADOLF HITLER.

APPENDIX XXIII

Organisation of the Command of the Armed Forces 1944

The Führer and Supreme Commander of the Armed Forces, also Commander-in-Chief of the Army

O.K.H.
Army High Command

O.K.W.
Supreme Command Armed Forces

Chief of the Army General Staff
(responsible for the Eastern theatre)

Operations Department
Organisation Department
Fortress Department
Foreign Armies West
Foreign Armies East
Training Department
Maps and Survey Department
Chief of Transport Services
Chief of Signal Services
Quartermaster General
Generals of Service Arms
(Inf., Arty., etc.)

Chief of the Armed Forces
Supreme Command
(Keitel)

Chief of the Armed Services
Command Staff
(Jodl)

(responsible for the OKW theatres)

Norway
Finland
Africa
Italy
France/Belgium/Holland
The Balkans

General
Inspectorate
of
Armoured
Troops

The Army
Groups

Armies

Corps

Divisions

Commander-in-Chief
of the
Air Force

General Air
Staff   Fleets

Defence of
the Reich

Commander-in-Chief
of the
Navy

Conduct of
Naval
Operations

Naval Group
Commands

The Fleets

Commander
of U-boats

Commander-in-Chief
of the
Training
Army
(after 21.7.44
Himmler)

Only the more important offices are shown. The Waffen SS and the Ministry of Armaments and War Production were directly subordinate to Hitler.

APPENDIX XXIV

War Establishment of a Panzer Division as of 15.10.35

1ST PANZER DIVISION

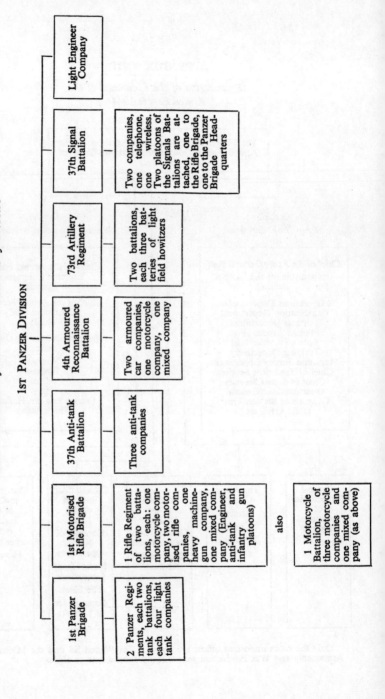

1st Panzer Brigade	1st Motorised Rifle Brigade	37th Anti-tank Battalion	4th Armoured Reconnaissance Battalion	73rd Artillery Regiment	37th Signal Battalion	Light Engineer Company
2 Panzer Regiments, each two tank battalions, each four light tank companies	1 Rifle Regiment of two battalions, each: one motorcycle company, two motorised rifle companies, one heavy machine-gun company, one mixed company (Engineer, anti-tank and infantry gun platoons)	Three anti-tank companies	Two armoured car companies, one motorcycle company, one mixed company	Two battalions, each three batteries of light field howitzers	Two companies, one telephone, one wireless. Two platoons of the Signals Battalions are attached, one to the Rifle Brigade, one to the Panzer Brigade Headquarters	

also

1 Motorcycle Battalion, of three motorcycle companies and one mixed company (as above)

APPENDIX XXV

War Establishment of 1st Panzer Division as of 9.5.40

1ST PANZER DIVISION
DIVISION H.Q.

| Panzer Brigade 1 | Rifle Brigade 1 | Anti-tank Battalion 37 | Armoured Reconnaissance Battalion 4 | Artillery Regiment 73 | Anti-Aircraft Battalion 83 | 2/Armoured Reconnaissance Squadron 23 | Signals Battalion 37 | Engineer Battalion 37 | Bugle Platoon 81 | Supply Battalion 81 | Administrative Services |

see (a) below — see (b) below — see (c) below — see (d) below — see (e) below — see (f) below — 9 Recce planes — see (g) below — see (h) below

(a)

PANZER BRIGADE 1

Panzer Regiment 1	Panzer Regiment 2	Supply, etc.
two tank battalions each two light, one medium companies, supply, etc.	two tank battalions each two light, one medium companies, supply, etc.	

(b)

RIFLE BRIGADE 1

Rifle Regiment 1 — Motorcycle Battalion — Heavy Infantry Gun Company

1st Battalion — 2nd Battalion — 3rd Battalion — Supply etc.

1st Battalion: Motorcycle Company, two Infantry Companies, Machine-Gun Company, Mixed Engineer, Anti-tank and Infantry Gun Company

3rd Battalion: Three Infantry Companies, Machine-Gun Company, Mixed Company

2nd Battalion: Motorcycle Company, two Infantry Companies, Machine-Gun Company, Mixed Engineer, Anti-tank and Infantry Gun Company

Motorcycle Battalion: Two Motorcycle companies, Machine-Gun Company, Mixed Company

Heavy Infantry Gun Company: (6 pieces)

(c)

ANTI-TANK BATTALION 37

1st Company — 12 light anti-tank guns

2nd Company — 12 light anti-tank guns

3rd Company — 12 light anti-tank guns

1st Company/Heavy Anti-tank Battalion 8 — 6 pieces

(d)

ARMOURED RECONNAISSANCE BATTALION 4

Armoured Car Company — 10 armoured cars

Armoured Car Company — 10 armoured cars

Motor-cycle Company

Mixed Company

Engineer Platoon

Supply etc.

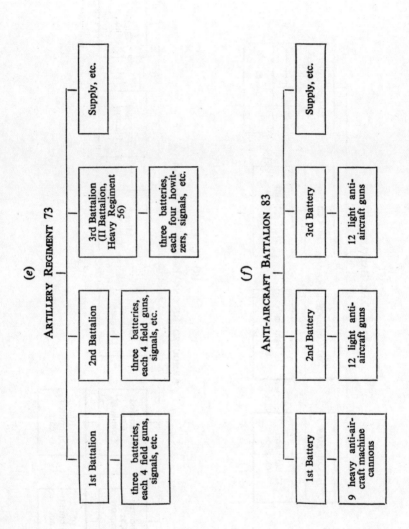

(e)

ARTILLERY REGIMENT 73

1st Battalion	2nd Battalion	3rd Battalion (II Battalion, Heavy Regiment 56)	Supply, etc.
three batteries, each 4 field guns, signals, etc.	three batteries, each 4 field guns, signals, etc.	three batteries, each four howitzers, signals, etc.	

(f)

ANTI-AIRCRAFT BATTALION 83

1st Battery	2nd Battery	3rd Battery	Supply, etc.
9 heavy anti-aircraft machine cannons	12 light anti-aircraft guns	12 light anti-aircraft guns	

(g)
SIGNALS BATTALION 37

Wireless Company | Telephone Company | Supply, etc.

(h)
ENGINEER BATTALION 37

Motorised Engineer Company | Motorised Engineer Company | Armoured Engineer Company | Two Bridging Columns | Light Engineer Column

INDEX

Adam, General, 72
Aisne, Battle of the, 123–6
Altrock, General von, 20
Amiens, Capture of, 112
Amsberg, Major von, 370
Amsberg, Colonel von, 18
Angern, Colonel, 71
Antonescu, Marshal, 364–6
Arnim, General von, 146, 156, 158, 222
Audörsch, Lt.-Col., 215
Axthelm, General von, 146

Bach-Zelewski, Group Leader von dem, 355–6, 358
Bacher, General, 146, 210
Bader, General, 68, 80
Badoglio, Marshal, 46, 141, 310
Balck, Lt.-Col., later Gen., 100, 102, 107–8, 112, 125, 127–8, 255, 261, 372, 374, 376, 385–6, 394
Barandon, Dr. Paul, 401–2, 421, 426
Barsewisch, Lt.-Col. von, 146, 160, 220
Bayerlein, Major later Gen., 120, 134, 142, 208, 323
Beaulieu, Charles de, 287
Beck, Foreign Minister, 437
Beck, Col.-Gen., 32–3, 36, 49, 50, 60, 87, 190, 301, 345, 348, 457, 462
Becke, Lt., 287
Becker, General, 30
Belfort, Capture of, 132–4
Below, Colonel von, 171, 340
Bergmann, General, 262
Berlin, General, 343
Bevin, Ernest, 285
Bialystok, Pocket at, 157–164
Bismarck, Prince, 30, 414, 435, 442, 454, 461
Bissing, Lt.-Col. Frhr. von, 186
Bittrich, Colonel, 219
Blomberg, General von, 29, 35, 47–8, 87, 436, 452, 464
Blücher, F.-M. Prince von, 455–6
Bock, F.-M. von, 50, 53, 56, 75, 122, 145, 166, 189, 192, 195–6, 198, 218, 252, 259, 264
Bolbrinker, Colonel, 292
Boltenstern, General von, 146, 176
Bonin, Colonel von, 343, 396–8
Bor-Komorowski, General, 35–6, 358
Bormann, Martin, 344, 362, 364, 416, 424, 449, 452
Botho-Wend zu Eulenburg, Graf, 83
Boulogne, Capture of, 114–16
Brahe, Battle of the, 70–1
Brandenberger, General, 380
Brandt, General, 38
Braubach, Lt.-Col., 81, 83
Brauchitsch, Lt.-Col., later F.-M. von, 21, 37, 48, 56, 60, 61, 126, 152, 166, 199, 200, 213, 262–3, 265, 267, 275, 465
Braun, Eva, 442, 452
Bredow, General von, 33
Bredow, Major von, 185
Brest-Litovsk, 1st Battle of, 81–2; 2nd Battle of, 153–4
Brockdorff, General Graf, 72
Bryansk, Battle of, 232–7
Buchterkirch, Lt., 206

Bug, Battle of the, 146–9, 153–4
Buhle, General, 304, 340, 361
Bünau, Lt. von, 130
Burén, Colonel, 23
Burgdorf, General, 340–2, 346, 364, 382, 400, 406, 416, 429, 452
Busch, Lt.-Col., later F.-M., 23, 92, 104, 336
Buschenhagen, General, 289
Büsing, Major, 206, 217, 269
Busse, General, 394, 427, 428

Calais, Capture of, 116–18
Cambrai, Battle of, 39
Cavallero, Marshal, 141
Chamberlain, Neville, 60, 435
Charles XII of Sweden, 142, 218, 440
Christen, Lt.-Col. von, 397–8
Churchill, Winston, 54–6, 60, 84, 120, 284–5, 438–9
Ciano, Count, 64–5
Clary-Aldringen, Prince, 59
Clausewitz, 378, 454, 456
Crinis, Professor de, 443

Daladier, 94, 435
Dalerus, Birger, 445
Dallmer-Zerbe, Lt.-Col., 156
Darré, Minister, 452–3
Deverill, Field-Marshal Sir Cyril, 46
Dietrich, Sepp, 50, 117–18, 272, 380, 413
Dirlewanger, 356, 448
Dnieper, Battle of the, 170–2
Dohna-Finckenstein, Count, 74
Dollman, General, 132, 134–5, 334
Domarus, Professor von, 274
Dönitz, Grand Admiral, 372, 413
Dorpmüller, Minister, 452
Dunkirk, British Evacuation from, 117–18

Eberbach, Col., later Gen., 230, 235, 242, 244–8, 292
Eckinger, Capt., 128, 133
Eden, Anthony, 60
Ehlermann, Lt.-Col., 99
Elnya, Battle of, 180–2, 196, 212
Eltz von Rübenach, Baron, 452
Engel, Colonel, 289
Epp, General Ritter von, 135, 137

Falkenhorst, General von, 76
Fegelein, SS. Brigade-Leader, 356, 358, 416, 452
Feldt, General, 145
Felix, Lt., 70
Feller, Lt.-Col., 156
Fessmann, General, 36, 46
Fischer, Colonel, 100
Ford, Henry, 316
Förster, General, 272
Forster, Gauleiter, 449
Frank, Governor-General, 355, 358, 450
Frank, Major, 217, 218
Franco, General, 140, 287
Franz, Major, 175
Frederick the Great, 74, 266, 406, 416, 425, 441–2, 454, 466

Frederick William I, 406
Frère, General, 111
Freyer, Lt.-Col., 292
Freytag von Loringhoven, Major Baron, 342
Freytag von Loringhoven, Col. Baron, 345
Frick, Minister, 452
Friessner, Col.-Gen., 354, 366, 373
Fritsch, General Frhr. von, 31, 33, 35–6, 46–9, 55, 87, 436
Fromm, General, 37, 63, 273–4, 289, 345, 349
Fuller, General, 20

Gall, Colonel, 76
Galland, General, 445
Gamelin, General, 108
Gärtringen, Frhr. Hiller von, 70
Gaulle, General de, 94, 109, 111
Gebhardt, Professor, 421
Gehlen, Col., later General, 343, 382, 384, 387, 413
Gercke, General, 343
Gerlach, Colonel von, 146
Gessler, Dr., 462
Geyer, General, 184–5, 188, 272
Geyr, von Schweppenburg, General Frhr., 49, 68, 145, 148, 157, 160–1, 168, 182, 192, 210, 213–14, 217, 220, 228, 230, 232, 234–5, 245, 247, 259, 324, 328–30, 332–4
Ghengis Khan, 383
Gille, General, 384–6
Glaise-Horstenau, von, 51
Gneisenau, General, 454–5, 461
Goebbels, Dr., 85, 267, 293–4, 324, 344, 416, 418, 448, 452
Goerdeler, Dr., 300–2, 344, 348
Goering, Hermann, 85, 98, 120, 304, 334, 344, 378, 412, 438, 444–6, 448, 452
Gollnik, Colonel, 82
Gothsche, General, 348
Gräser, General, 374
Graziani, Marshal, 141
Greiser, Gauleiter, 449
Grote, 278
Guderian, Heinz-Günter, 17, 58, 66, 83, 120
Guderian, Kurt, 17, 66, 72–3, 80, 83, 120, 132
Gürtner, Minister, 452

Haase, General, 123
Hacker, 278
Haeften, von, 345
Halder, Col.-Gen., 60, 90–1, 142, 198–200, 202, 206, 218, 275, 462
Halm, Colonel, 22
Hansen, General, 365
Harpe, Col.-Gen., 336, 374, 386–7, 390, 394
Hauenschild, Gen, von, 293
Hausser, Col.-Gen., 145, 164, 174, 209, 334
Heckel, Lt.-Col., 408
Heigl, Fritz, 21
Heinemann, General, 146
Heinrici, Gen., later Col.-Gen., 242, 244, 374, 422, 425
Heistermann von Ziehlberg, Gen., 347
Heitz, General, 47
Henderson, Nevile, 60
Hentzsch Mission, 107
Hess, Rudolf, 444, 452, 453
Hesse, Dr., 421
Heusinger, Col. later Gen., 189, 361
Hierl, 416, 449
Himmler, Heinrich, 51, 293, 303, 325, 344, 355–6, 358, 364, 383, 394, 403–6, 413–14, 419, 421–2, 426, 446–9, 452, 517

Hindenburg, Field-Marshal von, 29, 34, 87, 414, 434, 452, 455–6
Hippel, Colonel von, 105
Hirschberg, General von, 26
Hitler, Adolf, 29 et seq.
Hlond, Cardinal, 82
Hoare, Sir Samuel, 286, 287
Hoeppner, General, 64, 170, 259, 272–3, 348
Höring, Major, 22
Hörnlein, Col., 222
Horthy, Admiral, 57, 368, 378–9
Hossbach, General, 376, 400–1
Hoth, General, 145–6, 150, 158, 160, 162, 166, 170, 178–9, 180, 182, 189, 192, 503
Hube, General, 296
Hubitzki, General, 227
Hugenberg, Minister, 452
Hühnlein, Adolf, 30

Imredy, 57

Jakob, General, 360
Jänicke, Col.-Gen., 328
Jeschonnek, Col.-Gen., 303
Jodl, Col.-Gen., 199, 268, 289, 325, 339, 341, 351, 361, 366–7, 382–3, 385, 387–8, 393, 403, 406, 420–1, 423, 427, 429, 431, 439, 445, 464, 517
Jordana, 286
Jungenfeldt, Major, later Col. von, 230, 366
Juniville, Battle of, 125

Kahlden, Major von, later Lt.-Col., 213, 217, 252, 269
Kaltenbrunner, 346, 398
Kaminski, 356, 448
Kauffmann, Major, 292
Kaupisch, General, 66
Keitel, General Bodewin, 61, 261, 284
Keitel, General Wilhelm later F.-M., 48, 199, 264, 268, 287, 289, 294, 302, 304, 308–10, 327, 340–1, 345–6, 351, 361, 364, 368, 382, 415, 420, 429, 431, 464–5, 517
Kempfe, General, 226
Kempff, General, 108, 134, 226, 228, 233, 287, 302
Kesselring, Field-Marshal, 209, 379
Kiev, Battle of, 202–24
Killinger, Ambassador, 365
Kirchheim, General, 345–6
Kirchner, General, 98, 123, 133
Kleemann, Colonel, 215
Kleist, Col.-Gen. von, later F.-M., 91–2, 99, 101–2, 107, 109–10, 113–14, 118, 129, 216, 217–19, 233, 274, 316, 476, 478, 480, 484, 493, 503, 504–9
Klingenberg, Hauptsturmführer, 181
Klingspor, Captain, 23
Kluge, Col.-Gen. von, later F.-M., 65, 82, 147, 161–2, 166–7, 169, 171, 175, 179, 262, 264, 269, 272–3, 306–8, 312, 334, 338, 341, 369–70
Knesebeck, Lt.-Col. von dem, 397–8
Knobelsdorff, General von, 302
Knochenhauer, General von, 26
Koch, Reich Commissar, 289, 388
Kordt, Erich, 378
Korten, General, 345
Köstring, General, 151, 289
Krause, Lt., 188, 191
Krebs, Colonel, later General, 191, 415–16, 425–6, 428
Kreysing, General, 402
Kriebel, General, 345, 346

Krivochin, Brig.-General, 83
Kübler, General, 272
Küchler, General von, 75
Kuhl, General von, 41
Kuhn, Major, 347
Kühne, Lieutenant-Colonel, 22
Kuntzen, General, 306

Lammerding, SS. Brigade-Leader, 403, 421
Landgraf, Colonel, 112
Langermann und Erlencamp, Gen. Frhr. von,
   126, 130, 145, 182, 230, 235
Leeb, Col.-Gen., later F.-M. Ritter von, 132,
   134, 145, 195, 272
Lemelsen, General, 146, 149, 154, 156, 162, 169,
   228, 232, 254
Lenin, 432
le Suire, Lt.-Col. von, 62
Ley, Dr., 420, 450
Licht, Colonel, 171
Liddell Hart, Captain, 20, 295
Liebenstein, Lt.-Col. Frhr. von, 107, 142, 145,
   159, 182, 206, 217, 218, 227, 237, 244, 247,
   259, 269, 270, 272
Liese, Lt.-Col., 23
Linnarz, General, 284
List, Colonel General, 91, 110, 122, 124
Litvinov, 140
Loch, General, 124
Loeper, General von, 145, 209, 215, 268
Lörzer, General, 98, 101, 102, 104
Lossberg, Lt.-Col. von, 117, 439
Ludendorff, General, 87, 184, 455, 456
Luther, Dr. Martin, 264
Lüttwitz, General Frhr, Smilo von, 394
Lutz, Major, later General, 18, 19, 24–5, 28,
   33, 35–6, 38, 47, 49, 278

Mackensen, Field-Marshal von, 33, 34
Mackensen, General von, 123, 153
Maginot Line, 94, 96, 106
Mahan, Admiral, 440
Mannerheim, Field-Marshal, 368
Manstein, Gen. later F.-M. von, 85, 89, 90–1,
   109, 302–3, 306–7
Manteuffel, General von, 380–1, 421
Marras, General, 171
Martel, General, 20
Martinek, General, 191
Meier-Rabingen, General, 191
Meisel, General, 346, 397
Merz von Quirnheim, 345
Metz, General, 226, 233
Meuse, Battle of the, 101–8
Miklos, General, 378
Milch, Field-Marshal, 293
Minsk, Capture of, 158
Model, Lt.-Gen., later F.-M., 145, 182, 186,
   209–10, 215, 217–18, 306–7, 311, 336, 355–6,
   369, 376, 380, 415
Mölders, Colonel, 146, 161, 168, 256
Molotov, 139–42, 382
Moltke, F.-M. Graf von, 32, 378, 439, 454, 456–
   7, 461
Morell, Dr., 342, 442, 452
Müller, Dr., 281, 299–300
Müller, Colonel, 499
Müller, Gen. Friedrich-Wilhelm, 401
Müller, Bishop, 451
Müller, SS. Group-Leader, 346, 398
Munzel, Lt.-Col., 218
Mussolini, 33, 46, 140, 144, 310, 371, 432, 435,
   439

Nagel, Lt.-Col., 209–10, 213
Napoleon, 21, 74, 142, 171, 432, 440, 454, 456
Narev, Battle of the, 76–80
Natzmer, Colonel von, 21
Naumann, State Secretary, 418–9
Nedtwig, Colonel, 133
Nehring, Col., later Gen., 84, 100, 120, 130, 146,
   154, 168–9, 390, 393, 395, 398, 417, 499,
   508, 512
Neurath, Frhr. von, 452
Nicholson, Brigadier, 117

Ohnesorge, Postmaster, 452
Olbricht, General, 339, 345, 348
Orel, Battle of, 226–32
O'Rourq, Bishop, 82
Oshima, Ambassador, 412
Otto, General, 58

Papen, Franz von, 452–3
Paul of Yugoslavia, Prince, 65
Paulus, Col. later F.-M., 35, 49, 206, 274
Péronne, Capture of, 111
Pétain, Marshal, 134
Petter, Major, 19
Pirner, Captain, 27
Porsche, Prof., 277–8, 281–2, 299, 309
Potemkin, 383
Praun, Col. later Gen., 146, 343
Prien, General von, 289
Prittwitz, Colonel von, 105, 113

Rabenau, General von, 300–1
Raeder, Admiral, 287
Rauss, Col.-Gen., 376, 415, 420–1
Reichenau, General von, later F.-M., 29, 48
   55, 86, 87, 256, 464
Reinefarth, Police General, 425
Reinhardt, General, later Col.-Gen., 56, 106,
   108, 117, 122, 125, 127, 129, 259, 356, 376,
   384, 386–7, 400–1
Rendulic, Col.-Gen., 401
Ribbentrop, 65–6, 364, 366, 378, 402, 404–5,
   421, 426, 452
Richthofen, Field-Marshal von, 178, 261
Richthofen, Manfred von, 444
Riebel, Lt.-Col., 62, 122, 125
Roehm, Ernst, 33, 362, 452
Rommel, General later F.-M., 141, 174, 273,
   310, 329–34, 349, 369
Roosevelt, Franklin D., 284, 441
Rosenberg, Alfred, 450
Roslavl, Battle of, 186–9, 194–5
Röttinger, Captain, 62
Runciman, Lord, 59, 435
Rundstedt, Col.-Gen. von, later F.-M., 85–7,
   89–91, 105, 110, 120, 122, 127, 145, 256, 272,
   304, 324, 328–30, 334, 345–6, 369, 380, 385
Rust, Minister, 451, 452

Salaszy, 379, 417
Salmuth, General von, 76
Saucken, General von, 393–4, 398, 417
Saur, Chief Assistant, 276, 308–9
Schaal, General, 76, 98, 100, 106, 118, 145, 181,
   477, 486
Schacht, Hjalmar, 287, 452–3
Scharnhorst, General, 454–5
Schell, General von, 316–17, 320, 322
Schepman, 362
Schlabrendorff, Fabian von, 301
Schleicher, General von, 33, 434
Schlieffen, General von, 32–3, 378, 456–7, 461

"Schlieffen Plan," 89–90, 96–7, 456
Schmidt, General Rudolf, 49, 122–3, 127–8, 270
Schmidt, Ambassador, 365
Schmitt, Minister, 452
Schmundt, Colonel later General, 172, 174, 185, 189, 199, 261, 263–4, 272, 287–9, 295, 304, 308, 313, 340, 342, 345, 364, 452
Schneider, Colonel, 192
Schörner, General, later Col.-Gen., 316, 343, 352, 354–5, 366, 376, 394, 401
Schroth, General, 148, 154, 345–6
Schultz, General, 374
Schwerin von Krosigk, Graf, 452–3
Seeckt, Col. General von, 38, 457, 462
Seiss-Inquart, 51
Seldte, Minister, 452, 453
Seydlitz, General von, 400
Smigly-Rydz, Marshal, 438
Smolensk, Capture of, 180
Sodenstern, General von, 90
Speer, Albert, 276–7, 282, 293–4, 298, 304, 306, 308–10, 313, 407, 422–4, 426, 453
Speidel, General, 333
Sperrle, General, later F.-M., 101, 104, 334
Spitta, 113
Spoleta, Duke of, 144
Stalin, 85, 440
Stauffenburg, Graf, 344, 345, 348
Stemmermann, General, 258
Stiotta, Major von, 91
Stockhausen, General von, 146
Stottmeister, Colonel, 22
Strachwitz, Colonel Graf, 355
Strauss, Col.-General, 65–6, 72, 272, 361
Streich, General, 169–72
Stülpnagel, Gen. Heinrich von, 349
Stülpnagel, Lt.-Col. later Gen. Joachim von, 18, 25
Stülpnagel, General Otto von, 24, 25
Stumme, General, 330
Stumpff, General, 76
Stumpfl, General, 52
Stutterheim, General von, 98, 100–1

Theiss, Colonel, 53, 293
Thilo, Lt.-Colonel, 360
Thoma, General Ritter von, 180, 204, 209, 222
Thomale, Colonel, later Gen., 292, 294, 306, 309, 339–40, 387, 408, 413
Timoshenko, Marshal, 176, 218
Todt, Dr., 136, 267, 277, 453
Tolstoi, Count, 256–7
Toppe, Colonel, 343
Treskow, General von, 312, 345
Tschammer und Osten, von, 450
Tschischwitz, General von, 18–19, 21, 347

Tuchel Heath, Battle of the, 71–3
Tula, Battle of, 242–62

Udet, General, 304
Usinger, Colonel, 170–2

Vaerst, Colonel von, 105
Veiel, General, 49–51, 98, 110, 113, 127
Verdun, Battle of, 22
Viebirg, General, 146, 161
Vietinghoff genannt Scheel, Gen. Frhr. von, 145, 149, 174, 180, 220, 222
Volckheim, Lt., 20
Vormann, General von, 355, 376
Vörös, General, 368, 378, 399

Wäger, Lt.-Colonel, 22
Wagner, General, 343, 345
Waldeck, Lt.-Col. Prince Max zu, 292
Weber, Lieutenant, 128
Weber, General Ritter von, 154, 158, 162, 178, 180
Wechmar, Col. Frhr. von, 322
Weichs, Gen. Frhr. von, later F.-M., 35, 36, 373, 403
Weidling, General, 311
Weisenberger, General, 242, 244, 247
Weiss, Major, 287
Weiss, Col.-Gen., 376, 400
Weizenegger, Lt.-Col., 339
Weizsäcker, von, 72
Wenck, Major, later General, 23, 105, 110, 132–3, 343, 354, 384, 397, 409, 413–15, 421, 426
Wendland, Lt.-Col., 343
Wenig, Captain, 137
Westphal, General, 385
West Wall, 51
Weber, General, 444
Wietersheim, General von, 91, 106, 114, 118, 362
Wiktorin, General, 68, 78, 129
William I, Kaiser, 434
Wilkins, von, 66
Wilson, President, 432
Wimmer, Captain, 18, 19
Witzleben, F.-M. von, 348
Wöhler, General, 386, 418
Wolf, Major, 208
Wöllwarth, Major Frhr. von, 292

Xylander, General von, 386

Yefremov, General, 239

Zeitzler, Colonel, later General, 107, 275, 289, 306–7, 311, 323–4, 339–41
Zhukov, Marshal, 407
Zimmermann, Dr., 429

READ MORE IN PENGUIN

In every corner of the world, on every subject under the sun, Penguin represents quality and variety – the very best in publishing today.

For complete information about books available from Penguin – including Puffins, Penguin Classics and Arkana – and how to order them, write to us at the appropriate address below. Please note that for copyright reasons the selection of books varies from country to country.

In the United Kingdom: Please write to *Dept. EP, Penguin Books Ltd, Bath Road, Harmondsworth, West Drayton, Middlesex UB7 ODA*

In the United States: Please write to *Consumer Sales, Penguin Putnam Inc., P.O. Box 12289 Dept. B, Newark, New Jersey 07101-5289*. VISA and MasterCard holders call 1-800-788-6262 to order Penguin titles

In Canada: Please write to *Penguin Books Canada Ltd, 10 Alcorn Avenue, Suite 300, Toronto, Ontario M4V 3B2*

In Australia: Please write to *Penguin Books Australia Ltd, P.O. Box 257, Ringwood, Victoria 3134*

In New Zealand: Please write to *Penguin Books (NZ) Ltd, Private Bag 102902, North Shore Mail Centre, Auckland 10*

In India: Please write to *Penguin Books India Pvt Ltd, 11 Community Centre, Panchsheel Park, New Delhi 110017*

In the Netherlands: Please write to *Penguin Books Netherlands bv, Postbus 3507, NL-1001 AH Amsterdam*

In Germany: Please write to *Penguin Books Deutschland GmbH, Metzlerstrasse 26, 60594 Frankfurt am Main*

In Spain: Please write to *Penguin Books S. A., Bravo Murillo 19, 1º B, 28015 Madrid*

In Italy: Please write to *Penguin Italia s.r.l., Via Benedetto Croce 2, 20094 Corsico, Milano*

In France: Please write to *Penguin France, Le Carré Wilson, 62 rue Benjamin Baillaud, 31500 Toulouse*

In Japan: Please write to *Penguin Books Japan Ltd, Kaneko Building, 2-3-25 Koraku, Bunkyo-Ku, Tokyo 112*

In South Africa: Please write to *Penguin Books South Africa (Pty) Ltd, Private Bag X14, Parkview, 2122 Johannesburg*

INSPECTION COPY REQUESTS

Lecturers in the United Kingdom and Ireland wishing to apply for inspection copies of Classic Penguin titles for student group adoptions are invited to apply to:

Inspection Copy Department
Penguin Press Marketing
80 Strand
LONDON
WC2R 0RL

Fax: 020 7010 6701

E-mail: academic@penguin.co.uk

Inspection copies may also be requested via our website at:
www.penguinclassics.com

Please include in your request the author, title and the ISBN of the book(s) in which you are interested, the name of the course on which the books will be used and the expected student numbers.

It is essential that you include with your request your title, first name, surname, position, department name, college or university address, telephone and fax numbers and your e-mail address.

Lecturers outside the United Kingdom and Ireland should address their applications to their local Penguin office.

Inspection copies are supplied at the discretion of Penguin Books

READ MORE IN PENGUIN

PENGUIN CLASSIC BIOGRAPHY

 Highly readable and enjoyable biographies and autobiographies from leading biographers and auto-biographers. The series provides a vital background to the increasing interest in history, historical subjects and people who mattered. The periods and subjects covered include the Roman Empire, Tudor England, the English Civil Wars, the Victorian Era, and characters as diverse Joan of Arc, Jane Austen, Robert Burns and George Melly. Essential reading for everyone interested in the great figures of the past.

Published or forthcoming:

E. F. Benson	**As We Were**
Ernle Bradford	**Cleopatra**
David Cecil	**A Portrait of Jane Austen**
Roger Fulford	**Royal Dukes**
Christopher Hibbert	**Charles I**
	The Making of Charles Dickens
Christopher Hill	**God's Englishman: Oliver Cromwell**
Marion Johnson	**The Borgias**
James Lees-Milne	**Earls of Creation**
Edward Lucie-Smith	**Joan of Arc**
Philip Magnus	**Gladstone**
John Masters	**Casanova**
Elizabeth Mavor	**The Ladies of Llangollen**
Ian McIntyre	**Robert Burns**
George Melly	**Owning Up: The Trilogy**
Raymond Postgate	**That Devil Wilkes**
Peter Quennell	**Byron: The Years of Fame**
Lytton Strachey	**Queen Victoria**
	Elizabeth and Essex
Gaius Suetonius	**Lives of the Twelve Caesars** translated by Robert Graves
Alan Villiers	**Captain Cook**

READ MORE IN PENGUIN

PENGUIN CLASSIC HISTORY

Well written narrative history from leading historians such as Paul Kennedy, Alan Moorehead, J. B. Priestley, A. L. Rowse and G. M. Trevelyan. From the Ancient World to the decline of British naval mastery, from twelfth-century France to the Victorian Underworld, the series captures the great turning points in history and chronicles the lives of ordinary people at different times. Penguin Classic History will be enjoyed and valued by everyone who loves the past.

Published or forthcoming:

Leslie Alcock	**Arthur's Britain**
John Belchem/Richard Price	**A Dictionary of 19th-Century History**
Jeremy Black/Roy Porter	**A Dictionary of 18th-Century History**
Ernle Bradford	**The Mediterranean**
Anthony Burton	**Remains of a Revolution**
Robert Darnton	**The Great Cat Massacre**
Jean Froissart	**Froissart's Chronicles**
Johan Huizinga	**The Waning of the Middle Ages**
Aldous Huxley	**The Devils of Loudun**
Paul M. Kennedy	**The Rise and Fall of British Naval Mastery**
Margaret Wade Labarge	**Women in Medieval Life**
Alan Moorehead	**Fatal Impact**
Samuel Pepys	**Illustrated Pepys**
J. H. Plumb	**The First Four Georges**
J. B. Priestley	**The Edwardians**
Philippa Pullar	**Consuming Passions**
A. L. Rowse	**The Elizabethan Renaissance**
John Ruskin	**The Stones of Venice**
G. M. Trevelyan	**English Social History**
Philip Warner	**The Medieval Castle**
T. H. White	**The Age of Scandal**
Lawrence Wright	**Clean and Decent**
Hans Zinsser	**Rats, Lice and History**

READ MORE IN PENGUIN

PENGUIN CLASSIC MILITARY HISTORY

This series acknowledges the profound and enduring interest in military history, and the causes and consequences of human conflict. Penguin Classic Military History covers warfare from the earliest times to the age of electronics and encompasses subjects as diverse as classic examples of grand strategy and the precision tactics of Britain's crack SAS Regiment. The series will be enjoyed and valued by students of military history and all who hope to learn from the often disturbing lessons of the past.

Published or forthcoming:

Correlli Barnett	**Engage the Enemy More Closely**
	The Great War
David G. Chandler	**The Art of Warfare on Land**
	Marlborough as Military Commander
William Craig	**Enemy at the Gates**
Carlo D'Este	**Decision in Normandy**
Michael Glover	**The Peninsular War**
	Wellington as Military Commander
Winston Graham	**The Spanish Armadas**
Heinz Guderian	**Panzer Leader**
Christopher Hibbert	**Redcoats and Rebels**
Heinz Höhne	**The Order of the Death's Head**
Anthony Kemp	**The SAS at War**
Ronald Lewin	**Ultra Goes to War**
Martin Middlebrook	**The Falklands War**
	The First Day on the Somme
	The Kaiser's Battle
Desmond Seward	**Henry V**
John Toland	**Infamy**
Philip Warner	**Sieges of the Middle Ages**
Leon Wolff	**In Flanders Fields**
Cecil Woodham-Smith	**The Reason Why**